Palgrave Studies in Financial Services Technology

Series Editor
Bernardo Nicoletti
Rome, Italy

The Palgrave Studies in Financial Services Technology series features original research from leading and emerging scholars on contemporary issues and developments in financial services technology. Falling into 4 broad categories: channels, payments, credit, and governance; topics covered include payments, mobile payments, trading and foreign transactions, big data, risk, compliance, and business intelligence to support consumer and commercial financial services. Covering all topics within the life cycle of financial services, from channels to risk management, from security to advanced applications, from information systems to automation, the series also covers the full range of sectors: retail banking, private banking, corporate banking, custody and brokerage, wholesale banking, and insurance companies. Titles within the series will be of value to both academics and those working in the management of financial services.

More information about this series at
http://www.palgrave.com/gp/series/14627

Bernardo Nicoletti

Insurance 4.0

Benefits and Challenges of Digital Transformation

palgrave
macmillan

Bernardo Nicoletti
Temple University
Rome, Italy

ISSN 2662-5083 ISSN 2662-5091 (electronic)
Palgrave Studies in Financial Services Technology
ISBN 978-3-030-58425-2 ISBN 978-3-030-58426-9 (eBook)
https://doi.org/10.1007/978-3-030-58426-9

This Palgrave Macmillan imprint is published by the registered company Springer Nature Switzerland AG

The registered company address is: Gewerbestrasse 11, 6330 Cham, Switzerland

Foreword

I have known Bernardo Nicoletti since a long time: we have been collaborating in many challenges and countries around the world and from many positions. He already wrote some years ago another inspiring book: Digital Insurance, that I consider a prequel to this one, where he now tackles a new, yet connected, topic, "How to push and support digital transformation in insurance companies."

It was about time to have such a book. Indeed the revolution of industry 4.0 goes back to 2012, while in the meantime, many financial institutions have almost continued unchanged, almost unaware of what was happening around them. New companies and business models have been started, and other have failed, sometimes in a dramatic way. The digital world has disrupted entire sectors, such as newspapers, media recording, commerce, manufacturing, and others. It is now impacting heavily also on financial services.

Consequently, the concept of "digital transformation" is on the agenda of many CEOs and Board rooms. But apart from the buzzword, it is often not clear what it really means; financial services have often interpreted "digital transformation" only as a way to provide access to some products via digital channels, online or mobile. Digital transformation is much more than that: it is a change in the business models of the company. It is essentially putting the customer at the center of attention and using digital platforms to build a new business and operating model around that. Such a transformation involves all the dimensions of the business such as products, processes, people, partners, and platforms.

In the last few years, prophets started to make statements such as: "banking is necessary, but banks are not." This approach has spurred a certain number of studies to understand what digital transformation meant for banks. In the meantime, the other cornerstone of financial services, insurance has not changed much. The mantra for some was that insurance does not have many contact points with customers. Hence digital transformation was not that essential.

Bernardo claims that there is a need for a Copernican revolution in insurance too. It is necessary to put at the center of attention the customers and their needs. This approach is what this book describes and its relevance is that not only it tells you what to do but also how to do it. Bernardo applies the Galileo method, which has three steps, intuition, demonstration, and experiment, and this is the method applied in this book.

There are also certain exciting intuitions on how "insurance" should change, like the evolution from "products" to "services", and the fundamental importance of "platforms" and "ecosystem". Simultaneously, the book goes into detail on what to do with the support of methodologies, old or new, which Bernardo describes in detail. Finally, the text is full of real business cases where the digital transformation has been experimented and implemented.

I am happy to see that Bernardo has also considered the company I work for in some of these business cases. Indeed I believe that Allianz has had the intuition to implement what another guru of financial services, Chris Skinner, has written in his books: companies like Banks need in their board and executives not only bankers but persons with deep experience of technologies, and this applies also to Insurances.

The book stresses also another important aspect: the increasing importance for insurance companies of data and their management. The crisis caused by COVID-19 has only underscored this point and given us a new sense of urgency, but also shown us that we can re-engineer all function in a much more digital and agile way then we thought.

To date, insurers must use all the tools to grow, protect themselves, and better plan the future. The most effective way to do this is through the strategic use of data. Data is essential to understand the customer and protect the company from exposure and mitigate the associated risks.

In times of crisis, the mutuality role of insurance increases in importance. Unfortunately, in some cases also the probability of fraudulent transactions, dictated by despair, is higher.

Analysis tools will play an essential role in this recovery, providing insurers with all the information they need to limit their exposure, promote new offers, and enrich their services.

It is fascinating to go through the various chapters of this book because the insurance companies that have started to implement the digital transformation state that their work is only the beginning of what is necessary. There is a need for a continuous digital transformation.

Because the question for insurance companies is not "if" to do it, it is "when" to do it; the time is now, and the success will be with the hard work pioneers.

Munich, Germany

Fabio De Ferrari
Chief Operation Officer bei Allianz
Deutschland AG

Contents

1	**Introduction**	1
2	**Industry 4.0 and Insurance 4.0**	11
	Introduction	11
	Industry 4.0	13
	Main Components	18
	Soft	18
	Hard	19
	Significant Challenges	21
	Insurance 4.0	22
	Insurance World	23
	First Industrial Revolution. Insurance 1.0	25
	Second Industrial Revolution. Insurance 2.0	27
	Third Industrial Revolution. Insurance 3.0	28
	Fourth Industrial Revolution: Insurance 4.0	30
	Insurance 4.0 Model	34
	Cybernetics	34
	Communication	35
	Control	35
	Cooperation	35
	Connection	36
	Cognition	37

Coordination 38
Conclusions 40

3 **Business Model Canvas and Insurance 4.0** 41
Introduction 41
Business Model Literature 41
Business Model Canvas—Structure and Components 45
Value Propositions 48
Customer Proximity 48
Customer Partitions 52
Place or Channels 53
Platforms and Resources 53
Essential Processes and Activities 54
Partnerships and Collaboration 56
Pricing and Revenues 58
Payments for Costs and Investments 59
Business Models, Strategy, and Competitive Advantage 60
Application of the Model to the Insurance Industry 64
Competitive Advantages 67
Conclusions 68

4 **Propositions of Value for the Customer in Insurance 4.0** 69
Introduction 69
Insurance 4.0 and Value Network 71
Empowerment of Customers 73
Benefits and Challenges in Insurance 4.0 75
Loss Control 76
Behavioral Change 76
Risk Selection 76
Shared Economy 77
New Products to Add Value 79
New Insurance Products Developed Based on the Technologies Used 80
New Products Based on the Objectives 81
On-Demand Insurance 82
Usage-Based Insurance (UBI) 82
Peer-to-Peer Insurance 83

Cyber Insurance 84
Parametric Insurance 88
Business Interruptions Insurance 90
Other Services 91
Unit-Linked 98
Conclusions 99

5 Proximity to the Customer in Insurance 4.0 101
Introduction 101
Value Proposition and Customer Proximity 104
Customer Engagement 104
Claims 107
Consultant 109
Customer Relationships Management 4.0 109
Direct Interaction of Insurance with Customers 113
Customer Proximity Center 114
The Evolution of the Call Center 119
Model of the Characteristics of a Call Center Based on the Strategy of the Organization 121
Persons 123
Processes 126
Structure 127
Technology 127
Assessing the Quality in a Call Center 129
The Future of the Call Centers 134
Conclusions 136

6 Partition of the Customers in Insurance 4.0 139
Introduction 139
Customer Partition 142
Millennials 143
The Impact of Technology 145
Conclusions 146

7 Place or Channels in Insurance 4.0 147
Introduction 147
Insurance 4.0 and Distribution 149

	Choice of the Channel for the Distribution of Insurance Products	153
	Direct Digital Channels	160
	Online Intermediaries for Insurance 4.0	163
	Price Comparison Websites	165
	Value Comparison Websites	165
	Digital Brokers	166
	An Overview of the Italian Market	167
	The New Distribution Regulation: IDD—Insurance Distribution Directive	168
	Conclusions	171
8	**Platforms for Insurance 4.0**	173
	Introduction	173
	Classification of the Platforms	176
	Architecture for the Platforms	177
	General Architecture for Insurance 4.0 Platforms	179
	Lean and Digitize	180
	Benefits of Insurance 4.0 Platforms	181
	Challenges of Insurance 4.0	182
	Connection: IoT and Blockchain	182
	IoT	183
	IoT Architectures	184
	Application Areas for Insurance 4.0	185
	Challenges with the Internet of Things	189
	Blockchain	196
	Blockchain Architecture	197
	Application Areas of Blockchain Solutions in Insurance 4.0	200
	Benefits and Challenges of Blockchain Solutions	205
	Cognition: Cognitive Insurance	209
	Big Data Analytics	214
	Big Data Analytics Architecture	215
	Applications Areas of Big Data Analytics in Insurance 4.0	216
	Benefits and Challenges of Big Data Analytics	221
	Artificial Intelligence	222
	Artificial Intelligence Architecture	223
	Applications Areas of AI in Insurance 4.0	225

Benefits and Challenges of AI 231
Robots 234
Robots Architecture 234
Application Areas of Robots in Insurance 4.0 235
Robotic Process Automation 236
Benefits and Challenges of Robots 239
Communication 240
Cloud Computing 240
Architecture of Cloud Computing 241
Application Areas of Cloud Computing in Insurance 4.0 242
Augmented Reality 247
Augmented Reality Architecture 247
Application Areas of Augmented Reality in Insurance 4.0 247
Benefits and Challenges of Augmented Reality 248
Cybersecurity 248
Cybersecurity Architecture 250
Application Areas of Cybersecurity in Insurance 4.0 250
Benefits and Challenges of Cybersecurity 251
Insurance 4.0 and Platform Solutions 255
Conclusions 257

9 **Processes in Insurance 4.0** 261
Introduction 261
Basic Insurance Processes 263
Product Development Process 263
Marketing 264
Contracts Life Cycle 266
Smart Contracts 266
Application Areas of CLM in Insurance 4.0 272
Benefits and Challenges of CLM Solutions 279
Cybernetics: Underwriting 4.0 280
Underwriting Activities 280
Underwriting 4.0 282
Information Collection 282
Risk Analysis 284
Risk Assessment 284
Decision 285

Pricing 285
Implementation of the Decision 286
Monitoring of Risks and Lessons Learned 286
Insurance 4.0 and Underwriting 286
Resilience and Insurance 4.0 289
Resilience in Insurance 291
Agility 292
Basic Features of Resilience 294
Resilience Metrics 297
Challenges and Benefits 298
Collaboration: Claim Processing 4.0 299
Insurance 4.0 and Claim Processing 299
Command: Insurance Process Intelligence 300
Insurance Process Intelligence Components 301
Forecasting, Strategy, Planning, and Budgeting 301
Collaboration 303
Execution 304
Monitoring and Spend Analysis (Visibility) 305
Insurance 4.0 and Business Process Intelligence 305
Conclusions 306

10 Persons in Insurance 4.0 309
Introduction 309
New Working Models 312
Old and New Profiles 316
New Competencies for Underwriters 316
Data Scientists 317
Process Architects 318
Technologists 319
Ongoing Support and Maintenance Staff 319
Person Contribution to Insurance 4.0 320
Training 4.0 322
Why 323
What 323
Who 324
When 324
Where 324
How 325
Insurance 4.0 Roadmap 326
Conclusions 327

11	**Partnerships in Insurance 4.0**	329
	Introduction	329
	Insurance 4.0 and Partnerships	332
	Ecosystems	334
	Insurance in Team	342
	Persons and Organization	342
	Processes	343
	Platforms	343
	Security	344
	Partners Evaluation in Insurance 4.0	345
	Big Data	346
	Artificial Intelligence	347
	Mobility	347
	Cloud Computing	347
	Conclusions	347
12	**Pricing in Insurance 4.0**	349
	Introduction	349
	Revenue Streams	350
	Pricing	351
	Risk-Based Pricing	352
	Conclusions	354
13	**Payments for Costs and Investments in Insurance 4.0**	355
	Introduction	355
	Digitize and Lean Insurance	357
	Conclusions	359
14	**Insurance 4.0 and Digital Transformation**	361
	Introduction	361
	Digital Transformation	362
	Digital Transformation in the Literature	364
	The Age of Digitization	367
	Successful Transformation	369
	Challenges and Risks in Digital Transformations	371
	Resilient Solutions	373
	Innovation in the Insurance Processes	375
	Technology Acceptance Model	376

Roadmap for a Digital Transformation 380
Conclusions 385

15 Future of Insurance 4.0 and Insurtech 389
Introduction 389
Scenarios 390
Four Ps of Insurance Management 391
Platforms 391
Processes 395
Persons 396
Partnerships 397
Future Perspectives 398
Insurtech 399
Business Model of Insurtech Organizations 402
Open Insuring Model 405
Development of Insurtech Organizations 407
Threats of the Insurtech Organizations 409
Collaboration Between Insurtech and Incumbents 410
Social Media 418
Regtech Organizations 420
Digital Wholesale Insurance 423
Sustainable Insurance 425
Conclusions 429

16 Conclusions 433

Glossary 441

References 473

Index 521

Abbreviations

3P	Planet, Persons, Profit
ADAS	Advanced Driver Assistance Systems
AGV	Automated Guided Vehicle
AI	Artificial Intelligence
AK	Awareness and Knowledge
AMA	American Marketing Association
AMC	Annual Maintenance Contract
APF	Attitude Towards Innovation
API	Application Programming Interface(s)
AR	Augmented Reality
ASA	Associazione Svizzera d'Assicurazioni
B2B	Business-to-Business
B2C	Business-to-Consumer
B3i	Blockchain Insurance Industry Initiative
BAU	Business as Usual
BC	Behavioral Control and Before Christ
BC	Business Continuity
BCG	Boston Consulting Group
BDAQ	Big Data Analytics Quality
BI	Business Intelligence or Business Interruption
BPaaS	**B**usiness Process as a Service
BPI	Business Process Intelligence (BPI)
BPO	Business Process Outsourcing or Business Process Optimization
CAGR	Compounded Annual Growth Rate
CBR	Case-Based Reasoning
CC	Cognitive Computing

CCPA	California Consumer Privacy Act
CDO	Chief Digital Officer
CISO	Chief Information Security Officer
CLM	Contract Lifecycle Management
CNC	Computer Numerical Control
CPM	Critical Path Method
CPM	Corporate Performance Management or Critical Path Method
CPS	Cyber-Physical System
CRM	Customer Relationship Management
CSP	Content Service Platform
DB	Data Base
DIP	Pre-contractual Information Document
DM	Data Management
DPI	Digital Performance Index
DR	Disaster Recovery
ECM	Enterprise Content Management
EDI	Electronic Data Interchange
EMEA	Europe, Middle East, and Africa
EMS	Small and Medium Enterprises
ERP	Enterprise Resource Planning
ESG	Environmental, Social and Governance
EU	European Union
EVI	Early Partner Involvement
FTE	Full-Time Equivalent
GAFAM	Google, Amazon, Facebook, Apple, and Microsoft
GBP	British Pound Sterling
GDPR	General Data Protection Regulation
HCI	Human–Computer Interaction
HR	Human Resources (Department)
IA	Integrated Analytics or Intelligent Automation
IaaS	Infrastructure as a Service
IBIP	Insurance-based Investment Product
IBNER	Incurred but not enough Reported
ICT	Information and Telecommunication Technology
IIoT	Industrial Internet of Things
ILS	Insurance-Linked Securities
IoE	Internet of Everything
IoP	Internet of Persons
IoS	Internet of Service
IoT	Internet of Things
IP	Internet Protocol
IRDA	Insurance Regulatory and Development Authority
ISO	International Standard Organization

IVASS	Istituto per la Vigilanza sulle Assicurazioni
IVR	Interactive Voice Response
KPI	Key Performance (or Process) Indicators
KYC	Know Your Customer
M&A	Merger and Acquisitions
MNO	Mobile Network Operator
MR	Mixed Reality
MSP	Multi-Sided Platforms
NFC	Near Field Communication
NIST	National Institute of Standards and Technology
NLP	Natural Language Processing
NPS	Net Promoter Score
NQ	Non-Quality
NRMA	National Roads and Motorists' Association
OBD	On-Board Diagnostics
ODA	Operational Data Analytics
OT	Operations Technology
P&C	Property and Casualty
P4	Predictive, Preventative, Personalized, Participatory
PaaS	Platform as a Service
PAYD	Pay-As-You-Drive
PBI	Process Business Intelligence
PCW	Price Comparison Websites
PEF	Perceived Economic Factor
PHYD	Pay-How-You-Drive
POG	Product Oversize Governance
PROU	Perceived Ease of Use
PT	Perceived Trust
PU	Perceived Usefulness
QR	Quick Response Code
R&D	Research and Development
RATER	Reliability, Assurance, Tangibles, Empathy, and Responsiveness
RBNS	Reported but not Settled
RE	Real Estate or Reputation
RFID	Radio-Frequency Identification
ROPO	Research Online, Purchase Offline
RPA	Robotic Process Automation
SaaS	Software as a Service
SARS	Severe Acute Respiratory Syndrome
SIM	Subscriber Identity Module
SLA	Service Level Agreement
SMS	Short Message Service
SN	Shared Nothing

SP	Social Pressures
STP	Straight Through Processing
SWOT	Strengths-Weaknesses-Opportunities-Threats
TAM	Technology Acceptance Model
TCM	Total Cost Management
TQM	Total Quality Management
UAS	Unmanned Aircraft System
UAV	Unmanned Aerial Vehicles
UBI	Usage-Based Insurance
UK	The United Kingdom
ULIP	Unit-linked Insurance Plan
UMTS	Universal Mobile Telecommunications System
US or USA	United States of America
USD	United States Dollar
VCW	Value Comparison Website
VR	Virtual Reality
VUCA	Volatile, Unpredictable, Complex, and Ambiguous
WHO	World Health Organization
XML	Extended Messaging Language

List of Figures

Fig. 1.1	Impact of transformation on insurance	2
Fig. 1.2	Business model canvas	7
Fig. 2.1	Industry 4.0	16
Fig. 2.2	From supply chain to value network	32
Fig. 3.1	Value chain in insurance	43
Fig. 3.2	Traditional business model canvas	46
Fig. 3.3	Business model canvas (9 Ps)	47
Fig. 3.4	Porter's five forces of competitive advantage for insurance	62
Fig. 3.5	Business model for an insurtech organizations (example)	64
Fig. 3.6	Issurance issues	67
Fig. 4.1	From insurance to insuring	80
Fig. 5.1	Modified Chandler-Leavitt model	123
Fig. 5.2	Interaction with the customer in the proximity center (Adapted by the author from Bicheno, J., & Catherwood, P. [2005]. *Six sigma and the quality toolbox* [rev. ed.]. Buckingham: Picsie Books)	126
Fig. 5.3	Example of RATER assessment	132
Fig. 8.1	Insurance platforms transformation	174
Fig. 8.2	Insurance 4.0	175
Fig. 8.3	Lean and digitize	180
Fig. 8.4	Blockchain and insurance processes	204
Fig. 8.5	Cognitive solution	211
Fig. 8.6	Artificial intelligence in insurance	226
Fig. 9.1	Insurance processes	263
Fig. 9.2	Schema for smart contracts	266

Fig. 9.3	Blockchain framework for insurance	270
Fig. 9.4	Smart contracts and insurance 4.0	272
Fig. 9.5	Phases of underwriting	283
Fig. 9.6	Underwriting process	283
Fig. 9.7	Ecosystem coordination	288
Fig. 9.8	Artificial intelligence in underwriting	289
Fig. 9.9	Risk management cycle	290
Fig. 9.10	Basic aspects of resilience	295
Fig. 9.11	Resilience graph	298
Fig. 9.12	Insurance process intelligence	302
Fig. 10.1	New roles in insurance 4.0	316
Fig. 10.2	Management of risk in insurance	319
Fig. 10.3	Customer facing jobs in insurance 4.0	320
Fig. 11.1	Insurance 4.0 ecosystem	335
Fig. 13.1	Lean and digitize	359
Fig. 14.1	Technology acceptance model	378
Fig. 14.2	Innovation types	381
Fig. 14.3	Innovation types in insurance	382
Fig. 14.4	Digital transformation stages (Adapted by the author from https://www.slideshare.net/briansolis/the-six-stages-of-digital-transformation-by-brian-solis)	383
Fig. 15.1	The four Ps	391
Fig. 15.2	Multi-sided platforms	392
Fig. 15.3	Tools for remote working	397
Fig. 15.4	Business Model Canvas for an insurtech organization (example)	404
Fig. 15.5	Four waves of insurtech organizations (Adapted from https://www.digitalinsuranceagenda.com/thought-leadership/the-four-waves-of-insurtech/)	407
Fig. 15.6	Partnership components	417
Fig. 15.7	Social media benefits	419

List of Tables

Table 5.1 Evolution of the call center 124
Table 9.1 Smart contract applications in insurance 4.0 268

CHAPTER 1

Introduction

The global recession and the pandemic hit hard. It has impacted all organizations and functions. Figure 1.1 summarizes some of these challenges. Insurance has almost remained outside of the trend of digital transformations until now.[1] After the pandemic crisis, it is vital to develop and manage innovative strategies also in insurance.

Insurance companies have begun to innovate, create new business models, invest in emerging technologies, and partner with insurtech organizations, either financing or acquiring them.[2] Most of these innovations did not center on the concept of customer-centricity. Companies need to design and offer customers products and services relevant to new and old customers.

Unlike the new insurtech organizations, traditional companies have millions of customers and must build engagement and loyalty to retain and grow their customers. In Italy, in the past, only 14 percent of customers have bought policies online. The use of services such as

[1] Uusitalo, J. (2019). *Strategic insurance in the face of uncertainty*. Master's thesis, University of Jyväskylä, Finland.

[2] Generali. (2018, February 28). *Le assicurazioni "tutto connesso."* www.generali.com/it/info/discovering-generali/all/2018/A-fully-connected-insurance. Accessed 2 November 2019.

B. Nicoletti, *Insurance 4.0*, Palgrave Studies in Financial Services Technology, https://doi.org/10.1007/978-3-030-58426-9_1

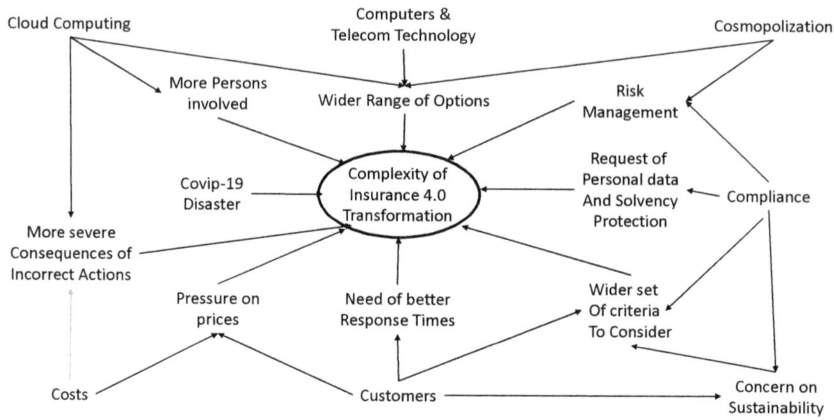

Fig. 1.1 Impact of transformation on insurance

micro-insurance or mobile claims management is only 2 percent.[3] The pandemic will bring a cultural transition to the customers. It is necessary to improve the proposals of insurance services also with the support of digital solutions.

Above all, it is critical to understand who are the insurance customers, and what their needs are, expressed or implicit.[4] Consultants Deloitte developed a survey called: "A demanding future - The four trends that define insurance in 2020." Through interviews with over 200 C-suite insurance managers, Deloitte identified and found some main trends throughout the EMEA area. They are the critical points for the future of insurance industry, or at least, for those companies that aim to continue growing.[5]

Deloitte says that the growth of the business for an insurance company will come from a change of approach. This approach must be transformed from merely protective to preventive and protective, with a range of new

[3] www.insuranceup.it/it/opinioni/deloitte-4-trend-per-le-assicurazioni-nel-2020/. Accessed 25 December 2019.

[4] Parasuraman, A., Berry, L. L., & Zeithaml, V. A. (1991). Understanding customer expectations of service. *Sloan Management Review*, *32*(3), 39–48.

[5] www2.deloitte.com/content/dam/Deloitte/uk/Documents/financial-services/deloitte-uk-insurance-trends-2019.pdf. Accessed 25 December 2019.

services and products, new business models, and more considerable attention to prevention on respect to claim management. Customer needs, knowledge, and expectations have expanded exponentially over the past decade. Companies need to adapt to their customers' needs. In an age of immediacy, continuous changes, and overwhelming choices in which loyalty is no longer a certainty, the sector must extend beyond its main products and services if it wants to maintain its customer base. It must substantially innovate and change its approach.

In a highly competitive environment, current companies can no longer rely on organic growth or internal innovation. As a result, mergers and acquisitions, equity partnerships, and collaborations are essential. The winners are the companies able to launch and grow an ecosystem, also with alliances with innovative startups, teaming up with insurtech organizations, and consolidating with their competitors. Merger & Acquisitions (M&A) activity will focus on key markets and products. Access and use technologies that allow improvements within the sector will come, also through acquisitions or partnerships. These potential opportunities require a holistic view of innovation. It would include distribution, new products, underwriting capacity, or improvements in the claim settlement process. The ability to integrate the assets acquired will be fundamental to determine the success of this strategy.

The winners should invest in innovative platforms. They should rethink and revise their business model. A rapidly changing market and evolving industry will require an unprecedented ability to do business. Technological changes are essential. They are not enough. Knowing these changes and using them in the best way are very different things. Companies should use solutions such as analytics, blockchain, artificial intelligence, internet of things, and cloud computing to their benefit. Insurance companies must be able to use the right technology for the right purpose and in the right combination with a revision of their entire business model, and mainly of their processes.

Insurance companies are pure service providers that are highly data-founded. Digitization can influence companies.[6] Already, large parts of the insurance industry are robustly affected by digitization. In particular, the distribution is becoming heavily digitized. Digitization will also strengthen other parts of the value network of the insurance industry.

[6] Prognos, A. G. (2017). *Digitalisierung in der Versicherungswirtschaft*. Studie. Hg. v. vbw Vereinigung der Bayerischen Wirtschaft e.V. München, Germany.

The digital change in various areas of the insurance value network should be systematically applied, taking into account several theses.[7] The three main business areas to grow in the post-pandemic area seem to be: liability insurance, vehicle insurance, and private health insurance.

A broader "fourth industrial revolution" based on technologies, such as cloud computing, telematics, the internet of things (IoT), mobile phones, blockchain solution, artificial intelligence/cognitive computing, and predictive modeling, affects the entire insurance business model. These new solutions enable new ways of communicating, information sharing, and ensuring.[8] It is crucial to understand how new digital solutions can help overcome the so-called information asymmetry.[9] So far, as a rule, the policyholder can better assess his/her risks than the respective insurance companies. Thanks to automatic detection features (e.g., motion profiles for health insurance or the driving behavior in motor insurance), insurance companies can evaluate the individual risks and take them into account in pricing insurance. The information asymmetry could potentially reverse in favor of insurance companies. As a result, there would be more customized rates: Good risks could be cheaper. Bad risks will get more expensive or simply not insured.

Digitization will change the profit and loss account of the companies in two ways:

- lower costs;
- additional revenues through new business models.

Digitization can impact on pricing and competition. The real question is whether the digitization-driven changes in distribution channels, competition, and so on, maybe allowed under new regulations. The compliance framework should not restrict competition. Instead, the customer and data protection should be at the center of considerations.

There is a need for a new vision of insurance. This vision is called insurance 4.0 in this book. New solutions have generated researchers' interest

[7] Prognos, A. G. (2017). *Digitalisierung in der Versicherungswirtschaft*. Studie. Hg. v. vbw Vereinigung der Bayerischen Wirtschaft e.V. München, Germany.

[8] Schmidt, C. 2018. *Insurance in the Digital Age*. The Geneva Association. Zurich. Switzerland, 1–20.

[9] Blomqvist, Å. (1991). The doctor as a double agent: Information asymmetry, health insurance, and medical care. *Journal of Health Economics, 10*(4), 411–432.

in very different fields: computer and management science, organization theory, law, and economics. An integrated vision is missing. This book shows why and how insurance 4.0 can change in an integrated way the insurance industry. Insurance 4.0 is potentially the engine and starting point of the changes the customers increasingly want and ask for digital services and solution models.

According to Deloitte, companies are too optimistic about the insurance industry's progress in adopting and using technologies. As a matter of fact, I, insurance companies are lagging behind many other sectors. Companies are not fully aware of the large-scale technological disruption that is about to fall upon them. This disruption might be generated by technology giants who are already entering other highly regulated spaces, such as banking. They have an unprecedented capacity for analyzing customer data and information. This capacity allows them to create easy-to-understand, flexible, and customer-centric insurance models.

Insurance 4.0 requires a change in the relationship with the customers. The insurance company uses digital solutions to automate processes and offer services via various channels to reduce costs and prices of services and meet the changing needs of customers. It is critical to transforming insurance companies through process improvement and automation management. To analyze how to do this, a vital entry point is insurance 4.0. Insurance 4.0 is not only a component of the initiative industry 4.0.[10] It is much more. It is a new original vision of insurance that makes it more agile, integrated, responsive to the customers, while adding a value to the organization. Insurance 4.0 represents the set of solutions that can support managers at all stages of the insurance processes. Insurance 4.0 refers to an organization that uses the fundamental principles of adaptive systems and complexity science to achieve success.

This book explores the problems and solutions in how insurance can add more value to the customers, how it can manage relationships, improve processes, and better manage resources, both internally or of

[10] Lasi, H., Fettke, P., Kemper, H. G., Feld, T., & Hoffmann, M. (2014). Industry 4.0. *Business & Information Systems Engineering*, *6*(4), 239–242.

the partners.[11] For analyzing these challenges, this book uses the business model canvas framework.[12] This framework is a powerful tool for the analysis of organizations and helps in modeling their strategies.

One of the principal objectives of the insurance 4.0 initiative is to implement agility. Agility is nowadays a much-used term in the management of organizations.[13] This development is essential. Agile management derives from lean management: a mantra of recent years. The need to be lean is not the goal that organizations must pursue. It is the way to be more agile and flexible. In other words, agility is the objective, while lean is a possible means to reach the goal.

The need for agility is a consequence of the turbulence of the current environment. Agility requires organizations that respond quickly to changes by adapting their configuration. Organizations can achieve agility by maintaining and modifying processes, products, and services to meet customers' needs. This objective is achieved by changing or at least improving, the business models. It requires to use in the best way the available resources within the ecosystem in which the organizations operate. Thanks to the agility, an organization can quickly adapt to the environment and market changes in effective, efficient, and economical ways.

Insurance 4.0 can provide support to the digital transformation of the organization. It aims to turn change into a habit of the organization's life. It has the objective to reduce or eliminate the organizational trauma that paralyzes many organizations that try to adapt to new markets, environments, technology, and solutions. Changes in the environment are perpetual. Insurance 4.0 can adjust and take advantage of emerging opportunities easily.

[11] This book uses the terms vendor or intermediary. It is replaced most of the times with "partners" as if the relationship fails, both the customer and the vendor/intermediary are damaged.

[12] Osterwalder, A., Pigneur, Y., Oliveira, M. A. Y., & Ferreira, J. J. P. (2011). Business model generation: A handbook for visionaries, game changers, and challengers. *African Journal of Business Management*, 5(7), 22–30.

[13] Nicoletti, B. (2017). *Agile insurance. Volume II: Designing and implementing a digital transformation*. London, UK: Springer International Publishing. ISBN 978-3-319-61085-6.

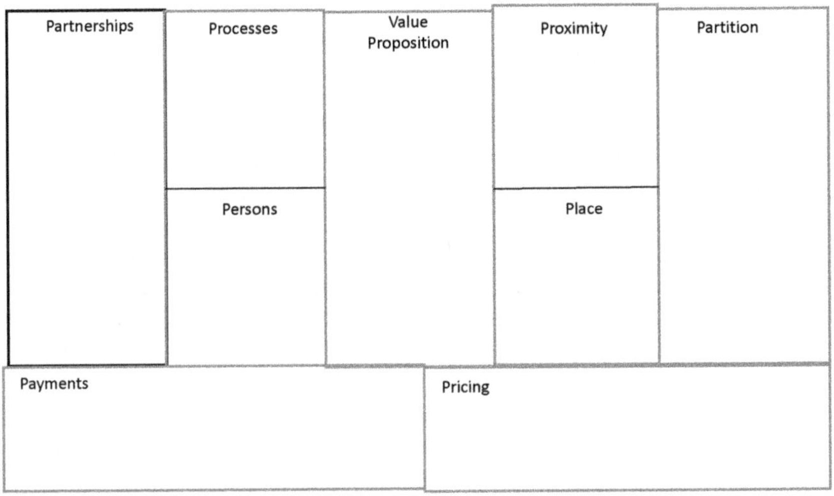

Fig. 1.2 Business model canvas

This book delves into these methods and techniques, treating the field of insurance 4.0 as an agile business model, involving all its components.[14] The organizations' transformation must cover all the components in the business model canvas, which this book indicates as the ten Ps (Fig. 1.2):

- Proposition of value;
- customer Proximity;
- market Partitions;
- Processes;
- Place or channels;
- resources and Platforms;
- Persons;
- Partnerships;

[14] Nicoletti, B. (2017). *Agile insurance. Volume II: Designing and implementing a digital transformation*. London, UK: Springer International Publishing. ISBN 978-3-319-61085-6. Nicoletti, B. (2017). *Agile insurance. Volume I: Adding value with lean processes*. London, UK: Springer International Publishing. ISBN 978-3-319-61082-5.

- Pricing and revenues;
- Payments for costs and investments.

The chapters of this book follow precisely the sequence of these ten Ps. The final part of the book includes how to manage the digital transformation of insurance 4.0 and a discussion on the future of insurance 4.0.

This book's thesis is that the function, discipline, and activity of insurance 4.0 can change insurance companies to support organizational efficiency, effectiveness, and economics within a long-term and sustainable perspective. The book reports several references to real organizations in very different areas to support this thesis.

This introduction analyzes the significance, development, and application of insurance 4.0, with particular regard to the digital transformation of insurance.

The Chapter 2 defines the goal of this book on insurance 4.0 and its relationships with industry 4.0. It also presents a model of the critical success factors of insurance 4.0.

The Chapter 3 aims to define the organization's business model concept since it is one of the main factors at the base of insurance 4.0. It also introduces the general framework of the business model canvas model used in the remaining part of this book. The chapter begins with an introduction to the insurance that is useful for those unfamiliar with this world.

The Chapter 4 deals with the proposition of value for the customer through insurance 4.0. It underlines the products and services provided or potentially offered by insurance companies within the framework of insurance 4.0.

The Chapter 5 deals with customer proximity. It underlines the importance of communication with the customer and building their user experience and journey. It examines in detail customer relationships applications and centers.

The Chapter 6 underlines the partition or segmentation of the market and how to choose the customers' target and how to satisfy them.

The Chapter 7 deals with distribution. It underlines the characteristics of the digital distribution typical of insurance 4.0. Digital distribution is the evolution of traditional distribution channels. Digital evolution is something that has an impact on different aspects of customers' lives and organizations. The latter needs to adapt to the new and increasingly demanding needs of customers (such as e-commerce).

The Chapter 8 deals with digital platforms. It examines in detail the technological innovations. The final part of this chapter deals with cyber-security and the privacy aspects in their double role of challenges and opportunities.

The Chapter 9 deals with the processes, with particular attention to the underwriting phase and the management of risks and contract management. It underlines the importance of resilience for the asset insured and an integrated approach to business re-engineering called insurance process intelligence.

The Chapter 10 deals with persons. It goes into the details of the new e-competencies and on the need for training 4.0.

The Chapter 11 deals with partnerships and examines the particular aspect of insurance ecosystems, whose importance is growing.

The Chapter 12 deals with the revenues and underlines the support to manage and innovate pricing in insurance 4.0.

The Chapter 13 deals with costs and investments. It underlines the importance of a lean and digitizes method for improvement.

The Chapter 14 deals with digital transformation. This chapter includes an introduction and a general picture of the management of a project for transformation to insurance 4.0.

The following chapter explores the future of insurance 4.0 and, in particular, underlines the characteristics and the perspective of the insurtech model.

The last chapter concludes and opens to future research on the subject.

The 2020 pandemic is pushing, even more, to embark on the digital transformation of the companies and become more agile, responsive, and connected enterprises. One legacy of the coronavirus crisis could be that it pushes more companies to move to insurance 4.0.

CHAPTER 2

Industry 4.0 and Insurance 4.0

Introduction

A saying attributed to Darwin argues that[1]:

> *It is not the strongest species or the most intelligent which survived, but one that is best suited to change.*

This statement also applies to organizations. They need to renew. Otherwise, the organizations would suffer or simply disappear. This chapter examines innovation in insurance. This book calls such innovation insurance 4.0.

Industry 4.0 is the convergence of information and communication technology (ICT) and automation of work and infrastructure. The term refers to a fourth industrial revolution. Its characteristics are advanced digitization within the organizations, based on the integration of ICT solutions with operational technologies (OT)[2] in intelligent objects (systems, processes, and products). This integration enables and transforms industrial production systems and services with products that can

[1] Huxley, T. H. (2018). *The darwinian hypothesis*. Bellevue, WA: Amazon Digital Press LLC.

[2] Piggin, R. (2014). Industrial systems: Cyber-security's new battlefront [Information Technology Operational Technology]. *Engineering & Technology, 9*(8), 70–74.

B. Nicoletti, *Insurance 4.0*, Palgrave Studies in Financial Services Technology, https://doi.org/10.1007/978-3-030-58426-9_2

control their production process independently. Besides the focus on digitization and automation, industry 4.0 provides support to technology innovations whose effects enable organizations to create new products, processes, modes of production, and business models.

Innovation is necessary to face new challenges for organizations. It is also essential to substantially improve the effectiveness, efficiency, and economics of the industries and to meet the growing needs of adding value and providing delight to their customers by each function in the organization. There is a need to improve relations and integration with the entire organization but also with its partners. If the partners are not satisfied, the organization cannot create a sustainable partnership in an extended value network perspective.

This book stresses the move from a supply chain or a value chain to a value network and uses the latter term throughout the book.[3] The value for the customers and the organizations is obtained by an ecosystem combining in a network organization, partners, customers, and regulators.

The innovation goals can be summarized in three aspects[4]:

3. Maximum utilization of the potential of new solutions

- Innovating by using new solutions such as cloud computing, the internet of things, mobile, artificial intelligence, and big data analytics, in all operations and channels;
- Standardizing wherever possible;

[3] The term value network has been used with a different meaning. Stabell and Fieldstad (Stabell, C. B., & Fjeldstad, Ø. D. [1998] proposed it. Configuring value for competitive advantage: On chains, shops, and networks. *Strategic Management Journal, 19*(5), 413–437). It is based on mediation technologies according to Thompson's typology (Thompson, J. D. [2017]. *Organizations in action: Social science bases of administrative theory*. London, UK: Routledge). It connects customers and customers who are interested in creating mutual relations and interdependence. The mediating technologies support relations between actors scattered over time and space. This model is similar to what has been called the platform approach (Zhu, F., & Iansiti, M. [2007]. *Dynamics of platform competition: Exploring the role of installed base, platform quality and consumer expectations*. Cambridge, MA: Division of Research, Harvard Business School).

[4] Hammer, M., & Champy, J. (2009). *Reengineering the corporation: Manifesto for business revolution, A*. Grand Rapids, MI: Zondervan.

2. Savings in the organization's resources

- Creating centers of excellence in the organization where it makes sense;
- Optimizing relationship with the partners;
- Automating and outsourcing, where the benefits/cost ratio is more significant.

1. Smarter partnership (fewer transactions and more value in each of them). This situation involves:

- Focusing on areas which contribute more to adding value to the customers and the organization;
- Consolidating partners and relate with them in an ecosystem vision;
- Outsourcing or automating the administrative parts of the functions and focusing on high value-added activities.

The move in these directions requires to push on better governance of the insurance processes and to define an innovation plan to:

- Reflect better priorities of the organization;
- Be more integrated and accessible to the customers and the entire ecosystem;
- Create efficiencies, increase revenues, and achieve savings for the organization.

Industry 4.0

The term industry 4.0 was published for the first time in 2011 when an association of representatives from industry, politics, and academia promoted the idea as an approach to improve the German manufacturing competitiveness.[5] The German government supported the idea,

[5] Schwab, K. (2017). *The fourth industrial revolution*. Currency: London, UK.

announcing that industry 4.0 was an integral part of its initiative "High-Tech Strategy 2020 for Germany."[6] A working group industry 4.0 developed the first recommendations for the implementation of industry 4.0, published in April 2013.[7] Industry 4.0 is the incorporation and management of intelligent products in an organization's processes, management, and information/digital. These processes in industry 4.0 interact with each other and across geographies and organizations.[8]

Industry 4.0 facilitates the vision of the future: the so-called "smart factory" or, in the case of insurance, "smart insurance." It requires and assists agile and effective organizations.

Industry 4.0 provides support to two essential developments. On the one hand, an action must be "pulled" by the customer that induces a change in operating conditions and the model. This aspect leads not only to changes in the organization but also to social, economic, and political changes. The most relevant changes are:

- Industry 4.0 pushes the entire organization for innovation. A high capacity for change is a critical success factor. This trend leads to an increasing customization of products. The ultimate goal is a "batch one" production;
- Because of market-changing characteristics, agility is essential in all the operations of an organization, to allow flexibility and capacity to be adaptive;
- Faster decision-making procedures are needed to meet the new requirements of the business model. The organizational structure must be as flat as possible;
- There is a boost in the organization's economic and ecological efficiency and social awareness for sustainability issues.

[6] Hermann, M., Pentek, T., & Otto, B. (2016, January). Design principles for industries 4.0 scenarios. In *2016 49th Hawaii International Conference on System Sciences (HICSS)* (pp. 3928–3937). IEEE.

[7] Hermann, M., Pentek, T., & Otto, B. (2016, January). Design principles for industries 4.0 scenarios. In *2016 49th Hawaii International Conference on System Sciences (HICSS)* (pp. 3928–3937). IEEE.

[8] Härting, R. C., Schmidt, R., Möhring, M., Reichstein, C., Neumaier, P., & Jozinovic, P. (2015). *Nutzenpotenziale von Industries 4.0: Einblicke Aktuelle Studienergebnisse*. Norderstedt, Germany: BOD-Books.on-Demand.

On the other hand, there is a push on new solutions based, for example, on mobility, tablets, mobile computers, advanced computers, automation applications, and so on. There is an increasing acceleration in their use. In industrial practice, these innovative solutions are still not yet widely used. These innovations allow to:

- Reduce the labor-intensive processes and allow the adoption of more automated solutions. Examples are increasing in process automation based on automated agents;
- Support mew solutions, such as simulation, artificial intelligence, digital security, or virtual reality, helping the increasing digitization of all sales and production, and the availability of advanced tools to support the organizations. Similarly, there is a more extensive network of technical and integrated components. The software allows organizations to collect and analyze data from the sensors or the tags attached to the assets;
- Monitor, manage, and maintain the items everywhere, including at the customer site.[9]

In short, the term industry 4.0 describes the integration of technology, information and communication technologies (ICT), and automation, in support of the changes in the sales and operational systems and consequently in all the processes. These developments have technology, process, organizational, and work implications.[10]

In a survey on the development, applications, and challenges of industry, 4.0, 235 German companies were involved. They worked in manufacturing, engineering, motor, electronics, information, and communication.[11] The survey shows that the companies planned to invest an average of 3.3 percent of their revenues in industry 4.0 by 2020. These investments refer to the critical areas in the value network: product development, planning, production, services, and distribution. The digitization

[9] Nicoletti, B. (2009). Sintesi Seminario RFID per l'Impiantistica. *L'Impiantistica Italiana, 6*(November–December), 1–7.

[10] Lasi, H., Fettke, P., Kemper, H. G., Feld, T., & Hoffmann, M. (2014). Industry 4.0. *Business & Information Systems Engineering, 6*(4), 239.

[11] Geissbauer, R., Schrauf, S., Koch, V., & Kuge, S. (2014). *Industry 4.0—Opportunities and challenges of the industrial internet*. PwCIL, Germany. www.pwc.de/industry4.0. Accessed 20 July 2019.

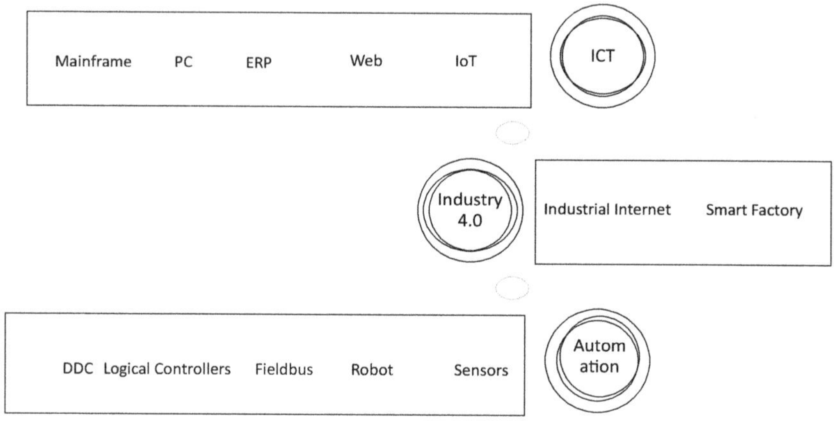

Fig. 2.1 Industry 4.0

of 80 percent of the value network should take place in the next few years, the productivity increased by 18 percent, and about 110 billion euros of revenue generated per annum.[12]

Figure 2.1 shows the industry 4.0 environment as a synthesis between ICT and automation. The following sections focus on how insurance 4.0 can provide support. Internet of things, cognitive technologies, and big data analytics are key drivers for the transformation of organizations to industry 4.0. They can increase profitability and competitiveness on a new level. Within value network ecosystems, the flow of information and data is a critical factor for organizational success or failure.[13] Deloitte, in its CPO Survey 2017, found that 50 percent of 480 respondents did not see short-term applications for automation and robotics (artificial intelligence, machine learning, chatbots, and so on) due to their concern

[12] Geissbauer, R., Schrauf, S., Koch, V., & Kuge, S. (2014). *Industry 4.0—Opportunities and challenges of the industrial internet*. PwCIL, Germany. www.pwc.de/industry4.0. Accessed 20 July 2019.

[13] Bucy, M., Hall, S., & Yakola, D. (2016). *Transformation with a capital T*. www.mckinsey.com/business-functions/mckinsey-recovery-and-transformation-services/our-insights/transformation-with-a-capital-t. Accessed 30 May 2020. Zhong, R. Y., Neman, S. T., Huag, G. Q., & Lan, S. (2016). Big data for supply chain management in the service and manufacturing sectors: Challenges, opportunities, and future perspectives. *Computers & Industrial Engineering, 101*(2016), 572–591.

on benefits introduced by these new solutions. However, in 2025, that percentage is expected to become only 7 percent.[14]

The Italian market for the industry 4.0 in 2018 stood at 3.2 billion euros, recording a 35 percent growth compared to 2017.[15] It was driven by the results of the investments made in 2017 (and invoiced in 2018). This increase benefitted of the grants of the National Industry 4.0 Plan. In a few years, the number of organizations moving to industry 4.0 solution grew by 140 percent. Seven hundred million euros go to "traditional" digital innovation projects (about 300 million euros more than the previous year). Industrial IoT, industrial analytics, and cloud manufacturing make up 85 percent of these figures. Eight hundred applications 4.0 were surveyed in Italy, on average, 4 per organization. The consolidated projects have brought flexibility and lower costs. The most comprehensive 4.0 technologies are ICT, in particular, the industrial IoT (the components for connecting machinery to the network), which, with a value of 1.9 billion euros in 2018, represents 60 percent of the market and records the most significant growth (+40 percent). They are followed by industrial analytics with 530 million euros (17 percent of the market, + 30 percent) and cloud manufacturing with 270 million euros (8 percent, +35 percent). Among the operational technologies, advanced automation gets the largest market share with 160 million euros and a growth of 10 percent, followed by additive manufacturing with 70 million euros. The advanced person-machine interface marks the most robust growth (+50 percent, 45 million euros). The last part of the market consists of consultancy and training activities related to industry 4.0 projects, estimated in 220 million euros (+10 percent). This figure is lower than expected. It shows that there is still much to do in competencies improvement awareness.

[14] www2.deloitte.com/bn/en/pages/operations/articles/cpo-survey-2017.html. Accessed 28 April 2019.

[15] www.corrierecomunicazioni.it/industria-4-0/rallenta-la-corsa-di-industria-4-0-nel-2019-crescita-in-calo-del-10-15/. Accessed 22 June 2019.

Main Components

Industry 4.0 includes a set of solutions enabling intelligent products and processes integrated with digital and physical components. It is changing products, processes, business models, organizations, and systems significantly.[16]

It is possible to define a model for industry 4.0.[17] It consists of several components. This book lists them for mnemonics reasons with words starting with "C":

The model classifies the industry 4.0 components in hard and soft. Hard components are based on the infrastructure. The soft components are more based on the software. For each of them, it is possible to show a solution capable of supporting its implementation within an industry 4.0 initiative. All these components require strict management tools (or Command to continue with words starting with C). In turn, specific solutions support them.

Soft

- Collaboration refers to the need to have all the machines, robots, and operators working together. Applications such as enterprise resource planning (ERP) are useful to provide support as automated as possible to all the management and operational processes.
- Controllership refers to the control processes and machines. They are essential to make them as much as possible independent from the need for human operators. Halfway between cybernetics and control, there are robots and autonomous driving vehicles. These advanced automated devices are critical to industry 4.0.
- Cybernetics refers to the use of computers, whether they are in a data center or distributed. The cyber-physical system (CPS) is a term that describes the unification of the digital world with the real (physical) flows in the processes.[18] The physical stages are accompanied by

[16] Schmidt, R., Möhring, M., Härting, R. C., Reichstein, C., Neumaier, P., & Jozinović, P. (2015). Industry 4.0-potentials for creating smart products: Empirical research results. In *The International Conference on Business Information Systems* (pp. 16–27). Springer, Cham, Switzerland.

[17] Nicoletti, B. (2017). *Agile procurement. Volume I: Adding value with lean processes.* London, UK: Springer International Publishing. ISBN 978-3-319-61082-5.

[18] Lee, J., Bagheri, B., & Kao, H. A. (2015). A cyber-physical systems architecture for industry 4.0-based manufacturing systems. *Manufacturing Letters, 3,* 18–23.

processes based on computers, using the concepts of digital twin,[19] ubiquitous computing,[20] and pervasive computing.[21] Robots and artificial intelligence systems are increasingly used in organizations. The cyber-physical system (CPS) includes automatic sensors and actuators used to collect and send data.

Hard

- Connection is essential to provide an integration of all activities. The internet of things, or rather the internet of everything, allows human operators, and even customers, to be part of the elements connected in the organization.[22] The internet of things (IoT) is the solution in the CPS that enables communication with other objects. IoT makes possible creating networks that incorporate the entire processes. Thus, it makes possible both horizontal and vertical integrations. The horizontal integration refers to the combination of ICT applications in the phases of the organization planning and operational processes, such as marketing, sales, operations, claims management, and between the various organizations in the ecosystem (value networks).[23] Industry 4.0 pushes on communication and cooperation with the distribution network, internal organization, and the partners and customers (output services). Vertical integration refers to the combination of different hierarchical levels, such as the planning organization, marketing management, operations management, quality control, and so on.
- Communication refers to the need to connect the computing devices and all machines in a local area network (LAN) or a wide area network (WAN), usually using the internet;

[19] Schleich, B., Anwer, N., Mathieu, L., & Wartzack, S. (2017). Shaping the digital twin for design and production engineering. *CIRP Annals, 66*(1), 141–144.

[20] Lyytinen, K., & Yoo, Y. (2002). Ubiquitous computing. *Communications of the ACM, 45*(12), 63–96.

[21] Saha, D., & Mukherjee, A. (2003). Pervasive computing: A paradigm for the 21st century. *Computer, 36*(3), 25–31.

[22] Ashton, K. (2009). That 'internet of things' thing. *RFID Journal, 22*(7), 97–114.

[23] Group, R. F. (2013). Acatech.mmendations-to-implement-the-strategic-initiative-Industrie-40-final-report-of-the-industr.html. Accessed 30 May 2020.

- Cognition means the intelligent use of data. All information systems, sensors, and numerical controls (all thanks to the integration connection tools) generate huge numbers of data, referred to as big data. These data should be analyzed. Big data analytics is essential in industry 4.0.[24] Data analytics, data mining, and distribution of big data are a critical support for big data analytics. They have the 9 V's characteristics: (Veracity, Variety, Velocity, Volume, Validity, Variability, Volatility, Visualization, and Value) needed to process the data from the CPS and add value to the organization.[25] The software to manage this data is essential for the implementation of appropriate computing system applications. It is also vital to assess data quality and governance, as also required by regulators. For this purpose, it is possible to use big data analytics quality (BDAQ) model. BDAQ is a hierarchical, multi-dimensional, and context-specific model.[26] Perceived technology, talents, and information quality are significant determinants of BDAQ and company performance.[27]
- Coordination is another essential additional component to ensure the governance (or Command) of the systems, machines, and processes. Proper design, management, and operation of all components included in the system can ensure coordination.

The model should also include two other components:

[24] Chiang, R. H., Grover, V., Liang, T. P., & Zhang, D. (2018). Strategic value of big data and business analytics. *Journal of Management Information Systems, 35*(2), 383–387. https://doi.org/10.1080//07421222.2018.1451950.

[25] Owais, S. S., & Hussein, N. S. (2016). Extract five categories CPIVW from the 9 V's characteristics of the big data. *International Journal of Advanced Computer Science and Applications, 7*(3), 254–258.

[26] Wamba, S. F., Akter, S., & De Bourmont, M. (2019). Quality dominant logic in big data analytics and firm performance. *Business Process Management Journal*. Quality dominant logic in big data analytics and firm. www.emerald.com/insight/content/doi/10.1108/BPMJ-08-2017-0218/full/html. Accessed 30 May 2020.

[27] Fosso Wamba, S., Akter, S., & De Bourmont, M. (2018). Quality dominant logic in big data analytics and company performance. *Business Process Management Journal*.

- Condivision, or sharing of data and documents, is vital to support industry 4.0. There are traditional and advanced tools to ensure such sharing. They are useful not only within the internal organization but also externally to connect with partners, intermediaries, and customers. The internet of services (IoS) enables partners to offer their services via the internet. It consists of participants, infrastructure services, business models, and the services themselves[28];
- Confidence or trust must be the cornerstone of the industry 4.0 solutions. The basis of trust is a stringent security policy. Cyber attacks would be extremely dangerous for a system based primarily on non-human agents, highly integrated components, and fragile units.

Significant Challenges

A characteristic of industry 4.0 is the increasing digitization and networking of products, processes, organization models, and value networks. It requires significant investments.

Price Waterhouse Coopers' Strategy & in 2015 surveyed 235 German industries and processes.[29] The respondents expected that industry 4.0 would lead to a significant transformation of their organizations. They estimated that the share of investments in industry 4.0 initiatives would represent more than 50 percent of their planned capital investments for the following five years. The survey also covered the challenges of industry 4.0. The first and foremost challenge is the funding of the investments required to deploy its solutions.[30] Other challenges are the unclear business case for new internet and industrial applications. Industry 4.0 pushes on communication and cooperation with the distribution network, internal organization, and the partners and customers (output services). The organizations must define the rules and standards for the industry 4.0 implementation. The challenges in ICT security should be addressed and

[28] Schroth, C., & Janner, T. (2007). Web 2.0 and SOA: Converging concepts enabling the internet of services. *IT Professional, 9*(3), 36–41.

[29] www.strategyand.pwc.com/cds. Accessed 30 May 2020.

[30] Koch, V., Geissbauer, R., Kuge, S., & Schrauf, S. (2014). *Industry 4.0: Opportunities and challenges of the internet industry*. www.strategyand.pwc.com/media/file/Industria-4-0.pdf. Accessed 30 May 2020.

resolved. There is a need that research centers, organizations, unions, and associations cooperate to support the expansion of the industry 4.0.[31]

Industry 4.0 requires integration with other organizations of their information systems, such as intermediaries.[32] All partners must have access to the data and be able to process them to support decision making. Linked data offers a solution in this respect.[33] Linked data is a method that allows to aggregate and collects data from distributed sources. To make this data accessible in the web,[34] the data must be published under the condition of "open" use for a specific category of users. This publishing allows the organizations to browse and navigate the data by any media, through deep linking,[35] and possibly aggregate them. Linked data is now a mature solution with great potential. It requires large numbers of data linked together. Linked data can provide a powerful representation of the investigation also into the insurance activities, in relationships (links).[36]

Insurance 4.0

The concept of insurance comes from the mutuality idea, sophisticated and elementary at the same time, to manage the uncertainty of the future, protecting from risks even remote but potential, and sharing the

[31] Zhong, R. Y., Xu, X., Klotz, E., & Newman, S. T. (2017). Intelligent manufacturing in the context of industry 4.0: A review. *Engineering, 3*(5), 616–630.

[32] Nicoletti, B. (2019). Digital transformation via open data in insurance. In A. L. Mention (Eds.), *Digital innovation harnessing the value of open data*. World Scientific, Singapore.

[33] Data, L. (2014). *Connect data distributed across the web*. http://linkeddata.org. Accessed 29 May 2020.

[34] Tomassetti, F., Rizzo G., Glass, A., Hardy, L., Torchiano, M., & Morisio, M. (2011). Linked data approach to the automation of the selection processes in systematic reviews. In *The Assessment and Evaluation in Software Engineering (EASE 2011), 15th Annual Conference. EIT* (pp. 31–35).

[35] The term deep linking in the context of the web is the use of hyperlinks linking to a specific, generally searchable or indexed, piece of web content into a website (e.g., "example.com/path/page"), rather than the website's home page (e.g., example.com. Accessed 20 May 2020).

[36] Bizer, C., Heath, T., & Berners-Lee, T. (2011). Linked data: The story so far. In *Semantic services, interoperability and web applications: Emerging concepts* (pp. 205–227). Hershey, PA: IGI Global.

costs between subjects with the same need.[37] Solidarity is at the basis of insurance. It has very positive aspects for the society.[38]

Insurance World

Insurance is the contract where the insurer receives a premium. It is then obligated to reimburse the policyholder, within the agreed limits, of the damage produced by a casualty, or to pay capital or a pension at the occurrence of an event related to life. In other terms, the contractor acquires a policy from an insurance organization through the execution of a contract. The contractor may coincide or not with the policyholder/beneficiary and, to receive the benefits of the insurance purchased, she/he must correspond, with a specific frequency, an insurance premium. Depending on the type of policy purchased, the contractor may benefit from different ceilings.

The insurance industry's basic principles are the need to ensure economic stability. There is a trustee relationship between policyholder and insurer, based on transparency. The process is that the customer pays a premium. If the accident is assured, the insurer must reimburse the damages covered by the contract.

There are many types of insurance products and services.[39] The main types of insurance are[40]:

- Property & Casualty (P&C) insurance contracts are carried out and conclude the occurrence of an event related to an event or an asset, physical or not, for example, a vehicle. The insurer is obligated to pay the policyholder a capital equivalent to the damage connected with a claim, normally up to a ceiling. These insurance contracts work on the indemnity principle, according to which compensation cannot anyway exceed in value the suffered damage;

[37] www.generali.com/it/what-we-do/what-is-insurance. Accessed 30 May 2020.

[38] Lehtonen, T. K., & Liukko, J. (2011). The forms and limits of insurance solidarity. *Journal of Business Ethics, 103*(1), 33–44.

[39] en.wikipedia.org/wiki/Category:Types_of_insurance. Accessed 30 May 2020.

[40] Adamo, S., & Di Cagno, N. (1994). *L'economia delle aziende di assicurazione: amministrazione e controllo*. Torino, Italy: Giappichelli.

- Life insurance contracts go on and conclude at the occurrence of an event related to life. The capital or guaranteed income depends on the agreement between the two parties.

There are also some compulsory insurance contracts:

- On motor vehicles;
- On boats;
- For races and competitions with motor vehicles.

Finally, it is critical to mention the regulation of the insurance industry. What happens in Italy is representative of many countries. IVASS, the Italian Institute for Insurance Supervision, is a body-endowed legal personality of public law that operates to ensure the adequate protection of policyholders by pursuing the healthy and prudent management of insurance and reinsurance organizations transparency and fairness to customers.[41] The Institute also pursues the stability of the system and the financial markets. To ensure the impartial exercise of its functions, the Institute has organizational, economic, and accounting autonomy. It acts based on the principles of transparency and economy. The Institute communicates its activity to the government, congress, and citizens through the dissemination of data and information on the institutional activity and its use of resources.

The need for insurance was born a long time ago. In prehistoric times, the man created food reserves to cope with the winter. Subsequently, with the introduction of the currency, the simple saving of money was not sufficient to cope with possible risky events. The insurance market was born thus, influenced by personal and social changes. The insurance market has undergone changes marked by the advent of new technologies that have revolutionized the world: from communication and transport to medicine and information systems. The insurance market is always constantly changing. It depends on the development of the other markets

[41] www.ivass.it/chi-siamo/index.html. Accessed 30 May 2020.

and the birth of new ones. An example in this direction is the cybersecurity insurance, which was born out of the development of information technology.[42]

Insurance organizations have continuously transformed over time. It is possible to divide the macro changes into four main periods. The periods correspond to the four industrial revolutions.[43] Changes after each revolution have been substantial and have also led to economic and social changes. In between subsequent disruptive changes, there has been a continuous improvement. The following pages detail these four waves of innovation in the industrial sectors and the insurance (called in this book as insurance 1.0, 2.0, 3.0, and 4.0).[44]

First Industrial Revolution. Insurance 1.0

Insurance was born several centuries before Christ (BC). Methods for transferring or distributing risks were practiced by Chinese and Babylonian traders as long ago as the 3rd and 2nd millennia BC, respectively.[45] Chinese merchants traveling dangerous river rapids distributed their wares across many vessels to limit the loss of any vessel's capsizing. The Babylonians developed a system recorded in the Code of Hammurabi, around 1750 BC, and practiced by early Mediterranean sailing merchants. If a merchant received a loan to fund his/her shipment, she/he would pay the lender an additional sum in exchange for the lender's guarantee to cancel the loan should the shipment be stolen, or lost at sea.

Circa 800 BC, the inhabitants of Rhodes created the "general average." This mechanism allowed groups of merchants to pay to ensure their goods shipped together. The collected premiums were necessary to reimburse any merchant whose products were lost during transport, whether due to storm or sinking.[46]

[42] Garrie, D., & Mann, M. (2014). Cyber-security insurance: Navigating the landscape of a growing field, 31. *The John Marshall Journal of Information Technology and Privacy Law, l*, 379.

[43] Schwab, K. (2017). *The fourth industrial revolution*. London, UK: Currency.

[44] Domingo Galindo, L. (2016). *The challenges of logistics 4.0 for the supply chain management and information technology*. Master Thesis, NTNU, Trondheim, Norway.

[45] Trenerry, C. F. (2009). *The origin and early history of insurance: Including the contract of bottomry*. Clark, NJ: The Lawbook Exchange.

[46] Trenerry, C. F. (2009). *The origin and early history of insurance: Including the contract of bottomry*. Clark, NJ: The Lawbook Exchange.

The genesis of modern homeowner insurance was the great fire of London, which in 1666 destroyed more than 13,000 homes.[47] Before that fire, insurance existed in various forms but lacked the rigor and formality present in today's policies. In the seventeenth century, for example, each policy covered just one peril. Companies spread the risk, distributing the losses of a few to a large number of premium payers.[48]

The industry, meant as organized and systematic labor, was born a long time ago. The manufacture of bricks in ancient Rome provides an example. The steam engine introduced by James Watt in 1782 sparkled the first significant industrial revolution.[49] Later it spread to Western Europe, North America, and then in the rest of the world. The change brought by this invention is essential. It allows the organization to turn jobs based only on manual tools and animal power in activities that use machines, infrastructure, and industrial production and transportation of both goods and persons.[50] This innovation made possible a significant increase in production capacity. The development of naval transport, the railways, and later the aircraft led to unprecedented changes. It significantly improved transportation capacity and the speed of production and transportation.

The first company to offer accident insurance during this first industrial revolution was the Railway Passengers Assurance Company, formed in 1848 in England to insure against the rising number of fatalities on the nascent railway system. Its name was Universal Casualty Compensation Company.[51] The company reached an agreement with the railway companies. Basic accident insurance was in a package deal along with travel tickets to customers. The company charged higher premiums for second- and third-class travel due to the higher risk of injury in the roofless carriages.

[47] Johnson, B. (na). *The great fire of London*. Historic UK Ltd. Company Registered in England No. 5621230, www.historic-uk.com/HistoryUK/HistoryofEngland/The-Great-Fire-of-London/. Accessed 11 December 2019.

[48] iotinsobs.com/. Accessed 11 December 2019.

[49] McNabb, D. E. (2016). *A comparative history of commerce and industry*. New York, NY: Palgrave Macmillan USA.

[50] Schwab, K. (2017). *The fourth industrial revolution*. London, UK: Currency.

[51] History of insurance. *Modern Insurance*. cpb-us-w2.wpmucdn.com/blogs.baylor.edu/dist/a/6818/files/2013/12/History-of-insurance-11gcwej.pdf. Accessed 18 November 2019.

Second Industrial Revolution. Insurance 2.0

Several discoveries characterized the second industrial revolution. The essential discovery was the introduction of electricity, and the second one was the telegraph. These innovations made possible radical advances in transportation and communication. Materials such as steel, copper, or aluminum became relevant in the construction of machines and products. Besides, the chemical industry expanded in a significant way.[52]

Other innovations characterized the second industrial revolution. These innovations helped to substantially reduce the purchase price of a large number of products. The introduction of the division of labor meant a revolution in the industry with the capability of mass production. It was the model for industrial plants for several decades. At the same time, Henry Ford pushed the idea of the assembly line.[53]

The insurance management began operating increasingly on a global or at least on a regional scale. By the late nineteenth century, governments began to initiate national insurance programs against sickness and old age. Germany built on a tradition of welfare programs in Prussia and Saxony that started as early as in the 1840s. In the 1880s, Chancellor Otto von Bismarck introduced old-age pensions, accident insurance, and medical care that formed Germany's welfare state.[54]

The British Liberal government issued in 1911 the National Insurance Act, a more extensive legislation.[55] This law provided British persons with the first contribution system of insurance against illness and unemployment. This system was greatly expanded after the Second World War under the influence of the Beveridge Report, to form the first modern welfare state.[56]

[52] Schwab, K. (2017). *The fourth industrial revolution*. Currency: London, UK.

[53] *The second industrial revolution*. ushistoryscene.com/. Accessed 28 December 2018.

[54] Hennock, E. P. (1997). The origin of the welfare state in England and Germany, 1850–1914: Social policies compared. Beck, H. (1997). *The origins of the authoritarian welfare state in Prussia: Conservatives, bureaucracy, and the social question, 1815–70*. Ann Arbor, MI: University of Michigan Press.

[55] Heller, M. (2007). The National Insurance Acts 1911–1947, the approved societies and the prudential assurance company. *Twentieth Century British History, 19*(1), 1–28.

[56] Lĝdemel, I. (1997). *The welfare paradox: Income maintenance and personal social services in Norway and Britain, 1946–1966*. Oslo, Norway: Scandinavian University Press.

Third Industrial Revolution. Insurance 3.0

The introduction of the computer marked the third industrial revolution. It is a device that separates hardware and software.[57] This separation allows excellent flexibility, technology innovations, and the introduction of entirely new types of solutions: The computer-based applications started to provide support to the organization's functions.

The containers (1956)[58] substantially simplified the transportation of goods, reducing the need for labor, and increasing security and time to delivery.

Actuarial and statistical applications were among the first application of the computer. Later other applications were introduced for the management and control of insurance processes.[59] As computers became more widespread in the insurance workplace, including the independent agent's office, new ways to unleash their potential use developed. Smaller computers became powerful. They could be linked together, or networked, to share memory storage, software, information, and communicate with each other.[60]

Independent agents started using more and more technology. From the early 1980s through the mid-1990s, most independent agents used desktop computer-based automation systems to improve efficiency and reduce costs.[61] Since 1970, Acord, an American not-for-profit standards-setting association for the insurance industry, has been involved in automation.[62] Companies, agents, vendors, solution providers, associations, and other interested parties are part of the association. They provide

[57] Rifkin, J. (2011). *The third industrial revolution: How lateral power is transforming energy, the economy, and the world*. London, UK: Macmillan.

[58] Cudahy, B. J. (2006). *Box boats: How container ships changed the world*. New York, NY: Fordham University Press.

[59] Nicoletti, B. (2014, 27 May). Lean and digitize e-procurement. In *Proceedings of the Public e-procurement in Europe: public Management, Technologies and Processes of Change*. Lisbon, Portugal.

[60] *A brief history of automation*. www.insurancejournal.com/magazines/mag-coverstory/2000/05/15/21633.htm. Accessed 30 May 2020.

[61] *A brief history of automation: The past, present and future*. www.insurancejournal.com/magazines/mag-coverstory/2000/05/15/21633.htm. Accessed 30 May 2020.

[62] Nelson, M. L., Shaw, M. J., & Qualls, W. (2005). Interorganizational system standards development in vertical industries. *Electronic Markets*, *15*(4), 378–392.

standard-forms and Electronic Data Interchange (EDI). Many vendors or solution providers base on them their automation systems.

In 1972, the first Acord form, a property loss notice, went into use. Over time, Acord's standards include forms, AL3 (Automation Level 3), XML, OLife, and ObjX. The forms are the point of sale, data collection tools, AL3 is Acord's Electronic Data Interchange (EDI) standard (or machine-to-machine, business-to-business, data transmission formats, or components), and OLife is a data integration standard. ObjX is "much more than EDI."[63]

In the 1980s when the number of personal computers in use increased substantially, Acord members asked for standardized electronic transmissions between the agents' computers and the insurance companies' computers.

Acord and the industry, working hand in hand, introduced one form accepted and used by many of those companies. These forms have contributed to reducing the costs out of the insurance distribution channels.

In the same manner that the industry came together with Acord forms, Acord also supported the development of Electronic Data Interchange (EDI) standards. Companies implemented automation and developed proprietary systems that they placed in their agents' offices. With the inception of the agency management vendors and Acord's standards implemented in those systems, the agents were conceptually able to eliminate those proprietary terminals and work through one system.

The more advanced companies set up websites that required the agents to go to them and enter the data. This situation forced the agents to move to a separate terminal in their office, connect to a website, and rekey the data that was already in their databases. A new standard was introduced called Extensible Markup Language (XML).[64] XML is a standard that enables connectivity between Web applications and agency management systems, in addition to business-to-business, business-to-customer, and so on. XML dramatically facilitates the exchange of information.

Today there are roughly 400 Acord forms. Although it is critical to note how many forms there are, what is even more critical is to note

[63] www.acord.org/. Accessed 28 December 2019.

[64] Schweiger, R., Brumhard, M., Hoelzer, S., & Dudeck, J. (2005). Implementing health care systems using XML standards. *International Journal of Medical Informatics, 74*(2–4), 267–277.

that these Acord forms have eliminated or prevented 80,000 proprietary forms. Thus, they were able to save the industry millions of dollars.

The insurance handles business on a worldwide basis, so it makes sense to be able to communicate on a global basis. As an example, companies write coverage for properties owned by persons all over the world. In turn, these companies work with other, domestic or international, companies or reinsurers to share the exposure.

Fourth Industrial Revolution: Insurance 4.0

The widespread use of telecommunications networks (mainly the internet) marked the beginning of a new revolution. The introduction of the internet of things (objects) (IoT) and advanced software applications combined with the automation of the machines in the operations environment introduced the fourth industrial revolution also in insurance.[65]

The fourth industrial revolution is not only smart and connected machines and systems. It has a much broader scope. Simultaneously there are waves of further breakthroughs in areas ranging from mobile phones to nanotechnology, from renewables to advanced sensors. It is the fusion of these technologies and their interaction across the physical, digital, and biological domain that makes the fourth industrial revolution essential and different from the previous revolutions.[66]

Industry 4.0 is the convergence of industrial operations technologies and information and communication technologies.[67] Industry 4.0 also relates to the convergence of the internet of things (IoT), the internet of persons (IoP), and the internet of everything (IoE).[68]

Insurance 4.0 is a disruptive innovation similar to the three previous revolutions. They have in common the use not of a single technology, but the interaction of several technologies whose effects create new modes

[65] Kagermann, H., Helbig, J., Hellinger, A., & Wahlster, W. (2013). *Recommendations for implementing the strategic initiative INDUSTRIE 4.0: Securing the future of German manufacturing industry; Final report of the Working Group 4.0 Industries*. Forschungsunion, Essen, Germany.

[66] Skilton, M., & Hovsepian, F. (2017). *The 4th industrial revolution: Responding to the impact of artificial intelligence on business*. Cham, Switzerland: Springer.

[67] Skilton, M., & Hovsepian, F. (2017). *The 4th industrial revolution: Responding to the impact of artificial intelligence on business*. Cham, Switzerland: Springer.

[68] Hermann, M., Pentek, T., & Otto, B. (2016). Design principles for industries 4.0 scenarios. In *2016 49th Hawaii International Conference on System Sciences (HICSS)* (pp. 3928–3937). IEEE.

of operation. The results have also influenced the organizations, the environment, and social functions.[69]

Underlying the initiative of insurance 4.0 is the internet. It allows reliable communication among machines, humans, and digital applications in real-time and cheaply. This enables the implementation of what is known as "smart insurance",[70] an advanced digitization within and between organizations or service operations websites.[71] The convergence of ICT and automation of machinery and infrastructure is at the base of insurance 4.0. It is characterized by advanced digitization within organizations in the same ecosystem, in the form of integration of internet technologies with the technologies of intelligent objects (systems and products). This integration enables and transforms insurance sales and operational systems in the direction of services that control their sales and operational processes. Besides the focus on digitization, insurance 4.0 is supported by innovative solutions whose quantitative effects create new services, processes, modes of operations, and business models. All of them support the customization of the products and services.[72]

Successful organizations increasingly do not just add value. They reinvent it. The critical strategic task is to reconfigure roles and relationships among a constellation of actors (vendors, partners, customers) to mobilize the creation of value by new combinations of players and services in an integrated ecosystem. This new organization paradigm has been called value constellation.[73] This new logic of value breaks down the distinction between products and services. It combines them into activity-based "offerings" from which customers can create value for themselves. As potential offerings grow complex, so do the relationships necessary to create them. This concept can be generalized. This book stresses the move

[69] Schmidt, R., Möhring, M., Härting, R. C., Reichstein, C., Neumaier, P., & Jozinović, P. (2015). Industry 4.0-potentials for creating smart products: Empirical research results. In *The International Conference on Business Information Systems* (pp. 16–27). Cham, Switzerland: Springer.

[70] Mcclellan Jr, R. E. (2006). Smart insurance. *Grower Talks, 70*(5), 76–78.

[71] Stock, T., & Seliger, G. (2016). Opportunities of sustainable manufacturing industry in 4.0. *Procedia CIRP, 40,* 536–541.

[72] Riecken, D. (2000). Personalized views of customization. *Communications of the ACM, 43*(8), 26–26.

[73] Normann, R., & Ramirez, R. (1993). From value chain to value constellation: Designing interactive strategy. *Harvard Business Review, 71*(4), 65–77.

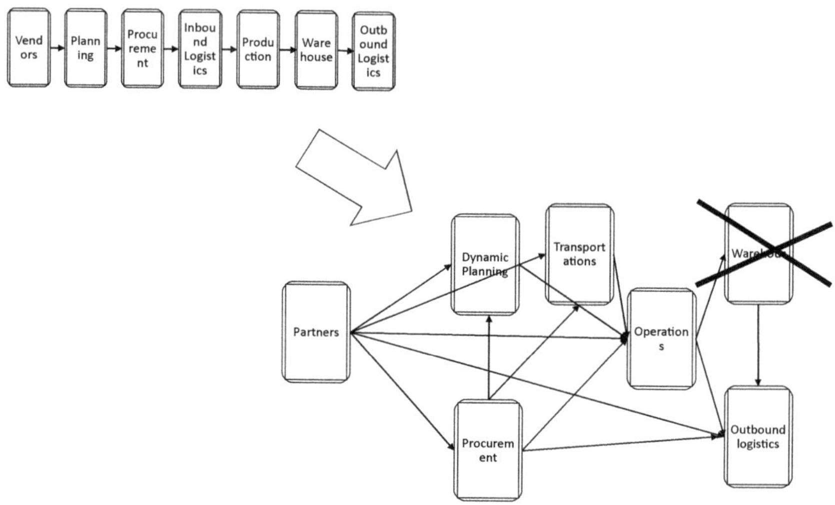

Fig. 2.2 From supply chain to value network

from a supply chain to a value network. This book uses such a term.[74] The value for the customers and the organizations is obtained by an ecosystem that combines in network organizations, vendors, customers, and public administrations (Fig. 2.2).[75]

Insurance 4.0 involves a change not only in operations but also in the rest of the organization. An essential function is marketing/sales. The continuous increase of global e-commerce requires not only cross-functional integration but also sophisticated integrative processes across

[74]The term value network has also a different meaning. Stabell and Fieldstad (Stabell, C. B., & Fjeldstad, Ø. D. [1998] proposed it. Configuring value for competitive advantage: On chains, shops and networks. *Strategic Management Journal, 19*(5), 413–437). It is based on mediation technologies according to Thompson's typology (Thompson, J. D. [2017]. *Organizations in action: Social science bases of administrative theory*. London, UK: Routledge). It connects customers and other parties that are interested in creating mutual relations and interdependence. The mediating technologies support relations between actors scattered over time and space. This model is similar to what has been called the platform approach (Zhu, F., & Iansiti, M. [2007]. *Dynamics of platform competition: Exploring the role of installed base, platform quality and consumer expectations*. Cambridge, MA: Division of Research, Harvard Business School).

[75]Nicoletti, B. (2017). *Agile insurance. Volume I: Adding value with lean processes*. London, UK: Springer International Publishing. ISBN 978-3-319-61082-5.

the organization.[76] The continuous transformation toward insurance 4.0 requires the improved exchange of communication and information through the insurance systems. Innovations can support the move toward insurance 4.0 by collecting and processing the relevant data over the whole value network while supporting intelligent decision making.[77]

The gradual movement of companies toward digitization earmarks the era of the fourth industrial revolution. In an insurance 4.0 environment, organizations can increasingly connect and integrate with partners (upstream) and intermediaries and customers (downstream) in a network through the internet of everything. Transparency of information can create virtual copies of the insurance processes. Cyber-physical systems can enable decentralized decision making. Finally, decision support systems (using mobile apps) or robo-advisors can assist and support. These principles are the basis of design principles for further digitizing insurance.[78]

Insurance 4.0 can benefit from the development of the internet of objects.[79] Technologies such as black boxes and automated guided vehicles allow the introduction of processes that do not require, or they need much less, human intervention and allow insurance to offer new services. The objective is to integrate automation and information and communication technology solutions.

The implementation of these types of processing solutions will take place over a long time. They require significant investments and special programs and training. The results are a substantial improvement in the insurance processes' performance and costs, their speeding, but above all, their flexibility, mainly in support of the insurance services customizations and extensions. IoT devices, made available on the network, combine

[76] Castillo, F. (2016). *Managing information technology*. Cham, Switzerland: Springer International Publishing.

[77] CFB Bots. (2018). *The difference between robotic process automation and artificial intelligence*. medium.com/@cfb_bots/thedifference-between-robotic-process-automation-and-artificial-intelligence4a71b4834788. Accessed 22 July 2019.

[78] Tham, C. K., & Luo, T. (2013). Sensing-driven energy purchasing in smart grid cyber-physical system. *IEEE Transactions on Systems, Man and Cybernetics Society, 43*(4), 773–784. Klötzer, C., & Pflaum, A. (2015). Cyber-physical systems as the technical foundation for problem solutions in manufacturing, logistics and supply chain management. In *October 2015 5th International Conference on the Internet of Things (IoT), IEEE* (pp. 12–19).

[79] Domingo Galindo, L. (2016). *The challenges of logistics 4.0 for the supply chain management and the information technology*. Master's thesis, NTNU, Trondheim, Norway.

with automatic storage and operations already widespread. Their further diffusion is limited because they are dedicated systems, in line with the shape and characteristic of the specific initiative they use. The goal is to introduce new solutions that provide additional services to the customers, make resource savings, save time in the communication, and, in particular, increase flexibility, and customization.

Insurance 4.0 Model

This section examines in detail the critical success factors for insurance 4.0 initiatives This book calls them the eight "Cs," related to the model of industry 4.0: Cybernetics, Communication, Control, Collaboration, Connection, Cognition, Coordination, and Confidence.

The following pages examine each of the "C" in the case of insurance 4.0. The following chapters consider the Confidence aspect.

Cybernetics

The base of the insurance 4.0 revolution is the shift from a supply chain model to that of a value network. Intelligent machines and computer applications link all the functions and allow the company to use and share real-time information. At the same time, it is necessary to streamline the insurance processes. Insurance 4.0 is the integration of information and communication technology and automation in support of insurance to improve the added value to the customer and the entire organization.

The "smart insurances" share real-time information among all stakeholders. They make insurance processes optimized and transparent. With the use of cybernetics in the insurance sector, it is necessary to develop a secure system to ensure that data are protected and are available at the right time and in the right place to support the insurance activities.

The management of insurance 4.0 lies on a vast network in which all parties involved (customers, intermediaries, and partners) have access. This network is possible by using an internet platform that handles all orders from customers, intermediaries, and partners in real-time.

Communication
An essential aspect of the paradigm of insurance 4.0 is the emphasis on ICT smart or intelligent systems.[80] There is a difference in respect to the support of the operations provided by the traditional applications.[81] One might expect that the "smart" adjective in the insurance sector is the basis for the automation of end-to-end insurance processes. It means a lot more. Insurance 4.0 solutions automatically recognize the demand for a specific service. They can generate a draft order to submit to the customer for approval. This request is automatically transmitted to the respective operator. In-depth automation is another difference between insurance 4.0 and traditional insurance. In technical jargon, it is a system without interruption in the processing (Straight Through Processing—STP, as it is called in the financial systems).[82]

Control
This factor of the insurance 4.0 model implies a substantial change in how insurance works today. It requires significant rethinking regarding the organization and competencies. Both need to be remodeled. Insurance 4.0 accelerates communication in an ever more tightly interconnected world. In the past, it was enough to be aware of some potential markets for offering and supplying insurance services. Insurance 4.0 requires an organization with a comprehensive and global approach. In this scenario, control is an essential factor that must be fully automated.

Cooperation
The productivity benefits resulting from traditional ICT application initiatives are a reduction in transaction and process costs. Insurance 4.0 allows the company to turn paper documents into digital ICT applications. Thus, there is a transformation from a labor-intensive activity into automated workflows and sustainable ICT processes. Insurance 4.0

[80] Schmidt, R., Möhring, M., Härting, R. C., Reichstein, C., Neumaier, P., & Jozinović, P. (2015). Industry 4.0-potentials for creating smart products: Empirical research results. In *The International Conference on Business Information Systems* (pp. 16–27). Cham, Switzerland: Springer.

[81] Wisner, J. D., Keong Leong, G., & Keah-Choon, T. (2006). *Principles of supply chain management*. Stamford, CT: Thomson Learning.

[82] Khanna, A. (2010). *Straight through processing for financial services*. Cambridge, MA: Academic Press.

should also support critical activities like the process of managing relationships with partners. The driving factors of insurance 4.0 collaborative productivity are the improvements in sales, operations, and design of new services.[83] Insurance 4.0 enables the development of faster processes of sales and operations. The organization can activate new product-service functions and improve the insurance organization.[84] Traditional ICT applications are focused on process efficiency. The objectives of insurance 4.0 are increased productivity, flexibility, and performance, which meet the high customization needs of today's customers.[85]

Connection
The handling operations define the efficiency of the services in their movement along with the value network. By optimizing the external information exchange and internal handling processes, it is possible to impact the structure of the insurance costs.

To help the physical connections, automated or semi-automated assets (like vehicles) are essential. In insurance 4.0, it is necessary to implement an automatic path between black boxes and insurance operations. The organization needs to consider the legal and insurance aspects beyond the technical considerations. Even partial automation of these pathways can have a sizable impact on insurance costs as it reduces the values of the document interchange and increases overall security and accuracy. Automated exchange of information facilitates their access and recording, allowing knowledge and availability of big data for analysis.

[83] Schuh, G., Powerful, T., Wesch-Powerful, C., Weber, A. R., & Prote, J. P. (2014). Collaboration mechanisms to increase productivity in the context of Industries 4.0. *Procedia CIRP, 19,* 51–56. https://doi.org/10.1016/j.procir.2014.05.016. Accessed 9 March 2020.

[84] Schuh, G., Powerful, T., Wesch-Powerful, C., Weber, A. R., & Prote, J. P. (2014). Collaboration mechanisms to increase to productivity in the context of Industries 4.0. *Procedia CIRP, 19,* 51–56.

[85] Kagermann, H. (2014). von Industries 4.0 Chancen nutzen. In T. Bauernhansl, M. T. Hompel, & B. Vogel-Heuser (Eds.), Produktion Industries 4.0. *Automatisierung und Logistik* (pp. 603–614). Wiesbaden, Germany: Springer.

Cognition
Data analytics are the most essential enabler for insurance 4.0.[86] The intelligent (smart) technologies and related algorithms allow the aggregation, processing, and analysis of large volumes of data from many heterogeneous sources. Using all these big data, the organization can improve its knowledge of the partners, markets, and customers, forecast market trends, and improve the shortcomings of processes and products. Big data analytics can allow managers to make better and more informed decisions. In a growing number of cases, big data analytics can automatically take operational decisions regarding insurance, such as premiums or claims.[87]

Analysis of the data and their intelligent use are critical success factors for the organizations that want to exploit the potential of insurance 4.0. The data analytics tools can also support the organization's partners in improving the sales, design, and performance of their businesses. The predictive analysis, on where and when to expect the next claims, offers the possibility to optimize the services.[88]

It is the organization's responsibility, ensuring that all the insurance opportunities for the organization use big data analytics. Insurance should work with customers to allow both the organization and its customers to benefit from the improvements resulting from a more effective, efficient, and economic organization's extended value network.

McKennon[89]
McKesson is a USD 179 billion healthcare services and information technology employing 70,000 persons and several partners. It uses a discovery and analytics platform to identify all of their insurance and sourcing

[86] Koch, V., Kuge, S., Geissbauer, R., & Schrauf, S. (2014). *Industry 4.0: Opportunities and challenges of the industrial Internet*. Strategy & PwC. www.strategyand.pwc.com/media/file/Industria-4-0.pdf. Accessed 30 May 2020.

[87] Nicoletti, B. (2014, February). Using operational analytics to achieve to digitized, visible supply chain. *Inbound Logistics*.

[88] Lee, J., Kao, H. A., & Yang, S. (2014). Service innovation and smart analytics for industry 4.0 and big data environment. *Procedia CIRP, 16*, 3–8.

[89] www.mckesson.com/. Accessed 20 June 2019.

contracts across the organization.[90] It stores the documents in a specific contract repository. It is possible to search the contracts easily and quickly in this repository, saving some staff time. The metadata from the contract analysis enables the organization to identify potential obligation risks and revenue opportunities and savings from otherwise hidden unfavorable payment and renewable terms.

Coordination

In the past, partners of the traditional ICT applications have provided considerable support for the exchange of information with the customers and the intermediaries.[91] Technology advances in an insurance 4.0 initiative greatly increase the potential to do so. The key change is the transition from an "exchange of information" to the "free flow of information" in the value network between the products, services, and related organizations.[92] It is necessary to coordinate effectively this exchange.[93] A free movement implies a higher degree of exchangeability of the data, a higher degree of automation in the exchange of information, and possibly also an integrated use of the data in the approach to big data analytics[94] or, in the future, based on the use of blockchain, as described in the following chapters.

[90] Burgess, A. (2017). *The executive guide to artificial intelligence: How to identify and implement applications for AI in your organization*. Cham, Switzerland: Springer.

[91] Kollmann, T. (2011). *E-Business: Grundlagen elektronischer Geschäftsprozesse in der Net Economy*. Wiesbaden, Germany: Gabler.

[92] Schlick, J., Stephan, P., Loskyll, M., & Lappe, D. (2014). Industries 4.0 in der praktischen Anwendung. In T. Bauernhansl, M. T. Hompel, & B. Vogel-Heuser (Eds.), *Industrie 4.0 to Produktion, Automatisierung und Logistik: Anwendung - Technologien – Migration* (pp. 57–84). Wiesbaden, Germany: Springer.

[93] Van Weele, A. J. (2010). *Purchasing & supply chain management: Analysis, strategy, planning and practice*. Andover, UK: Cengage Learning EMEA.

[94] Lee, J., Kao, H. A., & Yang, S. (2014). Service innovation and smart analytics for industry 4.0 and big data environment. *Procedia CIRP, 16*, 3–8.

These implications distinguish traditional insurance processes and insurance 4.0.[95] Insurance 4.0 improvements can be:

- Functional integration and cross-organization;
- Use of systems that reduce manual labor while increasing effectiveness and economics in insurance tasks.

Their implementation is through a flexible insurance approach based on the digitization and automation of processes and infrastructure.

In insurance 4.0, both the depth of integration (mainly among organizations and customers) and the automation potential of the entire insurance process are much more than those in the traditional insurance services. The latter is limited to facilitating the tasks using a computer application based on the personalized information and exchange of documents. The automation process, a higher degree of integration, and the use of artificial intelligence characterize insurance 4.0. This is different with respect to traditional insurance. Insurance 4.0 is based on the digitization and advanced automation within the organizations and functions of the ecosystem. It is not limited to the use of new and improved solutions.

Next to the degree of integration, relationships with intermediaries will be different in insurance 4.0 (e.g., around new services complimentary to the insurance services[96]). The impact of insurance 4.0 in the organizations is extensive and pervasive.

All these components of the model pose a substantial challenge and a potential change in working with insurance companies. They require a critical and holistic re-engineering of the organization and competencies, both of which should change synergistically.[97] Organizations need to create new job profiles, for example, for digital actuaries, contract experts on intellectual property, or data scientists to analyze relevant data, their

[95] Glas, A. H., & Kleemann, F. C. (2016). 4.0 The impact of industry on insurance and supply management: A conceptual and qualitative analysis. *International Journal of Business and Management Invention, 5*(6), 55–66.

[96] Essig, M. (2006). Electronic insurance—Konzeption und Anwendung. In J. Zentes (Ed.), *Handbuch Handel* (pp. 735–758). Wiesbaden, Germany: Gabler.

[97] Geissbauer, R., Weissbarth, R., & Wetzstein, J. (2016). *Insurance 4.0: Are the organization ready for the digital revolution?* www.strategyand.pwc.com/reports/insurance-4-digital-revolution. Accessed 18 December 2018.

management, and their use. Security will require a completely different set of capabilities and competencies to cope with cyberattacks.[98] To find these talents, new sources must be opened with the help of partners in insurance, such as partnership programs with universities and research centers. It is also useful to explore new channels such as social networks, social media, and similar. Larger organizations should consider establishing relationships with academia to conduct educational and informational activities, cross-functional training, proof of concepts, and workshops for partners. Only if the professionals who work in insurance have digital competencies (also named e-competencies[99]), an organization can fully benefit from the opportunities offered by insurance 4.0.[100]

Conclusions

This chapter presents the revolution of insurance, along with the four industrial revolutions. This chapter presents a model for industry 4.0 and its application in the case of insurance 4.0. The model underlines the critical factors that are at the basis of the success of an insurance 4.0 initiative.

[98] Zhu, B., Joseph, A., & Sastry, S. (2011, October). A taxonomy of cyber attacks on SCADA systems. In *2011 International Conference on Internet of Things and 4th International Conference on Cyber, Physical and Social Computing* (pp. 380–388). IEEE.

[99] Sternberg, R. J., Sternberg, R. J., & Grigorenko, E. L. (Eds.). (2003). *The psychology of abilities, competencies, and expertise*. Cambridge, UK: Cambridge University Press.

[100] Competence is an ability to apply knowledge, skills, and attitudes for achieving observable results. The European model of e-Competence (e-CF) provides a reference of 40 skills, as required and applied to the digital workplace transformation, using a common language for skills, abilities, and ability levels. For details, reference can be made to: Sanz, L. F., Gómez-Pérez, J., & Castillo-Martinez, A. (2018). *Analysis of the European ICT competence frameworks: In multidisciplinary perspectives on human capital and information technology professionals* (pp. 225–245). Hershey, PA: IGI Global.

CHAPTER 3

Business Model Canvas and Insurance 4.0

Introduction

The study of business models and their literature is associated with the relevance of value creation within organizations. Recent research has identified business model innovation and design as critical tools in the effective implementation of organizational strategy.[1] This book considers the business model canvas, as introduced by Osterwalder,[2] and applies it to insurance 4.0.

Business Model Literature

The term business model (BM) is widely used and applied to the organization, information technology, and management literature since the advent of the internet between 1996 and today.[3] The term business model has taken a particular relevance and usage recently even if the

[1] Pfeffermann, N., Minshall, T., & Mortara, L. (Eds.). (2013). *Strategy and communication for innovation*. New York, NY: Springer.

[2] Osterwalder, A., Pigneur, Y., Oliveira, M. A. Y., & Ferreira, J. J. P. (2011). Business model generation: A handbook for visionaries, game changers and challengers. *African Journal of Business Management, 5*(7), 22–30.

[3] Zott, C., Amit, R., & Massa, L. (2011). The business model: Recent developments and future research. *Journal of Management, 37*(4), 1019–1042.

B. Nicoletti, *Insurance 4.0*, Palgrave Studies in Financial Services Technology, https://doi.org/10.1007/978-3-030-58426-9_3

term is born from the studies of Peter Drucker.[4] In principle, the words "business model" identifies how an organization pursues its goals, and all processes are part of it. According to Peter Drucker, a business model can support in the analysis and transformation of organizations: Who is your customer, what does the customer value, and how do you deliver value at an appropriate cost?

A business plan is different from a business model. A business plan is a document about the planning of activities necessary to achieve an objective. A business model clarifies the functioning of the various components of the organization and how they can be successful in adding value to the customers and the organization.

There is not a single definition of the business model. The consensus is on the reasons why this term is used, that is, to explain how an organization generates value for its stakeholders, especially the customers. There are different definitions of the term, based on the point of view of those who use it. A possible definition for the business model is: "a statement, a description, a representation, an architecture, a conceptual tool or model, a structural template, a method, a framework, a pattern, and a set."[5] Following some other definitions.

"In the most basic sense, a business model is the method of doing business by which a company can sustain itself generating revenue." The business model clarifies how an organization can produce a margin by specifying where it is positioned in the value chain (Fig. 3.1) or better in the value network.[6]

"The business model can be defined as the description of how a business can create value through the value it proposes to its customers, its value architecture (including its resources and internal and external value network), and how it can capture the value to convert it into profit."[7]

"A business model is the method by which a company builds and uses its resources to offer its customers better value than its competitors and make money. It details how a company makes money now and how it

[4] Drucker, P. (1994, September–October). The theory of the business. *Harvard Business Review*, 95–104.

[5] timreview.ca/article/807. Accessed 30 May 2020.

[6] Rappa, M. (2000). *Managing the digital enterprise*. digitalenterprise.org/index.html. Accessed 30 May 2020.

[7] Lehmann-Ortega, L., & Schoettl, J. M. (2005). From buzzword to managerial tool: The role of business models in strategic innovation. *CLADEA, Santiago de Chile*, 1–14.

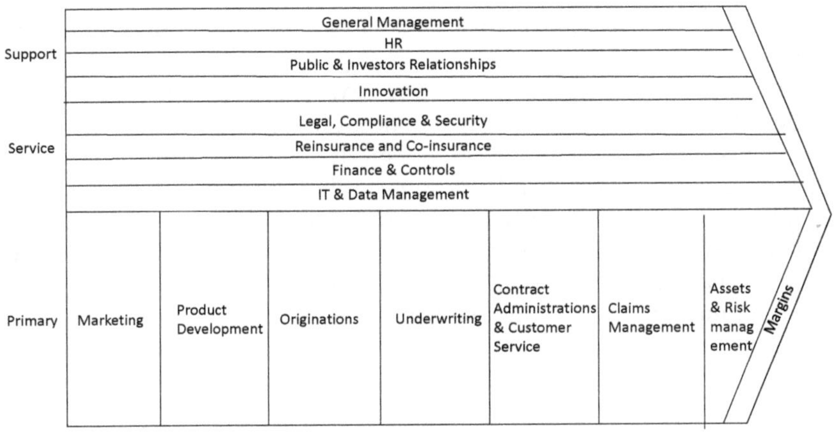

Fig. 3.1 Value chain in insurance

plans to do so in the long term. The model enables a company to have a sustainable competitive advantage to perform better than its rivals in the long term."[8]

"At its heart, a business model performs two essential functions: value creation and value capture. First, it defines a series of activities that yield a new product or service in such a way that there is net value created throughout the various activities. Second, it captures value from a portion of those activities for the company developing the model."[9]

The business models depend on four key questions "who the customers are, what is the company selling, how to make it, and how to realize a profit."[10]

Notwithstanding the several definitions of a business model, there are some standard features that the authors describe in their works: Rappa, for example, highlights the monetary aspect of the business model concept,

[8] Afhua, A., & Tucci, C. L. (2000). *Internet business models and strategies* (1st ed.). New York, NY: McGraw-Hill College.

[9] Chesbrough, H. W. (2006). *Open business models*. Cambridge, MA: Harvard Business Press.

[10] Gassmann, O., Frankenberger, K., & Csik, M. (2017). *Develop business models. 55 innovative concepts with the St. Gallen business model navigator* (2nd ed.). Miinchen, Germany: Carl Hansen.

which is also present in some other definitions.[11] Other authors as Chesbrough and Rosenbloom (2002) and Magretta connect the concept of business model to organizational strategy.[12] Chesbrough and Rosenbloom (2002) stress the mentioned concept in a technological innovation perspective, stating that "the business model is an intermediary between technology development and economic value creation."[13] Chesbrough (2007) states that it is critical also innovation in the business model itself to make revenue with it through the market.[14] Magretta defines business models as "stories that explain how enterprises work [...], A good business model begins with an insight into human motivations and ends in a rich stream of profit."[15] With this statement, Magretta refers to Peter Drucker and defines "a good business model" as the one that provides answers to his two questions. Other scholars, who focus on e-business, stress the value creation related to this specific typology of business. They describe the business model "as the design of transaction content, structure, and governance transactions."[16] In particular, they analyzed a sample of US and European e-business models to define the drivers of value creation. They state that: "A business model depicts the content, structure, and governance of transactions designed to create value through the exploitation of business opportunities."

[11] Afhua, A., & Tucci, C. L. (2000). *Internet business models and strategies* (1st ed.). New York, NY: MGgraw-Hill College. Mullins, J. W., Mullins, J. W., Mullins, J., & Komisar, R. (2009). *Getting to plan B: Breaking through to a better business model*. Cambridge, MA: Harvard Business Press. Teece, D. J. (2018). Business models and dynamic capabilities. *Long-Range Planning, 51*(1), 40–49.

[12] Magretta, J. (2002, May). Why business models matter. *Harvard Business Review*, 3–8. Chesbrough, H., & Rosenbloom, R. S. (2002). The role of the business model in capturing value from innovation: Evidence from Xerox Corporation's technology spin-off companies. *Industrial and Corporate Change, 11*(3), 529–555.

[13] Chesbrough, H., & Rosenbloom, R. S. (2002). The role of the business model in capturing value from innovation: Evidence from Xerox Corporation's technology spin-off companies. *Industrial and Corporate Change, 11*(3), 529–555.

[14] Chesbrough, H. (2007). Business model innovation: It's not just about technology anymore. *Strategy & Leadership, 35*(6), 12–17.

[15] Magretta, J. (2002, May). Why business models matter. *Harvard Business Review*, 3–8.

[16] Zott, C., & Amit, R. (2013). The business model: A theoretically anchored robust construct for strategic analysis. *Strategic Organization, 11*(4), 403–411.

Most of these scholars developed a specific explanation of what a business model is, based on the particular context. In this sense, Peter Drucker described the theory of the business, stating that it relates to the underlying assumptions on which the organization is built, and it is associated with the organizational behavior, organization's business scope, their customers, competitors, their values, their actions, the technology, its dynamics, and also about the organization's strengths and weaknesses.[17] Most of the later literature regarding the definition and use of business models have been developed, starting from this definition.

Until this point, the focus has been on the economic and monetary meaning of a business model. Other authors gave a different definition for all those organizations in which profit plays a less central role (such as socially oriented organizations and government organizations).

Diversified use of the business model concept for different purposes based on nature, necessity, and context, explains why there is no agreed-upon definition.

Business Model Canvas—Structure and Components

Before explaining the relation between business models, strategy, and competitive advantage, it is useful to go through the components that an organization must define to develop a good/excellent business model.

One of the most used techniques is visual thinking, which uses visual tools like Post-it, notes, pictures, sketches, and diagrams for building and defining business models.[18] Thus, it becomes simpler to discuss, brainstorm, and make changes to the model because it is concrete and tangible.

Figure 3.2 is the typical structure used to design a business model canvas (BMC), which could serve as a reference for every type of organization. It provides a standard method of evaluating, planning, thinking, and developing the activities necessary to add value to the customers.[19]

[17] Drucker, P. (1994). *The theory of the business*. Books, Google.com.

[18] Fielt, E. (2014). Conceptualizing business models: Definitions, frameworks and classifications. *Journal of Business Models, 1*(1), 85–105.

[19] Osterwalder, A., Pigneur, Y., & Clark, T. (2010). *Business model generation*. Hoboken, NJ: Wiley.

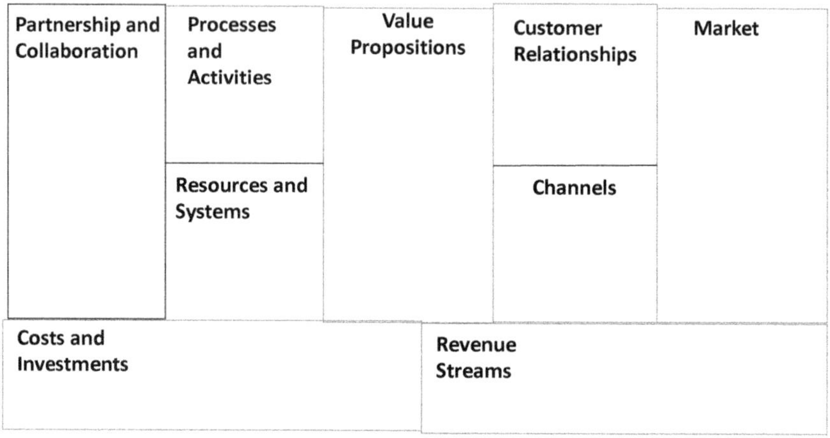

Fig. 3.2 Traditional business model canvas

It is based on Osterwalder book[20] and his later research on business models.[21] This scholar provides a template (a canvas) through which organizations can easily explain and define their business models. Nine building blocks compose it. Each one must be "answered," considering the specific organization and strategy in which it is applied. For this reason, it is critical to understand the meaning of each component of the canvas correctly.

This book uses the business model canvas version, as modified by the author (Fig. 3.3).[22]

The BMC is composed of nine segments. For a mnemonic reason, the parts start with nine Ps.

- Proposition of value or products;
- Proximity with the customer;

[20] Osterwalder, A. (2004). *The business model ontology a proposition in a design science approach*. Doctoral dissertation, Université de Lausanne, Faculté des hautes études commerciales. Lausanne, Switzerland.

[21] Osterwalder, A., Pigneur, Y., & Tucci, C. L. (2005). Clarifying business models: Origins, present, and future of the concept. *Communications of the Association for Information Systems, 16,* 1.

[22] Nicoletti, B. (2016). *Digital insurance*. London, UK: Palgrave Macmillan. https://doi.org/10.1057/9781137553270_8.

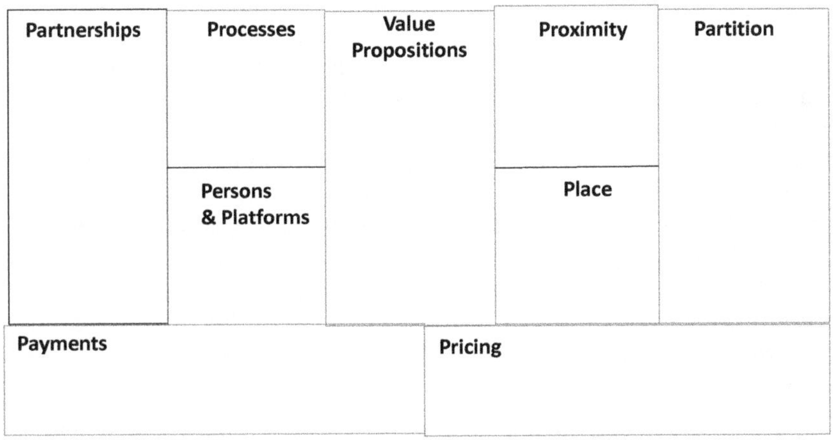

Fig. 3.3 Business model canvas (9 Ps)

- Partition of the customers;
- Place or channels;
- Platforms and resources;
- Persons;
- Processes;
- Partnerships;
- Pricing and revenues;
- Payments for costs and investments.

A business model canvas underlines the fact that the definition and the sequential application of a well-thought business model are an essential part of the business creation process. If properly designed, each of the nine building components of the business model canvas can become distinctive and robust components of an organization. They can contribute to the organization growth and success in the market. No component can be left out because they are all closely related.

The remaining part of this chapter analyzes each component.

Value Propositions

The value propositions represent all the products and services that an organization offers to its customers in all their possible uses. Customer satisfaction is a critical component that makes an organization successful. The customers are the ones who do word of mouth, thus bringing other customers, generating revenues, and assuming constant supporting behavior to the organization.[23] A successful value proposition must be unique. It must be clear to the decision-makers. It is about conquering the customer, influencing his/her choice, taking him/her to choose a product or service rather than another. This is the essential component that serves to distinguish one brand from another. The customer value proposition (CVP)[24] is about all those benefits that an organization promises to the customer when she/he chooses a service/product, in exchange for her/his payment It is critical to understand this concept and make value propositions an integral part of the business strategy. Without the economic return from the customer, an organization cannot last for long.

Customer Proximity

This segment includes three essential aspects: the 3 Cs: the target customers, the competitors, and the compliance with regulations:

- For whom does the insurance 4.0 initiative aim to create value?
- Who are its target customers and the competitors?
- Which are the rules it must respect?[25]

[23]Hassan, A. (2012). The value proposition concept in marketing: How customers perceive the value delivered by firms. A study of customer perspectives on supermarkets in Southampton in the United Kingdom. *International Journal of Marketing Studies, 4*(3), 68.

[24]Zhang, T. C., Gu, H., & Jahromi, M. F. (2019). What makes the sharing economy successful? An empirical examination of competitive customer value propositions. *Computers in Human Behavior, 95*, 275–283.

[25]Osterwalder, A., & Pigneur, Y. (2010). *Business model generation: A handbook for visionaries, game changers, and challengers*. Chichester, UK: Wiley.

1. Customer

Customers are the central components of an organization. They are specific types of persons or companies to whom propose goods or services. The customer is the person who is willing to pay for the company's services and products. It is critical to understand what type of products/services to develop and deliver during a business lifecycle.

Customer proximity describes the types of proximity an organization establishes with specific customers and/or customers' segments. These relations impact distribution channels. All the building blocks connect between them: no one of them can exist without the others. The type of customer proximity strongly influences the overall customer experience (a key component of competitive advantage). Empathy is an essential component of customer proximity.

Some questions to be answered to define the right customer relationship to build are:

- What type of relationship each customer or customer segment expects to establish with the organization, and how this relationship continues over time?
- How expensive is the development and maintenance of the relationship?
- How and how much is this relationship integrated within the organization's business?

Some types of relationships are as follows[26]:

- There is no real relationship between the organization and the customer. The organization interacts with the customer on an *ad hoc* transactional basis;
- Personal assistance refers to the interaction between the customer and a representative of the organization. The latter provides customer support for any need during the sales process and after the sale. This type of interaction can take place physically at the point of sale, or through virtual channels intermediaries, such as chats, emails, call centers, agencies, and so on;

[26] www.strategyzer.com. Accessed 9 March 2020.

- Long-term assistance means that a long-lasting and maybe even deep proximity exists between the organization and the customer. The organization interacts with the customer on a periodical basis and in the long term;
- Dedicated personal assistance refers to continuous interaction between the customer and a representative of the organization. In this case, the representative is always the same for the same customer. Thus, the relationship becomes more personal, and the customer has more confidence, establishing a long -term relationship;
- Self-service is a marketing technique that allows customers to choose and buy products and services, without the help of a salesperson. The self-service, in addition to facilitating the customer, enables the organization to reduce the operating costs, but it loses customer proximity;
- Automated services are a more advanced form of self-service because there is a customization component. The customer's characteristics are detected and based on these characteristics; specific information and support are provided;
- Communities are virtual communities where multiple users can get in touch with each other and exchange opinions and experiences about the same topic. To date, more and more organizations make these communities available to other persons, which is also a way to better know their customers.
- Co-creation is based on involvement and experience. It is an active, creative, and social process that involves customers creating new products and services. For example, many organizations in the video game industry ask persons to try out developing games, having direct feedback from which to take information on how to improve the products. Amazon.com invites customers to write reviews. YouTube.com solicit customers to create content for public consumption;
- Switching costs indicate how easy or difficult it is for a customer to switch to a different alternative. It is a measure of the lock-in, how much the customer is tied to a vendor, such as a bank or an insurance company.

The following motivations may drive customer proximity[27]:

- Customer acquisition
- Customer retention
- Boosting sales (upselling or cross-selling)
- Customer loyalty programs.

Allstate[28]
For Allstate Business Insurance, Earley Information Science developed "ABIe," a context-aware virtual assistant. It works through an online avatar (called "Abby") and provides Allstate agents with answers to questions.

2. Competitors

For the organizations, a competitor is any organization that offers or can offer the same or similar products or services within the same market sector.[29] The competition triggers a price lowering mechanism that serves to gain market share. It follows that organizations must try to be more and more efficient in reducing their costs.[30]

3. Compliance

Compliance is a term that identifies that organizational behavior is consistent with the laws, internal business policies, procedures, and any other regulation.[31]

[27] Geib, M., Reichold, A., Kolbe, L., & Brenner, W. (2005, January). Architecture for customer relationship management approaches in financial services. In *Proceedings of the 38th Annual Hawaii International Conference on System Sciences*, 240b-240b. IEEE.

[28] *KM World*. (2016, January). www.kmworld.com/Articles/Editorial/Features/Allstates-Intelligent-Agent-Reduces-Call-Center-Traffic-and-Provides-Help-During-Quoting-Process-108263.aspx. Accessed 10 January 2020.

[29] Porter E. M. (1990). *Competitive advantage of nations*. New York, NY: Macmillan.

[30] www.businessdictionary.com/definition/competitor.html. Accessed 30 May 2020.

[31] www.businessdictionary.com/definition/compliance.html. Accessed 30 May 2020.

Customer Partitions

To be able to serve its customers better, an organization needs to segment them.[32] Cluster analysis can help in this segmentation.[33] This method of analysis creates groups that, within them, are homogeneous, that is, having similar characteristics. For example, in business-to-customers marketing, organizations make the first segmentation based on a few necessary information: age, marital status, gender, and location. On the other hand, business-to-business marketing focuses on industry, the number of employees, products previously purchased from the organization, and location. Customer groups represent separate segments if[34]:

- Their requirements need and justify a distinct offer;
- They reach them through different distribution channels;
- They require different types of relationships;
- They have substantially different profitability;
- They are willing to pay for different aspects of the offer.

To be able to define these characteristics, an organization must collect information from customers. Several methods are used for this scope: surveys, telephone interviews, face-to-face, and so on.[35] The types of markets in which the organization is positioned can be mass market, niche market, segmented market, diversified markets, or multi-sided markets.

Choosing a customer segment to serve is a scoping decision that helps organizations focus on the customer opportunities most likely to generate success. Thus, the choice of the specific type of customers to serve is the first decision to be taken.

[32] Ericson, R. V., Doyle, A., Barry, D., & Ericson, D. (2003). *Insurance as governance*. Toronto, Canada: University of Toronto Press.

[33] Romesburg, C. (2004). *Cluster analysis for researchers*. Lulu.Com.

[34] www.shopify.com/encyclopedia/customer-segmentation. Accessed 30 May 2020.

[35] Sarstedt, M., & Mooi, E. (2014). A concise guide to market research. *The Process, Data, and, 12.*

Place or Channels

The distribution channels are the go-through whereby an organization decides to supply its products and services to a particular type of customer.[36] Depending on the type of customers, an organization can choose a specific distribution channel. The choice of channels is pivotal in strategic marketing decisions. This choice also affects the timing and costs of the distribution. It depends on different factors like:

- Typology of target customers;
- Type and size of the market;
- Value proposition;
- Type of products/nature of services and the need for support/maintenance;
- Type of operations;
- Costs and benefits;
- Competition.

The objective in choosing a channel is to reach as many customers as possible at the lowest possible cost. Thus, the organization chooses a channel when it is flexible, efficient, economical, and consistent with the organization type of business. The online channels are more and more used for their interesting characteristics.[37]

Platforms and Resources

The essential resources represent the critical assets of an organization. They are the resources (physical and non-physical) a company needs to operate its business, to maintain relations with the different customers' segments, to earn revenues, and to build a valid value proposition. The assets included in these resources are the persons, the materials, the structures, and the equipment necessary for the correct operation of the activity and to achieve the company's objectives.

[36] McDonald, M., & Wilson, H. (2016). *Marketing plans: How to prepare them, how to profit from them.* Hoboken, NJ: Wiley.

[37] Soopramanien, D. G., & Robertson, A. (2007). Adoption and usage of online shopping: An empirical analysis of the characteristics of "buyers", "browsers" and "non-internet shoppers". *Journal of Retailing and Consumer Services, 14*(1), 73–82.

The essential resources can be of four types: physical, intellectual, human, and financial:

- Physical resources are the most natural resources to identify. Tangible resources can be equipment, inventory, buildings, operational or services locations;
- Intellectual resources have a value higher than the physical ones. Brands are one of the essential resources of organizations. In addition to the trademarks, there are other intangible resources like business and market knowledge, copyrights, patents, and technology competencies;
- Human resources refer to employees and contractors who represent the engine of each organization;
- Financial resources include cash, lines of credit, and stocks, including stock option plans for employees.

The organization must answer the following question:

- Which are and what are the essential resources the organization's value propositions/distribution channels/customer proximity/revenue streams require?

Platforms represent how to enhance the resources. They are both information and telecommunication platforms and automation support.

Essential Processes and Activities

The essential processes and activities are a set of interrelated activities, carried out within the organization, that create value for the customers, contributing to building customer proximity, and adding value to the customers and the organization. Depending on the type of business model, the activities are different. During the process of defining these activities, an organization should consider:

- Value propositions;
- Distribution channels;
- Characteristics of the production, operations, and support
- Customer proximity;

- Revenue streams.

The essential activities create a bridge between value propositions and customer partitions' needs. Some types of essential activities engaged by the organizations are:

- Research & Development (R&D): It is the term commonly used to describe all the activities that an organization performs to create new processes/products/services or to improve current ones.[38] Typical functions of R&D are new product development, current product updates, quality assurance, and innovation;
- The marketing department of an organization plays an essential role in its growth and promotion.[39] Through the management of various promotional activities and their coordination, the company can attract more customers (or investors). Thus, it can increase its market share. Depending on the types of products/services offered by an organization, the marketing function may include different activities, such as designing and preparing promotional materials, monitoring and managing social media, producing external and internal communications, conducting campaign management for marketing initiatives, and so on;
- The operational activities create value for the customer through the production of the products or services. More specifically, operations are a process which transforms the inputs in outputs. This process is composed of manual, machinery, virtual activities, and so on. Operations are a value addition process. By definition, every operational activity must add value or be necessary for regulatory reasons.[40] Classical activities related to this function are: the selection of product, design, and operations processes, selecting right operations capacity, operations scheduling and planning, operations execution, quality, costs and inventory controls, maintenance, and replacement or disposition of assets and systems;

[38] Hall, B. H. (2006). *Contribution to the international encyclopedia of the social sciences* (2nd ed.).

[39] Epetimehin, F. M. (2011). Achieving competitive advantage in insurance industry: The impact of marketing innovation and creativity. *Journal of Emerging Trends in Economics and Management Sciences, 2*(1), 18–21.

[40] www.newagepublishers.com. Accessed 30 May 2020.

- Sales: A systematic approach involves a series of steps that enable a sales force to close deals, increase revenue and margins contribution, and make more sales through referrals.[41] The series of steps are customer-centric and help the sales force of a company to retain customers and increase sales volume and revenues. A sales process involves the following key steps: prospecting, qualifying, proposal presentation, handling negotiations, closing, follow-up for repeat business.[42]

Partnerships and Collaboration

Partnerships are the network of equity and capital suppliers, vendors, and intermediaries that make the business model work. A collaborative relationship between two or more organizations (irrespective of their size or how long they are on the market), who want to carry out joint projects or complement each other, is essential in the business model.[43] A contract normally defines the partnership relationship. The contract specifies how much each partner contributes to the expenses and the percentage of earnings.[44] When considering a partnership, the starting point is the benefits that such an agreement can bring to the business. The possible benefits connected with a partnership are[45]:

- Bridging the gap in expertise and knowledge: collaborating with other parties can give a wider range of expertise to different parts of the business. A correct partner may bring expertise and experience the organization may be lacking, or complementary competencies helping the growth of the company;
- A prospective partner can bring availability of cash into the company;

[41] www.nasp.com/article/D6BC485A-B705/how-to-define-a-sales-process-for-sales-success.html. Accessed 29 December 2019.

[42] Viio, P., & Grönroos, C. (2014). Value-based sales process adaptation in business relationships. *Industrial Marketing Management, 43*(6), 1085–1095.

[43] *Example of collaboration between two or more organizations*. florencedouglascenter.org/rocky-river/example-of-collaboration-between-two-or-more-organizations.php. Accessed 30 May 2020.

[44] www.businessdictionary.com. Accessed 20 April 2020.

[45] www.americanexpress.com/us/small-business/openforum/articles. Accessed 20 April 2020.

- A business partner would allow one company to share the financial burden for expenses and capital expenditures needed to run the business. This could result in substantial savings;
- Having a partner may afford the ease and flexibility to pursue more business opportunities. It might even eliminate the downside of opportunity costs;
- A partnership can bring in a set of new perspectives, vision, and culture that can help an organization to complement what they have or even replace it.
- A partnership can simplify the competition environment.

It is possible to establish different types of partnerships[46]:

- General partnership involves many general partners, all equally active in the management, in earnings and expenses to be addressed. If only one of the partners is liable, everyone else also has to contribute. It is precisely for this reason that this type of partnership is the least used;
- Limited partnership is a mix of general partners and limited partners. The latter has limited participation in comparison with the other partnerships;
- Limited liability partnership (LLP) is a mix between general partnership and corporation. All partners have a limited responsibility with regards to errors, omissions, negligence, incompetence, or malpractices committed by other partners or by their employees;
- Joint venture is typically a partnership of different businesses set up for a specific purpose (like making a particular deal) or for a limited period.

The components to consider when deciding whether an organization wants to make a partnership or not are[47]:

[46] www.thebalancesmb.com/selecting-a-business-partnership-398880. Accessed 20 April 2020.

[47] www.uwplatt.edu/files/entrepreneurship/Businesspercent20Modelpercent20Canvaspercent20Explainedpercent20Handout.docx. Accessed 30 May 2020.

- Key partners;
- Types of partners;
- Key vendors;
- Key resources or knowledge that an organization can pool with the partners;
- Key activities that partners perform;
- Key markets on which it might be possible to enter;
- Key competitor in the market space;
- Customer portfolio.

Pricing and Revenues

This component of the business model describes the earnings that the organization gets from selling products or services to the customers. The variables to be considered are the prices (fixed or dynamic) and the methods of payment. These are two essential aspects to make the business model sustainable. Revenue streams may be different and be generated from equally varied sources: from the sale of products to the payment of a fee, from the transfer of a license to brokerage commissions. For this component of the business model definition, an organization can identify customers' preferred payment system. Revenue streams are in two categories:

- Transaction revenue: it is a one-time payment for the product or provision of a service;
- Recurring revenue: it is an ongoing payment given to the organization.

The following questions should have an answer[48]:

- What benefits will convince customers to pay more for the product/service?
- What benefits are customers now paying for?

[48] *Revenue streams in business model canvas | cleverism*. www.cleverism.com/revenue-streams-in-business-model-canvas/. Accessed 30 May 2020.

- How are they paying for these benefits now?
- What mode of payment would they prefer?
- What percentage of the total earning does each revenue stream represent?

Payments for Costs and Investments

This component of the business model canvas defines the fixed and variable costs, and the investments that the company must support for the essential resources, activities, and partnerships. This component can be defined in smaller units, such as by product, service, product line, customer, cost center, or geographic region.[49] For specific organizations, containing costs may be an essential aspect, mainly if one of the company's objectives is to offer competitive prices Thus, the cost structure concept is a management accounting concept.[50] The critical components of the cost structures are:

- Product cost structure

  Fixed costs: Direct labor, operations overhead, general management dedicated to a product;

  Variable costs: Direct costs, commissions, operations supply, and piece-rate wages.
- Service cost structure

  Fixed costs: Administrative overhead;

  Variable costs: Staff wages, bonuses, payroll taxes, travel, and entertainment.
- Product line cost structure

  Fixed costs: Administrative overhead, operations overhead, and direct labor;

  Variable costs: Direct materials, commissions, and operations supplies.
- Customer cost structure

  Fixed costs: Administrative overhead for customer service and claims;

[49] *Cost structure—Accounting tools*. www.accountingtools.com/articles/what-is-cost-structure.html. Accessed 30 May 2020.

[50] www.accountingtools.com/articles/what-is-cost-structure.html. Accessed 15 April 2020.

Variable costs: Costs of products and services sold to the customer, product returns, credits taken, and early payment discounts taken.

Business Models, Strategy, and Competitive Advantage

Based on the previous overview of a business model's components, it is interesting to consider the strategies designed for a business model and the possible competitive advantages achievable. To this end, it is useful to start with the concept of strategy.

"*A satisfied customer is the best business strategy of all*".[51] These words of Michael LeBoeuf (an American business author and former management professor at the University of New Orleans) underline that a good strategy is strongly customer-oriented. This statement can be true for many organizations. Some organizations set profit and revenues as the main objective of their organization. In particular, these organizations focus their efforts on the financial results, leaving out the customer experience. Rarely they can succeed and become successful organizations at least beyond a short period. A real robust organization is one that achieves the same result by satisfying all aspects of a business, above all customer delight.[52]

The beginning of the modern study of strategy dates to the 1960s. Similarly, to the business model concept, there is still no unique definition of strategy. A historical review of the definitions used in the literature for the strategy concept shows that they are different due to the diversity of terms employed to explain it and the central basic ideas. One way to become aware of the core of a concept is to examine the context in which it was named for the first time.[53] The strategy is the core of strategic management. This area of research has not yet found a clear definition.

[51] Panda, S., & Rao, K. S. N. (2019, October). Customer acquisition and retention in non-banking finance companies (NBFC). *Journal of Mechanics and Continua and Mathematical Sciences, 14*(5). https://doi.org/10.26782/jmcms.2019.10.00045.

[52] Schneider, B., & Bowen, D. E. (1999). Understanding customer delight and outrage. *Sloan Management Review, 41*(1), 35–45.

[53] Evered, R. (1983). So what is strategy? *Long-Range Planning, 16*(3), 57–72.

the strategy is "the creation of a unique and valuable posi- ; a different set of activities."[54] From this definition, the ıing more than a set of critical actions aimed at positioning the organization in the market and achieving a robust and sustainable competitive advantage. The concept is to diversify with the competitors so that the organization can maintain and improve its position. What is needed is to introduce an innovation that can attract more customers. On the other hand, when one company successfully introduces a change in the market, other organizations tend to replicate it. An organization must be good at planning its strategy so that, even if the competitors replicate what it proposes, it can, always and in any case, provide something more than the others or introduce a strategy that provides a sustainable competitive advantage.

In this sense, Porter stated that the essence of strategy formulation is coping with competition.[55] Peter Drucker explains strategy through three assumptions[56]:

1. The environment in which the organization is;
2. The mission of the organization;
3. The core competencies needed to reach the mission.

Mintzberg defines strategy as a pattern in a stream of decisions.[57] As a consequence, it is critical to define the objective of these decisions.

Porter introduced the concept of competitive advantage. Porter starts from the following basic premises.[58]

- "The nature of the competition is different among industries and even among the segments of the same industry."

[54] Michael, P. O. R. T. E. R. (1996). What is strategy. *Harvard Business Review, 74*(6), 61–78.

[55] Porter, M. E. (1989). How competitive forces shape strategy. In *Readings in strategic management* (pp. 133–143). London, UK: Palgrave Macmillan.

[56] Drucker, P. (1994). *The theory of the business*. publicpurpose.com.au/wp-content/uploads/2016/05/Theory-of-the-Business-HBR-Sept1994.pdf. Accessed 20 April 2020.

[57] Mintzberg, H., & Waters, J. A. (1985). Of strategies, deliberate and emergent. *Strategic Management Journal, 6*(3), 257–272.

[58] Porter, M. E. (1990). *The competitive advantage of nations: With a new introduction*. New York, NY: Free Press.

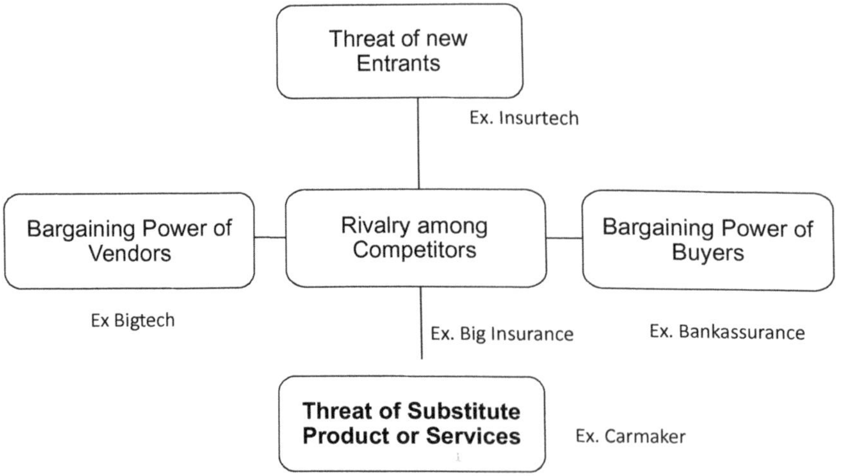

Fig. 3.4 Porter's five forces of competitive advantage for insurance

- "In the globalization context, a country can offer different competitive benefits for an organization, depending on if it is an origin country or a host country."

Porter, with his five forces model, explains the functioning of the competition in the market. He provides an essential basis for organizations to refer to when it is necessary to develop the business strategy. The five forces are (Fig. 3.4)[59]:

- Threat of new entrants;
- Threat of substitute products or services;
- Bargaining power of customers (buyers);
- Bargaining power of vendors;
- Intensity of competitive rivalry.

1. "Threat of new entrants refers to how high are the barriers to entry in a market." Some classic barriers to entry are:

[59] Porter, M. E. (2008). The five competitive forces that shape strategy. *Harvard Business Review, 86*(1), 25–40.

- Government policy;
- Capital requirements;
- Economies of scale;
- Product differentiation;
- Switching costs or sunk costs;
- Access to distribution;
- Customer loyalty to established brands;
- Industry profitability.

2. Threat of substitute products or services is about:

    - Buyer propensity to substitute;
    - Buyer switching costs;
    - Number of substitute products available in the market.

3. Regarding the bargaining power of customers, generally, it is so much higher as the more options of choice the buyers have.
4. Bargaining power of vendors: the power of organizations is less when they have only one (or at least a few) vendor available.
5. The intensity of competitive rivalry. In general, the level of intensity of competitive rivalry determines the competitiveness of a market.

These are the factors that play an essential role in the achievement of competitive advantage. The types of competitive advantage can be summarized as[60]:

- Cost leadership: the objective is to become the lowest-cost producer in the industry (generally achieved by producing on a large scale);
- Cost focus: it is about a lower-cost advantage;
- Differentiation focus: by differentiating within just one or a small number of target market segments organizations that want to achieve this type of advantage must be sure that customers have different needs. It is a niche marketing strategy;
- Differentiation leadership: it is about charging a premium price that more than covers the additional operational costs, and about giving customers clear motivations to prefer a product over the others.

[60] Porter, M. E. (1985). Technology and competitive advantage. *The Journal of Business Strategy*, 5(3), 60.

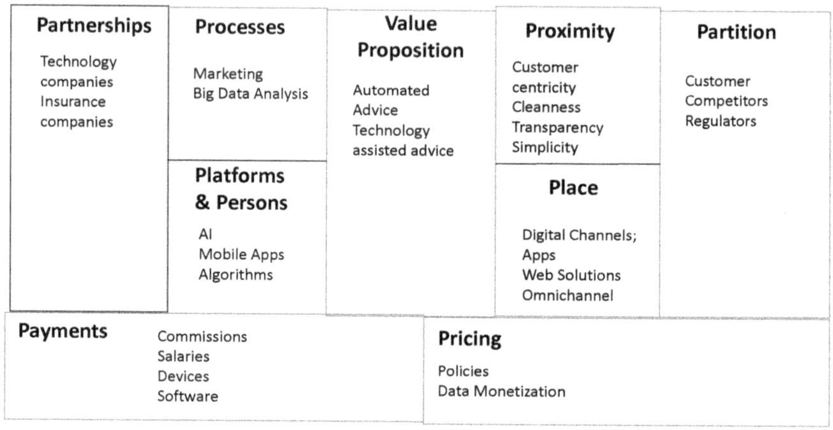

Fig. 3.5 Business model for an insurtech organizations (example)

It is possible to link them to the design of a business model through an analysis of the concepts of strategy and competitive advantage. It is easy to understand why these three aspects of an organization's management are robustly correlated with each other.

Application of the Model to the Insurance Industry

The insurance world is too varied to allow building a business model capable of fitting each of the organizations included in that definition. The value proposition, the market, and the structure of revenues and costs are distinctive aspects of every organization. This chapter does not discuss them. Figure 3.5 shows an example of a business model canvas for an insurance company. It is interesting to understand while in light of the business model presented in this book, insurance companies need to change their business model. This type of change is on the basis of the insurtech initiatives discussed in the following chapters. Insurance and insurtech organizations have several points in common. Although the former's financial base, in some cases, is significantly higher than the one of the latter, insurtech is the natural evolution of insurance according to the Darwinian principles of evolution.[61] Insurtech organizations are the

[61] Darwin, C. (2004). *On the origin of species, 1859*. London, UK: Routledge.

outcome of a still-on-going process of adaptation and mutual influence with the external environment.

The business model canvas aims to provide each company operating in the insurance industry with general and practical guidelines for being a successful organization.

According to the McKinsey organization, the drivers that can disrupt the insurance industry are (Fig. 3.5)[62]:

- Poor engagement: "Life companies have long struggled to engage prospective customers and nurture proximity with current ones. The product purse high customer interest but low engagement, leading to significant untapped demand."[63] The high degree of intermediation between insurance companies and customers does not help in reducing their distance. This situation is due to agencies, banks, independent financial advisors, and brokers vertically operating within the distribution channels. The low digitization of the whole industry does not match the expectations of the new types, and especially the new generation, of customers, such as the millennials. The expression of the millennials (or Generation Y) refers to this customer segment between 18 and 34 years. This segment is very active on the web, social media, and mobile phone. Generation Y represents a quarter of the world population,[64] It is a significant target also for insurance companies to try to conquer this market, as millennials are the customers of the near future. These customers do not rely on their private sphere, as family or friends, to get information. Millennials prefer online reviews or social communities like specialized forums and other online sites. With the radical diffusion of smartphones and other mobile devices, millennials affect the behavior of the old generation of customers. This is known as the

[62] www.mckinsey.com/~/media/mckinsey/industries/financial%20services/our%20insights/time%20for%20insurance%20companies%20to%20face%20digital%20reality/digital-disruption-in-insurance.ashxx. Accessed 30 May 2020. https://doi.org/10.26782/jmcms.2019.10.00045. 18 November 2019.

[63] Nicoletti, B. (2017). A business model for insurtech initiatives. In *The future of FinTech* (pp. 211–249). Cham: Palgrave Macmillan.

[64] www.ft.com/content/f81ac17a-68ae-11e8-b6eb-4acfcfb08c11. Accessed 30 May 2020.

"equalizing effect."[65] Its consequence may be severe for a static and low digitized industry like insurance that has traditionally targeted a predominantly non-digital natives market. The insurance companies that have shown a management mindset, a forward-looking attitude, and implemented digital solutions are relatively few. This situation opens the door to agile, digital-oriented innovators: like the insurtech organizations.

- Legacy cost and investment structures: New startups can deliver leading-edge propositions without incurring in transformation costs as it is for incumbent organizations. Traditional life insurance companies most likely have policies stipulated twenty, maybe thirty years ago, implying an inflexible set of customers and policies that are difficult and costly to change.
- Legacy ICT systems: The rigidity of their policies and customers goes together with the use of old processes and ICT systems. The combination of Legacy Cost Structures and Legacy ICT Systems has caused the total expense ratio to decline by only 0.5 percentage points (2000–2013) in several European markets.[66]
- Risk aversion: The insurance industry has often been static, averse to change and innovation: high product development cycles, low ICT investments, and slow delivery decisions have been severe bottlenecks for many companies trying to survive. Somebody has labeled companies as "slow fishes," operating in a "sea" built on stability and risk-reluctance.[67]

As the first step, it is interesting to position the four issues identified by McKinsey into the associated components of the business model canvas. This macro-area of the business model affects (positively or negatively) the issue taken into account (Fig. 3.6). The figure can provide insights into the factors that have or could create difficulties for the whole sector. It is possible to consider the different paths within the model presented

[65] www.mckinsey.it/idee/transforming-life-procurement-with-design-thinking. Accessed 30 May 2020.

[66] Average expense ratio (expense per GWP) from 2000 to 2013; unweighted average expense ratios of Austria, Belgium, France, Germany, Ireland, Italy, Netherlands, Portugal, Spain, Sweden, and the United Kingdom (McKinsey Global Insurance Pools).

[67] Nicoletti, B. (2017). A business model for insurtech initiatives. In B. Nicoletti (Ed.), *The future of FinTech* (pp. 211–249). Cham, Switzerland: Palgrave Macmillan.

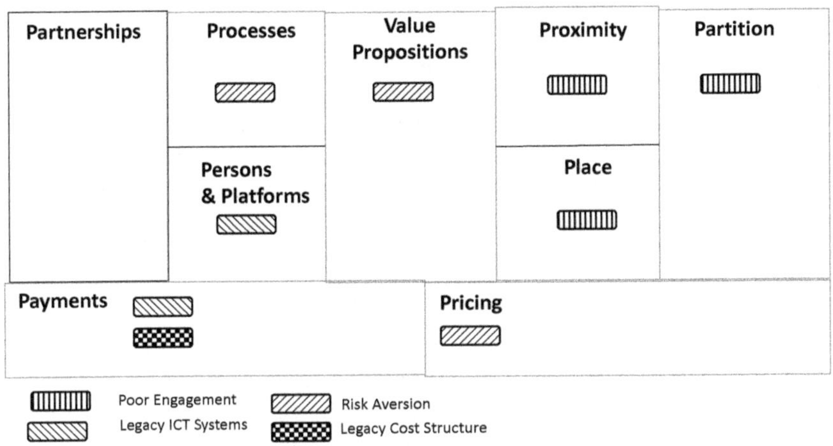

Fig. 3.6 Issurance issues

in this book. If it is possible to single out the adverse factors, it should be possible to find the possible remediation.

Competitive Advantages

The industry structure analysis is to investigate the industry-related environment.[68] An analysis concludes that by digitizing the profitability in the insurance industry tends to fall. Competition is intensifying not only from new providers but also between current companies. The customers get more control. The risk of substitution increases. These points are mutually dependent but, to some extent, mutually exclusive. It is critical than ever for the insurance companies that they differ by strategies. A precise objective is still missing; according to the analysis, the insurance industry is slowly catching up doing where it has slept and to position themselves strategically, either through cost leadership, differentiation, or focus/niche choice.

To limit a corporate strategy and digitization to a purely sectoral analysis is not enough. Internal factors, such as leadership, employee motivation, robust organizational structures, also play an essential role

[68] Hartung, T., & Rohatsch, N. (2018). *Einfluss der Digitalisierung auf die Unternehmensstrategie*. Munchen, Germany: München University.

and must be analyzed. The long-term winners are those companies using online activities as a growing supplement and not as an alternative to the mode of their current operations. The insurance companies must be willing to give up long-term planning by business cases and build on competencies such as risk-taking and agility. They should leave the comfort zone where some companies have been staying for over a hundred years.

Conclusions

By defining the nine components of the business model canvas, an organization can select its business model and market strategy. From that moment on, based on the choices made, the organization's positioning in the market may, or may not, result in competitive advantage (sustainable or not). To be robust, an organization must be able not only to reach a position of advantage but also to know how to keep it. From time to time, the company needs to rethink its strategy and then adapt and improve its business model to avoid being overwhelmed by competitors. It is not a simple objective because, speaking of change, other factors (mostly human) arise, determining the ability of an organization to adapt to new situations.

To conclude, a business model reflects the objectives of an organization, its strategy, and produces results through the market, in which the organization can gain a competitive advantage. Digitization changes how companies and customers interact (e.g., in sales, in customer service, and similar).[69] Insurance 4.0 combines digitization and automation, which influences all business processes (e.g., with the automated acquisition and processing of contracts) and the decision-making processes, including risk assessment (e.g., automated underwriting using tools of artificial intelligence), and big data analytics. Digitization changes current products (for instance, introducing online and connected insurance) and allows new product offerings (e.g., cyber risk insurance). The correct way to analyze such changes is by considering a business model canvas and work on it for the benefit of the customers and hence of the organization.

[69] Eling, M., & Lehmann, M. (2018). The impact of digitalization on the insurance value chain and the insurability of risks. *The Geneva Papers on Risk and Insurance-Issues and Practice*, *43*(3), 359–396.

CHAPTER 4

Propositions of Value for the Customer in Insurance 4.0

Introduction

Value is essential to meet customer needs[1] and to identify the best value network.[2] A potential customer would buy a particular product or service strongly connected with the value proposition connected with the product or the services. A customer can choose an organization rather than another (preferring it to the competitors) based on the value-adding of the company's solution. The offer must be irresistible. It should be an invitation so attractive that the customer cannot refuse it.

Several papers detail how to identify and measure customer value.[3] The real value of a company comes from the customer, without which the company itself would not have revenues. "Satisfying customers is the source of sustainable value creation."[4] For this reason, value propositions are very different across industries and market segments within an

[1] Soliman, M., & Saurin, T. A. (2017). Lean production in complex socio-technical systems: A systematic literature review. *Journal of Manufacturing Systems, 45*, 135–148.

[2] Welo, T., & Ringen, G. (2012). NPD practices in the Norwegian manufacturing industry: Assessing the relationship between key dimensions and performance. In *ISPIM Innovation Symposium, the International Society for Professional Innovation Management.*

[3] da Luz Peralta, C. B., Echeveste, M. E., Lermen, F. H., Marcon, H., & Tortorella, G. (2020). A framework proposition to identify customer value through lean practices. *Journal of Manufacturing Technology Management.*

[4] Kaplan, R. S., & Norton, D. P. (2004). The strategy map: Guide to aligning intangible assets. *Strategy & Leadership, 32*(5), 10–17.

B. Nicoletti, *Insurance 4.0*, Palgrave Studies in Financial Services Technology, https://doi.org/10.1007/978-3-030-58426-9_4

industry. Only when an organization receives the revenue through the customer's payment can consider having sustainable sales financing. In many cases, the priority has been giving value to the shareholders rather than to the customers.

One of the reasons why business models have become popular is that persons want to discover the best way to manage their business to add value to the customers and the organization at the same time. Drucker pointed out that making a profit is very often mentioned as the purpose of a firm, it "is not only false; it is irrelevant."[5] It may even be harmful. Profit-making is not the purpose. For Drucker, "there is only one valid definition of business purpose: to create a customer."[6] An organization can get customers only if it can fulfill what its target customers need. An organization defines its business through the value proposition it offers to its customers. This approach is exactly the bridge between the organization's purpose and the need and desires of customers. The business model is a vehicle to drive the employees, the management, and the company's stakeholders in this direction. Insurance companies need to build a value proposition around what modern customers care about[7]:

- speed and simplicity of purchase transaction;
- speed and simplicity with the claims process;
- price;
- on-demand availability when he or she needs help or have questions;
- overall convenience & customer experience;
- innovation.

With the adoption of a smart solution, the value proposition could improve substantially. In this respect, alliances are possible, potentially with device manufacturers and service providers that may provide an excellent customer value proposition.[8] With expansion from the core capability to complementary customer needs and with the adoption of the

[5] Swaim, R. W. (2011). *The strategic Drucker: Growth strategies and marketing insights from the works of Peter Drucker*. Hoboken, NJ: Wiley.

[6] Zehner, W. B., & Zehner, J. A. (2019). Marketing for science based organizations perspectives and questions. *Marketing of Scientific and Research Organizations*, *32*(2), 77–106.

[7] advisorevolved.com/insurance-agency-value-proposition/. Accessed 28 March 2020.

[8] iotinsobs.com. Accessed 20 May 2020.

smart solutions, the value proposition could improve substantially. Insurance companies can take the role of the orchestrators of an ecosystem that adds value for the policyholders.[9]

Insurance 4.0 and Value Network

Insurance 4.0 is the integration of the automation and digital world with several new solutions that enhance value for the customer, data availability, and business processes. It is fundamentally changing the value creation of the insurance industry.[10]

It is interesting to analyze the relationship between insurance 4.0 and the value network of an organization.

Because of insurance 4.0, information is becoming more relevant for the organization than the operational factors. To cope with this digital development, many organizations have started to move part of their business to the web. They have developed a type of relationship with customers based on innovative solutions and advanced communication tools.

Online business means initiating, arranging, and carrying out online business processes. In other words, it means interacting and exchanging services with the help of communication networks, mainly the internet, to achieve added value for the customers and the organization. Organizations, public institutions, and customers can be both service providers and service customers. What is essential is that the online business relationship generates added value, which may take either a direct or indirect financial benefit or an intangible contribution.[11]

The dematerialization of products and the remote working are transforming how companies position themselves in the value network due to reduced operational and transport costs and the different ways businesses engage with customers. These new market conditions can strengthen downstream organizations. Upstream companies can still gain added

[9] Smart Home Insurance—LinkedIn SlideShare. www.slideshare.net/matteocarbone/smart-home-insurance-14443835. Accessed 30 March 2020.

[10] Eling, M., & Lehmann, M. (2018). The impact of digitization on the insurance value chain and the insurability of risks. *The Geneva Papers on Risk and Insurance-Issues and Practice*, *43*(3), 359–396.

[11] Meier, A., & Stormer, H. (2009). *eBusiness & eCommerce: Managing the digital value chain*. Berlin/Heidelberg, Germany: Springer Science & Business Media.

value through the digital service if their offers, including components of uniqueness that are difficult to replicate or imitate from the competition.[12]

It is interesting to examine the impact of insurance 4.0 on the company. The three main categories of change in insurance 4.0 are[13]:

- Proximity: new solutions change how companies and customers interact. A later chapter on customer proximity deals with these changes;
- Business processes: new solutions allow automatizing, standardizing, and improving the effectiveness, efficiency, and economics of business processes. A later chapter on processes deals with these changes;
- Products: new solutions create opportunities to modify current products and to develop new ones. This chapter covers this subject.

The first impact on the value network is how insurance organizations interact with their customers (e.g., marketing, sales, and customer service) and adapt to their behavior. Customers traditionally needed personal interaction for product information or transactions. They can now get information online, which allow comparing products and prices via marketplace comparators.[14] More and more products can be purchased online without any personal interaction. A survey by Accenture done in 2016 has probed eighteen markets. The result is that 68 percent of persons prefer to use online channels to get info on insurance products and services.[15]

The second impact regards the digitization of all processes of the value network, leading to the automation of business processes (i.e., the automated processing of contracts, automatic reporting of claims, and so on)

[12] Vendrell-Herrero, F., Bustinza, O. F., Parry, G., & Georgantzis, N. (2017). Servitization, digitization and supply chain interdependency. *Industrial Marketing Management*, *60*, 69–81.

[13] Eling, M., & Lehmann, M. (2018). *The impact of digitization on the insurance value chain and the insurability of risks*. New York, NY: Springer.

[14] Saffer, D. (2010). *Designing for interaction: Creating innovative applications and devices*. Indianapolis, IN: New Riders.

[15] www.accenture.com/t00010101T000000Z__w__/gb-en/_acnmedia/PDF-50/Accenture-Distribution-Marketing-Survey-Insurance-Report.pdf. Accessed 1 January 2020.

and decisions (i.e., automated underwriting, claim settlement, product offerings, and so on).

A third impact is that digitization changes current products and allows new product offerings such as cyber risk insurance. Concerning new offerings, the requirements for protecting from cyber attacks in the USA and the European Union[16] have triggered the development of an insurance market for cyber risks, both in personal and commercial lines. The technological progress to date makes it possible to underwrite risks not considered until now. Smart contracts, that is programs that automatically execute the claim payment under predefined conditions stored in the blockchain, are fully digital and automatic products, implementing Straight Through Processing (STP), a characteristic of insurance 4.0.[17]

Empowerment of Customers

This section aims to clarify how insurance companies should deal with the empowerment of their customers and, at the same time, leverage them to achieve a competitive advantage.

Some issues influence the market negatively, mainly incumbent organizations tend to have[18]:

- poor engagement;
- risk aversion.

For new entrants and recent startups may be easier to design their businesses following the insurance 4.0 model. Incumbents may face significant transformation difficulties. They could end up with negative consequences if not well managed.

[16] An example is the GDPR in the European Union. gdpr-info.eu/. Accessed 1 July 2020.

[17] Eling, M., & Lehmann, M. (2018). *The impact of digitization on the insurance value chain and the insurability of risks*. Cham, Switzerland: Springer.

[18] www.mckinsey.it/idee/culture-for-a-digital-age. Accessed 20 March 2020.

A European-wide study,[19] commissioned by Fujitsu, helps in understanding the dimension of the change in the interaction between insurance companies and their customers.[20] This study underlines these facts[21]:

- More than a third of European customers would consider moving to a competing financial services institution if they did not get up-to-date technology to aid interactions;
- Nearly a third of customers are already embracing mobile payments. A fifth are already using wearables and cryptocurrency to pay;
- Nearly a fifth of customers would be ready to buy banking or insurance services from challengers such as Google, Facebook, and Amazon.

Another Fujitsu survey on insurance companies found that across Europe, 97 percent of those surveyed were willing to leave financial institutions use their personal data for marketing a broader range of services. This shift in customer mindset is massive[22]:

- Nearly three in five (59 percent) would be willing for their financial institutions to use their data to lower their mortgage premium;
- Nearly half (47 percent) of customers would allow financial institutions to use their data to recommend exciting products and services;

[19] Fujitsu EMEIA. (2016, May). *Banking on change: Consumers drive digital charge in financial services*. www.fujitsu.com/fts/about/resources/news/press-releases/2016/emeai-160504-banking-on-change-consumers-drive-digital.html. Accessed 25 August 2019.

[20] Seven thousand online consumers across the UK, France, Benelux, Spain, Germany, Switzerland, and Eastern Europe understand consumers' habits and views and opinions towards current Financial Services.

[21] Fujitsu EMEIA. (2016, May). *Banking on change: Consumers drive digital charge in financial services*. www.fujitsu.com/fts/about/resources/news/press-releases/2016/emeai-160504-banking-on-change-consumers-drive-digital.html. Accessed 25 August 2019.

[22] Fujitsu EMEIA. (2016, May). *Banking on change: Consumers drive digital charge in financial services*. www.fujitsu.com/fts/about/resources/news/press-releases/2016/emeai-160504-banking-on-change-consumers-drive-digital.html. Accessed 25 August 2019.

- More than two in five (44 percent) would find essential for financial institutions to use data to inform them about their spending habits and offer relevant advices;
- Nearly a third (36 percent) would like their data used by financial institutions to improve their credit rating.

Based on this survey, the move to insurance 4.0 appears as a natural evolution. Customers are going digital, although is not simple in some cases. Companies need to build or heavily modify their information and communication technology systems, make changes to their business models, renovate their culture, adapt their structure to the new business, and so on.

Companies can achieve growth by leveraging on several trends[23]:

- Mobility;
- Channels;
- Big data analytics;
- Internet of things;
- Blockchain.

Smart insured assets data can enable the insurer to assess and manage specific risks in these assets. The result, of course, is an excellent value proposition.

Benefits and Challenges in Insurance 4.0

There are several ways to get value from the data in insurance 4.0. Four "value-creation lever" categories are[24]:

- Loss control;
- Behavioral change;
- Risk selection;

[23] Classification modified by the Author to Vertafore. (2013). *7 technology trends transforming the insurance industry: How companies can achieve growth*. www.vertafore.com/~/media/Vertafore-Media-Library/Resources-Liabrary/Brochures/7-Trends-Transforming-the-procurement-Industry-062513_v2b.ashx. Accessed 20 May 2020.

[24] www.slideshare.net/matteocarbone/smart-home-insurance-144438351.

- Shared economy.

The following is a more in-depth discussion of each of these categories.

Loss Control
The prevention and mitigation potential of innovations can help in anticipating insurance claims and improve reimbursement evaluation. If carefully selected, smart data can allow for tangible economic benefits to claims management based on real-time, data-driven processes. The use of intelligent data can[25]:

- Anticipate the first notification of loss, making it almost in real-time;
- Reduce the timeline to address customer needs or settle claims;
- Enforce objectivity and automation of the claim management process; and
- Improve false claims detection.

Such improvements from innovative solutions can help in improving accuracy and loss adjustment expenses.

Behavioral Change
The more an insurer links customer behaviors and losses, the higher the opportunity to understand and promote safer and more secure practices while discouraging riskier ones. When a company adds rewards for safer actions to this equation, there is the additional benefit of improved loyalty from the more harmless customer. Companies can provide bonuses, possibly also financed by partners who are keen to access the insurer's customer base. This approach requires a successful orchestration of an ecosystem, where different partners provide tangible value to customers. Reward mechanisms, permitted by law, represent other ways to give back to customers in ways that are in tune with them.

Risk Selection
Smart solutions are useful directly or indirectly to select risks during the underwriting stage, improving the effectiveness of underwriting

[25] www.octotelematics.com/blog/the-power-of-insurance-iot-for-risk-management/. Accessed 26 March 2020.

activity. Data collection tools can also enhance the overall quality of the underwriting process.

An insurer must gather a sufficient number of smart data and study the correlation between newly-discovered risk factors and loss events. This discovery process is a trial and error process that adds new risk types to the current risk models. It can support continuous improvements and increasing sophistication of the risk models. Data can help identify the relevance of real-time property conditions as in the case of asset insurance (such as home or vehicle).[26]

- Completed maintenance;
- External weather conditions;
- Heating, ventilation, and air conditioning status;
- Plumbing conditions;
- Mechanical vibration;
- Mold presence;
- Roofing conditions; and
- Temperature of the asset (engine, pipes, roof, and walls).

Shared Economy

The sharing economy is connected with the loss of interest from customers in owning an object, such as a vehicle. There is a change in the insurance product since insurance does not ensure the vehicle owner. The new coverage is for a specific group of persons who use a shared asset. There is an entirely different risk of liability and claims. With the sharing economy, it is difficult to accurately assess the risk since it traditionally determines the premium based on experience.[27] Although many statistical and mathematical tools calculate the risk, there is still a lack of experience demonstrating the probability of accidents and their impacts statistically in the case of shared assets.

[26] Holler, J., Tsiatsis, V., Mulligan, C., Karnouskos, S., Avesand, S., & Boyle, D. (2014). *Internet of things*. Cambridge, MA: Academic Press.

[27] The Tragedy of the Sharing Economy—GoWander—Medium. medium.com/gowander/the-tragedy-of-the-sharing-economy-c3a45cb207cc. Accessed 40 March 2020.

This new business model presents challenges but, as usual, also opportunities for insurance companies. They would have access to an extensive number of small customers. A critical issue is that this will create new inefficiencies because companies can cash reduced premiums from each user in more significant numbers, which correspond to fewer but higher unit premiums than before. In this new scenario, companies are faced with many more partial users (or small users) and must assess their risks. In a shared economy, technology plays a vital role.[28]

The availability of large data on policyholders and the use of technologies such as the IoT and big data analytics enable the sharing economy platforms to offer more appropriate insurance products to customers' needs and with better rates, but not reduced earnings for the company.[29]

Digital technologies facilitate the use of business models of the sharing economy.[30] These models are growing. Companies are already offering in some country's insurance products arising from the sharing economy.[31] The sharing economy can and will change the character of Property and Casualty (P&C) insurance. The growing importance of the sharing economy's business models leads to insurance benefits amplified by the use of assets and less tied to the ownership of goods. There are tendencies where the price for the use of a shared asset includes insurance.[32]

Thanks to digital technology, the development of person-to-person (P2P) policies can replace and threaten traditional insurance companies. An opportunity is to collaborate with these P2P competitors and develop them into a type of intermediary of conventional insurance companies.[33]

[28] Traum, A. B. (2015). Sharing risk in the sharing economy: Insurance regulation in the age of uber. *Cardozo Public Laws, Policy, & Ethics Journal, 14*, 511.

[29] Campos, I. (2018, January 31). *How the sharing economy is changing the insurance industry*. www.capgemini.com/2018/01/how-the-sharing-economy-is-changing-theinsurance-industry/. Accessed 24 December 2019.

[30] Prognos, A. G. (2017). *Digitalisierung in der Versicherungswirtschaft. Studie*. München, Germany: Hg. v. vbw Vereinigung der Bayerischen Wirtschaft e.V.

[31] Campos, I. (2018, January). *How the sharing economy is changing the insurance industry*. https://www.capgemini.com/2018/01/how-the-sharing-economy-is-changing-theinsurance-industry/. Accessed 24 December 2019.

[32] Bughin, J., Chui, M., & Manyika, J. (2010). Clouds, big data, and smart assets: Ten tech-enabled business trends to watch. *McKinsey Quarterly, 56*(1), 75–86.

[33] Stern, F. (2015). The end of the automobile. *Allianz Journal*. www.allianz.com/en/press/allianz-journal/edition-02-15/150701_the-end-of-theautomobile/. Accessed 24 December 2019.

Rent'n'Share[34]

AXA gives high priority to many projects with insurtech organizations. In 2017, AXA Winterthur and Swisscom started a project called Rent'n'Share. Ownership of a vehicle is less essential.[35] With Rent'n'Share, Axa offers an alternative transparent, simple, and flexible hiring of a vehicle.[36] AXA Winterthur and Swisscom launched the project on the market as a separate company. With the "Rent'n'Share" project, AXA "became" a kind of startup. In cooperation with Swisscom, AXA has set up a sharing pool where vehicle owners can rent their vehicles on a long-term basis and get financial benefits.

New Products to Add Value

It is important to take into account that most companies do not have sufficient tools and methods to help them understand and forecast when to push appropriate products.[37]

A drastic way to look at new products is to consider that "insuring is necessary, insurance is not." It is critical to the basics of insuring, to understand which will be the products of success as soon as possible. The following pages will detail this concept in terms of new and growing products. A synthesis of some insurance products under this philosophy is in Fig. 4.1.

In the analysis of new products supported by insurance 4.0, it is possible to use two criteria. The first one is connected with the technologies used. The second criterion is based on the objective that the company wants to reach. This section analyzes these two opportunities.

[34] Ade, M. (2017, October). *Wenn Grossunternehmen zum Startup werden*. blog.axa.ch/unternehmen/startupkickstart-accelerator-intrapreneur-swisscom-axa/. Accessed 24 December 2019.

[35] *GM invests $500 million in Lyft and driverless car partnership*. www.mercurynews.com/2016/01/04/gm-invests-500-million-in-lyft-and-driverless-car-partnership/. Accessed 33 March 2020.

[36] Fuhrmann, K. (2017). *Insurer AXA & ICT provider Swisscom build intrapreneurship project rent'n'share*. magazine.startus.cc/insurer-axa-ict-provider-swisscom-build-intrapreneurship-project-rentnshare/. Accessed 24 December 2019.

[37] worldinsurancereport.com. Accessed 39 May 2020.

Value-Adding	Cases of Insurance
Improving the Value Proposition	On-Demand Usage-based Person-to-Person
Keeping the same value proposition And make incremental changes to the promises	Parametric Bsuiness Interruptions
Cross-selling products	Other Services Unit-linked Cybersecurity

Fig. 4.1 From insurance to insuring

New Insurance Products Developed Based on the Technologies Used

The chapter on the platforms for insurance 4.0 considers this classification in more detail. A brief recap is the following one. New solutions can support product development and sale. They can be based on big data analytics, possibly combined with the use of the internet of things (IoT), systems of interrelated sensors/devices, and blockchain ledgers, which allow for the development of smart contracts, capable of executing or enforcing by themselves without human intervention.

The collection and analysis of big data facilitate a better knowledge of potential customers and identify their risk profiles. They improve the competitiveness of the products and services offered by adapting offer customization to customers' needs in quality and price.[38] Big data analytics allow for processing, correlating, and analyzing the data available and drawing new information and forecasts from this process in real-time and with a known probability. The ability to collect and use big data analytics proves to be crucial to analyze the vast quantity of information, structured, and unstructured,[39] collected by telematics devices, social networks, and other sources (customer feedback, market research,

[38] Cappiello, A. (2020). The digital (R) evolution of insurance business models. *American Journal of Economics and Business Administration, 12*(1), 1–13.

[39] Anchen, J., & Dowe, A. (2019). Advanced analytics unlocking new frontiers in P&C insurance. *Sigma, 4,* 2–30.

and so on). Machine learning algorithms can improve the quality of data analysis used for customer segmentation and risk allocation.

New Products Based on the Objectives

This categorization considers the objectives that the company wants to reach with the introduction of new products. On the objectives for introducing new products, it is possible to distinguish among:

- How to act on the demand for insurance by improving the value proposition;
- Keeping the same value proposition and making incremental changes to the implied promise;
- Cross-selling products for insuring.

In the first category, there are mainly three types of insurance products:

- On-demand;
- Usage-based;
- Person-to-person.

The second category connects with the object of insurance by expanding the value proposition: Keeping the same value proposition, but making the implied promise more in-depth or broader for customers. In this category, there are mainly three types of insurance products:

- Cybersecurity;
- Parametric;
- Business Interruptions.

The third category is for cross-selling products of different types, not necessarily of the traditional insurance types. It creates a new value proposition. The organization makes a new promise to its customers regarding the value of its products and/or services. In this category, it is possible to list two types of products:

- Other services;
- Unit-linked insurances.

The following pages consider each one of these products.

On-Demand Insurance

According to KPMG, on-demand insurance is convenient for many customers since it offers the possibility to pay when required.[40]

The majority of the customers look to on-demand assurances positively and optimistically way. Young persons find that this type of insurance is beneficial for those who do not often use the asset (e.g., the car or the motorcycle). It is cheaper than the annual premium. If one day, a customer forgets to activate the insurance coverage, there is a risk of not being covered in the event of an accident. Some persons might not voluntarily activate the coverage. Apps can very well support this type of insurance by activating the insurance by simply touching an icon on the cell phone. Insurance companies might have a loss of revenue.

Usage-Based Insurance (UBI)

Usage-based insurance (UBI) allows the customer to save on insurance premiums and increase the fairness of premiums because the latter would be equivalent to the use of the asset. In the case of a vehicle, there could be a pay-as-you-drive (PAYD) insurance. Not everyone would be willing to enter into a policy of UBI. According to a survey conducted by Deloitte in 2014, about 50 percent of drivers around the world are not interested in using UBI.[41] According to the findings from this research, some insurance executives, and media reports regarding UBI programs, concluded that there is a significant customer segment that would not be interested in testing this type of insurance. The reasons for this position are that some persons do not want to share personal information with companies. This position connects partially with concerns about privacy. Some customers would not feel at ease with these controls. Other

[40] Merrey, P., & Kokins, A. (2017). *Will on-demand insurance become mainstream*. Assets. https://assets.kpmg/content/dam/kpmg/uk/pdf/2017/09/will-on-demand-insurance-become-mainstream.pdf. Accessed 30 May 2020.

[41] www2.deloitte.com/content/dam/insights/us/articles/telematics-in-auto-insurance/DUP-695_Telematics-in-the-procurement-Industry_vFINAL.pdf. Accessed 1 January 2020.

customers worry that hackers or thieves of mobile phones could have access to their data. Other customers are afraid that the information collected can be used one day by the judicial or police authorities.[42]

After the pandemic, the mood has completely changed. UBI looks particularly attractive to many persons, for instance, for the delivery, courier, and trade van fleets.[43] A van fleet owner will only need to pay a base subscription rate for the vehicles which are not out on the road. If they experience a sudden surge in demand, costs can go up to a threshold. So they will never pay more than the agreed limit. This method keeps insurance costs in line with workload and revenue.

Peer-to-Peer Insurance

The current social economy leads to a new way of insurance based on peer-to-peer relationships. Peer-to-peer insurance (P2PI) makes individuals pool together to share risk.[44] These types of insurance have grown mainly based on social networks. It covers the smaller losses that usually persons would have paid individually. If no such claims occur during the year, the pool members can get back a part of their premiums.

P&C insurance products are the most sold in this category. The significant growth of some trends, such as carpooling, could lead P2P insurance to play a central role within auto insurance.

P2PI works in this way:

- a group of persons join together to share risk;
- they pay a portion of their premiums into a mutual pool;
- they pay the balance of their premiums to an insurer;
- the mutual pool fund claims. The insurance company reinsures by funding claims that the peers cannot meet because they have finished

[42] Friedman, S., & Canaan, M. (2014). *Overcoming speed bumps on the road to telematics: Challenges and opportunities facing auto companies with and without usage-based programs*. www2.deloitte.com/content/dam/insights/us/articles/telematics-in-auto-insurance/DUP-695_Telematics-in-the-Insurance-Industry_vFINAL.pdf. Accessed 20 March 2020.

[43] member.fintech.global/2020/05/13/zego-extends-partnership-with-rsa-insurance-to-cover-van-fleets/. Accessed 30 May 2020.

[44] Greco, A. (2018). *Digital transformation and disruption*. Doctoral dissertation, NOVA—School of Business and Economics, Lisbon, Portugal.

their funds. Companies can also provide other services to the pool, such as policy administration or risks evaluations;
- The funds not spent at the end of the year are refunded to the peers, or used for next year. Thus, they generate savings that would have been profits for the company in a traditional insurance process.

Some European P2PI networks declared that they could save their members up to 80 percent[45] on their premiums and 1/3 on average in property insurance.[46] This saving depends on the fact that the pool is brought to commit fewer fraudulent claims than normal policyholders since making fraudulent claims members risk being thrown out of the pool. This network allows persons to assess risks for the pool more accurately than companies by sharing valuable insights that companies do not possess. This situation happens because some specific information on the insured persons could be available to the members of the pool. P2PI has lower costs since members pay each other small claims, eliminating part of the claims handling procedures. The customer acquisition cost (CAC) is more economical since the pool is doing the marketing by themselves, for example, through social networks. Of course, the bigger the pool, the bigger the savings.

Cyber Insurance

Cybersecurity is the practice of protecting computers, servers, applications, mobile devices, electronic systems, networks, and data from malicious attacks, unauthorized accesses, or data loss.[47] It depends on information and communication technology or operational technology (OT) security.[48] These terms apply in a variety of contexts, from the organization to a computing ecosystem,

In 2016, the annual global cost of cyber crime reached USD 575 billion, with 26 percent of organizations reporting a substantial loss of

[45] www2.deloitte.com/content/dam/Deloitte/uk/Documents/financial-services/deloitte-uk-insurance-disrupted.pdf. Accessed 20 March 2020.

[46] www.the-digital-insurer.com/dia/friendsurance-germany-makes-insurance-social-again/. Accessed 20 March 2020.

[47] Www.Kaspersky.Com/Resource-Center/Definitions/What-Is-Cyber-Security. Accessed 31 May 2019.

[48] Windelberg, M. (2016). Objectives for managing cyber supply chain risk. *International Journal of Critical Infrastructure Protection, 12,* 4–11.

at least 10,000 data records caused by the breach.[49] The average cost of a cyber attack in the USA is estimated at USD 7 million.[50]

McKinsey and the World Economic Forum surveyed executives. Sixty-five percent of respondents agreed with the statement; that the risk of a cyber attack is a significant issue that could have significant strategic implications over the next five years.[51] Cyber risks have long been among the top ten business risks across industries. Cyber insurance can cover data loss, theft, identity recovery, business interruption, and post-incident public relations, among other things. It has not yet reached maturity, mainly due to three factors[52]:

- Limited robust, publicly available data for underwriters;
- Rapidly evolving scale, scope, and characteristics of cyber attacks;
- The danger of compounded future losses.

Cyber insurance products were first introduced late in the 1970s.[53] These products initially extended traditional insurance policies for online banking to cover victims from losses caused by outsiders gaining physical access to computer systems.[54] Initial insurance policies for protecting policyholders against computer attacks only covered physical damage from cyber crime. With the internet, new forms of cyber crime caused an increasing number of losses or damage to intangible assets, including lost

[49] *Insurance beyond digital: The rise of ecosystems and platforms*. www.mckinsey.com/industries/financial-services/our-insights/insurance-beyond-digital-the-rise-of-ecosystems-and-platforms. Accessed 30 May 2020.

[50] Symantech. (2017, April). *Internet security threat report*. www-east.symantec.com/content/dam/symantec/docs/reports/istr-22-2017-en.pdf. Accessed 30 May 2020. Symantec. (2016, October). *Cost of cyber crime study and the risk of business innovation*. Ponemon Institute. Ponemon.Org. Accessed 30 May 2020.

[51] Chinn, D., Kaplan, J., & Weinberg, A. (2014, January). *Risk and responsibility in a hyperconnected world: Implications for enterprises*. World Economic Forum in collaboration with McKinsey & Company. McKinsey.com. Accessed 30 May 2020.

[52] https://www.businessinsurance.com/article/20190103/NEWS06/912325909/Business-Insurance-2018-Data-&-Rankings#. Accessed 10 October 2020.

[53] Majuca, R. P. Yurcik, W. & Kesan, J. P. (2006). *The evolution of cyber insurance*. arXiv preprint cs/0601020.

[54] Majuca, R. P. (2006). *Three essays on the law and economics of information technology security*. Urbana-Champaign, IL: University of Illinois.

data and information theft.[55] Since the data and information managed by organizations do not, in many cases, exist in physical form, those insured by traditional insurance policies failed to get coverage for their loss of data and information from companies.[56] The inability of initial cyber insurance policies to deal with this problem resulted in costly litigations between companies and cyber victims, and companies attempts to avoid including intangible losses in insurance coverage.[57] Adopting traditional insurance policies in information security is not an appropriate approach to be protected from Information and Communication Technology (ICT) or OT security risks.

Crane[58] and Gold[59] demonstrated that there is a significant risk that the insurance policies will not cover losses that occurred outside the specifically designated coverage area. The result has been that due to both increased ICT security risks and the failure of insurance to manage the new characteristics of cyber threats, the demand for insurance products mainly designed to target cyber space is rising.

Since late in the 1990s, several insurance policies (known as "early hacker insurance policies"[60]), specifically designed to target cyber losses, were introduced.[61] Several hardware/software companies teaming up with insurance companies offer these policies to cover for their products.[62] As a result, these policies were not stand-alone insurance products, but part of the hardware/software companies' risk management solutions

[55] Beh, H. G. (2001). Physical losses in cyberspace. *Connecticut Insurance Law Journal*, *8*, 55.

[56] Majuca, R. P. (2006). *Three essays on the law and economics of information technology security*. Urbana-Champaign, IL: University of Illinois. Norman, P. (2001). 12 Policing "high-tech" crime within the global context. *Crime and the Internet*, 184.

[57] Majuca, R. P. (2006). *Three essays on the law and economics of information technology security*. Urbana-Champaign, IL: University of Illinois.

[58] Crane, M. (2001). International liability in cyberspace. *Duke Law & Technology Review. CSI/FBI Computer Crime and Security Survey* (2005).

[59] Gold, J. (2002). Insurance coverage for Internet and computer related claims. *Computer and Internet Lawyer*, *19*, 8–16.

[60] Majuca, R. P., Yurcik, W., & Kesan, J. P. (2006). *The evolution of cyber insurance*. arXiv preprint cs/0601020.

[61] Since late in the 1990s, several insurance policies (known as "early hacker insurance policies"), specifically designed to target cyber losses, were introduced.

[62] Majuca, R. P. (2006). *Three essays on the law and economics of information technology security*. Urbana-Champaign, IL: University of Illinois.

to their customers. Further, these policies did not provide full insurance coverage.[63]

Increased internet risks and more robust compliance obligations can come from the continuous emergence of more sophisticated cyber insurance products.[64] There are several cyber liability laws which require a higher standard of compliance in certain ICT-related activities.[65] They require covering not only losses, such as physical damages that can be addressed by traditional insurance products. They also require coverage for intangible costs. The coverage of cyber insurance could include "DDoS attacks."[66] This could damage e-commerce sites, cause electronic theft of sensitive information, create virus-related damage, bring losses associated with internal networks crippled by hackers or rogue employees, impact privacy-related suits, and generate legal issues associated with copyright and trademark violations.[67] The cyber insurance market is expected to grow and reach USD 28.6bn by 2026, growing at a CAGR of 24.9 per cent from 2019 to 2026.[68]

Covering cyber risks could put companies in a challenging situation in which a traditional approach to risk aggregation might prove inadequate. Companies tend to think of coverage as their only cyber insurance product. They could establish a robust infrastructure by building partnerships with all the stakeholders. Companies should adopt a broader view of risk prevention through partnerships and aiming at insuring rather than just insurance. In other words, they could orchestrate risk management in a cyber risk ecosystem that includes companies but also cloud providers,

[63] Shim, W. (2010). *Interdependent risk and cybersecurity: An analysis of security investment and cyber insurance*. Michigan State University. Communication Arts and Sciences-Media and Information Studies.

[64] Majuca, R. P. (2006). *Three essays on the law and economics of information technology security*. Urbana-Champaign, IL: University of Illinois.

[65] Majuca, R. P. (2006). *Three essays on the law and economics of information technology security*. Urbana-Champaign, IL: University of Illinois.

[66] Denial-of-service (DDoS) attack is a cyberattack in which the hacker seeks to make a machine or network resource unavailable to its intended users by temporarily or indefinitely disrupting services of a host connected to the internet. www.us-cert.gov/ncas/tips/ST04-015. Accessed 25 March 2020.

[67] Gralla, P. (2001). Insurance for cyber attacks has yet to catch on. *Insurance for Online Attacks Has Yet to Catch on*.

[68] www.alliedmarketresearch.com/press-release/cyber-insurance-market.html. Accessed 30 May 2020.

cybersecurity specialists, and enterprises with confidential customer data. This cyber risk ecosystem could overlap with a broad spectrum of other ecosystems covering companies and individuals, which are still in the early stages of building resilience or border protection to cyber attacks. These alliances would enable companies to move both up the value network to prevention by using readiness diagnostics, preventive recommendations, and awareness campaigns. It could also help companies to move down the value network to post-breach response and support from specialist vendors after a successful attack. Both of these value-added service streams could build an insurer's significant role in risk prevention, intervention, and management.[69]

Parametric Insurance

Parametric insurance is a type of non-indemnity insurance contract, not identical to insurance policies written based on the valued policy principle.[70] Parametric insurance is an innovative approach to managing the protection gap. In recent years, there has been a rise in parametric insurance, insuring risks from natural catastrophe to human-made incidents, and physical asset protection to revenue or income protection.[71] Parametric insurance can offer an opportunity to solve some protection gap issues while making the insurance market more effective, efficient, and economical in managing claims.[72]

Parametric insurance (also known as index insurance) refers to an insurance contract under which the company becomes responsible for the payment of an *ex-ante* agreed or scheduled amount once a parameter arrives at a contract-defined threshold.[73] Any risk with only a loss

[69] These alliances would enable companies to move both up the value network to prevention (using readiness diagnostics and preventive recommendations) and down the value network to post-breach response and support (from specialist providers in case of attacks). Both of these value-added service streams could build an insurer's comprehensive role in risk prevention, response, and management.

[70] Sfetcu, N. (2014). *Insurance glossary*. Nicolae Sfetcu.

[71] Banks, E. (2005). *Catastrophic risk: analysis and management*. Hoboken, NJ: Wiley.

[72] Singer, A. W. (2019). The evolution of parametric insurance. *Risk Management*, *66*(3), 32–36.

[73] Lin, X., & Kwon, W. J. (2019, July). Application of parametric insurance in principle/regulation-compliant and innovative ways. Jean, *Application of parametric insurance in principle/regulation-compliant and innovative way*.

outcome, excluding speculative risks, is a candidate for parametric insurance in case there is a statistically significant correlation between the loss event and the insurance payout. Parametric insurance can cover the risks currently underwritten by indemnity, or valued policy principles. Examples of this type are direct property damages and consequential losses of revenue, and additional operating expenses caused by a natural or human-made accident. Parametric insurance can ensure those risks that are considered uninsurable in the traditional insurance market, such as a loss of revenue or a rise in operating expenses but without any direct physical damage to the insured property. The companies benefit from an immediate release of their capital holdings as parametric insurance claims are short-tailed by design. They do not incur any cost for claims evaluation or settlement. Buyers of parametric insurance benefit from an additional or new layer of insurance coverage and fast claim payments. Events like a pandemic have created a significant interest in this type of insuring.

There are challenges in parametric insurance policies.[74] The fundamental risk challenge is not going away. To mitigate the risk, the current parametric insurance product often uses double-trigger events or staggered payout structures. Thus, there would be a partial payout for a lower category of events and progressively higher payouts for more damaging events.[75]

Finding reliable third-party reporting agencies (also-called independent arbiters or "oracles") can be difficult, mainly when operating in emerging countries.[76] Another challenge to the expansion of parametric insurance is the lack of awareness and understanding among prospective policyholders. Companies need to convince risk managers that it works as published. This insurance product has other limitations, such as that it is hard to see a wide application to P&C) insurance.[77] It is not necessarily cheaper to buy than indemnification coverage.

[74] www.rmmagazine.com/2019/04/01/the-evolution-of-parametric-insurance/. Accessed 26 December 2019.

[75] *The evolution of parametric insurance—risk management*. Accessed 29 April 2020.

[76] documents.worldbank.org/curated/en/262691559115855583/Credit-Reporting-Knowledge-Guide-2019. Accessed 20 March 2020.

[77] *The evolution of parametric insurance—risk management*. www.rmmagazine.com/2019/04/01/the-evolution-of-parametric-insurance/. Accessed 40 May 2020.

If parametric insurance is purchased to supplement, rather than replace, conventional indemnity insurance, it can be a useful tool for risk managers. Its payouts are faster, with no gray areas, costly court disputes, or lengthy waiting periods once a loss is confirmed. Parametric coverage can provide a more efficient insurance product, making it an exciting option.[78]

CCRIF SPC[79]

Developed under the World Bank's technical leadership, the CCRIF SPC (formerly the Caribbean Catastrophe Risk Insurance Facility Segregated Portfolio Company) was set up in 2007 as the world's first regional fund providing parametric insurance to cover catastrophe-related losses. Panama was the twenty-first member country. Each nation benefits from quick payouts even before actual damages are assessed. Thus, they can get financial liquidity that is critical for recovery efforts. This motivation was behind the record USD 1.36 billion catastrophe bond issued by the World Bank last year. It relies on parametric triggers also to cover earthquake risk in Chile, Colombia, Mexico, and Peru.

Business Interruptions Insurance

Business interruption insurance (BI) is a valuable tool to transfer business disruption risk. BI insurance can protect from revenue loss. It is vital in the case of catastrophes or a pandemic.[80] Most insurers learned the lessons from the severe acute respiratory syndrome (SARS) outbreak of 2003 and introduced exclusion clauses for infectious diseases and epidemics/pandemics into most non-life products.[81]

BI can assist companies in resuming their regular operation. In the USA, in 2018, this type of insurance was launched as a specific parametric

[78] Singer, A. W. (2019). The evolution of parametric insurance. *Risk Management*, *66*(3), 32–36.

[79] www.rmmagazine.com/2019/04/01/the-evolution-of-parametric-insurance/. Accessed 26 December 2019.

[80] Zhen, X., Li, Y., Cai, G. G., & Shi, D. (2016). Transportation disruption risk management: Business interruption insurance and backup transportation. *Transportation Research Part E: Logistics and Transportation Review*, *90*, 51–68.

[81] home.kpmg/xx/en/home/insights/2020/03/do-insurers-have-covid-19-covered.html. Accessed 30 May 2020.

insurance product to compensate businesses from the risk of business interruption consequent damages to a pandemic/epidemic.[82] An index that measures the "common sense" in case of a pandemic occurrence is at the base of this product. The measures taken by public authorities represent a parameter to measure the scope of the event. The cover is a hybrid between a traditional insurance product and a parametric coverage since the economic damage is not clear upstream. It is paid according to the usual winding-up of the damage taken by the policyholder company.

The coronavirus epidemic is a tragedy waiting to happen: for years (the last time in 2019). The World Health Organization (WHO) declares that a new virus/flu epidemic is among the top 10 global threats in the coming years. There is a new and genuine risk to which the customer on a personal level is undoubtedly ready to purchase insurance protection. The businesses are interested in the policies for covering BI. These insurance type will grow over time. In parallel, it is necessary to improve assessments.

Assurely[83]

Assurely is an insurtech that creates and delivers insurance products for new and changing industries. The company's aim is to change how to access risks, how to transfer them, and how to manage them. Assurely's first product, TIgerMark™, protects issuers engaged in technology-enabled capital raising strategies such as crowdfunding or digital securities against investor complaints and lawsuits. TigerMark simultaneously provides trust, comfort, and safety to investors. They benefit from a simple, streamlined, and easy claims process to request their principal investment returned should the issuer misrepresent in their offering documents, steal, or misuse the funds.

Other Services

One new exciting opportunity for insurance companies is to change the service model. The change could be offering new services to improve

[82] www.nytimes.com/2020/03/05/business/coronavirus-business-insurance.html. Accessed 30 March 2020.

[83] www.assurely.com. Accessed 30 May 2020.

the attractiveness of their insurance policies. In the case of a vehicle accident or theft, there might be a prompt intervention in support, an offer of a replacement vehicle, or simply an automatic message to the default number or e-mail address, and so on. Insurance would become a virtual assistant: moving as suggested from insurance to insuring.[84] Thanks to this customer proximity, there could be an increase in the retention of the best-performing customers. The black boxes installed in the vehicle could help in the reconstruction of how an accident happened. It would be possible to cross the data of those involved to understand the dynamics better and analyze the social networks and other connections to highlight any fraudulent behavior.

A similar approach is applicable for home automation (the so-called domotics[85]), with the possibility to make a home, an office, a shop, a department of a factory, and so on, a technologically assisted place. It would be possible to insert smart sensors that can provide alerts or identify repetitive behaviors that may affect the likelihood of an accident and create potential losses in case of the occurrence, which prompted the customer to subscribe to the policy. The insurance provides as a service a monitoring system. The continuous risk management interconnected with sensors in security systems could detect in real-time fires, water leaks, intrusion attempts, power cuts, and so on.

It is possible to imagine offering similar services to detect accidental falls or other human accidents of the elderly or others who need a form of home care.[86]

Services within the insurance proposition are essential. Companies can support the solution of customer problems by delivering significant value propositions for their customers. Smart solutions make, for example, the following services possible:

- Tracking and optimization tools to reduce expenditures of resources like energy and water;

[84] assets.publishing.service.gov.uk/media/5421c2ade5274a1314000001/Final_report.pdf. Accessed 30 March 2020.

[85] Ligny, E. L., & Mohammadi, M. (2011). Innovations in domotics: Fulfilling potential or hampered by prevailing technological regime? *Construction Innovation*, *11*(4), 470–492. Accessed 30 April 2020.

[86] Sale, P. (2018). Gerontechnology, domotics, and robotics. In *Rehabilitation medicine for elderly patients* (pp. 161–169). Cham: Springer.

- Assets management platforms including certified service providers, such as housing insurance plumbers, engineers, carpenters, construction persons, and electricians or in the case of life insurance: doctors, hospitals, clinics, laboratories ambulance services, and so on;
- Remote monitoring and assistance to the policyholders;
- Emergency solutions to prevent and mitigate insured risks.

The classification of value-added services in insurance is[87]:

- Self-service: This category includes services where companies support customers with tools and techniques to manage better their insured risks, including the customer's property or their health.
- Advice and assistance: This category includes services that provide customers with fast support in case of need and with information that can help them manage their lifestyles, property, or funds better.
- Anticipation of customer needs: Some value-added services can fill gaps in the customers' journey by anticipating their needs and taking care of those needs by supplying coverage and detection of losses or incidents.[88]
- Collaboration and engagement: Value-added services for collaboration and engagement can support better customer proximity. By providing differentiated services, insurance companies can improve customer acquisition and retention.

The combination of insurance with these value-added services can enable companies to play a more significant and consistent role in the customer journey.[89]

There are several other options for increasing the value-adding services offered by companies to their customers. Services are an exciting option for cross-selling efforts of insurance companies. Insurance companies

[87] Radwan, S. M. (2019). *The impact of digital technologies on insurance industry in light of digital transformation*. www.joif.org/SystemFiles/Assets/The%20Impact%20of%20digital%20Technologies%20on%20Insurance%20Industry%20.pdf. Accessed 30 May 2020.

[88] *Insurance reinvented: Value-added services*. www.capgemini.com/wp-content/uploads/2017/07/value_added_services_in_insurance_2017_2_web.pdf. Accessed 22 April 2020.

[89] Lemon, K. N., & Verhoef, P. C. (2016). Understanding customer experience throughout the customer journey. *Journal of Marketing*, *80*(6), 69–96.

could monetize their ability to analyze data and manage risks. Companies have robust analytics capabilities compared with other industries. Analytics and actuarial sciences have been a standard component of the traditional insurance business model.[90] Digital ecosystems offer traditional companies' valuable opportunities to use analytics to evolve and expand their business models. They could facilitate the evolution of current insurance businesses by advancing risk assessments, for example, by considering security and safety measures such as connected-vehicle or connected-home solutions. Companies can also use analytics to enhance pricing and risk-accumulation control.

As different businesses generate growing volumes of data, risk management will demand an increasing amount of data modeling and advanced analytics. Because of their established analytics capabilities, companies in new digital ecosystems could offer analytics-as-a-service to other industry players.[91] This offering could include predictive modeling and optimization services that enable faster and smarter business decisions across all industries within the entire analytics value network.

Many consulting firms, including Bain,[92] McKinsey,[93] and Deloitte,[94] have identified services as an important topic for the insurance sector. The ecosystems using digital platforms could deliver an interconnected set of services to the customer in one integrated package with insurance. An insurer capable of distributing smart property management propositions to its customer base will strengthen the customer relationship. It could get access to more precious customer insights, and be able to orchestrate its ecosystem of partners. The company would compete as a

[90] www.businessinsurance.com/article/20190103/NEWS06/912325909/Business-Insurance-2018-Data-&-Rankings. Accessed 10 January 2020.

[91] www.mckinsey.com/industries/financial-services/our-insights/insurance-beyond-digital-the-rise-of-ecosystems-and-platforms. Accessed 20 March 2020.

[92] Ecosystems: How companies can reinvent customer relationships. *Bain*, 13 August 2018. www.bain.com/publications/articles/ecosystems-how-companies-can-reinvent-customer-relationships.aspx. Accessed 10 January 2020.

[93] *Insurance beyond digital: The rise of ecosystems and platforms*. McKinsey & Company. www.mckinsey.com/industries/financial-services/our-insights/insurance-beyond-digital-the-rise-of-ecosystems-and-platforms. Accessed 10 January 2020.

[94] Building new ecosystems in middle-market insurance. *Deloitte Insights*. www2.deloitte.com/insights/us/en/industry/insurance/new-ecosystems-middle-market-insurance.html. Accessed 10 January 2020.

platform sponsor capable of defining the platform strategy and the degree of openness that fits best with its corporate goals.[95]

An example of services possible in an ecosystem is assurbanking. This service is the opposite of bankassurance: the sale of insurance services in bank branches. Assurbanking is the sale of banking products, such as loans, in insurance agencies.[96]

American Family's Smart Home Journey[97]

In June 2014, American Family and Microsoft launched a startup accelerator.[98] The two companies' focus was on assisting startups working on the next generation of home automation products and services. During the following months, American Family and Microsoft met with more than 400 applicants to the accelerator. Microsoft Ventures and American Family selected ten startups.

To help these startups grow, Microsoft provided resources, including workspace on the Redmond, Washington, campus, dedicated mentors, and connections to specific valuable Microsoft customers. American Family offered insurance and analytics expertise and an optional USD 25,000 equity investment in each startup accepted into the program. These investments in early-stage emerging technology companies strengthened American Family's commitment to protecting policyholders proactively.

American Family was established as one of the insurance leaders in early-stage investing for the smart home.[99]

[95] Parker, G., & Van Alstyne, M. W. (2014, April). Platform strategy. *Boston University School of Management Research Paper No.* 2439323, p. 14.

[96] Filipan, M., Švarčan, A., Novinc, I., Šustić, T., Meaški, R., Draganić, A., & Mioč, A. (2019). *Analiza sistemskog rizika u osiguranju*. Doctoral dissertation, University of Zagreb, Faculty of Economics and Business, Department of Finance.

[97] iotinsobs.com/. Accessed 11 December 2019.

[98] Guggenheimer, S. (2014). *Microsoft and American family insurance launch startup accelerator for home automation*. blogs.microsoft.com/blog/2014/06/17/microsoft-and-american-family-insurance-launch-startup-accelerator-for-home-automation/. Accessed 30 May 2020.

[99] CB Insights (2018, March). The smart home startups companies: Have invested. *CB Insights Research*. www.cbinsights.com/research/smart-home-procurement-investment/. Accessed 30 May 2020.

To further improve understanding of the smart home customer value proposition, American Family's innovation unit set up a small demonstration home inside a warehouse into a smart home showcase. The warehouse was previously used only for adjuster training.[100] This space was used for testing product experiences from American Family Ventures' portfolio companies and other technology companies. Hundreds of employees, partners, and similar have toured the facility to touch and feel some of the latest smart home devices.

Since 2014, American Family offered employees technology products in very small-scale pilots to learn how effectively these devices meet customer expectations, mitigate risks, and improve the lives of homeowners. American Family has tested, in its lab and homes, dozens of smart devices including:

- light bulbs;
- security cameras;
- smoke and carbon monoxide detectors;
- thermostats;
- video-enabled doorbells;
- water flow meters;
- water leak detection sensors;
- water shutoff valves.

In 2015, American Family launched a pilot program and provided customers with some smart home products. In exchange, customers who agreed to be part of this program shared some data about whether the smart home products were on, working properly, and communicating through Wi-Fi. The American Family legal team issued a clear data privacy policy. American Family team members sent participants replacement batteries when the smoke alarm alerted for a low battery level. This service eliminated a chore for customers. The correct functioning of devices such as the smoke detectors can protect families and houses.

American Family found that customers expect technology to work right out of the box. American Family team members learned that many customers seeking technical support came to American Family, not the device manufacturer. For many customers, troubleshooting temporarily inoperable equipment is an unacceptable inconvenience.

[100] Higginbotham, S. (2016, December). Why insurance companies want to subsidize your smart home. *MIT Technology Review*. www.technologyreview.com/s/602532/why-insurance-companies-want-to-subsidize-your-smart-home/. Accessed 22 April 2020.

American Family team members learned to empathize and iterate quickly from experiment participant feedbacks. For example, one device manufacturer introduced a service triggered when its water sensor detected moisture. Despite evidence of false alerts, the manufacturer continued to inundate experiment participants with phone calls urging the use of its on-demand plumber service.

Several pilots and subsequent testing by American Family, and participation in the IoT Insurance Observatory since May 2017, have identified several paths to large-scale adoption.

Nexecur[101]

Company overview: Nexecur, a subsidiary of Groupe Credit Agricole since 1986, specializes in alarm systems and remote surveillance and assistance for homes, businesses, and the banking industry. Nexecur serves more than 145,000 customers throughout France.

The company sought to develop an agile new offering that would strengthen its role as an everyday life partner by alerting policyholders about potential hazards. The IoT-based offering would support Credit Agricole Groupe's growth strategy.

Improving operational efficiency and security alert accuracy is essential to the new mass-market product. Nexecur aimed to leverage its presence in the safe-home market to enter the fast-growing smart home domain and outpace the competition.

The company was determined to offer clients active, on-demand monitoring and at the same time enhance remote surveillance to reduce false alarms such as those caused by animals or fallen objects. The goal was to create an innovative, reliable, scalable, and secure smart home platform. In support of the Groupe's plan to grow its client base, this offering would boost Nexecur capabilities. It would help reduce operational costs and lay the groundwork for a scalable IoT platform road map to launch additional

[101] Capgemini. (2020). *Capgemini financial services analysis, 2020, World insurance report 2020 executive interviews*. www.capgemini.com/news/world-insurance-report-2020/. Accessed 30 May 2020.

smart home services related to smart home and traditional insurance and banking services. Examples include capabilities to anticipate potential floods, fires, or other climate or weather disturbances.

An integration team guides end-to-end, agile-mode development of the platform. Nexecur mobilized experts from various domains (hardware, UX/UI, architecture, IoT). The team mapped the omnichannel customer journey (web and mobile) and designed, developed, and tested appropriate protections. Implementation includes the development of a continuous integration platform.

Early indications are that the innovative IoT platform will speed up Nexecur's time-to-market capacity while improving customer experience with new on-demand service options particularly popular with millennials.

Unit-Linked

Wealth management products have been very successful and very lucrative for banks.[102] Insurance companies have launched products that are similar even if still with insurance characteristics. A Unit Linked Insurance Plan (ULIP) is a product that, differently from a pure insurance policy, provides investors insurance and investment under a single integrated plan.[103] These innovative life insurance products are becoming popular. They represent nearly a third of new business in Germany.[104] These insurance products also induce dynamic policyholder behavior. Their volatile value, complexity, dynamic policyholder behavior, options, and guarantees can have an unexpected influence on the solvency capital requirement. It is critical to consider these products in Solvency II's framework, even if today Solvency II framework focuses on traditional insurance products.[105]

[102] Stulz, R. M. (2019). Fintech, bigtech, and the future of banks. *Journal of Applied Corporate Finance, 31*(4), 86–97.

[103] www.investopedia.com/terms/u/unit-linked-insurance-plan.asp. Accessed 20 January 2020.

[104] Helfenstein, R., & Barnshaw, M. (2003). Unit-linked life insurance in Western Europe: Regaining momentum? *SwissRE Sigma*, 3. Enz, R. (2006). *World insurance in 2005: Moderate premium growth, attractive profitability*. Swiss Reinsurance Company. M¨Arten, G., & Daalmann, S. 2009. *Fondsgebundene Ver-Sicherungsprodukte Mit Garantien Trotzen Der Finanzmarktkrise*. Stamford, CT: Towers Perrin.

[105] Rae, R. A., Barrett, A., Brooks, D., Chotai, M. A., Pelkiewicz, A. J., & Wang, C. (2018). A review of solvency II: Has it met its objectives? *British Actuarial Journal, 23*.

Innovative life insurance services differ from traditional life insurance products in some fundamental aspects and require an in-depth risk examination,[106] Both companies and policyholders expect the value of an innovative life insurance product to be somewhat volatile. The volatility depends on the fact that the capital is normally invested in risky assets, compared to the fixed-income-oriented investment strategies of traditional life insurance products. Innovative life insurance products normally do not have a simple structure and contain a broad range of options and guarantees.[107]

Conclusions

The central theme of this chapter is: insurance companies should move from pure insurance to insuring services. This move could create a myriad of new products and services. On the other side, this should be the main target of any company. The aim should be to add value to the customers. In so doing, they would also ensure value for the shareholders and the employees.

[106] Kochanski, M. (2010). Solvency capital requirement for german unit-linked insurance products. *German Risk and Insurance Review (Grir)*, *6*(2), 33–70.

[107] Gatzert, N. (2009). Implicit options in life insurance: An overview. *Zeitschrift Für Die Gesamte Versicherungswissenschaft*, *98*, 141–164.

CHAPTER 5

Proximity to the Customer in Insurance 4.0

Introduction

Financial institutions have several characteristics different from manufacturing organizations.[1] A one-to-one transfer of the principles of industry 4.0 from manufacturing to the financial services sector is not suitable due to their differences.[2]

- Nature/type of goods and services: banks and insurance providers offer information-processing services predominantly. They are services that collect, produce, and process information.[3] Products resulting from such information processing service processes are generally not tangible (even though employees process documents) and remain somewhat not completed defined for both customers and companies.

[1] Nicoletti, B. (1979, November–December). Aziende di servizio: opportunità e problemi. *Sviluppo e Organizzazione, 10*(56), 19–32.

[2] Leyer, M., & Moormann, J. (2014). How lean are financial service companies? Empirical evidence from a large scale study in Germany. *International Journal of Operations & Production Management, 34*(11), 1366–1388. https://doi.org/10.1108/ijopm-06-2013-0296.

[3] Davies, M. N. (1994). Bank-office process management in the financial services: A simulation approach using a model generator. *The Journal of the Operational Research Society, 45*(12), 1363–1373.

B. Nicoletti, *Insurance 4.0*, Palgrave Studies in Financial Services Technology, https://doi.org/10.1007/978-3-030-58426-9_5

- Production process: processing information services are independent of a specific location. Digital data can travel around the world within seconds. The type of work is different from manufacturing, where typically a tangible product is assembled in one or a few specific locations. Generic tasks for information processing services range from support over processing transactions to mostly administrative work.[4]
- Customer integration: a core element of information-processing service processes is the direct involvement of customers in the service delivery, unlike in manufacturing industries.[5] Customers participate at specific points in time during the service process so that they can use the services.[6] The service delivery will take longer if the required customer input is not available on time.

The last item in this list is essential. In a business model, it is necessary to dedicate particular attention to customer proximity or relationships. A necessary aspect of financial services is that customers mainly acquire services that solve their real "pain points."[7] Online or mobile apps can deliver remotely real value once the initial difficulty of using them is over.

In the case of insurance, customers appreciate tools that help them[8]:

- Understand the risks;
- Monitor progression of those risks; and
- Receive insight to mitigate damages.

[4] Davies, M. N. (1994). Bank-office process management in the financial services: A simulation approach using a model generator. *The Journal of the Operational Research Society, 45*(12), 1363–1373.

[5] Corrêa, H. L. Ellram, L. M., Scavarda, A. J., & Cooper, M. C. (2007). An operations management view of the services and goods offering mix. *International Journal of Operations & Production Management, 27*(5), 444–463.

[6] Leyer, M., & Moormann, J. (2012). A method for matching customer integration with operational control of service processes. *Management Research Review, 35*(11), 1046–1069.

[7] iotinsobs.com. Accessed 11 December 2019.

[8] Rejda, G. E. (2011). *Principles of risk management and insurance*. Chennai, India: Pearson Education India.

Companies have promoted safer and more secure behaviors for years. New technologies are enabling higher awareness, whether an asset is used or not and how it is used.

When customers share data with insurance companies, companies can use new opportunities to encourage safer and more secure behaviors through education and positive reinforcements. Companies can use customer data to provide rewards for safe and secure practices.[9] This market fit applies also outside traditional insurance.[10]

Security and safety services, built on information coming from smart devices, can lead to the prevention or mitigation of specific losses. For this objective, it is necessary to have[11]:

- secure, trusted relationships;
- broad distribution of secure and reliable smart devices;
- large quantities of data streaming from the apparatus;
- algorithms that derive insights from these data; and
- capabilities to deliver effective and efficient actions in the field.

Technological change is not just something inevitable in the market for financial services, and insurance availability of advanced technical infrastructure is a critical factor of success and competition. This factor is so relevant that, according to Gartner Group,[12] the insurance companies that will not expand and upgrade their technological facilities in the coming years will decline and move to inevitable failure. The solutions that will help companies to achieve the goals are products for managing marketing campaigns, data mining products, systems for rating, and risk analysis internet-based, and solutions for the automation of sales force and business processes.[13]

[9] www.naic.org/insurance_summit/documents/insurance_summit_2017_CIPR_16.pdf. Accessed 3 January 2020.

[10] Vitalitydrive—Telematics Based Car Insurance from Discovery. *The Digital Insurer*. www.thedigital-insurer.com/dia/vitalitydrive-telematics-based-car-insurance-from-discovery/. Accessed 3 January 2020.

[11] Yan, Z., Zhang, P., & Vasilakos, A. V. (2014). A survey on trust management for Internet of Things. *Journal of Network and Computer Applications*, *42*, 120–134.

[12] www.gartner.com—Articles and research. Accessed 20 March 2020.

[13] A survey conducted by Accenture/Siebel has shown that insurance companies are devoting a growing share of investment to develop CRM programs. Cantù F.—CRM in

Value Proposition and Customer Proximity

The nature of customer interactions has changed, thanks to technology. Currently, insurance companies mainly focus on pushing for new deals and contracts, with customers who passively are recruited and are not fully aware of what they are signing up. This symptom is characteristic of the so-called information asymmetries.[14] Customers are taken care of by intermediaries (such as agencies, banks, and brokers). They have been the leading players in a "sales heavy" model.[15] The market is moving in favor of a customer weight much more relevant. Insurance companies are getting more and more aware of this. They are moving to a different relationship and more interactive engagement with the customers. Relations are developing toward "interaction," where customers are becoming active and central players in an environment that is becoming "customer-pulled."

There are also changes in what concerns policy and underwriting processes. Customers are now expecting completely different approaches, mainly supported by innovations, such as big data analytics and online portals.

A hybrid blend of digital and emotional connection offers a balanced approach to personalized engagement.[16]

Customer Engagement

In the past years, companies focused mainly on higher up the customer purchase intention. The new objective of marketing departments or marketing agencies is to create and possibly increase the Customer Engagement Value (CEV).[17] In insurance companies, the value of retaining customers starts to become essential over the past years.

insurance in Lamonica, S., Piraccini, M., & Venegoni. D. (2002). *Customer relationship management*. Milano, Italy: IPSOA.

[14] Binks, M. R., Ennew, C. T., & Reed, G. V. (1992). Information asymmetries and the provision of finance to small firms. *International Small Business Journal*, *11*(1), 35–46.

[15] web.bi.no/forskning/papers.nsf/0/b723c0570c4026eac12575b0004a329a/$FILE/2009-04-Jensen.pdf. Accessed 20 August 2016.

[16] worldinsurancereport.com. Accessed 30 May 2020.

[17] Kumar, V., Rajan, B., Gupta, S., & Dalla Pozza, I. (2019). Customer engagement in service. *Journal of the Academy of Marketing Science*, *47*(1), 138–160.

Extending the contract period is essential because a premium is due normally every year. The focus shifts partially from increasing the purchase intention to engaging customer loyalty and extending the value of the customer in contract length in years. In the past, companies tried to challenge in the market on the price, trying to be the cheapest. Now there is mainly a focus on maintaining an increased Customer Engagement Value, which partly depends on attracting purchasing power.[18]

The results of studies indicate that interactions have a positive influence on the evolution of the Customer Engagement Value factor.[19] Adding one interaction increases the chance of positive evolution of the CEV factor by 28.8 percent. In the case of single interactions, interactions via the telephone and direct communication have the most significant contribution. For a series of interactions, an interaction strategy combining the above interaction channels increases the chance of positive evolution of the Customer Engagement Value by 14.5 percent.

Ernst and Young (EY) reports about customer proximity in the EY's Global Consumer Insurance Survey 2014.[20] This survey involved approximately 24,000 persons in 30 countries around the globe about their relationships with insurance providers. This survey confirms that strengthening customer proximity and achieving customer-centricity in core operations are a must for the insurance industry across product classifications, geographies, and operating models. EY asked customers to mention the essential characteristics during an ongoing relationship.[21] "Value for money" and "brand reputation" were among the most relevant factors. The research shows that service and experiential factors, such

[18] Lee, S. K. (2018). A customer touch point management system for effective service communication. *Business Communication Research and Practice, 1*(1), 46–49. https://doi.org/10.22682/bcrp.2018.1.1.46. Shaw-Ching Liu, B., Petruzzi, N. C., & Sudharshan, D. (2007). A service effort allocation model for assessing customer lifetime value in service marketing. *Journal of Services Marketing, 21*(1), 24–35. https://doi.org/10.1108/08876040710726275.

[19] Westervoorde, P. M. (2020). *Using customer interactions to understand the customer engagement value: A predictive study in the B2B insurance industry.* Master's thesis, University of Twente, Enschede, Netherlands.

[20] www.ey.com/Publication/vwLUAssets/ey-2014-global-customer-insurance-survey/$FILE/ey-global-customer-insurance-survey.pdf. Accessed 1 January 2020.

[21] Key findings from the EY Global Consumer Insurance Survey 2014. www.ey.com/Publication/vwLUAssets/ey-2014-global-customer-insurance-survey-america/$FILE/ey-global-customer-insurance-survey-america.pdf. Accessed 20 May 2020.

as "easy to understand, clear communications," and "being easy to deal with," are almost as highly valued. For life products, "financial stability" is essential. For non-life insurance, "being easy to deal with" and "being responsive" are more relevant.[22]

The customer does not always know where she/he wants to get from insurance. Companies (or their intermediaries) have problems with confusing and inconsistent questions from the customers. Companies should help potential customers toward identifying their needs and the most suitable product to cover their risks through a consultancy service, transparent, clear, and correct. On the other hand, it is challenging to make total clarity without hitting the sensitivity of the customer that might feel overstated. The customer could perceive the company's advice as forced and intrusive, aimed at increasing the premium in the insurance policy, rather than to understand his/her doubts. On the other hand, there are other customers who, undoubtedly in possession of some insurance knowledge, approach the company with a particular attitude, convinced to know everything. This type of customer creates some barriers to achieving a piece of valid and correct advice like the most confused and unprepared customers. The communication in the relationship between them and the company often risks to get stranded on controversy and misunderstandings.[23]

The insurance companies and the intermediaries must always look for new solutions to propose to the customers. It is necessary to evolve and not to remain anchored to traditional risk-based insurance products. Robust customer proximity not only directly contributes to the user experience but also provides access to customer information. This access is an absolute necessity in a world where ecosystems are essential.[24] Companies can harness customer adoption of new solutions to create opportunities for better and more frequent customer interactions (e.g., through wearables) and improve efficiency through sensor-based automation (such as trigger-based claims payments and apps).

[22] Reimagining customer proximity—Key findings from the EY Global Consumer Insurance Survey 2014.

[23] Giudici, G. (2008). *Intermediazione Assicurativa e Mercato*. Milano, Italy: FrancoAngeli.

[24] www.businessinsurance.com/article/20190103/NEWS06/912325909/Business-Insurance-2018-Data-&-Rankings. Accessed 10 January 2020.

It is important to digitize and optimize the customer journeys. This activity includes improving access to data to drive customer insights, streamlining onboarding, enabling direct communications with customers, allowing self-service for claims and amendments, and so on. In the spirit of insurance 4.0, companies can extend the customer journey by integrating additional tools and services from other exciting providers to further deepen their capabilities and increase revenue streams.

Companies must offer a broader portfolio of products for remaining relevant to customers looking for high degrees of customization. It is critical to have innovative portfolio management techniques and the establishment of product factories. This is essential for designing better products and delivering them to the market faster and in customer-proximity.[25]

Claims

An essential moment for customer proximity is at the time of a claim. Insurance 4.0 programs may drive innovation in back-office processes, such as fully automated claims management processes. They can also enable innovation by removing technology barriers. For example, better-integrated data from sensors deployed within vehicles or buildings can add exciting services, like an alarm to a garage or provide data for smarter underwriting.[26]

The development and technological progress are essential not only to introduce new and attractive products to the market but also to improve everyday work so companies can save time and resources. The magazine of Swiss RE, Sigma, called the impact of digitization on the distribution of insurance as a "quiet revolution."[27] In the last decade, there has been a robust acceleration of technological change. The penetration of the internet and social networks has grown significantly. A growing part of online activity goes through smartphones. According to the Pew Research

[25] Digital transformation in insurance—EY—US. www.ey.com/Publication/vwLUAssets/Digital_transformation_in_insurance/$FILE/ey-digital-transformation-in-insurance.pdf. Accessed 30 May 2020.

[26] www.ey.com/Publication/vwLUAssets/ey-digital-transformation-in-insurance/$FILE/ey-digital-transformation-in-insurance.pdf. Accessed 30 May 2020.

[27] www.swissre.com/dam/jcr:b8010432-3697-4a97-ad8b-6cb6c0aece33/sigma3_2019_en.pdf. Accessed 10 January 2020.

Center,[28] the average rate of individuals in emerging countries who claim to use the internet occasionally and owning a smartphone has gone from 45 percent in 2013 to 54 percent in 2015 and more in the following years. The increase is mainly due to large emerging economies, such as Malaysia, Brazil, and China. This research probed also the customers' opinion on using an app to notify a claim to insurance with the photo of the damage. This app can provide an estimate of the cost of the accident, thanks to artificial intelligence tools capable of analyzing the images. Sixty-six percent of survey participants were ready to use such an app, compared with 34 percent opposed. Some persons would use it only for small damages, for simple cases, or to estimate the cost of the accident. They would then ask for a second opinion from a mechanic or an expert.

For the policyholder, the benefits of this app are the speed and comfort of a claim-notification process. They could avoid filling a large part of the paper bureaucracy. Another advantage is to have an instant quotation of the damage. Thus, it is possible to compare the proposal with the one of a repair shop. Some customers say it could be useful, but it would have to evaluate the actual functioning of this app because it might not be accurate in estimating the damage.

Zurich Insurance UK[29]

Zurich Insurance UK offers its customers an app that allows them to report a claim directly to the accident. The customer can simply send documents and images via the app. This mode speeds up the process for about two days. The app also provides advice on the risks to avoid or mitigate the damage. It allows the policyholder to request an update on the status of his/her claim. The notification process of an accident is simple, fast, and efficient.

[28] Pew Research Center is a nonpartisan fact tank that informs the public about the issues, attitudes, and trends shaping the world. They conduct public opinion polling, demographic research, content analysis, and other data-driven social science research. www.pewresearch.org/global/database/. Accessed 30 May 2020.

[29] Zurich Insurance. (2013, February). *Zurich launches home and motor claims app*. www.zurich.co.uk/en/about-us/media-centre/general-insurancenews/.2013/zurich-launches-home-and-motor-claims-app. Accessed 12 December 2019.

Consultant
For customers, the benefits of the service offered by a consultant, be it an agent or a contact center of the company, are the convenience, fast troubleshooting, and the easy reachability of the person. Human relationships are essential. If the customer has had relations with the consultant for a long time, there is trust in him/her. The disadvantage, however, is to have to wait maybe even a few days to get an appointment, especially if the consultant is on leave or sick.

Customer Relationships Management 4.0

To support customer proximity, an insurance company needs to set up a customer relationship management system (CRM). CRM applications are a category of software that covers a broad set of applications. This software helps businesses manage customer data and customer interactions, access business information, automate sales, marketing, and customer support. At the same time, a CRM can help in managing employee, vendor, and partner relationships.[30] CRM covers the front end with the customer and the sales force. Typically, large corporations use CRM software. Some software products scale to a business of any size, but the use of CRM in small companies is limited.

A CRM can help in several aspects of customer proximity[31]:

- To meet the policyholder's needs, which involves creating a propensity scoring (i.e., a dashboard to evaluate the insurance services the customer uses). This solution allows offering to the customer services designed for his/her needs. A CRM helps with the more profitable policyholders by defining the best customer retention strategy,[32] behavioral scoring would allow knowing immediately early signs of worsening relations with the customer. Scoring of attrition can provide the reasons for the balking of the customer.

[30] Nicoletti, B. (2016). *Cloud computing & procurement*. ACM—International Conference Proceedings Series (ICPS) & ACM Digital Library ISBN ACM ICPS to ICC.

[31] Coviello, A. (2008). *The impact of ICT in the insurance industry: The role of Customer Relationship Management*. www.itais.org/proceedings/itais2012/pdf/002.pdf. Accessed 22 March 2020.

[32] Xing, L., & Syriac, N. D. (2019). The influence of customer relationship management on customer retention in the insurance sector, Malaysia. *INTI Journal*, *2019*(47).

- To know and retrieve the policyholder's global potential, considering the possibility of a customer who could manage his/her savings across several financial institutions. The scoring potential is based on how likely a customer establishes relationships also with a competitor;
- To know and integrate the riskiness of the insured to minimize the risk by improving the quality of the portfolio, supporting the launch of new products and services, and increasing business productivity. This increase would be possible by using the information derived from a better understanding of the customer. This approach could reduce costs and increase productivity in handling requests through a better distribution of workloads in the contact organization and improve the effectiveness of processes and touchpoints with the customer.

Implementing a CRM system provides the company with a logical step to move toward a marketing one-to-one. It is possible to use a model (called 5Cs) to define the process of implementing a CRM in the insurance industry[33]:

1. Close to the customer: to identify and understand his/her needs and expectations.
2. Clear vision: to have a plan for future activities, identifying a development model.[34]
3. Consistency with the vision: to govern the activities of a CRM to achieve the target goals and define the instruments for monitoring the effectiveness, efficiency, and/economics of the processes of active references.[35]
4. Support to Continuous improvement: to define processes and procedures and continually identify areas for improvement.

[33] Turchetti, G. (2004). *New scenarios of insurance marketing*. Milano, Italy: FrancoAngeli.

[34] Productivity in handling requests through a better. www.coursehero.com/file/p1m96qe4/productivity-in-handling-requests-through-a-better-distribution-of-workloads/. Accessed 30 May 2020.

[35] Productivity in handling requests through a better. www.coursehero.com/file/p1m96qe4/productivity-in-handling-requests-through-a-better-distribution-of-workloads/. Accessed 30 May 2020.

5. Connection to the rest of the company to define integrations of the CRM program with all the different areas of improvement of the customer proximity.

The diffusion of CRM systems in the insurance industry is progressing, albeit not as fast as necessary. It is causing a discontinuity in the traditional culture of the companies and their models. Companies need to take more effective customer focus, improve and enrich customer service offerings, streamline production processes and administrative systems, and reorganize the intermediary networks and sales in opportunities offered by the CRM.

These initiatives meet obstacles in the persistence of a corporate culture primarily focused on products rather than customer needs. It requires an adequate capacity for investments in technological equipment and operating systems and a significant effort to integrate new professional competencies necessary to implement and successfully manage change processes.

In this perspective, investment in talents and employee training and intermediaries is a insurance 4.0's top priority to meet the challenge of a CRM and improve its effectiveness, efficiency, economics, and competitiveness. There are several guidelines for use and invest in CRM.[36] There are plenty of diversified solutions applicable to the diversity and multiplicity of automation needs in insurance. CRM will have a high rate of growth. It still suffers a stiffness resulting from the legacy of previous traditional ICT systems developed in the past with inflexibility in changing their logic and technologies.

CosmosDirekt[37]

CosmosDirekt, established in 1982, started selling insurance products via telephone in Germany. As soon as the Internet became available also to the

[36] Coviello, A. (2008). *The impact of ICT in the insurance industry: The role of Customer Relationship Management*. www.cersi.it/itais2012/pdf/002.pdf. Accessed 20 March 2020.

[37] Coviello, A., & Di Trapani, G. (2016). Ict and new service experience in Italian insurance industry. In T. Russo-Spena & C. Mele. (2019). *Proceedings of the 26th RESER Conference 2016*, Naples, Italy, 512–530.

public, CosmosDirekt opened its first website form. The website provides information to customers. It also allows to do purchases and after-sales operations remotely, in a self-service model.

Today CosmosDirekt is the market leader of directly sold life products not only in Germany but within continental Europe.

Hi Oscar[38]

Oscar Health[39] has raised more than USD 700M, 32.5 USD of which by Alphabet (parent company of Google).[40] Its goal is to revolutionize health insurance by transforming the value proposition in building a strong and direct connection with customers.[41] This approach makes more human the entire private health insurance operations: "*It aims to make its customers love health insurance — as opposed to seeing it as a necessary evil — and put Oscar at the center of people's health and wellness needs.*"[42]

Oscar's strategy focuses primarily on customer experience, brand, and simplicity since competing on scale, price, and distribution was going to be harder when considering the size of incumbents. Oscar saw its potential niche in customer satisfaction, considering that the health insurance industry's characteristic is a modest Net promoter score (NPS) of 12 out of 100.[43]

[38] www.hioscar.com. Accessed 23 March 2020.

[39] money.cnn.com/2018/08/14/technology/google-oscar-health-insurance/index.html. Accessed 20 March 2020.

[40] Greco, A. Thesis. www.slideshare.net/AngelicaGreco/thesis-final-87203889. Accessed 30 May 2020.

[41] Greco, A. Thesis. www.slideshare.net/AngelicaGreco/thesis-final-87203889. Accessed 30 May 2020.

[42] CB Insights. (2017, January 3). *Insurance tech startups raise $1.7B across 173 deals in 2016*. www.cbinsights.com/research/2016-insurance-tech-funding/. Accessed 20 March 2020.

[43] Shaw, R. (2008). Net promoter. *Journal of Database Marketing & Customer Strategy Management*, *15*(3), 138–140.

Direct Interaction of Insurance with Customers

There are other ways in which insurance companies are interacting with customers. Chatbots represent an exciting approach. A chatbot, short for chatterbot, is a computer program that simulates human conversation through voice commands or text chats or both.[44] Chatbot is an artificial intelligence (AI) feature that can be embedded and used through any significant messaging applications. The chat programs such as WhatsApp, Facebook Messenger, and Instagram are used daily by many persons. Mainly young persons prefer to send a message rather than making a call.[45] For this reason, the app messaging has become the leading platform for the chatbot, as Facebook did with Facebook Messenger.

Chatbots support standardized customer interactions. It can also provide computer-generated advice about the type of insurance coverage customers can buy.[46] An example of a chatbot is the virtual assistant Kate, launched by US Geico insurance.[47] It responds to questions from customers regarding insurance policies and payments. Another example is spixii, an automated insurance agent who interacts with customers through an app or other messaging platforms (Facebook Messenger, and Skype). It helps customers to buy the appropriate insurance cover for their needs.[48]

Chatbots can help customers to deal quickly and on a 24*7 basis with specific standard chores such as buying insurance, obtaining documents, filing claims, or having simple questions answered. Chatbots simulate conversation with human users. They can help to save time and effort. Customers expect personalized product offers based on the history of interactions. More sophisticated predictive models can provide this type

[44] www.investopedia.com/terms/c/chatbot.asp. Accessed 20 April 2020.

[45] Ade, M. (2018, May 14). *Il suo nome è bot, chatbot*. www.axa.ch/it/ueber-axa/blog/trend/chatbot-digital-ux-cx-axa-chatbot.html. Accessed 10 January 2020.

[46] Albrecher, H., Bommier, A., Filipović, D., Koch-Medina, P., Loisel, S., & Schmeiser, H. (2019). Insurance: Models, digitization, and data science. *European Actuarial Journal*, *9*(2), 349–360.

[47] Nordman, E., Director, C. I. P. R., DeFrain, K., Hall, S. N., Karapiperis, D., & Obersteadt, A. (2017). How artificial intelligence is changing the insurance industry. *CIPR Newsletter*, 2.

[48] Kumaresan, A., Saurav, S., & Raghunanda, K. (2017). *Top 10 trends in property & casualty insurance 2018*. www.capgemini.com/wpcontent/uploads/2017/12/property-and-casualty-insurance-trends_2018.pdf. Accessed 21 December 2019.

of functionality.[49] These points of contact also help collect relevant information about customers to enrich the database storing these services. If the chatbot is coupled with a machine learning application, more data would help in improving the performance of the chatbots.

Usually, customers are eager to prove the chatbot. Most of the persons would use it only in case of straightforward requests, not for critical issues. Other customers are willing to consider this technology when the technology has matured further. According to the policyholder, chatbots are secure, easy to use, and efficient. They are a good source to have instant information at any time. The lack of human contact represents the negative side. They would prefer to talk to a counselor for privacy reasons. A chatbot does not inspire confidence or security. Some believe it is too soon for such a technology. This situation will change.

Trov, an insurtech startup, sells on-demand policies to protect personal assets, also characterized by the use of a chatbot to manage claims.

Chatbots can also help in claim management. According to Gartner, in a few years, 85 percent of customer interactions will go through chatbots.[50] Claims management via chatbot automates the initial reporting process and makes it available and easy to use 24*7.

Customer Proximity Center

Customer proximity and experience are critical in the strategy of the organizations and hence in insurance 4.0.[51] A survey shows that 66 percent of managers indicate customer relationships as the third most crucial source of sustained economic value for the organization,[52] One of the ways organizations use to relate with customers is the call center. Call centers are

[49] Hong, S. J., & Weiss, S. M. (2001). Advances in predictive models for data mining. *Pattern Recognition Letters*, *22*(1), 55–61.

[50] How AI Can Solve Fast-Food Labor Problems|*QSR magazine*. www.qsrmagazine.com/outside-insights/how-ai-can-solve-fast-food-labor-problems. Accessed 30 April 2020.

[51] Sheth, J. N., Parvatiyar, A., & Sinha, M. (2015). The conceptual foundations of relationship marketing: Review and synthesis. *Journal of Economic Sociology = Ekonomicheskaya sotsiologiya*, *16*(2), 119–149. Kohlbacher, F., & Herstatt, C. (2010). *The silver market phenomenon: Marketing and innovation in the aging society*. Springer Science & Business Media.

[52] IBM. (2013, July 6–9). *IBM BusinessConnect 2013: Realize the art of the possible*. Bucharest, Romania.

changing over time due to several factors. One of the most important factors behind the change in call centers is the organization's strategy.

A call center is typically an operational center that interacts with the customers in a variety of ways, from issue resolutions, user guidance, administrative support, billing, provisioning, up to technical support, claims issues, and more. Call centers, or contact centers[53] or voice operation centers[54] are globally approximately 800,000.[55] They represent a profitable business. In some countries, the labor market cannot meet the demand for call center agents, often called Customer service representatives (CSR). This industry is also continuously changing. Information and communication technology (ICT) has drastically improved operations, helping cut costs, among other benefits.[56] Call centers today are multichannel communication centers that provide several types of services using various media.[57] Outsourcing operations is also a significant trend in the industry.[58] Most organizations have outsourced their call centers to external contractors, often offshoring the services ("co-sourced"). Other organizations decided to keep the call centers in house or outsource only part of the services. An example of a growing service provided by call center is the support to online access by the customer to the companies'

[53] Koole, G., & Mandelbaum, A. (2002). Queueing models of call centers: An introduction. *Annals of Operations Research*, 113(1–4): 41–59.

[54] Jack, E. P., Bedics, T. A., & McCary, C. E. (2006). Operational challenges in the call center industry: A case study and resource-based framework. *Managing Service Quality*, *16*(5), 477–500.

[55] Aksin, O. Z., Armony, M., & Mehrotra, V. (2007). The modern call center: A multi-disciplinary perspective on operations management research. *Production and Operations Management*, *16*(6), 665–688.

[56] Aksin, O. Z., Armony, M., & Mehrotra, V. (2007). The modern call center: A multi-disciplinary perspective on operations management research. *Production and Operations Management*, *16*(6), 665–688.

[57] Jack, E. P., Bedics, T. A., & McCary, C. E. (2006). Operational challenges in the call center industry: A case study and resource-based framework. *Managing Service Quality*, *16*(5), 477–500.

[58] Ren, Z. J., & Zhou, Y.-P. (2008), Call center outsourcing: Coordinating staffing level and service quality. *Management Science*, *54*(2), 369–383.

internet sites.[59] Organizations have redefined the role of their call centers. They are often their only point of contact with the customers.[60]

Call centers can be categorized as inbound—receiving the calls—or outbound—making the calls—and mixed[61]:

- Inbound services manage incoming requests, such as information about products and services of the organization, technical assistance (help desk), counseling, after-sales service, complaints handling, and so on;
- Outbound services (outgoing) are used by the organizations to reach out to their existing or potential customers for direct sales by phone, perform surveys on the degree of customer satisfaction, campaigns advertise, debt collection, complete the sales process, and so on.

A great set of review articles is included in a tutorial and review published by Mandelbaum on telephone call centers.[62]

There is an essential aspect of the evolution over time of the call centers. The call center has moved from managing the non-quality (of the products or the services of the organization) to the management of the value of the product or service for customers. It is an important evolution (or almost a copernican revolution). It is consistent with the management shift in thinking of the organization not as a provider of a product or service, but as a value-adding to the customer. Therefore, the customer experience with the organization, including the call center, has become central to the organization strategy.

Quality of the service in a call center has been evaluated often on how long the customer is waiting and whether or not the information provided

[59] Aksin, O. Z., de Véricourt, F., & Karaesmen, F. (2008). Call center outsourcing contract analysis and choice. *Management Science, 54*(2), 354–368.

[60] Aksin, O. Z., Armony, M., & Mehrotra, V. (2007). The modern call center: A multi-disciplinary perspective on operations management research. *Production and Operations Management, 16*(6), 665–688.

[61] Aksin, O. Z., Armony, M., & Mehrotra, V. (2007). The modern call center: A multi-disciplinary perspective on operations management research. *Production and Operations Management, 16*(6): 665–688. Koole, G., & Mandelbaum, A. (2002). Queueing models of call centers: An introduction. *Annals of Operations Research, 113*(1–4), 41–59.

[62] Gans, N., Koole, G., & Mandelbaum, A. (2003). Telephone call centers: Tutorial, review, and research prospects. *Manufacturing and Service Operations Management, 5*(2), 79–141.

met the customer's needs. This section challenges this view. Johnston's Customer Processing Operation model already identified several factors that influence customer expectations and their perceptions of the call center's quality.[63] A more general measurement of the quality of the services is along several dimensions.[64]

The configuration and the quality of the call center depend on the strategy of the organization. This chapter presents a model which can be used to select the best configuration of the call centers in a specific organization strategy.[65]

The operations management academic community has dedicated much time and research to the service operations in the last decades.[66] Services have grown to represent the most significant industrial sector in Western economies.[67] Organizations are paying close attention to the ways products and services are delivered and on the customer experience as a way to develop competitive advantages.[68] Academics researched different aspects of service delivery.[69]

[63] Bicheno, J., & Catherwood, P. (2005). *Service quality concepts: Six sigma and the quality toolbox* (pp. 132–150). Buckingham: PICSIE Books.

[64] Parasuraman, A., Zeithaml, V. A., & Berry, L. L. (1985). A conceptual model of service quality and its implications for future research. *Journal of Marketing, 49,* 41–50. Bicheno, J., & Catherwood, P. (2005). *Service quality concepts: Six sigma and the quality toolbox* (pp. 132–150). Buckingham: PICSIE Books.

[65] Nicoletti, B. (2015, March). Optimizing innovation with the lean and digitize innovation process. *TIM Review.*

[66] Johnston, R. (1994). Operations: From factory to service management. *International Journal of Service Industry Management, 5*(5), 49–63. Heskett, J. L. (1987). Lessons in the service sector. *Harvard Business Review, 65*(2), 118–126.

[67] Heskett, J. L. (1987). Lessons in the service sector. *Harvard Business Review, 65*(2), 118–126. Haynes, R. M., & DuVall, P. K. (1992). Service quality management: A process-control approach. *International Journal of Service Industry Management, 3*(1), 14.

[68] Johnston, R. (1994). Operations: From factory to service management. *International Journal of Service Industry Management, 5*(5), 49–63.

[69] Nicoletti, B. (1984, November). La gestione delle aziende di servizio. *Aggiornamenti IFAP,* No. 26, 6–10. Shostack, G. L. (1984). Designing services that deliver. *Harvard Business Review, 62*(1), 133–139. Schlesinger, L. A., & Heskett, J. L. (1991). Customer satisfaction is rooted in employee satisfaction. *Harvard Business Review, 69*(6), 148–149. Tseng, M. M., Qinhai, M., & Su, C. J. (1999). Mapping customers' service experience for operations improvement. *Business Process Management Journal, 5*(1), 50. Johnston, R. (2005). Service operations management: From the roots up. *International Journal of Operations and Production Management, 25*(12), 1298. Heskett, J. L., Jones, T. O., Loveman, G. W., Sasser, W. E., & Schlesinger, L. A. (2008). Putting the service-profit

Gronroos presented two dimensions, the technical aspect—what service provides, defined as the outcome of the process—and the functional point—how the service is delivered, the process quality dimension.[70] Gronroos also introduced the concept of corporate image and its impact on customer perceptions.[71] Lehtinen and Lehtinen (1991) added three other dimensions parallel to Gronroos's ones: physical quality—product and material support, and interactive quality—the interaction with the customer—and corporate quality—how customers perceive the organization.[72] A significant further contribution was the inclusion of the corporate image dimension.[73]

A certain number of authors considered the possible evolution of the call centers. Jon Anton (2000) wrote that customers desire improved access to their vendors. Anton reviews how organizations have responded to this requirement. He looks at the past, present, and future information needs of the customers and how they have been met. He forecasts the future technological developments which will change the type of interactions and the availability of information.

Along with traditional research areas, Aksin et al. paid particular attention to the new management challenges originated in connection with emerging technologies, to behavioral issues associated with both call center agents and customers, and to the patterns of interactions between call center operations and sales and marketing. They identified a handful of themes for future investigation while also pointing out several particular

chain to work. *Harvard Business Review, 86*(7), 118–129. Allon, G., & Federgruen, A. (2008). Service competition with general queuing facilities. *Operations Research, 56*(4), 827–849. McGuire, K. A., Kimes, S. E., Lynn, M., Pullman, M. E., & Lloyd, R. C. (2010). A framework for evaluating the customer wait experience. *Journal of Service Management, 21*(3), 269. Carmon, Z., & Shanthikumar, J. G. (1995). A psychological perspective on service segmentation models: The significance of accounting for consumers' perceptions of waiting and service. *Management Science, 41*(11), 1806–1816.

[70] Gronroos, C. (1982). *Strategic management and marketing in the service sector*. London, UK: Chartwell-Bratt. Gronroos, C. (2001). The perceived service quality concept—A mistake? *Managing Service Quality, 11*(3), 150.

[71] Gronroos, C. (2001). The perceived service quality concept—A mistake? *Managing Service Quality, 11*(3), 150.

[72] Lehtinen, U., & Lehtinen, J. R. (1991). Two approaches to service quality dimensions. *Service Industries Journal, 11*(3), 287–303.

[73] Kang, G. D., & James, J. (2004). Service quality dimensions: An examination of Gronroos's service quality model. *Managing Service Quality, 14*(4), 266.

research opportunities.[74] Moss et al. (2006) suggested a more nuanced account of changing job structures in the call centers that incorporate market, institutional, and agency factors.[75]

Additional references are in scholar.google.com/scholar?q=call+centers+&hl=en&as_sdt=0%2C15&as_ylo=2009&as_yhi=2014.

The Evolution of the Call Center

The call center evolves for many reasons. For instance, the fact that organizations have to cope with the high costs of maintaining the technology and the commitments of the agents. There are three trends in the call center management[76]:

- Increase in the scale and scope of the call center operations. Customers' expectations for quality service from the call centers are higher than in the past. In today's marketplace relationships, quality, convenience, speed, precision, and value are critical competitive advantages;
- Diffusion of multichannel communication centers where several channels provide a wide variety of services to customers. For example, phones, internet, e-mails, webchats, and social networks are all used to maximize opportunities for customer contacts;
- Outsourcing of call center operations also to emerging countries. Advanced telecommunications systems have enabled organizations (for instance, financial services) outsourcing their call centers to nearshore or offshore locations (for instance, India, other countries in Asia, or North African countries).

[74] Aksin, O. Z., Armony, M., & Mehrotra, V. (2007). The modern call center: A multidisciplinary perspective on operations management research. *Production and Operations Management, 16*(6), 665–688. Hawkins, L., Meier, T., Nainis, S., & James, H. (2001). *The evolution of the call center to customer contact center*. Information Technology Support Center, White Paper.

[75] Moss, P., Salzman, H., & Tilly, C. (2006). Under construction: The continuing evolution of job structures in call centers. *Industrial Relations*.

[76] Williams, G. (2003). Call center operations: Profiting from teleservices. *Consulting to Management, 14*(2), 57–58.

In light of all these changes, it is interesting to see how the denominations of the call centers has changed;

- Initially, organizations used the terminology "call centers." The idea was to provide the customers with the possibility to "call" somebody to represent the issues, complaints, and get advice on how to resolve them. It was indeed a passive way to see the relationships with the customers;
- Later many call centers started to be called Contact Center. This name shows a critical aspect of the call center: it is a contact point between the organization and the customers. This name emphasized how the organization "see" the call center as being at the border of the organization;
- The next step was to call the call centers Customer Service. This denomination introduced the concept of service to the customers. It was still very much an internal view of the relationships and a passive way to approach the relationships with the customer;
- Call centers are requested to do more non-traditional tasks with fewer resources. The more traditional roles of the call centers (such as collections and customer support) are still relevant. More strategic functions (such as improving the customer experience and moving from service to sale) have become more critical. The denomination of the call centers changed to Customer Care. The idea was that it was essential to care for the customers;
- In some cases, the call centers are called the Customer Support Center. The idea is that the customers needed support in the use of the products/services provided by the organizations, which implied that they were not user friendly!;
- Another way to call the call centers is Customer relationships point (CRP) or Customer proximity center. This expression underlines the fact that the call center is a point of relationships with the customer. It is one of the most important point for customer proximity in insurance 4.0. It must be the place to add value to the customers and to the organization. The name CRP underlines the fact that the interaction with a call center is a significant "customer experience." The underlying idea is that the organization provides an experience rather than just a product or a service. In this respect, the call center is more and more an active part of the organization. It is a crucial

point where it is possible to push Service to Sale (S2S). These organizations that view call centers as a key contact point to their customer base want to transform the customer support paradigm by shifting the call center from a cost center to a strategic revenue builder. In other words, the relationships with the customer are an essential moment of selling additional services and products to the customers.

Model of the Characteristics of a Call Center Based on the Strategy of the Organization

It is possible to examine in more details the relevant functions in insurance 4.0 in the customer relationships centers:

- The customer experience. Now more than ever, the customer experience is the top priority of the organization: the interaction becoming richer. It is possible to use powerful and differentiated tools. The call center is a channel where the customers meet the business (efficiently, effectively, and economically with a favorable mix of technology and professionalism of the operators). The "environment" should support a better knowledge of the customer needs and, on the other side, of the potential offerings of the organization to satisfy them. The intermediation role and the functions performed in the call centers are considerably more complex than in the past;
- A multi-media interaction. Today's customer relationship centers, through the technologies available, enable omnichannel, the integrated and coordinated management of all contact points with the customer: agencies, salesforce, postal mail, telephone, mobile, e-mail, and online;
- The management of the information on the product and the customer. In the case of insurance, the quality of products/services derives directly from the quality of the process that generates them. It must be constructed throughout the service process and controlled through activities of measurement and monitoring of the characteristics that influence the quality. The results of these activities are the source of information based on which to evaluate the quality of products/services and the effectiveness, efficiency, and economics of the processes in the organization. The analysis of these data and the comparison with the levels of quality and productivity

expected can help to trigger initiatives for the improvement of the organization's products/services.

It is interesting to refer to two models to analyze the changes in the call centers. Chandler described corporate strategy as the definition of long-term goals and objectives, the adoption of courses of action and related allocation of resources required to achieve the goals. He defined structure as the instrument of the organization through which strategy is managed. Changes in an organization's approach lead to new management, operational, and administrative problems. They, in turn, require a new or remodeled structure for the successful implementation of the new strategy. Chandler's thesis argued that new organizational forms are a derivative of policy.[77]

Leavitt offered a new approach to looking at organizations. Leavitt stated that every organization comprises four interactive components: People, Task, Structure, and Technology. The interactions between these four components are the basis of the success of an organization. The graph showing the relationships between these four components resembles a diamond. For this reason, the model is called Leavitt's diamond. Leavitt emphasized that any change in one of these elements directly affects all the other parts. They need to transform to accommodate the change. Leavitt's diamond is an integrated approach. It is widely used for managing organizational change.

This chapter considers a model shown in Fig. 5.1, based on the combinations of the Chandler and Leavitt models. This model replaces the "Tasks" in the Leavitt model with "Processes" "Technology" with "Platforms," and "People" with "Persons/Partners," since it seems more appropriate.

Based on this model, the evolution of the call center is summarized in Table 5.1, it is necessary to take into account that:

- The column of the years is purely indicative of the year at the introduction of the model;
- New call center models have been added over time. The previous models have not disappeared;

[77] Chandler Jr., A. D. (1962). *Strategy and structure: Chapters in the history of the American industrial enterprise*. Cambridge, MA: MIT Press.

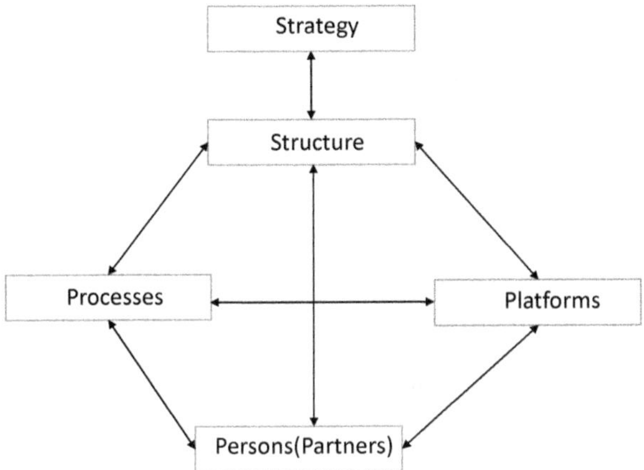

Fig. 5.1 Modified Chandler-Leavitt model

- The model underlines the main characteristics. It might be interesting to consider more details.

It is interesting to analyze in more depth each of the components of these models and how they interact with each other.

Persons
The persons are the operators of the call centers. It is necessary to consider the employees not only as operators. One should also consider their skills, professionalism, efficiency, experience, knowledge, and productivity. The human factor is essential. The ability of the operator to present all information and details is central to assess the competence and the quality of the service provided. However, the operator's approach (formal or informal, cold or warm, and so on) is also critical. The perception of the operator's ability to connect with the customer and express empathy is essential.

Another critical factor is the operator's ability and willingness to follow up. Many customers feel that it is very important if the service provided during the call would not end there since it was not complete. The relationship with the customers is at the heart of any strategy for call centers. New technologies for ICT are an outstanding support structure for their development (see the column on platforms in Table 5.1). However, it

Table 5.1 Evolution of the call center

Years	*Denomination*	*Description*	*Strategy*	*Structure*	*People*	*Technology*	*Assessment*
1960	Call Center	The aim was to provide the customers the idea that they could "call" somebody to describe the issues and get advices on how to resolve them.It was born as a branch of the Claim Office	Claims avoding. Resisting	Operations	Low skilled	Telephone	Call volumes Talk time Holding time
1970	Contact Center	This name shows one important aspect of the call center: the fact that it is the contact point between the organization and the customers. This name emphasized the way the organization "saw" the call center as the border of the organization	Product centric. Passive	Operations	Medium skilled	PABX	Call waiting Number of contacts Average duration of the call
1980	Customer Services	This denomination introduced the concept of service. It was still very much an internal view of the relationships and a passive way versus the customer	Service centric. Passive	Operations	Professional	ACD—Automatic Call Distribution	Customer Dedication Claim resolution

Years	*Denomination*	*Description*	*Strategy*	*Structure*	*People*	*Technology*	*Assessment*
1990	Customer Support Center	The idea here is that the customer should be supported in their activities	Sale centric. Passive-Active	Sales	Supportive and caring people	IVR—Interactive Voice Response	First call resolution Average duration of the call queu duration Hang-ups
2000	Service to Sale	The idea is to use the contact to service but also to sell more services and products. At the same time perform also campaign	Marketing centric. Active-Passive	Marketing Offshoring	Sales persons	CTI—Computer Telephony Integration Campaign Manager Call recording	Customer Satisfaction Ability to up-sale/cross-sale
2010	Customer Relationships (CR)	This expression underlines the fact that the call center is a point of relationships with the customer. It is one of the most important points to do Customer Relationships Management. It must be the place to add value to the customers and to the organization	Customer Centric. Active	Outsourced or Cosourced	Relationships persons	UCC—Unified Communication and Collaboration (voice-over-IP, email, Chat, fax)	Customer experience in the IVRs, queues and with agents (through surveys at the end of the call) Customer Retention
2020	Virtual Call Point (CRP)	More and more CR are becoming distributed, thanks to the technology more and more available	Network Centric. Proactive	Automatic Telework Self Service	Technical, Coach	Automation IVR, queue and speech analytics Social Networks Geo-location	Value for the customer per call

is only through the acquisition of qualified professionals, with distinct operator professional skills, that strategies are transformed into a real competitive advantage.

The central professional figures, the activities, and the required skills are essential. These skills include both the management skills (the ability to interact with people and manage the relationships) and the technical and professional skills (the ability to provide clear support to the customer) for all professionals involved in the effective operations of a call center. Hence the importance of education and training as a critical tool for building and maintaining excellent professionals.

Processes

This component refers to the processes, which can include goals in addition to tasks. It would consist of the consideration of two aspects: how things are done; and what they need to achieve.

It is critical to focus more on the qualitative aspects of the processes than the actual tasks and goals. When looking at the activities in the operations, one should consider their relevance and their benefits. When examining goals, it is critical to think about the yield and productivity characteristic of the process of interaction with the customers in the call center (Fig. 5.2).

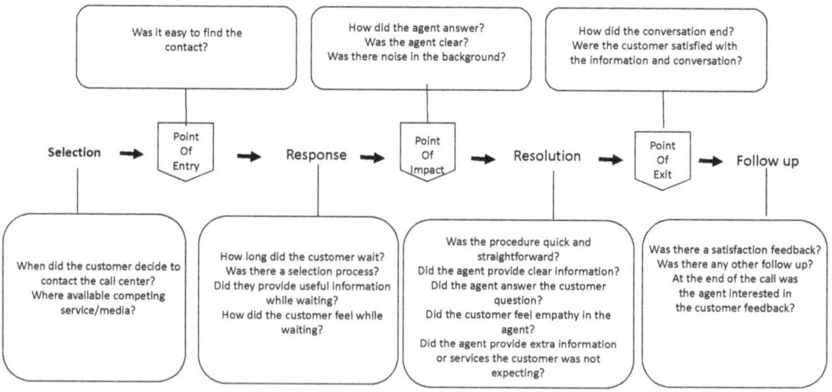

Fig. 5.2 Interaction with the customer in the proximity center (Adapted by the author from Bicheno, J., & Catherwood, P. [2005]. *Six sigma and the quality toolbox* [rev. ed.]. Buckingham: Picsie Books)

Structure
The patterns or structural component of Leavitt's diamond includes not only the hierarchical structure, but also the relationships, communication, and coordination among different management levels, sections, and people in the organizations. These aspects include the flow of authority and responsibility inside the organization. The structure needs to be modified when changes are made to the strategy but also to any other component of the diamond.

Technology
Platforms or technology is the component that supports or facilitates the people implementing the activities in the processes. Computers, networks, telephone equipment, interactive voice response (IVR), robo-advisors, software applications, and others are all parts of the technology. Technology like all the other components of the Leavitt's diamond needs to be changed when any other component is modified.[78]

The most significant development in the customer relationships will be in the technology: both in terms of the tools to support from the call center and from the use of pervasive technology to reduce the need for a manned call center and allow the customer to do self-service or assisted-service through robo-advisors. Artificial intelligence promises substantial supports with tools like chatbots, machine learning, natural voice processing, and so on.

The technical aspects of the services play a significant role during the call. The volume and quality of sound and voice, both during the waiting time and the actual service, are among the primary aspect. A secondary point is the simplicity of the initial selection process in the call. Traditional IVR selection choices will be replaced by natural voice processing.

There are several tools developed to help in automating the call centers. One of the most effective tools is operational data analytics (ODA).

Data analytics is the discovery and communication of meaningful patterns in the data and the information available to the organization.[79]

[78] *Leavitt's diamond: An interactive approach to change*. www.brighthubpm.com/change-management/122495-a-look-at-the-components-of-leavitts-diamond/. Accessed 30 May 2020.

[79] LaValle, S., Lesser, E., Shockley, R., Hopkins, M. S., & Kruschwitz, N. (2011). Big data, analytics and the path from insights to value. *MIT Sloan Management Review*, *52*(2),

Data analytics can be applied in areas rich with stored or accessible information, as possible in a customer relationship center. Data analytics works on the simultaneous application of statistics, computer programming, and operations research to analyze why, what, when, where, who performs and possibly makes decisions on the best way to proceed. Data analytics tends to be more productive by visualizing the data to communicate insights. Organizations may apply analytics to business data to describe, forecast, and make decisions to improve a call center's customer-centric performance.

ODA is particularly crucial in supporting the call centers. ODA is analytics done, possibly in real or near real-time to help operational business processes. By way of contrast, investigative analytics is done according to the timing requested by research, not the speed of operational business processes. There can be mixed cases, such as when the analytics are highly urgent yet otherwise investigative. ODA is becoming interesting also because of the possibility of process data in memory.[80]

The objective of ODA is to implement the cycle:

- Enterprise automation;
- Sensors to get actual data in real-time;
- Analytics to suggest (or take) actions to improve.

ODA is strongly connected to the lean and digitize approach.[81] The improvement of a process, the reduction of cycle times, and the cutting of waste require the knowledge of the processes and especially the measure of its performance (KPI—Key Process Indicators). This improvement requires to have data, facts, on the process. With modern systems and sensors, the amount of data available is vast, Hence the need to combine in a synergic way the leaning of the operations with their digitization. Once we know the process, it is critical to manage it minute by minute. This requires moving from business intelligence to business process intelligence: from analyzing data to managing the processes operationally.

21–31. Davenport, T. H., & Kim, J. H. (2013). *Keeping up with the quants: Your guide to understanding and using analytics*. Cambridge, MA: Harvard Business Press.

[80] Plattner, H., & Zeier, A. (2012). *In-Memory data management: Technology and applications*. Berlin/Heidelberg, Germany: Springer Science & Business Media.

[81] Nicoletti, B. (2012). *The methodology of lean and digitize*. Abingdon, UK: Gower.

Voice analytics is becoming more and more feasible and accessible.[82] It is a powerful way to help measure quality in a call center, especially in self-help. The way it could work is[83]:

1. Entire end-to-end call analytics. New solutions should reveal the quality and performance of each segment of the customer experience with the customer relationships center;
2. Measure Performance. It reveals specific performance measures based on success and failure in Voice Self-Service as well as with the operators;
3. Automatic measures of caller experience;
4. Analysis of First Call Resolution by task;
5. Measurement of KPI by comparing the call flow design intent with actual caller behavior;
6. Focus on meeting business goals, whether they are cost savings, customer experience improvements, improving training and skills routing, or increasing revenues;
7. Linking design decisions to operational costs.

At the same time, ODA, used in the customer relationship centers, can become more and more one of the most important agents to improve the design of products and services using information collected in a call center in a terotechnological approach.[84]

Assessing the Quality in a Call Center

A critical aspect of the evolution of the call centers is their assessment needs to change. This aspect is obviously taking into account that strategy changes over time and among organizations.

The call center is a service. The representation of the provision of a service in a workflow (see a simplified workflow in Fig. 5.2).

[82] Imran, A., Pandharipande, M., & Kopparapu, S. K. (2013). SpeakRite: Monitoring speaking rate in real time on a mobile phone. *International Journal of Mobile Human Computer Interaction (IJMHCI)*, *5*(1), 62–69.

[83] Nicoletti, B. (1979). Maintenance strategies. *Terotechnica*, No. 16, 1–11. Amsterdam, Holland.

[84] Nicoletti, B. (1979). Maintenance Strategies. *Terotechnica*, No. 16, 1–11. Amsterdam, Holland.

Before examining the quality of the call center, it is interesting to see how the concept of quality of service has changed over time.

As the management consultant Drucker once said: "If you can't measure it, you can't manage it." Hence the importance of the diagnostic tools to assess and monitor the quality of the service over time.[85] Shostack (1984) argued that it is not possible to ensure quality and uniformity in services without a detailed design. She developed a blueprint to identify the processes involved in delivering a service.[86] By visually seeing the steps involved in the service delivery, an organization can identify the timings, the costs involved, and the possible failure points.[87] Besides according to the method of lean and digitize, it is possible to identify the waste in the processes and their possible redesign and automation.[88] Another diagnosis framework stems from SERVQUAL's five dimensions of quality.[89] Parasuraman et al. (1985) developed the service quality model to identify the "gaps" on the service provider's side that cause the discrepancy between the customer's expectations and perceptions.[90] Some authors have raised concerns about the application of this model,[91] highlighting the excessive broadness of the five dimensions.[92]

[85] Oliver, R. L., & Rust, R. T. (1997). Customer delight: Foundations, findings, and managerial insight. *Journal of Retailing, 73*(3), 311–336. Ghobadian, A. Speller, S., & Jones, M. (1994). Service quality concepts and models. *International Journal of Quality and Reliability Management, 11*(9), 43.

[86] Shostack, G. L. (1984). Designing services that deliver. *Harvard Business Review, 62*(1), 133–139.

[87] Shostack, G. L. (1984). Designing services that deliver. *Harvard Business Review, 62*(1), 133–139.

[88] Nicoletti, B. (2012), *The Methodology of Lean and Digitize*. Abingdon, UK: Gower.

[89] Parasuraman, A., Zeithaml, V. A., & Berry, L. L. (1985). A conceptual model of service quality and its implications for future research. *Journal of Marketing, 49*(4), 41–50.

[90] Parasuraman, A., Zeithaml, V. A., & Berry, L. L. (1985). A conceptual model of service quality and its implications for future research. *Journal of Marketing, 49*(4), 41–50.

[91] Johnston, R. (1995). The determinants of service quality: Satisfiers and dissatisfiers. *International Journal of Service Industry Management, 6*(5), 53.

[92] Johnston, R. (1995). The determinants of service quality: Satisfiers and dissatisfiers. *International Journal of Service Industry Management, 6*(5), 53. Finn, D. W., & Lamb, C. W. (1991). An evaluation of the SERVQUAL scales in a retailing setting. *Advances in Consumer Research, 18*, 483. Asubonteng, P., McCleary, K. J., & Swan, J. E. (1996). SERVQUAL revisited: A critical review of service quality. *The Journal of Services Marketing, 10*(6), 62.

Johnston (1987) developed a framework to assess the service quality from the customer's point of view.[93] The Customer Proximity Operation outlines the steps and activities in the delivery of the service and highlights the threats to achieving an excellent customer experience.[94] It is necessary to give special attention to what Carlzon defined "moments of truth," where a customer assesses the perceived quality during the delivery of the service.[95] This model seeks to identify the elements that create the customer's perception, even if it does not provide practical means for improving service quality.[96]

High service quality results in better organizational performance and, thus, higher margins[97] even during economic downturns.[98] Given the nature of services, there is no easy way to assess or measure the quality of the service per se. Quality is a multidimensional concept. For Parasuraman et al. (1988), service quality is the difference between the customers' expectations and their perceptions after the service.[99] This chapter presents a model which can be used to select the best configuration of the call centers in a specific organization strategy. It has been used in the call center context.[100] The service quality work and SERVQUAL

[93] Johnston, R. (1995). The determinants of service quality: Satisfiers and dissatisfiers. *International Journal of Service Industry Management, 6*(5), 53. Bicheno, J., & Catherwood, P. (2005). *Service quality concepts: Six sigma and the quality toolbox* (pp. 132–150). Buckingham: PICSIE Books.

[94] Bicheno, J., & Catherwood, P. (2005). *Service quality concepts: Six sigma and the quality toolbox* (pp. 132–150). Buckingham: PICSIE Books.

[95] Carlzon, J. (1987). Putting the customer first: The key to service strategy. *McKinsey Quarterly, 3,* 38–51.

[96] Ghobadian, A., Speller, S., & Jones, M. (1994). Service quality concepts and models. *International Journal of Quality and Reliability Management, 11*(9), 43.

[97] Parasuraman, A., Berry, L. L., & Zeithaml, V. A. (1991). Perceived service quality as a customer-based performance measure: An empirical examination of organizational barriers using an extended service quality model. *Human Resource Management, 30*(3), 335–364.

[98] Fornell, C., Rust, R. T., & Dekimpe, M. G. (2010). The effect of customer satisfaction on consumer spending growth. *Journal of Marketing Research (JMR), 47*(1), 28–35.

[99] Parasuraman, A., Zeithaml, V. A., & Berry, L. L. (1988). SERVQUAL: A multiple-item scale for measuring consumer perceptions of service quality. *Journal of Retailing, 64*(1), 12–40.

[100] Staples, W., Dalrymple, J., &, Bryar, R. (2002). Assessing call centre quality using the SERVQUAL model. In *7th International Conference on ISO* (Vol. 9000).

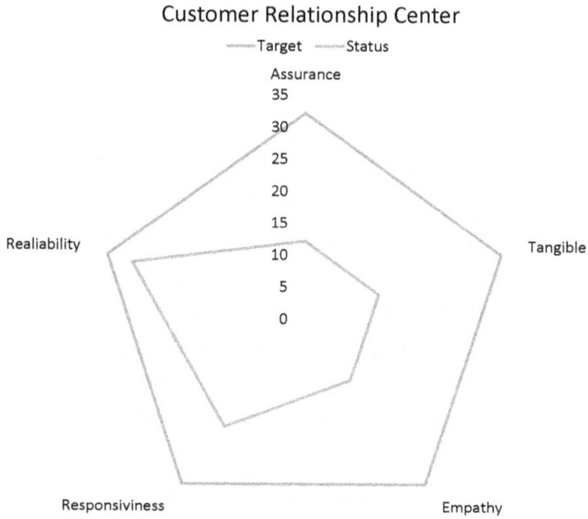

Fig. 5.3 Example of RATER assessment

scale developed by Parasuraman and his group has some limitations as an effective tool to measure service quality issues. The refined model considers only five of them with the acronym of RATER: Reliability, Assurance, Tangibles, Empathy and Responsiveness (see an example in Fig. 5.3).[101] In the case of a call center, the interpretation of the RATER dimensions could be:

- Reliability. This dimension is based on the differences between calls;
- Assurance. This dimension assesses the agents' ability to answer the customer questions or solve their problems, as well as their skills to provide trust, confidence, and security[102];
- Tangibility. This dimension includes the technical aspects of the call center service: the quality of the sound, the clarity and speed of the agent's voice and accent, and so on;

[101] Bicheno, J., & Catherwood, P. (2005). *Service quality concepts: Six sigma and the quality toolbox* (pp. 132–150). Buckingham, UK: PICSIE Books.

[102] Bicheno, J., & Catherwood, P. (2005). *Service quality concepts: Six sigma and the quality toolbox* (pp. 132–150). Buckingham, UK: PICSIE Books.

- Empathy. This dimension measures both the ways the agents engage with the customer, and whether they make an effort in really helping the customers;
- Responsiveness. This dimension assesses the agents' response to a special request (for instance, details on the next bills due), and their willingness to follow-up.

Focusing on the customer relationships center operation, many authors studied the call centers' operational challenges, often with a multidisciplinary approach. In the research on services, authors have mostly focused on call centers' queuing models,[103] human resources management,[104] and methods to forecast volumes of incoming calls.[105] Service quality in call center operations is not easy to assess. Koole and Mandelbaum presented a simplified model suggesting measuring service quality in call centers along two dimensions: qualitative aspects—the psychological size, often prioritized in marketing and social sciences—and quantitative issues—analytical approach, relating to the operational capabilities.[106] Performance measurement systems for call center employees often use this model. The appraisal of operators takes place on both the quantitative dimensions—number of calls, call duration, customer evaluation, and so on—and qualitative ones—adherence to policies, content, follow-up on customers, and so on.[107] Most often, organizations prefer to measure

[103] Koole, G., & Mandelbaum, A. (2002). Queueing models of call centers: An introduction. *Annals of Operations Research, 113*(1–4): 41–59. Gans, N., Koole, G., & Mandelbaum, A. (2003). Telephone call centers: Tutorial, review, and research prospects. *Manufacturing and Service Operations Management, 5*(2), 79–141.

[104] Bain, P., & Taylor, P. (2004). Call centers and human resource management: A cross-national perspective. *Employee Relations, 26*(5). Cezik, M. T., & L'Ecuyer, P. (2008). Staffing multiskill call centers via linear programming and simulation. *Management Science, 54*(2), 310–323.

[105] Weinberg, J., Brown, L. D., & Stroud, J. R. (2007). Bayesian forecasting of an inhomogeneous Poisson process with applications to call center data. *Journal of American Statistical Association, 102*(480), 1185. Taylor, J. W. (2008). A comparison of univariate time series methods for forecasting intraday arrivals at a call center. *Management Science, 54,* 253.

[106] Koole, G., & Mandelbaum, A. (2002). Queueing models of call centers: An introduction. *Annals of Operations Research, 113*(1–4), 41–59.

[107] Aksin, O. Z., Armony, M., & Mehrotra, V. (2007). The modern call center: A multidisciplinary perspective on operations management research. *Production and Operations Management, 16*(6), 665–688.

critical performance only on quantitative measures, like the waiting time or duration of calls. Technology helps in this respect. This method ignores the hidden drawbacks of low-quality service:

- Most customers will not complain, but they will either change the service provider or complain with other customers[108];
- Most dissatisfied customers will call back, with operational consequences, such as system overloading.[109]

Many organizations publish annual reports on the level of customer complaints received and solved. They somehow draw a link between these numbers and their customers' satisfaction. Even if the handling of complaints is crucial, as complaining customers show stronger brand loyalty, and service quality. Customer satisfaction have more complex dimensions.[110]

This chapter states (and describes in Table 5.1) that the assessment of the quality of a call center supporting insurance is strictly related to the strategy of organization

The last column in Table 5.1 represents different ways to assess quality in a call center according to the changes in the strategy.

The Future of the Call Centers

It is interesting to look at the future of call centers. The trend is to design and implement the customer relationships centers for self-help.[111] The effort that some organizations' customers are making is to first change their attitude on respect to the customer relationship center: from the "welfare" approach (the center is necessary to solve problems, and at any cost) to cooperating, proactively with the center. This issue is economic

[108] Mitchell, V. W. (1993). Handling consumer complaint information: Why and how? *Management Decision*.

[109] De Véricourt, F., & Zhou, Y. P. (2005). Managing response time in a call-routing problem with service failure. *Operations Research*, *53*(6), 968–981.

[110] Fornell, C., & Wernerfelt, B. (1987). Defensive marketing strategy by customer complaint management: A theoretical analysis. *Journal of Marketing Research (JMR)*, *24*(4), 337.

[111] Mohapatra, S. (2013). Understanding E-commerce product design strategy. In *E-Commerce Strategy* (pp. 113–125). New York, NY: Springer US.

and a question of mentality. Some customers and companies are already on this path due to the substantial cost savings that it brings. The tools which can help are the technologies of self-diagnosis, automatic identification of failure, the connection with control systems, and databases of statistical information of the non-quality made available to the customer. These new tools focus less on the need for a relationships center and more on optimizing the system and preventing malfunctions.

An approach of this kind has its counterpart in the formalization of *ad hoc* contracts in which the recognition by the company of this activity of self- help by the customer can save up to 40 percent in the prices of some contracts. On their part, companies are pushing the customers toward this type of solution. Companies agree: the higher the ability of the customer to self-service the product the more companies can expand their radius of action. This approach allows companies to achieve a double objective: financial and strategic. The goal is for this support, more and more complex, in some cases touching the boundary of advice and sale. It is therefore much more profitable than the traditional support.

It is interesting to deepen the financial objective associated with a strategy of this type. In particular, it is interesting to explore the concept of complex support on respect to simple advice. It is moving from servicing products to the provision of a service. There is a growing need by the companies to optimize the performance of the system. To do this, the support service must move in direction of a constant monitoring and remote control that allows the tuning of the system, as well as the prevention of faults and not only the interventions after the onset of the problem.

The call center should seek more and more to improve the efficiency of the customers' use of insurance services. All this implies that it is necessary to:

- Change processes;
- Get suggestions from the customers for the optimization of the services,
- Activate a presence that in the event of a claim provides the customer with the continuation of its use of the insured asset without harm; and last and not least
- Change completely the characteristics of the call center to be much more active and "outbound."

All this should be a target for the insurance 4.0 customer relationships center. One aspect which requires attention is the fact that self-help makes it more difficult to measure the quality of the service offered to the customers. To evaluate the service, It is necessary to do in-depth surveys with the customers or some type of remote monitoring or automatic feedback on the service provided.

More investigation is necessary to assess the quality of the service provided by the customer relationships centers, as today's customers expect excellent levels of service quality.

Conclusions

Insurance 4.0 requires different customer relationships.[112] New solutions present opportunities to better satisfy the customer expectations.[113] Customer satisfaction is undoubtedly increased by the possibility of managing the use of insurance cover and claims independently, anywhere, and at any time.[114] Customers desire new ways of purchasing insurance and managing risk, including more fit-for-purpose cover and services, and more immediate delivery. Customers wish to interact through various channels when searching for and purchasing insurance products. These customers greatly influence the evolution of online services, which changes the traditional "face-to-face" business model. The spread of information, and mainly of comparators websites, can diminish the loyalty of the policyholder. This diffusion may be exacerbated if increasing automation brings progressive de-customization of the

[112] Cappiello, A. (2020). The digital (R) evolution of insurance business models. *American Journal of Economics and Business Administration*, *12*(1), 1–13.

[113] Larsson, A., & Broström (2019). Ensuring customer retention: companies' perception of customer loyalty. *Marketing Intelligence and Planning*. https://doi.org/10.1108/mip-02-2019-0106.

[114] Akroush, M. N., & Mahadin, B. K. (2019). An intervariable approach to customer satisfaction and loyalty in the internet service market. *Internet Research*. Demong, N. A. R., Othman, A. K., Yunus, N. H., & Amran, N. A. W. (2019). Service quality factors and customer satisfaction on life insurance services. *Journal of Islamic Management Studies*, *2*(1), 22–31. Kaewsawad, S., & Li, Z. (2019, September). The effects of service quality of customer service on total customers' satisfaction in case of buying life insurance via the online channel. In *Proceedings of the IWEMB 2018: Second International Workshop on Entrepreneurship in Electronic and Mobile Business* (p. 119). BOD GmbH DE.

insurer/policyholder relationships. The increasing lack of human relationships due to the dissemination of digital distribution must move toward new digital-ready models of insurance intermediation, which require customer-proximity and continuous market research.

Through the integration of data from offline as well as online sources, insurance companies can understand better their customers. It allows them to approach in an holistic way their customers and understand their expectations from initial inquiry to buy the policy and finally to the use of their services.[115] Insurance 4.0 compels each organization to restructure its marketing and sales procedure, build long-term customer relationships, and win more deals with a robust CRM in place.

CRM solutions are a valuable marketing tool that allows companies to gain loyal customers. New solutions such as big data analytics can help quite a bit. CRM is a tool that enables marketing departments to make detailed reports according to the customers' changing preferences.

Higher customization of services and communication with the market involves developing an integrated communication strategy to better reach the customers to:

- Understand customer requirements and preferences;
- Create customers' new needs and anticipate them;
- Increase loyalty; and
- Monitor and oversee reputational dynamics that could otherwise escape of control.

This chapter underlines that the assessment of the quality of a call center is strictly connected with the strategy of the organizations. The strategy of the organizations has changed over time and so have the call centers. Therefore, also the parameters used to assess the quality, effectiveness, efficiency, and economics of a call center have changed.

The chapter presents a model of the evolution of the call center and presents some parameters used to assess the quality of the call center in each of its evolutionary stage. The different models in the evolution of the call center have deep consequences on the management of all the

[115] Industry 4.0 and Why There's a Need for an Effective CRM. blog.markgrowth.com/industry-4-0-and-why-theres-a-need-for-an-effective-crm-software-91963b865a73. Accessed 30 May 2020.

components of the call center as listed in the works of Chandler and Leavitt.

The future will see some fundamental changes in the relationships with the customer. One of the main drivers will be the technology: both in terms of better support to the call centers and in terms of self-help aids in the products and services. There will be more and more attention to improve the reliability, robustness, usability, and the support to the customer experience in the use of services. As an example, data centers will move more and more to the cloud.[116] The result will be an increasing importance of the call centers. On the other side, the increased use of mobile devices will make simpler the connection with the call centers but will require substantial changes in the design and deployment of services.[117] These aspects will greatly influence the quality of the service provided to the customers and its assessments.

Call centers will become more and more central in improving the customer experience. The models suggested in this chapter help in selecting the best strategy and implementation of a call centers in connection with the strategy of the organization.

[116] Nicoletti, B. (2013). *Cloud computing and financial services*. London, UK: Palgrave Macmillan.

[117] Nicoletti, B. (2014). *Mobile banking: Evolution or revolution*. London, UK: Palgrave Macmillan.

CHAPTER 6

Partition of the Customers in Insurance 4.0

Introduction

Insurance 4.0 business model analyzes whether the digitization leads to a segmentation of the market into a price competition or quality competition. Digitization increases the transparency of the non-complex insurance products. Their distribution channel is direct. As a result, the competition will intensify. On the one hand, there might be a fierce price competition with standardized products and high comparability. On the other hand, the premium providers might generate an intensive quality competition.

The objective of digitization is to move and possibly arrive at a market segment of one customer. Insurance organizations should include the distribution of personalized value propositions to their customers within the boundaries of their business plans. Several solutions may support this approach. For example, the internet of things: can help businesses into the delivery of personalized value propositions. Another example is wearables, such as fitness products or smartwatches. By tracking and monitoring the leading health indicators, these devices can send that information to an insurance company. In turn, the insurance company is then capable of providing better and tailored services, such as proposing simple incentives to decrease premiums or provide more services at a moderately higher price.

B. Nicoletti, *Insurance 4.0*, Palgrave Studies in Financial Services Technology, https://doi.org/10.1007/978-3-030-58426-9_6

To develop a customer-oriented strategy, an insurance company must, first of all, understand who the target customer is. Some additional questions can help[1]:

- Which are the company's most profitable customers? What makes them profitable?
- Why do they buy from the company and not from its competitors?
- What percentage of the total population of the target market is represented by these customers? Is it possible to find more customers with the same profile?
- How can the company make these customers buy more from the company?
- How will the company manage the less profitable customers to reduce the costs they require?

The answers to the above questions are shaping a customer segmentation analysis. Until the company understands who its profitable customers are, it will not be able to use the customer relationships management system (CRM) correctly. CRM can help in many ways, such as analysis of data associated with customers' costs and revenues, customer behavior related to products and services, identifying profitable customers, and those with potential. CRM cannot replace human labor that can develop a unique strategy for acquiring and building relationships with interesting customers and retaining them in the long term.

Generali[2]

With its "Vitality" accounts and policies, Generali has begun to encourage its customers to use recording equipment (Fitness trackers, wearables), which can provide insurance with the available data. In return, Generali gives insurance discounts and provides the customers with permanently lower rates. The benefits can be interesting.

[1] Matis, C., & Ilies, L. (2014). Customer relationship management in the insurance industry. *Procedia Economics and Finance, 15*(14), 1138–1145.

[2] Prognos, A. G. (2017). *Digitalisierung in der Versicherungswirtschaft. Studie*. Hg. v. vbw Vereinigung der Bayerischen Wirtschaft e.V. München, Germany.

In health insurance, there are only some providers who link their products with telematics. Generali offers Vitality as an innovative wellness program.[3] According to Generali, policyholders do not want insurance just to pay claims. Customers search for "real values at all times" from their companies.[4] Policyholders want to live a healthier lifestyle and be rewarded for it. As a health management program globally, Vitality motivates, rewards, and supports policyholders and offers new possibilities for various stakeholders. Ultimately, Generali thinks that Vitality will change how those persons view and engage with insurance.[5]

Vitality was launched in 1997 by the Discovery Group in South Africa. It is one of the world's most extensive wellness programs. Users of Vitality, South African insurer Discovery's health-and-wellness-management program, have 28 percent shorter hospital stays and 10 percent fewer chronic conditions than those who do not use it. These results are probably due to a combination of selection effects and actual behavior change.[6] The combination of components provides the possibility to reduce the information asymmetry.[7] Many experts estimate the Vitality data of Generali more as a marketing tool rather than an effective new service. It does not add value. On the contrary, many customers like to experiment with such insurance service.

The offer of Vitality has expanded globally to the UK, the USA, and across Asia, with over 3.5 million members in 2016.[8] In July 2016, the program started in Europe (with Germany first,[9] followed by France[10]). Generali Vitality combines actuarial, behavioral, and clinical tools in a step-by-step program that helps members improve their health through wellness

[3] See for more information. generalivitality.com. Accessed 30 May 2020.

[4] Generali. (2017). Introduction to vitality. generalivitality.com. Accessed 30 May 2020.

[5] Generali. (2017). Introduction to vitality. generalivitality.com. Accessed 30 May 2020.

[6] *Integrated Annual Report*. Discovery, 2018. discovery.co.za. Accessed 21 March 2020.

[7] Blomqvist, Å. (1991). The doctor as double agent: Information asymmetry, health insurance, and medical care. *Journal of Health Economics*, *10*(4), 411–432.

[8] All information provided by Vitality on its website: generalivitality.com. Accessed 30 May 2020.

[9] www.generali.com/media/press-releases/all/2016/Generali-Vitality-better-health-starts-today. Accessed 30 May 2020.

[10] www.generali.com/media/News/Generali-launches-Generali-Vitality-in-France. Accessed 40 May 2020.

activities and a healthy lifestyle.[11] Members receive rewards for getting more healthy. This has a positive impact on the mortality and morbidity experience in the insurance business and society.[12] Empirical evidence for that is still rare. The unsolved problem is to find a group of persons to which to compare the group of users of such health programs. There is a large selection bias of persons willing to give their health data to be used within insurance contracts (usually they are much healthier than the average population). That is why a random group of persons is not a reliable control group.

In Germany, Generali offers Vitality for new customers of term life or occupational disability insurance policies with either Dialog Life Insurance-AG or Generali Life insurance AG, respectively.[13] The issue in Germany is that such a product violates the German insurance laws if insurance company use the policyholders' data for the premium of health insurance contracts.

Customer Partition

Market segmentation involves the grouping of customers with similar needs and purchasing behavior into segments, each of which can be reached by a different marketing program.[14] The concept is useful to reconcile different customer needs with limited company resources. It allows product and marketing proposals to be adjusted to suit different customer groups.[15] The theoretical basis for market segmentation comes from the economic pricing theory. This theory indicates that margins are maximized when prices that discriminate segments are set.[16]

[11] *Market segmentation: A tool for improving customer*. jetems.scholarlinkresearch.com/articles/Market%20Segmentation.pdf. Accessed 5 April 2020.

[12] Generali. (2017). Introduction to vitality. generalivitality.com. Accessed 30 May 2020.

[13] Generali. (2017). Introduction to vitality. generalivitality.com. Accessed 30 May 2020.

[14] *Market segmentation: A tool for improving customer*. jetems.scholarlinkresearch.com/articles/Market%20Segmentation.pdf. Accessed 30 May 2020.

[15] Wind, Y. (1978, August). Issues and advances in segmentation research. *Journal of Marketing Research, 15*, 317–337. American Marketing Association.

[16] Frank, R., Massy, W., & Y. Wind (1972). *Market segmentation*. Upper Saddle River, NJ: Prentice-Hall.

One possible segmentation is based on the risk. Another traditional segmentation is on three significant types of insurance market segments[17]:

1. Life cycle segmentation classifies financial customers into household according to the stages in their life cycles[18];
2. Psychographic segmentation uses customers' lifestyles and personality differences to determine variances in customer demands;
3. Social Class Segmentation uses demographic information to analyze customers. Segmentation in insurance was basically along demographic lines. The approaches to this segmentation are:
   i. Geographic;
   ii. Demographic;

The other segments that need special attention are:

i. Students
ii. Women.

Millennials

An exciting segment, especially for insurance 4.0, is relative by the so-called millennials. With millennials (or Generation Y), the reference is to the customer segment relative to individuals born between 1981 through 1996. This segment is very active on the web, social media, and mobile phones. Generation Y represents a quarter of the world population.[19] It is a significant challenge for insurance companies trying to gain this market, as they are the customers of the future. Insurance 4.0 changes not only

[17] Epetimehin, F. (2011). *Market segmentation as a strategy for goal attainment in the insurance industry*. SSRN 1749663.

[18] Haas, R. W., & Berry, L. L. (1972). Systems selling of retail services. *Bankers' Monthly (USA)*, 276–283.

[19] How companies can appeal to millennials in 2018|Insurance. www.insurancebusinessmag.com/au/news/breaking-news/how-companies-can-appeal-to-millennials-in-2018-86282.aspx. Accessed 20 April 2020.

the insurance market but also the relationship with the customers.[20] This segment uses digital solutions and buy services via various channels.

Customers today, mainly the millennials but not only, want instant control of everything and to have more and more innovative products and services. Many millennials living in big cities do not own a car. The on-demand insurance supports these changes in the customer. It offers the possibility to pay the insurance based on the actual usage of the vehicle insurance.[21]

Trov[22]

AXA UK has a partnership with Trov. This insurtech organization offers an easy-to-use app that allows persons to provide on request specific insurance for assets for a limited period of particular use, not included in the annual premium. A policyholder can enable and disable the insurance coverage with a simple click, in case of an incident. A chatbot offers rapid assistance.[23] This type of flexible and affordable insurance is aimed primarily at millennials resident in the UK. Trov is changing not only how persons purchase insurance but the kinds of things they want to ensure. With the swipe of a button, one can turn insurance protection on and off. This technology makes insurance affordable for demographics like millennials, giving them the ability to access protection for essential items like cameras, mobiles, or laptops. It also responds to the customer's desire for instantaneous and straightforward access to services.

[20] Nicoletti, B. (2016). *Digital insurance*. London, UK: Palgrave-Macmillan (also translated in Chinese). https://doi.org/10.1057/9781137553270_8.

[21] Zarei, S., & Fallahi, A. R. (2019). *Pay-as-you-drive insurance pricing model*. arXiv preprint, arXiv:1912.09273.

[22] Kumar, C. (2017, September 29). *Digital Innovation: How AXA is changing insurance for its customers?* www.axa.com/en/spotlight/story/chelsie-digital-innovation. Accessed 10 January 2019.

[23] Chatbot is a robot that communicates with the customer via chat. Goyal, P., Pandey, S., & Jain, K. (2018). Developing a chatbot. In *Deep learning for natural language processing* (pp. 169–229). Berkeley, CA: Apress.

The Impact of Technology

Technology is one of the essential components to consider when dealing with the insurance industry.[24] Insurtech organizations are entirely aware of the strategic benefits of this lever: Start-up Bootcamp has analyzed over 1000 companies to identify the areas where technology can have significant effects.[25] Insurance is one of them.

Insurance companies have used information and communication technology (ICT) for a long time. Still, ICT has not been relevant in insurance companies as it has been in other financial institutions like the banks. ICT is becoming more and more essential for insurance companies. There are several reasons why this is happening. Several forces can drive this innovation:

- Markets (3C's: Customers, Competition, Compliance)
- Technology
- Design.

This chapter examines new solutions that can help in segmenting the customers. ICT technology can help, and it does not still stop in its development. Several aspects are relevant:

- Mobility;
- Big data analytics;
- Internet of things;
- Cognitive Technologies (Robots and artificial intelligence);
- Blockchain;
- Cloud Computing.

It is interesting to examine the technologies more visible to the customers (that are also a driving force).

Mobility is expanding at very high rates, even in the presence of the economic crisis, which is still affecting many economies in the world.

[24] Startupbootcamp. (2015). *So, what is an Insurtech startup?* www.startupbootcamp.org/blog/2015/october/so-what-is-an-insurance-startup-infographic.html. Accessed 19 August 2019.

[25] www.ey.com/Publication/vwLUAssets/EY-UK-FinTech-On-the-cutting-edge/$FILE/EY-UK-FinTech-On-the-cutting-edge.pdf. Accessed 30 May 2020.

The use of smartphones and tablets is expanding. The total number of mobile phones is almost equal to the world population.[26] The sales of smartphones and tablets are expanding faster than tablets and laptop computers. Mobile is influencing the sales of insurance products heavily. In some cases, it is the ideal solution. An example is travel insurance.

Big data analytics are technologies significant for insurance companies. Two uses stand up among the many ones: marketing support and risk management. These two technologies promise to move ICT from being systems of records to a system of engagement.[27] In other words, ICT can move from being just a big archive to the operational support of decisions in the insurance companies, such as the decision if to accept re-insurances, decide on the premium on new risks, and so on.

The internet of things is relevant in the case of insurance companies for the possibility to base on it customized services for the customers, such as the pay on consuming or based on the policyholder's health fitness and lifestyle.

The following chapters give further insights into these areas when they focus on applying the business model presented in this book. Nevertheless, it should now be clear how much potential might be unleashed by the extensive use of technology within the insurance industry and the possibility to implement more partitions of the market.

Conclusions

This chapter explores the concept of insurance partition of the market, its justification, and the business model canvas application. The chapter provides a list of the various segments that make up the business model canvas applied to the insurance market. It is critical to understand how the insurance world works and the main processes and resources necessary for the insurance business to occur. Attention is placed, in particular, to new ways to partition a market in transformation. This chapter also underlines the relevance of the millennial market.

[26] www.pewresearch.org/global/2019/02/05/smartphone-ownership-is-growing-rapidly-around-the-world-but-not-always-equally/. Accessed 20 March 2020.

[27] www.forbes.com/forbes/welcome/?toURL=www.forbes.com/sites/joshbersin/2012/08/16/the-move-from-systems-of-record-to-systems-of-engagement/&refURL=www.google.it/&referrer=www.google.it/. Accessed 20 August 2016.

CHAPTER 7

Place or Channels in Insurance 4.0

Introduction

This chapter analyzes insurance 4.0 from the points of view of distribution processes and channels. The initial analysis is in general. Then the chapter focuses the attention on the insurance marketplace and direct distribution. The chapter also looks at new regulations laid out by IVASS IVASS is the Italian regulator for the insurance organizations.[1]

All organizations have limited control over their external environment, which has recently shown some exciting developments. These developments are connected mainly with technology, but their solution embraces the entire business model. It is interesting to examine two aspects of the distribution of insurance products:

- to understand all the components that have significantly changed the insurance sector after years of technological stalemate;
- to analyze the levers on which insurance companies should rely on the short-medium term for the distribution of their products and services.

[1] IVASS is the Italian regulator for the insurance organizations. It is now part of the Central Bank of Italy (Banca d'Italia). www.ivass.it. Accessed 30 May 2020.

B. Nicoletti, *Insurance 4.0*, Palgrave Studies in Financial Services Technology, https://doi.org/10.1007/978-3-030-58426-9_7

As a whole, the insurance industry is positioned several years behind on the digital maturity curve compared to the financial services industry altogether. In turn, this is behind many other sectors. Going away from technological issues, an interesting point to analyze is the changed expectations and needs of the insurance customers, be they prospects or policyholders. Ubiquitous smartphones, open-source software, and cloud computing have substantially reduced experimentation and engagement with customers.[2] Lower barriers to company creation have given birth to insurtech organizations. These are mainly startup companies that rely on the latest technology to improve insurance customer experiences. Insurtech organizations are emerging rapidly[3] to collect on opportunities to disrupt the insurance market in areas where incumbent companies' legacy systems do not satisfy customers. Several new insurance startups, mainly in the Property and Casualty (P&C) domain,[4] are delivering new policyholder insurance offerings and significantly simplifying the procurement experience.

Digital transformation has had a significant impact on business distribution models. This book concentrates on the insurance sector. It is interesting to analyze the change of channel management in this specific case. Today's multi-channel presence of insurance organizations allows customers to perform search and operations of insurance services over multiple channels. Compared with other industries, for insurance customers, the adoption and utilization of digital channels are lagging, with a large part of policies sold over the traditional intermediary channels. New trends have emerged recently. Digital adoption does not depend anymore from the age. It is now common across generations.[5] Extended pandemic lockdowns in 2020 forced a generalized learning and extensive use of digital channels for day-to-day transactions. Everyone is digital is becoming a global slogan.[6] Customers are adopting online

[2] Internet Trends Report. 2018. *Kleiner Perkins*. www.kleinerperkins.com/perspectives/internet-trends-report-2018/. Accessed 10 January 2020.

[3] WebSight Design. "Financial technology partners—The only investment bank focused exclusively on financial technology." FT Partners|Financial Technology Investment Bank San Francisco. www.ftpartners.com/fintech-research. Accessed 10 January 2020.

[4] myhippo.com or www.kin.com or www.lemonade.com. Accessed 11 December 2019. Accessed 10 January 2020.

[5] REPORT. (2020). www.capgemini.com/de-de/wp-content/uploads/sites/5/2020/05/WorldInsuranceReport2020_Web.pdf. Accessed 30 May 2020.

[6] worldinsurancereport.com. Accessed 40 May 2020.

channels as the preferred medium searching for insurance products in advance of their actual purchase. In addition to pure traditional and digital customers, this behavior leads to a further customer group, the so-called search-shoppers. They utilize one channel for search and another one for purchase.[7]

Insurance 4.0 and Distribution

Despite the growth of digital technology and the growing customer literacy level with e-commerce, traditional insurance partners continue to dominate the distribution on a global scale. Agents, brokers, and other intermediaries such as banks, had relatively stable share, from 60 to 70 percent of premiums collection, in most insurance markets. Their role is mainly essential in the sale of life insurance products, with more sophisticated products that require the support of a consultant or a broker. The distribution of insurance services could be the domain that will be affected more by digital technologies, in particular in the sales of vehicles and housing (or other standardized products). In Europe, while sales through e-commerce of non-financial sectors are rising at double-digit rates, the average proportion of direct insurance via the internet is small. Some insurance companies in advanced economies are unable or unwilling to offer the opportunity to purchase via the web. They prefer the traditional channels not to make enemies the agents or simply because they do not want to invest in advanced technology.[8]

Beyond e-commerce developments, digital technologies have essential effects on all distribution processes: both on how products and services are delivered or supplied, and, more generally, on how organizations interact with their customers. While in the past, customers relied almost exclusively on their insurance agent or broker for every need, today's customers are increasingly autonomous. They use media and different sources for searching, learning from, and eventually purchase an insurance product. Digitization has expanded the range of services available to

[7] Mau, S., Cvijikj, I. P., & Wagner, J. (2018). Understanding the differences in customer portfolio characteristics and insurance consumption across distribution channels. *University of Lausanne*, 56–58.

[8] www.assinews.it/07/2017/impatto-della-digitalizzazione-sulla-distribuzione-assicurativa-ancora-rivoluzione-tranquilla/660042393/. Accessed 20 March 2020.

customers in various channels, including the web, e-mail, live chat, mobile application, text messages, forums, and social.

This evolution toward a multi-touch and omnichannel distribution model is a phenomenon present mainly in the advanced markets for now. It is also starting in emerging economies. Digital technology provides many options for customers. Mobile channels for communication allow subscribing to the premium payment debited on the operator's card or to an electronic wallet. Thus, the settlement of claims and their payment becomes more accessible and affordable.

The technology is not taking out the agents and brokers. It has created new types of partners. At the same time, traditional partners evolve and make use of new technologies to improve how they interact with customers, either in person or remotely.

Sales and distribution are undoubtedly the value network components that are being affected most by new solutions. The application of digital technologies has vastly changed the service delivery processes, their use, and, above all, the interactions with the customers. By reducing interaction time thanks to the digitization of distribution channels, insurance companies can improve their effectiveness, efficiency, and economics with cost reduction and better pricing policies. They can consolidate/expand their market share thanks to the careful management of customer relations.

E-commerce innovation, upon which direct insurance is dependent, experienced explosive growth in several developed countries. This growth offers three distinct benefits: reduced transaction costs, capacity to provide products to customers any time (24*7), and access to any customer in the world, by abolishing every distance and physical barriers.[9] The distribution of insurance services implies more and more close interaction between companies and customers. This relationship becomes an

[9] Kraemer, K., Gibbs, J., & Dedrick, J. (2002). *Impacts of globalization on e-commerce adoption and firm performance: A cross country investigation*. Irvine, CA: University of California, Center for Research on Information Technology Organization. Humphrey, J., Manshell, R., Pare, D., & Schmitz, H. (2003). *The reality of e-commerce with developing countries*. www.gapresearch.org/production/publications.html. Accessed 30 May 2020. United Nation Conference on Trade and Development. (2002). *Ecommerce and development report*. United Nations. UNCTAD. Yap, A., Das, J., Burbridge, J., & Cort, K. (2006). A composite-model for e-commerce diffusion: Integrating cultural and socio-economic dimensions to the dynamics of diffusion. *Journal of Global Information Management, 14*(3).

integral part of the distribution process itself. During the stages of acquisition and use of the insurance services, more or less frequent contacts are necessary between the customer and the company.[10] The robust interaction between the insurance company and customers is also underlined by the fact that the service does not exit the insurer's sphere of availability and proves to be continually influenced and activated by the latter.[11] This situation happens even when it enters the user's sphere of availability. In the initial stage of delivery, the service's use becomes at any time (e.g., in the case of on-demand insurance). The user's conduct may influence the distribution and use of the service (e.g., in the case of increases in risk or moral risk behavior).

An interactive process is taking place between the two parties. They together contribute to the creation and maintenance of the insurance relationship. The very nature of the insurance product, and the consequent interrelation between supply and demand, ensure that the service distribution and delivery system represent one of the critical factors for the success of the company's strategies. The interdependence in insurance among the production, distribution, and consumption phases makes the distribution system fundamental in the characteristics of the service, and its qualification with the customer.

Product differentiation can be implemented through a technological, relational, or organizational change that affects the constituent elements of the distribution system and modifies the customer's use of the product.[12] The technological evolution becomes critical when renewing insurance services' distribution and operations processes and their innovation.[13]

[10] Dumm, R. E., & Hoyt, R. E. (2003). Insurance distribution channels: Markets in transition. *Journal of Insurance Regulation, 22*(1), 27–48.

[11] Normann, R. (2001). *Reframing business: When the map changes the landscape*. Hoboken, NJ: Wiley.

[12] Nightingale, P. (2003). Innovation in financial services infrastructure. In L. V. Shavinina (Ed.), *The international handbook on innovation* (pp. 529–547). Oxford UK: Elsevier Science Ltd. Pires, C. P., Sarkar, S., & Carvalho, L. (2008). Innovation in services—How different from manufacturing? *The Service Industries Journal, 28*, 1339–1356.

[13] Coelho, F., Easingwood, C., & Coelho, A. (2003). Exploratory evidence of channel performance in single vs. multiple channel strategies. *International Journal of Retail & Distribution Management, 31*(11), 561–573.

In addition to making a significant contribution to the rationalization of insurance services' distribution systems, digitized channels make possible their differentiation and innovation.[14] More specifically, the changes introduced by technology may involve the product/service in the strict sense—with the introduction of new products—or the production and distribution process of the product/service. In the latter case, technological progress modifies the components of the traditional distribution system and the relationships established between different processes.

Overcoming the direct link with sales staff implies more robust intervention and higher involvement of the customer in the distribution of many services.[15] In the insurance sector, the distinction between product innovation and process innovation is not always clear. The finished product and the different phases of its distribution system are often strictly related. The differentiation and modernization of the production and distribution processes have significant effects on the service's qualitative and functional characteristics. They become a unique element. The different technological solutions significantly innovate the distribution process and affect the degree of novelty of the service itself.

In light of these considerations, information and communication technology is not only a tool for streamlining procedures and saving costs. It is a factor of differentiation and innovation of the product/service and its distribution process to achieve sustainable competitive advantages.[16]

The growing utilization of information technology allows for the expansion of distribution channels, including online ones. It promotes the intermediary's transformation with its physical and functional configuration and its role in the relationship with the customer. The expansion of operational boundaries, financial innovation, and changing requirements

[14] Coelho, F., & Easingwood, C. (2005). Determinants of multiple channel choice in financial services: An environmental uncertainty model. *Journal of Services Marketing, 19*(4), 199–211.

[15] Badoc, M. (1986). *Marketing pour le banque et l'assurance europeennes*. Paris, France: Les Editions d'Organization. Eiglier, P., & Langeard, E. (1987). *Servuction, le Marketing des Services*. Paris, France: McGraw Hill.

[16] Kabadayi, S., Loureiro, Y. K., & Carnevale, M. (2017). Customer value creation in multichannel systems: The interactive effect of integration quality and multichannel complexity. *Journal of Creating Value, 3*(1), 1–18.

of the market leads to the emergence of right conditions for diversification, and for a specific specialization of the distribution systems.[17] This trend leads to a careful assessment of the composition and coordination of the entire distribution system related to the services offered and to the market segments served.

Choice of the Channel for the Distribution of Insurance Products

Distribution channels have different functional characteristics that depend directly on the type of service offered, and the features of the market segments served.[18] The different nature of the requirements expressed by the various customers' partitions, and the consequent specificity of the services offered, require unique methods of delivery, which relate to specific distribution channels.[19]

The choices for the design of distinct delivery systems depend on the analysis of the features and competitive dynamics of the strategic business areas in which the company operates. These business areas depend on the following critical elements:

- Customers' partitions;
- Needs they express (types of services); and
- Satisfaction of these needs (production-distribution processes).

Insurance products are between two extremes: simplicity and low unit added value, on the one hand, high complexity, and significant added value, on the other hand.[20]

[17] Heinhuis, D., & de Vries, E. J. (2009). Modeling customer behaviour in multichannel service distribution. *Enterprise Applications and Services in the Finance Industry, 35*, 47–63.

[18] Normann, R. (2001). *Service management: Strategy and leadership in service business* (3rd ed., p. 256). Hoboken, NJ: Wiley. ISBN-10: 0471494399.

[19] Coelho, F., & Easingwood, C. (2008). An exploratory study into the drivers of channel change. *European Journal of Marketing, 42*(9/10), 1005–1022.

[20] Cappiello, A. (2018). *Technology and the insurance industry: Re-configuring the competitive landscape*. Cham, Switzerland: Palgrave Macmillan.

The first category includes all services characterized by simple operations with minimum customization content. It is easily standardized. Examples are vehicle insurance, home insurance, and so on. In some cases, these products are mandatory by law, so they tend to be in large quantities and with standard characteristics. The demand for these services is characterized mainly by price and comfort: the latter referring to the proximity of the distribution point and transaction execution speed. The insurance company must develop for the distribution of such services relatively inexpensive distribution systems. New solutions can help quite a bit in this direction.

The complex, or specialist services, have opposite characteristics. They require a high degree of customization and bring high added value. Examples are life insurance, pension products, and especially unit-linked insurances. Customers are sensitive to the quality of these services and personal relationships. These services require assistance and consultancy services before, during, and after the purchase by the customer. In this case, it is not easy to automate the operations, as they impact the degree of relationship. The company must have distribution and delivery systems that allow for the development of unstructured and high-content service relationships. For the placement of these sophisticated services, companies must provide high-quality channels with substantial customization and operational flexibility. It is advisable to use a distribution system implying the right level of contact with the customer. This system can be at the level of intermediaries or, better, through dedicated distribution networks.[21]

The complexity of the distribution systems increases with the complexity of the service provided and the relationship with customers. In general, the most sophisticated distribution systems are used for the distribution of services with higher specialist content and characterized by the highest value-added. This case takes place in the case of life insurance policies with relatively high costs by the customer. For these services, new solutions should improve the efficiency and effectiveness of the intermediaries, not necessarily to replace them. The latter is happening instead with the relatively simple products, such as vehicle or travel insurance.

The distribution systems characterized by a lower level of complexity and a small added value are adapt to simple services, such as non-life insurance policies. Technology allows for standardization and widespread

[21] Cappiello, A. (2018). *Technology and the insurance industry: Re-configuring the competitive landscape*. Springer.

distribution systems. These systems provide benefits in the cost structure. As a consequence, they support competitive strategies based on price. Thus, it is possible to effectively reach customer expectations, increase the distribution of sales points, reduce waiting times, and expand service hours.[22] The internet makes all this possible.

It is possible to offer a service that has reached a specific degree of diffusion and simplification through automated procedures. In the case of lesser-known, even if simple to use, products, it is critical to have direct contact with the customer. The products can be delivered through a channel that allows for a specific number of interactive relationships to facilitate promotional activities, service demonstrations, and excellent customer proximity. This situation takes place, for example, with unit-linked products. For these products, the empathy and trust generated by direct relationships between a consultant and the policyholder are important. It is necessary the flexibility in the approach and to assures professional responses. In this type of service, the creativity to define strategies and interventions to the events is critical.[23]

The increasing diversification of the services offered requires a corresponding specificity of the distribution systems. Specialization of the latter can be carried out within the same distribution channel (in particular at the agency or other financial institutions), or give rise to relatively dedicated channels. The choice between direct and indirect distribution depends on several factors, including but not limited to the size of the company, the geographic extent of the markets served, the competitive dynamics related to them, the type of products/services offered, and the features of the demand segments.

The selection of the various types of distribution channels is robustly influenced by the product policies chosen by the company, the features of the segments served, and by inheritance factors. The latter is relative mainly to the current distribution structure. This structure creates constraints and conditions the strategic choices relating to rationalizing and restructuring of the entire distribution system, including the enlargement of the types of distribution channels.

[22] Thornton J., & White L. (2001). Customer orientations and usage of financial distribution channels. *Journal of Services Marketing, 15*(3), 168–185.

[23] Magnani, N. (2020). *Robot*. Milano, Italy: Utet.

The adoption of a distribution system that provides for the use of a broader range of distribution channels is characterized by higher specialization, besides efficiency, effectiveness, and economics. The higher specificity of the channel is suited to satisfying the target market's needs more appropriately and optimizing the customer relationship. With more channels, it becomes difficult to implement politics of cross-selling, but only upselling.

Innovation allows for the activation of new distribution systems and channels for specific combinations of services offered/customer segments served. These distribution channels are a real innovation in the distribution systems that, in the past, were closely connected with physical channels.[24] The automation, and possibly, outsourcing of some production-distribution processes and easily standardized services brings an improvement in the operational efficiency, effectiveness, and economics of the company distribution system.

Besides encouraging the optimization of the structure of the distribution network and reducing its costs, the use of channels based on new solutions allows for the improvement of service quality, such as performance, speed, and precision. It can satisfy better the expressed or implied customer requirements.

Insurance 4.0 unlocks new competitive and marketing opportunities. It allows for remote interaction with the user. The automation contributes to a progressive de-customization of the insurer-customer relationships. This situation is mainly true for the intangible nature of the insurance service. It can be easily evaluated in its qualitative aspects at the time of use. The components of the service distribution system have a significant impact on the quality perceived. This impact results with the combination of different elements such as ease of access and convenience of the interaction, time frames, reduction of material errors, transparency, cost-effectiveness of the relationship, professionalism, and courtesy of

[24] Stepanek, L., & Roman, P. (2017). Urban insurance industry ideas of the second millennium. *Ecoforum, 6*,1(10).

the intermediaries.[25] Technological innovation offers the opportunity to improve many of these aspects. It can increase the frequency of customer interactions, offering the possibility to increase customer loyalty and the potential of cross-selling.[26]

The fragmentation of contact points, due to the expansion of digital channels and the customer's economic and cultural evolution, contributes to reducing customer loyalty. It makes it more challenging to establish a lasting relationship. The de-customization of the link pushes to evaluate the quality of the service on technical and economic considerations and less on personal/emotional factors.[27]

Another aspect to consider is the increasing competition between insurance companies, and the possible overlapping of areas of expertise made possible by the growing spread of technology knowledge.

The company should manage the technological variable not only from a purely productive perspective (to streamline procedures and reduce operating costs) but also in marketing to improve the brand. The loss of direct contact with customers is undoubtedly a negative factor. It is necessary to balance the need for a personalized relationship with customers through automation benefits. A marked standardization of elementary services, associated with higher specialization of the company-customer link, can reach such balance. It is critical to adopt a personalized approach to the customers according to the logic of mass customization.[28] Through a more precise identification of different needs and requirements, higher customization is possible in the distribution of

[25] Normann, R. (2001). *Service management: Strategy and leadership in service business* (3rd ed.). Hoboken, NJ: Wiley. ISBN-10: 0471494399. Kotler, P. (2001). *A framework for marketing management*, Upper Saddle River, NJ: Prentice Hall. Donnelly, J., Berry, L. L., & Thompson, T. W. (1985). *Marketing financial services: A strategic vision*. New York, NY: Dow Jones Irwin.

[26] Accenture. (2017). *The future of insurance distribution: New models for a digital customer*. www.accenture.com/_acnmedia/pdf-38/accenture-reimagine-procurement-pov-final.pdf. Accessed 21 March 2020.

[27] Reicheld, F. F. (1996). *The loyalty effect*. Boston, MA: Harvard Business School Press. Schwarz, G., Naujoks, H., Goossens, C., Whelan, D., Schwedel, A., & Singh H. (2014). *Customer loyalty and the digital transformation in P&C and life insurance*. www.bain.com/insights/customer-loyalty-and-the-digical-transformation-in-p-and-c-and-life-procurement/. Accessed 20 March 2020.

[28] Bardakci, A., & Whitelock, J. (2003). Mass-customization in marketing: The consumer perspective. *Journal of Consumer Marketing*.

services and communication with the customers. It is needed to strive for continuous improvement in the approach to contact with the reference market. It is necessary to renew and innovate the relationship with customers to cover as much as possible their expectations.[29]

Customers expect to communicate and be involved with the company at any time, wherever they want, and with any device. They accept to use innovative services if they are more interactive and improve communication. Companies modify the distribution by offering a digital experience omnichannel[30] and customizing their products and services.[31] In the past, customers would choose a channel (mobile phone, agency, and so on) and stick to it until finishing their transaction. Now, these paths are becoming more complex. They include several channels at a time (agency, television, personal computers, social media, smartphones, and so on). Each channel constitutes a hub making the multichannel access essential and an opportunity that insurance companies must carefully consider. To improve interactions with customers, insurance should push on all communication channels, such as apps, social media, and web pages, and adjust them continuously.[32]

The purchase of the policy is not necessarily completed in the same place where customers look for information.[33] Marketers call it the "ROPO effect." It is an acronym that expresses the behavior of those who, before shopping, search for information online, but then buy offline.[34]

[29] Hänninen, N., & Karjaluoto, H. (2017). The effect of marketing communication on business relationship loyalty. *Marketing Intelligence & Planning*.

[30] An omnichannel strategy enables customers to use channels seamlessly and interchangeably and experience the channels uniquely. Mirsch, T., Lehrer, C., & Jung, R. (2016). Channel integration towards omnichannel management: A literature review. In *20th Pacific Asia Conference on Information Systems (PACIS)* 2016. Chiayi, Taiwan.

[31] Insurance Europe. (no date). *Digitalisation. The benefits of digitalisation*. www.insuranceeurope.eu/digitalisation. Accessed 20 January 2020.

[32] Barwitz, N. (2020). The relevance of interaction choice: Customer preferences and willingness to pay. *Journal of Retailing and Consumer Services*, *53*, 101953.

[33] www.assinews.it/07/2017/impatto-della-digitalizzazione-sulla-distribuzione-assicurativa-ancora-rivoluzione-tranquilla/660042393/. Accessed 20 March 2020.

[34] repository.upb.edu.co/bitstream/handle/20.500.11912/4507/Omnichannel%20Shopping%20Patterns.pdf?sequence=1&isAllowed=y. Accessed 28 April 2020.

AXA[35]

The development of the app MyAXA is an example of how insurance uses digital innovation to meet customer needs. With this app, policyholders can access and manage their contract information directly from their mobile phones. Another example is the establishment of the Social Media Command Centers. These centers use sophisticated technology to monitor what is present on social media, incorporate the concerns, demands, and customer feelings, and act accordingly.[36] Social networks are also an active listening and communication channel. For example, AXA France has partnered with Facebook Messenger to offer young customers 100 percent digital experiences and make faster customer service, error-free, and customized. Customers may request information on products and services, as well as information on required documents or certificates.[37] The benefit of the chatbot is that it can assist customers 24*7, collect their geographical and social data, better understand their needs, and offer custom quotes. The customer journey is automated and effortless.

In the past, the promotion of insurance contracts tool place through billboards, television commercials, newspaper advertising, and other media.[38] The new channels of promotion are sponsoring, specialized articles, and social networks (such as Facebook and LinkedIn). Some communication channels are most appropriate for a particular type of customer. For example, Facebook is suitable for individuals. For insurance contracts with organizations, the channel is LinkedIn, because it is a professional social network.

[35] Kumar, C. (2017, September). *Digital innovation: How AXA is changing insurance for it customers?* www.axa.com/en/magazine/chelsie-digital-innovation. Accessed 30 May 2020. www.axa.com/en/spotlight/story/chelsie-digital-innovation. Accessed 11 December 2019.

[36] Kumar, C. (2017, September). *Digital innovation: How AXA is changing insurance for its customers?* www.axa.com/en/spotlight/story/chelsie-digital-innovation. Accessed 11 December 2019.

[37] AXA. (2016, April). *AXA, the first insurance brand to adopt Facebook Messenger*. www.axa.com/en/newsroom/news/axa-adopts-facebook-messenger. Accessed 30 May 2020.

[38] tesi.supsi.ch/2609/. Accessed 11 December 2019.

Many studies tried to understand if and how customers differ over different channels and which factors drive channel selection.[39] The objective of these studies was to provide evidence on customer behavior within and across individual channels.

Direct Digital Channels

Direct insurance is the sale of insurance products and services without the use of intermediaries (insurance agents, banks, and brokers)- Technological evolution supports this relative innovative channel for insurance distribution.[40] Through the direct channel, insurance companies sell their products to their customers by telephone, internet, mail, or interactive television and bypass the intermediaries. By doing this, they can significantly reduce their expenses ratio by subtracting the commission costs (10–20 percent or more of the product) and limiting their administrative expenses through paperless processing procedures.[41] Early research by the consultants Price Waterhouse Coopers showed that the average transaction carried out directly by a financial services company can cost half when done over the telephone on respect of over the branch network and one-tenth when conducted over the internet.[42] These cost reductions are significant for insurance companies to survive in some very price-sensitive markets such as vehicle insurance. The price war regarding that product

[39] Elliott, M. T., Fu, F. Q., & Speck, P. S. (2012). Information search and purchase patterns in a multichannel service industry. *Services Marketing Quarterly*, *33*(4), 292–310. Punj, G. (2011). Effect of consumer beliefs on online purchase behavior: The influence of demographic characteristics and consumption values. *Journal of Interactive Marketing*, *25*(3), 134–144. Robertson, A., Soopramanien, D., & Fildes, R. (2007). Household technology acceptance: Heterogeneity in computer adoption. *AMCIS 2007 Proceedings*, 77. Montoya-Weiss, M. M., Voss, G. B., & Grewal, D. (2003). Determinants of online channel use and overall satisfaction with a relational, multichannel service provider. *Journal of the Academy of Marketing Science, 31*(4), 448–458.

[40] Tzanis, S. (2012). *Direct Insurance: The determinants of success*. Doctoral thesis, University of St. Gallen, St. Gallen, Switzerland.

[41] Bates, I., & Atkins, D. (2007). *Management of insurance operations*. Kent, UK: Institute of Financial Services.

[42] Page, Y. (2000). *E-commerce in insurance*. London: Informa.

has reduced profit margins and, for instance, has resulted in underwriting losses of 25 billion Euros during the period 1997–2007.[43]

Overcoming the direct relationship with sales staff implies more robust interventions and higher involvement of the customer in the distribution of many services.[44] In the insurance sector, the distinction between product innovation and process innovation is not always clear. Since the finished product and the different phases of its distribution system are often strictly combined, it is not difficult to detect how the differentiation and innovation of the production and distribution processes have significant effects on the qualitative and functional characteristics of the service. They are a unique element. The different technological solutions significantly innovate the distribution process and affect the degree of novelty of the service itself.

To upgrade communication methods and improve sales activities, insurance companies focus on the design of mobile apps, websites, and official pages on the main social networks. They are attempting to implement distribution methods and customer relationship management through chatbots and robo-advisors, which are sophisticated technological systems. Customers demand clarity and transparency in the contract. A plus of digital channels is the possibility for the customer to access more information online.

Accenture surveyed in 2016 the opinions of the customers from eighteen markets. They found that 68 percent of persons prefer to use online channels to get information about insurance products and services.[45] Over time, there has been an increase in the number of visits to online portals, especially during the pandemic. On the other side, many persons (even young) still give importance to human contacts. This percentage is around 41 percent in the Italian market.[46] Prospects tend to use the online portal at first for a quote. Later on, when there is confidence

[43] www.insuranceeurope.eu/sites/default/files/attachments/European%20Motor%20Insurance%20Markets%202019.pdf. Accessed 30 April 2020.

[44] Badoc, M. (1986). *Marketing pour le banque et l'assurance europeennes*. Paris, France: Les Editions d'Organization. Eiglier, P., & Langeard, E. (1987). *Servuction, le Marketing des Services*. Paris, France: McGraw-Hill.

[45] Generali. (2018, 28 February). *Le assicurazioni "tutto connesso."* www.generali.com/it/info/discoveringgenerali/all/2018/A-fully-connected-insurance. Accessed 11 January 2020.

[46] Casadei, M. (2020, June 1). La Conversione al digitale chiede fiducia. *Il Sole 24 Ore*.

in the consultant, the customer contacts him/her for clarifications and confirmation.

To sum up, the benefits of direct insurance for companies are[47]:

- Savings on brokerage commission;
- Possibility of spending the money they save on advertising their brand and attracting the customers directly;
- No assigning of the core processes of underwriting and claims management to the intermediaries;
- More flexibility in segmentation and pricing
- Avoidance of the conflict of interest that an intermediary might have in both underwriting and claims management;
- Underwriting alterations are not possible;
- Direct collection of the premiums;
- Security of payment;
- Better cash flow;
- More time to invest the premiums;
- 100 percent ownership of the customer;
- Increase in the company's value;
- Improvement in customer retention management.

Apart from the companies, the policyholders benefit from direct insurance as well[48]:

- Attractive prices thanks to the lower operating costs;
- Instant coverage on a 24*7-hour basis;
- A faster route for telephone or internet;
- Direct access to information and access the private customer area. These channels are fast and direct because they are available to the customers any time and saves on printing paper.
- The market structure can determine the success or failure of direct insurance in a country to a large extent.

[47] Tzanis, S. (2012). *Direct insurance: The determinants of success*. Doctoral thesis, University of St. Gallen, St. Gallen, Switzerland.

[48] Tzanis, S. (2012). *Direct Insurance: The determinants of success*. Doctoral thesis, University of St. Gallen, St. Gallen, Switzerland.

Direct insurance can optimize its possibilities of success when promoted in a country that has a culture conducive to innovations (macroeconomic level) because direct insurance is an innovative method of buying insurance. The country should also have an insurance market structure that facilitates the development of direct insurance (market level). A facilitating market structure is where brokers are the leading channel of insurance distribution or the agents, and where insurance regulation encourages market competition. The latter is necessary since direct insurance's significant advantage is its better pricing. Direct insurance cannot succeed under restrictive competition regulations that protect the traditional insurance players from new ones entering the market. The insurance company that sells directly should have no conflict with other channels of distribution of its group (microeconomic level). This situation will give the direct insurance company the freedom to price its products cheaply than the other, indirect insurance companies. Thus, they can gain a significant market share. This situation, in turn, will reduce their costs and hence increase their competitiveness.

Online Intermediaries for Insurance 4.0

According to OECD, internet partners are those middlemen that facilitate transactions between third parties on the internet.[49] This way, they provide access, host, transmit, and index content, products, and services (also based on the internet) from third parties.[50]

Thanks to incumbents' legacy, customer ownership has not been a problem, until now. The competition was coming just from other traditional insurance companies. Companies felt safe to pass customer contacts to partners. Customer access and ownership are essential to earn higher profits.[51] To succeed and beat the competition, companies have to offer superior products and services. They cannot rely anymore on their reputation and legacy.

[49] www.oecd.org/internet/ieconomy/44949023.pdf. Accessed 22 March 2020.

[50] Greco, A. (2018). *Digital transformation and disruption*. Doctoral dissertation, NOVA—School of Business and Economics, Lisbon, Portugal.

[51] McKinsey. (2017). *Now, customer access and ownership are crucial to gain higher profits*. www.mckinsey.com/~/media/mckinsey/business%20functions/operations/our%20insights/how%20to%20capture%20what.%20the%20customer%20wants/customer-first-personalizing-the-customer-care-journey.ashx. Accessed 30 May 2020.

Another component to consider in the distribution of insurance products is web marketplaces (or comparators). Online marketplaces form now an integral part of the landscape of insurance distribution. They act mainly as "virtual" agencies. These channels enable customers to compare different insurance products, get instant quotes, and subscribe to the chosen policy directly online on the portal of the marketplace or on the platform of the insurer to which the customer can be re-directed by the web marketplace. Until now, the comparators are mainly successful in the UK and the Netherlands. They have become essential also in Germany, Italy, Spain and, to a lesser extent in France.[52]

Vehicle insurance was one of the products sold through marketplaces. Now, comparators offer products from other industries, such as insurance travel and housing, or even social security covers. There are also comparative platforms with insurance products aimed at small businesses. The marketplaces are evolving their offerings looking to go beyond the tariff comparison and to propose additional services such as product evaluation, requirements analysis, and consultancy. With the increased availability of personal and smarter methods of analysis and assessment of risk profiles, the potential of customized insurance products increases. This situation implies that the simple comparison of insurance loses interest in favor of personal advice to help customers choose the best coverage for risks, which may change over time,[53] Web marketplaces are moving from "virtual agencies" to "virtual brokers." The use of robo-advisors (examined in another chapter) will make this virtual consultancy very powerful.

There are three main online partners that incumbents should consider: Price Comparison Websites (PCWs), Value Comparison Websites (VCWs), and Digital Brokers.

[52] The comparators are mainly successful in the UK but have become important also in Germany, Italy, Spain and, to a lesser extent in France.

[53] www.assinews.it/07/2017/impatto-della-digitalizzazione-sulla-distribuzione-assicurativa-ancora-rivoluzione-tranquilla/660042393/. Accessed 11 January 2020.

Price Comparison Websites

According to a Deloitte definition, Price comparison websites (PCW) help users to quickly find insurance by aggregating policies from multiple insurance companies and display them based on quoted price.[54] Customers use platforms like Comparis, Bonus.ch, or Segugio.it. They are sometimes recommended by friends and family to consult and compare the estimates and have a general idea of prices. The customer has a chance to save because they can see the best prices. The problem is that the choice is made mainly on the premiums.

With the increase in the use of PCWs, there will be a commoditization of some of Europe's largest markets[55] by making customers more price-sensitive and allowing low-cost companies to gain market share.

Value Comparison Websites

Value Comparison Websites (VCW) help customers purchase a policy through a comparison of value instead of price. This type of intermediary is customer-centric. They can meet customer needs by explaining the value of insurance policies that are often not well known. VCWs might become the preferred distribution channel. According to a Deloitte survey, over a quarter of health, home, and motor insurance customers stated that it is difficult for them to work out if insurance is excellent for the money.[56] If persons start using this tool more, they will get a more in-depth understanding of insurance products and get more consciousness when making purchases.

[54] Insurance disrupted General insurance in a connected world, 2015. www2.deloitte.com/content/dam/Deloitte/global/Documents/Financial-Services/gx-fsi-insurance-disrupted.pdf. Accessed 20 March 2020.

[55] www2.deloitte.com/content/dam/Deloitte/de/Documents/strategy/20161116Europeanpercent20motorpercent20study-DE-englisch.pdf. Accessed 20 March 2020.

[56] www2.deloitte.com/content/dam/Deloitte/us/Documents/life-sciences-health-care/us-lchs-dig-deep-hidden-costs-112414.pdf. Accessed 30 May 2020. Accessed 30 May 2020.

Digital Brokers

A broker has contracts with several companies. He/she gets commissions paid by the companies who offer the coverage. As a general rule, when a broker agrees to sell a policy to a customer and obtains a commission in return, the broker has a duty toward the customer to act with reasonable care, competence, and diligence. In particular, in the German insurance market, insurance brokers may provide advisory service of higher quality and better suited to the needs of the customers than that of insurance agents.[57] Digital brokers are a new type of online intermediary that often operates by using social media.[58] Specifically, this solution has a better focus on market niches until now poorly-served by insurance companies.[59]

The potential in attracting a significant number of customers of this type of intermediary lies in the fact that digital brokers can offer them substantial savings and customized products. Many brokers declared that it could save up to 19 percent by using their collective procurement power.[60]

Digital brokers should not alarm companies. The latter should look at them as a great business opportunity since these platforms can identify reasonable risks, by indicating to companies the users to whom direct their offerings. Digital brokers tend to possess a more in-depth and more robust relationship with customers than traditional companies.[61]

Companies should act promptly, considering that for now, digital brokers are just partners. Soon they could turn their customer insights into valuable reasons to start underwriting.

[57] Guillem, M. A. L. (2020). The customer orientation service of Spanish brokers in the insurance industry: The advisory service of the insurance distribution channel bancassurance. *Sustainability*, *12*(7), 1–22.

[58] Röschmann, A. Z. (2018). Digital insurance brokers—old wine in new bottles? How digital brokers create value. *Zeitschrift für die gesamte Versicherungswissenschaft*, *107*(3), 273–291.

[59] Greco, A. (2018). *Digital transformation and disruption*. Doctoral dissertation, NOVA—School of Business and Economics, Lisbon, Portugal.

[60] Catlin, T., & Lorenz, J. T. (2017, March). *Digital disruption in insurance: Cutting through the noise*. Digital McKinsey.

[61] Greco, A. (2018). *Digital transformation and disruption*. Doctoral dissertation, NOVA—School of Business and Economics, Lisbon, Portugal.

Bought by Many[62]

Bought By Many (BBM) is the first digital broker in Europe. It raised USD 7.5M in Jan 2017. It serves, for example, persons with heart conditions who need travel insurance.[63] Customer acquisition comes from the analysis of social media users' patterns and other online behaviors (e.g., by analyzing the "likes"). BBM had a young driver group with over 10,000 members in May 2015. BBM acquires customers by applying affinity marketing, social media, and Search engine optimization (SEO). BBM has a top ranking on Google for 6100 niche insurance search terms.[64]

An Overview of the Italian Market

Technological innovation and the use of new connection tools into customers' hands are rewriting the dynamics of development and sustainability of the insurance industry. A digital study insurance in Italy, The Time to Act Is Now made by The Boston Consulting Group, in collaboration with Google, has an exciting picture of the phenomenon and discusses the opportunities that will open up in the sector.[65]

This study by The Boston Consulting Group, in partnership with Google highlights the growing recourse to the internet to decide to buy the insurance. The study estimates that premiums influenced by the search were worth 36 billion euros in 2015.[66] The use of searches is mainly for deciding which insurance to buy and is directly impacting the business. This situation is actual even when the final purchase is offline (ROPO, Research online, purchase offline).

In this context, mobile devices play an essential role. As early as 2015, 24 million Italians were using a smartphone. By 2018, the estimate rises to 37 million. Insurance searches performed by smartphone (on auto, life,

[62] boughtbymany.com/. Accessed 30 May 2020.

[63] www2.deloitte.com/content/dam/Deloitte/de/Documents/strategy/20161116Europeanpercent20motorpercent20study-DE-englisch.pdf. Accessed 20 March 2020.

[64] Stanley, M. (2015). *Insurance Tech Ecosystems*. https://goo.gl/N3QH45. Accessed 22 March 2020.

[65] www.bcg.com/it-it/perspectives/123863. Accessed 31 March 2020.

[66] www.corrierecomunicazioni.it/digital-economy/cloud/assicurazioni-boston-consulting-group-ricerche-online-in-italia-su-del-128-in-5-anni/. Accessed 11 January 2020.

health, home) grew by an average of 155 percent a year for the past six years.[67]

The Italian market for insurance differs depending on life and non-life solutions chosen by customers.

The agents retain a larger share of the insurance market, even if with an amount underestimated for brokers, which often intermediate insurance solutions not directly to the insurance organization, but rather via agents. Agents and brokers have 86.3 percent market share on P&C (where the insurance is critical). The agents show a slight reduction in brokerage percentage in the previous year (−2.7 percent). There is specific stability in the market share for this distribution mode.[68] In five years, there were no significant changes, if not a few decimal percentage units.

The New Distribution Regulation: IDD—Insurance Distribution Directive

The implementation of the European Directive 97/2016/EU intervenes on the brokerage insurance business segment. It influences insurance distribution.[69] This directive regulates, more broadly, the insurance distribution business by introducing more efficient systems and simplified log management and supervision of organizations and intermediaries. It accurately represents a significant increase in the customer protection and, in many respects, consolidates European law principles and rules that are already in some nation's regulation.[70]

The Italian regulatory agency for insurance (IVASS) issued three regulations[71]:

[67] www.corrierecomunicazioni.it/digital-economy/cloud/assicurazioni-boston-consulting-group-ricerche-online-in-italia-su-del-128-in-5-anni/. Accessed 23 March 2020.

[68] www.ilpuntopensionielavoro.it/site/home/assicurazioni/assicurazioni-e-tecnologia-lintermediario-restera-indispensabile.html#_ftn6. Accessed 23 March 2020.

[69] eur-lex.europa.eu/legal-content/en/TXT/?uri=CELEXpercent3A32016L0097. Accessed 31 March 2020.

[70] www.ivass.it/normativa/focus/distribuzione-assicurativa/index.html. Accessed 23 Mach 2020.

[71] www.assinews.it/08/2018/ivass-line-regolamento-recepimento-dellidd/660054950/. Accessed 23 Mach 2020.

- Regulation n. 40 on the distribution of insurance and reinsurance;
- Regulation n. 41 on transparency, publicity, and realization of products;
- Regulation n. 39 on sanctions.

"Regulation n. 40 on the distribution of insurance and reinsurance" brings a discipline regarding the rules of market access, the conduct of such activities, conducted in the sales phase to customers, even in the case of remote placement and promotion, professional training of operators. The regulation does not apply to the provisions concerning additional products IBIPs (insurance-based investment products) or POGs (Product Oversight Governance), without prejudice to the applicability to the distribution of all insurance products, including IBIPs, general rules of conduct detailed under this compliance intervention.

IVASS believes that the regime applicable to the POGs and the IBIPs from October 1, 2018 is defined by the CAP and the European Commission's delegated Regulations Nos. 2017/2358 and 2017/2359.

These regulations include, in particular:

- Opportunity for the broker to make publicly available information concerning the main rules of conduct of intermediaries (Annex 3), including through technological equipment;
- Possibility for the contractor to communicate with the distributor, on the use of specific assumptions, via the website;
- Discipline in detail of the website's contents, social network profiles, or any other applications, when used by the distributor to the task of placing or only the promotion of insurance distribution business.

The "Regulation n. 41 on transparency, publicity, and realization of products" introduces the pre-contractual information documents (DIP) with a from the simplified format and standardized content, to aid comprehension and comparison of the insurance products (life and non-life) by customers, and the requirement of digital control of contracts on insurance services. Compliance intervention replaces, updating the principles of EU law and the subsequent news of the French insurance code, regulation 35, pursuing four main objectives:

- revision of the pre-contractual information for all products, through the preparation of new simplified and standardized documents replacing the current securities note and summary, if provided;
- strengthening digitization through: (i) the enhancement of the capabilities of the so-called housing insurance (reserved areas on the websites of organizations); (ii) substitution, on customer choice, of paper communications with communications that use digital media; (iii) lower newspaper publisher obligations;
- strengthening of the contractor's protection, particularly regarding the information in the course of the contract and the arrangements for preparation of contractual documents;
- simplification on the regulation text and additional adjustments necessary based on current legislation, in coordination with the regulation on distribution.

Regarding the pre-contractual information, the text introduces the same articulation envisaged by the CAP and, in light of European standardized documents, prepares the more standardized templates in place of the current notes: DIP-on Damages; DIP-DIP's life, the life; DIP-on all risks; additional DIP IBIP.

The Regulation pursues the objective to enhance the digitization of the insurance market, through:

- review of the rules for private internet areas (housing insurance) by introducing the obligation to enable contract management for undertakings authorized in Italy and, limited to contracts relating to insurance mandatory liability insurance for the circulation of motor vehicles and boats, for EU organizations; the restricted areas may also be present via mobile application and website;
- enhancement of website with content expansion for the benefit of users and businesses (publication of the information set of all products, free distribution to assist to contractors, management regulations split up, and the information on conflicts of interest and ethical and sustainable finance, until now included in the pre-contractual information paper);
- introduction of digital management requirement of contractual details to facilitate the collection of data to support the effective management of the target customers and identify the identity of

the beneficiary of the life insurance policies, helping to contain the phenomenon of dormant insurance;

- the elimination of the obligation to publish in newspapers for yields on mutual funds and segregated funds and mutual funds, and more general forecasting mode of communication envisaged by the code that can be chosen by the customer, paper or digital.

Special attention is given in strengthening policyholder protection rules. There are provisions to facilitate the simplification of contract further, to ensure the comparability of conditions in case of changes in contract course (Amendment of the interest rate guaranteed exercise of the options, processing of the contract), and to reduce the phenomenon of dormant insurance. It was also governed by the preparation and management of contractual documentation when multiple individuals realize the insurance product.[72]

The "Regulation n. 39 on sanctions" innovates the sanctioning procedure, defining the criteria for identifying the "relevance" of the offense, the notion of turnover for the application of financial penalties, and the assessment of multiple crimes. It introduced the principle of "relevance" of the crime, which replaced that of absolute lack of prejudice to the timely exercise of supervisory functions or for the interests of the policyholders and other persons entitled to insurance benefits.

Conclusions

This chapter covers the resources used by insurance in their distribution. It included the strategies, the types of customers, and the relationships, partnerships and collaborations, costs, investments, and revenues. The chapter does not intentionally cover another component of the business model canvas, the one related to the partnership with intermediaries. Another chapter considers the convergence of this with insurance 4.0.

This chapter also analyzes the impact of technology on traditional insurance intermediation processes. It is possible to explain such an

[72] www.assinews.it/08/2018/ivass-line-regolamento-recepimento-dellidd/660054950/. Accessed 2 May 2020.

effect on the light of the framework of Porter's Value Chain.[73] Requirements for new digital solutions are challenging legacy systems. Modern solutions offer options for innovative services distribution. Digitization has a profound impact on all phases of the value network of the processes. It provides benefits by reducing asymmetric information, properly combining the right pricing, responsive risk management, appropriate underwriting, improved claim management, and fast and reliable distribution systems.

[73] Cappiello, A. (2020). The digital (R) evolution of insurance business models. *American Journal of Economics and Business Administration*, *12*(1), 1–13.

CHAPTER 8

Platforms for Insurance 4.0

Introduction

An increasing number of insurance companies now consider investments in digitation as a priority, since the sector has lagged behind its financial services peers in adopting digital technologies owing to regulations, cultural resistances, and investments involved.[1] Many incumbent companies are working to upgrade their digital capabilities, mainly to improve customer engagement and collect data for managing new and old risks. In some cases, companies have increased spending on research and development to foster in-house innovation.

A platform is a group of technologies that are used as a base upon which other applications, processes, or technologies can be developed. In this chapter, the term is used to indicate any information and communication system or automation support. In this sense, the support from the platforms has increased over time (Fig. 8.1).

The integration of traditional computing platforms with advanced automation platforms characterizes insurance 4.0. The Boston Consulting Group (BCG) listed the enabling technologies for industry 4.0[2]:

[1] Watson, W. T. (2017). *New horizon: How diverse growth strategies can advance digitisation in the insurance industry*. www.mergermarket.com/info/new-horizons-how-diverse-growth-strategies-can-advance-digitalisation-insurance-industry. Accessed 30 May 2020.

[2] Lu, Y. (2017). Industry 4.0: A survey on technologies, applications and open research issues. *Journal of Industrial Information Integration, 6*, 1–10.

B. Nicoletti, *Insurance 4.0*, Palgrave Studies in Financial Services Technology, https://doi.org/10.1007/978-3-030-58426-9_8

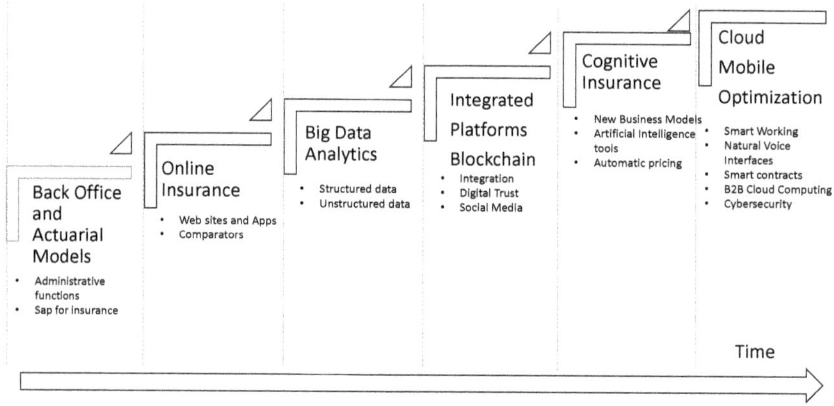

Fig. 8.1 Insurance platforms transformation

- Inputs
  - Internet of things
  - Mobility.
- Process automation
  - Blockchain;
  - Big data analytics and business intelligence (analysis, management, evaluation, and extrapolation of data of interest for the organization);
  - Intelligent automation;
  - Cognitive insurance;
  - Process automation.
- Output
  - Robot(ic) process automation.
- Support
  - Cloud computing;
  - Cybersecurity and Data Privacy.

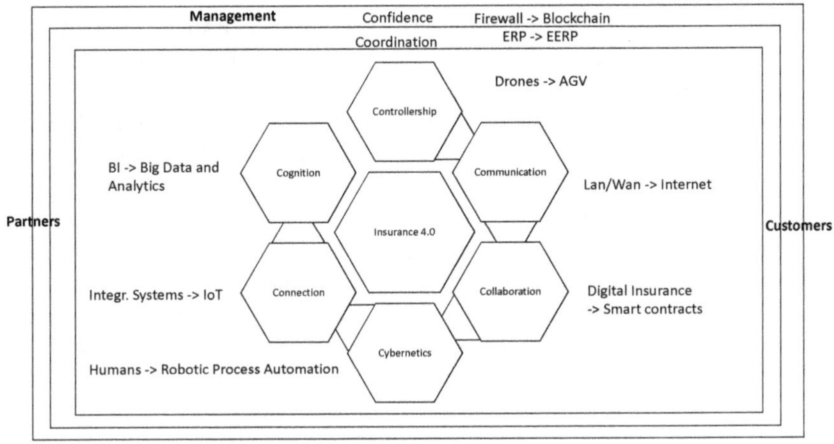

Fig. 8.2 Insurance 4.0

The design of the hardware architecture should have the following significant features: modularity, easy implementation, and the use of broad technologies and devices. In network, it is critical to ensure easy access to the customers, to the intermediaries, and to the employees when working remotely. All these connections should assure the maximum security.

This chapter examines the significant technology platforms and their use in insurance 4.0. The order corresponds substantially to that suggested by BCG.[3] This chapter starts with architectural consideration related to digital insurance, which can be considered the foundation for insurance 4.0. These platforms are classified, taking into account the model of the 8 Cs presented in Chapter 2 (Fig. 8.2).

The opportunity for insurance companies to use better platforms is significant.[4] When used properly, these solutions can provide information and insights to support strategic decision-making but also marketing, selling, and operational processes. They can help with the accurate tracking and reporting of revenues, costs, and risks. Some of the more

[3] Lu, Y. (2017). Industry 4.0: A survey on technologies, applications and open research issues. *Journal of Industrial Information Integration, 6,* 1–10.

[4] assets.kpmg/content/dam/kpmg/pdf/2012/07/the-power-of-insurance-a-global-survey-of-insurance-functions.pdf. Accessed 13 May 2019.

transactional tasks can be automated. Thus, the insurance company can focus on its strategic tasks and deliver a better contribution to the performance of the organization.

The digitization of insurance processes has several benefits.[5] Apart from the overall increase in organization performance, it supports administrative tasks and complex decision-making processes. Digitization improves organizational effectiveness, efficiencies, and economics. It is the basis for establishing new business models, services, and products. Digitizing insurance processes comes with challenges from the current procedures and processes. The company must overcome these difficulties to fully use the improved characteristics of insurance 4.0 as an asset.[6]

Each company must allocate part of its budget into technology investments. An essential question is on the amount that should be invested and in which technology. These two questions help in understanding the peculiarities of the environment in which each business organization operates. No rule-fits-all exists. Specificity is always modifying and changing the outcomes of company actions.

Classification of the Platforms

A classification of the platforms considers three different attributes related to the level of the physical automation, the type of the interfaces, and the decisional processes.[7]

Referring to the first attribute of the level of automation, the platforms can be manual, partially automated, or completely automated.

The second attribute relates to the type of interfaces and capability of an object or an asset to collect and transmit data. According to this attribute, there might be non-connected objects with data collected manually or reading a barcode. The second type of platform includes smart objects which sense and store data through sensors and Real feeding

[5] Härting, R. C., Reichstein, C., & Sochacki, R. (2019). Potential benefits of digital business models and its processes in the financial and insurance industry. In *Intelligent decision technologies 2019* (pp. 205–216). Singapore: Springer.

[6] Bienhaus, F., & Haddud, A. (2018). Procurement 4.0: Factors influencing the digitization of procurement and supply chains. *Business Process Management Journal, 24*(4), 965–984.

[7] Tappia, E., & Moretti, E. (2019). La Ricerca dell'Osservatorio Contract Logisitcs "Gino Marchet." *Euromerci*, 4–5, 34–37.

Identification devices (RFID).[8] The third type of platforms includes the storage and movements systems which may also send and transmit structured information among the resources

The third attribute differentiates the platforms based on the decisional processes. Traditionally, the decisions were taken in a centralized way, sometimes with the support of ICT applications. In insurance 4.0, the decisional operations should be mostly decentralized, with the assets self-configuring, in standard situations, without the intervention of external agents, or completely automated. In the latter case, the platforms have an extensive decisional autonomy. They can evaluate the context and make appropriate decisions, possibly in an automated way.

Architecture for the Platforms

It is interesting to analyze the developments in the platforms relevant to insurance 4.0. This chapter refers to them as the seven "C"s[9]:

- Cloud computing;
- Communication increasingly mobile;
- Cognition, meaning how to improve the knowledge of the organizations through the tools referred to as big data analytics;
- Cybersecurity to assure protection from un-authorized accesses and security of data privacy.

The following chapters analyze the three remaining Cs:

- Collaboration, through the so-called social networks;
- The use of external Contractors;
- Costs to be more and more reduced, despite the challenging economic and competitive situations.

Each of these trends is a robust change agent in the insurance processes:

[8] Ahson, S. A., & Ilyas, M. (2017). *RFID handbook: Applications, technology, security, and privacy*. Boca Raton, FL: CRC Press.

[9] This classification is related but not the same of the model of the 8 Cs presented in Chapter 2.

- Cloud computing is the use of computing resources, accessed through networks and payments for services provided and charged based on use. The impacts on insurance are significant since they open new horizons for marketing and accessing computing resources;
- Communication pushes toward interactions anywhere, anytime, and on any device;
- Cognition technologies are characterized by tools such as big data analytics, which supports the analysis of the insurance processes. This analysis is much easier than in the past, thanks to the increasing availability of a large number of data, information, and documentation;
- New collaboration tools make it possible to develop integration along with the value network;
- Need to be lean pushes the use of external resources, such as partners, for a better ecosystem. In this case, the difficulty is to evaluate the partners.
- Reduction of costs is pressing in these times of deep and prolonged crisis and strong local and global competition. The pressure on the insurance companies becomes very strong to implement competitive pricing and reduce costs.
- Cybersecurity is the practice of defending computers, servers, applications, mobile devices, electronic systems, networks, and data from malicious attacks or un-authorized accesses.[10] It should be a substantial part of the information and communication technology or operational technology implementation.[11]

An interesting concept at the basis of industry 4.0 is the "digital twin."[12] The vision of the digital twin refers to a full physical and functional description of a component, service, or system.[13] A digital twin includes

[10] www.kaspersky.com/resource-center/definitions/what-is-cyber-security. Accessed 31 May 2019.

[11] Windelberg, M. (2016). Objectives for managing cyber supply chain risk. *International Journal of Critical Infrastructure Protection, 12,* 4–11.

[12] Schleich, B., Anwer, N., Mathieu, L., & Wartzack, S. (2017). Shaping the digital twin for design and production engineering. *CIRP Annals, 66*(1), 141–144.

[13] Boschert, S., & Rosen, R. (2016). Digital twin—The simulation aspect. In P. Hehenberger & D. Bradley (Eds.), *Mechatronic futures: Challenges and solutions for mechatronic systems and their designers* (pp. 59–74). New York, NY: Springer International Publishing.

more or less all information that could be useful in the current and subsequent life-cycle phase. From a product life-cycle management point of view, there is a robust need to integrate all life-cycle data artifacts into a comprehensive management system.[14] Various actors can use this system for querying data, such as on an insurance product performance. The digital twin supports also design optimization and operational system improvement.[15]

This chapter examines the most relevant of these platforms, one at a time to analyze which are their possible support of insurance 4.0.

Mattereum[16]

Mattereum represents a real innovative blockchain-based business model. It also highlights how insurance is critical. This venture uses blockchain to describe an immutable, high fidelity record, or digital twin, of real-world entities and concepts.

Mattereum uses digital twins on the blockchain. The twin is an abstract idea connected with the notions of governance, ownership, and legal obligations.[17] An investor can fractionally own a USD 9M Stradivarius violin on Mattereum's platform. The platform autonomously handles voting rights, transfers of ownership, and dispute resolution. Once again, because this model is autonomous and new, there is a heightened customer perception.

General Architecture for Insurance 4.0 Platforms

It is critical to underline the connection of the platforms to the processes and the groundwork for the development of insurance 4.0. The following sections describe these aspects.

[14] Rosen, R., von Wichert, G., Lo, G., & Bettenhausen, K. D. (2015). About the importance of autonomy and digital twins for the future of manufacturing. *IFAC-Papers OnLine, 48*(3), 567–572.

[15] Mobley, R. K. (2002). *An introduction to predictive maintenance.* Amsterdam, Netherlands: Elsevier.

[16] mattereum.com. Accessed 11 January 2020.

[17] Kim, H., & Mehar, M. (2019). Blockchain in commercial insurance: Achieving and learning towards insurance that keeps pace in a digitally transformed business landscape. SSRN 3423382.

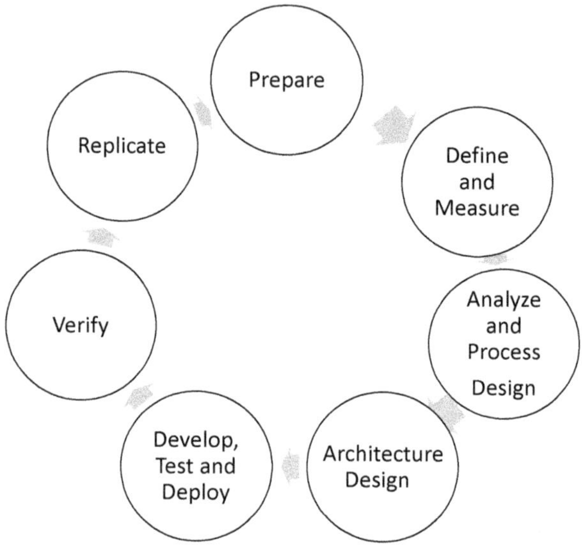

Fig. 8.3 Lean and digitize

Lean and Digitize

The correct implementation of insurance 4.0 combines process optimization and automation by using the method of Lean and Digitize, as shown in Fig. 8.3.[18]

This approach is useful, as demonstrated in many organizations. In some past attempts to introduce insurance 4.0, the organizations have not given proper importance to the improvement of the processes. Equal attention is necessary for the persons affected by the transformation, and the partners that are essential counterparts.

The introduction of insurance 4.0 requires a cultural change. It is necessary to make the insurance processes integrated, simpler, and more immediate to manage. It is critical to transfer the benefits to the staff to guarantee success.

[18] Nicoletti, B. (2012). *Lean and digitize: An integrated approach to process improvement*. Farnham, UK: Gower Publishing. ISBN-10: 1409441946.

The development of digital insurance is expanding.[19] It can be an essential starting point for insurance 4.0. It is also important to have a clear vision of the final target architecture and to implement it through several generations.

The development of innovative platforms changes how organizations work. There are still challenges connected with the reliability of connections, security, and interoperability.

Benefits of Insurance 4.0 Platforms

The use of innovative platforms in insurance 4.0 brings a series of benefits, such as flexibility and cost reduction. The main reason for such use has been economics. Insurance 4.0 is much more than just a new solution or a cost-saving model. It can change the culture of the organization, products, processes, structure, and business models.[20]

Insurance 4.0 platforms are a digital and automatic integrated way to manage insurance. Organizations should implement some form of digital insurance on the cloud. Their benefits are a more extensive choice of customers and partners. Digital insurance leads to lower costs, better quality, improved delivery, shorter cycle times, and reduced total cost of ownership, time- and cost-savings, and convenience. When using insurance 4.0 platforms, the primary sources of increase in the margins came until now from the reduction of costs (automated marketing processing, more cost-effective offers, and similar). In the future, there should be increased attention to improvements in the earnings.[21]

The emergence of internet platforms, such as eBay, Amazon, and Alibaba, has progressively provided data to economists and Information and Telecommunication Technology (ICT) experts. Thus, it is possible to conceptualize and analyze aspects such as the structure of the information needed in the e-marketplace, the nature of forces affecting price formation, the main performance dimensions, the degree of participation from both sides of the market (customers and companies), and the

[19] Nicoletti, B. (2016). *Digital insurance*. London, UK: Palgrave Macmillan (also translated in Chinese). https://doi.org/10.1057/9781137553270_8.

[20] Nicoletti, B. (2012). *Lean and digitize: An integrated approach to process improvement*. Farnham, UK: Gower Publishing. ISBN-10: 1409441946.

[21] Timmers, P. (1998, September 9). Business models for electronic markets. In *CommerceNet Research Report*.

level of competition.[22] This data shows that the benefits connected with insurance 4.0 platforms are substantial. There is still plenty of room for expansion. Companies have not yet made full use of innovative models and tools to streamline their value networks, to increase transparency and speed, and to reduce administrative cost and contract prices. Insurance 4.0 platforms can bring significant savings and additional revenue. Such a change process requires a new management culture and new tools. Several authors have analyzed the critical lines of change to pursue. They have shown that digital insurance and, mainly, e-commerce are the appropriate tools to implement such changes. These solutions, in connection with Business Process Intelligence (BPI), can support significant improvements to cope with the strategic and tactical challenges of insurance.[23]

Challenges of Insurance 4.0

The challenges connected with insurance 4.0 are the needs of:

- Customer-centricity;
- Cultural changes;
- Development and availability of the applications, platforms, network, and infrastructure;
- Security, privacy, and trust issues;
- Reliability;
- Governance of the processes;
- Talents and training.

Connection: IoT and Blockchain

The connection is an essential aspect of insurance 4.0. Several solutions can support it. Two are mainly relevant: internet of things (IoT) and Blockchain.

[22] Oppong, S. A., Yen, D. C., & Merhout, J. W. (2005). A new strategy for harnessing knowledge management in e-commerce. *Technology in Society, 27*(3), 413–435.

[23] Castellanos, M., De Medeiros, A. A., Mendling, J., Weber, B., & Weijters, A. J. M. M. (2009). Business process intelligence. In *Handbook of research on business process modeling* (pp. 456–480). Hershey, PA: IGI Globa.

IoT

Internet of things defines the network of equipment and devices connected to the internet, equipped with software capable of exchanging data with other related objects.[24] The objectives of these devices are the collection of data and information, the issue of commands, and the monitoring of activities.

The two main features of a "connected object" are:

- an internet protocol (IP)[25] address on the network;
- the ability to exchange data over the same network without the need for human interventions.

Gartner estimates that the connected objects are 25 billion in 2020.[26] Other sources estimate that connected devices are between 8 and 10 billion.[27] In 2025, connected objects across the world are expected to be 75.4 billion.[28] The internet of things is increasingly present in the daily lives. In the near future, connected devices, such as computers, smartphones, and tablets, will represent only a third of all objects connected because in addition to the tools mentioned above, there will also be connected cars, wearable devices, smart homes, and so on.[29]

[24] Atzori, L., Iera, A., & Morabito, G. (2017). Understanding the Internet of Things: Definition, potentials, and societal role of a fast evolving paradigm. *Ad Hoc Networks, 56*, 122–140.

[25] Stevens, W. R. (1993). *The protocols* (TCP/IP illustrated, Vol. 1). Boston, MA: Addison-Wesley Professional.

[26] www.gartner.com/en/newsroom/press-releases/2017-02-07-gartner-says-8-billion-connected-things-will-be-in-use-in-2017-up-31-percent-from-2016. Accessed 10 March 2019.

[27] www.forbes.com/sites/forbestechcouncil/2018/03/16/developing-the-connected-world-of-2018-and-beyond/. Accessed 25 April 2019.

[28] Kumaresan, A., Saurav, S., & Raghunanda, K. (2017). *Top 10 trends in property & casualty insurance 2018*. www.capgemini.com/wpcontent/uploads/2017/12/property-and-casualty-insurance-trends_2018.pdf. Accessed 3 May 2020.

[29] Generali. (2018, febbraio 28). *Le assicurazioni "tutto connesso."* www.generali.com/it/info/discoveringgenerali/all/2018/A-fully-connected-insurance. Accessed 20 May 2020.

IoT Architectures
IoT devices, also known as microcontrollers, are more and more connected but with limited resources. They must continually communicate with each other in a synchronized manner according to precise protocols. They collect data using the sensors, store them in data structures, generally in the cloud or on edge computers,[30] where they are analyzed. From them, the organization gets information fed back into the real world to use them for the planned objectives. They become push messages on mobile apps, browser charts, quick response (QR) codes, and so on. The entire ecosystem of hardware/software objects that is part of an IoT project is based on an architecture composed of connected components.

There is not one single architecture in the internet of things. At a high level, it is necessary to take into account:

- Hardware items;
- Communication protocols;
- Cloud computing services;
- Possibly middleware;
- Data storage;
- Software applications.

The communication can be:

- Short-range: they communicate on the network through Bluetooth, cable, or Wi-Fi and require gateways/hubs for the connection into the network (usually the internet);
- Long-range: they communicate on the wide-area network thanks to their Subscriber Identity Modules (SIM).[31]

[30] Salman, O., Elhajj, I., Kayssi, A., & Chehab, A. (2015, December). Edge computing enabling the Internet of Things. In *2015 IEEE 2nd World Forum on Internet of Things (WF-IoT)* (pp. 603–608). IEEE.

[31] The name comes from the acronym Subscriber Identity Module (SIM). It is a smart card inserted into a mobile phone or a tablet and allows the device to securely store the IMSI, a unique number associated with all users of cellular GSM or UMTS networks. It becomes the subscriber's identity.

Elasticity, scalability, power, and reduced costs characterize cloud computing. It can enable IoT. One of the reasons for the close connection between cloud computing and IoT depends on the fact that the technology of intelligent devices is still in the process of expanding and developing by innovative organizations. The central aspect that makes it so interesting is the blend of cloud computing, IoT, and the data that IoT can generate. This data can be analyzed to draw relevant conclusions about customers, market trends, risks, and so on.

Application Areas for Insurance 4.0

IoT applications are classified into three degrees of maturity:

- Consolidated applications;
- Experimental applications;
- Embryonic applications.

The consolidated applications are the simplest. Applications under development are those that are closest to the paradigm of the internet of things. The plans for the future are embryonic applications.[32]

IoT supports "intelligence" in information processing systems. Through the internet of things, objects can be controlled remotely. They are capable of transmitting data from which the organization can extract useful information on the functioning of assets or bodies, and the interactions between these objects and those who use them (e.g., the customer). Hence the criticism regarding security and data privacy for IoT, and the need for transparency in the processing of personal data.

The applications of the internet of things can be:

- Automotive industry for new applications for vehicles. Smart vehicles will diffuse with autonomous or assisted driving. In the meantime, it is possible to monitor connected vehicles. This feature allows insurance by-usage or to provide additional services such as monitoring of the vehicle and alerts for possible incidents.

[32] Ma, T., & Zhang, C. (2011, December). On the disruptive potentials in internet of things. In *2011 IEEE 17th International Conference on Parallel and Distributed Systems* (pp. 857–859).

- Industry biomedical with IoT applied to health management, such as remote management of individual health and patients.
- Facility automation or technology applied to the facilities, to manage for example refrigerators, washing machines, phones, and so on.
- Robotics engineering is a technology that allows for the robots to execute tasks performed normally by humans.

Among the factors that enable innovation at the insurance level, there are platforms to support collaboration between all stakeholders (internal and external). They enable IoT devices or other devices to collect and retrieve data. It is possible to "see" the data, define what they are "doing," and finally "imagine" a vision of the future of insurance.

These platforms are precious insurance collaborators.[33] They allow the organization to synchronize, integrate, and make digitally available real-time information to all concerned. There are success factors and critical aspects of each component of the IoT. IoT can support platforms that allow the organization to incorporate many insured assets, even the smallest, with optimized management and reduction of the associated risks and costs.

The risks that need to be insured are changing significantly for two primary reasons. Tracking and predictive technology improvements reduce uncertainty.[34] For example, connected vehicles have fewer accidents and breakdowns. Predictive maintenance reduces business interruptions. Wearables help ensure a healthier lifestyle. Substantial changes in risk distribution and actuarial models are aggravating more this trend. A resulting demutualization could shift the focus to predicting and managing the risks of individuals rather than market segments. As a consequence, premiums come under pressure, reducing what has traditionally been a rather stable revenue stream. The expansion to new markets could replace lost revenues. Companies must take a more holistic view of the developments and opportunities available.

IoT-based health and home insurances are emerging. They are available just in some markets. There is an excellent potential for disruption.

[33] Yan, M. R., Chien, K. M., & Yang, T. N. (2016). Green component insurance collaboration for improving supply chain management in the high technology industries: A case study from the systems perspective. *Sustainability, 8*(2), 105.

[34] www.reportlinker.com/market-report/Insurance/8495/Insurance?gclid=EAIaIQobChMIsZL4ia-t7AIVlcx3Ch2ogwt4EAMYASAAEgIjzPD_BwE. Accessed 10 January 2020.

New types of services need to be able to provide more than one benefit and not just focus on lowering premiums.[35] The pandemic crisis may have a number of long-term positive effects on the sector. As the pressure on health services rises due to the number of patients during a pandemic, there is likely to be a rise in remote health services. The use of IoT devices will rise together with the possibility of offering consultancy to patients via phone or online video services. This helps health care to reach more remote and less affluent populations including the under- or un-insured. Making health care more available and accessible means that, in some small ways, companies may benefit from learnings and actions taken during the 2020 pandemic.[36]

IoT can help customers to avoid or minimize losses. The potentials are several. In home insurance, thanks to IoT, persons can, for example, close a leaking water pipe just using their smartphone.

Another application of the IoT could be for companies to change their business model: from life benefits to coach health advisors, promoting well-being. Thus, they will be able to gain new and better customer segments. Services that will focus on fitness and quality of life could specifically target millennials, who might be unaware of the need for life insurance yet. According to a Deloitte report, many customers are willing to use these types of services.[37] Many more could do in the future. The disruption may occur with a shift in risk assessment from "what has happened" to "what could happen."[38] This analysis will lead companies to predict why and when things could to happen, using data to improve sales conversion ratio by continually adjusting prices and policies.[39] Companies must move fast in developing and adopting these types of solutions. This

[35] Greco, A. (2018). *Digital transformation and disruption*. Doctoral dissertation. NOVA—School of Business and Economics. Lisbon, Portugal.

[36] home.kpmg/xx/en/home/insights/2020/03/do-insurers-have-covid-19-covered.html. Accessed 30 May 2020.

[37] www2.deloitte.com/tr/en/pages/financial-services/articles/innovation-in-insurance-internet-of-things-iot.html. Accessed 5 May 2020.

[38] Greco, A. (2018). *Digital transformation and disruption*. Doctoral dissertation, NOVA—School of Business and Economics, Lisbon, Portugal.

[39] Price Waterhous Coopers. (2015). *Insurance 2020 & beyond: Necessity is the mother of reinvention*. www.pwc.com/sg/en/insurance/assets/insurance-2020-and-beyond.pdf. Accessed 30 March 2020.

way, first-movers will be able to gain a higher number of data and consequently precious insights and benefiting from network effects. They will be likely to be better positioned on respect to competition.

Individual Offers
Thanks to telematics,[40] customers will have the opportunity to enter into new types of policies, such as usage-based insurance, designed to pay the premium based on mileage or driving behavior.[41] Sensors and other devices will continue to grow in the future

Value-Added Services
Online platforms compare the prices of various insurance, makes it easy for customers to change company if they are not satisfied with the service or simply trying to get a lower price. Companies must put at the center of their strategy the customers and their loyalty.[42] Traditionally, companies were in contact with the customer only at the time of the sale, including renewals, and during the unpleasant compensation claim process. IoT allows companies to use real-time relevant data to design value-added services. There is a better customer engagement thanks to the interaction fast and individual supported by IoT.

[40] The definition of telematics is "the set of technical and methodological solutions adopted to allow the processing to remote data or to communicate with applications residing on remote computing systems and connected".

[41] Generali. (2018, February). *Le assicurazioni "tutto connesso."* www.generali.com/it/info/discoveringgenerali/all/2018/A-fully-connected-insurance. Accessed 40 March 2020.

[42] Friedman, S., & Canaan, M. (2014). *Overcoming speed bumps on the road to telematics: Challenges and opportunities facing auto companies with and without usage-based programs.* www2.deloitte.com/content/dam/insights/us/articles/telematics-in-autoinsurance/DUP-695_Telematics-in-the-procurement-Industry_vFINAL.pdf. Accessed 30 March 2020.

Challenges with the Internet of Things
"By 2025, IoT is expected to be pervasive, with connected "things" driving a data explosion with sensors embedded in vehicles, buildings, and wearable devices so much so that a family of four could have more than 100 connected devices."[43]

The challenges are in these connected areas[44]:

- Value and impact;
- Processes and policies;
- Services;
- Applications;
- Sensors and devices;
- Infrastructure;
- Regulations, privacy, and security.

The suggested approach is either improving or expanding.

Improving requires increasing the quality level of the current business. With connected vehicles, telematics allows UBI (usage-based insurance). These offerings definitively change the customer perception of vehicle insurance. Improving means also adapting to all those technologies and features (such as advanced driver assistance systems (ADAS) to be implemented widely.

Expanding refers to one of the most effective benefits presented in a previous chapter: new value propositions. Companies should be able to identifying new behaviors and requirements of the customers, delivering new tailored products and services.

In this context, it is critical to understand how the internet of things changes the collection, analysis, and distribution of large numbers of data (big data analytics) to make them convertible into information to support activities and business decisions. Everything should comply with the rules established by the law and the regulations by the authorities guaranteeing the protection of personal data.

[43] Kearney, A. T. (2014). *The internet of things: Opportunity for Companies*. www.atkearney.com/documents/10192/5320720/Internet+of+Things+-+Opportunity+for+Companies.pdf/4654e400-958a-40d5-bb65-1cc7ae64bc72. Accessed 30 May 2020.

[44] www.iot-now.com/tag/a-t-kearney/. Accessed 30 May 2020.

Some of the opportunities with IoT for insurance companies are the following ones[45]:

- The pricing model will be increasingly customized and no longer be based only on actuarial evaluations (backward-looking) but on the analysis of behavioral predictions (forward-looking).[46] It is possible to move from static to dynamic pricing updated with increasing frequency. Premiums would change with the evolution of the risk profile of the customers. Thus, it would be possible to move the focus from pricing to the customer service model.
- The distribution model should follow the same approach in the delivery of service customization, prevention, and risk reduction, improvement of claims management with a better reconstruction of the dynamics of claims, and reduction of fraud and litigations. This situation is possible thanks to the connection of objects and their traceability. The study of the collected data provides information at the level of individuals. It will, in short, extend the black box mechanism for vehicles. There would be a reduction in the premium if the customer agrees to install the black box in the vehicle, to other assets and/or the person.

For the application of more customized rates, the consequences are[47]:

- Higher initial costs for the evolution of tariff models;
- Cannibalization of the current portfolio;
- Risk of potential distortion in insurance, due to the absence of the principle of mutuality.

[45] www.agendadigitale.eu/infrastrutture/come-cambieranno-le-assicurazioni-nell-internet-delle-cose_2384.htm. Accessed 30 July 2016.

[46] www.theactuary.com/features/2019/03/seeing-the-bigger-picture/?utm_source=slipcase&utm_medium=affiliate&utm_campaign=slipcase. Accessed 5 May 2020.

[47] ebrary.net/79680/business_finance/internet_things. Accessed 5 May 2020.

Connected Vehicles

AXA Switzerland[48]

AXA Switzerland experimented, in collaboration with the German technology startups ThinxNet, a new advanced offer, called AXARyd. This offer includes an advanced GPS, innovative features, and an informative app. Users of the app receive at any time battery status information, on gasoline, on distance traveled, and their driving style. Customers with a good driving can receive benefits in the form of virtual bonus points usable with various partners such as Salt and Tesla. The project aims to raise awareness among drivers on a prudent driving style. Another innovative feature is the reporting of an incident directly through the app. The user can communicate via the app directly with the Service Center AXA. The benefit is to be able to take necessary actions quickly after an accident. This offer is free for AXA customers.

According to the Allianz Risk Barometer 2018, the increasing interdependence ensures that the autonomous driving vehicles connected are more vulnerable to technical failures or cyber-attacks. For example, if a hacker tampers with the vehicle, the latter becomes a sort of weapon.[49]

The connected vehicle can share access to the internet via the supplied devices, both inside the same vehicle, and externally, between two vehicles. The connected vehicle market is growing. It will grow more in the coming years. According to IHS Markit, in 2030, the number of these vehicles on the road will amount to around 789 million.[50] North America

[48] AXA. (2018, April 26). Un'offerta comune di AXA e ThinxNet nel settore delle connected car. www.axa.ch/content/dam/axa/newsdesk-it/index.html#/news/unofferta comune-di-axa-e-thinxnet-nel-settore-delle-connected-car-303991. Accessed 5 April 2020.

[49] Allianz Global Corporate & Specialty. (2018). *The rise of artificial intelligence: future outlook and emerging risks*. www.agcs.allianz.com/assets/Insights/Artificial%20Intelligence/Artificial_Intelligence_Outlook_and_Risks.pdf. Accessed 5 May 2020.

[50] Elliott, A. (2017, December). *The Internet of Things is changing the way we view the world*. www.zurich.com/en/knowledge/articles/2017/12/the-internet-of-things-isc hanging-the-way-we-view-the-world. Accessed 30 March 2020.

is currently the largest market of connected vehicles.[51] Some experts estimate that by 2020 Europe could occupy the first place in the connected vehicle market. These vehicles make it possible to ensure that the vehicle has a sufficiently safe distance from other vehicles, warn the driver in the event of failure of the vehicle, provide automatic driver assistance, automatically call for help in case of an accident, and so on. They can improve road safety substantially.[52]

The connected vehicle can share information with the outside world. Through these smart devices, companies can understand what and how a person is driving. Some of the online services offered directly by the vehicle manufacturers are real-time navigation, roadside assistance, in case of an incident or a malfunction, and vehicle tracking. Insurance 4.0 includes the black box technology, which collects information on the distance, geographic location using GPS, the speed, type of road, and so on. Some companies offer the possibility for the customers to install in the vehicle black box.[53] To win customers, IoT could provide valuable information to users, targeting new market niches. It could tell environmentally-friendly persons how to reduce their carbon footprints by changing how they usually drive. Such a connected vehicle tells drivers how they can minimize risks both by analyzing how they drive and by advising routes where the environment is safer. In time, they might become compulsory.

Both customized products and the provision of additional services allow to meet customer needs and increase customer engagement. They can also engage customers in accident mitigation proactively. They can prevent or minimize damage and reduce compensation costs.[54] For example, usage-based insurance offers a higher discount to those who

[51] A report published by Digital Journal, North America is the largest market of connected cars.

[52] Allianz Partners. (2017, December). *Market for connected cars set for global expansion by 2020*. allianzpartners-bi.com/news/market-for-connected-cars-set-for-globalexpansion-by-2020-9dc9-333d4.html. Accessed 3 May 2020.

[53] Allianz Insurance plc. (2015). *The future of mobility: Changes in vehicle technology*. www.allianzebroker.co.uk/content/allianzebroker/en_gb/application/content/documents/news-and-insight/commercial/future-ofmobility/_jcr_content/documentProperties/currentDocument.res/acom6027.pdf. Accessed 30 March 2020.

[54] Generali. (2018, February). *Le assicurazioni "tutto connesso."* www.generali.com/it/info/discoveringgenerali/all/2018/A-fully-connected-insurance. Accessed 30 March 2020.

drive responsibly. This way, it is possible to encourage persons to drive better. Another example of proactive risk mitigation is the additional services which are possible thanks to the connection. This application can send mobile messages to an app for providing feedbacks on how to improve their driving style or receive alerts in case of traffic or risky road conditions.

According to research by Amodo, customer engagement could change the behavior of drivers driving. The participants in this research have used the Amodo's Mobility Platform and the app on the customers' smartphones. The platform can collect data through sensors and then compute the security rating of the driver based on factors such as speed, acceleration, and braking. Some insurances have used gamification (game experience) to encourage persons to use the app. This research has shown that telematics technology can prevent risks, encouraging safer driving.[55]

In this area of operations, it will be likely for companies to partner with sensors manufacturers and companies that own the data (like auto manufacturers or health equipment producers). To find the right partners, companies have to strategically think on the best way to position themselves in the IoT ecosystem. For example, they could leverage trustability and reliability qualities, taking into consideration the increasing concern of customers on data collection and analysis by other companies. The most attractive companies will be the ones that will provide risk assessment services, and roadside and medical assistance.

Autonomous Driving Vehicles

The evolution of autonomous driving is of high importance for traffic safety and also to insurance companies. With autonomous driving vehicles, there will be increased safety in the roads since human errors are eliminated: Although the potential is excellent, there is no certainty of being able to prevent all accidents, because the vehicle could be the cause.

[55] Amodo. (no date). *Customer communication & engagement with purpose*. www.amodo.eu/custengagment/. Accessed 31 March 2020. Novic, M. (2018, August). *Maritime Financial Group licensed Amodo's connected mobility platform for a pioneering UBI initiative in the region*. www.amodo.eu/maritime-launched-their-copilott-app/. Accessed 31 March 2020.

Apple, Google's Waymo, and Tesla are competing to automate cars one function at a time.[56] Most of the traditional automotive players seem to be at a disadvantage in the mobility industry. They face a pressing need to reimagine their roles.[57] Some are starting to see opportunities to move toward an ecosystem mindset. Tesla has launched its insurance program. Toyota has invested USD 1 billion in the Toyota Research Institute, which aims to use artificial intelligence to address the problems across the mobility ecosystem.[58] The institute defines its mission as making automobiles safer, more affordable, and more accessible to everyone, regardless of age or ability, and expanding the benefit of mobility technology beyond automobiles, for example, to in-home support of older persons and those with special needs.

Tesla Motors[59]

California based Tesla Motors launched an insurance offering in August 2019, available initially only for Tesla vehicle owners in some USA states. The company leverages the advanced technology, safety, and serviceability of its electric cars to provide personalized pricing that traditional insurers cannot offer.

Testa accesses its extensive real-time vehicle data as well as information about driver behavior (including camera recordings and sensor readings) to develop highly personalized, value-added services for the future. It can estimate the risks of accidents and repair costs accurately. Testa's strategy to insure its own vehicles is a strong differentiator to its customers. It reinforces the feeling of belonging to a unique community and, thus, exponentially increases customer retention.

While traditional insurers would charge a relatively high premium for Testa cars because they do not have much historical information about electric vehicle repair costs, Tesla knows them. By vertically integrating insurance into its offering, Testa brings down its products' total cost of ownerships.

[56] www.vox.com/future-perfect/2020/2/14/21063487/self-driving-cars-autonomous-vehicles-waymo-cruise-uber. Accessed 30 March 2020.

[57] www.reportlinker.com/market-report/Insurance/8495/Insurance?gclid=EAIaIQobChMIsZL4ia-t7AIVlcx3Ch2ogwt4EAMYASAAEgIjzPD_BwE. Accessed 10 January 2020.

[58] global.toyota/en/detail/10171645. Accessed 30 May 2020.

[59] Testa. (2019, August). *Introducing testa insurance*. www.testa.conn/bLoci/introducing-testa-insurance. Accessed 30 May 2020. Zarifis, A. (2020). Why is Testa selling Insurance and what does it mean For drivers? *The Conversation*. theconversation.com/profiles/alex-zarifis-777544. Accessed 30 May 2020.

There are several potential new and current risks with autonomous driving cars[60]:

- Malfunctions or not planned occurrences;
- A hacker manipulates the brakes of a vehicle and causes the vehicle to accelerate and causes a collision;
- Autonomous driving does not reduce all risks. A rock can affect the car's windshield. Even with the most advanced technology, it will be impossible to avoid current threats such as damage by hail, floods, accidents with animals, and so on. Insurance companies will continue to have to deal with this type of claims;
- Self-driving cars will have to operate on existing highways, roadways and city streets, which were not built for such vehicles;
- If the vehicle in autonomous driving is in a dangerous situation, where an accident is inevitable, and the only two alternatives available would have in both cases a negative aspect, what would be the maneuver "right" to choose?
- Self-driving cars can increase drivers' exposure to electromagnetic field radiation.

Also with all these risks, vehicles in autonomous driving will increase road safety, but accidents will not disappear. Mixed traffic will initially be present (contemporary movement of vehicles automated, partially automated, and traditional). This situation brings new challenges. There may be more accidents. Companies have not yet collected experiences regarding the likelihood of accidents and their causes, as to date, due to fully automated vehicle.[61] The timing for their widespread adoption and their significant impact on the insurance companies will take time, on the

[60] www.axa.ch/content/dam/axa/newsdesk-it/index.html#/pressreleases/axa-crashtests-la-guida-autonoma-divide-i-pareri-2119011. Accessed 5 May 2020. irgc.org/wp-content/uploads/2018/09/IRGC-workshop-Autonomous-Cars_15-16June-Background-Paper-13June.pdf. Accessed 5 May 2020. www.vesttech.com/top-3-possible-dangers-of-self-driving-cars/. Accessed 5 May 2020.

[61] AXA. (2017, August). *AXA Crashtests: La guida autonoma divide i pareri*. www.axa.ch/content/dam/axa/newsdesk-it/index.html#/pressreleases/axacrashtests-la-guida-autonoma-divide-i-pareri-2119011. Accessed 30 March 2020.

one hand for a purely technological issue and on the other for the need for a change of the complex regulatory system tied to this market.[62]

AXA XL[63]
AXA XL launches an insurance solution for self-driving cars. It is a solution which allow companies working on this technology to manage and transfer specific risks.

The policy is available in various countries and offers essential coverage for third party liability, damage to insured property, and theft of the vehicle: There are modular coverage options: Liability for damages during the contractor's custody or control. liability for damages; cyber-attack; liability for damage/personal injury, expenses for data recovery. Available extensions include: liability coverage provided by law; extension for Cyber risk; Crisis Management service and response to them; extension for loss of turnover.

Since 2016 AXA XL has collaborated with Oxbotica, an ICT company that deals with independent robotics and autonomous systems. In 2017, AXA XL joined the consortium Driven to help implement a fleet of "driverless cars" between Oxford and London. In 2018, AXA XL established the Global Autonomy Center of Excellence, a multidisciplinary center. It announced the creation of an insurance solution to support the adoption of autonomous vehicles technologies.

Blockchain

The critical success factors of insurance 4.0 are six words that begin with "C": Cybernetics, Communication, Control, Partnership, Connection, and Cognition. Two other factors are relevant for insurance processes. They are two additional Cs: Condivision, or sharing, and getting Confidence or trust. Deriving from the new interconnected and automated insurance 4.0 ecosystems, trust plays a vital and essential role in the entire

[62] Cambosu, D. (2017, July). *Tecnologie digitali, ecco quelle che hanno davvero impatto sulle assicurazioni (infografica)*. www.insuranceup.it/it/business/tecnologie-digitali-ecco-quelle-che-hannodavvero-impatto-sulle-assicurazioni-infografica_1603.htm. Accessed 30 March 2020.

[63] www.aziendabanca.it/notizie/polizza-auto-guida-autonoma. Accessed 26 March 2020.

ecosystem. Within traditional insurer-policyholder relationships, trust is a dominant factor based on the interactions between both parties and external factors.[64] Considering value network ecosystems, the factor of trust must be maintained mutually between more than two parties, since other stakeholders appear, such as the vehicle manufacturers. This situation challenges organizations in their traditional behavior. It requires a change in organizational culture[65] and solutions used,

An emerging solution can provide support to both Condivision and Confidence. It is called the blockchain. Blockchain solution can enhance customer trust by providing a more prominent level of honesty and integrity of prices and claims. In a survey, 86 percent of respondents affirmed the significant impact of blockchain solutions on the insurance industry. 54 percent of them even predicted the transformation of the industry, citing potential benefits that can be obtained in speeding claim processes, simplifying and upgrading administrative procedures, and record-keeping, offering more transparency in addition to fraud reduction.[66]

Blockchain Architecture

Blockchain is a computerized open ledger in which it is possible to record every transaction in the network for a specific application.[67] Blockchain is available for all participants. They can see and check the transactions in the ledger. If registered, a participant may also enter new data. There is a log that allows standard visibility of operations and services. The shared vision and access eliminate the need for data transfer between organizations. One can also imagine blockchain as a "digital trust."[68] This synthetic expression indicates that the blockchain is a set of reliable data, because

[64] Lesch, W. C., & Brinkmann, J. (2011). Consumer insurance fraud/abuse as co-creation and co-responsibility: A new paradigm. *Journal of business ethics*, *103*(1), 17–32.

[65] Harshak, A., Schmaus, B., & Dimitrova, D. (2013). *Building a digital culture: How to meet the challenge of multichannel digitization*. www.strategyand.pwc.com/media/file/Strategyand_Building-a-Digital-Culture.pdf. Accessed 27 January 2019.

[66] cognizantsnapshot.com.au/blockchain-insurance-risk-not-reap-not/.

[67] Zheng, Z., Xie, S., Dai, H. N., Chen, X., & Wang, H. (2018). Blockchain challenges and opportunities: a survey. *International Journal of Web and Grid Services, 14*(4), 352–375.

[68] Nofer, M., Gomber, P., Hinz, O., & Schiereck, D. (2017). Blockchain. *Business & Information Systems Engineering*, *59*(3), 183–187.

its authenticity is based on the consensus of a large number of actors. Not coincidentally, the birth of the blockchain was in support of the Bitcoin, a virtual currency. A currency requires Condivision and Confidence in the possibility of using it.[69]

From a technical point of view, a blockchain is a secure database among many users. It is managed through a global network of independent servers. They provide a shared vision. The blockchain solutions are in the cloud. It is easy to access from any location. Blockchain solutions can manage products and partner quality certificates, proof of ownership, references of a specific company, contracts, purchases, and so on.

Blockchain solutions can be classified as a development over time of the Data Management (DM 4.0), in the sequence:

- DM 1.0 Dataset in an application;
- DM 2.0 Database/Data Communication architecture (DB/DC)
- DM 3.0 Relational Database
- DM 4.0 Blockchain in the cloud.

Blockchain solutions have also developed over time. It is possible to distinguish four stages[70]:

- The deployment of cryptography and distributed architectures in liquidity-related applications, such as currency transfer and digital payment systems, has formed the technology layer supporting the creation of blockchain 1.0. The first application was a virtual currency Bitcoins;
- Blockchain 2.0 allowed the use of blockchain in other fields on respect to crypto currency only,
- Blockchain 3.0 relies on smart contracts to develop autonomous decentralized organizations that have their legal procedures defined upstream by network members;

[69] Wolf, R. A. (2016). Virtual currencies, M-payments and VAT: Ready for the future? In *Bitcoin and Mobile Payments* (pp. 231–249). London, UK: Palgrave Macmillan.

[70] Swan, M. (2015). *Blockchain: Blueprint for a new economy*. Newton, MA: O'Reilly Media.

- Blockchain 4.0 makes the technology useful in a real-life business context (industry 4.0) with the characteristics of traceability, transparency, and security.

The multiplication of tenures in blockchain solutions guarantees the accuracy of the registration. Each participant controls a complete copy of the ledger. The discrepancies resolution mechanisms ensure that all copies reflect an identical story. Although permits can be managed with a reasonable degree of control, by default, each authorized participant can view all transactions. Transparency is an essential feature of blockchain solutions.

The characteristics of a blockchain solution are essentially[71]:

- Distributed database. Each party on a blockchain has access to the entire database and its complete history. No single party controls the data or information. Every party can verify the records of its transaction partners directly, without an intermediary.
- Peer-to-peer transmission. Communication occurs directly between peers, not through a central node. Each node stores and forwards information to all other nodes.
- Transparency with pseudonymity. Every transaction and its associated value are visible to anyone with access to the system. Each node, or user, on a blockchain, has a unique 30-plus-character alphanumeric address that identifies it. Users can choose to remain anonymous or provide proof of their identity to others. Transactions take place between blockchain addresses.
- Irreversibility of records. Once a transaction is entered in the database, the accounts are updated. The records cannot be modified since they are linked to every transaction record that came before them. Blockchain includes several computational algorithms and solutions to assure that the recording on the database is permanent, chronologically ordered, and available to all other participants on the network.

[71] Iansiti, M., & Lakhani, K. R. (2017). The truth about blockchain. *Harvard Business Review, 95*(1), 118–127.

- Computational logic. The digital nature of the ledger implies that the blockchain transactions can be tied to computational logic and, in essence, programmed. Users can set up algorithms and rules that automatically trigger transactions between nodes.

Application Areas of Blockchain Solutions in Insurance 4.0

Blockchain solutions are of great interest to the insurance industry.[72] Several thousand solutions based on blockchain have been developed around the world, roughly 10 percent of which are estimated to be applicable to the insurance industry.[73] Price Waterhouse Coopers shows that blockchain solution can transform the insurance value network by helping to cut acquisition, management, documentation, and compliance costs.[74]

Companies have recognized the potential of the blockchain solutions. The interest in Insurtech has risen rapidly in recent years. There is a significant increase in investment in startups that work on research for insurance companies or in partnerships with other companies.

The idea of a decentralized, secure, and transparent ledger distributed among users can be relevant to many different fields. The insurance industry, with its highly complex processes, could be a significant beneficiary of the technology. Blockchain solutions could completely change the insurance value network[75]:

- Development/acceleration of new products/markets for which business models are difficult to define beforehand;
- New approaches to underwriting, contracts, and claims management, mainly through a combination of smart contracts and the internet of things (IoT);

[72] Yıldırım, İ. (2020). Blockchain in the insurance industry: Use cases and applications. In I. Williams (Ed.), *Cross-industry use of blockchain technology and opportunities for the future* (pp. 117–130). Hershey, PA: IGI Global.

[73] McKinsey & Company. (2017). Blockchain solution in the insurance sector. In *Proceedings of the quarterly meeting of the Federal Advisory Committee on Insurance (FACI)*. New York, NY.

[74] Lorenz, J. T., Münstermann, B., Higginson, M., Olesen, P. B., Bohlken, N., & Ricciard, V. (2016, July). Blockchain in insurance—Opportunity or threat? *McKinsey Co.* 1–9.

[75] Price Waterhouse Coopers. (2017). *Blockchain, a catalyst for new approaches in insurance, Part 1 and 2.* www.pwc.com/gx/en/industries/financial-services/publications/blockchain-a-catalyst.html. Accessed 30 May 2020.

- Overhaul of how to work on insurance agreements;
- New reinsurance approaches, possibly internal reinsurance, via smart contracts;
- Transformation of asset management with automated settlement and delivery of intangibles.

E-aggregators are an emerging business model that companies should consider. Thanks to them, they offer better prices due to reduced commissions when compared to the traditional agent-based model. They could also provide better information to customers. By using blockchain solutions, customers will be able to smooth and speed up data verification processes and reduce privacy concerns considering that it will not be possible to give data to a third party without the customer's permission.

Blockchain solutions can identify frauds since they help in detecting falsified damage reports, theft, and medical reports, by authenticating the validity of the documents, controlling police reports and claim histories, and verifying identities. Some of the European insurance incumbents' giants (Aegon, Allianz, Munich Re, and Swiss Re) collaborated in a pilot project named Blockchain Insurance Industry Initiative (B3i) to improve the knowledge of this disruptive technology.[76] A startup from the UK is working on a blockchain solution in support of Know-your-customer (KYC).[77] This solution will help financial institutions to prevent money laundering by driving down the costs and the time requested by this process. The objective is to avoid customers to provide the same information on their identity and source of wealth to different institutions. When KYC is in place and the data is verified, individuals will be able to provide a private key to the companies to get them access to the encrypted information when necessary.

While blockchain offers many promises for traditional insurance providers, several challenges remain and deserve to be mitigated. First, new players enter the market and compete with established players.

[76] www.mckinsey.com/~/media/McKinsey/Industries/Financialpercent20Services/Ourpercent20Insights/Timepercent20forpercent20insurancepercent20companiespercent20topercent20facepercent20digitalpercent20reality/Digital-disruption-in-Insurance.ashx. Accessed 30 March 2020.

[77] www.mckinsey.com/industries/financial-services/our-insights/the-promise-of-blockchain. Accessed 30 March 2020.

According to the Price Waterhouse Coopers report, 90 percent of companies fear competition from insurtech organizations.[78]

The adoption of blockchain solutions also raises issues of governance and regulation. The establishment of a specific form of "decentralization"[79] requires defining, implementing, and maintaining, over time, a specific system of governance and management.[80] It is necessary to define a new decision-making mode, a new way of thinking about the strategy.

A Price Waterhouse Coopers study on the topic shows that while 56 percent of insurance companies recognize the importance of blockchains, 57 percent still do not know how to respond and capitalize on this opportunity.[81]

One area in which blockchain solutions are available is insurance-linked securities (ILS). They are investment instruments that enable the transfer of insurance risk to financial markets.[82] For example, Solidum Partners, a Zurich based investment management firm, who specializes in ILS, was the first to issue an ILS securitization on a private blockchain in 2017.[83] Blockchain solutions have proved to be a cost-effective platform for settlement in the ILS space. Less clear is whether smart contracts are viable for the more significant part of reinsurance type risk transfers. The reason is

[78] Price Waterhous Coopers. (2017). Opportunities await: How InsurTech is reshaping insurance, Global FinTech Survey, PricewaterhouseCoopers, London. www.pwc.com/gx/en/industries/financial-services/fintech-survey/insurtech.html. Accessed 30 May 2020.

www.pwc.fr/fr/assets/files/pdf/2016/06/pwc_assur_tech.pdf, 2016. Accessed 17 June 2019.

[79] M. Atzori. (2015, December). Blockchain solution and decentralized governance: *Is the State Still Necessary?* https://doi.org/10.2139/ssrn.2709713. Accessed 2 May 2020.

[80] Swan, M. (2015). *Blockchain: Blueprint for a new economy.* Newton, MA, USA: O'Reilly Media.

Porru, S., Pinna, A., Marchesi, M., & Tonelli, R. (2017). Blockchain-oriented software engineering: Challenges and new directions. In *Proceedings of the 39th International Conference on Software Engineering Companion* (pp. 169–171). EEE Press.

[81] Price Waterhous Coopers. (2017). *Chain reaction: How blockchain solution might transform wholesale insurance.* https://www.pwc.com/gx/en/industries/financial-services/publications/blockchain-technology-might-transform-wholesale-insurance.html. Accessed 30 May 2020.

[82] Albrecher, H., Bommier, A., Filipović, D., Koch-Medina, P., Loisel, S., & Schmeiser, H. (2019). Insurance: Models, digitization, and data science. *European Actuarial Journal, 9*(2), 349–360.

[83] Sandor, R. L. (2018). *Electronic trading and blockchain: Yesterday, today and tomorrow.* Singapore: World Scientific Publishing.

because, for example, reinsurance is still mostly indemnity based. It relies on complex contracts that require loss adjustment to take place before settlement. As a result, at least for the moment, large-scale automatic settlement does not seem to be within reach. Some signs of progress have been made, for example, by the Blockchain Insurance Industry Initiative (B3i) already mentioned.[84]

SafeShare Insurance[85]

Insurance for the sharing economy needs to be flexible and responsive to customer needs. The distributed ledger approach, developed by Z/Yen Group, offers the opportunity to coordinate the provision of products between counter-parties in near real-time and to cut the cost of this coordination substantially.[86]

SafeShare Insurance, a British company, provides another example of advanced underwriting. It uses Bitcoin's underlying blockchain solution to confirm counterparty obligations. Blockchain solution facilitates the delivery of a flexible and responsive product to customers at a reasonable price.

Blockchain solutions can help in the automatic discover of claims. The startup Everledger uses the blockchain to create a distributed ledger that records the detail of precious stones like diamonds.[87] This ledger allows insurance companies (and potential purchasers) to check the history of any individual stone, including previous claims. Thus, it helps insurance companies to prevent, detect, and counter fraud.

It is possible to use blockchain together with connected devices: the vehicle's black box, a wearable, or an installed equipment in the house sensor, to detect an anomaly and sends an alarm. A blockchain would end up in the workflow associated with the complaint, or pre-complaint, on automatic problem identified by the connected device.

[84] b3i.tech/home.html. Accessed 30 March 2020.

[85] www.safeshareinsurance.com/. Accessed 30 March 2020.

[86] www.metrognomo.com/pressrelease_mar2016/. Accessed 30 March 2020.

[87] www2.deloitte.com/content/dam/Deloitte/ch/Documents/innovation/ch-en-innovation-deloitte-blockchain-app-in-insurance.pdf. Accessed 30 March 2020.

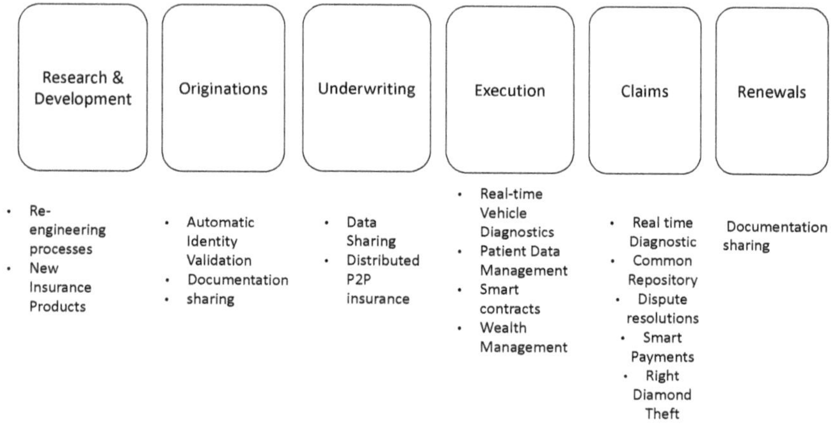

Fig. 8.4 Blockchain and insurance processes

Another example of a possible application of blockchain solutions is the "peer to peer" insurance. In this business model, a group of individuals ensure each other by sharing the premium, similar to what Friendsurance does.[88] A portion of the premiums paid goes to the company for the coverage of higher gravity claims. The remaining part is kept in a fund of mutuality to take care of lower claims. Each participant signs a commitment to contribute to the mutuality fund. The blockchain will store securely all the data. The award is not paid immediately but saved in the blockchain. The contribution from each individual is transferred at the bottom of the mutuality only in the event of a claim.

There are several other possible applications of blockchain, in all sectors of insurance. Figure 8.4 shows the typical high-level process of insurance. Blockchain could be useful throughout the entire cycle. It is possible to use Blockchain at the time of the origination, to verify the identity of the customers or to limit the risks of fraud.

88 www.friendsurance.com/. Accessed 30 March 2020.

It is interesting also to consider the combination of blockchain and IoT in supporting use cases in claims management and in smart contract.[89] IDC forecasts that 20 percent of all IoT deployments will have basic levels of blockchain services enabled.[90]

Benefits and Challenges of Blockchain Solutions

Blockchain solutions need a change in the applicable legal framework.[91] Consensus protocols, which specify the rules governing the proper use and management of blockchain solutions, are already in themselves an agreement between the parties. They remain in the hands of the coders and left to the adherence of the participants. There is no supervision by a legal regime appropriate and adapted, for example, to an international context.

Blockchain solutions also need to overcome several technical limits before being able to be transposed on a large scale. The technology comes with barriers to large-scale implementation, such as platform development, scalability.[92] It is difficult to assess its impact on insurance companies due to the complexity, ambiguity, inevitable transition, and implementation challenges associated with blockchain solutions.

The use of blockchain solutions should help new players enter the market and new markets to appear, mainly in emergent countries. By simplifying use and increasing transparency, it will also help to improve customer satisfaction. Although the upside is significant, it is necessary to take into account of several risks. These include competition with insurtech organizations and a legal framework that will need to evolve.

[89] Rabah, K. (2018). Convergence of AI, IoT, big data and blockchain: A review. *The Lake Institute Journal, 1*(1), 1–18.

[90] Mishra, D. K., Dey, N., Deora, B. S., & Joshi, A. (Eds.). (2020). *ICT for competitive strategies: Proceedings of 4th international conference on information and communication technology for competitive strategies (ICTCS 2019), December 13th–14th, 2019*. Udaipur, India: CRC Press.

[91] Lorenz, J. T., Münstermann, B., Higginson, M., Olesen, P. B., Bohlken, N., & Ricciardi, V. (2016, July). Blockchain in insurance—Opportunity or threat? *McKinsey & Co*, 1–9.

[92] Beck, R., Czepluch, J. S., Lollike, N., & Malone, S. (2016). Blockchain-the gateway to trust-free cryptographic transactions. In *ECIS* (p. 153). World Economic Forum. (2016). Top 10 emerging technologies of 2016. www3.weforum.org/docs/GAC16_Top10_Emergng_Technologies_2016_report.pdf. Accessed 30 March 2020.

Insurance companies are laggards to the financial world in the examination of the potential use of blockchains. There are exceptions. Lloyds is considering the redesign of its operating model with blockchain.[93] The real impact of this technology on insurance will take several years, even if the life cycles of new technologies are becoming shorter.[94] Another trend noted in the report is that some companies, such as Aviva, Allianz, and MetLife, are bringing FinTech and other technology organizations together in innovation labs.[95] Their effort is to engage customers in ways that are more meaningful across online and mobile platforms and improve policy handling and claims-payment processes.[96]

Blockchain Insurance Industry Initiative (B3i)[97]
The Blockchain Insurance Industry Initiative (B3i) was established in October 2016. The five founding members Aegon, Allianz, Munich Re, Swiss Re, and Zurich joined forces to explore the possible applications of blockchain solutions in insurance.[98] In June 2017, the partners welcomed ten more primary insurers and reinsurers[99] as new members.[100] B3i members are from Asia, Europe, and the Americas. The original Central European venture has become a worldwide initiative.

[93] Nicoletti, B. (2019). Digital transformation via open data in insurance. *Digital Innovation: Harnessing the Value of Open Data, 4,* 113.

[94] Kumar, S., & Phrommathed, P. (2005). *Research method* (pp. 43–50). New York, NY: Springer US, and www2.deloitte.com/content/dam/Deloitte/dk/Documents/finance/CIOs-struggle-to-stay-ahead-POV.pdf. Accessed 5 August 2016.

[95] Nicoletti, B. (2017). A business model for insurtech initiatives. In *The Future of FinTech* (pp. 211–249). Cham, Switzerland: Palgrave Macmillan.

[96] www.insurancenetworking.com/news/innovation/insurtech-companies-are-the-new-fintech-leaders-37470-1.html. Accessed 30 May 2020.

[97] b3i.tech/home.html. Accessed 30 May 2020.

[98] www.munichre.com/de/media-relations/publications/company-news/2016/2016-10-19-company-news/index.html. Accessed 30 May 2020.

[99] XL Catlin, Hannover Re, Achmea, Generali, SCOR, Ageas, Sompo Japan, RGAs, Tokio Marine, Liberty Mutual.

[100] www.munichre.com/de/media-relations/publications/company-news/2017/2017-02-06-company-news/index.html. Accessed 30 May 2020.

One focus of the initiative is in exploring whether the blockchain solutions can be used to support the exchange of data between companies and reinsurers efficient and to simplify the retrocession within the group of members.[101] B3i develops standards and procedures for an industry-wide use. The results should get efficiency gains for the economy of insurance.[102] In addition to the joint research, the initiative acts as a platform for exchanging experience with blockchain and other technologies, and other pilot schemes or research results.[103]

Tradle[104]

Every financial institution can access the Tradle network and eliminate the Know your customer (KYC) checks that they are forced to do today. Thanks to Tradle, KYC checks can be shared among financial institutions reducing the costs of KYC, which normally are very high.[105]

Tradle uses a blockchain solution. This American startup has provided an answer to the question on where it is better to store the personal information with its high resilience to potential hackers and cyber-attacks.[106] Allowing the partner financial institutions to share data about their customers, such as the document's identity, the partner company of the financial institutions can offer a rapid and streamlined process for subscribing a product without asking data already available. Blockchain could save and guarantee document exchange and communications. This data certification would be in full compliance also with European private data laws.

[101] www.munichre.com/de/media-relations/publications/company-news/2017/2017-02-06-company-news/index.html. Accessed 30 May 2020.

[102] www.munichre.com/de/media-relations/publications/company-news/2016/2016-10-19-company-news/index.html. Accessed 28 March 2019.

[103] www.munichre.com/de/media-relations/publications/company-news/2016/2016-10-19-company-news/index.html. Accessed 28 March 2019.

[104] tradle.io/. Accessed 28 March 2019.

[105] www.newsbtc.com/2015/08/24/tradle-integrating-blockchain-technology-with-kyc-requirements/. Accessed 26 August 2016.

[106] www.munichre.com/en/reinsurance/magazine/topics-online/2016/04/automated-life-procurement/index.html. Accessed 30 July 2016.

Tradle can store information with high resilience to potential hackers and cyber-attacks.[107] It has created a platform to compensate for the limitations of normal blockchain solutions, such as low throughput of the transactions, data storage limits, absence of transactional semantics, and high costs for processing.

Trust in Motion (TIM) is an application of Tradle.[108] It allows users to initiate a secure line of communication and go on-the-record for the exchange of confidential documents, checks, assignments, and agreements. The resulting recordings are stored securely and irrevocably with high resilience to hackers, unauthorized accesses, and a remarkable ability to respond to many requirements.

SCOR[109]

SCOR initiated in June 2016 a Proof of concept (PoC) for the exchange of reinsurance accounts using a blockchain solution. The PoC started under the Ruschlikon Initiative, a worldwide network of around 50 companies, reinsurers, and brokers focused on executing e-administration to optimize the market productivity. Helped by the startup ChainThat, in two months, SCOR implemented exchanges of technical reinsurance accounts between two brokers and SCOR via a private blockchain.

BudgetChain—Allianz[110]

At Allianz, accounting relies on paid invoices for all the departments, except the ICT department. Hence, there is no global vision of the paid invoices. There is no vision over the details and advancement on the use of a project budget on a daily or even monthly basis.

[107] Grisoni, A. (2016). If companies look to blockchain, Bank Organization Also, Mar: 66:67.

[108] www.trust-in-motion.com/. Accessed 11 September 2018.

[109] www.scor.com/en/our-solutions-0. Accessed 8 March 2020.

[110] Sayegh, K., & Desoky, M. (2019). *Blockchain application in insurance and reinsurance*. France: Skema Business School.

As it is critical to monitor the internal use of the allocated budget for different projects, Allianz used an MS Excel worksheet, Allianz had 30 different Excel files used by a steering committee. It was a complicated process.

Some departments have up to 10,000 invoices. There were possible errors in the MS Excel files, since the tool is not very reliable and painful to keep up to date. However, there is a real need to monitor the use of the internal budget for each department of the company level.

BudgetChain is a tool that enables cost tracking relative to the budget. It is based on blockchain. The tool enables users to enter the invoices from the first interaction with the vendor till the end. The state of the invoice follows the advancement of each operation.

The pilot project involved 15 users. At steady state, it engaged 50 users at the end of 2018. The benefit of such a tool is its ability to share the information between the budget managers and the budgetary management. Thus, it is possible to have a global vision of all the departments.

It is a cheap, user-friendly tool. A private blockchain hosts the tool with a protocol of validation. Currently, Allianz has four nodes that are hosted by OVH but accessed only by Allianz. Two-thirds of the nodes must validate the transactions to approve them. The solution can be replicated for all the departments.

Cognition: Cognitive Insurance

The lean approach originated in Japan around 1946. At that time, the use of computers was nil or very limited. The expression lean was introduced in the USA by groups associated with the organization and management of human resources.[111]

At the same time, the computer was born and developed independently. Only in the nineties, the two solutions started to be analyzed together.[112] The computer applications at the time were rather rigid and not suited to supporting the idea of slenderness and agility associated with

[111] Nicoletti, B. (2013). *Lean insurance*. Milano, Italy: FrancoAngeli.

[112] Nicoletti, B. (2012). *Lean and digitize: An integrated approach to process improvement*. London, UK: Gower Publishing.

lean principles. Over time, computer applications have become more flexible. In recent decades, the concept of computer applications, open and integrated with other solutions, have become popular. Solutions based on blockchain are an example of how information technology has become a powerful tool of integration also inter-organization. The agility of the organization became much more valuable,

The real development of agility can benefit significantly from the so-called artificial intelligence or augmented intelligence[113] (AI), and, in particular, from cognitive solutions. The set of cognitive technologies are products that can capture data and continually learn how humans would do, but using data at a vast scale.[114] These technologies with the acquired data (including unstructured data) start understand meanings, reasons, context, and possible impacts. Cognitive technologies can generate hypotheses, arguments, and recommendations. These technologies can perform tasks that now only humans could do. They allow persons to focus on the most innovative and critical activities.

Mainly attractive are these solutions in insurance 4.0: the so-called cognitive insurance.[115] It is another step in the insurance 4.0 transformation (Fig. 8.5).

The platforms presented in this section represent the next generation of insurance applications. They provide intelligent automation, predictive analytics, and proactive interventions. Artificial intelligence and machine learning work with the different components of IoT architecture layers as components of sophisticated cognitive insurance platforms.[116] Many solutions and techniques (e.g., deep learning, neural networks, and natural language processing (NLP)) are part of these components. These tools move beyond traditional rule-based algorithms to create autonomous systems. These systems understand, learn, forecast, adapt, and operate autonomously. They give rise to "intelligent" implementation. These implementations can include physical devices (e.g., robots,

[113] Zheng, N. N., Liu, Z. Y., Ren, P. J., Ma, Y. Q., Chen, S. T., Yu, S. Y., & Wang, F. Y. (2017). Hybrid-augmented intelligence: Collaboration and cognition. *Frontiers of Information Technology & Electronic Engineering*, *18*(2), 153–179.

[114] Fekete, N. (2016, June 20). What artificial intelligence can do for you? *Insurance Leaders*.

[115] Schoenherr, T. (2018). System capability and technology. *CPSM Study Guide*, 3rd.

[116] Vermesan, O., & Bacquet, J. (Eds.). (2017). *Cognitive hyperconnected digital transformation: Internet of things intelligence evolution*. Gistrup, Denmark: River Publishers.

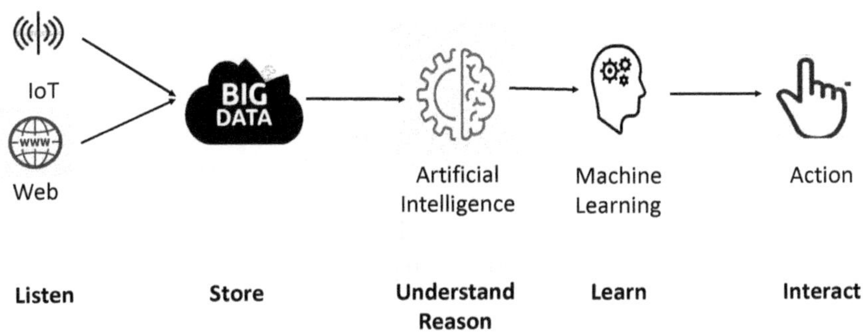

Fig. 8.5 Cognitive solution

autonomous vehicles, industrial electronics, and so on) and application and services (e.g., virtual personal assistants, smart advisors, and so on). In this context, the platforms deliver a new class of intelligent applications and objects. They provide embedded intelligence for a wide range of processes, software platforms, and service solutions in support of insurance 4.0.

Some of the initial applications of cognitive insurance are:

- Replace the humans in complex repetitive tasks of insurance;
- Provide integrated support in the acquisition of new partners;
- Automatically provide prices, create new business models, and evaluate customers;
- Manage emergencies, due to difficulties in insurance from a specific event or territory;
- Integrate with the robots for the implementation of automated and integrated solutions to support the insurance processes in the so-called robotic process automation (RPA).[117]

[117] Madakam, S., Holmukhe, R. M., & Jaiswal, D. K. (2019). The future digital work force: Robotic process automation (RPA). *JISTEM-Journal of Information Systems and Technology Management*, 16. Syed, R., Suriadi, S., Adams, M., Bandara, W., Leemans, S. J., Ouyang, C., & Reijers, H. A. (2020). Robotic process automation: Contemporary themes and challenges. *Computers in Industry*, *115*, 103162.

The possibility to use cognitive insurance from mobile phones and tablets can further benefit its use[118]:

- Allow to navigate through multiple insurance channels and systems;
- Recommend a corresponding product in the best possible way to the demands by adding transparency to the buyer;
- Recommend actions on selecting insurance services from catalogs;
- Allow interacting in natural language for improved user experience.

The benefits associated with cognitive insurance are several:

- Increasing workforce productivity and reducing the need for their education and training;
- Logging on to a more abundant and significant set of data;
- Allowing the organization to discover hidden information;
- Automating repetitive tasks;
- Improving underwriting timings and their accuracy;
- increasing efficiency in providing customized information suited to circumstances.

Groupama[119]

When Groupama Insurance began deploying smart sensors into customers' vehicles, the primary purpose was cutting down on theft and fraud by knowing where the vehicles were at all times. If policyholders opted into this internet of things system, known in the industry as telematics insurance, they could receive annual premium discounts of 15–25 percent.

At the same time, Groupama found that knowing a vehicle's location, speed, and acceleration could spot crashes in real-time. If one appeared

[118] Balasubramanian, R., Libarikian, A., & McElhaney, D. (2018). *Insurance 2030—The impact of AI on the future of insurance*. McKinsey & Company.

[119] Chaban. A. A. V. (2019, August). *How IoT insurance is helping Groupama reduce claims and accidents*. www.ibm.com/blogs/industries/telematics-iot-auto-insurance-data-groupama/. Accessed 12 December 2019.

severe enough (50 or higher on a 100-point impact scale), dispatchers would contact the customer. If no one answered, emergency services would be immediately sent.

On approximately 200 occasions a month, first responders are deployed, according to Groupama. They arrive faster than they otherwise might do. This rapid response has helped prevent some injuries from becoming severe or even fatal.

Saving lives was only the beginning of the results from the telematics program, which Groupama Assicurazioni (the Italian affiliate of Paris-based Groupama Group) has branded as G-Evolution. The service has also helped customers navigate safer, use more direct routes, reduce reckless driving, protect vehicles from criminals, and keep an eye on families.

The biggest surprise was how many policyholders in privacy-sensitive Italy signed up for the service: more than a third have opted in since the 2015 launch. Some of this early adoption is attributable to the unique challenges of vehicle ownership in Italy, mainly in the southern half of the peninsula from Abruzzo down through Sicily, where organized crime persists.

The precise location of a vehicle helps with theft, GPS detection, underlying telematics insurance, can also reveal even the subtlest frauds. For example, G-Evolution can tell if a customer who had a legitimate accident, maybe a head-on collision, then tries lump in previous damage, say to the rear bumper. Telematics data of the vehicle's precise movements at the time of the crash and in the past are fed into an algorithm and then combined with traditional inspection tools to help validate claims.

The offerings have grown alongside the growth in data. Groupama can now help customers navigate their routes based on weather patterns or road closures. There is hope that this could prevent crashes. If G-Evolution's algorithm knows a specific driver likes to speed through a mainly crash-prone section of the A51 outside Milan, which is dangerous with the rain, the tool could suggest the driver to slow down or even take a different route.

Such services would not be possible without robust data. This requirement led Groupama to move its telematics operation in-house in April 2017 in Rome, Italy.

The social benefits extend to the broader society, as well. G-Evolution is collecting data on potholes and other infrastructure problems, which Groupama plans to share with local governments. Such repairs both improve rides and prevent damages to vehicles.

Since lower rates reward good driving behavior, G-Evolution has demonstrated an impact on aggressive driving, with speeding and dangerous braking significantly reduced. According to Groupama data, at least 800 crashes have been avoided a year among G-Evolution drivers.

Thanks to the myriad features of telematics insurance, Groupama is on track to reduce claim expenses around 10–15 percent annually.

The following sections consider the three main technologies of cognitive insurance

- Big data analytics;
- Artificial intelligence; and
- Robots.

Big Data Analytics

Big data analytics is characterized by the so-called 5 V[120]:

- Volume: there should be a relatively high number of data;
- Variety there should be data of all types;
- Velocity or speed: at which data are generated and the speed with which they move in the value network;
- Veracity or accuracy: that is the reliability of the information and decisions arising from there;
- Value: the data should be able to add value.

More than a quarter of the digital data are transmitted in real-time. Among these data, more than 95 percent is generated by the connected objects. According to a 2019 IDC publication, the total volume of digital data will increase substantially.[121] It is interesting to analyze how to manage and use so many data.

[120] Corlosquet-Habart, M., Janssen, J., & Wiley, J. (Eds.). (2018). *Big data for insurance companies*. Hoboken, NJ: Wiley.

[121] www.idc.com/getdoc.jsp?containerId=TEA003093&pageNumber=0&pageSize=10. Accessed 21 March 2020.

The opportunity is that real-time customer data is packed with valuable details which can help companies gain actionable insight into policyholder preferences that can propel engagement to the next level. Based on customer data, insurers can revisit their portfolios with a keen eye on products that accommodate customers' current needs and demand for usage-based insurance. Meaningful data mined from all policyholder touchpoints can help companies map the customer journey to enhance offerings and promotional timing. A hybrid blend of digital and emotional connection offers a balanced approach to personalized engagement.

Big Data Analytics Architecture

Integrated analytics (IA) can analyze large number of data by applying multi-dimensional layers and statistical analysis criteria.[122] These analyses allow to move from primary data to information and from information to knowledge through aggregation processes, statistical inference,[123] and multivariate analysis.[124] The applications of integrated analytics can support functionality of different types.[125]

- Descriptive analytics can, for example, contextualize the behavior of the customers, grouping them into homogeneous classes;
- Predictive analytics can predict the future behavior of the customers based on their past behavior and the specific context as shown by the descriptive algorithms;
- Prescriptive analytics, or decision-making, allow relating all the components of a decision to try to predict the outcome and support the underwriters in decision making.

The analytics are models for data analysis. They are mainly valuable in areas rich in data. This situation is increasingly standard due to the use of

[122] Chen, Q., Hsu, M., & Liu, R. (2009, August). Extend UDF technology for integrated analytics. In *International conference on data warehousing and knowledge discovery* (pp. 256–270). Berlin/Heidelberg, Germany: Springer.

[123] Casella, G., & Berger, R. L. (2002). *Statistical inference* (Vol. 2). Pacific Grove, CA: Duxbury.

[124] Var, I. (1998). Multivariate data analysis. *Vectors, 8*(2), 125–136.

[125] www.digital4.biz/insurance/ufficio-acquisti-digitale-cose-quali-benefici-del-insurance-4-0/. Accessed 9 March 2019.

pervasive information systems also for insurance. This analysis can be the production of:

- Statistics;
- Reports; or
- Executive dashboards.

These outputs allow the organization to gain better management visibility and eventually take actions. The analytics may require the processing of vast masses of data (called in this case, big data).[126] Big data can serve as a basis for the formulations of strategy and risk assessments of different customers for several categories.[127] Master data is the gathered, cleaned, and stored data.[128] Reliable master data is crucial for several applications.[129]

Applications Areas of Big Data Analytics in Insurance 4.0
Getting a good data governance and management should be primary focuses of the insurance industry. Extracting value from data is central in this business.[130] Risk assessment is done based on statistical models built on large databases, that over time have become more and more complex to manage.

Insurance companies have essentially three main imperatives[131]:

- Profitable growth delivered through valuable customer acquisition and retention, cross-selling, and upselling. For this component, it is

[126] McAfee, A., Brynjolfsson, E., Davenport, T. H., Patil, D. J., & Barton, D. (2012). Big data: The management revolution. *Harvard business review*, 90(10), 60–68.

[127] Capgemini. (2018). *Digital insurance Research 2018: Uncovering the solutions that bring you forward*. www.capgemini.com/nl-nl/wp-content/uploads/sites/7/2018/10/CapgeminiDigital-insurance-Research-2018_web-version1.pdf. Accessed 24 July 2019.

[128] Berson, A., & Dubov, L. (2007). *Master data management and customer data integration for a global enterprise*. McGraw-Hill. Accessed 24 July 2019.

[129] Capgemini. (2018). *Digital insurance Research 2018: Uncovering the solutions that bring you forward*. www.capgemini.com/nl-nl/wp-content/uploads/sites/7/2018/10/CapgeminiDigital-insurance-Research-2018_web-version1.pdf. Accessed 24 July 2019.

[130] *Big Data Analytics—The Future of FinTech: Integrating*. ebrary.net/79679/business_finance/data_analytics. Accessed 20 March 2020.

[131] *Big Data Analytics—The Future of FinTech: Integrating*. ebrary.net/79679/business_finance/data_analytics. Accessed 20 March 2020.

critical to delight the customer and manage the distribution, be it direct or through intermediaries;

- Risk managed through excellent underwriting, capital efficiency, and operational risk management. For this component, strict cooperation between risk, sales, and finance departments is essential;
- Operational efficiency achieved through cost reduction, claims management, and productive strategies. The support of resources is essential for this component.

Big Data Analytics can help with all these three imperatives.[132]

In the case of pension planning, these capabilities can be transformed in a way for companies to be interactive at reducing expenses when the retirement time comes.[133] Customers will thus be able to conduct a financial trade-off between how much they want to save and when they will retire. All in all, this will help to open the path for tailored customer solutions. This effective way of managing persons' financial affairs will lead to adjust automatically change in income or to decide to switch some pension contribution to be able to pay forward a mortgage. Looking to data will improve the speed of servicing, drive down costs, and pave for better precision, customization, and adaptation. According to a Price Waterhouse Coopers survey, more than 30 percent of the insurance's senior management lacks the competencies to make alone the most of this new information and capabilities.[134]

Digital companies (BigTech), such as Google or Amazon, are built on a data-driven mantra. They are starting to enter the insurance market. Companies cannot afford to respond slowly. Companies possess valuable historical data, that, if properly managed, will help them beat the competition that is coming from these digital newcomers. The latter players collect vital data insights coming from all sort of channels (i.e., social networks, credit card history, and so on). They can know, for example, how fast persons drive, how they take breaks, and their online behaviors

[132] Boobier, T. (2018). *Advanced analytics and AI: Impact, implementation, and the future of work.* Hoboken, NJ: Wiley.

[133] www.oecd.org/pensions/Technology-and-innovation-in-the-insurance-sector.pdf. Accessed 2 May 2020. Pfau, W., Tomlinson, J., & Vernon, S. (2017, November). Income by Integrating Retirement Plans, IRAs, *Stanford Center on Longevity and Home Equity.*

[134] www.pwc.com/mu/pwc-22nd-annual-global-ceo-survey-mu.pdf. Accessed 2 May 2020.

on social media, which are more critical data when compared to the age, zip code, past accident records, and so on.[135]

Companies need to think about the implication that technology giants such as Google and Amazon may have for their business. These big players have access to millions of customers' data. They have the right competencies and tools to analyze those data. They might target tailored products offered at low-risk customers. This situation will have tremendous consequences for the companies' business model since premiums, collected from low-risk policyholders, contribute to the claims of high-risk ones.

The diffusion of internet, social networks, IoT, ICT, and other solutions has burst interest in data governance and management across the insurance industry. Companies have always investigated on new ways and methods that can better and more accurately evaluate risks. An effective, efficient, and economic data management is critical for a proper setting of policy premiums. In doing this activity, the premium should be based on[136]:

- Coverage, taking into account the characteristics of the person/asset/business insured;
- Assessments of the risks, setting premiums at a level that covers the insured risk;
- Potential margins depend on the cost structure of the insurance organization;
- Fitting the budget of customers is a critical point for companies, for targeting specific market segments;
- Competition, taking into account the competition present in the same market segment and channel.

The massive volumes of data generated in the last decades have shifted the attention of insurance companies to the data governance and management. Their focus is on those huge, diverse, and complex data that can be extracted from a variety of sources, such as documents, videos, photos,

[135] www.mckinsey.com/~/media/mckinsey/industries/financial%20services/our%20insights/time%20for%20insurance%20companies%20to%20face%20digital%20reality/digital-disruption-in-insurance.ashx. Accessed 2 May 2020.

[136] Big Data Analytics—The Future of FinTech: Integrating. ebrary.net/79679/business_finance/data_analytics. Accessed 2 April 2020.

chats, emails, and so on.[137] This data is unstructured. They have considerable values for the companies. Unlike structured data, which are stored in a fixed format in a field within a record or a file, as a spreadsheet or as a database, it is much more difficult for a company to extract information from unstructured data.[138] They should not miss this opportunity to get competitive advantages by exploiting unstructured data. Those companies that are willing to leverage big data analytics should look also to other tools. The management of unstructured data can be done with non-relational databases.[139] This technology deploys advanced and sophisticated technologies able to manage large quantities of unstructured data. D3.js is an example of these new technologies.[140] It indicates the relevance of data design in documents and supports the internet of data.[141]

According to the Puneet Bharal and Amir Halfon,[142] the suggested approach for insurance companies is an hybrid one. The suggestion is to combine relational and non-relational databases.[143] The objective would be pushing the paradigm to the limit while leveraging big data analytics with leading-edge technologies.

Advanced analytics is the autonomous or semi-autonomous analysis of information through sophisticated tools and techniques, to get a more in-depth understanding of the data.[144] Advanced analytics is different from

[137] Big Data Analytics—The Future of FinTech: Integrating. ebrary.net/79679/business_finance/data_analytics. Accessed 20 May 2020.

[138] Big Data Analytics—The Future of FinTech: Integrating. ebrary.net/79679/business_finance/data_analytics. Accessed 3 April 3030.

[139] Wu, X., Zhu, X., Wu, G. Q., & Ding, W. (2013). Data mining with big data. *IEEE Transactions on Knowledge and Data Engineering, 26*(1), 97–107. Big Data Analytics—The Future of FinTech: Integrating. ebrary.net/79679/business_finance/data_analytics. Accessed 20 March 2020.

[140] d3js.org/. Accessed 2 May 2020.

[141] Fan, W., Chen, Z., Xiong, Z., & Chen, H. (2012). The Internet of data: A new idea to extend the IOT in the digital world. *Frontiers of Computer Science, 6*(6), 660–667.

[142] Bharal, P., & Halfon, A. (2013). Making sense of big data in insurance. www.marklogic.com/resources/making-sense-of-big-data-in-insurance/resource_download/whitepapers/. Accessed 5 August 2016.

[143] Big Data Analytics—The Future of FinTech: Integrating. ebrary.net/79679/business_finance/data_analytics. Accessed 30 April 2020.

[144] Johansson, S., & Vogelgesang, U. (2016). Automating the insurance industry. *The McKinsey Quarterly.*

a traditional analysis since it not only considers the historical data. The method collects and analyzes data in real-time and can perform predictive analysis of future risks. The data analysis allows improving risk assessment as predictive models are developed. Using them, insurance companies can compute the probability of claims and consequently enhances the determination of the pricing of insurance products.[145] The most advanced form of advanced analytics is based on artificial intelligence.

It is possible to identify the top seven use cases of big data analytics in insurance[146]:

- Customer Insights;
- Customer Experience and journey;
- Policy premiums setting;
- Risk management;
- Fraud detection;
- Automation and smarter labor; and
- Finance support.

There are some new solutions to manage also open data. These are data which are freely available in internet. Most of the times they are loaded by public administrations and foundations. Examples of open data are meteorological data or special events like disasters.[147] They can generate advantages on respect to the competition.[148] Getting a good handle on them should be one of the focus of the insurance industry. Extracting value from data is central in insurance. On this respect, it is sufficient

[145] Generali. (2018, February). *Le assicurazioni "tutto connesso."* www.generali.com/it/info/discoveringgenerali/all/2018/A-fully-connected-insurance. Accessed 31 March 2020.

[146] Senousy, Y. M. B., Mohamed, N. E. K., & Riad, A. E. D. M. (2018, December). Recent trends in big data analytics towards more enhanced insurance business models. *International Journal of Computer Science and Information Security (IJCSIS), 16*(12).

[147] Ortmann, J., Limbu, M., Wang, D., & Kauppinen, T. (2011, January). Crowdsourcing linked open data for disaster management. In *Proceedings of the Terra Cognita Workshop on Foundations, Technologies and Applications of the Geospatial Web in conjunction with the ISWC* (pp. 11–22). Big Data Analytics—The Future of FinTech: Integrating. ebrary.net/79679/business_finance/data_analytics. Accessed 20 April 2020.

[148] Nicoletti, B. (2019). Digital transformation via open data in insurance. In A. L. Mention (Ed.), *Digital innovation harnessing the value of open data*. Singapore: World Scientific.

to consider the assessment of risks.[149] This is performed with actuarial models built on large databases, not easy to manage.

Benefits and Challenges of Big Data Analytics

The true value of big data is on finding the best use of these data: the so-called data monetization.[150] For this reason, in this book, the expression used is big data analytics. It is the correct expression to underline the immense power coming from being able to analyze structured and unstructured data, such as social media posts, videos, photos, email, social networks, chats, sounds, and so on. There are more and more channels for data collection (such as the IoT and social media) via cloud computing.[151] Thanks to the tool of big data analytics, these large numbers and complex data can be transformed into knowledge and value. Thus, companies can make better decisions. For example, the data collected by sensors and related devices on an insured asset are useful to understand the cause of an accident but also to help in attributing the responsibility to the correct party,

Insurance companies are focusing more and more on big data analytics to detect cases of fraud and analyze web content to gain new customers. Thanks to this technology, companies can better understand customers, and offer tailor-made solutions based on the actual behavior of the customer, placing the customer in a broad category. Big data analytics allows a micro-segmentation of risks.[152]

The use of big data analytics also has a specific number of risks.[153] There might be problems with customer privacy. The data are collected

[149] Big Data Analytics—The Future of FinTech: Integrating. ebrary.net/79679/business_finance/data_analytics. Accessed 20 April 2020.

[150] Thomas, R., & McSharry, P. (2015). *Big data revolution: What farmers, doctors and insurance agents teach us about discovering big data patterns*. Hoboken, NJ: Wiley.

[151] Nicoletti, B. (2013). *Cloud computing & financial services*. London, UK: Palgrave Macmillan (also translated in Chinese).

[152] Eling, M., & Lehmann, M. (2018). The impact of digitization on the insurance value chain and the insurability of risks. *The Geneva Papers on Risk and Insurance-Issues and Practice, 43*, 359–396. https://doi.org/10.1057/s41288-017-0073-0.

[153] www.corrierecomunicazioni.it/digital/42773_come-cambiano-le-assicurazioni-ai-tempi-dei-big-data.htm. Accessed 30 July 2016.

with potentially invasive tools.[154] There is the risk of an increase in the market position against anticompetitive regulations. There is the danger to disseminate customers. The information from the policyholders and the new solutions can create barriers for entry of new competitors. Incumbents can benefit from such restrictions. The restriction would penalize the companies that are not able to compete in the collection and use of the data. There are possibilities of anti-competitive consequences on the use of big data analytics. On the other side, companies not using these solutions would find difficult to utilize marketing strategies based on data on the customers, available with these new technologies.[155]

Artificial Intelligence

Artificial intelligence (AI), better called augmented intelligence, is the ability of computers to solve complex problems, react like human beings, and show intelligent behaviors.[156] AI can also be defined as: the scientific study of the computational principles behind thought and intelligent behavior.[157]

AI can process huge volumes of data faster, and possibly better than the ability of humans.[158] It includes algorithms that enable machines to show creative competencies. The capabilities of artificial intelligence activities arrive to machine learning. This tool can extract knowledge and models from a series of observations and learn from them.[159]

[154] Big Data Analytics—The Future of FinTech: Integrating. ebrary.net/79679/business_finance/data_analytics. Accessed 30 May 2020.

[155] Big Data Analytics—The Future of FinTech: Integrating. ebrary.net/79679/business_finance/data_analytics. Accessed 20 March 2020.

[156] Burgess, A. (2017). *The executive guide to artificial intelligence: How to identify and implement applications for AI in your organization*. Cham, Switzerland: Springer.

[157] Skilton, M., & Hovsepian, F. (2017). *The 4th industrial revolution: Responding to the impact of artificial intelligence on business*. Cham, Switzerland: Springer.

[158] Allianz Global Corporate & Specialty. (2018). *The rise of artificial intelligence: Future outlook and emerging risks*. www.agcs.allianz.com/assets/Insights/Artificialpercent20Intelligence/Artificial_Intelligence_Outlook_and_Risks.pdf. Accessed 12 December 2019.

[159] Cambosu, D. (2018, June). *Intelligenza artificiale, perché è sempre più importante per l'insurance*. www.insuranceup.it/it/business/intelligenza-artificiale-perche-e-sempre-piuimportante-per-l-insurance_1925.htm. Accessed 30 March 2020.

Artificial Intelligence Architecture

With artificial intelligence, computers can learn, plan, recognize, and solve problems by themselves. Artificial intelligence solutions have three characteristics[160]:

- Artificial intelligence operates intentionally. Artificial intelligence algorithms can use real-time data, structured or unstructured, to support sophisticated analysis and decision making. It uses sensors and digital data to combine information from a variety of different sources and analyze them instantly.
- Artificial intelligence works together with machine learning and data analytics. It has intelligence. Machine learning collects data and looks for underlying trends or small signals. When it spots something relevant for a practical problem, the software can extract that knowledge and use it to analyze specific issues and recommend or even take actions automatically.
- Artificial intelligence can adapt. Artificial intelligence can learn and make decisions. The AI system can collect a large number of data and use its advanced algorithms to learn and achieve experience from similar situations. Then, they can forecast the upcoming situations and suggest or take actions.

A possible classification of the artificial intelligence models is the following[161]:

- Machine Learning. It is a set of algorithms used to make a system artificially intelligent, enabling it to recognize patterns from large datasets and apply past findings to new data. Machine learning can be explained in further detail by separating it into three categories:
  - supervised learning;
  - unsupervised learning; and
  - reinforcement learning.

[160] West, J. R. A. D. M. & Allen, J. (2018). How artificial intelligence is transforming the world. www.brookings.edu/research/how-artificial-intelligence-is-transforming-the-world/. Accessed 2 June 2019.

[161] Krishnamoorthy, C. S., & Rajeev, S. (2018). *Artificial intelligence and expert systems for engineers*. Boca Raton, FL: CRC Press.

Most practical applications of machine learning involve supervised learning algorithms.[162]

- Neural Networks. It is a type of algorithms which is a subfield of machine learning using several layers of neural networks (algorithms that mimic the human brain) and requiring intense supervised or unsupervised learning;
- Rule-Based Reasoning. It is a set of algorithms used as a way to store and manipulate knowledge to interpret information in a useful way;
- Natural Language Processing. It is the interaction in human language, including Natural Language Understanding (Sentimental Analysis, Conversational AI bots.) and Natural Language Generation;
- Computer Vision. It is the capability in support of a machine to see and visually sense the environment around it. Computer vision is concerned with the automatic extraction, analysis, and understanding of useful information from a single image or a sequence of images;
- Cognitive Search. It collects, analyzes, and gives meaning to different types of data using rule based or machine learning algorithms often in a way that is similar to human cognition with the objective of making decisions in complex situations;
- Predictive Analytics. It combines the use of data, statistical algorithms and machine learning techniques to identify the likelihood of future outcomes based on historical data and improve the confiability of the predictions.

The strengths of artificial intelligence depend mainly on machine learning. Machine learning enables computer programs automatically to improve their performance at some tasks through experience.[163] This field connects with pattern recognition and statistical inference. Several pieces of research in machine learning have focused on classification, the task of developing a model, from a set of previously classified examples,

[162] Richman, R. (2018, July). AI in actuarial science. *SSRN*. ssrn.com/abstract=3218082. Accessed 30 May 2020.

[163] Pham, D. T., & Afify, A. A. (2005). Machine-learning techniques and their applications in manufacturing. *Proceedings of the Institution of Mechanical Engineers, Part B: Journal of Engineering Manufacture, 219*(5), 395–412.

that can correctly categorize new cases from the same population. The classification has a wide range of applications, including manufacturing, telecommunications, marketing, and scientific analysis. Many insurance problems fall under the category of classification. Insurance professionals need to assign a class label to an object or a situation based on the specific values of a set of parameters.

Machine learning solutions include inductive-learning algorithms such as decision-tree induction and rule induction, instance-based learning, neural networks, genetic algorithms, and Bayesian-learning algorithms.[164] Among several machine-learning solutions developed for classification, inductive learning is the most commonly used in real-world application domains. Inductive learning techniques are fast compared to other techniques.[165] Inductive learning techniques are simple. They allow generating models easy to understand. Inductive learning classifiers obtain similar and sometimes better accuracies compared with other classification techniques.

Applications Areas of AI in Insurance 4.0

Artificial intelligence application determines significant changes in the insurance industry, mainly in the risk assessment models, pricing policy, payment of compensation notifications, and customer management (Fig. 8.6).[166] According to the World Insurance Report 2017, for 69 percent of companies, artificial intelligence is essential. Eighty percent of respondents indicated that they are already investing in this technology or plan to do so in the next three years.[167]

One of the areas that have been the focus of artificial intelligence applications in virtually all business sectors is the customization of the

[164] Pham, D. T., & Afify, A. A. (2005). Machine-learning techniques and their applications in manufacturing. *Proceedings of the Institution of Mechanical Engineers, Part B: Journal of Engineering Manufacture, 219*(5), 395–412.

[165] Michalski, R. S. (1983). A theory and method of inductive learning. In *Machine learning* (pp. 83–134). Berlin/Heidelberg, Germany: Springer.

[166] Cambosu, D. (2018, June 22). *Intelligenza artificiale, perché è sempre più importante per l'insurance*. www.insuranceup.it/it/business/intelligenza-artificiale-perche-e-sempre-piuimportante-per-l-insurance_1925.htm. Accessed 10 May 2020.

[167] Kumaresan, A., Saurav, S., & Raghunanda, K. (2017). *Top 10 trends in property & casualty insurance 2018*. www.capgemini.com/wpcontent/uploads/2017/12/property-and-casuality-insurance-trends_2018.pdf. Accessed 19 January 2020.

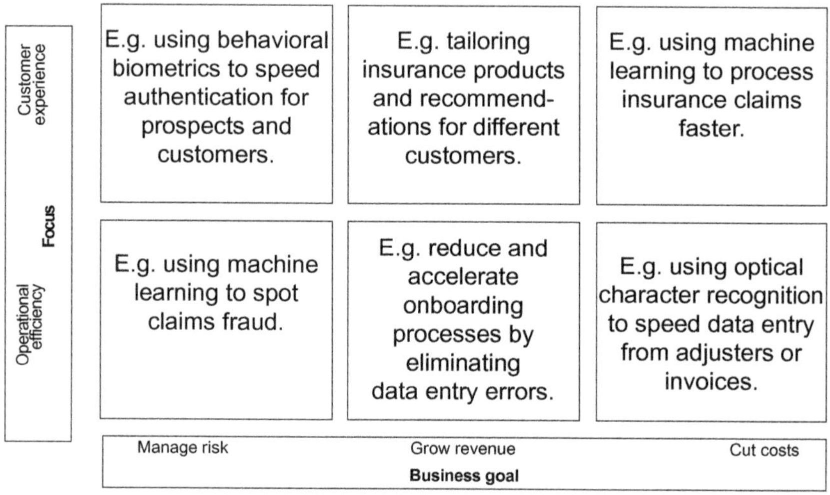

Fig. 8.6 Artificial intelligence in insurance

interaction with customers, including the customization of product offerings.[168] Traditionally, insurance companies have been robust at selling insurance but not necessarily in cultivating customer relations after the initial sale. This approach must change since customers extrapolate from their experience with other product and service providers and expect similar experiences from companies. Cultivating customer relations and customer ownership will be an essential field on which incumbent companies and newcomers will fight to gain access to and keep profitable business. Next to technical underwriting competencies, superior products and services will be the critical success factors.[169]

[168] Albrecher, H., Bommier, A., Filipović, D., Koch-Medina, P., Loisel, S., & Schmeiser, H. (2019). Insurance: Models, digitization, and data science. *European Actuarial Journal*, *9*(2), 349–360.

[169] McKinsey. (2017). Digital disruption in insurance: Cutting through the noise. www.mckinsey.com/~/media/mckinsey/industries/financial%20services/our%20insights/time%20for%20insurance%20companies%20to%20face%20digital%20reality/digital-disruption-in-insurance.ashx. Accessed 30 May 2020.

A natural area of application of AI is automated underwriting.[170] Companies tend to rely on past data to assess and price risks. Much of these data relevant for implementing an artificial intelligence approach to underwriting is in an unstructured form. They are emails, handwritten documents, or pictures. Hence, to exploit data, it needs to be available in a digital form. This operation will typically involve scanning and the use of image processing or natural language processing capabilities. The challenges are relevant.

Claim management is undoubtedly one of the insurance pillars and also one of its significant problems, both for the complexity of its management and for its delicacy, being the most critical touchpoint with the customer. The management of the claim is, for a company, the moment of truth in its relationship with the customer. Concerning the latter, the entire payment process must be effective, fast, transparent, and satisfactory. Nothing is more critical for the loyalty of the customer. The challenge is even more demanding today since the expectations of customers have evolved. The expectations are growing, what was once a hope for the customer, is now a fair expectation.[171] A claim which, if managed in a bad way, leads the interested party to change the company as quickly as changing a channel on TV.

Some examples of supervised learning that are common in the actuarial field are "the fitting of generalized linear models to claims datasets to forecast the frequency and severity of claims, or to policyholder datasets to forecast lapse rates."[172] Supervised learning models can be either simple linear regression models or more complex models. Unsupervised learning is the portion of machine learning that concerns the recognizing of sequences and patterns. "The task of unsupervised learning is to find meaningful patterns using only X, which can be then used to further understand the data, or, in some cases, model it".[173] Reinforcement

[170] Albrecher, H., Bommier, A., Filipović, D., Koch-Medina, P., Loisel, S., & Schmeiser, H. (2019). Insurance: Models, digitization, and data science. *European Actuarial Journal*, *9*(2), 349–360.

[171] Claim management, how technology turns it around. www.insuranceup.it/en/scenarios/claim-management-how-technology-turns-it-around/. Accessed 30 April 2020.

[172] Richman, R. (2018, July). AI in Actuarial Science. *SSRN*. ssrn.com/abstract=3218082.

[173] Richman, R. (2018, July). AI in Actuarial Science. *SSRN*. ssrn.com/abstract=3218082.

learning is a part of machine learning that does not yet relate to actuarial science. Its definition is "learning what to do—how to map situations to actions—so as to maximize a numerical reward signal."[174]

Supervised learning relies on a training data set that can be used by a machine to learn how to forecast or classify new data input. Input data needs to be enriched by organizing it according to the desired output categories, to build the training set. Insurance, and mainly reinsurance, is very much expertise driven. In other words, much of the claims experience has to be interpreted against changing conditions, including evolving judicial decisions. Since the classification leading to the training set has to be undertaken by experts, implementing supervised machine learning method is expensive and time-consuming. A possible way of overcoming this difficulty could be to combine machine-learning methods with a traditional expert system-approach. Another exciting direction would be to capture expert knowledge during regular business activity. At any rate, more fundamental research seems required to explore the possibilities of weakly supervised and unsupervised method.

Wüthrich used machine learning techniques (CART)[175] to forecast the number of reported but not settled (RBNS) claims.[176] Baudry and Robert used some other machine learning methods (including the so-called ExtraTrees algorithm).[177] Their forecast flows can compute RBNS and Incurred but not enough reported (IBNER) reserves separately, run the full reserving process as of any date as required. AI can compute reserves along with any time granularity, learn from any subsample of historical data defined by the user, and learn from any subspace of features specified by the user.

Technologies such as artificial intelligence augmented and virtual reality are opening up new scenarios. They will change the ways of work. It is possible to envision the emergence of mixed teams, composed of humans and smart technologies. Thus, it is possible to combine human

[174] Sutton, R, S., & Barto, A. G. (2018). *Reinforcement learning: An introduction* (2nd ed.). Cambridge, MA: MIT Press.

[175] A Classification and Regression Tree (CART), is a predictive model, which explains how an outcome variable's values can be predicted based on other values.

[176] Wüthrich, M. V. (2018). Neural networks applied to chain-ladder reserving. *European Actuarial Journal, 8*, 407–436.

[177] Baudry, M., & Robert, C. Y. (2017). *Non-parametric individual claim reserving in insurance* (Working paper).

experience with machine learning. This is the opinion of 43 percent of Italian manufacturing SMEs that have already adopted or intend to introduce innovative technologies/processes, including ICT security, AI, cloud computing, collaborative robotics, and the internet of things.[178]

Actuaries could have a key role in data selection and minimization, in setting goals and managing ethical and reputational risks.[179] AI-powered pricing solution can enable insurance companies to improve their margins and get market share with pricing models that are created and updated in short times. The technology embeds all of the steps within the pricing process into a single solution, automating the model building. The AI applications must be able to "justify" their solutions rather than working as black boxes, while giving users complete control on the models.[180]

The market for artificial intelligence is vast. The market size for machine learning in 2016 was USD 61.34 million. The forecast is to grow to USD 3.75 billion by 2021, with a CAGR of 43.7 percent from 2016 to 2021.[181]

The last examples of using artificial intelligence are when AI is combined with data: these are the so-called content service platforms (CSP).[182] Modern CSP with advanced AI capabilities or integrations can allow companies to automate fraud detection. For instance, the system can look at an image of a vehicle that was involved in an accident. It can read the license plate number. A CSP can compare accident damage across different sets of photographs and perform analyses based on existing information within the company's systems. This allows more informed decisions about different areas of a claim, such as comparing and contrasting with other images of the same make and model with similar damage to provide better damage estimates. It is possible to use

[178] www.mecspe.com/en/comunicati-stampa-en/osservatorio-mecspe-focus-nazionale/. Accessed 5 August 2019.

[179] Albrecher, H., Bommier, A., Filipović, D., Koch-Medina, P., Loisel, S., & Schmeiser, H. (2019). Insurance: Models, digitization, and data science. *European Actuarial Journal*, *9*(2), 349–360.

[180] Corea, F. (2019). *Applied artificial intelligence: Where AI can be used in business*. Cham, Switzerland: Springer International Publishing.

[181] www.marketsandmarkets.com. Accessed 10 June 3019.

[182] Nielsen, P., & Aanestad, M. (2006). Control devolution as information infrastructure design strategy: A case study of a content service platform for mobile phones in Norway. *Journal of Information Technology, 21*(3), 185–194.

this information to send it to the repair network to determine whether those estimates are in line or out of line with previous work or even find suspicious activity within their repair network.

AI solutions can have many applications in insurance are, for example, image classification for claims and text analytics for servicing customer queries. Insurance services of claims processing and new business preparation. These new technologies will further drive automation and improvement in insurance processes.

Fukoku Mutual Life Insurance[183]

Fukoku Mutual Life Insurance thanks to an Artificial intelligence (AI) solution believes it will increase productivity by 30 percent and see a return on its investment in less than two years.[184] The company would save about 140 million (m) yen (GBP 1 m) a year after the 200 m yen (GBP1.4 m) in labor-cost savings. The installation of the AI system took place in 2017. Its maintenance costs around 15 m yen (GBP 100 k) a year.[185]

The system is based on IBM's Watson Explorer. This tool, according to the tech firm, possesses "cognitive technology that can think like a human", enabling it to "analyze and interpret all of data, including unstructured text, images, audio, and video."[186]

The technology will be able to read tens of thousands of medical certificates and invoices in the length of hospital stays, medical histories, and any surgical procedures before calculating payouts.

While the use of AI will thoroughly reduce the time needed to compute Fukoku Mutual's payouts, which reportedly totaled 132,000 during the current financial year, the sums will not be paid until a member of the staff approve them.

[183] www.theguardian.com/technology/2017/jan/05/japanese-company-replaces-office-persons-artificial-intelligence-ai-fukoku-mutual-life-procurement. Accessed 10 January 2020.

[184] Japanese company replaces office workers with artificial. www.theguardian.com/technology/2017/jan/05/japanese-company-replaces-office-workers-artificial-intelligence-ai-fukoku-mutual-life-insurance. Accessed 30 April 2020.

[185] Japanese company replaces office workers with artificial. www.theguardian.com/technology/2017/jan/05/japanese-company-replaces-office-workers-artificial-intelligence-ai-fukoku-mutual-life-insurance. Accessed 30 April 2020.

[186] Japanese company replaces office workers with artificial. www.theguardian.com/technology/2017/jan/05/japanese-company-replaces-office-workers-artificial-intelligence-ai-fukoku-mutual-life-insurance. Accessed 30 April 2020.

Benefits and Challenges of AI

AI can bring several improvements to Claim Management:

- Improve efficiency. The settlement of insurance claims is only one aspect of the claims management process. The time necessary for the management of an accident involves several phases that begin with the reporting of the accident. Here, the customer experience is crucial. The subsequent steps determine whether the claim is correct (i.e., whether it falls under the policy coverage), authentic, and how much the insurance company will pay. Insurance customers expect the company to be quick and satisfactory, both by its side and not a problem in the problem. Reducing the time needed to settle insurance claims is essential. Most of the customer complaints depend on these events.[187] Reduce claims time is also a way to improving the service, increasing the level of satisfaction, and providing the company a competitive advantage. AI would allow insurance 4.0 to manage potentially the management of the whole claim process, starting from the user, and with a high level of automation, speeds up the process, and reduces the costs.
- Reduce Fraud. Another essential aspect is the contribution that artificial intelligence can make to fraud detection. Paying fraudulent claims costs money to the companies. The insurance industry transfers these costs to its customers. Honest customers bear the cost of fraud.
- Reduce operating and staff costs and expenses. As mentioned above, the digitization of the entire claim management process leads to improving the efficiency of the process with customer satisfaction. But it also allows reducing the company's operating costs: process automation, and use of collaborative digital tools.

Data privacy and data availability remain potential obstacles for companies.

[187] Claim management, how technology turns it around. www.insuranceup.it/en/scenarios/claim-management-how-technology-turns-it-around/. Accessed 30 April 2020.

The Startups for Claim Management Solutions

An analysis of over 2500 insurtech startups in Europe shows that only 15 percent of companies are dealing with claims related to the settlement of claims and the fight against fraud. The remaining 85 percent focuses on new distribution channels, new insurance products or risk assessment. The reason is that claims and fraud are the links in a value network. They require the combination of advanced technologies and specialist knowledge and do not always go hand in hand.[188]

There are several examples of insurtech in this sector.

The New Yorker Lemonade Insurance Company is among the most funded startups. It states to be able to solve a claim in three seconds, via chatbot. Lemonade Insurance Company initially offered developers access to its renters, condo, and homeowners' insurance through its application programming interfaces (API)[189] platform. It expands the use cases supported by the API as the company introduces new insurance products.[190]

Cove, a New Zealand startup, has built the entire process from purchase to claim on chatbot technology. The founders believe that artificial intelligence can make insurance matters more human.

Spixii, an Italian-French startup, already in 2016 had conquered Open-F @ b Call4Ideas 2016 with its chatbot.

It uses a technology of growing importance for claim management_ image recognition.

For many years, with the arrival of digital, taking photographs has become much simpler and less expensive than before. This solution has enormous potential in claim management. It provides to customers higher control in a long and not always clear process. The Italian startup Insoore has partially picked up this opportunity by offering insurance companies an innovative system to acquire vehicle images. It has leveraged crowdsourcing, to implement a platform that connects companies with

[188]Claim management, how technology turns it around. www.insuranceup.it/en/scenarios/claim-management-how-technology-turns-it-around/. Accessed 30 April 2020.

[189]www.mulesoft.com/resources/api/what-is-an-api. Accessed 2 May 2020.

[190]Catlin, T., Lorenz, J. T., Nandan, J., Sharma, S., & Waschto, A. (2020). *Insurance beyond digital: The rise of ecosystems and platforms*. www.mckinsey.com/industries/financial-services/our-insights/insurance-beyond-digital-the-rise-of-ecosystems-and-platforms. Accessed 21 March 2020. Insurance ecosystems and platforms: How companies can turn. www.mckinsey.com/industries/financial-services/our-insights/ecosystems-and-platforms-how-companies-can-turn-vision-into-reality. Accessed 30 April 2020.

thousands of detectors to make photographic documentation of insured vehicles. If the photos comply with the acceptance criteria, the insurance company accepts the survey. Insoore transfers the reward to the user's account. Human operators verify the conformity of the images.

The British startup Tractable is specialized in artificial intelligence applied to examine accidents and help in disaster recovery. This startup has automated these exams using a database of over 130 million images of destroyed cars. It has trained its systems to recognize the type of damage that a vehicle has suffered and to forecast the likely cost of the repair. This information is then communicated to the insurer.

Artificial intelligence, machine learning, and data science are technologies that can guarantee a definite improvement in the management of claims mainly if implemented in the whole process. The French startup Zelros has developed an end-to-end platform which embraces the entire back office activity of a company, helping staff manage sales and claims. Zelros' algorithms help to extract and make sense of information, reducing themes, and improving decisions. Investors of this startup, Astorya VC, write on its blog: "Insurance employees (claims managers, sales agents, underwriters of risks) make daily decisions based on data relating to policyholders. However, insurance companies usually work on several ICT systems and databases (CRM, policy administration, risks, and so on) and limit access to only the necessary employees. Most employees do not have access to these datasets or have to access many systems to collect detached information manually." It is a complex process. Thanks to technology (PNL, AutoML, SHAP, SHAP, and so on), Zelros allows insurance managers to access customer data scattered in many silos through a simple messenger (or a plug-in for any corporate messenger). By asking questions about the company's data sets, companies receive customer information or AI-based sales suggestions. Thanks to artificial intelligence algorithms, in some cases, the answers arrive even before the question. The algorithm classifies claims based on the level of complexity, calculating fraud or eligibility scores, and anticipating the type of resolution.

The British startup, Rightindem, offers companies a solution based on the customer experience. It claims to be able to help companies provide the claims service that their customers expect today. It is a critical tool (also in the form of a chatbot) that the company makes available to the customer, making it autonomous in the management of the claim. The system allows customers to easily describe, in natural language, how the accident occurred, and to add photos and supporting videos, helping them to present and manage the complaint more quickly and transparently.

Claim management requires a high effort in time and human resources. It is necessary to coordinate many entities (that is, the policyholder, the insurer, the adjuster, the mechanic). Easy access to information is often lacking. A Lithuanian startup called Claims Control and a Dutch Openclaims offers collaboration platforms that bring together all entities involved in claims management. This situation allows for quick and easy access to information, sharing photos, and keeping all communications in one place.

A very thorny and expensive problem for companies is insurance frauds. French Shift Technologies has developed software-as-a-service (SaaS) that uses big data and artificial intelligence, designed to detect potential insurance fraud and automate claims. The company's software uses mathematical models and algorithms to detect fraudulent behavior. It supports claim managers in a much more accurate and faster decision-making process. By working with many insurances and consequently having data from several databases, Shift can continuously improve its algorithms and continuously improve in detecting insurance fraud.

Robots

The use of software robots is very interesting also for insurance companies.[191] They have agents or programs with an appropriate level of artificial intelligence.

Robots Architecture

Robots are capable of replicating some human actions. As an example, software robots can carry out data entry tasks or interact with the interface of a management system as would a human operator do. It is possible to train a specific type of software robot called robotic process automation (RPA). Over time, the software robots should be able to learn and improve its performance through machine learning techniques.[192]

[191] Perona, M. (2019). *Procurement 4.0, the check list for purchasing digital*. www.digital4.biz/insurance/ufficio-acquisti-digitale-cose-quali-benefici-del-insurance-4-0/. Accessed 9 March 2019.

[192] Mohri, M., Rostamizadeh, A., & Talwalkar, A. (2018). *Foundations of machine learning*. Cambridge, MA: MIT Press.

Application Areas of Robots in Insurance 4.0

There are several areas of application of software robots in support of insurance. By combining artificial intelligence (AI), machine learning, and advanced robotic process automation (RPA) systems, insurance companies can handle policy inquiries and applications more quickly and accurately. Smart email management systems can filter and redirect incoming emails and reply to standard inquiries and requests. Automated call-center and web-chat services significantly improve the quality of customer services.[193]

Robots and artificial intelligence could be relevant in the insurance industry. Robo-advisors could suggest the best policy to adopt for a specific customer. Robotic process automation could help in the several activities that require the combination of what to do and perform it.

The following pages examine some of these applications.

Robo-Advisors[194]

Price comparison and distribution websites in support of insurance processes are becoming widespread. There also efforts to develop websites that provide financial guidance tailored to the policyholder's income and needs. This solution can be achieved with higher automation through algorithms for products with investment and/or saving components. These supports are called Rob-advisor. Their capabilities are[195]:

- Understanding customer needs and preferences, gathering customer information, assessing risk tolerance, and considering outside accounts;
- Proposing a policy, developing a financial plan, selecting asset allocation;
- Implementing the policy, opening accounts, transferring assets, and
- Monitoring and adjusting the policies with quarterly or even continuous performance reviews, dashboards and status alerts, market updates, and research.

[193] insuranceblog.accenture.com/intelligent-automation-gives-companies-a-big-opportunity-to-boost-the-quality-of-their-customer-service. Accessed 24 December 2019.

[194] www.oecd.org/pensions/Technology-and-innovation-in-the-procurement-sector.pdf. Accessed 5 April 2020.

[195] www.accenture.com/t20160509t220506__w__/us-en/_acnmedia/pdf-17/accenture-wealth-management-rise-of-robo-advice.pdf. Accessed 5 April 2020.

In comparison with robo-advice, human interaction brings benefits in personal long-term relations. They can develop trust and understanding between a policyholder and financial advisor/broker/agent, in particular in times of financial difficulty.

Robo-advice has the ability to prepare a business plan addressing multiple goals, including retirement, protection needs, estate planning, and health/long-term care coverage. Robo-advice has privacy, which some may feel more comfortable with, given the sensitivity in discussing money matters.

Robo-advice capabilities offer benefits to insurance companies as a way of expanding their presence in wealth management while allowing agents to maintain their focus on insurance sales.[196] The costs of this type of service would be sufficiently low to support also low-income customers. In the investment advisory sector in the USA, for example, financial advisers generally charge one percent of the assets under management as fees. The latter charge is more of the between 15 and 35 basis points of assets under management charged by investment robo-advisors.[197] In comparison, in the UK, for example, Santander's branch-based investment advice fees are 2.5 percent of assets invested, with a minimum investment of GBP 500 and a maximum of GBP 150,000.[198]

Robotic Process Automation

The robotic process automation (RPA) is the use of robots (based on software or physical) for the automation of simple and repetitive tasks.[199] Examples of such uses are data transfer from multiple input sources like email and spreadsheets to systems of record like enterprise resource planning (ERP) and Customer relationship management (CRM) systems.[200] Thus, the organization can free the time of their expert professionals.

[196] www.accenture.com/_acnmedia/PDF-2/Accenture-Wealth-Management-Rise-of-Robo-Advice.pdf. Accessed 30 May 2020.

[197] investorjunkie.com/robo-advisors/cost-comparison/. Accessed 5 April 2020.

[198] www.santanderbank.com/us/personal/banking/santander-select. Accessed 2 May 2020.

[199] Anagnoste, S. (2017, July). Robotic automation process-next major revolution in back-office operations improvement. *Proceedings of the International Conference on Business Excellence, 11*(1), 676–686. De Gruyter Open, Berlin, Germany.

[200] Lacity, M. C., & Willcocks, L. P. (2016). A new approach to automating services. *MIT Sloan Management Review, 58*(1), 41.

Robotic process automation applies specific technology and methods to use a computer as a "virtual Full Time Equivalent (FTE)" rather than a person to process current application software such as enterprise resource planning's, claims applications, and databases in the same way that a person today processes a transaction.[201] The past years saw a substantial increase in the introduction of robotic process automation in back offices and shared service operations.[202]

The combination of RPA and IoT is interesting. IoT solutions produce a vast amount of data. The agent in RPA could analyze them in real time and possibly take actions if properly programmed.[203]

Ladenburg[204]

Ladenburg Thalmann Financial Services Inc. is a publicly-traded diversified financial services company based in Miami, Florida. They launched $ymbil[SM], a self-service investment platform that matches customers of Ladenburg affiliated advisors to a diversified portfolio consistent with their risk tolerance. With a minimum investment of USD 500, $ymbil allows customers to fund their accounts and start investing in a short time. $ymbil[SM] uses a proprietary scoring method to recommend portfolios in multiple risk categories. The portfolios use globally diversified asset allocations and tactical decisions to capitalize on market conditions and unique investment opportunities.

Drones

Unmanned Aerial Vehicles (UAV) or drones can help for safe operation in remote and potentially dangerous locations.[205] One of the expected applications of drones is in intralogistics processes, monitoring

[201] Sutherland, C. (2013, October). Framing a constitution for robotistan. *Hfs Research*.

[202] Willcocks, L., & Lacity, M. (2016). *Service automation, robots and the future of work*. Stratford, CT: SB Publishing.

[203] Grieco, L. A., Rizzo, A., Colucci, S., Sicari, S., Piro, G., Di Paola, D., & Boggia, G. (2014). IoT-aided robotics applications: Technological implications, target domains and open issues. *Computer Communications, 54*, 32–47.

[204] www.businesswire.com/news/home/20160321005351/en/Ladenburg-Thalmann-Launches-ymbil---Robo-Advisor-Platform. Accessed 20 August 2016.

[205] Radivojević, G. & Milosavljević, L. (2019). The Concept of Logistics 4.0. *4th Logistics International Conference*, 23–25 May. Belgrade, Serbia.

of logistics activities, and delivery of goods to end-users.[206] Drones could help in monitoring facilities, infrastructures, and equipment, inventory management, and checking incoming vehicles on receiving gates.[207]

Insurance companies could use drones.[208] They have begun experimenting with UAVs. Drones could help in the adjustment for property claims.

Drones have some exciting features which could be exploited by companies. They are small, easy to maneuver, and do not require an airport runway for launching. Thanks to these characteristics, they are much cheaper to use than human-crewed aircraft. Drones are also pretty fast, so they can move more quickly over a large geographic area than humans.

Some potential uses of drones for companies are the following ones[209]:

- Inspecting the damage to large structures, such as warehouses. One of the most common uses for drones by companies is rooftop inspections, for example, if they have suffered fire damage. An adjuster can use a drone equipped with a camera to capture very detailed images even of parts of the roof that are not accessible to a human. Allstate insurance stated that the use of drones with their customers who had storm damage was a big step forward.[210]
- In some states, laws and regulations require periodic inspections of boilers and pressure vessels. Commercial boilers can be several stories high. They are difficult to inspect because of their size and potentially dangerous interiors.
- Examining areas affected by a significant disaster, such as a flood or earthquake. These areas might be hazardous for adjusters to enter.

[206] Bamburry, D. (2015). Drones: Designed for product delivery. *Design Management Review*, *26*(1), 40–48.

[207] Kiickelhaus, M., & Chung, G. (2018). Logistics trend radar, DHL *Customer Solutions & Innovation*, Germany. www.dhl.com. Accessed 14 July 2019.

[208] www.thebalancesmb.com/how-drones-change-procurement-industry-4125242. Accessed 12 January 2020.

[209] www.thebalancesmb.com/how-drones-change-procurement-industry-4125242. Accessed 13 January 2020.

[210] Lokuge, S., & Sedera, D. (2020). *Fifty shades of digital innovation: How firms innovate with digital technologies* (Completed Research Paper).

Adjusters can use camera-equipped drones to capture still photos or videos of damaged property to process claims.

- Conducting property insurance inspections. Drones are mainly useful if the insured property is extensive or difficult to reach. A drone's camera can be equipped with special lenses to detect problems that are not visible to the human eye.
- Deterring insurance fraud. When a hurricane or other incident occurs, some policyholders file claims for damage that existed before the incident took place. Companies can disprove some claims by comparing drone camera images taken before the event with those taken after it has occurred.

The combination of more than one technology provides exciting products. Interesting solutions combine drones with artificial intelligence. Thus, it is possible to assess the damage, analyze the data, and compute repair costs.

Benefits and Challenges of Robots

A potential benefit of drones is higher customer satisfaction. Drones can take more photos in less time than a human. By using drones to capture loss data, companies can process claims more quickly, cheaper, and accurately. Quicker and more accurate claims processing, as a result of automated damage assessment, data handling and loss analysis, accelerate turnaround times and can significantly enhance customer experience. Time-consuming activities such as checking for possible fraud can be speeded up with the use of intelligent automation solutions with predictive analytics capabilities to identify and scrutinize dubious claims.

Robots can cut operating costs substantially. With the use of intelligent automation technology, it is possible to help a company reduce its data handling time by 40 percent and cut its processing costs by as much as 80 percent.[211] The dramatic improvement in processing accuracy enabled the company to step up the number of times its staff spent addressing customer needs by 43 percent.

[211] insuranceblog.accenture.com/intelligent-automation-gives-companies-a-big-opportunity-to-boost-the-quality-of-their-customer-service. Accessed 10 April 2020.

Robots also have some disadvantages and criticalities. These generally fall into three categories: special regulations, the costs of setting up a program, and the risk of third-party lawsuits.

Companies must comply with robot regulations.

- For example, FAA rules allow drones to fly during daylight hours only. Drones can fly no higher than 400 feet off the ground and no faster than 100 miles per hour. The aircraft must remain in the visual line of sight of the remote operator. The person flying the plane must have a remote pilot certificate with a small Unmanned aircraft system (UAS) rating. If the drone operator does not have such a certificate, he or she must operate under the supervision of someone who does.
- Companies will incur costs to establish a robotic program. They will need to buy or lease the robots and create internal rules governing their use.

Communication

There are big innovations in communication. The following pages consider two of them, very different from each other:

- Cloud computing;
- Augmented reality.

Cloud Computing

Cloud computing is a set of technologies that allow processing and/or storing data through the use of distributed hardware/software virtualized in the network (usually internet).[212] Customers pay for the services on a pay-per-use basis, like the provision of other utilities, such as electricity or gas. The provider fully manages the service (be it private, community, public, or hybrid). The customer needs only an access device and

[212] Nicoletti, B. (2013). *Cloud computing and financial services*. London, UK: Palgrave Macmillan (also translated in Chinese).

an internet connection. The users can access the cloud from anyplace, anytime, and on any device.

Architecture of Cloud Computing
Nist, the American standardization institute, defines cloud computing as a model to enable, via the network, the widespread access, easy, and upon request, to a shared set of configurable computing resources (e.g., networks, servers, memory, applications, services, and cybersecurity). The resources can be requested and promptly released with minimal management effort or interaction with the service partners. The Nist cloud computing model is composed of five essential characteristics, three service modes, and four deployment models.[213]

There are many types of cloud computing services. The most popular are:

- In the Software as a Service (SaaS) model, the service provider contributes with the full software suite (including the applications and their updates). The customer cannot change or modify the software but only configure it in a self-service mode. For this service, the user pays a fee based on usage or a monthly charge (that can move upwards or downwards based on usage);
- Platform as a Service (PaaS) offers an entire platform (operating system, servers, relational database, but not applications) to customers for several purposes. As with SaaS, the platform is managed and kept stable and current by the service provider. Both in-house and remote staff can access the platform. This solution enables all persons in the organization to view, edit, and share data no matter their location. Each user has the option to utilize only the services they need. These services tend to be very customizable.
- Infrastructure as a Service (laaS) is an infrastructure on-demand service with servers, storage, network components, and so on. The service provider owns the equipment and is responsible for its deployment, operations, upgrade, and maintenance.

[213]Nicoletti, B. (2013). *Cloud computing and financial services*. London, UK: Palgrave Macmillan (also translated in Chinese).

Cloud computing is expanding fast. The use of cloud computing in European organizations was around 26 percent in 2018 Large organizations use cloud computing more (56 percent of organizations with 250 or more persons) of smaller companies (23 percent of organizations with number of employees between 10 and 49).[214] There are many scopes to research this area.[215] Emerging countries have a significant interest in cloud computing. In these countries, the current infrastructure is still weak in a certain number of cases. Cloud computing can provide almost instantaneously working environments. It requires only a good telecommunication infrastructure (fixed or mobile).

With new and advanced tools like internet of things, the number of data created is enormous. In that situation, centralized computing in the cloud would increase the network costs substantially. For this reason, whenever it is possible, it is good to have some processing and storage done locally. This solution is called edge computing.[216] Edge computing allows integrating more functions into intelligent devices and gateways closer to the edge. This solution reduces latency and improves response times. By moving some of the intelligence to the edge, the local devices can generate value when there are challenges related to transferring data to the cloud. Think, for example, to vessels or to remote locations, such as in the desert, where it is necessary to use satellite communication, which is still rather expensive. There are different edge computing paradigms, such as transparent computing and fog computing, fully described in the literature.[217]

Application Areas of Cloud Computing in Insurance 4.0

Cloud computing frees companies from fixed location data centers. They combine very well with the previous technologies, based very much on the internet. For example, the reinsurance business becomes easier, thanks to cloud computing.

[214] Eurostat (2018, December), *the EU Statistical Office*.

[215] Nicoletti, B. (2013). *Cloud computing and financial services*. London, UK: Palgrave Macmillan (also translated in Chinese).

[216] Vermesan, O., & Bacquet, J. (Eds.). (2017). *Cognitive hyperconnected digital transformation: Internet of things intelligence evolution*. Gistrup, Denmark: River Publishers.

[217] Zhang, Y., Ren, J., Liu, J., Xu, C., Guo, H., & Liu, Y. (2017). A survey on emerging computing paradigms for big data. *Chinese Journal of Electronics, 26*(1), 1–12.

The additional computing power in the cloud can support more sophisticated risk modeling to improve financial planning, actuarial reserving, and risk management activities. It can enable the creation of a complete risk profile by using customer's real-time and historical data to improve productivity in the actuarial department and cut losses.

In the insurance industry, cloud computing can help manage risks and fraud. In the cloud, it is possible integrating all risk data, such as risk and control assessments, loss events, and key risk indicators within a single environment. Thus, it is possible to make better decisions about the business risk and compliance context. With cloud computing, it is possible:

- Run simulations of complex risk, interest rates, and reserve requirement without investing heavily in server farms, which would remain idle for most of their time.
- Improve sales with cloud-based analytics of customer behavior and opinions, thanks to information pushed to the mobile devices of agents.
- Measure, aggregate, and report risk-based solvency capital to regulators and other key stakeholders in a repeatable, auditable fashion.

Cloud technologies can help to identify fraud and undesirable behavior. They can also help isolate recovery opportunities throughout the claims process. It is possible to identify and mitigate claims. Some of them might have a higher likelihood of being fraudulent. Undertake this detection earlier in the lifecycle across a broader range of fraud schemes would be particularly useful. The additional computing power in the cloud can support more sophisticated risk modeling to improve financial planning, actuarial reserving, and risk management activities. It can enable the creation of a complete risk profile by using customer's real-time and historical data to improve productivity in the actuarial department and cut losses.

With cloud computing, startup companies or traditional companies in emerging markets can use proven applications and resources. This solution can lower the cost of entering new markets. Business process as a service (BPaaS) can help automate systems and workflow, standardize processes, and optimize information inputs and retrieval. The scalability and dynamic provisioning that cloud computing provides can help companies meet peak demands for actuarial and financial workloads or the computational services needed for compliance. With cloud computing, companies can ramp up quickly to handle service peaks without a significant difference in service.

The pandemic crisis could also push to move more systems and applications to the cloud. In this area, companies have lagged other sectors. With more persons working remotely, having systems in the cloud offers much greater bandwidth and capacity than if staff are accessing on-premise servers remotely. This is an opportunity for the insurance industry and could be the catalyst for this movement. Actuarial modeling software, for example, often sits on individuals' computers, as there are deemed to be security issues with putting it in the cloud. But with cloud computing this type of applications not continuous and with spike are the ideal for the cloud.[218] Security could be even more on respect to on-premise due to the high professionalism and tools that cloud processing vendors can provide.

Nationwide[219]

In the last 80 years, Nationwide has grown out of a small mutual auto insurance company owned by policyholders into one of the larger financial services companies in the USA. It has more than 38,000 employees. The headquarters are in Columbus, Ohio. This company is the number one provider of public-sector retirement plans and the seventh-largest motor insurance company in the United States. Nationwide's 3000 distributed servers were inefficient and costly. To increase business agility and reduce growing costs, Nationwide started a virtualization transition that ultimately led to cloud computing.[220] They consolidated their distributed server landscape on Linux virtual servers running on mainframes. They created a multi-platform private cloud optimized for all its various workloads. This deployment in the cloud reduced power, cooling, and floor space requirements by 80 percent. It reduced expenditure on a distributed

[218] home.kpmg/xx/en/home/insights/2020/03/do-insurers-have-covid-19-covered.html. Accessed 30 May 2020.

[219] www.nationwide.com. Accessed 30 May 2020.

[220] www.enisystems.com/eninew/latest/blue/news/IBMSystem_z_Software_Virtualization_Virtualization_Server_Smarter_Computing.pdf. Accessed 25 April 2015.

server landscape, saving an estimated USD 15 million over the first three years.

B2B Cloud

An interesting use of cloud insurance is the so-called B2B cloud computing.[221] This solution helps to address an essential aspect of insurance 4.0 the collaboration and the integration among partners, such as, for example, agents and customer organizations. This solution is attractive when:

- There is a need for frequent exchanges of information between different organizations;
- Organizations that need to cooperate are distant from a geographical point of view;
- There are standard formats for the connection of various ICT solutions.

A situation of this type allows implementing a partnership B2B outsourcing and management of an ecosystem. This situation is typical in insurance. It would greatly alleviate the insurance processes thanks to the possibility of collaboration via computers and networks.

The best solution might be, at least initially, a hybrid B2B. This solution would allow the organization to connect directly with its most essential partners. At the same time, the organization may use a B2B cloud to communicate with the remaining partners. The cloud makes it easier to build an insurance social network to improve collaboration between the partners.

Cloud insurance promotes shared collaboration and a greener environment while reducing the need for expensive equipment. It also provides other benefits in connection with the proposed architecture:

- Flexibility;
- Security and data privacy;

[221] Kim, J., & Shunk, D. (2004). Matching indirect insurance process with different B2B e-procurement systems. *Computers in Industry*, 53.

- Lower capital investment and (potentially) expense cost savings;
- Easiness of access, implementation, and usage;
- Resources elasticity and expandability (such as workforce and energy savings);
- Increased efficiency.

BIMA[222]

BIMA uses mobile technology to provide insurance services in emerging markets, which the technology permits with lower entry costs. In many countries, in Africa in particular, mobile phones are widely used not only for telecommunications, but also for accessing banking and payment services. The diffusion of mobile phones (penetration of 70 percent of the population) and the acceptance of the technology for financial assistance helped BIMA to expand its health services in 16 markets. The success of this model enabled BIMA to reach profitability in several markets. BIMA sells a range of personal insurance products, including accident, life, and hospitalization cover. The main innovation of BIMA is the creation of a proprietary back-end platform. This platform creates a tool for registration and payment. Policyholders register using their handset to fill in some identification details. This process takes approximately two minutes. Payment of the premiums takes place with an automatic deduction of prepaid airtime credit. This unlock an interesting payment channel that simplify access to insurance. A trained agent staff takes care of the distribution. BIMA agents make the initial contact with potential policyholders. They inform on the products and about all aspects of the policy, including basics like the cost (just a few cents a day) and the coverage. Post-sale, the customer will receive a confirmation SMS plus a monthly reminder of their coverage status and amount to be deducted. For claims, policyholders call customer support that will help them to file their claim forms. The claim is paid in cash within 72 hours of the completed claim.

The license of BIMA is primarily as an insurance intermediary and/or a licensed micro-insurance provider, where applicable, and not an underwriter. Data is in Sweden and is protected under Swedish data protection regulation. BIMA has raised USD 75 million in equity so far. In 2015, BIMA closed its series C funding round with USD 38 million raised from

[222] www.oecd.org/pensions/Technology-and-innovation-in-the-procurement-sector.pdf.

current investors, including Investment AB Kinnevik, LeapFrog Investments, and Millicom. This situation follows a successful B series funding of USD 22 million and USD 15 million of capital invested before these rounds.

Augmented Reality

An Augmented reality (AR) system has the following characteristics[223]:

- Combines real and virtual objects in a visual environment;
- Align real and virtual objects with each other; and
- Runs interactively, in three dimensions, and in real-time.

Augmented Reality Architecture

In virtual reality, the computer-generates a simulation of a three-dimensional image or environment. A person using special electronic equipment (usually a helmet with a screen inside, or glasses or gloves fitted with sensors) can interact in a seemingly real or physical way with this simulated environment.[224]

Application Areas of Augmented Reality in Insurance 4.0

Augmented reality (AR) solutions have the potential to change significantly how promotion of insurance services take place. A certain number of companies have started using a real-world view combined with computer-generated information.[225]

Insurance companies are exploring the capabilities of AR. They are making the first steps toward determining their key priorities and

[223] Azuma, R. T., Baillot, Y., Behringer, R., Feiner, S. K., Julier, S., Andmacintyre, B. (2001). Recent advances in augmented reality. *Computer Graphics and Applications, 21*(6), 34–47.

[224] Oxford Dictionaries online; www.oxforddictionaries.com/definition/english/virtual-reality Accessed 30 March 2020. How augmented and virtual reality are changing the. assets.kpmg/content/dam/kpmg/xx/pdf/2016/10/how-augmented-and-virtual-reality-changing-insurance-landscape.pdf. Accessed 30 April 2020.

[225] jasoren.com/how-augmented-reality-impacts-the-insurance-industry-7-use-cases-of-ar-applications/. Accessed 24 January 2020.

goals with this type of solution. Insurtech organizations cooperate with augmented reality developers to build brand new solutions that would allow them to increase the proficiency of their business.

Providing interactive user experience and ensuring both customer entertainment and engagement are some of the uses of AR in insurance 4.0. Companies can use augmented reality to alert their customers about possible dangers, estimate claim, clarify insurance plans.[226] They also use AR for marketing and brand promotion purposes. Some use cases of these solutions in the insurance industry are Australia's NRMA (National Roads and Motorists' Association) Insurance[227] and the USA's Liberty Mutual Insurance using vehicle crash and breakdown simulations.[228] Using AR, Zurich Insurance provides staff training; Axa Insurance use AR as an advertising tool.[229]

Benefits and Challenges of Augmented Reality
Augmented reality solutions can improve how companies provide their services. Providing interactive user experience and ensuring both customer entertainment and engagement are not the only AR use cases for companies. They can use augmented reality to warn their customers about dangers, estimate damage, and explain insurance plans.

Cybersecurity

Cybersecurity is relative to the organization and collection of resources, processes, and infrastructures used to protect cyberspace and cyberspace-enabled systems from occurrences of malicious attacks and impact on the

[226] Augmented reality in the insurance industry—Jasoren. jasoren.com/how-augmented-reality-impacts-the-insurance-industry-7-use-cases-of-ar-applications/. Accessed 24 January 2020.

[227] www.nrma.com.au/. Accessed 5 April 2020. Augmented reality in the insurance industry—Jasoren. jasoren.com/how-augmented-reality-impacts-the-insurance-industry-7-use-cases-of-ar-applications/. Accessed 30 April 2020.

[228] assets.kpmg/content/dam/kpmg/xx/pdf/2016/10/how-augmented-and-virtual-reality-changing-insurance-landscape.pdf. Accessed 5 April 2020.

[229] www.businessfirstonline.co.uk/other-articles/liberty-it-launches-new-augmented-reality-game/. Accessed 5 April 2020.

property rights.[230] Fewer organizations rely on management and operations systems that are unconnected or stand alone.[231] In insurance 4.0, there are robust connections between several systems, which tend to make the system more fragile. This situation makes it more difficult the data protection in the various processes that the organization holds either internally or externally. As a result, secure and reliable communications, sophisticated identity, and access management of machines and users are essential.[232]

A UK government survey estimated that in 2014, 81 percent of large corporations and 60 percent of small businesses suffered a cyber-security breach. The average cost of a cyber security breach is GBP 600 k-GBP 1.15 m for large businesses and GBP 65 k-115 k for small- and medium-sized companies.[233]

The type, number, and specificity of data collected from billions of devices through the IoT and big data create concern among users regarding their privacy and between organizations about the confidentiality and integrity of their data.[234] Solutions must provide transparency on what data is used and how, and ensure they are adequately protected. Some organizations sign contracts with partners that offer products (such as IoT) without realizing that the organizations are authorizing the use of their data for commercial purposes by third parties.

[230] Craigen, D., Diakun-Thibault, N., & Purse, R. (2014). Defining cybersecurity. *Technology Innovation Management Review*, *4*(10).

[231] Lezzi, M., Lazoi, M., & Corallo, A. (2018). Cybersecurity for Industry 4.0 in the current literature: *A reference framework. Computers in Industry, 103,* 97–110. Rübmann, M., Lorenz, M., Gerbert, P., Waldner, M., Justus, J., Engel, P., & Harnisch, M. (2015). Industry 4.0: the future of productivity and growth in manufacturing industry. *Boston Consulting Group (BCG) Report.*

[232] Rodrigues, M., Sousa, B., & da Costa, J. B. (2019). The improvement of the supply chain channel based on digital transformation: An exploratory study in the Sustainable Industry 4.0 *4th Regional Helix- Book of Abstracts* Parallel Session 4, Porto, Portugal.

[233] www.abi.org.uk/Insurance-and-savings/Products/Business-insurance/Cyber-risk-insurance. Accessed 20 April 2020.

[234] Kozlov, D., Veijalainen, J., & Ali, Y. (2012, February). Security and privacy threats in IoT architectures. In *Proceedings of the 7th International Conference on Body Area Networks, 256–262. ICST (Institute for Computer Sciences, Social-Informatics and Telecommunications Engineering).*

Cybersecurity Architecture

Cybersecurity is a big problem with insurance 4.0. For example, organizations that collect data from billions of devices using IoT must be able to protect such data from unauthorized access. They also face new categories of risks that the internet of things can introduce. These types of platforms create significant dangers of cyber-attacks.

Application Areas of Cybersecurity in Insurance 4.0

Stephens and Valverde (2013) researches demonstrate the growing importance of security in insurance, mainly concerning several virtual information flows and automated transactions.[235] There is a concern for cybersecurity in insurance 4.0 overall and possible risks for organizations in cases of a malicious attack.[236] It is critical to extend the developments of security and related security systems within insurance 4.0. It is necessary to use a standard approach and include all insurance stakeholders. It is critical to create standard solutions and systems to secure a value network ecosystems against external violence[237] or internal attacks.

Insurance companies started to introduce new solutions using advanced digital monitoring.[238] Some examples are GPS based motor insurance (e.g., Unibox[239] in Italy and insurethebox[240] in the UK). Other exciting initiatives are relative to various forms of regular monitoring regarding lifestyle in the health insurance sector (e.g., "Generali

[235] Stephens, J., & Valverde, R. (2013). Security of e-procurement transactions in supply chain reengineering. *Computer and Information Science, 6*(3), 1–20.

[236] Barron, S., Cho, Y. M., Hua, A., Norcross, W., Voigt, J., & Haimes, Y. (2016, June 10). Systems-based cybersecurity in the supply chain. *IEEE Systems and Information Engineering Design Symposium (SIEDS)*, 20–25.

[237] Johnson, T.A. (2013). *Cybersecurity: Protecting Critical Infrastructures from Cyber Attack and Cyber Warfare*, CRC Press, Boca Raton, FL.

[238] Albrecher, H., Bommier, A., Filipović, D., Koch-Medina, P., Loisel, S., & Schmeiser, H. (2019). Insurance: Models, digitization, and data science. *European Actuarial Journal, 9*(2), 349–360.

[239] www.unipolsai.it/unibox-auto. Accessed 30 May 2020.

[240] www.insurethebox.com/. Accessed 30 May 2020.

Vitality"[241] or "Dacadoo"[242]). In some other cases, they are on-demand-insurance contracts using only a digital sales and approval process (e.g., "Lings"[243] or "Trov"[244]). These concepts can help to decrease the effects of adverse selection and moral hazard. In particular, a reduction of agency costs is possible via self-selection by the policyholders. The technology allows for real-time hints and incentives for loss-prevention. It is possible to escape transaction costs, and specific types of ex-post moral hazard (e.g., insurance fraud) with the help of new forms of digital monitoring. Insurance companies must evaluate if they need to execute awareness campaigns on cybersecurity also with their customers.

Insurtech organizations support the introduction and improvement of new products. Insurance for cyber risks would be an example.[245]

Benefits and Challenges of Cybersecurity

For criminals, the new platforms, and mainly the internet of things, represent an interesting opportunity with plenty of poorly protected devices to commit identity theft and infiltration in the ICT systems of the organizations. It is critical to defend access to these devices. Organizations have limited experiences and tools to detect or fix these types of attacks.[246]

In connection with the use of these advanced solutions to control the physical activity, whether it be in offices or vehicles, the consequences related to a security breach go beyond even the unauthorized release of information. They may cause catastrophes. The first malicious campaign, based on IoT as its driver, saw more than 750,000 phishing

[241] Eling, M., & Kraft, M. (2020). The impact of telematics on the insurability of risks. *The Journal of Risk Finance.*

[242] Bayındır, L. (2017). A survey of people-centric sensing studies utilizing mobile phone sensors. *Journal of Ambient Intelligence and Smart Environments, 9*(4), 421–448.

[243] Albrecher, H., Bommier, A., Filipović, D., Koch-Medina, P., Loisel, S., & Schmeiser, H. (2019). Insurance: Models, digitalization, and data science. *European Actuarial Journal, 9*(2), 349–360.

[244] Yan, T. C., Schulte, P., & Chuen, D. L. K. (2018). InsurTech and FinTech: Banking and insurance enablement. In *Handbook of blockchain, digital finance, and inclusion* (Vol. 1, pp. 249–281). Cambridge, MA: Academic Press.

[245] Klahr, R. (2017). *Cyber security breaches survey.* Doctoral dissertation, University of Portsmouth, Portsmouth, UK.

[246] Atzei, N., Bartoletti, M., & Cimoli, T. (2017, April). A survey of attacks on Ethereum smart contracts (sok). In *International Conference on Principles of Security and Trust* (pp. 164–186). Berlin/Heidelberg, Germany: Springer.

and spam emails launched from 100,000 everyday objects. The cyber-attack, detected by Proofpoint, a provider that operates in security as a service, occurred between 23 December 2013 and 6 January 2014. There were several waves of malicious emails intended for businesses and individuals of all the world.[247] The news of this attack went quickly around the globe. It has created an alert on the use of new technologies. The forecast is that IoT devices will grow more than four times the number of connected computers. Their weak points in security can have a significant impact on the business and the goals of the organizations.

Cybersecurity is also relevant for insurance companies as a new product to offer to the market. Cyber risk insurance is relative to the losses relating to damage to, or loss of information from, information and communication technology (ICT) systems and networks.[248] Cyber risk policies can include substantial assistance and management of the incident itself. This is essential when there are possible or real reputational damage or regulatory enforcement. Even more, it is critical before executing the policy a thorough examination of the cybersecurity systems of the customer. Eventually, in the future, such an assessment could become part of the (chargeable) services provided by the companies to their customers on cybersecurity.

Data Privacy[249]

Data security and data privacy is a significant concern with the use of advanced platforms. Transferring data to the insurer can perform disadvantages to policyholders in other insurance segments and areas outside the insurance market. Reports on new concepts of digital monitoring are negative (with reputational effects on the insurance business). Persons tend to assume that insurance companies aim only to focus on profitable and low-risk customer groups and do not want to provide insurance for others. To manage these aspects and to avoid reputational risks, companies could stick to a self-compliance framework and define which data to use for which scope. They should limit their risk classification and pricing

[247] www.proofpoint.com/us/proofpoint-uncovers-internet-things-iot-cyberattack. Accessed 30 March 2019.

[248] What are the different types of Losses Covered. *SecureNow*. securenow.in/insuropedia/what-are-different-types-losses-covered-cyber-risk-insurance/. Accessed 30 May 2020.

[249] iotinsobs.com/. Accessed 11 December 2019.

factors to specific criteria only. This situation would mean that personal, and especially, sensitive information could not be collected or used by providers of insurance products. Data protection is, in particular in the health sector, a central issue. Genomic data pose sensitive privacy problems.[250] This type of data is inherently able to identify a person cannot be changed, have unique statistical regularities, contain sensitive and personal information to individuals and their relatives. As a consequence, their theft or loss can expose individuals to discrimination. A cooperation of five Swiss research groups across the ETH university in Zurich, including the Swiss Data Science Center has been formed for a "Data Protection for Personalized Health (DPPH)".[251] The central goals of the research lab are to:

- Address the main privacy, security, scalability, and ethical tasks of data for allowing effective P4 (predictive, preventative, personalized, participatory) medicine;
- Define an ideal balance between usability, scalability, and data protection; and
- Evaluate a suitable set of computing tools.

The compliance scenario for data privacy is getting clearer. In Europe, the regulations to monitor are the General Data Privacy Regulation ("GDPR"), the Personal Data Privacy Regulation, and the European Data Protection Regulation.[252] In the USA, The California Consumer Privacy Act (CCPA) allows enforcing actions since July 1, 2020.[253]

The European regulation on data protection, which came into force on 25 May 2016, had and will have a relevant impact on the insurance

[250] Naveed, M., Ayday, E., Clayton, E. W., Fellay, J., Gunter, C. A., Hubaux, J. P., & Wang, X. (2015). Privacy in the genomic era. *ACM Computing Surveys (CSUR), 48*(1), 1–44.

[251] labdpph.ch. Accessed 19 March 2020.

[252] Carey, P. (2018). *Data protection: A practical guide to UK and EU law*. Oxford, UK: Oxford University Press.

[253] oag.ca.gov/privacy/ccpa#:~:text=The%20California%20Consumer%20Privacy%20Act,that.%20is%20collected%20by%20businesses.&text=The%20Attorney%20General%20cannot%20bring,CCPA%20until%20July%201%2C%202020. Accessed 1 July 2020.

industry. It aims to strengthen customer rights and provides for substantial penalties for those who break the rules.[254] The European regulation sets standard rules on the right of customers to know who has access to their personal data and how and why they are used. The users have more control over the data. Companies can no longer use data based on tacit consent. They must ask the customer's explicit consent. Companies need to tell from what sources they got personal information, who and for what purpose will have access to this information, and what is the legal basis for legitimizing the use of these data.[255]

A Gartner report states that by 2022, 70 percent of privacy breaches depend on a lack of privacy engineering.[256] To protect the personal information stored, transmitted, or simply accessed through smart devices, vendors and companies must use encrypted data. The National Association of Insurance Commissioners stated the following[257]:

> The increasing use of smart devices does present several risks and challenges for companies. As smart applications are becoming more ubiquitous, more opportunities for cybercriminals and fraudsters open up. With data transferred back and forth from system to system, the risk of interception increases. New smart products may also lead to new types of applications and claims fraud. As a result, IoT may require an expansion in data security and fraud protection. Additionally, data privacy is a key concern. The European Union's recent GDPR and the State of California CCPA impose enhanced data protection obligations on companies who process or store data.

[254] Ponce de León, M. (2018, May 20). Protección de datos: las aseguradoras apuran el plazo de adaptación a las nuevas exigencias. www.expansion.com/empresas/2018/05/20/5b01966e22601db97f8b4613.html. Accessed 3 March 2020. European data protection: Impact of the EU data-protection. voxeu.org/article/european-data-protection-impact-eu-data-protection-regulation. Accessed 30 April 2020.

[255] EU Data Protection Rules. ec.europa.eu/info/priorities/justice-and-fundamental-rights/data-protection/2018-reform-eu-data-protection-rules/eu-data-protection-rules_en. Accessed 14 March 2020. ec.europa.eu/commission/priorities/justice-and-fundamental-rights/dataprotection/2018-reform-eu-data-protection-rules_es. Accessed 14 March 2020.

[256] www.gartner.com/en/documents/3877564/build-for-privacy. Accessed 3 March 2020.

[257] www.slideshare.net/matteocarbone/smart-home-procurement-144438351. Accessed 14 March 2020. Smart Home Insurance. www.slideshare.net/matteocarbone/smart-home-insurance-144438351. Accessed 30 April 2020.

Insurance companies should recognize the relevance of gaining and maintaining customers' trust. Maintaining customers' personal data confidential should be a top priority for all company employees and intermediaries. Data security is very essential as data transparency. Consequently, the collection, use, and disclosure of data must be compliant at all times with all applicable laws and regulations relative to data privacy, data security, data governance, and the protection of personal data.[258]

Insurance 4.0 and Platform Solutions

It is interesting to report the results of some experiments on these new solutions in insurance 4.0, even if in an industrial sector different from insurance.[259] From the point of view of monetized benefits, in some applications, it is estimated the possibility of reducing over 37 percent of the number of employees. The results were considered in two different perspectives: organizational and in processes.[260] The organizational analysis allows sharing the benefits between the back-office categories, middle-office, and front-office.[261] The analysis shows that the most significant impacts in savings is 89 percent and occurr in the back office. The sector examined is mainly characterized by repetitive and standardized activities that corresponds well to insurance 4.0 solutions such as Robotic Process Automation. The activities in the front-office need higher creativity and relational capabilities. They allow savings of just 7 percent of the staff. Finally, the middle-office could bring a saving of 75 percent of the staff.

The benefits in the processes can be divided into the strategic, tactical, and transactional activities. In some cases, the results are in line with the

[258] Burdon, M. (2020). *Digital data collection and information privacy law*. Cambridge, UK: Cambridge University Press.

[259] www.digital4.biz/insurance/strategie/insurance-4-0-la-check-list-lufficio-acquisti-digitale/. Accessed 9 March 2019.

[260] www.digital4.biz/insurance/strategie/insurance-4-0-la-check-list-lufficio-acquisti-digitale/. Accessed 9 March 2019.

[261] Perona, M. (2019). insurance 4.0, the check list for Purchasing Digital. www.digital4.biz/procurement/ufficio-acquisti-digitale-cose-quali-benefici-del-insurance-4-0/. Accessed 9 March 2019.

findings at the organizational level.[262] A transactional level application is significant enough to generate savings of 90 percent of the current job content. This level includes all routine and repetitive activities based on the adoption of analytics solutions. At the tactical level, the analysis shows a reduction of 36 percent in total employment. Finally, the strategic level could bring a saving of 24 percent of the total, showing a less effective response.

The projects of insurance 4.0 bring tangible benefits, mainly in flexibility and cost reduction. The main benefits declared by the organizations with projects, that have been active for over a year, are the improved operational flexibility (47 percent), the increase in plant efficiency (38 percent), the reduction in design times (34 percent) and the opportunity to develop innovative products (33 percent).[263] The challenges, most perceived by organizations in the development of insurance 4.0 applications, are the difficulties in the use of new technologies and the adoption of standards (59 percent), organizational issues and competencies management (41 percent), change management difficulties (20 percent), and dissatisfaction with the current solutions available in the market (17 percent).

These results refer to one implementation in a large organization. They demonstrate the benefits potentially associated with the insurance 4.0. The maximum potential savings have been achieved with the RPA technology applied to the activities with lower intellectual content or relational. The benefits can be got in those transactional and execution types activities, typically belonging to the back-office or at the middle-office. The activities with the largest intensity of relationship or that require higher intellectual contribution, usually of a strategic type and concentrated in the front-office, are expected to provide potentially fewer benefits with the introduction of insurance 4.0 solutions. In this case, it is more challenging to replace human labor with the solutions presented in this chapter.

The non-financial benefits are made up of quality increases due to increased accuracy of processes and better results. With the platforms discussed in this chapter, the organizations can analyze a sample of data

[262] www.digital4.biz/insurance/strategie/insurance-4-0-la-check-list-lufficio-acquisti-digitale/. Accessed 9 March 2019.

[263] www.digital4.biz/insurance/strategie/insurance-4-0-la-check-list-lufficio-acquisti-digitale/. Accessed 9 March 2019.

much larger and define a more accurate resulting confidence interval. The solutions considered in this chapter can improve the compliance and consistency of the organization's activities to the regulations, procedures, and codes of conduct. This is possible thanks to codified and standardized processes. It is potentially possible to minimize the likelihood of errors in the execution of activities and/or of non-compliance to the internal procedures.

A challenge with the introduction of insurance 4.0 is the use of advanced platforms.[264] Results of this type are due to the backwardness in the technologies used in support of the insurance in many small- and medium-sized insurance companies (SMEs). The reason, in this case, is mainly due to the persistence of the traditional functional organization prevalent in the SMEs. Another reason for the fact that still few SMEs adopt insurance 4.0 platforms internally is due to the availability in the market of solutions mainly suited to large organizations. These solutions are expensive, complex, and of no immediate use. SMEs would need cheap and easy to implement and use platforms (that would allow the organizations to manage their business and the primary activities of the insurance cycle). From this point of view, cloud computing offers exciting possibilities for a more widespread use of these solutions. Cloud computing makes simple the acquisition and implementation, activation, and management of new advanced solutions.

Conclusions

This chapter considers the leading platforms that support insurance 4.0. The list is not exhaustive and it is dynamic. Over time, new solutions will be introduced. The greatest successes come with a combination of more than one technology. The examples are several. Think about the mobile phone or smartphone. It is a combination of a telephone with a computer. This rule also applies for insurance 4.0. Thanks to the combination of information technology with automation technologies, insurance 4.0 can bring big benefits, but also challenges, such as cybersecurity.

Insurance 4.0 is the integration of the analog and digital worlds with new technologies that enhance customer interaction, data availability,

[264] www.logisticaefficiente.it/procout/supplychain/approvvigionamenti/maturita-insurance-italia-europa-risultati-parte-1.html. Accessed 10 March 2019.

and business processes.[265] The new platforms are also in the fields of data acquisition and analysis (artificial intelligence, big data, internet of things), data storage and processing (blockchain, cloud computing) and communication (apps, chatbots, robo-advisor, web pages, social networks, messenger, video calls, and video platforms).

Platform solutions are robust tools that open up many possibilities for insurance and reinsurance companies. The traditional insurance and reinsurance model suffer from various common problems; fraud, expensive premiums, claim denials, complex procedures (involving many parties), lack of data about the policyholder's history. This situation leads to unsuitable offers, costly unnecessary procedures, and delay in the claim payout. This latter point is particularly damaging for the image of insurance companies.

The different use cases reported in this chapter underlines the possibility with insurance 4.0 of significant procedure cuts (automated, coupled with smart contracts, IoT). The adoption of these solutions enables record-keeping, real-time tracking, data sharing, simplification of interactions between several parties, KYC optimization, speeding processes, facilitating audit, and improved risk assessment.

There is interest from big companies to invest in platform solutions. Market competitors are pushing to tackle the technology better, working with startups, to evolve, and be at pace.

Some companies can obtain significant cost cuts. Bearing in mind the competitive market, these companies can use the reduction of costs to decrease their premiums. It will soon be a mandatory *crawling-effect* to be able to catch up and survive during this shift. It will undoubtedly not happen overnight. Insurance ecosystems are getting stronger, involving more companies not only in Japan, USA and Europe but in the rest of the world as well, with platform solutions consortiums. They will reinforce the relationship of the different actors of the sector (companies, reinsurers, intermediaries). It has a potential impact on the market as a whole by changing the working paradigms and establishing collaborative ecosystems. Platform solutions can transform the whole value network of the insurance and reinsurance parties.

[265] Eling, M., & Lehmann, M. (2018). The impact of digitalization on the insurance value chain and the insurability of risks. *The Geneva Papers on Risk and Insurance-Issues and Practice, 43*(3), 359–396.

The adoption of these platforms requires further automation and integration. Persons and assets are more connected. The question is if the society is ready to shift and give up much personal information to companies? Data sharing is a focal and sour point due to data privacy.

The shift to the platforms presented is challenging also in big well-established companies. It requires significant adjustments and reorganization within the company.

CHAPTER 9

Processes in Insurance 4.0

Introduction

The global recession has hit, and it is hitting hard. It impacts all the main functions of the organizations in every industry. Under this scenario, insurance management should consider four main priorities:

- Attention to the effectiveness, efficiency, and economics of the insurance processes;
- Willingness to invest in improving the competencies and capabilities of the staff in all the insurance functions;
- Ability to analyze and better manage the available data; and
- Capability to strengthen and improve collaboration and partnerships.

In defining processes for insurance 4.0, it is critical to take the following principles into account[1]:

- Modeling: The focus is on making processes adaptive and easily configurable so they could evolve quickly rather than according to rigidly defined or controlled procedures;

[1] Baiyere, A., Salmela, H., & Tapanainen, T. (2020). Digital transformation and the new logics of business process management. *European Journal of Information Systems*, 1–22.

B. Nicoletti, *Insurance 4.0*, Palgrave Studies in Financial Services Technology, https://doi.org/10.1007/978-3-030-58426-9_9

- Infrastructural logic: The emphasis is on an infrastructure's capability to transform to accommodate continuous change requests rather than being a pre-mapped infrastructure;
- Agential logic: Actors should take decisions in ambiguous situations with effective supports. The emphasis is on swift reaction and response in engaging with challenges or opportunities.

The processes of future companies will be data-driven and real-time. Insurance is about information and not about goods. Data are at the basis of the information on the insured asset. For companies, it is critical to have adequate processes and tools to collect, secure, manage, and analyze them to take strategic action. This transformation requires a structured approach to measuring the value created, systematically monitoring the measurements of the value added, and using a solid methodologys. Insurance 4.0 products require a constant process of monitoring and fine-tuning.

Companies in the future will be able to sense, understand, and act in real-time on value creation mechanisms. The ability to work on real-time data will support the prevention of casualties and mitigating risk in the assets or the health of the policyholders.

Insurance is usually the coverage of a physical asset or a person. Smart sensors should provide relevance, convenience, and a sense of security for the policyholders. This reason justifies why processes should connect to an ecosystem of services for monitoring. There are three key moments in this process:

- Installation, connection, and management of the monitoring devices;
- Actions to prevent and mitigate accidents; and
- Service partner support.

Companies' desire to proactively prevent or mitigate losses, with the support of data from digital devices, requires the certainty of timely and accurate data. The higher the ambition of value creation, the higher the necessity of a guaranteed and reliable data flow. This situation requires certainty of the correct installation of devices, proper connection, and effective operations during the insured period.

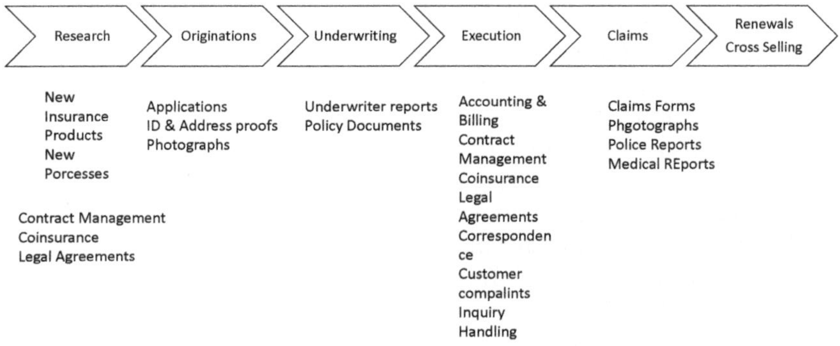

Fig. 9.1 Insurance processes

The more a company promises its customers, the more robust its processes must be in such a way to be able keep the promises. Prevention and mitigation require concrete actions to show alerts or messages on a digital front end. This solution requires sophisticated processes and persons in the field who can act in a timely way and partner effectively and effecitvely for prevention or remediation.

With this approach, for example, American Family is developing a robust ecosystem that is shaping its smart home insurance platform.[2] Understanding individual customer needs, providing complimentary or otherwise discounted smart devices, and integrated brick & mortar services for homeowners are only the start of ways to implement new processes to add value to the customers.

Basic Insurance Processes

This chapter deals with another component of the business model canvas. It is relative to the key processes and activities, which include a multiplicity of aspects and elements that should perform a proper analysis (Fig. 9.1).

Product Development Process

A process, without which an organization cannot exist, is the development of the products that the company should and would like to sell. For the

[2] www.slideshare.net/matteocarbone/smart-home-insurance-144438351. Accessed 30 May 2020.

insurance organizations that cover various dimensions, normative environments, and countries, the process of product development expresses the strategy of the company, the proposal of value, and the competitiveness position. It deals with a creative and interdisciplinary activity that turns an opportunity of market and technical ability into products that respond to the distribution and demands of the customers. At the same time, these products should add value to the company.

The most effective organizations are the organizations that complete most product development efforts in a short time, from idea generation to the launch of the products.[3]

The organizations aim to become more agile, and the innovation accelerates for being in sync with markets in continuous evolution, normative standards, and long-term growths. The results of product development are crucial for the sustainability of the organizations.

A survey of North American life insurance organizations shows that the insurance companies' strategies differ according to some organizational parameters, such as size, life, annuity, and region.[4] Several companies have specified their product development strategies (low-cost leadership, niche market leadership, or broad market leadership) reacting quickly to market changes.

Marketing

In insurance, marketing has a crucial role to satisfying the offer and the demand because the insurance products are intangible, and they exist only in the form of promises.[5] To sell a promise requires trust, a view that the buyer of the services will realize if an accident takes place.

Four core components (4Ps or marketing mix): product, price, place (distribution), and promotion, comprise marketing[6]:

[3] www.rgare.com/docs/default-source/newsletters-articles/understanding-product-development-overview.pdf?sfvrsn=d29da788_0. Accessed 30 May 2020.

[4] www.aberdeenstandard.com/docs?editionId=6a779e3b-5f1e-4c6a-96ab-7205d148ab60. Accessed 30 March 2020.

[5] Zekaj, B. (2016). Marketing in insurance industry, marketing functions in insurance industry. *European Journal of Multidisciplinary Studies, 1*(5), 33–39.

[6] Borden, N. H. (1965). The concept of the marketing mix. In G. Schwartz (Ed.), *Science in marketing* (pp. 386–397). New York and Hoboken, NJ: John Wiley.

- The first product is insurance, but other products could be connected: investments, services, prevention, and so on. Most companies do not sell single products. Companies tend to sell product lines or brands. They are all interconnected in the mind of the customers[7];
- The most critical component in the insurance market is the price of the service or product offered by the insurer;
- Place or distribution of insurance products can be through either direct and/or indirect channels. The former is the case of insurance selling directly to the end customer. The latter is selling through intermediaries;
- Promotion is a process of communication between providers and customers to create a definite belief in the buyers for products and services offered by the insurance company. Promotion is a continual process of communication by insurance providers for current and potential customers. According to Kotler, promotion includes all the tools of the marketing system, whose task is to communicate with potential buyers.[8] Organizations with the highest ratings and working traditions will undoubtedly have the normally a better position for the sale of their products. If this organization does not have adequate communication with customers, it will miss the sale of insurance products.[9]

There are other relevant aspects apart from the four Ps. They are described in specialized books.[10]

[7] A Review of Marketing Mix: 4Ps or More? pdf. 123doc.net/document/1151536-a-review-of-marketing-mix-4ps-or-more-pdf.htm. Accessed 5 May 2020.

[8] Zekaj, B. (2016). Marketing in insurance industry, marketing functions in insurance industry. *European Journal of Multidisciplinary Studies, 1*(5), 33–39.

[9] Zekaj, B. (2016). Marketing in insurance industry, marketing functions in insurance industry. *European Journal of Multidisciplinary Studies, 1*(5), 33–39.

[10] Goi, C. L. (2009). A review of marketing mix: 4Ps or more? *International Journal of Marketing Studies, 1*(1), 2; Möller, K. (2006). The marketing mix revisited: Towards the 21st century marketing by E. Constantinides. *Journal of Marketing Management,* 22(3), 439–450; Fakeideas. (2008). *Revision: Reviewing the marketing mix*. fakeideas.co.uk/2008/03/07/revision-reviewing-the-marketing-mix. Accessed 30 March 2020.

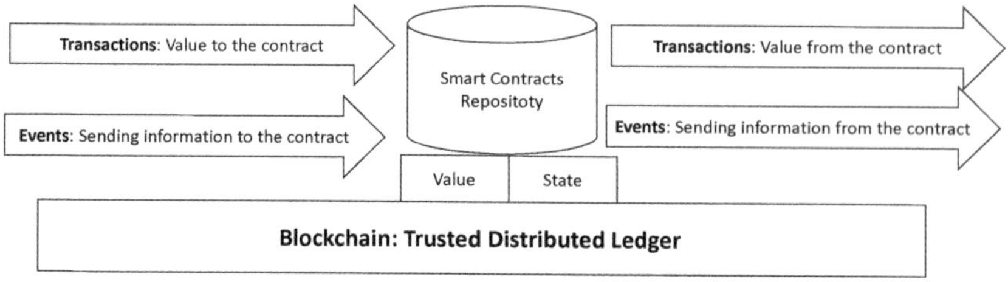

Fig. 9.2 Schema for smart contracts

Contracts Life Cycle

An insurance process often neglected is the Contract Lifecycle Management (CLM). This process is the proactive management of a contract from its creation to its renewal or termination. The implementation of an effective CLM can lead to significant improvements in savings, efficiency, and customer satisfaction. Understanding and automating the CLM can also limit the exposure to litigation and improve compliance with legal requirements.

The CLM process can be managed in insurance 4.0 using the support of commercial software, available and robust. The contract management software is a program or a set of programs related to the storage and management of legal agreements with partners or customers, such as contracts, leases, and license agreements. A contract management software's relevant objective is to simplify the contract administration and reduce the workload by providing a single, unified view of processes and documentation associated with each contract.[11]

Smart Contracts

One of the most exciting implementations of blockchain solutions is the so-called intelligent or smart contract. This solution aims to make contracts "live" with the automatic application of some specific contractual provisions for self-execution in a blockchain solution (Fig. 9.2). In the context of insurance 4.0, these programs can be self-executing intelligent contracts that manage the flows of funds based on the automatic

[11] searcherp.techtarget.com/definition/contract-management-software. Accessed 30 April 2020.

application of the contract terms. Thus, it is possible to apply effectively, efficiently, economically, and ethically (that is correct) contractual arrangements through a digital application. Potentially, there would be no need for human involvement for the execution of an agreement. It is possible to develop contracts which algorithmically enforce the rules of the transaction independently. All interactions related, for example, to the payment of a claim in parametric insurance, can be automated according to fixed rules and agreements.

Smart Contracts Alliance lists 12 smart contact use cases (Table 9.1)[12]:

- Digital Identity: controlling the access and action of the individuals;
- Records: for storing digitized filing, enabling auto-renewal and release processes;
- Securities: enabling automated payments of dividends and removing operational risks;
- Trade Finance: faster approvals and payment initiation;
- Derivatives: enforcing a standard set of rules and conditions for a transaction;
- Elimination of duplicate recording and verification processes of each party;
- Financial Data Recording: resulting in the uniform, accurate, transparent recording of financial data;
- Mortgages: enabling automated payment processing and release of a mortgage;
- Land Title Recording: deterring fraud and transparency of property transfers;
- Supply Chain: providing reliable tracking of the goods from the factory to the store;
- Clinical Trials: increasing visibility while preserving privacy;
- Cancer Research: improving data sharing across sectors while maintaining patient privacy.

The potential savings could be significant. A smart contract allows a reduction of the administration costs, the reconciliation, and the elimination, or at least decrease, of the potential errors. It would be possible to reduce the risks

[12] Gatteschi, V., Lamberti, F., Demartini, C., Pranteda, C., & Santamaría, V. (2018). *Blockchain and smart contracts for insurance: Is the technology mature enough?*

Table 9.1 Smart contract applications in insurance 4.0

Field	*Application*
Claims management	The smart contract will allow complete automation of the complaints' payment procedure and thus shortening of the payment periods for the insured. Instead of reaching several weeks to several months to be compensated, customers will be reimbursed almost instantly. Using the smart contract is relevant in the case of socalled "parametric" risks in which the measurement of a specific and tangible event can automatically generate compensation to the insured. This is the case for meteorological risks for example: in these cases, the payment is activated by foreseeable natural disasters (wind speed, the location of a hurricane, and magnitude of an earthquake ...)
Parametric insurance	Using the smart contract is relevant in the case of socalled "parametric" risks in which the measurement of a specific and tangible event can automatically generate compensation to the insured. This is the case for meteorological risks for example: in these cases, the payment is activated by foreseeable natural disasters (wind speed, the location of a hurricane, and magnitude (wind speed, the location of a hurricane, and magnitude of an earthquake ...)
Connected objects	The deployment of connected objects in our daily life (cars, home ...) is at the origin of the development of new insurance products based on the smart contract. The placement of sensors at homes makes it possible to measure the losses (pipeline breaks, power failure or device failure) and send this information to the smart contract, which triggers an automatic compensation
Peer to Peer insurance	The peer-to-peer defines a computer network model that is peer-to-peer between computers that distribute and receive data. In this network, comparable to the client-server network, ach client becomes a server. The peer-to-peer allows multiple computers to communicate with each other over a network
Policy management	In China, two companies (Ant Financial and Blue Cross) are handling the claim coronavirus via blockchain platforms, it offers a proven evidence of how the digital transformation is able to support companies in the management of new challenges, including health-related
Pandeia and epidemia	Use of blochchain solutions for health coverage, business and travel, as such forms of protection well be reconciled with the use of blockchain system and parametric nature instruments (ie in which the compensation is paid on the basis of the trend of indices/objective parameters)

(continued)

Table 9.1 (continued)

Field	*Application*
Policy management	The use of blockchain technology and smart contract streamlines the process of issuing and management of policies and makes fast and reliable the assessment of damages to policyholders. In addition, for the verification of the event of the accident, for example, using third-party sources, and certified public that allow you to open the practice of liquidation and will automatically be redeemed upon the occurrence of certain events (such as flight delay in the trip covers or severe weather events in the covers). In this way the consumer will not have to deal with all the bureaucratic steps for the claims report, the recognition of the damage and the amount of the amount will automatically be credited
Adjustment of insurance premiums	One potential application is for the automatic adjustment of the insurance premium to the conduct of the policyholder. By linking other of technologies with the Internet of Things, this is, for example, for the car insurance possible. The car can record the driving style of the policyholder about telemetric sensors. Via the Internet-based connectivity object[1] the recognized and recorded data driving style can be forwarded via the Internet to the insurer then. The preprogrammed Smart Contract can process the received data and automatically adapt the insurance premium to the policyholder in the event of a risky or low-risk driving style [2]. A "personalized" premium adjustment is possible also in the United assurance of ships. About GPS location of the transport means can be communicated to the insurer. the ship is in a dangerous place, such as in an area at high risk of piracy (as off the coast of Somalia in the Horn of Africa) [1] That send data from the Internet and receive objects [2] Djazayeri, A. (2016, December). Rechtliche Herausforderungen durch Smart Contracts. *jurisPR-BKR Anm*, 1, 4

and disputes related to contractual relationships. Smart contracts, with the support of a blockchain solution, could provide retrieval modes of information and agreements to handle claims in a transparent manner, responsive, and irrefutable. Contracts and complaints may be recorded on a blockchain solution and validated by this solution, ensuring the payment of only valid claims[13] (Fig. 9.3[14]).

[13] Deloitte. (2016). Blockchain: Democratized confidence in *tech trends 2016*: Innovating in the digital age.

[14] Adapted by the author from *Blockchain solution and its potential in taxes*, Deloitte (2017).

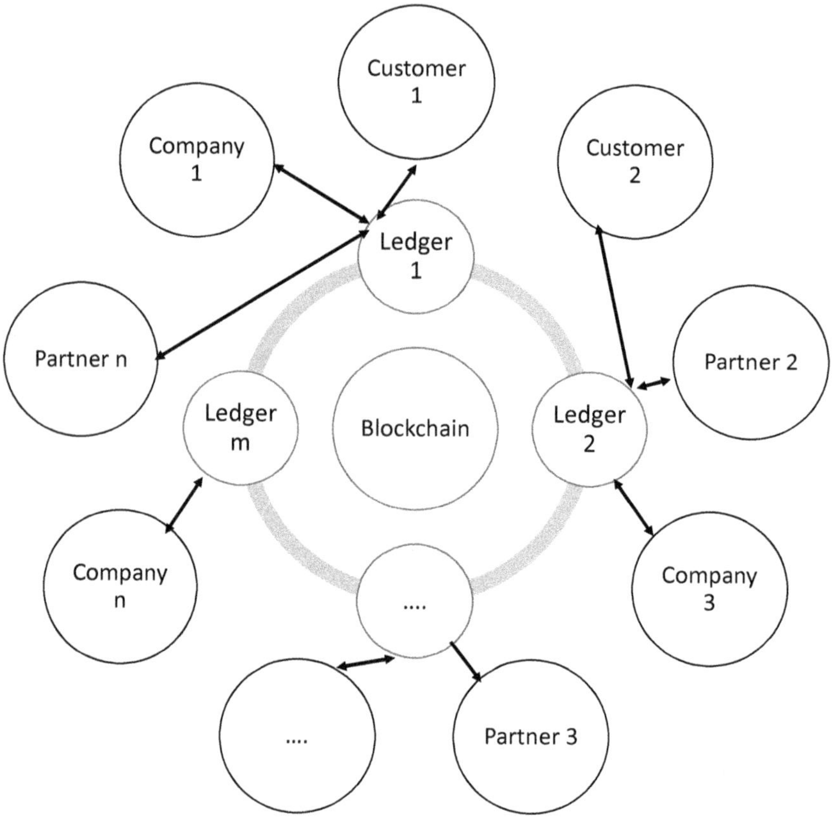

Fig. 9.3 Blockchain framework for insurance

A smart contract ceases to be a static document filed on a server computer.[15] The contract manages itself. The contract could become empowered to execute contractual agreements throughout the life of the contract. A smart contract, as an object, will know things about itself.[16] It will know its economic value. A contract management software's relevant objective is to simplify the contract administration and reduce the

[15] Chesebro, R. (2015). *A contract which managed itself*. Working Paper. University Fort Belvoir, VA.

[16] Morabito, V. (2017). *Business innovation through blockchain: The B3 perspective* (pp. 101–124). Cham, Switzerland: Springer.

workload by providing a single, unified view of processes and documentation associated with each contract. With further developments in smart contracts, the contract would be able to interact with other objects. This solution would allow all stakeholders to learn from the same source movements of funds between customers, partners, and financial institutions, and when funds need to be released. If a problem occurs, such as unspent funds with the contractor, which is no longer in business, the contract would know how to handle an event of this or similar type.[17]

Wekeep[18]

Wekeep is a French startup that offers to pool protection premiums for non-compulsory insurance, within a smart contract signed by the concerned parties. In case of a claim, a settlement is established on two conditions: endorsement of the policyholder of the concrete information and validation of other parties via a vote. In such an agreement, nobody has the power of decision making; it is instead the decision of the majority with no central organization that holds control over decisions. To settle the case, the majority must validate the data provided.

Many software firms offer CLM systems, as presented in this section. Typical functions are supports to:

- Creation of the contract, based on current contracts or third-party agreements;
- Contracting;
- Store contracts;
- Contract negotiation;
- Handling of several types of contracts;
- Approval of contracts;
- Complete contract monitoring;
- Optimization of the contracts;
- Management of contractual processes;
- Alerts of the relevant dates;
- Integration with other documents;

[17] www.kinno.fi/en/smartlog. Accessed 30 May 2020.

[18] Price Waterhouse Coopers. (2017). *Blockchain, a catalyst for new approaches in insurance*. www.pwc.com/gx/en/industries/financial-services/publications/blockchain-a-catalyst.html. Accessed 30 May 2020.

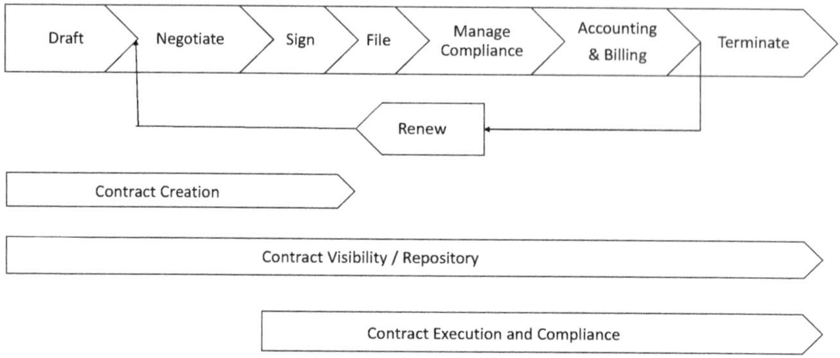

Fig. 9.4 Smart contracts and insurance 4.0

- Termination of the contracts or their renewal and extension.

Application Areas of CLM in Insurance 4.0

The main functions of a Contract Lifecycle Management (CLM), to automate contract management, are (Fig. 9.4)[19]:

1. Capture: The first step in a CLM consists of centralizing all current paper contracts into a single central point accessible online to all persons authorized to do so. The organizations must have a clear idea of which contracts they have. Otherwise, the organizations do not have a complete view of their potential exposure to risks;
2. Tracking: The next step is to acquire the data from the contracts. The objective is to keep track of all the essential data so as not to miss any of them. This activity applies to both the old contracts and the new contracts;
3. Preparation of new contracts with monitors in place. The focus is on accelerating the process of creating a new contract. The authoring process involves creating contract templates and libraries

[19] Nicoletti, B. (2017). *Agile procurement: Volume II: Designing & implementing a digital transformation*. London, UK: Springer International Publishing, ISBN 978-3-319-61085-6.

to allow users to connect to them and create new contracts quickly but controlled;

4. Drafting: The drafting of a contract can occur in two ways. First, it is appropriate to empower users in the organization by creating self-service draft contracts based on intelligent templates pre-approved by the legal department. Second, the organization can simplify the work of the legal department when they prepare complex offers or review and modify contracts;
5. Approval: Organizations need an approval workflow to ensure that the risky contracts are reviewed and approved by the correct parties. Some risks need to be approved by the legal department, some by the management, others by specific organization's entities such as underwriting officers, legal representatives, and so on. Ideally, simple contracts should be pre-approved, once the clearance on the pricing is defined;
6. Negotiation: The typical negotiator needs to include a list of potential problems of control for each type of business. Thus, it is possible to track the variations compared to the original or last draft, and a way to capture and report these differences;
7. Execution: When the contract is finalized and agreed upon, it must be signed (physically and increasingly digitally) from all subjects and the signed copies filed. Someone has to ensure that the final approved version is not modified in any way after sending texts around for their execution;
8. Analysis: Organizations with many contracts need to analyze these contracts for potential risks, rights, and obligations. Executives, lawyers, and professionals working in risk management need reports and alerts to manage the most common threats. Potential threatening clauses should have contingency scenarios. Fast access to the terms and contractual information allows persons to react quickly to new situations and address the risks related, for example, to the time factor;
9. Management: Capabilities such as monitoring of complex contracts with more applications, additions, amendments, and specifications for the management of changes or evolutions of the initial agreements are critical and help prevent errors, litigations, or similar actions. Management includes also alerts on relevant dates included in the contracts;

10. Termination or automatic renewals. Reminders of upcoming deadlines and closing tasks of contracts or basis for their renovation or extensions are critical not to incur in penalties;
11. Post-closing: Support for any claims or disputes with the availability of the history of the contract and all its variations and respect over time.

Startup organizations and investors focused in the past on the payments processing and banking business. They are increasingly interested in insurance solutions.[20] Insurance companies invest in insurtech organizations or take the initiative to explore the opportunities and the potential of the smart contracts.

Smart contracts pre-programmed actions ran automatically when one or more of the agreed and coded condition(s) has occurred. Because of this structure, smart contracts can automate critical processes of insurance. In addition to this, smart contracts can guarantee security. Such security is necessary for the processing of transactions between parties.[21] Smart contracts are exciting applications of the blockchain solution for the insurance industry.[22] They ensure the execution of the terms of a contract through the use of cryptographic code.[23] Smart contracts can manage complex rules among large numbers of policyholders. It can help develop peer-to-peer insurance. Parametric insurance (the insurance linked to an index, such as rainfall, temperature, or humidity) could be

[20] Stoeckli, E., Dremel, C., & Uebernickel, F. (2018). Exploring characteristics and transformational capabilities of insurtech innovations to understand insurance value creation in a digital world. *Electronic Markets, 28*(3), 287–305.

[21] Jacobs, C., & Lange-Haustein, C. (2017). Blockchain und smart contracts: zivil-und aufsichtsrechtliche Bedingungen. itrb IT-*Rechtsberater*, Bd, *17,* 9–15.

[22] Price Waterhouse Coopers. (2017). Blockchain: *A catalyst for new approaches in insurance.* www.pwc.ch/en/publications/2017/Xlos_Etude_Blockchain_UK_2017_Web.pdf. Accessed 30 March 2020.

Deloitte. (2016). *Blockchain applications in insurance.* www2.deloitte.com/content/dam/Deloitte/ch/Documents/innovation/ch-en-innovation-deloitte-blockchain-app-in-insurance.pdf. Accessed 30 March 2020.

McKinsey & Company. (2017). Blockchain solution in the insurance sector. In *Proceedings of the Quarterly Meeting of the Federal Advisory Committee on Insurance (FACI).* New York, NY.

[23] Lorenz, J. T., Münstermann, B., Higginson, M., Olesen, P. B., Bohlken, N., & Ricciardi, V. (2016 July). Blockchain in insurance—Opportunity or threat? *McKinsey Co.*, 1–9.

facilitated and be an alternative, for example, to traditional agricultural insurance policies.[24]

Smart contracts allow reducing administration costs for reconciliation and errors. Smart contracts could provide customers and insurance companies with the ways to manage claims in a transparent, responsive, and indisputable manner. The process would be[25]:

- The smart contract includes an option condition and related claims. The individuals involved are anonymous, but the agreement is in the public ledger;
- A triggering event, such as an expiration date and strike price, is hit. The contract executes automatically based on the coded terms, validated by the network, ensuring the payment only of valid claims[26];
- Regulators can use the smart contract to monitor the activity in the market.[27] At the same time, they can maintain the privacy of individual actors' positions.

One potential application is the automatic adjustment of the insurance premium to the conduct of the policyholder. By linking other technologies with the internet of things, this is possible, for example, for vehicle insurance. The vehicle can record the driving style of the policyholder using telemetric sensors. Via the internet-based connectivity object,[28] the recognized and recorded data on the driving style are forwarded to the insurer. The pre-programmed smart contract can process the received

[24] Skees, J. R., Barnett, B. J., & Collier, B. (2008, April). Agricultural insurance background and context for climate adaptation discussions. In *Prepared for the OECD expert workshop on economic aspects of adaptation.*

[25] www2.deloitte.com/content/dam/Deloitte/ch/Documents/innovation/ch-en-innovation-deloitte-blockchain-app-in-insurance.pdf. Accessed 30 March 2020.

[26] Blockchain and Cryptocurrencies. www.carolinascashadventure.com/resources/Documents/2018/Presentations/CCA%202018%2007A%20-%20Wells%20-%20Blockchain%20and%20Cryptocurrencies.pdf. Accessed 5 May 2020.

[27] Michael, J., Cohn, A. L. A. N., & Butcher, J. R. (2018). Blockchain technology. *The Journal*, *1*(7). Accessed 5 May 2020.

[28] That sends data from the Internet and receives objects.

data. They can automatically adapt the insurance premium to the policyholder in the event according to a high-risk or low-risk driving style.[29] A personalized premium adjustment is also possible in the insurance of ships. With GPS, the location of the transport can be communicated to the insurer. The company will know in real-time that the vessel is in a dangerous place, such as in an area at high risk of piracy.

Blockchain solutions can also help with processing payment transactions in the insurance industry. For example, the payment of the insured sum could be automatically initiated by the smart contract as soon as the registered loss event was verified. In the case of a digitally verifiable loss event, such as damage to the vehicle that was detected by sensors and reported to the insurer with internet of things. Theoretically, with the help of artificial intelligence, real-time payments would be possible when the loss event occurrs.

InsurETH[30]

InsurETH is a flight delay insurance, wherein the insurance amount for delayed or canceled flights is paid automatically through a smart contract. The payment of the insurance premium and the off-payment of the sum insured take place in the virtual currency "ether" because the InsurETH insurance is on the public blockchain "Ethereum."[31] This insurtech organization uses the historical delay or flight cancellation data of the global flight database. Based on the flight data of the last three months, the flight delay or cancellation failure probability is determined

[29] Djazayeri, A. (2016, December). Rechtliche Herausforderungen durch smart contracts. *jurisPR-BKR Anm*, 1, 4.

[30] insureth.mkvd.net. Accessed 24 November 2019. Accessed 5 May 2020.

[31] www.etherum.org. Accessed 24 November 2019. Accessed 5 May 2020.

and adjusted by the estimated result's potential payout. The postponement or cancellation of the insured flight is monitored and the smart contract automatically determines the policyholder-amount insured's payment to the policyholder.

Dynamis[32]
Startup Dynamis offers private unemployment insurance based on the principle of reciprocity. The policyholders are also partnering in the insurance and are also responsible for processing claims. It is possible to manage claims via social networks such as LinkedIn. These serve to verify the identity of the policyholder and to verify the unemployment or unemployment status. All members of the insurance company must belong to the same social network. Using the public blockchain "Ethereum," the policyholder receives a monthly payment in the cryptocurrency "ether." Insofar, the majority of the other policyholders have verified the unemployment. The system of mutual verification and recognition makes other partners unnecessary.

Fizzy[33]
A typical insurance model based on smart contracts is that of parametric insurance.[34] This is an insurance linked to an index

[32] dynamisapp.com/vision.html. Accessed 24 November 2019.

[33] Haapio, H., de Rooy, R. O. B. E. R. G., & Barton, T. D. (2018 February). New contract genres. In *Data protection/legaltech: Proceedings of the 21th International Legal Informatics Symposium IRIS*, 455–460.

[34] Cohn, A., West, T., & Parker, C. (2017 April). Smart after all: Blockchain, smart contracts, parametric insurance, and smart energy grids, cite as: 1 Geo. L. Tech. Rev. 273. www.Georgetownlawtechreview.Org/Wp-Content/Uploads/2017/04/Cohn-West-Parker-1-GEO.-L.-TECH.-REV.-273.pdf. Accessed 30 March 2020; Carter, M. (2018). *Parametric insurance: Breaking the mold of traditional insurance*, available online. www.ibm.com/blogs/insights-on-business/insurance/parametric-insurance-breaking-the-mold-of-traditional-insurance/. Accessed 30 March 2020.

[35] such as the weather (temperature, level of rain) or delays data. The smart contract concluded between the farmer and the company can, for example, stipulate that the payment takes place after 30 days without rain. The smart contract uses reliable external data, such as rainfall data from the meteorological service. This solution allows the smart contract to automatically trigger payment after 30 days of drought without the intervention of an expert or need for reporting or receipt of a policyholder's claim.

In September 2017, Axa launched an insurance product that genuinely meets the needs of new customers, called Fizzy. The goal was to provide travelers with an automated flight delay product that relies on third-party flight delay data and immediately proceeds with the compensation. There is no need of long questionnaires, claims, and waiting for payment. This product links to an Ethereum-based platform that analyzes data sources to find information on delayed flights.[36] If these flights correspond to a current insurance policy, Fizzy automatically triggers a payment. It is a revolutionary product not only regarding the technology used but also regarding its vision and market approach.

Fizzy is filling a gap and resolving recurring issues related to flight delays, including many exclusions typically found in traditional insurance contracts. Besides the strictly parametric aspect of its product, Axa aims to strengthen its customers' trust by transferring algorithmic processing on the Ethereum blockchain. The underlying message is that once subscribed, the insurance becomes somehow autonomous, without any company's intervention.

Axa delegates the indemnification decision to an independent network, reinforcing the customer's confidence. Fizzy is independent of the penalty for flight delays provided by airlines on the basis of the European regulation EC 261-2004 in case of delay higher than 3 hours. Sometimes, travelers can combine these two options.

[35] Carter, M. (2018). *Parametric insurance: Breaking the mold of traditional insurance*, available online. www.ibm.com/blogs/insights-on-business/insurance/parametric-insurance-breaking-the-mold-of-traditional-insurance/. Accessed 30 March 2020.

[36] Axa 2018, The Dawn of Insurtech, available online. www-axa-com.cdn.axa-contento-118412.eu/www-axa-compercent2F175cb5f3-54a5-457e-b80b-bea9d67b173c_axin005_gb.pdf. Accessed 30 March 2020.

Benefits and Challenges of CLM Solutions

Smart contracts can also help in the control of process flows, the administration of insurance protection, or the authentication and verification of identities, processes, and documents. The benefits are the possibility to avoid a further review or manual administration of the claims. Blockchain and smart contracts can simplify and accelerate the processing, checking, and ascertaining claims, shortening the processing time of claims as a whole. Such scenarios are not fictitious. There are already companies that offer innovative insurance solutions using smart contracts.

The CLM software category is expected to grow, on average, between 15 and 20 percent.[37] The reasons are several. The implementation of the CLM can lead to significant improvements in savings and efficiency. These solutions do more than merely creating a legal archive. They optimize and automate contracts. They allow the organization to follow up and support the management of all the stages of the contract life cycle.

Some specific benefits to support a business case for their evaluation are[38]:

- Rationalize the authoring process. Use of clauses, libraries, and improved collaboration mode;
- Create time for contract operations substantially reduced compared to the old ways of service. There are substantial savings in time and costs adopting the CLM;
- Automate the tracking of compliance. The integration with transactional systems ensures the issuance of orders with correct economic clauses. It enables organizations to demand the agreed discounts or benefits associated with the volumes;
- Reduce total administrative costs. This reduction enables the resources of insurance and legal entities to focus on more critical and complex tasks that add more value to the organization.

[37] www.digitaljournal.com/pr/3814597. Accessed 30 March 2019.

[38] www.bearingpoint.com/files/0553_WP_EN_Vertragsmgt_final_web.pdf. Accessed 30 March 2019.

In perspective, there will be several self-adaptive contracts.[39] They will act without a significant intervention of the persons. They will allow the organization to implement more flexible and faster contracts. They will require higher decentralization, an agile approach, and autonomous interaction. There are liability issues, such as technological failure or the rigidity of the contracts, that result in less flexibility to correct errors once the contract has been closed.

Other challenges are the absence of regulations and especially of standards. There are regulations of the economic activity in the financial sector at both national and European levels through comprehensive compliance provisions. Smart contracts obtain compliance relevance when individuals or companies are connected with the financial sector. On the use of smart contracts there are still many compliance uncertainties and unanswered questions. Similarly, there are not a common unified European approaches for a standardized compliance treatment of smart contracts.

Cybernetics: Underwriting 4.0

Underwriting is the process of reviewing and selecting risks that an insurer might cover, under what terms, and assigning those an expected cost and level of riskiness.[40] An insurance company will evaluate the risks of a potential policyholder based on a certain number of actuarial factors. The target of such an underwriting process is to give a price for insurance based on its risk.[41]

Underwriting Activities

The underwriting activities are essential for insurance companies. It is the assessment of the assets or the persons. Based on that assessment, the company will decide whether to insure or not the asset of the person

[39] Platform Industries 4.0: Aspects of the Research Roadmap for Application Scenarios. www.plattform-i40.de/I40/Redaktion/EN/Downloads/Publikation/aspects-of-theresearch-roadmap.pdf?__blob=publicationFile&v=10. Accessed 20 March 2020.

[40] Dorfman, M. S. (1998). *Introduction to risk management and insurance*. Upper Saddle River, NJ: Prentice Hall.

[41] investinganswers.com/dictionary/u/underwriting. Accessed 12 January 2020.

according to risk analysis. If the applicant is accepted, the following step is the determination of the cover price.[42]

The risk management process in insurance is a crucial aspect to consider in insurance 4.0. The definition of "risk" given by CIPS (Chartered Institute of insurance and Supply) is the "likelihood of an undesired result."[43] A more specific definition in the case of insurance is that the risk is a potential disruption in insurance processes in dealing with services, products, and/or resources. Common types of threats in the insurance are fraud, costs, partner quality, and delivery times.[44]

The insurance company approves the customer application and prices and should also consider the standards used to determine the policyholder's acceptance. These standards should be reasonable and not discriminatory. Regulation is an essential factor in this process.[45] A risk indicates the situation in which a future event may bring a claim. For example, the threat that faces the driver of a vehicle is to remain involved in an accident and suffer financial or physical damage. There are three broad categories of dangers linked to the vehicle: the person risks, asset risks, and liability.

The risk is the object of the pivotal insurance processes. It must depend on a particular condition, a potential of the fulfillment of an adverse event. When one considers a level of insurance risk, there is a paradox. The hope is that a given accident never occurs. There must be the possibility of its occurrence. Otherwise, there would be no need for insurance. Always according to this condition, it is not insurable a dead risk. The risk must already manifest but still possible over time.[46]

[42] Araujo, M. (2017, November 28). *What is insurance underwriting?* www.thebalance.com/what-is-insuranceunderwriting-2645778. Accessed 25 December 2019.

[43] www.cips.org/en/cips-for-business/knowledge-for-business/cips-risk-index/. Accessed 10 March 2019.

[44] Trkman, P., & McCormack, K. (2009). Supply chain risk in turbulent environments—A conceptual model for managing supply chain network risk. *International Journal of Production Economics, 119*(2), 247–258.

[45] California insurance continuing education. www.webce.com/catalog/courses/california-insurance-continuing-education. Accessed 12 January 2020.

[46] Favaron, F. (2015). *La tariffazione nelle assicurazioni contro i danni*. Venezia: Tesi di Laurea, Università Ca' Foscari. dspace.unive.it/bitstream/handle/10579/7024/822544-1182021.pdf?sequence=2. Accessed 22 March 2020.

It is critical also to consider reputational risks that can impact the insurance as an organization. These risks connect with improper operations in the company's or partner's organizations.[47]

In the Agreement of Basel for financial services, operational risks are the risk of losses due to inadequacy or failures of processes, human resources, and internal systems or from external events.[48]

Risk management requires several key activities: analysis, assessment, mitigation, monitoring, and lessons learned. These actions provide a structured and effective way to address the issues of risk management. These actions are essential since prevention is always better than cure. The rest of this chapter goes into detail on these aspects.

The underwriting activity has two main components: risk assessment and pricing. To be more precise, there are also other less important components of the underwriting process, some of which are disccussed in the following sections.

Underwriting 4.0

The term underwriter usually refers to an employee who evaluates the insurance required on specific cases, selects whom to accept, and determines the cover price, the terms, and conditions of the policy.[49] The traditional underwriting process is well defined. It includes several phases. The following pages list the most relevant of them (Fig. 9.5). The phases constitute a process (Fig. 9.6).

Information Collection

The underwriting process begins with the receipt of an insurance proposal. It is necessary to collect all the information necessary to assess risks related to assets or persons in the proposal. It is possible that

[47] Supplies of palm oil to Unilever alleged to contribute to the destruction of Indonesia's rainforests (April 2008). Mattel forced to recall children's toys due to safety issues following the sourcing of components from China (August 2007).

[48] Remains, A., & Sironi, A. (2011). *The financial crisis and Basel 3: Origins, aims and structure of the new regulatory framework (No. 1)*. Carefin Working Paper. www.bis.org/publ/bcbs195.pdf. Accessed 10 March 2019.

[49] Araujo, M. (2017, November 28). *What is insurance underwriting?* www.thebalance.com/what-is-insuranceunderwriting-2645778. Accessed 25 December 2019.

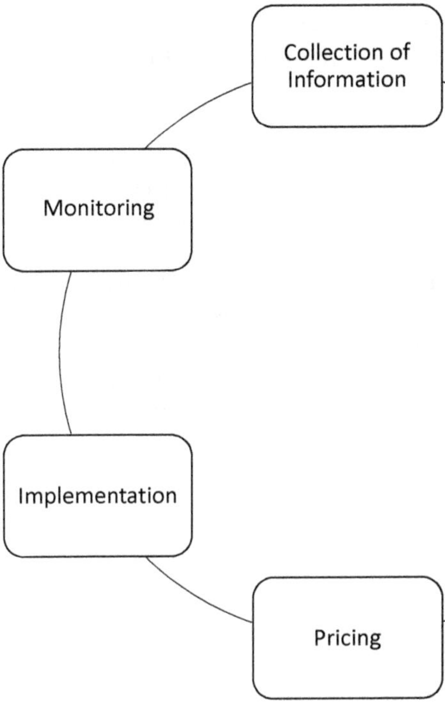

Fig. 9.5 Phases of underwriting

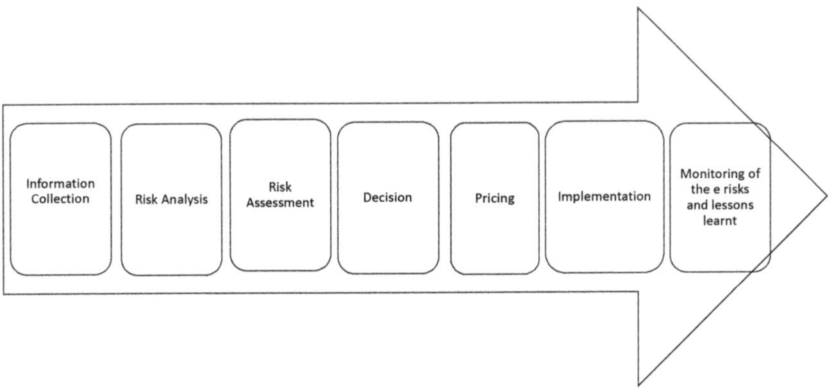

Fig. 9.6 Underwriting process

there might be a need for additional documentation, such as surveys and reports. The underwriting office will require them if necessary.

Risk Analysis
Risk analysis is the process of identifying all potential actions that can create problems.[50] It is an essential activity to be used, for example, to define the insurance strategy or the plans for individual categories of insurance.

The risk analysis can be a simple or very formal process. The latter approach is more appropriate for projects or insurance initiatives of high value and high risks, such as moving to a new data center or using a new vendor solution. The analysis can also be informal, using an iterative or intuitive process, less or more significant for the insurance. It can also be reactive, such as in response to a crisis.

Risk Assessment
Risk assessment refers to the determination of the probability of the occurrence of a risk, the potential impact that may have on the processes, and ways to try to anticipate or forecast its occurrence.[51] This evaluation is not an easy task, considering that insurance is a complex system, applied to many varied sectors.

The probabilities of occurrence of risk are analyzed based on two components: the likelihood that the risk occurs (measurement based on experiences or the presence of factors that may affect the likelihood) and severity of the loss potential (economic impact). The risk predictability is also essential.[52] To determine the probability that the insured will notify a claim in the future, the underwriter must consider criteria such as age, gender, asset characteristics, and applicant status.[53]

[50] Hallikas, J., Karvonen, I., Pulkkinen, U., Virolainen, V. M., & Tuominen, M. (2004). Risk management processes in vendor networks. *International Journal of Production Economics, 90*(1), 47–58.

[51] Baird, I. S., & Thomas, H. (1985). Toward a contingency model of strategic risk-taking. *Academy of Management Review, 10*(2), 230–243.

[52] Kitchens, F. (s.d). Financial implications of artificial Neural Networks in automobile insurance underwriting. *International Journal of Electronic Finance, 3,* 311–319. https://doi.org/10.1504/ijef.2009.027853.

[53] California Insurance CE. (no date). *Insurance underwriting*. www.ceclass.com/164.pdf. Accessed 30 March 2020. Accessed 30 April 2020.

Highly predictable risks may have a reduced impact. It might not be worth taking costly actions to control or avoid these risks. On the other hand, low-probability risks can have a significant effect and can require some efforts. The cost of control and the mitigation, or elimination of the risks need a careful assessment.

Decision

Depending on the risk assessment, the underwriter decides whether to accept the proposal totally or partially or reject it. Companies agree to ensure risks that have different levels of risk. The acceptance takes place under different conditions, for example, by applying a higher premium or applying exclusions.

Pricing

If the insurance proposal is accepted, the following step is to determine the premium that the policyholder will have to pay. The insurance company performs a risk classification, which means that persons with a similar risk level are assigned to the same category and pay similar premiums. Persons who are considered high risk must pay a higher premium than those with a lower probability of being involved in an accident.[54] This step's objective is to adequately define a premium for the insured commensurate reward to its level of risk.[55] In the calculation of premiums, the insurance company must ensure that it has the financial capacity to cover current and future costs and to generate profits.[56] If the policyholders pay too low a premium for the risks they pose, insurance could struggle to fulfill contractual obligations. Similarly, if companies apply too high premiums, it will be challenging to sell policies. The main objective of the underwriting, and generally any business for profit, is to

[54] Manulife Insurance. (no date). *What you need to know about insurance underwriting*. manulife.ca/wps/wcm/connect/3ef82954-404f-4cce-bebd-0813142c3848/ins_under_whatyouneed.pdf?MOD=AJPERES&CACHEID=3ef82954-404f-4cce-bebd-0813142c3848. Accessed 20 March 2020.

[55] The Institutes. Risk and Insurance Knowledge Group. (no date). *Underwriting*. The Institutes. Risk and Insurance Knowledge Group. www.theinstitutes.org/Comet/programs/ins24/assets/pdf/INS24.pdf. Accessed 22 March 2020.

[56] Parodi, P. (2016, October). *General insurance pricing*. www.cii.co.uk/knowledge/resources/articles/basic-concepts-and-techniques-ofthe-pricing-process/43681. Accessed 22 March 2020.

generate profit, add value for the customer, and increase the number of customers.

Implementation of the Decision

Completed the analysis, the next step is the registration of the policyholder and the person or asset information into the system for recording the policy. The registration is necessary for the accounting processes, monitoring, and producing statistics.

Monitoring of Risks and Lessons Learned

Like most competencies, effective risk management improves with experience and practice. It is critical to monitor the trend of the risks. Periodically, it is necessary to review what happened or is expected to arrive. Evaluation should focus on what the organization can learn and implement as improvements in working processes.

Monitoring and measurement are not a single task but a process. Their implementation should be a structured process.

When the insurance policy is issued, the underwriter monitors the risk exposure to ensure that the results achieved are satisfactory. The monitoring is carried out at contract renewal, usually every year and/or if there is a notice of a claim. If the insured has had several claims during the last period, the insurance company can increase the premiums or refuse to renew the policy. This type of decision making is still regulated by the governments to prevent abuses by the insurance companies.[57]

Insurance 4.0 and Underwriting

Insurance 4.0 can provide effective, efficient, and cost-effective risk management in insurance.[58] The insurance companies assess the risks and determine the premiums, using actuarial models that are now evolving and improving. Companies now have access to much more information about their customers. This possibility allows forecasting the likelihood of claim notices more accurately. Companies usually collect documentation at the underwriting time. Reliance only on these documents does

[57] California Insurance CE. (no date). *Insurance underwriting*. www.ceclass.com/164.pdf. Accessed 20 March 2020.

[58] Rigby, D., & Bilodeau, B. (2011). *Management tools & trends*. London, UK: Bain & Company.

not allow having a clear and detailed risk policy. Thanks to digitization, it is possible to collect data through different channels, such as social media and chatbots.[59] The risks can be analyzed using sophisticated algorithms and artificial intelligence.

Companies are investing in artificial intelligence, such as machine learning. AI is capable of giving meaning to the large number of data collected in real-time via the IoT, sensors, and online platforms. It allows companies to have a more precise risk assessment and pricing.[60] Artificial intelligence tools can automate and speed up the underwriting process and with machine learning they can improve over time, almost automatically. For example, a digital underwriter can determine whether for the proposed insurance an underwriter person should require a more in-depth analysis or whether to issue a policy automatically (Fig. 9.7).[61]

Thanks to customized procedures, the organization can access, combine, clean, and compare all relevant data, structured and unstructured, from internal and external sources of data, including third parties or open data. Based on these data, it is possible to take a series of actions:

- Develop automatic rules for controlling and monitoring after the initial identification and use a closed-loop learning system[62];
- Through an advanced study, analyze the insurance data model, specific scenarios for the insurance. Once done that, use an extensive set of predefined rules developed using the experience and expertise of professionals in the coverage;

[59] Kostelník, P., Pisařovic, I., Muroň, M., Dařena, F., & Procházka, D. (2019). Chatbots for enterprises: Outlook. *Acta Universitatis Agriculturae et Silviculturae Mendelianae Brunensis, 67*(6), 1541–1550.

[60] Cambosu, D. (2017, marzo 24). *L'abc dell'insurtech, le parole dell'innovazione nelle assicurazioni*. www.insuranceup.it/it/scenari/l-abc-dell-insurtech-le-parole-dell-innovazionenelle-assicurazioni_1544.htm. Accessed 30 March 2020; Reilly, M. (2016 July). *The future of the underwriting process in the digital age*. insuranceblog.accenture.com/future-of-underwriting-process-in-digital-age. Accessed 30 March 2020.

[61] Aggour, K., Bonissone, P., Cheetham, W., & Messmer, R. (2006). Automating the underwriting of insurance applications. *AI Magazine*, 36–50. www.aaai.org/ojs/index.php/aimagazine/article/view/1891/1789. Accessed 30 April 2020.

[62] Johannsdottir, L. (2014). Transforming the linear insurance business model to a closed-loop insurance model: A case study of Nordic non-life insurers. *Journal of cleaner production, 83,* 341–355.

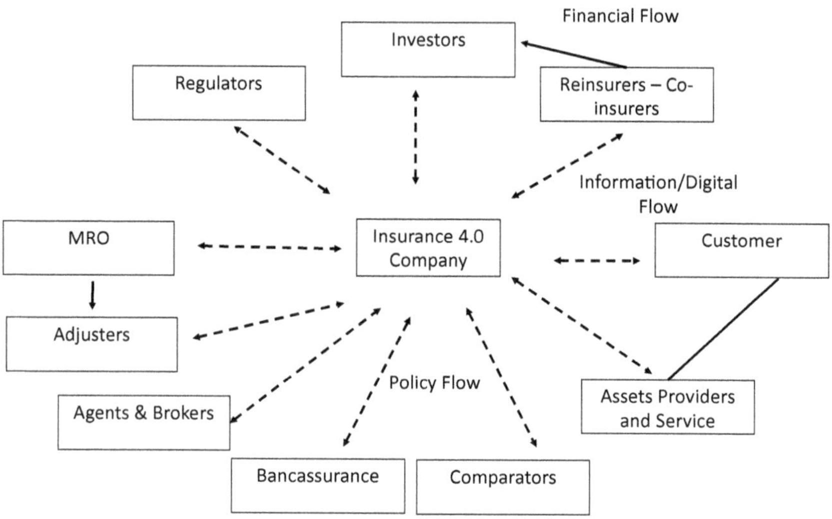

Fig. 9.7 Ecosystem coordination

- Monitor transactions in real-time with an online scoring engine that uses a hybrid analytical approach (including organizational rules, anomaly detection, predictive modeling, and analysis of associative links) to detect suspicious activity;
- Combine alerts and monitoring and alarm systems. This action may be associated with standard data and provide a better view of the insurance risks;
- Analyze also social networks beyond the processing of individual invoices, payments, and purchase orders, to evaluate all activities and related relationships in the ecosystem;
- Promote collaboration, compliance, and efficiency with easy-to-use interfaces that provide search and interactive visualization components.

Figures 9.8 and 9.9 shows an integrated scheme for the ICT support to risk management in insurance 4.0.

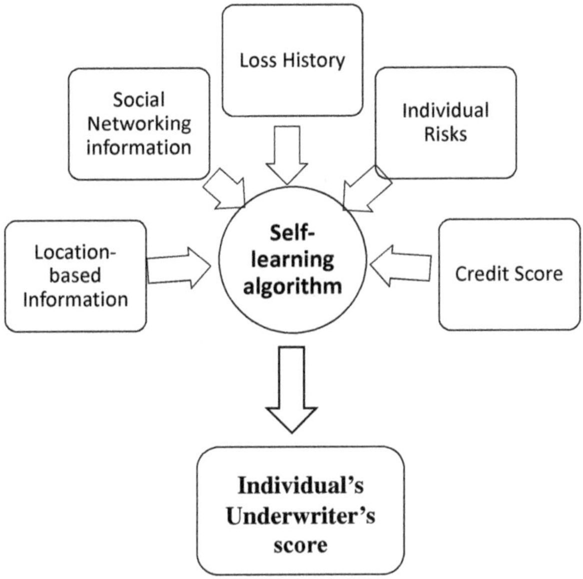

Fig. 9.8 Artificial intelligence in underwriting

Resilience and Insurance 4.0

The environment is increasingly turbulent and difficult to predict. Insurance 4.0 has the objective in supporting risk management in companies to:

- Add value to the customer;
- Focus on the core business of the organization;
- Gain in flexibility.

This objectives should be combined with a resilient insurance. The resilience of a system is its ability to withstand a significant break in degradation within adequate parameters and to recover within an acceptable time.[63] To study resilience is essential from both the underwriting point of view and the general insurance processes. Insurance 4.0 combines

[63] www.igi-global.com/dictionary/system-resilience/51260. Accessed 26 March 2019.

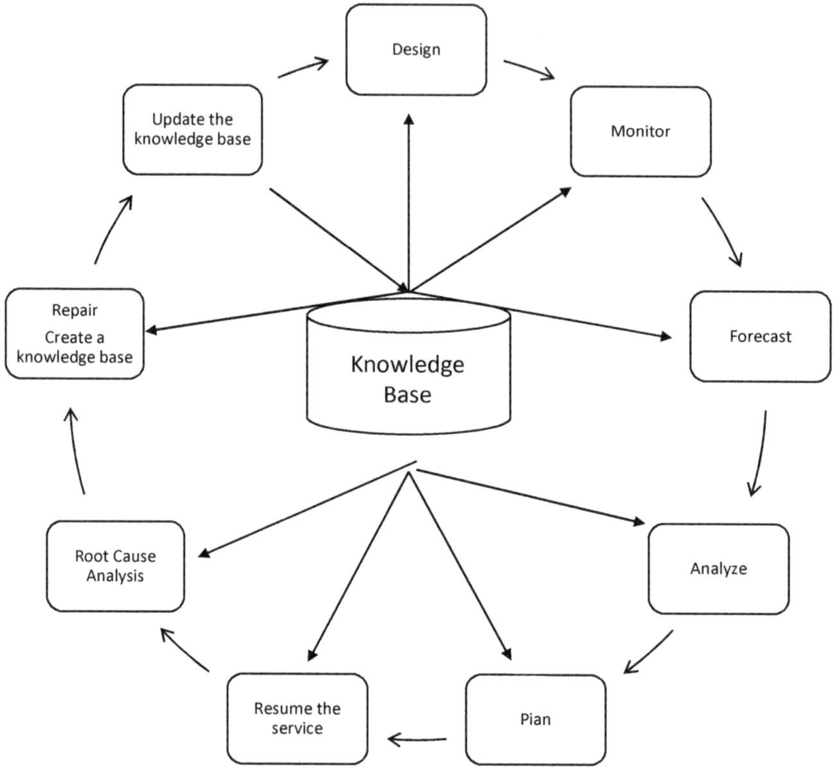

Fig. 9.9 Risk management cycle

automation and information systems. Their collapse could generate a big issue for the operation of the company. This section focuses on operational risks, mainly connected with the resilience of the assets to be insured. The Basel Agreement for financial services defines operational risks as the risk of losses due to inadequacy or failures of processes, persons, and internal systems, or from external events.[64]

Insurance 4.0 must take essential precautions to ensure the reduction as much as possible of the operational risks of the insured assets that

[64] Remains, A., & Sironi, A. (2011). *The financial crisis and Basel 3: Origins, aims and structure of the new regulatory framework (No. 1)*. Carefin Working Paper.

impact the organization's operations. If part of the activities is insured, it is critical to ensure their resilience. This requires a careful examination of the insured assets by the organization and the characteristics, competencies, and capabilities of the policyholder. They must be resilient. In other words, they must be able to consider the potential risks and disasters and be prepared to reduce their impacts and respond effectively.

A compelling case is represented by insurance 4.0. To evaluate the risks that an organization may incur, it is interesting to assess the resilience of the asset insured. Thus, it is possible to determine better risks. Besides risk evaluation, it is also possible to offer customer service on how to reduce their risks. The risks may be very different.

Resilience in Insurance

Several studies have emphasized the importance of resilience in the case of physical assets insured. There are essential services such as the provision of energy, transport, and health, which take place through complex infrastructures where robust assets play a crucial role.[65] These issues, if not adequately governed, can cause instability and business interruptions due to the occurrence of events of varying severity. The potential consequences can have a high or very high impact on the customer organizations and, in some cases, on the whole community. Some studies highlight the key drivers and best practices for insurance for the correct governance of the business continuity and for keeping the service levels of the critical infrastructure, with particular reference to the protection of critical information infrastructure.[66]

It is critical the ability to recover and to develop a shared understanding of the definition, theory, and managerial implications, in particular, of cyber risks and the related resilience of the potential actions.[67] It is necessary to provide targeted solutions to the challenges in developing a

[65] Carrozzi, L. (2009). *Insurance management for the protection of critical infrastructure*. Master thesis in Insurance Management, University of Tor Vergata, Rome, Italy.

[66] White House. (2013). *Critical infrastructure security and resilience*. Washington, DC: White House.

[67] White House. (2015, April). Cyber-resilience in the supply chains. *Technology Innovation Management Review*.

cyber-resilience, tools, and methods for responding to outages or claims in the assets or business insured and making available some good practices.

It is critical to analyze the role of insurance in identifying problems and managing intra- and inter-organization problems generated by the pursuing resilience in the organizations.[68] Ensuring the resilience in the insured assets in a turbulent environment requires the engagement of the internal and external components of the entire ecosystem inside or connected with an organization. Some studies have revealed that insurance activities can contribute significantly to the creation of resilience in the organization's processes. The literature has identified some intra- and inter-organizational issues. They could have an impact on the strength of the insurance. It is possible to identify the possible actions that insurance should take to verify and, in a proactive mode, help to improve or reinforce the resilience connected with the insured assets or the business itself.

Agility

In general, resilience refers to the ability of a material to deform elastically, to bend in front of stress without being permanently changed. Organizations should have resilience in meeting the growing challenges of socioeconomic environments.[69] Insurance companies should take an active role in understanding how prepared a policyholder is for a significant damage and how much the policyholder has focused on damage mitigation and the documentation and actions on the recovery process.[70] A robust recovery plan can help companies to better understand the policyholder's risk and its preparation in preventing the losses and mitigate the impacts after their occurrence.

[68] Pereira, R. C., Christopher, M., & Lake Da Silva, A. (2014). Achieving supply chain resilience: The role of insurance. *Supply Chain Management: An International Journal, 19*(5/6), 626–642.

[69] Hallegatte, S. (2014). *Economic resilience: Definition and measurement*. Washington, DC: The World Bank.

[70] Insurance Considerations in Operational Resilience. www.irmi.com/articles/expert-commentary/insurance-considerations-in-operational-resilience. Accessed 5 May 2020.

A comprehensive enterprise recovery plan can help to identify and measure the exposure at each insured asset or location.[71] It can provide a meaningful method to respond should a claim occur.[72] The recovery plan can also help identify and measure the exposures for losses to the customers and the company. It can be invaluable to understand the specific need for contingent business interruption or personal disabilities exposure. The plan may also be helpful to understand the exposure for specific insurance aspects assets, such as product recall insurance, cyber liability coverage, and political risk insurance.[73]

The previous resiliency characteristics underline the need for agility. This feature is essential to increase the flexibility of an organization to deal with unexpected events or even catastrophes.[74]

The base of risk is uncertainty. It exists in all operations. Despite the best plans, any organization is always susceptible to the risk of unpredictable events. Organizations must have the flexibility to manage these risks. The best way to cope with them is to increase flexibility and to have an agile organization. Agility means that the operations are sufficiently flexible to effectively address the risks occurrences, efficiently, economically with conditions of rapid response, and, if necessary, implement remediation changes.

In practice, it is often difficult to forecast the details of events that can be dangerous. Agility is often the best response. It is achievable in several ways, such as the ability to short-delivery times, so that to get all the changes or remediation be completed quickly, with a rapid recovery from outages. Standardization can help a lot. Standardized processes can be used interchangeably in different operations if it becomes necessary. An agile organization can reduce resources, solving delivery problems, reducing the impact on the ongoing activities, and so on.

The essential point for agility is that operations should be able to switch from one service to another without the availability of new resources. The

[71] Insurance Considerations in Operational Resilience. www.irmi.com/articles/expert-commentary/insurance-considerations-in-operational-resilience. Accessed 30 May 2020.

[72] www.irmi.com/articles/expert-commentary/insurance-considerations-in-operational-resilience. Accessed 20 January 2020.

[73] Baumgärtner, S., & Strunz, S. (2014). The economic insurance value of ecosystem resilience. *Ecological Economics, 101,* 21–32.

[74] Waters, D. (2011). *Supply chain risk management: Vulnerability and resilience in logistics*. London, UK: Kogan Page Publishers.

process must be as much as possible standard so that they can easily switch between the products with:

- Wildcard collaborators trained to move toward areas of deficiency through rapid reprogramming of the operations;
- Diversion of the work and resources away from areas of surplus to areas with shortages or outages;
- Operations that can move between different positions when there is an urgent need for a capacity increase, for example, by moving ICT services from one data processing center to another one. This solution is possible in many instances with cloud computing;
- Simultaneous development to accelerate new methods and products, flexible partners, use of multiple sources with different characteristics to meet the diverse needs, and various types of contracts with built-in flexibility.

Basic Features of Resilience

Some features are essential to ensure the resilience of an asset or process to insure. They are distinct. In reality, they are very interconnected. Some authors have considered them in the case of resilience in general.[75] There are nine actions to evaluate the resilience in the case of insurance. They are named with words starting with nine C (from the initials of their main aspects) (Fig. 9.10):

- Contract. This feature refers to the need for a precise agreement between the company and the policyholder, or more precisely to their commitments for the continued use of the asset or process. It is at the base of all the other features, which must be stated and defined in the contracts;
- Command. This feature is essential for risk management. The resilient organization must have effective leadership of resilience, both internally and from the partner side. The management must be able to make decisions before, during, and after a disaster, an attack, or an emergency. It must also be efficient and ready to intervene in a

[75] Gulati, R. (2010). *Reorganize for resilience: Putting customers at the center of your business*. Cambridge, MA: Harvard Business Press.

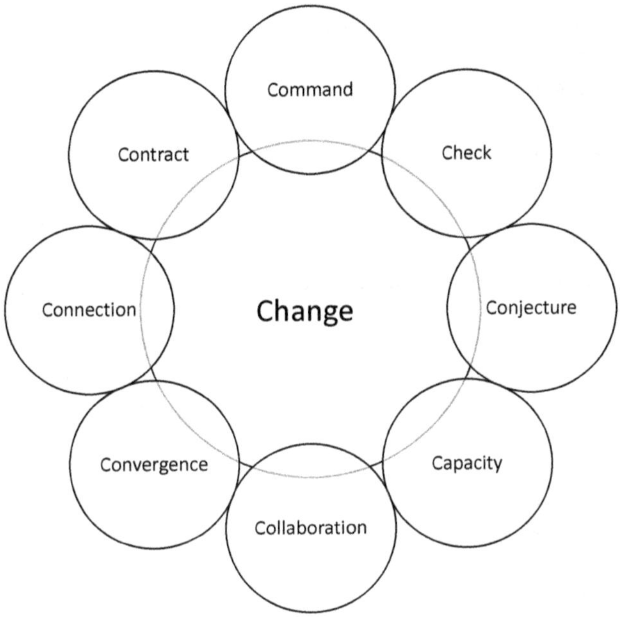

Fig. 9.10 Basic aspects of resilience

timely and cost-effective way. The risks and potential disasters should be managed in line with the objectives of ensuring continuity in the organization's profitability;

- Check. The control system connects with the ability to have good process governance. It implies a robust and detailed plan that the policyholder must verify. It must also take into account the unpredictable. It should include the "what if" and consider the management of what might happen;
- Conjecture. The conjecture implies the ability to predict or anticipate the occurrence of a disaster. It is critical to consider the risks starting in the design of a solution. Prevention is better than cure.[76] The base of conjectures is the attempt to prevent a damaging event, reducing the consequences if it does happen, and finally getting

[76] Güller, M., & Henke, M. (2018). *Resilience assessment in complex supply networks, revisiting supply chain risk*, 73–98. https://doi.org/10.1007/978-3-030-03813-7_5.

compensation from third parties if necessary. To be more precise, it is critical to carefully evaluate the best options for mitigating the damages from risk after it occurs. Policyholders and companies should explicitly include the effects of risks in their decisions. It is necessary to consider the risks associated with pushing too hard on the organization's leanness, on excessive efficiency, or on some other objectives that inadvertently increase vulnerability. The best design needs a balance between strengths and average efficiency measures. For example, a single path through the activities in a process can create a vulnerability. If something happens at one point in the trail, the whole process is at risk. How to avoid these risks requires, for example, designing a process with parallel trails or provide backup assets. Thus, the flows move from a disrupted path to one that is usually operating. It is also necessary to carry out continuous monitoring of services to assure their resilience;

- Capacity. Organizations often work to be lean and reduce waste, such as over-capacity or the number of resources. This approach is good, but the organization cannot overdo it. There is a need to ensure the ability to recover and not be too lean. The organization must have some more additional capacity available in case of an emergency;
- Collaboration. One of the essential ways to ensure resiliency is through the integration process, with several members in the ecosystem who work together to solve common problems, even if they might belong to different organizations. Without a basic level of cooperation, it is almost impossible to move towards a truly integrated process;
- Convergence in the processes. The visibility is beneficial for risk management. It can also bring other benefits, including the merging of operations. In other words, the services should converge toward common standards. Then, they become the normal mode of operation. Other initiatives have the same effect, in particular, quality assurance and risk management;
- Connection. The resilience requires flexible connections but capable of acting in support of unanticipated events. The links or networks must be, from the informatics and telematics capacity, in such a way

as allowing continuity using a backup, if necessary. Relationships, also have a commercial value, with the possibility of using other organizations' resources to allow continuity in the provision of services in emergency conditions;

- Change. Change management requires agility. It needs the right mix of bureaucracy, coordination, and speed that distinguish the most effective organizations.

Resilience Metrics

The metrics of the KPIs (key process indicator or key performance indicators) of the resilience must measure customer satisfaction. Customers must be able to appreciate the reduction in the severity of the occurrence of the risk, its minimum possible impact, and its duration.

It is possible to show what happens in the occurrence of risk with a chart that illustrates how the appearance of risk could affect the business continuity of an organization in sales, operational levels, margins, and/or quality of customer service. It is possible to generalize the so-called resilience triangle[77] model. The KPIs, which measure the resilience, are present in what it is called the "graph of resilience" (Fig. 9.11).[78] The graph shows the several stages of the performance of the system response. After a process has degraded, due to the occurrence of a risk, the actions need to be taken to restore service as soon as possible (if necessary with a work-around). Next, the organization needs to identify the root causes and restore the necessary performance. The "graph of resilience" visually shows these phases by tracing the organization's response over time. The graph displays in scale the impact and the duration of the negative performance of the processes or sub-processes.

The depth of the graph represents the severity of the interruption, that is, its duration and the impact of the damage associated with the disaster. The length of the graph represents the service recovery time and the root cause's determination and remediation. These KPIs influence the pricing of insurance.

[77] Carvalho, H., Barroso, A. P., Machado, V. H., Azevedo, S., & Cruz-Machado, V. (2012). Supply chain redesign for resilience using simulation. *Computers & Industrial Engineering, 62*(1), 329–341.

[78] Nicoletti, B. (2016). Resilience and outsourcing. *PMWORLD, 2,* 16.

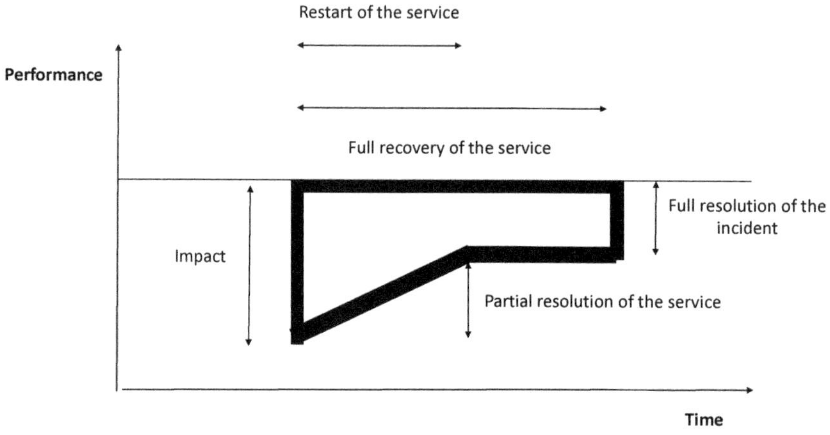

Fig. 9.11 Resilience graph

The graph resilience is essential for insurance. Its objective is to negotiate with the customers the reduction of the central area in Fig. 9.11. For this purpose, the contract should define the maximum permissible values for the parameters shown in Fig. 9.11.

Challenges and Benefits

To cope with the risks of the insured assets, be them property or life, it is critical to adopt a well-defined strategy for resilience. This strategy requires:

- Understand the critical risks associated with the asset or process insured, and how they can be either a technical or an organizational issue that could have an impact on the continuity of the customer's business, and create considerable damage in reputation and financial position;
- Consider radical changes that guarantee improvements in the creation of a more resilient asset or the environment;
- Analyze how actions on the nine "Cs," indicated in this section, can improve the underwriting;

- Find out how at all levels, the active engagement of the customer and partner organizations and management can make progress toward better resilience.

Collaboration: Claim Processing 4.0

Insurance 4.0 solutions (such as smart contracts) can improve the claim processes. They could trigger the claims and payment processes for damage caused in the insured asset, which is detected and controlled by sensors linked to the internet of things. Thus, it would be possible to avoid complaints about the causes of damage and calls to quest the progress of a claim.[79]

Insurance 4.0 aims to improve the transparency of the contracting as well as the claims management process, including fraud detection. It provides higher clarity to where the premiums paid go.

Innovation and new technologies can affect the value of insurance companies, with accompanying competition policy considerations. Policies that have customized coverage and simplified claims processes can have access to market segments that otherwise would not be able to access financial protection.[80]

Improvements in communication networks and processing capacity led to faster payment processes.[81] Online platforms can process claims in shorter times.

Insurance 4.0 and Claim Processing

The aspects connected with claim processing in insurance 4.0 are several[82]:

[79] The promise of blockchain | McKinsey. www.mckinsey.com/industries/financial-services/our-insights/the-promise-of-blockchain. Accessed 5 May 2020.

[80] www.oecd.org/pensions/Technology-and-innovation-in-the-procurement-sector.pdf. Accessed 30 March 2020.

[81] Technology and innovation in the insurance sector. www.oecd.org/pensions/Technology-and-innovation-in-the-insurance-sector.pdf. Accessed 5 May 2020.

[82] The Impact of Digitalization on the Insurance Value Chain. slideheaven.com/the-impact-of-digitalization-on-the-insurance-value-chain-and-the-insurability-o.html. Accessed 5 May 2020.

- Fraud investigation via artificial intelligence;
- Claim settlement using artificial intelligence and big data;
- Fraud prevention through data analytics;
- Automated calculation and payment of the loss using blockchain solutions;
- Storage of the information for automatic payout;
- Apps in digital devices;
- Customers' claims.

Big data analytics is also useful to detect and reduce fraudulent claims. These claims are estimated to be around 10 percent of all submitted requests. Their impact is approximately USD 40 billion in the USA alone.[83] Some of the biggest insurance companies, including Allianz, AXA, and AIG, are already starting to use the power of big data analytics to reduce fraud by adopting technologies such as voice biometrics, call behavior, and artificial intelligence.

At a risk management level, several data analytics solutions exist that could assist companies. These include integrated geospatial analytics tools, geospatial analysis, data quality management tools, and claims/exposure matching.[84] In particular, claims processes could benefit from the use of pictures taken and filed via smartphones and concierge services to smooth the process.

Command: Insurance Process Intelligence

It is critical to maximize the value provided by insurance 4.0 to the end customers and the organization. In the current volatility, there is the danger that some variables come into play and disrupt programs. It is critical to increase organizational agility. It is necessary to act on the processes and platforms. This means:

[83] Big data analytics is useful for detecting and reducing fraudulent claims that are estimated to be around 10 percent of all submitted claims, with an impact of approximately $40 billion in the US alone (EY, 2017).

[84] www.oecd.org/pensions/Technology-and-innovation-in-the-procurement-sector.pdf. Accessed 30 March 2020.

- Modernizing and improving the effectiveness and efficiency of the platforms and processes of insurance (underwriting, claims, and so on);
- Optimizing price/quality ratio and ensuring the standard quality of insurance and ancillary services;
- Rationalizing value for money on services offered;
- Creating a network of communication with the insurance ecosystem.

To achieve all these objectives with insurance 4.0, it is critical to adopt a business process intelligence model, also referred to as insurance process intelligence.[85] It is business intelligence focused on the optimal management of the insurance processes. It has a significant innovative aspect. Business intelligence primarily analyzes information and, in some cases, allows simulations (what-if analysis).[86] Insurance process intelligence adds the management of the workflows connected with the processes.[87] The next sections detail this approach.

Insurance Process Intelligence Components

Insurance process intelligence has several components summarized in the following pages (Fig. 9.12).

Forecasting, Strategy, Planning, and Budgeting

In the integration in a single solution strategy, planning, and monitoring with that of business intelligence, it is critical to have a collaborative platform. The platform should provide at the same time analytical and planning features. It is critical to design and implement processes and systems to support, facilitate, and make consistent in a flexible way all the planning processes (long, medium, and short term) that the organization intends to use and put under control.

[85] Yıldırım, İ. (2020). Industry 4.0 and its effects on the insurance sector. *Business Management and Communication Perspectives in Industry 4.0*, 251–266. IGI Global, Hershey, PA.

[86] Turban, E., Sharda, R., & Delen, D. (2010). *Decision support and business intelligence systems*. Google Scholar.

[87] Nicoletti, B. (2018). Processes in Agile procurement. In *Agile procurement* (pp. 113–147). Cham, Switzerland: Palgrave Macmillan.

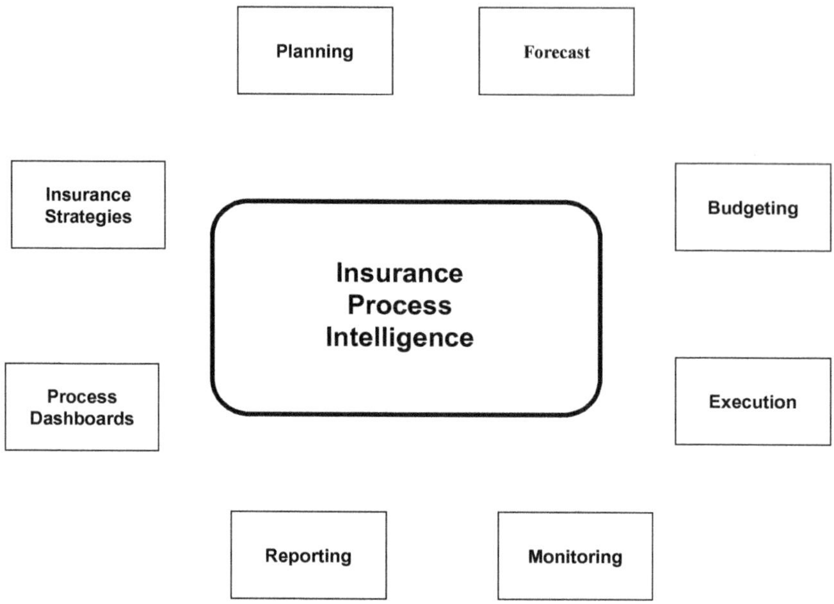

Fig. 9.12 Insurance process intelligence

The forecasting, strategy, planning, and budgeting modules, through collaborative management of scenarios and other features targeted to the analysis of the consequences of decisions, aim to:

- Analyze and share future results;
- Simulate alternative hypotheses;
- Prepare and validate more targeted planning.

These modules must be complemented by a performance management component (Enterprise Performance Management) that supports the planning and control processes, both on strategies and on operations, in line with the organization's objectives.[88]

[88] Qingping, L. (2006). The enterprise performance evaluation for maximizing the enterprise value based on stakeholder theory [J]. *Accounting Research, 3*, 56–62.

The platform must support insurance processes while providing unique flexibility innovatively. This solution is possible thanks to native integration with business intelligence:

- Forecast the flow of processes over time;
- Plan and control both the strategy and the operations;
- Plan from an economic and financial point of view;
- Budget;
- Simulate the consequences of possible choices;
- Manage profitability and costs;
- Produce synthetic dashboards for monitoring the ongoing activity.

The solution must be flexible. It must permit:

- Adapting to any need or requests from the insurance planning function;
- Providing a workflow aimed to collect the approvals, as stated in the organization's procedures.

The finance and control department using the platform must be able to:

- Communicate the organization's strategy;
- Implement and monitor its performance;
- Feel its influence in all organizational levels necessary to ensure that plans are effectively executed.

Collaboration

The collaboration process must allow the organization to adopt new ways of collaboration, inside and outside the organization, to support insurance 4.0. The traditional insurance support applications (ERP, CRM, and so on) provide structured information but do not allow activation of unstructured collaborative mechanisms "data-driven" where persons, including the partners, interact, negotiate, decide, and finally execute.[89]

[89] Anderson, C. (2015). *Creating a data-driven organization: Practical advice from the trenches*. Sebastopol, CA: O'Reilly Media, Inc.

An essential difference between an insurance process intelligence solution and all other collaboration platforms is that traditional collaborative methods focus on persons. Insurance process intelligence must allow the organization to target the collaboration on data, documents, and processes.

The key objective is to have a platform that can provide collaborative capabilities and execution of the processes of insurance 4.0 contextual information and relevant documents. It should allow insurance 4.0 to become more agile. This agility enables the organization to seize the opportunities that the market offers and to ensure that insurance processes cannot become inflexible, preventing the organization from adapting to increasingly rapid changes in markets and supply.

The collaborative platform must be able to integrate structured and unstructured data and provide collaborative capabilities and performance transactional capabilities able to connect internal actors with customers and partners.

The system must provide some of the following collaboration features:

- Automatic management of workflows;
- Instant messaging;
- Remarks;
- Alert signals;
- Exchange of documents;
- Collaborative work;
- Unified search and if possible semantic searches[90];
- Mobility tools (cellular phones, tablets, and similar).

Execution

With the support for executing processes, the insurance process intelligence system should allow the professionals of insurance 4.0 to integrate information, decisions, and actions. It should be possible to implement a collaborative judgment (e.g., the process of a claim) with a single mouse click or a mobile app. Contextually, it should be possible to record the information directly in the analysis system that has generated the decision.

[90] Guha, R., McCool, R., & Miller, E. (2003). Semantic search. In *Proceedings of the 12th International Conference on World Wide Web*, 700–709. New York City, NY: ACM.

These features allow to:

- Integrate processes monitoring in real-time all the key performance indicators (KPI) of the insurance. They are the critical variables placed under observation. Their correlation can generate intelligence;
- Use intelligence, built in the system, to handle unplanned events collaboration by providing all actors in the ecosystem of the organization (including partners and intermediaries) the optimal guidelines to maximize the critical performance indicators defined for specific processes;
- Close the loop by running or triggering the actions necessary to implement the decision taken by the insurance 4.0 professionals or by the system itself.

Monitoring and Spend Analysis (Visibility)

The insurance process intelligence solution must offer concrete and timely decision support. It must provide not only a magnifying glass of the data on the assets and persons insured by the organization. It should also be a way to maximize the return from utilizing internal resources and assets through integrated collaborative mechanisms.

The insurance business intelligence solution must provide the opportunity for all the persons and institutions involved to make collaborative decisions based on the information and, at the same time, propagate decisions on processes directly in the assay system using native functionality.

Insurance 4.0 and Business Process Intelligence

From a technology point of view, the business process intelligence solution must be an integrated platform that uses a single development environment, unified security management, and process descriptions. The administration of these components should allow managing and supporting analyzing, planning, knowledge sharing, and process execution, using a collaborative environment. This integration allows the organization to drive the execution of decisions, to optimize them, and, above all, to be able to consider the overall objectives in every step of the decision-making process.

There are technologies and vendors of application software packages with powerful integrated collaborative analytical engines. They can produce dashboards, reports, evaluation grids, alert signals with short deadlines, and on which to activate, when necessary, modes of collaboration needed for sharing information.[91]

Conclusions

This chapter reviews the transformation of processes that support insurance 4.0. The chapter does not cover all the insurance processes but those critical in helping insurance 4.0.

Innovation in insurance can take many forms. Often, but not always, technology helps. It is critical to improve processes. The solutions will be a combination of processes and platforms. The essential thing is to select the solution/(s), which suits the organization's needs. It is critical not to forget that the organization who hesitates to change has lost. This statement is true in organizations and personal life.

One of the most relevant changes in the insurance 4.0 processes is in the shift in the insurability of the risks.[92] The availability of big data impacts information asymmetry (depending on if this is possible to access the customer data) and risk pools, which will be smaller and with more homogeneity.[93] Insurance 4.0 can change loss frequency and severity (sale, operations, and administration costs could decrease. Values insured could increase due to a more expensive built-in technology).[94] New technologies could also increase threats through connectivity (cyber risks), raising many legal and ethical questions.

The chapter dedicates attention not only to risks but also to resilience. Resilience is an important subject for two reasons. Insurance companies

[91] Commercial packages are available to cover all or part of the business process intelligence.

[92] Eling, M., & Lehmann, M. (2018). The impact of digitalization on the insurance value chain and the insurability of risks. *The Geneva Papers on Risk and Insurance-Issues and Practice, 43*(3), 359–396.

[93] The Impact of Digitalization on the Insurance Value Chain. slideheaven.com/the-impact-of-digitalization-on-the-insurance-value-chain-and-the-insurability-o.html. Accessed 30 May 2020.

[94] The Impact of Digitalization on the Insurance Value Chain. slideheaven.com/the-impact-of-digitalization-on-the-insurance-value-chain-and-the-insurability-o.html. Accessed 12 June 2020.

should analyze better the capability of the policyholder to reduce the probability of the risks and especially their potential impact. Besides, in a changing role of companies toward services, they should be able to provide services to policyholders on how to improve their resilience, not only for business continuity but also on the assets and persons insured. An example on this respect is Generali Vitality, which aims to improve the lifestyle of the policyholders rather than just insuring the health.[95]

[95] Bitter, P., & Uphues, S. (2017, September). Big Data und die Versichertengemeinschaft–«Entsolidarisierung»durch Digitalisierung. *ABIDA-Dossier*.

CHAPTER 10

Persons in Insurance 4.0

Introduction

Organizations must re-engineer with a lean and digitize[1] approach all processes and activities. The use of new solutions allows the organization to have an integrated view. This approach facilitates decisions that affect the entire value network. The use of innovative solutions removes the discontinuity in the value network. It allows the companies to coordinate in smooth way processes and activities. The objective is to increase productivity and ease of use. In this phase of transformation, the determining factors are the persons. To further extend and deepen innovation and adopt advanced solutions, the role of the persons emerges as decisive. E-competencies are essential.[2]

Insurance 4.0 requires critical resources for the new approach in the organization's Value Propositions/Distribution Places and Channels/Customer proximity/Revenue Streams. This chapter frames the insurance sector's various categories to better understand the talents necessary for insurance 4.0.

[1] Nicoletti, B. (2012). *Lean & digitize: An integrated approach to process improvement*. Farnham, UK: Gower Publishing. ISBN-10: 1409441946.

[2] Dobozy, E. & Ifenthaler, D. (2014, May). Initial teacher education by open and distance modes: A snapshot of e-competency experiences in Australia. *eLearning Papers: Digital Literacies & eCompetencies, 38*, 57–67.

B. Nicoletti, *Insurance 4.0*, Palgrave Studies in Financial Services Technology, https://doi.org/10.1007/978-3-030-58426-9_10

There has been a concern that digital transformation will lead to a reduction in employment. On the contrary, employment levels have been remarkably robust in Germany in the last few years when looking at the number of those employed as well as volume of working hours, notwithstanding industry 4.0 transformation.[3]

Resources represent the real engine of the insurance organizations and their partners. The human resources selection is a process which should start from the needs of the organization. It aims to understand the potential gaps in talents and the need for the insertion of a new or current person in an insurance 4.0 organizational context. Mainly relevant are the persons in contact with the customers and the prospects. They are critical profiles in the insurance organization. An example is a consultant who, starting from the knowledge of the services offered, assists, advises, and then places the policy to the customer. The personnel selection and training processes are critical factors since the personnel competencies determine the success of the transformation to insurance 4.0.

Persons represent a challenge but also an essential opportunity. In launching an insurance 4.0 initiative, companies should be ready to build up the required capacities and competencies to support the organizational vision and mission from a more strategic and innovative perspective. The new role of insurance 4.0 as a vital network node within its ecosystems influences the management of value-adding services. This approach requires to rethink tasks, functions, and responsibilities of all insurance parties. It is also necessary to set up cross-functional interdisciplinary roles to speed up transactions and processes to stay at the cutting edge of new solutions. These roles need to drive future organizational success in the most efficient, effective, and efficient ways based on sustainable and diversified service offerings.[4]

Insurance 4.0 needs persons properly prepared, formed, and trained in insurance 4.0 processes and solutions. This is a challenge since most current employees in the organizations and their partners started working

[3] Eichhorst, W., Hinte, H., Rinne, U., & Tobsch, V. (2017). How big is the gig? Assessing the preliminary evidence on the effects of digitalization on the labor market. *mrev management revue, 28*(3), 298–318.

[4] Bienhaus, F., & Haddud, A. (2018). Procurement 4.0: factors influencing the digitization of procurement and supply chains. *Business Process Management Journal, 24*(4), 965–984.

when industry 4.0 does not even exist as a concept. Insurance 4.0 is an opportunity to revitalize the interests of these persons and provide opportunities for talents. For this reason, this chapter focuses on the training for insurance 4.0: training 4.0.

Companies compete for talents. Startups or technology companies attract them more. Companies must prioritize recruiting a workforce that considers the future of the world's demographics. The workforce will be diverse across education and experience, personalities, cultural needs, and preferences. The inclusion of all those differences can generate new learnings and ideas for improving business results. Talents are more mobile than ever. Millennials and Generation-Z[5] expect to work in corporate cultures that provide good opportunities to move in the organization and work collaboratively for projects that inspire and give challenges.[6]

According to Italian entrepreneurs, investments in training represent the best strategy to enhance human capital in the organization (49 percent).[7] There are still some stereotypes that are present mainly among young persons. The latter see work in the organization as tiring and manual (64 percent), repetitive, not very creative, with not much space for personal fulfillment (48 percent), little social recognition (41 percent), and even a technologically backward place (29 percent). All these factors make it difficult for organizations to fill specialized profiles. Industry 4.0 can contribute to resolving some of these difficulties by improving substantially the workplace.

A survey of the Italian market for industry 4.0[8] was directed to organizations that had started using 4.0 solutions in their processes. The survey found the need to manage the impact on the entire organization. Most of the organizations pay attention to the process and flow changes (54.2 percent of the sample), personnel activities and work methods (45.3

[5] Gen Y, or Millennials, were born between 1980 and 1994. Gen Z is the newest generation to be named and was born between 1995 and 2015. Shatto, B., & Erwin, K. (2017). Teaching millennials and generation Z: Bridging the generational divide. *Creative Nursing, 23*(1), 24–28.

[6] Singh, A. P., & Dangmei, J. (2016). Understanding the generation Z: The future workforce. *South-Asian Journal of Multidisciplinary Studies, 3*(3), 1–5.

[7] www.mecspe.com/en/comunicati-stampa-en/osservatorio-mecspe-focus-nazionale/. Accessed 5 August 2019.

[8] www.corrierecomunicazioni.it/industria-4-0/rallenta-la-corsa-di-industria-4-0-nel-2019-crescita-in-calo-del-10-15/. Accessed 22 June 2019.

percent), and technical competencies (42.7 percent). Less than 20 percent focused on roles, managerial and relational competencies, and expected behaviors. Companies' focus on organizational aspects is in 18.8 percent of the cases at the start of the project for the introduction of industry 4.0 and in 20.8 percent during its development.

Often, the promoter of the 4.0 initiatives is a top manager (43.8 percent of the sample) or the operations or plant manager (35.4 percent). The involvement of innovation or research and development (R&D) functions throughout the project's entire development. The human resources (HR) function is involved in very few cases in the several phases of insurance 4.0. Only in 6.8 percent, it was involved in all the steps in the transformation. In 27.1 percent, it was only informed at the start of the project. In 23.4 percent, it did not have a role in any activity of the industry 4.0 initiative. The involvement of operators was also limited: only 7.8 percent of organizations involved them in all phases of the industry 4.0 initiative. Twenty-five percent did not assign any role to the operators. In only 26.6 percent of the cases, operators received information on the 4.0 strategy.

Fifty-seven percent of organizations have taken steps to identify 4.0 competencies shortages and started the actions necessary to fill them. Three out of ten consider them adequate as many are working to improve them. There is robust participation of the entrepreneurs, top managers, and project managers 4.0 in the decision to evaluate the competencies necessary for industry 4.0. The HR managers have been kept in most cases in the background. They acquire importance only in the implementation phase.

New Working Models[9]

Insurance 4.0 also requires remote or smart working. This way of working is becoming the new or next normal, at least in insurances and other businesses, after the pandemic. There could be similar events in the future: another pandemic, a financial crisis, and a significant industry disruption. Companies need to be prepared and agile enough to manage in the short- and long-term future.

[9] https://home.kpmg/xx/en/home/insights/2020/04/insurance-workforce-transformation-through-covid-19.html. Accessed 30 May 2020.

Many companies are generally handling the remote working well. Some areas are more challenges than others:

- Health checks for life insurance;
- Person management;
- Call centers due to the increased activities connected with inquiries from policyholders, more and more interfacing companies online;
- Front office areas like sales, marketing, and distribution.[10] These sectors have traditionally had more face-to-face interactions with customers, especially with the agents. They must now adapt to a mediation of the technology[11];
- Policy endorsements and signatures;
- Sophisticated underwriting (specialty risks life insurance, commercial businesses, and so on);
- Sophisticated claims adjustments and handling;
- Reinsurance reporting;
- Settling and billing (mostly due to access to systems and complexity) and possible billing disputes;
- Compliance assessments and audit;
- Finance resources availability;
- Outsourced processes.

It is interesting to examine the KPMG model of the Talent Risk Framework. It identifies five areas critical for managing and staffing a workforce in times of significant changes. They are "The 5 C's"[12]:

- Capacity: Are there sufficient resources in the right locations. Are they staffed to do what the company needs them to do?

[10] The future comes early—KPMG Global. https://home.kpmg/xx/en/home/insights/2020/04/insurance-workforce-transformation-through-covid-19.html. Accessed 12 June 2020.

[11] The future comes early—KPMG Global. https://home.kpmg/xx/en/home/insights/2020/04/insurance-workforce-transformation-through-covid-19.html. Accessed 12 June 2020.

[12] https://assets.kpmg/content/dam/kpmg/ca/pdf/2020/03/managing-talent-risk-en.pdf. Accessed 30 May 2020.

- Capability: What are the critical competencies and skills required to ensure that the workforce operates effectively and efficiently in a sustainable way?
- Connectivity: How to teach and ensure that teams be connected and motivated? Are they committed to this new emerging environment?
- Cost: How much will the workforce cost to run as you ensure business continuity?
- Compliance: What are the regulatory implications of remote working for an extended period?

The gaps coming up are not so much connectivity or technology gaps. They are relative to persons, management skills, and processes. Many companies are coping well with moving to remote connectivity. Others have not been able to cope at the correct level, also for telecommunication network problems.

The more in-depth challenge is to manage the remote workforce to achieve the right capacity in the right areas. This challenge has already shown itself in the vast surge that many companies have experienced during the last pandemic in inquiries and claims for travel and health cover. This situation is in contrast to other areas (such as vehicle insurance), which have declined. Companies need the flexibility to respond and react quickly. They need a flexible workforce in which the use of resources is more flexible.

Remote working requires the creation of a distributed model, especially for insurance distribution. The model must bring the flexibility and functionality organizations needed to operate in a highly uncertain environment. It is something that many companies need to learn fast. Many times, insurance organizations are relatively traditional, with a high emphasis on presence in person. The impression is that teams of persons need to be present together in the same place for the business to function. The pandemic shows that teams can be set up and engaged in different ways and still be very productive. Pandemic is also pushing to adopt smaller, leaner, and especially more effective teams. These teams break down large functions into small working groups who can self-organize, highly effectively connect, and react quickly to changing requirements. The difficulty is that until now the work in a team has not been very much present in insurance companies and their intermediaries.

There are several challenges in this new working model. In some cases, remote working struggles to replicate some of the benefits of face-to-face interaction. Many customers report that the creativity and spontaneity, the snowballing of ideation, that occur when a group of persons comes together to discuss an issue or a problem are not easy to reproduce virtually. There is a disappearance of the water fountain effect or the casual meeting in the corridor, where persons informally meet and talk. In some cases, social networks or groupware can help. Still, persons refrain from putting in writing or communicate remotely some observations or information. These situations need further work and exploration to see whether there are solutions that can help.

Remote management is the most challenging part of running a remote workforce. Organizations must make efforts in supporting managers and team leaders and in how they are helping their staff. Managing a team where most of all the persons are working remotely is challenging. It is necessary to ensure that persons feel motivated and supported. It is essential to help them perform at their creative best, looking after individuals' mental and emotional well-being in a new and challenging time, setting goals, and assessing performance. There is no real roadmap for this on the scale that future remote working will require. Targets and performance measures are especially hard to set in such a dynamic time—without a doubt, pay and reward decisions will be especially difficult in this new environment.

It is critical to establish a correct picture of running a remote workforce compared to an onsite team. A more flexible and remote workforce can lead in the longer term to consider other aspects of the compensation. In the future, the overall organization-wide distribution of time spent in the office against time working remotely is expected to be around 50-50. Some staff may come into the office one or two times a week or a month.

Security is particularly important in the case of remote working. Hackers have taken the opportunity to monetize on the pandemic. Persons working from home do not have access to the cyber security defense infrastructures that they would have at work. As a result, there has been an increase in phishing, scams, and ransomware attacks that leverage remote working.

Working remotely also raises several challenging compliance issues that need to be managed. Data security becomes a critical concern, with a need to ensure that staff only use approved communication and data transfer methods. Compliance with regulated or business-critical processes remains vital. Management must ensure that the necessary online approval processes are in place. They should consider whether any new actions need to be introduced for compliance requirements to continue to be respected.

Old and New Profiles

In connection with insurance 4.0, there is a need to:

- Review the current competencies;
- Introduce new competencies, especially e-competence.

Some examples of new competencies are below (see also Fig. 10.1).

New Competencies for Underwriters

Addressing the risks in insurance 4.0 requires new processes and platforms. Persons are also essential. The role of the underwriters should take into account the threats in insurance management. It is necessary to:

- Promote the organization's needs for risk management in insurance;
- Bring an added value to the organization's decisions by conducting a careful assessment of risks in the insurance connected with the commercial strategies;
- Analyze and assess risks (old and new);

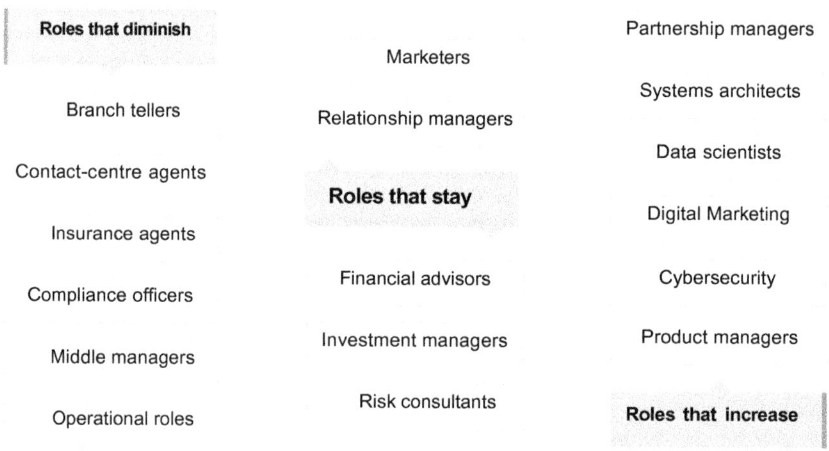

Fig. 10.1 New roles in insurance 4.0

- Inquire about the prospects and their assets to assess the chances of customers creating problems in what is insured;
- Be fully aware of a series of contractual strategies and tactics that can be applied when the organization defines and negotiates contracts to avoid or mitigate risks.

To address in an effective, efficient, and economical way risk management, the underwriters should have the following competencies[13]:

- Knowledge of business processes and market characteristics;
- Management of priorities;
- Knowledge of the methods and risk management tools and processes;
- E-competencies;
- Care of the details;
- Analytical and open mind;
- Objective approach.

Data Scientists

Organizations need to create new job profiles, for example, data scientists for relevant data analysis, management, and mining. Data scientists need in-depth domain knowledge and a broad set of analytical competencies.[14] Developing a broad set of analytical competencies requires consistent investments in time.

Data scientists are highly-trained scientists. They are also innovators able to sift new perspectives on general tendencies out of the available data.[15] A data scientist analyzes data from several and diverse sources.[16]

[13] www.cii.co.uk/media/1921347/c13j_8582_job_role_and_competency_framework_v2.pdf. Accessed 20 May 2020.

[14] Waller, M. A., & Fawcett, S. E. (2013). Data science, predictive analytics, and big data: A revolution that will transform supply chain design and management. *Journal of Business Logistics, 34*(2), 77–84.

[15] Molino, J. L., & Sedkaoui, S. (2016). *Big data, open data and data development*. Hoboken, NJ: ISTE Ltd. and John Wiley & Sons.

[16] Big Data, Open Data and Data Development—Slidelegend.Com. https://slidelegend.com/big-data-open-data-and-data-development_59b99b031723dde15b68a08e.html. Accessed 20 May 2020.

He or she examines the different tasks to attain a general understanding of the phenomenon it describes and enables a company to develop competitive advantages.

For the search of these talents, it is necessary to use non-traditional sources. Academic's partnership programs and research centers can help in these searches. It is also useful to explore new channels, such as social networks, social media, and top-performing employees. Only if insurance personnel have e-competencies can an organization fully benefit from the opportunities provided through digitization and automation.[17]

Process Architects

The process architects analyze current processes ("As-Is") and design future state processes ("To-Be") in support of insurance 4.0. The processes are associated with many factors of technology related to insurance 4.0, like robots, IoT, AI, and human interventions and interactions. There are different types of processes, including long-term and short-term processes. The process architects are responsible for defining new centralized or decentralized processes.[18] First, they need to understand the current process flow and identify the gaps in the process activities, system components, task handling, time requirements, and cost reductions along with systems effectiveness, efficiency, and economics. She/he and the business analysts are responsible for process re-engineering and process automation. The process architects design the consistent methods, processes, and standards of insurance 4.0.

Particular attention should be devoted to underwriting, which is one of the most critical processes. It requires new profiles to manage that process (Fig. 10.2).

[17] Competence is a demonstrated ability to apply knowledge, skills, and attitudes for achieving observable results. The European e-Competence Model (e-CF) provides a reference of 40 competencies as required and applied at the digital transformation workplace, using a common language for competencies, skills, and capability levels. More in www.ecompetencies.eu/wp-content/uploads/2014/02/European-e-Competence-Model-3.0_CEN_CWA_16234-1_2014.pdf. Accessed 30 May 2020.

[18] Cho, E. S. Cha, J. E., & Yang, Y. J. (2004, May). Marmi-Re: A method and tools for legacy system modernization. In *International Conference on Software Engineering Research and Applications* (pp. 42–57). Berlin/Heidelberg: Springer. The Future Digital Work Force: Robotic Process Automation. www.scielo.br/scielo.php?script=sci_arttext&pid=S1807-17752019000100300. Accessed 10 May 2020.

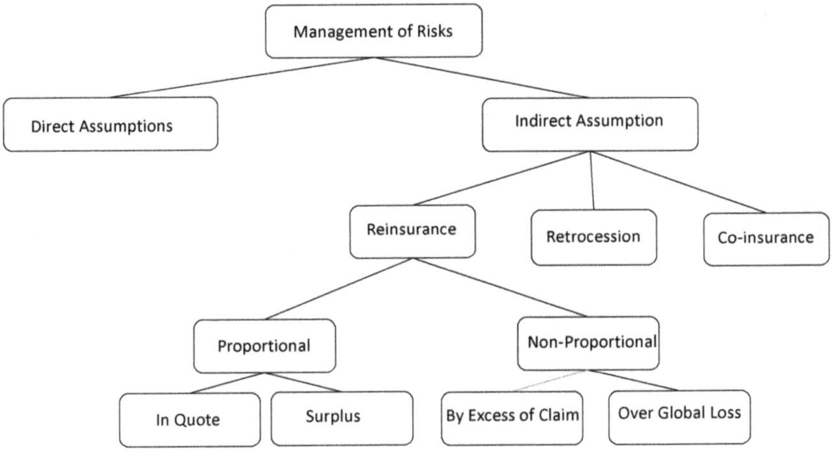

Fig. 10.2 Management of risk in insurance

Technologists

Technologists develop solutions that translate business logic into digital and automation platforms. Usually, a technologist is an engineer who specializes in a specific technology or who uses technology in a particular field.[19] An insurance 4.0 initiative will usually include a team of dedicated developers in a low-cost location to activate the program. The technical competencies required for insurance 4.0 tools are relatively less sophisticated compared to traditional application development. Usually, they need open-minded technology experts in several areas of digitization and automation.

Ongoing Support and Maintenance Staff

There is a need for a staff that executes newly automated tasks, provides maintenance, supports, and updates the solutions when necessary. This process generally happens through an annual maintenance contract (AMC) with the software vendor or vendors. They should debug the

[19] Pramanik, H. S. Kirtania, M., & Pani, A. K. (2019). Essence of digital transformation—Manifestations at large financial institutions from North America. *Future Generation Computer Systems, 95,* 323–343.

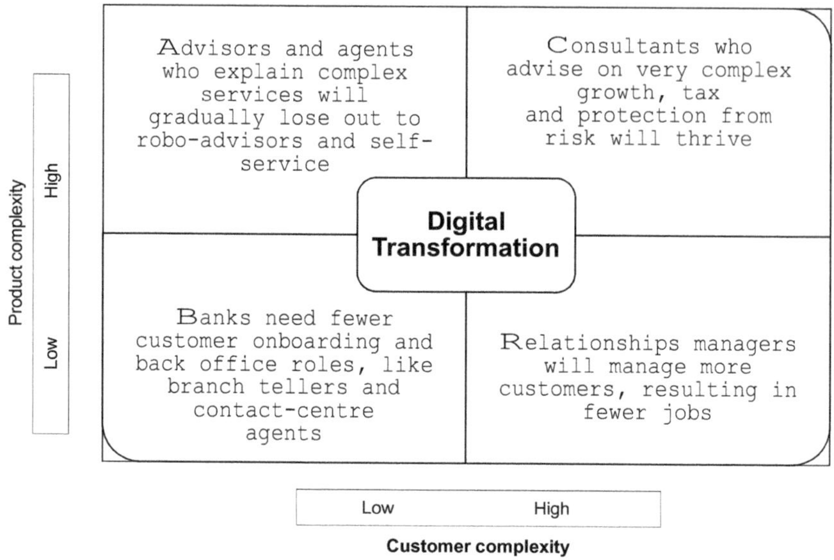

Fig. 10.3 Customer facing jobs in insurance 4.0

errors if there are any fault and failure in the system and application software. They give technical support 24×7 round the year. Typically, external vendors provide this support. In this way, it is possible to reduce the in-house professional persons' recruitments costs and time. There would not be any training costs also.

The customer-facing jobs are particularly relevant (Fig. 10.3).

Person Contribution to Insurance 4.0

Persons in the organization must contribute at two levels to insurance 4.0:

- Employees are the base of organizational procedures and processes. They must be close to the transformation into insurance 4.0. Persons are affected by this transformation for the changes in the working processes and platforms. Persons have the chance to be part of a successful transformation by identifying areas for improvement. The results of a survey[20] show that employees are partly undecided based on the micro-level perspective, which technologies can leverage insurance 4.0. On the macro-level perspective, the employees understand and highlight the importance of digital transformation as a success factor for the organization's future;

- At the management level, the insurance 4.0 transformation and increasing global connectivity with cross-functional teams push the management to creating a working environment able to free the potential of creativity and innovation in all the staff. The role of the managers is on one side to guide employees through the process of the transformation to insurance 4.0. On the other hand, it is critical to create time and space for the persons to accomplish this change process and to ensure sustainable long-term success. Managers need to identify the bottlenecks and challenges on the macro-level perspective and define appropriate actions to resolve them. This roadmap is the correct one for ensuring an efficient, effective, and economical operation within the entire organization.

Some leaders are still working hard to match the desired agility and expectations, along with the essential information and communication security on the insurance 4.0 roadmap.[21] Some organizations have already introduced a new profile, called Chief Digital Officer (CDO), to support insurance 4.0.[22] The job of the CDO is to overcome the lack of agility, business focus, and inflexible nature of some of the current staff. The managers need to lead from the front and collaborate more closely with the concerned staff and managers. There is also the need for support from the top management to help redefine the middle managers' role.

[20] Bienhaus, F., & Haddud, A. (2018). Procurement 4.0: Factors influencing the digitization of procurement and supply chains. *Business Process Management Journal, 24*(4), 965–984.

[21] Sharma, A. (2020). Industry 4.0—An opportunity to revivify the IT function. cio.economictimes.indiatimes.com/news/corporate-news/industry-4-0-an-opportunity-to-revivify-the-it-function/73078237. Accessed 28 January 2020.

[22] Horlacher, A., & Hess, T. (2016, January). What does a Chief Digital Officer do? Managerial tasks and roles of a new C-level position in the context of digital transformation. In 2016 49th Hawaii International Conference on System Sciences (HICSS), 126-5135. IEEE.

Training 4.0

Insurance 4.0 is associated with the convergence and integration between traditional ICT and automated systems. Some aspects that characterize industry 4.0, and hence insurance 4.0, are[23]:

- Cooperation. New solutions enable the creation of virtual teams through which organizations exchange data, information, and documents;
- Connectivity. Insurance 4.0 enables horizontal and vertical integration in the value network and ensures visibility of information in all network links;
- Adaptiveness. The system of connected digital and automation resources must be flexible. It must be able to respond to changes in the environment (requests, customers, users, partners, and so on);
- Integration. In the digital world, the combination of the insurance systems involves connecting different computer systems, software applications, machinery automation, physically or functionally, to coordinate the insurance flows;
- Autonomous. Smart objects, physical or virtual, that have the possibility of communicating are present in the insurance 4.0 solutions;
- Cognition. Application of devices and systems for the automation of tasks requires human competencies, knowledge, perception, and cognitive competencies (planning, reasoning, and learning).

Insurance 4.0 launched at the level of an organization requires a great effort and rethinking of education and training. To analyze the requirements of training 4.0, it is interesting to follow the sequence suggested by Rudyard Kipling to describe the phenomena: 5 W and 1 H.[24] It is useful to examine the Why, What, Who, When, Where, and How in this case of training 4.0. It is appropriate to spend special attention to the insurance issues since they are different from manufacturing industries.

[23] Kayikci, Y. (2018). Sustainability impact of digitization in logistics. *Procedia Manufacturing, 21,* 782–789.

[24] Kipling, R. (2013). *Just so stories*. Scott Valley, CA: CreateSpace Independent Publishing Platform.

Why

Underlying insurance 4.0, there are some components of the organizations. They are the 4Ps: processes, platforms, persons, and partnerships. Persons are essential to architect, design, develop, monitor, and control new solutions. Hence, the importance of educating and training persons on the insurance 4.0 vision involves the most significant number of persons. It is critical to developing their e-competencies. E-competencies are the ability to design and use with confidence advanced solutions.[25] The competencies of insurance 4.0 are useful to all persons and, in particular, to those who occupy managerial positions in insurance 4.0.

E-competencies are the basic competencies in information, communication, and automation solutions. They are skills essential to retrieve, assess, store, produce, present, exchange information, communicate, and participate in collaborative networks also via the web.[26]

What

Training 4.0 must relate the persons to the other three Ps: processes, platforms, and partnerships. Some persons believe that insurance 4.0 is only automation and digitization. It is critical to review the processes and re-engineer them in the direction of the insurance 4.0 robust organization goals.

Attention should go in providing training in small- and medium-sized organizations through practical research and tailor-made knowledge transfer. The items to consider are several, such as automation and process re-engineering, both accompanied by the business model transformation.

The training and the application of insurance 4.0 should be made in teams. It is critical to promote training on how to improve teamwork and make it more effective, efficient, and value-adding.

[25] Arballo, N. C. Núñez, M. E. C., & Tapia, B. R. (2019). Technological competencies: A systematic review of the literature in 22 years of study. *International Journal of Emerging Technologies in Learning (iJET), 14*(04), 4–30.

[26] www.aicanet.it/competenza-digitale. Accessed 30 March 2020.

Who

Training 4.0 must be for at all levels and roles of the organization. It should not be limited to persons working on automation and ICT. On the contrary, it is necessary to develop e-competencies in all areas.

Insurance professionals must take into account the insurance 4.0 approach. Management, staff, strategy, maintenance, marketing, sales, and administration should be involved in the insurance 4.0 training.

The partners, at least those critical to the organization, such as the intermediaries and agents, should attend the training. It is useful to start with an activity of "train the trainers,"[27] that is, training other trainers or at least the key users throughout the organization. The number of persons involved in the organization in an insurance 4.0 transformation could be very high. Training trainers in the organization can help reduce costs and foster the creation of "evangelists" who spread good practices across the organization.

When

Ideally, training for insurance 4.0 should start in schools and universities. It is also essential to train the persons already employed by the organizations for their conversion and active support to the initiative.

Insurance 4.0 requires new competencies and capabilities. As a result, persons in the organization should be involved well before the start of an insurance 4.0 initiative.

Where

The ideal location for training 4.0 is in or near the organization's premises. Training on the job with frequent applications and interactions is essential. Training limited to the classroom would not achieve the purpose of the transformation. If the organization is unable to prototype and do proofs of the concept of insurance 4.0, the organization can

[27] Pearce, J., Mann, M. K., Jones, C., van Buschbach, S., Olff, M., & Bisson, J. I. (2012). The most effective way of delivering a Train-the-Trainers program: A systematic review. *Journal of Continuing Education in the Health Professions, 32*(3), 215–226.

use training as the playground to make the first successful small implementations of insurance 4.0. Thus, it would be possible to strengthen the participants in the importance and mainly the viability of insurance 4.0.

How

The approach suggested in this chapter for training 4.0 is holistic and integrated.

Apart from the training in the classroom and on the job, it would be essential during the training to include visits to other organizations that have successfully implemented insurance 4.0. A visit to German organizations or research centers can be useful. An excellent research center on industry 4.0 is the Fraunhofer-Gesellschaft, the largest organization for applied research in Europe.[28] It is a nonprofit German research organization. The institute collaborates with the industry to promote research that generates benefits for the whole society. This research institute was the first in Germany to work on the concept of industry 4.0 and to experience it successfully.

A visit to research centers would be useful also to expand the network of relationships. It can help in drawing on funds allocated to research and competence centers for the development and testing of insurance 4.0 within the organizations.

[28] www.fraunhofer.de. Accessed 26 April 2020.

Insurance 4.0 Roadmap

It is critical to consider the roadmap to migrate from the traditional insurance organization toward the application of the paradigm of insurance 4.0. There are three necessary steps to lead this change giving the correct value to the persons[29]:

1. Develop appropriate education and training programs. The design must be an integrated process. It starts to create awareness and sensitivity from the top management downward. It should disseminate the knowledge of insurance 4.0 going top down to the more operational layers of the organization. This approach must be consistent with the insurance company's strategy and, in general, with its policy. Digital competencies and e-competencies are essential at all levels[30];
2. Redesign how persons work and interact. Digitize and automate a process involves not only adopting new and advanced methods and techniques to perform the same activities as before, with higher efficiency, effectiveness, and economy. The organization needs to push on accelerating the organizational changes and the insurance 4.0 transformation. It should completely redesign the work experience of the persons within the organization and the critical intermediaries;
3. Attract new talents from the labor market. The transition from a traditional to a digital operating model, no matter how well prepared, tends to result in a non-negligible percentage of failures. The innovative way of working (new roles, new competencies, new

[29]This section follows the guidelines introduced and pioneered by Prof. Marco Perona and presented in www.digital4.biz/insurance/strategie/insurance-4-0-la-check-list-lufficio-acquisti-digitale/. Accessed 9 March 2019.

[30]In 2006, the European Parliament proposed a first definition of "Digital Competence" in the "Recommendation of the European Parliament and of the Council of December." It includes eight critical competencies for lifelong learning. "Digital competence is to be able to use with confidence and critical Information society technologies (IST) for work, leisure, and communication. It is built on primary competencies in ICT (Information and Communication Technology): the use of computers to retrieve, assess, store, produce, present and exchange information, and to communicate and participate in collaborative networks via the Internet."

relationships and partnerships, new tools, and so on) can be challenging to be accepted and integrated within their jobs by some persons in the organization.

Conclusions

New profiles, education, and training are essential for insurance 4.0. It is necessary to address them holistically. It is necessary to take into account all aspects and addresses in a consistent and integrated framework.

To consolidate a culture supporting insurance 4.0 is necessary to take into account five essential competencies. They would be essential in implementing correctly insurance 4.0 in the organization:

- Ability to manage innovation in person-digital-automation relationships;
- Digital value network and ecosystem management;
- Application of lean business 4.0[31];
- Core competencies in safety management and cybersecurity both in the ICT domain and in operations technology (OT) domains.[32]

The Osservatorio del Politecnico di Milano (Italy) conducted a survey that tracks the profile of some Italian organizations in their knowledge of industry competencies 4.0.[33] Half of the organizations knew about industry 4.0 or claimed to have assessed their competencies for industry 4.0. These news are positive. It is in a context where another 25 percent say they want to do it soon. The survey revealed that the training was for persons engaged in operations, employees, and profiles directly involved in the work on digitization and automation systems. The sensitivity in the

[31] Elg, M. Gremyr, I. Hellström, A., & Witell, L. (2011). The role of quality managers in contemporary organizations. *Total Quality Management & Business Excellence, 22*(8), 795–806.

[32] Hickson, D. J. Pugh, D. S., & Pheysey, D. C. (1969). Operations technology organization structure: An empirical reappraisal. *Administrative Science Quarterly*, 378–397.

[33] www.industry4business.it/osservatori/osservatorio-industria-4-0-industrial-iot-analytics-e-cloud-manufacturing-spingono-il-mercato-a-24-mld-con-un-30/. Accessed 25 May 2019.

training courses does not stop at the operational floor. Instead, managers and entrepreneurs should be involved in the roadmap to e-competencies 4.0.

The survey was useful to determine some essential aspects of training 4.0. The training of internal staff (24 percent) and external acquisition (11 percent) of the competencies required are the two great feedbacks from organizations engaged in the 4.0 transformation. The survey creates some concerns on the marginal role of the HR function in this training. Only 12 percent of the sample involved human resources function in guiding and directing the training roadmap to the insurance 4.0 transformation. For 70 percent of the survey participants, HR either was not involved or only in a marginal way.

CHAPTER 11

Partnerships in Insurance 4.0

Introduction

This book does not use the term vendor, intermediaries, agents, and similar but partners. There are several reasons for the use of this terminology. The first reason is that the partners can be of very different types: distributors of products, services, and systems, partners external or from the same group of companies or even from the same organization, or academic research institutions, consultants, and so on. The real reason to use the word "partner" is that all the mentioned external parties are real partners. A partner is a person, natural or legal, with which the organization works together in activities in which sales and operations require the participation of more than one person and more than one skill. A partner is an ally. If the delivery is unsuccessful, both the partners and the customers suffer in their reputation, if not directly from a financial point of view. In the case of insurance 4.0, the partners play an essential role in the value network, because of their relevance and close interconnection.

There are many types of partners of insurance companies:

- Reinsurers and capital markets are a sort of vendors. Without the protection of reinsurers, significant risks or huge portfolios could not be insured. The capital markets provide the required rate of return on the investment of the insurance premiums;

B. Nicoletti, *Insurance 4.0*, Palgrave Studies in Financial Services Technology, https://doi.org/10.1007/978-3-030-58426-9_11

- Intermediaries, agents, claim adjusters, maintenance operators, and brokers can also be described as partners. They are still a very essential part of the insurance distribution and operations[1];
- New types of partners are the vendor of new solutions, such as the internet of things (IoT), artificial intelligence (AI), or similar;
- Finally, the insurtech organizations introduce new products, services, and processes. They can also be valuable partners.

For an insurer to realize the potential value of the digital transformation, it must include partners in their migration to insurance 4.0.[2] As companies integrate smart insurance product technology, such as IoT, into core offerings, forging partnerships open up many possible benefits. Not only will these devices provide companies with higher awareness of insured assets and lives. The companies will find in them opportunities to mitigate potential losses and develop new services. The ecosystem for these services, combined with artificial intelligence (AI), will add value to the data generated. Robust partnerships with hardware or software original equipment manufacturers and platform providers, committed to continuous improvement, are also essential.

Some companies are already providing some of the capabilities discussed in the previous chapters to customers. Many potential partners for companies have designed business models to allow for experimentation and piloting. These solutions enable an insurance company to plug into a program, develop its offering using the appropriate number of resources and planning, and quickly get scale.

Coordinating partnerships that are best in class to deliver an engaging insurance offering to the market might be challenging. It can bring many benefits. Such an alliance can move quickly (as opposed to building internal capabilities from scratch) and allow opportunities to test and learn to improve the program. The key to successfully manage these new partnerships is to bring partners to the standards of the insurance carrier's brand. There is also the need for internal resources that work with partners to bring them to the appropriate standards.

[1] Hartung, T., & Rohatsch, N. (2018). *Einfluss der Digitalisierung auf die Unternehmensstrategie*. München, Germany: München University.

[2] iotinsobs.com/. Accessed 11 December 2019.

Advanced solutions will generate an increase in the market for digital products.[3] The role of partners of such virtual components and the decline of partners' importance in physical components are very likely.

Insurance 4.0 push on an increasing emphasis on the importance of partners. The activities that insurance 4.0 organizations must implement are quite different from the past. Insurance 4.0 requires partner developments, partner design engagements, use of full-service providers, selection of integrated partners, long-term partner relationships, strategic cost management, enterprise resource planning, integrated internet connections, and shared databases as ways of creating new value within the value network.[4]

The integration of operations with partners enables organizations to capture the benefits from the exchange of information. Vanpoucke et al. reported that ICT use is an essential foundation for integration with partners in an insurance 4.0 perspective.[5]

Outsourcing helps the organization to achieve higher levels of value creation for the final customer.[6] Drivers of outsourcing come from organizational initiatives, improvement focus, financial and cost objectives, growth objectives, search of flexibility, or need of critical resources not available internally. A wide range of core and non-core essential processes of an organization are increasingly outsourced. These processes cover a broad spectrum of sectors and operations, enabling host organizations to world-class capabilities. In the past, insurance companies have outsourced processes like underwriting and claims. To be successful, insurance 4.0 requires the insurance managers to professionally monitor whichever part of insurance value network contact should go to the partners.[7]

[3] Porter, M. E., & Heppelmann, J. E. (2014). How smart, connected products are transforming competition. *Harvard Business Review, 92*(11), 64–88.

[4] Rodrigues, M., Sousa, B., & da Costa, J. B. (2019). The improvement of the supply chain channel based on digital transformation: An exploratory study in the sustainable industry 4.0. *4th Regional Helix-Book of Abstracts*. Parallel Session 4, Porto, Portugal.

[5] Vanpoucke, E., Vereecke, A., & Muylle, S. (2017). Leveraging the impact of supply chain integration through information technology. *International Journal of Production Management, 37*(4), 510–530.

[6] Ghodeswar, B., & Vaidyanathan, J. (2008). Business process outsourcing: An approach to gain access to world-class capabilities. *Business Process Management Journal, 14*(1), 23–38. https://doi.org/10.1108/14637150810849382. Accessed 15 June 2020.

[7] Hood, J., & Stein, W. (2003). Outsourcing of insurance claims: A UK case study. *The Geneva Papers on Risk and Insurance—Issues and Practice, 28*(3), 510–520.

Insurance 4.0 and Partnerships

In partnerships, insurance 4.0 consists of an adjustment rather than an entirely new approach. The organization must take into account the increasing importance given to partners and to the relationships with them. To achieve this, some organizations have tried not only to meet their needs but to get a higher degree of flexibility with their partners through increased visibility into their internal insurance flows and administrative aspects.

There are three different fields for redefining innovation: the simplification and digitization at the level of transactions, the assignment of benefits, and the degree of use of the partners.[8]

The restructuring process consists of a complete organizational change. In a globalized ecosystem, there is a need for a new partnership between the different areas of an organization, mainly by supporting partners in the financial sectors, such as re-insurers or capital markets. This solution is necessary to make useful innovations in insurance. It is critical an innovation upstream of the organizations in which partners take on an essential role. This type of change requires cooperation and robust communication with the partners. The term restructuring of insurance is necessary because this new partnership brings insurance professionals to perform tasks that they did not do in the past. In particular, they need to sell insurance 4.0 solutions upstream of the organization and to its partners and downstream to agents and customers.

The redefinition and restructuring in insurance 4.0 can be beneficial for the partners and the organization's customers.[9] The internal restructuring of the organization is not sufficient without the close involvement of the partners. Considering the redefinition of insurance, this is only possible with a change in the organization. The latter is only possible with a redefinition of innovation. For example, in some organizations, the adjustment of performance evaluations and the new collaboration between insurance and finance functions allow both the redefinition and restructuring

[8] Wuttke, D. A., Blome, C., Foerstl, K., & Henke, M. (2013). Managing the innovation adoption of supply chain finance—Empirical evidence from six European case studies. *Journal of Business Logistics, 34*(2), 148–166.

[9] Wuttke, D. A., Blome, C., Foerstl, K., & Henke, M. (2013). Managing the innovation adoption of supply chain finance—Empirical evidence from six European case studies. *Journal of Business Logistics, 34*(2), 148–166.

of insurance processes. The tasks must align with the effective adoption of insurance 4.0. At the same time, this alignment is possible with the restructuring process. The organization's missions should consider the adoption of insurance 4.0 as a tool to improve the performance of the organization. As for the involvement of partners, some organizations have realized that besides this alignment on the objectives, the participation of the partners requires the redefinition of the organization. This redefinition must also be done considering the needs of the partners. This involvement not only enables a more straightforward process redesign. It facilitates the alignment of the different functions by better communicating with various partners. Some surveys have confirmed that this involvement has promoted the link between restructuring and redefinition and did not directly enhance the effectiveness of insurance 4.0.[10] After the redefinition and restructuring process, the adoption of insurance 4.0 can become a routine for the organization. Some organizations have put in place this innovation. They are working to make innovation a habit. The companies including their partners need to convince all those responsible for the effectiveness of the organization to adopt insurance 4.0 gradually but entirely.

In this spreading action of insurance 4.0, the functional managers play an essential role. These actors should be in direct communication with the insurance organization network operators to get more awareness of the decisions to involve more partners.

The benefits that an organization can provide to the partners are several. The company can represent a lever for the adoption by the partners of the insurance 4.0 approach. This diffusion depends on trust. Based on trust, the partners can accept the migration to insurance 4.0. Another essential factor in the spread of insurance 4.0 to the partners is the power of the insurance organizations on the partners. Some organizations can impose the adoption of an insurance 4.0 approach to their partners. The insurance leverage of the power of relationships and trust with the partners are vital components for organizations that want to adopt insurance 4.0.

[10]Wuttke, D. A., Blome, C., Foerstl, K., & Henke, M. (2013). Managing the innovation adoption of supply chain finance—Empirical evidence from six European case studies. *Journal of Business Logistics, 34*(2), 148–166.

Organizations should promote the sustainability of insurance 4.0. The value of this innovation often revolves around the initiative of an organization that has chosen to innovate. Change does not only optimize the relationships between partners and customers. It also facilitates the continuity of the partnerships. If large organizations expand the perspective of the value network members, the benefits are risk-sharing in exchange for more reliable revenues and more stable relationships.

Ping An[11]
Ping An is a giant Chinese insurer with more than one million employees and agents. Its single customer portal called One Account offers also services from other partners such as healthcare consultations, auto sales, real estate listings, and banking services to more than 350 million online customers. This activity also generates customer traffic for Ping An's core services. It helped the company to become the world's most valuable insurance brand.[12] Ping An serves an enormous and dynamic customer market, making the company a directionally relevant example for global insurance organizations that seek to replicate its success in other markets.

Ecosystems

This section examines the rise of ecosystems and the implications for companies principally from a distribution point of view. An ecosystem is "an interconnected set of services (or products) that allows users to satisfy a variety of needs in one seamless experience."[13] Ecosystems live around customer needs. They are different from simple partnerships across industry boundaries to bring together digitally accessible services or products. An ecosystem can provide customers with an end-to-end experience. Ecosystems will generate globally USD 60 trillion in revenue

[11] Ping An. (2017). Ping An becomes the world's most valuable insurance brand. brandfinance.com, Accessed 10 March 2020.

[12] brandfinance.com/press-releases/ping-an-becomes-the-worlds-most-valuable-insurance-brand/. Accessed 30 May 2020.

[13] Catlin, T., Lorenz, J. T., Nandan, J., Sharma, S., & Waschto, A. (2018, January). Insurance beyond digital: The rise of ecosystems and platforms. McKinsey.com. Accessed 20 May 2020.

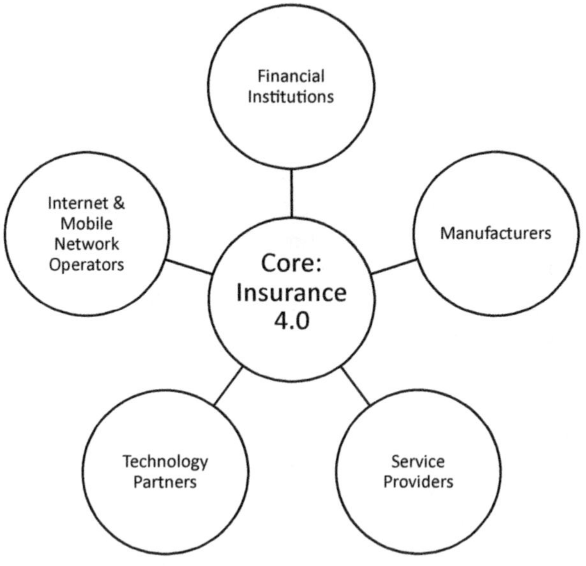

Fig. 11.1 Insurance 4.0 ecosystem

by 2025.[14] This revenue will constitute 30 percent of global sales in that year.[15] According to a July 2018 survey by DXC Technology, 22 percent of European companies said they were already part of an ecosystem that could provide additional services to customers. Another 46 percent said that becoming part of an ecosystem would be a high priority[16] (Fig. 11.1).

Although today's challenges may cause apprehension, insurance companies are not alone. It is time for insurers to embrace open ecosystems. They need to collaborate with mature insurtech organizations and

[14] *Insurance ecosystems and platforms: How companies can turn*. www.mckinsey.com/industries/financial-services/our-insights/ecosystems-and-platforms-how-companies-can-turn-vision-into-reality-. Accessed 10 May 2020.

[15] Catlin, T., Lorenz, J. T., Nandan, J., Sharma, S., & Waschto, A. (2018, January). *Insurance beyond digital: The rise of ecosystems and platforms*. McKinsey.com. Accessed 20 May 2020.

[16] DXC Technology. (2019, July). *Advancing digital insurance: A survey on the digital maturity of the European insurance industry*. dxc.technology. Accessed 10 May 2020.

third-party specialists to develop innovative solutions and enable quick market successes.[17]

In a given ecosystem, there are two ways for a company to get involved: orchestration and participation.[18] Orchestration means assembling various services into a transparent customer journey. Some companies, such as the Chinese Ping An, arrange their ecosystems using their subsidiaries.[19] Their common name is "builders." Others create partnerships to integrate non-insurance services into the insurer's domain to ensure scalability. Other companies simply participate in current ecosystems orchestrated by other players. Their objective is often to gain access to the ecosystem for lead generation. As an example of the latter, Maersk has teamed up with Zurich Insurance Plc to launch Maersk Cargo Insurance, a product to protect customers' goods against physical loss or damage.[20] Maersk Cargo Insurance covers goods from the time they are first moved for loading until the completion of unloading at destination, from and to almost every country in the world. Regardless of the transport or carrier used, customers can get peace of mind knowing their shipment is insured from door to door, and from departure to arrival.

Participation tends to generate less value and forfeit the customer interface. It is easier to achieve for a single use case and can bring benefits. Orchestration generally requires a significant investment in capital and resources. It is not a strategic option for all companies, such as the smaller ones.

Each role has its benefits. In practice, these roles are not clear-cut. An insurer can play both characters at the same time across different ecosystems.

[17] worldinsurancereport.com/. Accessed 30 May 2020.

[18] Catlin, T., Lorenz, J. T., Nandan, J., Sharma, S., & Waschto, A. (2020). *Insurance beyond digital: The rise of ecosystems and platforms*. www.mckinsey.com/industries/financial-services/our-insights/insurance-beyond-digital-the-rise-of-ecosystems-and-platforms. Accessed 21 March 2020.

[19] www.the-digital-insurer.com/china-in-depth-ecosystems-in-china/. Accessed 15 June 2020.

[20] www.coverager.com/maersk-teams-up-with-zurich-to-offer-maersk-cargo-insurance/. Accessed 20 June 2020.

To succeed in an ecosystem, companies need to take a hard look at their traditional roles and business models. They must evaluate opportunities to integrate with organizations in other industries.[21] They should consider partnerships to achieve this objective. This spirit is in tune with the insurance 4.0 model.

Companies must also understand how ecosystems will shift value propositions. They need different transformation management to get all the benefits connected with insurance 4.0 and reduce the risks related to this innovation. Adopting an ecosystem mindset will not be easy for many companies. Those that understand this evolving landscape can take the first steps to create new margins sources.

For companies, shifting from industry to an ecosystem perspective requires a significant change in their business models. Companies act primarily as risk aggregators. Traditionally, they have a passive and limited relationship with customers. This approach increases their exposure to disintermediation, disaggregation, commoditization, and invisibility. If companies do not want to lose their customer proximity and channels, they should change their business models. Adopting an ecosystem perspective could reinforce companies' market strategies.[22] This approach implies re-evaluating the traditional business model and considering partnerships both within and outside the industry. The industry has already seen several high-profile partnerships between established companies and tech and analytics startups.[23]

Ecosystems need different transformation management to get all the benefits connected with insurance 4.0 and reduce the risks related to this innovation.[24] The options include offering innovative mixed solutions in

[21] fwww.the-digital-insurer.com/insurance-beyond-digital-the-rise-of-ecosystems-and-platforms/. Accessed 10 January 2010.

[22] *Digital disruption in insurance: Cutting through the noise.* (2017). www.mckinsey.com/~/media/McKinsey/Industries/Financialpercent20Services/Ourpercent20Insights/Timepercent20forpercent20insurancepercent20companiespercent20topercent20facepercent20digitalpercent20reality/Digital-disruption-in-Insurance.ashx. Accessed 29 January 2020.

[23] www.the-digital-insurer.com/insurance-beyond-digital-the-rise-of-ecosystems-and-platforms/. Accessed 10 January 2010.

[24] www.mckinsey.com/industries/financial-services/our-insights/insurance-beyond-digital-the-rise-of-ecosystems-and-platforms. Accessed 11 January 2020.

insurance and services with partners from other industries (e.g., predictive maintenance and preventive care).[25] Companies could also enhance how they manage their risks by exploiting information based on sensor data from other industries. Companies could also draw on their analytics expertise to offer proprietary data and analytics solutions to third parties.

Defining and implementing an ecosystem strategy require continuous dedication and commitment. Executives aiming to consider an ecosystem strategy should focus on a couple of areas. The total value at stake is going to be up for pick up for all players in the distribution economy. All players must identify and prioritize the specific ecosystems in which they can and want to play. An ecosystem strategy requires robust performance across multiple dimensions, including culture, technology, and customer proximity. Companies should determine the critical capabilities that can help them with differentiation in an ecosystem. Then, they should evaluate whether their organization can accept a new approach or not. Moving to an ecosystem requires the insurance 4.0 company to become more and more a coordinator of a complex network.[26]

IoT-based health and home insurance only recently emerged and is used by a relatively small number of European companies.[27] There is great potential for disruption. These new types of services need to provide more than one benefit and not just focus on lowering premiums. For example, to win customers, IoT could provide valuable information to users, targeting new market niches. It can inform environmentally-friendly persons how to reduce their carbon footprints by improving their way to drive. These new devices could inform drivers on how to minimize their risks by analyzing how they drive and advising them to take safer routes. Ecosystems can help to achieve these goals. Besides, they can help customers to avoid or minimize losses. The potentials are endless: in home insurance, thanks to IoT, persons can, for example, receive alerts and shut off a leaking water pipe using their mobile phones.[28]

[25] Bouwman, H., de Vos, H., & Haaker, T. (Eds.). (2008). *Mobile service innovation and business models*. Berlin and Heidelberg, Germany: Springer Science & Business Media.

[26] Chang, H. H., Chou, P. B., & Ramakrishnan, S. (2009, October). An ecosystem approach for healthcare services cloud. In *2009 IEEE International Conference on e-Business Engineering* (pp. 608–612). IEEE.

[27] Greco, A. (2018). *Digital transformation and disruption* (Doctoral dissertation). Lisbon, Portugal: Nova—School of Business and Economics.

[28] breadware.com/blog/iot-applications-and-examples/. Accessed 5 March 2020.

Another application of the IoT could be for companies to change their business model: from life benefits to coaching health advisors and promoting well-being.[29] They will be able to enter new customer segments. For example, if an insurance company would add services that will focus on health, they could specifically target millennials, which usually might be unaware or not interested in the need for life insurance. According to a Deloitte report, many customers are willing to use these types of services. Many more could do so in the future.[30] The disruption may occur in the sense that there would be a shift in risk assessment from "what has happened" to "what could happen."[31] This authoritative analysis can allow companies to forecast why and when things are going to happen. Exploiting data available could help companies improve the sales conversion ratio by continually adjusting prices and policies.[32]

Companies need to move fast in developing and launching these types of solutions based on IkT devices. First-movers will gain a more significant amount of data and, as a consequence, useful insight. Network effects will help them to reach these targets.[33] They will be likely to be better positioned in the competition environment. In this area of operation, it will be possible for companies to partner with sensor manufacturers and companies that own the data (like vehicle manufacturers, health equipment producers, and so on).[34]

To find the right partners, companies have to think about the best way to position themselves in the IoT ecosystem strategically. For example, they could leverage trust and reliability qualities, considering

[29] Spender, A., Bullen, C., Altmann-Richer, L., Cripps, J., Duffy, R., Falkous, C., & Yeap, W. (2019). Wearables and the Internet of Things: Considerations for the life and health insurance industry. *British Actuarial Journal*, *24*.

[30] *Insurance disrupted: General insurance in a connected world*. (2015). www2.deloitte.com/content/dam/Deloitte/global/Documents/Financial-Services/gx-fsi-insurance-disrupted.pdf. Accessed 29 January 2020.

[31] Jacobson-Wright, N., Latham, I., & Frost, F. (2019). *Guidance for care homes—Implementing Namaste Care*. eprints.worc.ac.uk/8987/1/Guidance-for-Care-Homes-V3-updated.pdf. Accessed 15 July 2020.

[32] www.pwc.com/gx/en/insurance/publications/assets/pwc-insurance-2020-and-beyond.pdf-. Accessed 29 January 2020.

[33] Cai, J., De Janvry, A., & Sadoulet, E. (2015). Social networks and the decision to insure. *American Economic Journal: Applied Economics*, *7*(2), 81–108.

[34] Oztemel, E., & Gursev, S. (2020). Literature review of Industry 4.0 and related technologies. *Journal of Intelligent Manufacturing*, *31*(1), 127–182.

the increasing concern of customers on data collection and analysis by other organizations. The most attractive companies will be those that will provide risk assessment services and roadside and medical assistance.[35]

Due to their technology, robust organizational requirements, ecosystem, and platform business models are not easy to build up and scale.[36] If successful, ecosystems enable new sources of growth, help attract and retain customers, and make products more viable through prevention and assistance. Companies could benefit from robust economies of scale and growth through resources that they do not necessarily need to possess themselves.

Ping An[37]

Ping An of China is an example of an ecosystem orchestrator in the insurance industry. The company goes beyond selling insurance products, offering its customers an ecosystem of services such as Ping An Good

[35] Greco, A. (2018). *Digital transformation and disruption* Doctoral dissertation. Lisbon, Portugal: NOVA—School of Business and Economics.

[36] Catlin, T., Lorenz, J. T., Nandan, J., Sharma, S., & Waschto, A. (2020). *Insurance beyond digital: The rise of ecosystems and platforms*. www.mckinsey.com/industries/financial-services/our-insights/insurance-beyond-digital-the-rise-of-ecosystems-and-platforms. Accessed 21 March 2020.

[37] Catlin, T., Lorenz, J. T., Nandan, J., Sharma, S., & Waschto, A. (2020). *Insurance beyond digital: The rise of ecosystems and platforms*. www.mckinsey.com/industries/financial-services/our-insights/insurance-beyond-digital-the-rise-of-ecosystems-and-platforms. Accessed 21 March 2020.

Doctor, PingAnfang, and Autohome to address their health, housing, and mobility needs more comprehensively. By stocking the ecosystem with its subsidiaries, this approach generates a substantial number of new customers and increases current-customer loyalty. Ping An's online car-purchasing platform, Autohome, has almost 30 million unique visitors each day. It generates one-third of customer leads for the insurance company's P&C and financial services businesses.[38]

Zubie[39]

Zubie is active in the connected vehicle business. It makes a vehicle-tracking and engine-diagnostic device that plugs into a vehicle. It can help to track how well the driver is driving. The company has a partnership with the insurance provider Progressive. The agreement enables Zubie customers see how much Progressive would charge them based on the driving data that Zubie collects.[40] Driving habits affect their premiums.

Progressive has been a pioneer in usage-based pricing. It wants to get out of the business of sending customers hardware to discover their driving habits. Under a program called Snapshot, Progressive customers can get an appliance device that plugs into their cars' on-board diagnostics (OBD) ports. This device enables sharing driving data with the company.[41]

Progressive is interested not only in vehicle data, but also weather data and GPS data that could pinpoint the likelihood of accidents or how a person drives. In perspective, there might be an interest in sensor data about persons.

As for Zubie, this is one of the first options available under a new perks program it is building for its members. The members have the opportunity

[38] "Form 20-F," United States Securities and Exchange Commission, April 12, 2019. ir.autohome.com.cn.

[39] gigaom.com/2014/09/04/connected-car-company-zubie-signs-deal-with-progressive/. Accessed 33 January 2020.

[40] *Connected car company Zubie signs deal with progressive.* gigaom.com/2014/09/04/connected-car-company-zubie-signs-deal-with-progressive/. Accessed 16 June 2020.

[41] *Connected car company Zubie signs deal with progressive.* ngigaom.com/2014/09/04/connected-car-company-zubie-signs-deal-with-progressive/. Accessed 15 July 2020.

to send their data to Progressive in order to pay less for insurance and get other types of service. Zubie collects a monthly fee for its device to offset the cost of providing a cellular data connection.

Insurance in Team

The correct approach in insurance 4.0 is to consider the four Ps: processes, platforms, persons, and partnerships. Lately, there is much talk of teamwork in insurance due to the increasing importance and complexity of the value network. Insurance work has always been teamwork. This feature is now increasingly appreciated and valued. The support tools help the management of persons, processes, and platforms. Insurance takes a new role as team coordinator. It seems appropriate to analyze this view. The current insurance model will change in a future perspective with regard to functions, responsibilities, and stakeholders. The change is also pushed by increasing digitization and its opportunities, supported by ecosystems and other trends outlined in this book.[42]

Persons and Organization

Insurance 4.0 is teamwork. Teamwork can be within the insurance ecosystem. It can also refer to the collaboration within the organization. For example, in the case of a project, it is critical to have in the project team members, subject matter experts of insurance services and processes. They would be members of the project full- or part-time based on the size of the project. For organizations that are part of a group, it is interesting to work within the group to achieve synergies in the standard policies. In the case of organizations that are not part of the same group, the organization can team up with other organizations in the same ecosystem.

[42] Sengupta, S. (2013). 10 trends in supply chain management. *Supply Chain Management Review, 17*(4), 34–39.

Processes

In the insurance team, teamwork can be very effective in supporting the marketing of insurance. In this case, the participation of many persons with diverse experiences can be of great support. Similarly, the participation of partners can be of great help in sharing the experiences with other intermediaries and in selecting future partners.

Platforms

The support that the information and communication technology (ICT) can provide for teamwork is growing and improves over time. For insurance 4.0, it is useful that the ICT platform includes three essential aspects of the collaboration:

- Communication is the backbone of the teamwork. An insurance platform supporting teams uses a variety of media, chats, email, video and audio conference calls, and so on, at several levels of sophistication;
- Coordination is based on rules, explicit or implicit, to enable several components of the team to operate in synergy. Typical tools in the insurance 4.0 teams are group calendars and automatic software packages for planning and document sharing;
- Cooperation implies the sharing of a context that varies with the characteristics of the initiatives developed by the working team.

In the past, the platforms for the teamwork were proprietary. Today many standardized commercial solutions are available. Examples are the organization chat or the so-called groupware.[43] The latter term describes methods and tools that enable users with workstations connected via a network to:

- Communicate in several ways: from the exchange of messages (email, chats, and similar) voice calls, and videos on a computer screen;
- Allow Condivision of multimedia documents (text, data, images, and sounds);

[43] Kadir, B. A., & Broberg, O. (2020). Human well-being and system performance in the transition to industry 4.0. *International Journal of Industrial Ergonomics, 76*, 102936.

- Co-work on the same application programs, whether it is a simple spreadsheet or a complex application to schedule jobs in which different team members take part;
- Get Consensus on decisions at several stages of the process, using tools that facilitate discussion and idea generation, such as online brainstorming sessions.

Intra-organization and inter-organization can exploit cloud computing solutions. Organizations that have an advanced approach to cloud computing tend to maximize their benefits through hybrid solutions. This approach enables organizations to effectively use these solutions as a means to integrate information across the organization. It also allows the organization to use cloud computing to interact effectively, efficiently, economically, and in total transparency with its partners.

An exciting variation of the distribution models of cloud computing is the so-called cloud B2B.[44] This solution helps to address the cooperation and integration between the insurance companies and their partners and customers.

Security

In teamwork, it is necessary to consider cybersecurity protection and tracking of information, and how much transparency of data with all partners and customers should take place.

There are some things to consider for data security and confidentiality. The benefits of teamwork can be significant, from the standpoint of effectiveness, efficiency, and economy. The most significant benefits are the increase in the effectiveness of the insurance organization: in response times and also in the satisfaction of the customers.

[44] Nicoletti, B. (2013). *Cloud Computing and Financial Services*. London, UK: Palgrave Macmillan (also translated in Chinese).

Allianz X and Debeka[45]

Allianz X is the digital investment unit of German insurance company Allianz Group. Debeka is an insurance and financial services provider based in Koblenz, Germany. According to Allianz X, the company SDA SE platform enables companies to efficiently integrate their current ICT systems and processes. The platform helps in getting external partners and service providers on board. At the same time, they continue to have full ownership of their data and analytics. The company is said to achieve that by incorporating service-dominant architecture into its open-source platform. The potential of service-dominant architecture in the insurance industry is significant.[46] It will bring demand-driven customer communication to a new level with the insurance 4.0 transformation.

By making use of SDA SE's platform, insurance providers, irrespective of their sizes, can introduce their services quickly and in real-time, operationalize their digital strategy, and bolster customer touchpoints.

Insurance companies tend to primarily rely on in-house approaches and own architectures for the insurance 4.0 transformation. These isolated solutions have several disadvantages. They cover in great depth the value network, they are expensive, and several times do not consider the know-how in the market.[47]

Partners Evaluation in Insurance 4.0

The subject of the assessment of the partner (or Partner Rating) is essential. It is relevant to the processes of insurance 4.0 as it allows:

- Better selection of the partners;

[45] www.nsinsurance.com/news/sda-se-open-industry-allianz-x-debeka/. Accessed 10 January 2020.

[46] *Allianz X and Insurance Firm Debeka Invest in Insurtech*. www.crowdfundinsider.com/2019/11/154647-allianz-x-and-insurance-firm-debeka-invest-in-insurtech-sda-se-open-industry-solutions-an-open-platform-for-developing-digital-ecosystems/. Accessed 15 July 2020.

[47] *Allianz X and Insurance Firm Debeka Invest in Insurtech*. www.crowdfundinsider.com/2019/11/154647-allianz-x-and-insurance-firm-debeka-invest-in-insurtech-sda-se-open-industry-solutions-an-open-platform-for-developing-digital-ecosystems/. Accessed 25 July 2020.

- Correction also during the operations of any defects or inadequate performance;
- Involvement of the entire ecosystem in the insurance processes.

The assessment of the partners should take place at different times:

- Before the organization starts working with a partner, at the time of its selection;
- During the provision of services or the supply of services;
- At the end of the service.

Everybody in any organization agrees with the previous statements. Rarely, the process is followed throughout the life of a partnership. For example, in the evaluation at the end of a period, getting from several internal operators a proper and written assessment is challenging. The problem is that persons are often over-committed and do not have time or do not prioritize the partners' assessment.

One may wonder whether the insurance 4.0 transformation can also support the assessment of the partners. This is essential since, in many cases, the percentage of total sales or claims over total amounts brought by the partners is increasing over time.

It is worthwhile to see how the most meaningful solutions in insurance 4.0 can help assess the partners.

Big Data

IoT collects many data also on the partners and their products or services. For claims, IoT can help collect data on road service assistance. Other electronic tools are available to gather data on insured assets. The customer relationship center provides an example. More and more organizations are using applications that enable the creation of a ticket to record incidents, problems, service and change requests, and knowledge management processes. Many of these tools can produce dashboards on compliance with the agreements on the levels of service. Therefore, the organization can automatically record data on the partner performance, compliance with the contracts, and mainly the trends. Thus, the organization can evaluate the partners and, if necessary, take action before the situation goes out of control.

All these data can be stored using big data analytics. In this way, it is easy to access or produce statistical reports on performance.

Artificial Intelligence

Big data analytics allows the organization to connect with artificial intelligence tools. These applications can provide operational and management level support. They can also be used to evaluate partners and support them for better delivery if they do not reach the agreed performance.

Mobility

Whenever there is a need for a manual assessment of the partner performance, organizations can use simple apps on mobile phones to collect data on the partners' performance. In this case, the apps can also remind the employees of the need for the partners' assessment, which will require only a few clicks.

Cloud Computing

Cloud computing extends the use of the tools mentioned above virtually to the entire organization, even when employees are very mobile.

Conclusions

Porter states that the source of competitive advantage is the skillful management of connections in the value network.[48] It is possible to generalize the statement to an ecosystem. Other authors add that the complexity of offers increases with the complexity of the partnerships necessary to deliver these offers.[49] As a result, strategic activities should be oriented on the reconfiguration of roles and relationships with the partners to provide new forms of value for the customer. The purpose of partnerships in insurance 4.0 needs to change substantially.

[48] Porter, M. E., & Heppelmann, J. E. (2014). How smart, connected products are transforming competition. *Harvard Business Review, 92*(11), 64–88.

[49] Normann, R., & Ramirez, R. (1993). From value chain to value constellation: Designing interactive strategy. *Harvard Business Review, 71*(4), 65–77.

Organization's operations are increasingly a network in which the different paths allow advanced customization of the product. The objective of insurance 4.0 is not merely delivering services to add value to customers and the organization. In this new vision, insurance companies need to work as a coordinator of a network of partners (the ecosystem). The ecosystem must work as one team. With this in mind, the assessment of the partner is an essential aspect. The relationships with the partners should be of mutual value. Assessments should ensure the continuous improvement or, at the extreme, the fixing or closing of the partnerships.

CHAPTER 12

Pricing in Insurance 4.0

Introduction

A Gartner survey found that 65 percent of respondents expect their companies' use of technology to support revenue growth rather than cost reduction.[1] One-quarter of respondents say that increased revenue from new customers will be the primary outcome of their use of the latest solutions in the next few years. Roughly one-fifth of respondents expect new solutions to increase engagement with current customers (21 percent) or to add revenue from new products or business models (19 percent). Another 21 percent of respondents believe that reduced costs through automation and digitization will be the most likely outcome of their companies' use of new solutions.

One of the significant benefits, with the adoption of insurance 4.0, is the possibility for companies to forecast risks and customer demand with higher precision than ever before, transforming companies' value proposition from "reactive claims payer" to "preventive risk advisors"[2] lowering prices, and better shaping their targets.

[1] www.mckinsey.com/business-functions/mckinsey-digital/our-insights/managing-the-fallout-from-technology-transformations?cid=other-eml-alt-mip-mck&hlkid=bf4d7318c abc44d99ce3ad00689ae9fc&hctky=2743882&hdpid=eac0bc3c-8635-4f36-a0ed-4322b5 1bbc6a. Accessed 9 March 2020.

[2] Price Waterhouse Coopers. (2017 [2015]). *Disruption is the new reality in the global insurance industry*. goo.gl/oh8Htt. Accessed 10 May 2020.

B. Nicoletti, *Insurance 4.0*, Palgrave Studies in Financial Services Technology, https://doi.org/10.1007/978-3-030-58426-9_12

Revenue Streams

For insurance companies, a large part of sales is coming through intermediaries. These partners manage the relationships with the policyholders and businesses. Their compensation is with a fee or commission for placement/broking of an insurance policy. Supports include introducing policyholders to the company, getting quotes from companies, and advising on which insurer would provide the required cover for the best value/price.[3] Intermediaries can also earn revenue by performing several other services for companies, such as underwriting, policy administration, claims processing, loss prevention, risk management consulting, employee benefits consulting, and captive management services. The amount of remuneration for these services often depends on the intermediary's performance.

Captive management services might include business planning, compliance, financial accounting, management reporting, and insurance underwriting.[4] Under IFRS and US GAAP, insurance intermediaries gain revenue from transactions based on the stage of completion. The revenue standards require an insurance intermediary to recognize revenue as services are provided to the customer, using the amount expected in exchange for the services.[5] Insurance intermediaries need to assess their contracts to determine the timing and amount of revenue to recognize under the revenue standards. The model requires a contract-based approach under which the following steps apply[6]:

1. Identify the contract with the customer;
2. Identify the performance obligations in the contract;
3. Determine the total transaction price;

[3] Price Waterhouse Coopers. (2017 [2015, June]). *In-depth: A look at current financial reporting issues*. www.pwc.com/hu/hu/szolgaltatasok/ifrs/ifrs_15/irfs_by_industries/insurance.pdf. Accessed 10 May 2020.

[4] PWC. (2015). *In-depth: A look at current financial reporting issues*.

[5] Price Waterhouse Coopers. (2017 [2015, June]). *In depth: A look at current financial reporting issues*. www.pwc.fr/fr/assets/files/pdf/2016/06/pwc_in_depth_insurance_entity_may2016.pdf. Accessed 10 May 2020.

[6] Price Waterhouse Coopers. (2017 [2015, June]). *In depth: A look at current financial reporting issues*. www.pwc.fr/fr/assets/files/pdf/2016/06/pwc_in_depth_insurance_entity_may2016.pdf. Accessed 10 May 2020.

4. Allocate the total transaction price to each performance obligation in the contract;
5. Recognize as revenue when (or as) each performance obligation is satisfied.

Pricing

For insurance 4.0, it is critical to use new solutions for a more adequate pricing of risks.[7] In particular, it is possible to reduce information asymmetries.[8] On the one hand, the main challenges are in respect of the customer interface and on the other in the early response to the actions from potential new competitors. Yields for the policyholder in the modern world of insurance mainly benefits (in the form of lower premiums or more individualized offers), if they are willing to provide the insurance company their data.

Pricing is essential for customers. Technology can help quite a bit. Simon-Kutcher in August 2017 conducted a quantitative study on the main reasons pushing policyholders to change their companies. He found that: 29 percent is "price too expensive", 20 percent "premiums getting higher without justification", 16 percent "given cover is not adapted to policyholders needs", 7 percent "claim is mismanaged", and so on.[9] Within the same study, the benefits of signing online insurance are 53 percent due to "lower prices", 51 percent for "simplicity and rapidity", 23 percent "customization of the offer to customer needs".

New risk evaluation methods enable insurance companies to use more effective pricing models. They can also not use any more traditional models for computing claims reserves, based on statistical-actuarial methods of historical data analysis. Companies are beginning to use predictive models that detect the customer risk profile in real-time,

[7] Prognos, A. G. (2017). *Digitalisierung in der Versicherungswirtschaft. Studie.* München, Germany: Hg. v. vbw Vereinigung der Bayerischen Wirtschaft e.V.

[8] Browne, M. J., & Doerpinghaus, H. I. (1993). Information asymmetries and adverse selection in the market for individual medical expense insurance. *Journal of Risk and Insurance*, 300–312. Eling, M., & Lehmann, M. (2018). The impact of digitization on the insurance value chain and the insurability of risks. *The Geneva Papers on Risk and Insurance-Issues and Practice*, *43*(3), 359–396.

[9] Sayegh, K., & Desoky, M. (2019). *Blockchain application in insurance and reinsurance.* France: Skema Business School.

thanks to advanced solutions.[10] Smart analytics, predictive modeling, and connected telematics devices assist companies in designing their services and setting premiums based on how policyholders behave, rather than using general proxies. Therefore, companies can make policy and claim management more effective and efficient.[11] As new risks come up in real-time, companies can improve the management of eligibility, underwriting, and monitoring policy risks.

Information can also be analyzed and processed by algorithms to accurately compute the claims reserves in the event of a claim. Thus, insurance companies can use the resources available in a more effective, efficient, and economical way, directing them toward investments with a better return rate.

If the core business of insurance is risk selection and the price determination for taking them, the current trend toward the use of big data analytics can substantially modify the data type itself, how data is analyzed, claim management, and relationships with customers.

Risk-Based Pricing

The growing availability of data about policyholders, collected via sensors and smart devices, enables a more granular underwriting and monitoring of individual risks. Smart analytics is the term used to describe a more systematic use of data.[12] To this end, both structured data from a range of sources (such as sensors, written documents, and data on the internet) and unstructured data, taken from conversations or letters, are collected. Software solutions recognize patterns in the data and cluster them. They can provide companies with more detailed insights into the characteristics and needs of their customers.

The opportunity to collect and analyze a large variety of data in real-time is transforming insurance processes, such as claims. They enable

[10] Cappiello, A. (2020). The digital (r)evolution of insurance business models. *American Journal of Economics and Business Administration, 12*(1), 1–13.

[11] OECD. (2017). *Technology and innovation in the insurance sector*. Organization for Economic Cooperation and Development.

[12] Parziale, L., Avramenko, A., Chan, S., de Valence, F., Dziekan, C., Dziekan, M., & Roik, N. (2010). *IBM smart analytics cloud*. IBM Redbooks. Cappiello, A. (2018). Technology and insurance. In *Technology and the insurance industry* (pp. 7–28). Cham: Palgrave Pivot.

companies to improve fraud detection, cut loss-adjustment costs, and reduce or eliminate personal interactions. Artificial intelligence and big data analytics help to perform claim management correctly: This type of analysis makes it possible to prevent false accident frauds, automate claims calculations, and better manage correct payments.[13]

By lowering the accident rate, the relationship between the policyholder and the company changes: There are interactions not only in the event of an accident. Companies can become partners in loss prevention. In this regard, innovation applied to claims management has a dual positive effect: It reduces the cost of indemnities (both administrative costs and the total number of allowances, reduced thanks to fraud prevention). It increases customer satisfaction thanks to faster payment procedures and claims management available anytime, anywhere, and with any device.[14]

Advanced solutions and wearable technologies can provide data in real time along the entire policy life cycle, such as driving behaviors and health measures of policyholders. The combination of rich customer data, advanced solutions, and improved computing power makes it possible to compute premiums based on the actual use of the insured assets and conduct of the policyholder. Companies can use the real-time data captured through advanced devices and powerful analytics to reassess the current risks and re-compute the premium for current threats at regular intervals. Companies can develop customized products with pricing adjusted to individual risk levels and an accurate selection of them.[15] Companies with innovative pricing models and information about individual risks can better identify the lowest-risk customers. Self-informed, higher-risk customers may seek out less sophisticated providers offering more attractive rates based on fewer data. In this environment, late adopters of new technology would be more susceptible to adverse selection.[16]

[13] Cappiello, A. (2020). The technological disruption of insurance industry: A review. *International Journal of Business and Social Science*, *11*(1).

[14] Cappiello, A. (2020). The digital (r)evolution of insurance business models. *American Journal of Economics and Business Administration*, *12*(1), 1–13.

[15] Porter, M. E., & Heppelmann, J. E. (2014). How smart, connected products are transforming competition. *Harvard Business Review*, *92*(11), 64–88.

[16] Porter, M. E., & Heppelmann, J. E. (2014). How smart, connected products are transforming competition. *Harvard Business Review*, *92*(11), 64–88.

Conclusions

New risk models allow for innovation in pricing approaches in insurance.[17] These models allow companies to include data recorded in the insured assets into premium calculations. An insurance product providing continuous monitoring of risk exposure during the coverage period makes it possible to price each risk at a sufficient rate.[18] Until smart data is incorporated into premium calculations, some insurance companies, such as American Family, offer a smart home technology discount to encourage the use of solutions to help prevent threats and losses before they occur.[19] As with risk selection, the relevant regulatory authorities must approve pricing processes.

[17] Abdou, D. S. (2019). Using big data to discriminate charged price in the car insurance industry: Evidence from United States. *Proceedings of Business and Economic Studies*, *2*(6).

[18] www.slideshare.net/matteocarbone/smart-home-procurement-144438351. Accessed 14 March 2020.

[19] www.amfam.com/insurance/home/smart-home. Accessed 14 March 2020. Smart Home Insurance—slideshare.net. www.slideshare.net/matteocarbone/smart-home-insurance-14443835. Accessed 18 June 2020.

CHAPTER 13

Payments for Costs and Investments in Insurance 4.0

Introduction

Companies generally invest in two different ways:

- Compulsory investments in the face of commitments made against policyholders. These are law-constrained investments that are the cover of insurance liabilities. These are the main guarantee for the customers. As a consequence, they must comply with specific characteristics:
  - Be quickly monetizable in anticipation of indemnification;
  - Allow the maintenance of a profitable asset;
  - Provide for an appropriate risk-return combination;
  - Reflect and satisfy the congruence between financial needs and possibilities[1];
  - Diversify to minimize the systematic risks.[2]
- Free investments decided and implemented based on considerations within the organization.[3] Their function and purpose distinguish them in these ways:

[1] www.econ.uniurb.it. Accessed 10 May 2020.

[2] Brealey, R. A., Myers, S. C., Allen, F., & Sandri, S. (2007). *Principi di Finanza Aziendale* (Quinta edizione). Milano, Italy: McGraw-Hill.

[3] Lusvarghi, V. (1990). *La gestione dell'impresa di assicurazione*. Padova, Italy: Cedam.

B. Nicoletti, *Insurance 4.0*, Palgrave Studies in Financial Services Technology, https://doi.org/10.1007/978-3-030-58426-9_13

- Strengthen and extend the structure and the financial stability of the organization;
- Generate income;
- Guarantee the solvency for compensations;
- Create a solvency image and solidity toward the market of potential customers and investors.

The situation of unit-linked insurance is different since, in that case, the investments are also agreed with the customers.

The difficult financial situation might tempt companies to suspend investment and cut costs. The crisis creates an incentive to do the reverse: invest in how they operate and create a more agile, digitally-enabled business. This way is the only one to prepare for the future. Companies should embrace the flexible and remote working necessary across all sectors due to the economic and pandemic crisis. The crisis provides companies the opportunity to test and ensure that their businesses have sufficient infrastructure to move to the "new normal" with, for instance, support more staff working off-site and according to flexible ways—now and for the future.[4]

The guiding principles of finance are the optimum reallocation of the wealth collected, pursuing a reasonable combination of risk-return, and maintaining the assets of ownership. This activity is complementary to technical-insurance management, which relates to the coverage of the risks assumed. It represents the core business of insurance organizations.

In the case of technical-insurance management, it is necessary to distinguish organizations' business activity in two areas: P&C and life-management. This distinction is essential as it represents two different critical strategies.[5] The recruitment and management of risks within organizations are possible in two ways:

[4] home.kpmg/xx/en/home/insights/2020/03/do-insurers-have-covid-19-covered.html. Accessed 30 May 2020.

[5] Fontana, F., & Caroli, M. (2009). *Economia e gestione delle imprese*. Milano, Italy: McGraw-Hill.

- Direct assumption: in this case, the organization stipulates the contract directly with the end customer. The company takes the premium and, in the event of an accident, provides for its management and indemnifies the insured;
- Indirect intake[6] can be divided into three typologies:
  - Reinsurance: represents the operation whereby an insurance organization frees itself of part of the risk assumed by its customers, transferring it to another insurance organization (a reinsurance company). The goal of this system is to achieve efficient management of the risks and be able to increase the customer base;
  - Retrocession: a transaction in which a reinsurer transfers risks it has reinsured to another reinsurer[7];
  - Co-insurance: represents the contractual situation in which two or more organizations compete for the same risk in percentages. In the event of a claim, the underwriting insurance organizations must pay the compensation in proportion to the insured quota to the co-insurance company.[8]

Digitize and Lean Insurance

Insurance 4.0 aims to optimize the value provided by the insurance function. The information is sometimes uncertain. In the current volatility, there is the difficulty of forecasting some variables that can come into play and distort the programs. It then becomes essential to increase agility. To accomplish this, it is necessary to act on the processes and platforms. This means:

[6] Selleri, L. (2003). *Impresa di assicurazione e strategia del valore*. Milano, Italy: Etas.

[7] www.irmi.com/term/insurance-definitions/retrocession. Accessed 18 June 2020.

[8] www.treccani.it. Accessed 10 May 2020. Accessed 30 May 2020.

- Modernizing and improving the efficiency of insurance processes;
- Optimizing the price/value ratio, ensuring the services' quality and ancillary services at a reasonable cost;
- Rationalizing spending on goods and services;
- Creating a communication network with the entire ecosystem.[9]

This chapter goes beyond and proposes the insurance 4.0 approach based on a method indicated as lean and digitize.[10] Unlike traditional methods, this one focuses on organizational and operational aspects. This method argues that the transformation project must include two phases:

- The process improvements through the use of lean six sigma method, with the realization of the aspects that do not require automation, such as new organizational and operational models, elimination of unnecessary activities, layout optimization, and so on;
- The improvement of the management and operational processes with their digitization and automation.

Based on the research and experiences made, the lean and digitize method can be summarized as follows (Fig. 13.1). The method has six macro phases and 20 + 1 steps.[11] At the end of each macro phase, there is a progress control indicated, according to six sigma terminology, tollgate (exit control).

[9] This last aspect has been defined as not a line or a system but a "sea": Luccini, S., & di Giovanni, G. (2010). *Niente di più facile, niente di più difficile* (Fausto Lupetti ed.). Milano, Italy.

[10] Nicoletti, B. (2012), *Lean and digitize: An integrated approach to process improvement*. Farnham, UK: Gower Publishing. ISBN-10: 1409441946.

[11] Nicoletti, B. (2012), *Lean and digitize: An integrated approach to process improvement*. Farnham, UK: Gower Publishing. ISBN-10: 1409441946.

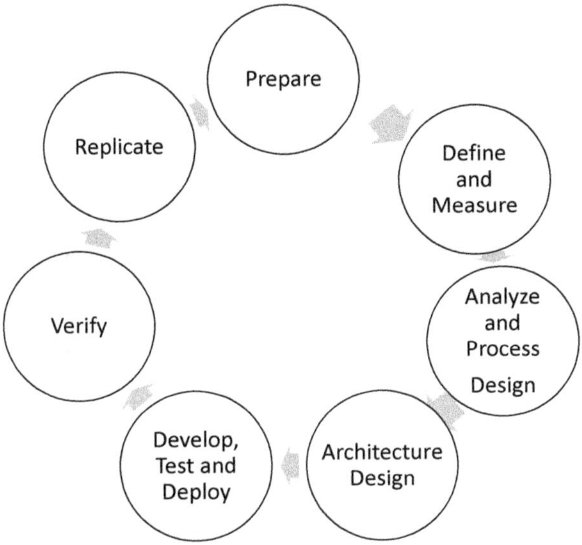

Fig. 13.1 Lean and digitize

Conclusions

In the modern highly turbulent times, it is critical to maintain the necessary agility. This approach means strict control of the costs and investments. This chapter examines the structure of investments in insurance companies. This chapter suggests using the lean and digitize method to reach the objectives of agility, feasibility, and profitability, which insurance 4.0 must ensure.

CHAPTER 14

Insurance 4.0 and Digital Transformation

Introduction

Digital transformation indicates the changes in the business models associated with digital solutions in all aspects of a company.[1] There are four essential dimensions in a digital transformation: the use of technologies, changes in value creation, structural changes, and financial aspects.[2] This chapter focuses on the application of digital transformation to insurance companies. The approach is holistic, covering the entire business model. It underlines the relevance of three features in the digital transformation[3]:

- Light touch processes that are structured to be modifiable rather than rigidly fixed;
- Infrastructural flexibility that allows for flexible flows and configurability of process flows; and
- Mindful actors that are enacting the business models, evaluating them, and their corresponding actions based on the relevant circumstances of the context.

[1] it.wikipedia.org/wiki/Trasformazione_digitale. Accessed 30 May 2020.

[2] Matt, C., Hess, T., & Benlian, A. (2015). Digital transformation strategies. *Business & Information Systems Engineering, 57*(5), 339–343.

[3] Baiyere, A., Salmela, H., & Tapanainen, T. (2020). Digital transformation and the new logics of business process management. *European Journal of Information Systems,* 1–22.

B. Nicoletti, *Insurance 4.0*, Palgrave Studies in Financial Services Technology, https://doi.org/10.1007/978-3-030-58426-9_14

According to a McKinsey Global Survey, 99 percent of executives claimed that they had pursued a large-scale technology transformation in the past two years.[4] While doing so, many executives experienced cultural and talent gaps and weak partnerships between ICT and the rest of the business. Overcoming these issues requires companies to reskill persons, reset culture, produce closer ICT–business relationships, and rigorously measure technologies' value-added capabilities.

Digital Transformation

Sergio Balbinot, at the time President of Insurance Europe, said that European regulations must adapt to digitization. The rules in customer protection should enable innovation so that companies can continue to meet ever-changing customer requirements.[5]

When working on digital transformation, it is useful to consider the experiences and errors done by other organizations. Some statistics are impressive. According to a study by McKinsey, the rate of change is "unprecedented."[6] Nearly 80 percent of the companies in a survey have started a path in this direction over the last years. Fifty percent believe they will have to change even more by 2023. In the motor, engineering, and aerospace sectors, 85 percent of respondents expect that new solutions based on artificial intelligence, internet of things, and data-driven business models will completely transform their businesses.

The consulting company Bain & Company recommends that companies invest between 2 and 5 percent of their turnover in digitization.[7]

[4] www.mckinsey.com/business-functions/mckinsey-digital/our-insights/managing-the-fallout-from-technology-transformations?cid=other-eml-alt-mip-mck&hlkid=bf4d7318cabc44d99ce3ad00689ae9fc&hctky=2743882&hdpid=eac0bc3c-8635-4f36-a0ed-4322b51bbc6a. Accessed 9 March 2020.

[5] Associazione Svizzera d'Assicurazioni. (2017, June). *Il settore assicurativo internazionale discute a Zurigo il tema della digitalizzazione*. www.svv.ch/it/newsroom/il-settore-assicurativo-internazionale-discute-zurigo-il-tema-della-digitalizzazione. Accessed 20 April 2020.

[6] McKinsey. (2018, October). Unlocking success in digital transformations. *McKinsey White Paper.*

[7] www.bain.com/insights/rebooting-a-digital-solution-to-trade-finance/. Accessed 29 February 2020.

A survey of the digital performance index (DPI)[8] on 343 companies in eight industrial sectors found that in 2018 only 6 percent of companies were able to improve their financial performance as a result of their digital investments or convert them into revenue growth. There are several reasons why this happened. According to a Bain & Company study, most companies do not have a holistic digital transformation strategy.[9] According to the same survey, the companies that have this comprehensive strategy grow at a rate of 50 percent more than their competitors. They are 30 percent more profitable. The ICT costs are reduced by 20 percent on average. The lessons learned are that it is possible to succeed in digital transformation. The condition is that the company must have a clear strategy in this regard. This strategy must be holistic. It must consider the technological platforms and consider all the components of the business model, and especially processes, persons, and partnerships. The role of partnerships for the success of the digital transformation is essential. Digital transformation affects all areas of a company: products and services. As such, insurance companies have a unique role to play in developing the digital transformation.

In a VUCA world (Volatile, Unpredictable, Complex, and Ambiguous), organizations need to rethink how insurance companies can interact with digital solutions to overcome business challenges and exploit market opportunities.[10] Some organizations mix different generations of personnel to create a pool of innovative digital know-how and experienced resources. This approach can contribute to change the whole culture of the organization and amplifies how persons work in teams, both with internal staff and partners.

[8] Digital Performance Index is an Accenture index that assesses the level of digital investment and progress across four business functions: planning, manufacturing, selling, and management. www.accenture.com/_acnmedia/pdf-64/accenture-digital-performance-index.pdf. Accessed 20 April 2020.

[9] www.bain.com/insights/leading-360-degree-digital-transition/. Accessed 29 February 2020.

[10] www.mindtools.com/pages/article/managing-vuca-world.htm. Accessed 4 March 2020.

Digital Transformation in the Literature

Digital transformation is the subject of many studies. Many scholars have tried to explain which are the impacts of this digital evolution in the organization of the companies.[11] Dehning et al. defined some criteria about the phenomenon, based on the organizational function/process impacted[12]:

- Business capabilities, processes, and relationships;
- Acquisitions;
- ICT uses on internal processes.

Lucas et al. propose seven specific dimensions for describing a technology-driven transformation: change in processes, creation of new organizations, change in relationships, change in user experience, change in markets, change in the number of customers, and disruptive impact. A technology must impact three or more of these dimensions to be transformational.[13]

The digital (r)evolution[14] is often (but not only) implemented through digitization. It is "the ability to turn current products or services into digital variants, and offer benefits over tangible products."[15] The media industry experienced a digital shift with the dematerialization from physical products to online products. Internet and social networks enable access to a new field of potential customers and strengthen ties with current customers. Digital transformation also has an organizational impact on persons. Job roles evolve in line with the change of activities.

[11] Lucas, H. C., Agarwal, R., Clemons, E. K., El Sawy, O. A., & Weber, B. (2013). Impactful research on transformational information technology: An opportunity to inform new audiences. *MIS Quarterly*.

[12] Dehning, B., Richardson, V. J., & Zmud, R. W. (2003). The value relevance of announcements of transformational information technology investments. *MIS Quarterly*.

[13] Lucas, H. C., Agarwal, R., Clemons, E. K., El Sawy, O. A., & Weber, B. (2013). Impactful research on transformational information technology: An opportunity to inform new audiences. *MIS Quarterly, 37*(2), 371–382.

[14] Cappiello, A. (2020). The digital (r)evolution of insurance business models. *American Journal of Economics and Business Administration*. https://doi.org/10.3844/ajebasp.2020.

[15] Gassmann, O., Frankenberger, K., & Csik, M. (2014). *The St. Gallen Business Model Navigator*. www.im.ethz.ch/education/HS13/MIS13/Business_Model_Navigator.pdf. Accessed 3 January 2020.

Decision-makers must take into account the evolution and, in some cases, the revolution, on knowledge and competencies.[16]

To succeed in the digital transformation, it is essential to have clear what it means and which would be the objectives in the specific company and situation examined. Digital transformation can impact the whole insurance ecosystem. The impacts in operational processes can be of two types[17]:

- Transformation of processes necessary for exploiting new technologies: digitization creates the opportunity to transform the company, both in user experience and business model;
- Organizations can decide to undertake the digitization of a specific process in full.

Continuous innovation has become part of life in a short time and thoroughly changing in nature. Thanks to the mobile network, persons are always in connection with the rest of the world. Thanks to smartphones, persons can access information anywhere and share thoughts and files with friends, acquaintances, and anyone else. A revolution of this size requires a parallel change in customer usage and product use by the customer. The main driver of evolution in the organizations requires the adding value to the customers and takes into account their increasing needs.

Digital transformation is not an option. It is now essential for any corporate reality that top and medium management should understand that must pursue a digital transformation to remain competitive in a world that moves faster between old and new forms of interactions and sales.

Digital transformation is not just about adopting new technologies.[18] Digital transformation is a change in the corporate culture and the definition of the business model of the organization. The digital transformation

[16] Kohli, R., & Johnson, S. (2011). Digital transformation in latecomer industries: CIO and CEO leadership lessons from Encana Oil & Gas (USA) Inc. *MIS Quarterly Executive, 10*(4), 141–156. Liu, D. (2012). Competitive business model in audio-book industry: A case of China. *Journal of Software, 7*(1), 33–40.

[17] Henriette, E., Feki, M., & Boughzala, I. (2015). Information systems in a changing economy and society. In *MCIS Proceedings*.

[18] *Why digital transformation matters*. www.bons.io/blog/why-digital-transformation-matters. Accessed 20 June 2020.

consists of a radical shift in the organizations, from processes and information flows to business models to fully exploit the opportunities offered by new solutions, media, and channels of communication and distribution. It is a radical change that impacts the entire organization. It needs a robust approach, a rigorous method, and appropriate application tools. It requires a long-term vision and an in-depth analysis of the short, medium, and long terms steps that the organization should take. It is critical to analyze the specific situation. Without a redesign of the business processes, there is a danger to using these extraordinary means in a much less efficient, effective, and economical way than their potential.[19]

The Altimeter Group, referring to organizations that have made or are making efforts to implement the digital transformation, states that the first and most significant objective is to provide a better experience for the digital customer. It is about "the re-alignment of, or new investment in, technology and business models to more effectively engage digital customers."[20] Digital transformations require to rethink how to connect with the customers, offering an experience aligned with their requirements. Customers now have more information on insurance services than in the past. They can use and compare a large number of sources with increasing ease. They know the characteristics of the services and the competition. They purchase with a higher awareness than in the past. The phases of the insurance process previously occurred at separate times and through different channels. There is now an immersion in an almost continuous process that takes place more and more in the virtual world.[21] When it is not closed in the digital environment, the customer requires consistency and continuity across all channels. An omnichannel approach can provide this feature.[22]

[19] www.hyphen-italia.com/cosa-significa-trasformazione-digitale/. Accessed 30 May 2020.

[20] Solis, B., Li, C., & Szymanski, J. (2014). *Digital transformation: Why and how companies are investing in new business model to lead digital customer experience*. Altimeter Group. (2014). www.altimetergroup.com/disclosure. Accessed 12 December 2019.

[21] docplayer.it/6872-La-trasformazione-digitale-aggiungere-tecnologia-al-business-per-ottenere-l-effettomoltiplicatore.html. Accessed 30 May 2020.

[22] Juaneda-Ayensa, E., Mosquera, A., & Sierra Murillo, Y. (2016). Omnichannel customer behavior: Key drivers of technology acceptance and use and their effects on purchase intention. *Frontiers in psychology, 7*, 1117.

The Age of Digitization

According to Accenture, digital is re-imagining the human experience.[23] It is remaking how persons live, work, play, and connect. Everything is being rethought, simplified, and improved, even what, in the past, persons have taken for granted.

Digital transformation is revolutionary in the face of life in all its aspects. It is a process that can potentially bring significant benefits for organizations and also to the persons. It requires a considerable effort from individuals who, before the advent of digitization, were used to different processes, streams, and work activities. Similarly, as in private life, many things have changed: sociality, connection with persons, trends, and so on. The new technologies have become part of living in a short time and without having time to realize it, thoroughly, changing their habits. Through the mobile network, persons are in continuous connection with the rest of the world. With a smartphone, it is possible to access information everywhere and share thoughts and information with friends, contacts, and anyone interested. A revolution of this magnitude results in a parallel change in customer manners and product usage. It is precisely the realignment toward new and increased customer expectations, which is the primary driver of the evolution in how to do business. Digital transformation is not limited to innovative companies, to young digital startups, or Silicon Valley giants. It is a process that is important for organizations of any size and operation in the most diverse markets. Those who stay behind incurs in penalties. Potentially, an insurance startup with small capital and no experience, through the launch of an innovative solution, can change the insurance market and capsize the companies' market positioning. It can cause the disappearance of dominant players with many years of experience. Being digital is vital for the survival of the organization itself.

The implementation of innovative solutions is not sufficient to ensure the success of the organization. It is vital to redesign the basis of the organizational structure, adapting it to the digital age regulations. It is necessary to imagine a new organization able to capture the opportunities that digital transformation makes available. This process must cover every

[23] www.accenture.com/t20160128t000639__w__/us-en/_acnmedia/accenture/conversion-assets/dotcom/documents/global/pdf/technology_7/accenture-interactive-digital-transformation.pdf. Accessed 12 December 2019.

aspect of the organization, from the organization chart to the corporate culture, from the business model to the leadership style, and finally to the company vision and culture itself.

The digital transformation can generate new players to create markets that did not exist before. These new realities are born out of business opportunities made possible from innovative solutions and creative approaches. Every organization is different from another depending on the core business, the sector, and the market. The digital transformation can be implemented in a different way and with different objectives. Digital transformations have already dramatically changed some areas. Examples are in several industry, that has seen multinational corporations disappear, like Blockbuster[24] and its retailers, or Nokia,[25] or Kodak,[26] due to their inability to adapt their business model to the changes in the customers' evaluation of products.

The success of a digital transformation can come from providing a better user experience for the digital customer through realignment, investing in, technology and business models to engage more effectively, efficiently, and economically with the customer at every touchpoint in the customer journey.[27] One of the first reasons for digital transformation is the need to rethink the way of interacting with the customer. It offers an experience aligned with his/her expectations formed in the daily and almost continuous use of innovations. It changes rapidly, and that changes how the customers interpret the tools they enter into contact. The first and more pressing obligation of organizations is to understand and act based on the new habits of customers (starting from the purchasing process, up to the experience of use) and change their way of interacting with them.

[24] Zhu, K. (2001). Internet-based distribution of digital videos: The economic impacts of digitization on the motion picture industry. *Electronic Markets, 11*(4), 273–280.

[25] Alibage, A., & Weber, C. (2018, August). Nokia phones: From a total success to a total Fiasco: A study on why Nokia eventually failed to connect people, and an analysis of what the new home of Nokia phones must do to succeed. In *2018 Portland International Conference on Management of Engineering and Technology (PICMET)* (pp. 1–15). IEEE.

[26] Lucas, Jr., H. C., & Goh, J. M. (2009). Disruptive technology: How Kodak missed the digital photography revolution. *The Journal of Strategic Information Systems, 18*(1), 46–55.

[27] Edelman, D. C., & Singer, M. (2015). Competing on customer journeys. *Harvard Business Review, 93*(11), 88–100.

In this digital age, the customers are much more aware of the characteristics of the product/service they are interested in. They often know the competition. This trend leads organizations to revise their marketing strategies completely. In the past, it was possible to push the sale talking to the customer and showing the products available. Online interactions cannot easily replicate this type of selling approach. It is necessary to find new ways to convince the customer to purchase. Efforts can no longer be directed only to increase customer awareness concerning the insurance services or to make them accessible online. They must also be able to catch customer interest through an ever-increasing social and economic approach and journey.

Successful Transformation

There are three significant transformation models in a successful company-wide digital transformation[28]:

- Step-wise. Transforming to an insurance 4.0 organization can appear as a step into the dark for senior management. This transformation model is the most common. It shows a distinction between the aspiring, designing, and piloting phase and the scale and improve phase. Many organizations run multiple rounds of pilots and iterations before fully committing to scaling up across the entire or substantial part of the organization. Often, this process takes several years, as managers and the organization become familiar with the insurance 4.0 approach and proves that ways of working can add value to their organization.
- Big-bang. An increasing number of organizations get firm conviction early on going on with a digital transformation.[29] They fully commit upfront to move the whole organization into insurance 4.0. Managers from these organizations plan the execution of all steps of the change as quickly as possible.

[28] www.mckinsey.com/business-functions/digital-mckinsey/our-insights/five-moves-to-make-during-a-digital-transformation. Accessed 20 May 2019.

[29] *The journey to an agile organization*|McKinsey. www.mckinsey.com/business-functions/organization/our-insights/the-journey-to-an-agile-organization. Accessed 10 May 2020.

- Emergent. It is impossible to plan out an insurance 4.0 transformation in details from the start. Most insurance 4.0 roadmaps have new approaches. Some organizations have chosen to implement their entire agile transformation through an emergent, step-wise, bottom-up approach.[30] In this approach, an aspiration from the top managers sets a clear direction. It is necessary a significant effort to build an insurance 4.0 culture and capabilities among the management.

It is interesting to look at the structure of digital and analytics transformations points for some key moves at particular steps of a transformation.[31] These points are essential to assuring success to the change.[32] These actions have suggestions in such a way that other organizations can plan and implement digital transformations successfully.[33]

For starters, who report the highest levels of success in pursuing digital transformations, their organizations focus on a few digital themes tied to performance outcomes.[34] In defining their transformations' scope, these successful organizations boldly establish company-wide efforts and build a new organization. They also create an adaptive design that allows the transformation strategy and resource allocation to adjust in the course of the initiative. They adopt insurance 4.0 execution practices and mindsets by pushing risk-taking and collaboration across all parts of the organization. In these successful efforts, leadership and accountability are clear for each stage of the transformation.

[30] *The journey to an agile organization*|McKinsey. www.mckinsey.com/business-functions/organization/our-insights/the-journey-to-an-agile-organization. Accessed 20 June 2020.

[31] *The journey to an agile organization*|McKinsey. www.mckinsey.com/business-functions/organization/our-insights/the-journey-to-an-agile-organization-. Accessed 20 June 2020.

[32] www.mckinsey.com/business-functions/digital-mckinsey/our-insights/five-moves-to-make-during-a-digital-transformation. Accessed 19 May 2019.

[33] *Five moves to make during a digital transformation*| McKinsey. www.mckinsey.com/business-functions/mckinsey-digital/our-insights/five-moves-to-make-during-a-digital-transformation. Accessed 20 June 2020.

[34] www.mckinsey.com/business-functions/digital-mckinsey/our-insights/five-moves-to-make-during-a-digital-transformation. Accessed 19 May 2019.

Challenges and Risks in Digital Transformations

Insurance 4.0 and digital transformation can provide significant benefits to insurance companies. Digital transformation has not been successful in some organizations.[35] It is important to find ways to overcome such a situation. This section covers a particular class of risks connected with insurance 4.0 and digital transformation. It is critical to push for digital transformation.[36]

There are several risks associated with digital technology. They must be analyzed and taken into account. They are called operational risks. Operational risk is the risk of losses deriving from inadequate or broken processes, personnel, internal systems, or due to external events.

The main risk is the occurrence of a disaster that could put the organization's continuity at risk. The more an organization depends on digital and automation technologies, the more it is necessary to protect the company from these situations, due to dependence on digital technologies. The organization is in danger of cyber attacks. The use of advanced solutions can also lead to data loss. It is possible losing data due to the interruption of processes for human errors but also problems in the software and hardware. Hackers can cause damages in the case of ICT systems and especially in IoT. The risks can also be internal to the organizations. The risks can be due to a slowing down in the case of procedures, with long transaction responses and batch jobs. That can be due to infrastructural sizing problems or buggy software implementations.

Digital transformation also involves migration from manual procedures or old ICT procedures. These migrations can lead to errors or interruptions of the processes. The consequences can be significant for the organization. The use of new methods requires training of the operators who must use and manage them. This process is neither easy nor immediate. The use of information technology tends to create a dependency on ICT procedures, even with the loss of knowledge of the corresponding manual processes.

All the mentioned causes can create much damage. The temporary use of manual procedures in the absence of the availability of ICT procedures

[35] Bughin, J., LaBerge, L., & Mellbye, A. (2017, February). The case for digital reinvention. *McKinsey Quarterly.*

[36] Nicoletti, B. (2020). *Procurement 4.0 and the digital revolution.* London, UK: Palgrave Macmillan.

can be simply not feasible or forgotten. ICT procedures cannot be easily modified or updated. Such difficulty is actually in the case of internally developed applications (so-called legacy applications). These difficulties of updating are also real in the case of ICT solutions acquired from outside. In these cases, the dependency on the vendor can be very penalizing if software updates are needed.

The situations described require an effort to manage risks, both in the case of projects and in the business as usual. The analysis of operational risks is an integral part of the activity of the company. Its timely and correct management minimizes potential negative impacts on critical (tangible/intangible) company assets and possibly adverse consequences on the corporate strategy. The following activities are necessary:

- Risk assessment on all areas subject to risk (with particular attention to cross-departmental risks) at least once a year;
- Creation of a risk register. The operational risk committee should revise and approve its content regularly;
- Creation and follow-up activities by an operational risk committee on the strategies implemented to mitigate the vulnerability areas.

ISO 9000[37] and ISO 27000[38] have implicit the concept of risk. The new revisions of these standards make more explicit risk management, developing it within the entire management system. Risk-based thinking is essential and must be part of the culture of prevention and improvement. It is necessary to question the possible obstacles and their consequences on the business, on the processes, and on the entire organization. The activities for risk assessment are part of the cycle[39]:

- Definition of risk management policies;
- Identification, assessments (probability of occurrence, impact, and forecastability), and risk analysis;

[37] *A risk based thinking model for ISO 9001:2015*. rube.asq.org/audit/2015/01/a-risk-based-thinking-model-for-iso-9001-2015.pdf. Accessed 10 May 2020.

[38] *ISO/IEC 27000—Key international standard for information security revised*. www.iso.org/news/ref2266.html. Accessed 30 June 2020.

[39] Boneva, M. (2018). Challenges related to the digital transformation of business companies. In *Innovation Management, Entrepreneurship and Sustainability (IMES 2018)* (pp. 101–114). Prague, Czech Republic: Vysoká škola ekonomická v Praze.

- Risk treatment and finding remedies;
- Monitoring and measurement;
- Evaluation of the performance of the processes (to identify residual risks);
- Continuous improvement.

This process is not easy. Sometimes the company does not have the internal competencies. Planning and governance may require the use of resources outside the organization. It is essential not to forget that there are risks also in the digital transformation. If a risk becomes real, the consequences might be high. In most cases, there is a tendency to consider risks only in a negative sense. Risk-based thinking can also help identify opportunities.

Resilient Solutions

With the spread of insurance 4.0 functionality, the organization can connect all their computer and automation applications with monitoring and management tools to support the insurance processes. One can imagine the automatic construction of a black or gold list of customers and partners. The information gathered can be shared in real-time directly with the partners in the same ecosystem.[40]

In this future environment, the resilience of the ICT and automation system becomes essential.[41] It must be an integral part of assessing potential risks, services, systems, and even more in the evaluation of the possible solutions. The researchers are developing products with autonomic computing, the ability of a computer system of self-care, or self-unlock.[42] The products or services can autonomously detect and remedy failures/recover. These solutions enable, for example, large ICT systems, aimed at providing services 24*7, to meet their targets with little or no human intervention. Achieving self-care requires automated

[40] Rajola, F. (2019). *Customer relationship management in the financial industry organizational processes and technology innovation.* Berlin and Heidelberg, Germany: Springer-Verlag.

[41] Nicoletti, B. (2016). Resilience & outsourcing. *PMWORLD*, N. 2, 2016, p. 16.

[42] Montani, S., & Anglano, C. (2008). Achieving self-healing in service delivery systems software through case-based reasoning. *Applied Intelligence, 28*(2), 139–152.

testing as it is possible using Jenkins' continuous integration[43] and the implementation and maintenance of domain knowledge in the form of problem determination, diagnosis, and repair models.[44] Case-based reasoning (CBR) is a learning paradigm that reduces many types of these bottlenecks thanks to automatic knowledge acquisition.[45] Besides, the application of the CBR for the diagnosis and remediation in software systems looks promising. In this field, most errors are new occurrences of known issues. It is more challenging to develop an autonomic solution in the case of services with a strong human presence in the service provision. It is not impossible. Most likely, the future holds some exciting developments in this area thanks to artificial intelligence.

One other exciting architecture is the so-called shared-nothing architecture (SN).[46] This architecture is independent and self-sufficient at each node. There is no point of contention in the entire system. More specifically, none of the nodes share memory or space on the memory devices. The exciting part of this system is the fact that there is no single point of failure. This system is very scalable and reliable.

Digital resilience will be available in the more distant future. It is the ability to design customer applications, business processes, technology architectures, and related cybersecurity defenses with the protection of critical information and assets of the organization in mind and the assurance of continuity of service.[47]

[43] Smart, J. F. (2011). *Jenkins: The definitive guide: Continuous integration for the masses*. Sebastopol, CA: O'Reilly Media, Inc.

[44] Yiran, W., Tongyang, Z., & Vidong, G. (2018, May). Design and implementation of continuous integration scheme based on Jenkins and Ansible. In *2018 International Conference on Artificial Intelligence and Big Data (ICAIBD)* (pp. 245–249). IEEE.

[45] Kolodner, J. (2014). *Case-based reasoning*. Burlington, MA: Morgan Kaufmann.

[46] Chaisuriya, S., Keretho, S., Sanguanpong, S., & Praneetpolgrang, P. (2018, January). A security architecture framework for critical infrastructure with ring-based nested network zones. In *2018 10th International Conference on Knowledge and Smart Technology* (KST) (pp. 248–253). IEEE.

[47] Kaplan, J. M., Bailey, T., O'Halloran, D., Marcus, A., & Rezek, C. (2015). *Beyond cybersecurity: Protecting your digital business*. Hoboken, NJ: Wiley.

Innovation in the Insurance Processes

Though the insurance industry has been one of the slowest sectors in adopting digital transformation, the digitization process is affecting insurance companies significantly. It is forcing them to radically change corporate culture, services and procedures, customer relationships, and relations with the sector's various stakeholders and competitors. Few companies are working on updating their business model with a real digital transformation. This book has the objective to change this situation.

Several media articles and studies attempt to investigate the impact of digitization applied to the insurance sector.[48] There is some analysis of the strategic implications of new solutions on cost structures, business processes,[49] customer satisfaction,[50] human resources,[51] and newly emerging risks.[52]

Digital transformation will deeply modify the financial and insurance ecosystem, impacting all activities in the insurance value network, from

[48] Segev, I., & Vickers, A. (2017). *What the new world of insurance could look like*. McKinsey and Company. www.mckinsey.com/business-functions/mckinsey-digital/our-insights/digital-blog/what-the-new-world-of-insurance-could-look-like. Accessed 26 February 2020. Muller, F., Naujoks, H., Singh, H., Schwarz, G., Schwedel, A., et al. (2015). *Global digital insurance benchmarking report*. Bain and Company. McKinsey. (2016). *Making digital strategy a reality in insurance*. www.mckinsey.com/business-functions/mckinsey-digital/our-insights/making-digital-strategy-a-reality-in-insurance. Accessed 26 February 2020. Willis Towers Watson. (2017). *New horizon: How diverse growth strategies can advance digitization in the insurance industry*.

[49] KPMG. (2019). *Insurtech 10: Trend for 2019*. EY. (2018). *Can commercial companies transform, cut costs and accelerate growth?*

[50] Larsson, A., & Broström, E. (2019). Ensuring customer retention: Companies' perception of customer loyalty. *Market Intelligent Planning*. https://doi.org/10.1108/mip-02-2019-0106. Moneta, A. (2014). The customer-centric insurer in the digital era. *Accenture White Paper*.

[51] Johansson, S., & Vogelgesang, U. (2015). Insurance on the threshold of digitization: Implications for the life and P&C workforce. *McKinsey and C. Whitepaper*.

[52] Singh, A., & Akhilesh, K. B. (2020). The insurance industry-cybersecurity in the hyper-connected age. In K. Akhilesh & D. Möller (Eds.), *Smart technologies* (pp. 201–219). Singapore: Springer. Egan, R., Cartagena, S., Mohamed, R., Gosrani, V., Grewal J., et al. (2019). Cyber operational risk scenarios for insurance companies. *British Actuarial Journal, 24*, 1–34. https://doi.org/10.1017/s1357321718000284. Biener, C., Eling, M., & Wirfs, J. H. (2015). Insurability of cyber risk: An empirical analysis. *Geneva Papers Risk Insurance—Issues Practice, 40*, 131–158. https://doi.org/10.1057/gpp.2014.19.

product development to pricing/underwriting, sales and distribution, policy and claims management, and asset and risk management.[53] The new insurance 4.0 scenario can enable incumbent companies to set up or become part of unique ecosystems, generated by the development of connections among traditionally separated sectors and new partners and competitors.

For an effective, efficient, and economic innovation in insurance, it is critical to adopt an open innovation structure. The steps necessary in this direction are[54]:

- Innovating or redefining the organization's structure;
- Clarifying roles and responsibilities in the organization;
- Making sure that innovation is diffused and accepted by the critical stakeholders;
- Reaching fast a steady state for the changes introduced;
- Implement a continuous improvement program working toward perfection.

Technology Acceptance Model

It is relevant in the introduction of insurance 4.0 to analyze a model developed to assess the acceptance of new technology solutions: the so-called technology acceptance model (TAM).[55] Some studies have used this model to assess the acceptance of internet and mobility

[53] Eling, M., & Lehmann, M. (2018). The impact of digitization on the insurance value chain and the insurability of risks. *The Geneva Papers on Risk and Insurance—Issues and Practice, 43*, 359–396. https://doi.org/10.1057/s41288-017-0073-0.

[54] Zafar, A., & Kantola, J. (2018). Relationship between company's performance and factors involved in the innovation selection of providers. In *International Conference on Applied Human Factors and Ergonomics* (pp. 194–205). Cham, Switzerland: Springer. Wuttke, D. A., Blome, C., Foerstl, K., & Henke, M. (2013). Managing the innovation adoption of supply chain finance—Empirical evidence from six European case studies. *Journal of Business Logistics, 34*(2), 148–166.

[55] Davis, F. D. (1989). Perceived usefulness, perceived ease of use, and user acceptance of information technology. *MIS Quarterly, 13*(3), 319–340.

technologies,[56] and supply chain.[57] Authors have applied TAM to new technologies also for the insurance sector.[58]

TAM states that the critical determinants for the adoption and use of new technologies are[59]:

- Perceived usefulness (PU) is the degree to which persons think that using a specific innovation allows their organization to improve performance. The PU measures include the increase in performance, productivity, efficiency, overall usefulness, time savings, and an increase in work productivity;
- Perceived ease of use (Peou) is the degree to which a person believes that the use of a new solution requires little effort. The Peou measures include the ease of control, ease of use, simplicity, clarity, and flexibility.

Both these factors have a significant and direct effect on an organization planning to adopt insurance 4.0 and its tools. These two beliefs create a favorable disposition or intention toward the use of technology and consequently influence its use.

It is possible to generalize the TAM model.[60] There are other factors to take into account when considering insurance 4.0 from the TAM perspective. Despite the benefits of insurance 4.0, overcoming the trust issues is,

[56] Kim, Y., Park Y. J., & Choi, J. (2016). The adoption of mobile payment services for fintech. *International Journal of Applied Engineering Research, 11*(2), 1058–1061. Chen, M. C., Chen, S. S., Yeh, H. M., & Tsaur, W. G. (2016). The critical factors influencing Internet services finances satisfaction: An empirical study in Taiwan. *American Journal of Industrial and Business Management, 6*(6), 748–762.

[57] Kamble, S., Gunasekaran, A., & Arha, H. (2019). Understanding the blockchain solution adoption in supply chains—Indian context. *International Journal of Production Research, 57*(7), 2009–2033.

[58] Tzanis, S. (2012). *Direct insurance: The determinants of success*. Dissertation of the University of St. Gallen, Switzerland.

[59] Song, Y. W. (2019). *User acceptance of an artificial intelligence (AI) virtual assistant: An extension of the technology acceptance mode*. Doctoral dissertation. The University of Texas at Austin, Austin, TX.

[60] Nicoletti, B. (2017). *The future of FinTech*. Cham, Switzerland: Palgrave Macmillan. Bin, M. A., Pyeman, J. B., Ali, N. B., Abdul, N. B., & Khai, K. G. (2018). Determinants of supply chain finance adoption among Malaysian manufacturing companies: A proposed conceptual framework. *International Journal of Education and Research, 6*(4), 237–248.

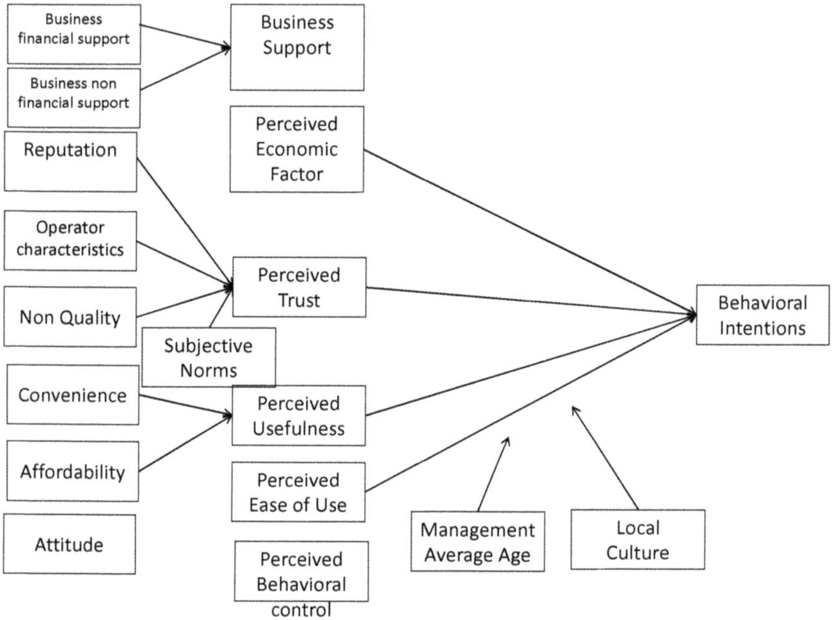

Fig. 14.1 Technology acceptance model

for example, a significant challenge for the adoption of insurance 4.0. In the case of organizations, mainly small- and medium-sized enterprises, research has extended the TAM model to include the theory of planned behavior[61] and examined the influence of several possible factors.[62]

A comprehensive model for TAM should include (Fig. 14.1)[63]:

[61] Ajzen, I. (1991). The theory of planned behavior. *Organizational Behavior and Human Decision Processes, 50*(2), 179–211.

[62] Bin, M. A., Pyeman, J. B., Ali, N. B., Abdul, N. B, & Khai, K. G. (2018). Determinants of supply chain finance adoption among Malaysian manufacturing companies: A proposed conceptual framework. *International Journal of Education and Research, 6*(4), 237–248.

[63] Schierz, P. G., et al. (2010, May–June). Understanding customer acceptance of mobile payment services: An empirical analysis. *Electronic Commerce Research and Applications, 9*(3), 209–216. Nicoletti, B. (2014). *Mobile banking*. London, UK: Palgrave Macmillan.

- Behavioral intentions (BI) arise from the adoption of insurance 4.0, namely the propensity to embrace a new solution;
- Perceived economic factor (PEF) has a substantial and immediate effect for small- and medium-sized enterprises in adopting insurance 4.0;
- Perceived usefulness (PU) has a significant and direct effect on an organization's intention to adopt an innovation. It is determined by the level of convenience (CON) and the affordability (AFF) arising from moving to insurance 4.0;
- Perceived trust (PT) has a significant and direct effect on the intention of an organization to adopt insurance 4.0;
- Characteristics of the digital operation (Maintenance and Operations—MNO);
- Non-quality of service provided by the vendor of the new solutions (NQ);
- Awareness and knowledge (AK) shown, or the realization, perception, or knowledge of a situation or facts;
- Possible support organizations can be of two types: (1) Financial assistance, such as the availability of subsidies, working capital, and concessions. (2) The non-financial support includes courses, consulting, management, distribution, research, and development[64];
- Reputation (RE) based on the perception of reliability, credibility, social responsibility, and reliability of the organizations offering insurance 4.0[65];
- Attitude toward insurance 4.0 refers to the favorable or unfavorable evaluations of the organization to innovation (APF—Attitude toward the innovation)[66];
- Subjective norms relate to perceived social pressures that influence the behavioral intention of an organization (SP—Social Pressures)[67];

[64] Yusoff, M.-N. H., & Yaacob, M. R. (2010). The government business support in the new economic model. *International Journal of Business and Management, 5*(9), 60–67.

[65] Fombrun, C. J. (1996). *Reputation: Realizing value for the corporate image*. Cambridge, MA: Harvard Business School Press.

[66] Ajzen, I., & Fishbein, M. (1980). *Attitude understanding and predicting social behavior*. Upper Saddle River, NJ: Prentice-Hall.

[67] Ajzen, I., & Fishbein, M. (1980). *Attitude understanding and predicting social behavior*. Upper Saddle River, NJ: Prentice-Hall.

- Perceived behavioral control (BC) refers to the ease or difficulty of performing the behavior associated with the specific innovation.[68]

Roadmap for a Digital Transformation

It is interesting to analyze how innovative solutions can become business as usual in an organization. A study suggests how foundational technologies and their business use cases evolve.[69] The first factor to consider is novelty. This factor is the degree to which a solution is new. The more radical the innovation is, the more effort will be required to ensure that users understand which problems are possible and how it can help to solve them. The second factor is complexity. This factor is the level of the ecosystem coordination needed. Its measurement depends on the number and diversity of parties necessary to work together to add value to the new solution.

The same study developed a framework that maps innovations against these two contextual dimensions, dividing them into quadrants. Each quadrant represents a stage of technology development.[70] Identifying in which one a change falls into can help managers understand its challenges, the level of collaboration and consensus needed, and the legislative and compliance requirements.[71] This mapping also suggests which types of processes and infrastructure are necessary to adopt innovation. Managers and professionals can use this model to assess the state, for example, of a new solution, such as blockchain, applied to insurance 4.0 development in the organization, and to evaluate strategic investments in their innovation solution capabilities.

In this model, the stages in the innovative solution introduction are (Fig. 14.2)[72]:

[68] Ajzen, I. (1991). The theory of planned behavior. *Organizational Behavior and Human Decision Processes, 50*(2), 179–211.

[69] Iansiti, M., & Lakhani, K. R. (2017). The truth about blockchain. *Harvard Business Review, 95*(1), 118–127.

[70] *Blockchain for and in logistics: What to adopt and where*. www.mdpi.com/2305-6290/2/3/18/htm. Accessed 20 June 2020.

[71] The truth about blockchain. *Harvard Business Review*. hbr.org/2017/01/the-truth-about-blockchain. Accessed 10 May 2020.

[72] Iansiti, M., & Lakhani, K. R. (2017). The truth about blockchain. *Harvard Business Review, 95*(1), 118–127.

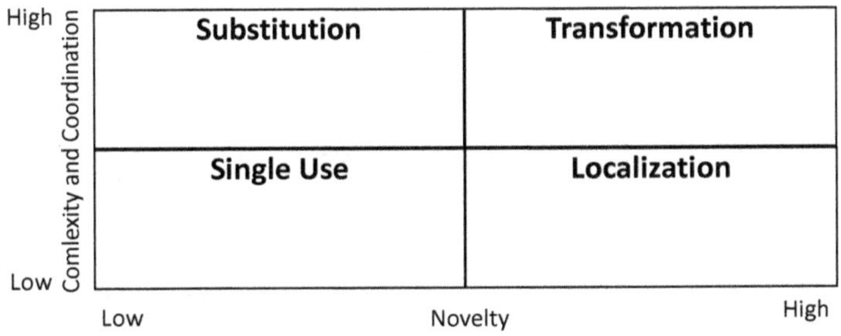

Fig. 14.2 Innovation types

- Single use. The first quadrant refers to low-novelty and low-coordination applications that create better, less costly, and highly focused solutions.
- Localization. The second quadrant includes innovations that are high in novelty. They need only a limited number of users to generate immediate value. As a consequence, it is easy to promote their adoption.
- Substitution. The third quadrant contains applications that are small in novelty because they build on current single use and localized applications. They need high coordination since they involve broader and increasingly public uses. These innovations aim to replace whole ways of doing business. There are high barriers to their adoption.
- Transformation. The last quadrant includes completely innovative applications that, if successful, could change the very nature of economic, social, and even legislative systems. They involve coordinating the activities of many actors and gaining institutional agreement on standards and processes. Their adoption requires significant social, legal, legislative changes, and challenges.

In the case of the blockchain solutions applied to insurance 4.0, the potential applications at each one of the previous steps could be (Fig. 14.3):

- Low Novelty and Low Complexity—Single Use. Blockchain solution in the health industry has the potential to take over the full register of patients. Implementing such technology in the health industry

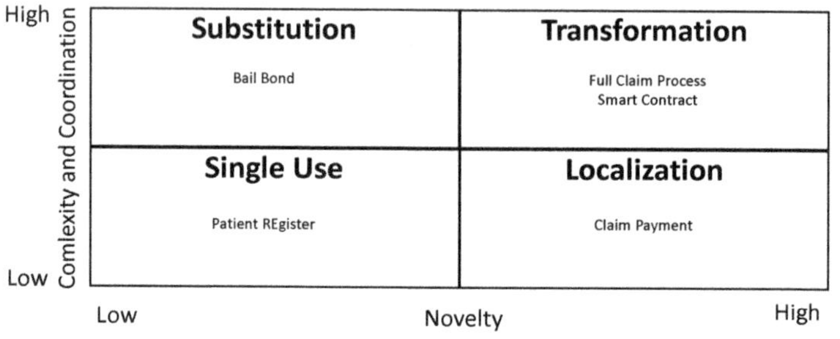

Fig. 14.3 Innovation types in insurance

would facilitate access to the entire history of patients. It would speed up the insurance procedure, allowing patients not to worry about administrative procedures while taking care of their health;

- High Novelty and Low Complexity—Localization. Many insurance processes are performed by brokers, companies, and reinsurers to determine the ultimate beneficial ownership and parties involved in the case of a claim payment. The broker often deals with several reinsurers, which further increases the involved parties and complicates the overall check process. A blockchain solution could register the integrity of customers' data for which only the customer has the encrypted keys, in full respect of compliance and privacy issues. In this case, the customers hold the keys to present for the next company with whom they want to be insured. The goal of such a solution is to reduce costs, delays, and time spent on this use case.
- Low Novelty and High Complexity—Substitution. A sinister cannot be void until the payment of the claim in full. For example, if a ship hits a port and ends up causing damage, a bail bond is to be established. The issue is that these letters are made on paper and need to be physically void. It is a complicated process, mainly in emergent countries. A blockchain solution can facilitate the process by registering the bail bond and linking it to the claim process voiding it automatically as soon as the payment of the claim takes place. It could be specified in the insurance contract's additional terms either by a receipt confirmation from the port's bank or "confirmation of final settlement request."

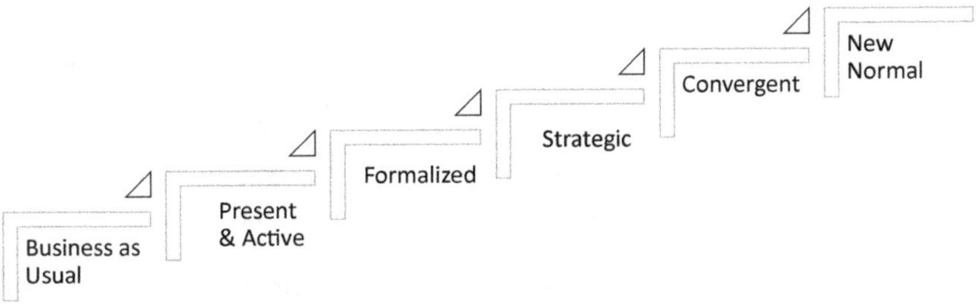

Fig. 14.4 Digital transformation stages (Adapted by the author from https://www.slideshare.net/briansolis/the-six-stages-of-digital-transformation-by-brian-solis)

- High Novelty and High Complexity—Transformation. In case of a claim, usually, several parties (companies, reinsurers, brokers, adjusters) are involved except for the Lloyds market that designates a lead underwriter to be responsible for the process and handle the claim. These different parties need to work on different processes which add up unnecessary costs. A blockchain solution can assure the integrity of data involved in the claim process and make it available correctly and immediately to all underwriters and the claim broker.[73] This solution could facilitate the whole process, as each member can view in real-time and contribute their requirement without interacting and waiting for responses. It would potentially reduce administrative costs as it is no longer necessary to send the same information several times to the different parties. The blockchain solution can be an independent entity or an extension of the "contract lifecycle."

Altimeter defines six stages of digital transformation (Fig. 14.4)[74]:

- Phase 1: Business as usual, where organizations operate with a current legacy perspective of customers, processes, metrics, business

[73] Sayegh, K., & Desoky, M. (2019). Blockchain application in insurance and reinsurance. *France: Skema Business School.*

[74] Solis, B. (2016). *Six stages of digital transformation.* www.slideshare.net/briansolis/the-six-stages-of-digital-transformation. Accessed 4 March 2020.

models, and technology, under the assumption that it remains the solution to digital relevance. This initial phase is the analysis and definition of the tools that govern an organization, its processes, and its activities.

- Phase 2: Present and Active, where small experiments foster digital literacy and creativity throughout the organization. At the same time, they aim to improve and amplify specific touchpoints and processes. In this phase, it is necessary to identify processes that need a change, decide and start doing research, and test the possible new ways of working.
- Phase 3: Formalized, where experimentation becomes intentional while executing in more promising and capable levels. Innovations become more challenging. As a result, change agents need executive support for new resources and technology.
- Phase 4: Strategic, where individual groups recognize the strengths in collaboration since their research, work, and shared insights contribute to new strategic plans for digital transformation ownership, efforts, and investments.[75] In this phase, there is the definition of the various areas of action and the financial resources needed to support the planned implementation.
- Phase 5: Converged, where a dedicated digital transformation team leads strategy and operations based on business and customer-centric objectives. The organization's new structure takes shape as roles, expertise, business models, processes, and systems support and sustain the change.
- Phase 6: New normal, where digital transformation becomes business as usual with executives and strategists recognizing that change is constant. There is the implementation of a new ecosystem to identify and act upon technology and market trends in the pilot and, eventually, at scale. In this phase, there is also an extension to other companies in the group or the partners.

Collectively, these phases act as a digital maturity model to drive a successful digital transformation. Digital customer experience plays a

[75] *Digital transformation: A guide to digital transformation*. rejolut.com/digital-transformation/. Accessed 20 June 2020.

pivotal role in guiding business evolution, in addition to technology and other market factors.[76]

In a survey of the Italian market, the participating organizations planned to concentrate investments in industrial IoT (48 percent), industrial analytics (39 percent), and advanced automation (33 percent). Considering a 3–5-year horizon, the priorities become advanced automation, cloud processing, and additive manufacturing.[77] Artificial intelligence and blockchain solutions are not yet relevant in the next few years' investment plans, with some exceptions for large organizations. This situation will change momentarily.

Implementing a full digital transformation is not easy for incumbent companies since they still have to devote the bulk of their resources to maintaining current processes and attending the existing business.[78] Transforming a company requires moving front and back offices in a synchronized fashion to ensure that the new approach has higher acceptance and swift implementation. A similar transformation is required by the partners in the company' ecosystem. On the other side, incumbent insurance companies have the funds and the resources to invest in a full-scale digital transformation.

Conclusions

This chapter shows which factors affect the adoption of insurance 4.0 and how insurance organizations can propagate. The adoption of insurance 4.0 is different from the adoption of traditional innovations. In this type of change, there is a need for redefining insurance 4.0. In doing so, the organization needs the involvement also of the partners in its ecosystems. This change is made possible through a process of restructuring, able to align different sectors such as insurance marketing, sales, and operations. The reorganization of these sectors should push toward the same goal, which is the effective adoption of insurance 4.0. This adoption is a new

[76] www.prophet.com/2016/04/the-six-stages-of-digital-transformation/. Accessed 29 February 2020.

[77] www.corrierecomunicazioni.it/industria-4-0/rallenta-la-corsa-di-industria-4-0-nel-2019-crescita-in-calo-del-10-15/. Accessed 22 June 2019.

[78] Albrecher, H., Bommier, A., Filipović, D., Koch-Medina, P., Loisel, S., & Schmeiser, H. (2019). Insurance: Models, digitization, and data science. *European Actuarial Journal, 9*(2), 349–360.

concept for many companies. Over time, this adoption should become a routine.

Few organizations are achieving the results expected. McKinsey Global Survey confirms that the rate of success of digital transformations is alarmingly low.[79] About eight in ten respondents in one of its surveys stated that their organizations had begun digital transformations in recent years. Just 14 percent say their efforts have reached sustained performance improvements. Only 3 percent of the respondents report complete success at supporting their change.

This chapter explores the factors assuring the success of digital transformation and details the action to take. The implementation of insurance 4.0 requires a strategy and an integrated design of several aspects of insurance. It is a vision which should cover at the same time its business model, including:

- Proposition of value;
- Proximity;
- Partition of the customers;
- Place of channels;
- Processes;
- Platforms;
- Persons;
- Partnerships;
- Correct Pricing; and
- Payments for costs and investments.

This book looks at all these aspects and analyzes the changes necessary for the overall design of insurance 4.0.

Digital transformation can have impacts on customers and on the organization itself of companies. However, to better understand this phenomenon's magnitude, it is necessary to explore other vital concepts. They can lead to a higher awareness of innovation, mainly applied to the insurance market. The next chapter analyzes these concepts at the basis of future developments.

[79] www.mckinsey.com/business-functions/digital-mckinsey/our-insights/five-moves-to-make-during-a-digital-transformation. Accessed 19 May 2019.

Based on the topics discussed in this chapter, it becomes clear the importance and impact of the digital transformation in the life cycle of insurance organizations and their partners, such as intermediaries, agents, and brokers. At the same time, digital transformation becomes more critical to the distribution of services and the channels. The insurance regulator, for instance, Ivass in Italy, recognized the increasing incidence of digitization in internal and external processes to insurance organizations and issued new regulations to take into account these changes and especially protect the customers.[80]

An interesting question is if, with insurance 4.0, the insurance industry will lose parts of their value network to other sectors.[81] Companies from other industries may have better access to the customer or the corresponding data. It is useful to follow very closely such a threat. Customers are increasingly willing to buy insurance from non-traditional firms such as bigtech organizations or product manufacturers (for instance, Tesla).[82] Still, at the moment, it seems unlikely that bigtech organizations, for example, will take over substantial parts of the insurance value network. This situation happens because a realistic return on equity is too small to justify investments. More attractive alternatives exist (investment in other businesses, cooperation with incumbent insurance companies, and so on). Regulation and lack of expertise serve as entry barriers. This consideration only holds for today, very likely not for the future.

[80] www.ivass.it/pubblicazioni-e-statistiche/pubblicazioni/relazione-annuale/2017/Relazione_IVASS_2016_en.pdf?language_id=3. Accessed 14 March 2020.

[81] Eling, M., & Lehmann, M. (2018). The impact of digitalization on the insurance value chain and the insurability of risks. *The Geneva Papers on Risk and Insurance—Issues and Practice, 43*(3), 359–396.

[82] worldinsurancereport.com/. Accessed 30 May 2020.

CHAPTER 15

Future of Insurance 4.0 and Insurtech

Introduction

This chapter deals with the future of insurance 4.0. The great physicist Niels Bohr said: "It is very difficult to predict, mainly the future."[1] For surviving as persons and organizations, it is critical to predicting the future in the best possible way. This observation holds in general. It is even more so in the case of insurance, because of its close links with the external environment. This interrelationship becomes more robust in the case of insurance 4.0.

Potentially, it is also possible that competitors would come from outside the insurance world (e.g., the large internet companies, the so-called bigtech organizations).[2] Bigtech organizations can find ways to overcome the structural barriers to market entry in insurance.[3] They have robust financial strength and data and information essential for risk calculations. Compliance and administrative burden are so high that widespread market entry of insurtech or bigtech organizations as digital insurance companies is unlikely. Big internet or bigtech organizations may

[1] Camussone, P. F. (2017). Digital for job: The future of work: technology. *Digital World, 2,* 1–15.

[2] Frost, J., Gambacorta, L., Huang, Y., Shin, H. S., & Zbinden, P. (2019). BigTech and the changing structure of financial intermediation.

[3] Prognos, A. G. (2017). *Digitalisierung in der Versicherungswirtschaft. Studie.* Hg. v. vbw Vereinigung der Bayerischen Wirtschaft e.V. München.

B. Nicoletti, *Insurance 4.0*, Palgrave Studies in Financial Services Technology, https://doi.org/10.1007/978-3-030-58426-9_15

occupy part of the value network currently covered by the incumbent insurance companies. From the perspective of the insurance companies, mainly the loss of direct customer proximity would be a significant danger.

Insurance will evolve in the short and medium terms. Insurance 4.0 not only changes current markets and business models.[4] The new technological possibilities, new solutions, and new services may also bring other substantial changes. Insurtech organizations with new business models beyond the core markets *of* the established insurance companies, open up an entirely new scenario.

Scenarios

To predict it is necessary to define possible scenarios. A prediction might be simple for the short term. Slower growth, pandemic, and other difficulties worldwide will make it challenging to resume the pre-crisis operational levels of 2008 or even 2019. At the same time, globalization is in crisis. There are several reasons. The acceleration of globalization was probably too fast. The result has been a revival of localism and sovranism (a new term used to avoid the word nationalism which evokes bad past times).

These changes will also be reflected in the organizations and so on insurance. The examination of what could happen to insurance 4.0 is fascinating referring to the classic four Ps of the marketing mix: product, price, promotion or advertisement, and place or location.

From the product point of view, dematerialization is prevailing. This trend pushes the services toward sharing economy, sharing of material goods, and consumption, but also from the organizations' perspective. Outsourcing is the traditional mode of sharing economy for organizations. The expectation is that working in complex ecosystems outsourcing will grow.

From the price perspective, the trend will be the inclusion in the economic balance of a product or service some factors not strictly connected with the price, but with the financial gains in general. The expectation is that insurance companies will finance significant campaigns to reduce the costs and hence be able to reduce the premiums to beat the competition and increase the market share.

[4] Prognos, A. G. (2017). *Digitalisierung in der Versicherungswirtschaft. Studie.* Hg. v. vbw Vereinigung der Bayerischen Wirtschaft e.V. München.

Fig. 15.1 The four Ps

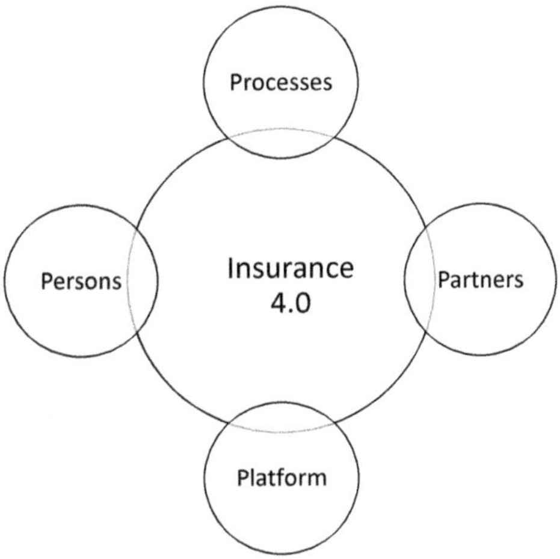

In promotion, it is interesting to note the diffusion also in the insurance of some multimedia promotion to the customers.

The last P of these four aspects, the place and the facilitation in the selling and the delivery of insurance will expand through online and mobile channels with a push to an omnichannel approach.[5]

Four Ps of Insurance Management

The organization can try to identify how the future looks from the perspective of some of the Ps, introduced in this book's approach to the insurance business model. In particular, how the future looks like for possible developments in the platforms, processes, persons, and partnerships (Fig. 15.1).

Platforms

One exciting development is the increasing diffusion of innovative platforms as a business model. A multi-sided platform (MSP) is a business model that allows multiple participants (producers and customers) to

[5] Hu, T. I., & Tracogna, A. (2020). Multichannel customer journeys and their determinants: Evidence from motor insurance. *Journal of Retailing and Consumer Services, 54*, 102022.

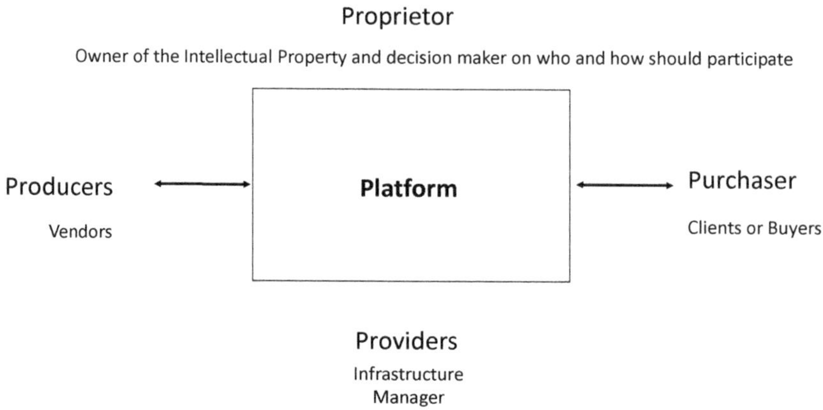

Fig. 15.2 Multi-sided platforms

connect and interact with one another and create and exchange value.[6] These solutions are telematics platforms that allow the matching of other 4 Ps (Fig. 15.2):

- The Proprietor of the platforms: those that have identified and funded this type of online information systems;
- The Provider of the platforms provides the infrastructure, the service, and the software supporting the platform;
- The Producers provide the products and the services, made available on the platform;
- The Purchasers buy the products or the services on the platform.

These roles are interchangeable. For example, Producers can become Purchasers and vice versa.

These platforms are usually in the cloud, to which all other applications will migrate over time. From a data management point of view, the support can be provided by a blockchain solution.[7] In a short time, this

[6] Van Alstyne, M. W., Parker, G. G., & Choudary, S. P. (2016). Pipelines, platforms, and the new rules of strategy. *Harvard Business Review, 94*(4), 54–62.

[7] Nicoletti, B. (2017). *The future of fintech.* London, UK: Springer International Publishing. ISBN 978-3-319-51414-7.

solution has been appreciated for its capability to innovate the work in groups substantially. The insurance team can benefit the most. Blockchain solutions are an open online ledger in which it is possible to record every transaction in the network for a specific application. The blockchain is available for all participants. They can see it and check it. A standard log allows typical visibility of operations and services. This capability automates the secure exchange of data transfer among organizations. Blockchain solutions could help in the exchange of documentation, such as the policies, warranties, claims, and other documents in insurance 4.0. The blockchain solution can certify the documents as accessed from all sides.

These platforms are indicated in the literature as multi-sided platforms.[8] MSPs have two critical features beyond any other characteristics (such as indirect network effects or non-neutrality of fees)[9]:

- They enable direct interactions between two or more distinct sides. Direct communication means that two, or more, different parties retain control over the critical terms of the connection, as opposed to the intermediary taking control of those terms.[10] Where the interactions involve trading, the critical terms of the communication are the pricing, bundling, marketing, and delivery of the goods or services traded, the ability to determine the nature and quality of services offered, the terms and conditions, and so on.
- Each side has an association with the platform. Association means that users on each side consciously take platform-specific actions necessary for them to interact with each other directly.[11] The actions

[8] Hagiu, A., & Wright, J. (2015). Multi-sided platforms. *International Journal of Industrial Organization, 43,* 162–174. Eling, M., & Lehmann, M. (2018). The impact of digitization on the insurance value chain and the insurability of risks. *The Geneva Papers on Risk and Insurance—Issues and Practice, 43,* 359–396. https://doi.org/10.1057/s41288-017-0073-0.

[9] *Multi-sided platforms* (Harvard Business School Working Paper). hbswk.hbs.edu/item/multi-sided-platforms-. Accessed 10 May 2020.

[10] Hagiu, A., & Wright, J. (2015). Multi-sided platforms. *International Journal of Industrial Organization, 43,* 162–174.

[11] Hagiu, A., & Wright, J. (2015). Multi-sided platforms. *International Journal of Industrial Organization, 43,* 162–174.

could be a fixed access fee (e.g., buying a policy), an expenditure of resources (e.g., spending time and money on learning how to develop apps using the cellular phone's APIs), or an opportunity cost (e.g., joining a loyalty program).[12]

For more details, refer to the literature on the applications of MSP in insurance.[13] To describe the relationship constellations between MSP and traditional companies: MSP in the insurance value network can[14]

- Increase competition among traditional companies;
- Facilitate coordination among companies, customers, and other stakeholders;
- Enable cooperation with companies; and
- Improve collaboration among insurers and other organizations.

Taken as a whole, value creation in the insurance industry is undergoing a massive transformation due to the emergence of MSPs. This change has three main implications for the insurance industry: specialization, modularization, and higher complexity of the value network. It might become increasingly difficult for traditional insurance companies to structure and coordinate their value network and their distribution and communication activities (e.g., omnichannel). They even might give up essential activities of value creation and customer interaction to MSPs or other new players in the market. In the worst case, traditional insurance companies might become suppliers of only basic insurance services.

The insurance industry's MSPs are likely to promote the decrease of information asymmetries among traditional insurance companies, customers, and other stakeholders in the value network. Customers can interact with many suppliers and channels to access or assess information, compare or buy insurance services, and interact with their insurance companies. New ways of customer interactions might promote the birth

[12] Alonso R., Dessein W., & Matouschek N. (2014). *Organizing to adapt and compete* (Working paper). University of Southern California, Los Angeles.

[13] Pousttchi, K., & Gleiss, A. (2019). Surrounded by middlemen—how multi-sided platforms change the insurance industry. *Electronic Markets, 29*(4), 609–629.

[14] Pousttchi, K., & Gleiss, A. (2019). Surrounded by middlemen—how multi-sided platforms change the insurance industry. *Electronic Markets, 29*(4), 609–629.

of new products or business models. Consequently, shifts in the value network and changing customer behaviors might lead to new constellations of customer ownership.

The society's growing reliance on digital technologies is not only reshaping customer expectations. It is also redefining boundaries across industries. Companies cannot avoid this occurrence. As traditional industry borders disappear, the future of insurance stands to be significantly influenced by platforms[15] and ecosystems.[16] The most successful organizations in the digital era, including Alibaba, Amazon, and Facebook, were all designed on platform business models. Their bases are ecosystems. An ecosystem is an interconnected set of services that allows users to fulfill a variety of needs in one integrated experience.[17] Customer ecosystems currently emerging worldwide tend to concentrate on requirements such as travel, healthcare, or housing. Business-to-business (B2B) ecosystems generally revolve around a specific decision-maker, for example, marketing and sales, operations, procurement, or finance professionals.[18] Ecosystems are an opportunity for insurance companies to sell more services integrated with other products or services.

Processes

Processes will become increasingly integrated. For too long, companies have leaned processes only with organizational or logistic measures. The lean and digitized method will become more used to make processes thinner and integrated into an increasingly digital world.[19]

[15] www.mckinsey.com/industries/financial-services/our-insights/insurance-beyond-digital-the-rise-of-ecosystems-and-platforms. Accessed 10 January 2020.

[16] Komninos, N. (2019). *Smart cities and connected intelligence: Platforms, ecosystems and network effects*. Google books.

[17] Global Banking Practice. *The ecosystem playbook: Winning in*.... www.mckinsey.com/~/media/mckinsey/industries/financial%20services/our%20insights/winning%20in%20a%20world%20of%20ecosystems/winning-in-a-world-of-ecosystems-vf.ashx. Accessed 22 June 2020.

[18] www.mckinsey.com/industries/financial-services/our-insights/insurance-beyond-digital-the-rise-of-ecosystems-and-platforms. Accessed on 10 May 2020.

[19] Nicoletti, B. (2012). *Lean and digitize: An integrated approach to process improvement*. Farnham, UK: Gower Publishing. ISBN-10: 1409441946.

Persons

There will be fewer persons in insurance companies. They will work more as consultants for customers or for other functions of the organization rather than doing operational work. Significant roadblocks for companies include talent management and inadequacy in talent strategy.[20] Many organizations lack proper competencies to upgrade their insurance business model to insurance 4.0.

Remote work will become very much diffused after the pandemic outbreak. Efforts to contain the spread of pandemic pushed insurance company staff, from actuaries to underwriters to claims managers, to work remotely.[21] Smart working will become the new normal for many types of jobs. Companies should ensure that employees can access the necessary files and conduct business from remote locations. Chief information security officers (CISOs) need to establish new cyber security protocols to permit the secure exchange of confidential information among employees connecting from outside the office.

Many organizations are setting policies around remote access. As companies move toward remote protocols, chief information officers, chief technology officers, and CISOs should ensure that offsite workers have access to at least the following technology capabilities:

- A laptop or desktop computer, preferably equipment issued by the company;
- A virtual private or zero-trust network to securely and remotely connect to critical business applications;
- Collaboration tools (groupware) to help with audio, video, and screen-sharing;
- An adequately equipped and staffed ICT support team to answer employees' questions and help them continue to do their jobs remotely (Fig. 15.3).

[20] SAP Ariba. (2018). *CPO survey 2018—What's the next big thing in insurance*. www.ariba.com/resources/library/library-pages/cpo-survey-2018. Accessed 1 August 2019.

[21] www2.deloitte.com/content/dam/insights/us/articles/6702_covid-19-insurance/DI_COVID-19-insurance.pdf. Accessed 5 April 2020.

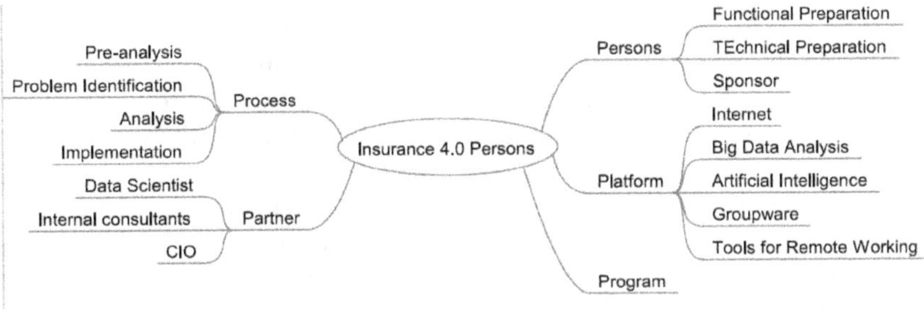

Fig. 15.3 Tools for remote working

Partnerships

From the perspective of critical partners, future changes will be substantial. There will be a move more and more from intermediaries to partners. There will be a consolidation of the partners and their integration in ecosystems. The importance of the partner location, and then to the proximity (physical or virtual) to the customers of the partners, will be relevant.

The digitization of the contracts is evolving rapidly. Smart contracts will become more used.[22] They are computer-based protocols and telecommunications that facilitate, manage, or enforce, the negotiation or execution of a contract. They allow data storage shared between virtual organizations parties of the agreements. It is necessary to guarantee the protection of the data, once the data is in the system. This type of warranty can come from the use of blockchain solutions that are at the basis of smart contracts. The smart contracts usually have an advanced user interface. They often simulate the logic of standard contractual clauses. Many types of contractual terms can be partially or fully automated, self-actuating, or both. The smart contracts can ensure more security to the current agreements and reduce the transaction costs associated with insurance.

Insurance companies should connect more and more automatically with their intermediaries. This connection is the correct and secure way after the terrible experience of the pandemic. Companies that have

[22] Nicoletti, B. (2012). *Lean and digitize: An integrated approach to process improvement*. Farnham, UK: Gower Publishing. ISBN-10: 1409441946.

invested in advancing their digital capabilities will be in good contact with their distribution partners, who, in turn, should offer faster, more professional, and more comprehensive services to their customers.[23]

After the COVID-19 experience, companies should enhance planning and training in anticipation of a potentially longer-term social distancing mode. This new mode will transform how intermediaries stay in contact with their customers, how they prospect for referrals, and how they serve customers who may be experiencing financial strain. With excellent digital tools, this can be an opportunity for productive planning, training, and outreaching across the company, intermediary, and customer stakeholder groups. In times of uncertainty and financial stress, it is essential for all the financial services to maintain communication and be able to serve in an excellent way.[24]

Companies may have additional circumstances to consider to accommodate claims adjusters. Often, they need to travel to perform their jobs, both locally and to more distant locations. That could be problematic in a pandemic scenario. An example of a project that can impact the future of underwriting activity is the app designed by Zurich insurance in Switzerland.[25] The app can send a photo of the vehicle at the time of the conclusion of a policy. Thus, the possible customer does not have to send a copy of the insurance gray paper, must not communicate the vehicle's model, and how many accessories have the vehicle because the company recognizes its model through the photos. The company directly provides an estimate based on the security level determined by the vehicle's degree of automation.

Future Perspectives

A significant issue, mainly in vehicle insurance, is the sharing economy. The other considerable idea is the cooperative ecosystem involving various digital partners. In these sectors, sharing and cooperation will be critical

[23] file:///C:/Users/18HW010075/Downloads/DI_COVID-19-insurance.pdf. Accessed 5 April 2020.

[24] *Impact of COVID-19 on insurers*. Deloitte Insights. www2.deloitte.com/us/en/insights/economy/covid-19/impact-of-covid-19-on-insurers.html. Accessed 22 June 2020.

[25] Varela Tomè, M. A. (2018). *Le nuove tecnologie digitali: opportunità e rischi per il settore assicurativo auto* (Doctoral dissertation). Scuola Universitaria Professionale della Svizzera Italiana.

to success. Another trend is a collaboration with insurtech organizations. In the strategy of all the significant insurance groups there are relevant ideas concerning the potential of innovation initiatives. They need them; otherwise, the companies might not be able to keep up with the new environment.

Artificial intelligence and blockchain solutions are still at an early stage. Companies are examining the areas in which they can apply this technology. These tools will become more and more sophisticated. Somebody believes that they will become the basis of the fifth industrial revolution: insurance 5.0.[26]

Car Digital Dossier[27]
In 2017, AXA Winterthur developed a Car Digital Dossier in collaboration with the AdNovum software company and other partners. It is a blockchain solution and collects all relevant data on the entire life cycle of a vehicle. This information can be used not only by the owner of the vehicle but also by manufacturers, dealers, companies, repair shops, and offices. For the customer, the benefits are to have a virtual booklet, completely transparent, and counterfeit-proof. The Car Digital Dossier facilitates the used market, as it will record all the processes a vehicle has undergone. Thus, the customer can be sure about the state in which the vehicle is reversed, simplifying the repairs,[28] The Car Dossier opens up new possibilities in pricing, service, and more efficient claims management.

Insurtech

Fintech companies are reshaping the financial services industry, providing customers with innovative value propositions. Forward-looking strategies

[26] Özdemir, V., & Hekim, N. (2018). Birth of industry 5.0: Making sense of big data with artificial intelligence, "the internet of things" and next-generation technology policy. *Omics: A Journal of Integrative Biology*, *22*(1), 65–76.

[27] Ade, M. (2017, December). *AXA Winterthur punta sulla tecnologia Blockchain*. www.axa.ch/it/ueber-axa/blog/trend/axa-adnovum-blockchain-mobilita-futuro-mobility.html. Accessed 14 March 2020.

[28] Ade, M. (2017, December). *AXA Winterthur punta sulla tecnologia Blockchain*. www.axa.ch/it/ueber-axa/blog/trend/axa-adnovum-blockchain-mobilita-futuro-mobility.html. Accessed 14 March 2020.

and advanced business models back them. This section considers insurtech organizations, the insurance-specific branch of fintech organizations,[29] related to digital technology applied to the insurance sector.[30] This terminology includes any technology-driven innovation in the insurance industry: software, applications, processes, products, and services.[31]

Fintech startups have relentlessly targeted some areas of financial services, mainly in payments. They are now directing their efforts also to insurance companies. Nine out of 10 insurance executives polled by consultant Price Waterhouse Coopers reckon that at least part of their business is at risk—a higher proportion than in any other finance area.[32]

The insurance industry, according to Price Waterhouse Coopers, has not shown relevant changes for decades.[33] During the last decades, technology has fueled transformation and innovations in every sector, carrying around innovative applications and cutting-edge business models.[34] The

[29] Price Waterhouse Coopers. (2016). *Insurtech: A golden opportunity for companies to innovate.* www.PwC.com/us/en/insurance/publications/assets/PwC-top-issues-insurtech.pdf. Accessed 31 July 2016. Scheuffel, P. (2016). Taming the beast: A scientific definition of fintech. *Journal of Innovation Management, 4*(4), 32–54.

[30] Nicoletti, B. (2017). *The future of FinTech*. Cham, CH: Springer.

Chishti, S., & Barberis, J. (2016). *The FinTech book: The financial technology handbook for investors, entrepreneurs and visionaries*. Chichester, UK: Wiley. Drummer, D., Jerenz, A., Siebelt, P., & Thaten, M. (2016). *FinTech: Challenges and opportunities—How digitization is transforming the financial sector*. Dusseldorf: McKinsey. Mackenzie, A. (2015). The fintech revolution. *London Business School Review, 26*(3), 50–53. OECD—Organisation for Economic Co-operation and Development, 2017. Technology and Innovation in the insurance sector.

[31] Baumann, N. (2018). *A catalyst for change—How fintech has sparked a revolution in insurance.* www2.deloitte.com/content/dam/Deloitte/global/Documents/Financial-Services/gx-fsi-cataylst-for-change. Accessed 20 March 2020.

Chester, A., Hoffman, N., Johansson, S., & Braad Olesen, P. (2018). *Digital insurance in 2018—Commercial lines InsurTech: A pathway to digital.* www.mckinsey.com/industries/financial-services/our-insights/html. Swiss Re Institute. (2017, June). *Technology and insurance: Themes and challenges.*

[32] blogs.reuters.com/breakingviews/2016/07/13/fintech-bigger-and-dicier-for-companies-than-banks/. Accessed 29 July 2016.

[33] Price Waterhouse Coopers. (2016, March). *Insurtech: A golden opportunity for companies to innovate.* www.PwC.com/us/en/insurance/publications/assets/PwC-top-issues-insurtech.pdf. Accessed 10 May 2020.

[34] Nicoletti, B. (2017). *The future of fintech.* London, UK: Springer International Publishing. ISBN 978-3-319-51414-7.

size of its investments in insurtech organizations, if compared to fintech initiatives for the banking and payment sectors, follows the same pattern.

Insurtech organizations are gaining an increasing market share in the insurance sector. Investments have increased exponentially, from 130 million dollars in 2011 to 6.7 billion in 2019.[35] Additional growth of insurtech organizations is expected to continue after this terrible pandemic. This trend should push the fundraising from 175 billion dollars in 2016 to 235 billion dollars in 2021.[36] The investments show homogeneity on a global scale: Forty-six percent of all investments are in the USA, 40 percent in Europe, Middle East, Africa (EMEA) area, and 14 percent in the Asia-Pacific area, with the prospect of progressive growth in the latter regions over the next few years.[37]

Insurtech organizations are growing despite the high level of regulation characterizing the insurance sector. The presence of entry barriers instead is not allowing access to the market to the so-called bigtech organizations such as Google, Facebook, and Amazon.[38] Without players in a robust dominant position, the sector can develop gradually and widely, giving insurtech organizations the time and space to get funding and develop new solutions.

Insurtech organizations are innovating the insurance value network mainly through technology but not only. The insurance industry is ready for technological disruptions. Transformations that occurred in the financial services industry have also affected the insurance companies. Customers' expectations and requirements have increased significantly. Companies should be able to fit this changing environment by adapting

[35] https://www.mckinsey.com/industries/financial-services/our-insights/insurtech-the-threat-that-inspires. Accessed 10 May 2020.

[36] Kaesler S. (2019, May). *A new industry model for InsurTech.* www.mckinsey.com/industries/financial-services/our-insights/insurance-blog/a-new-industry-model-for-insurtech. Accessed 10 May 2020.

Statista. (2019, December). *Outlook: Digital market outlook.* Retrieved from Statista Web site: www.statista.com/outlook/digital-markets.

[37] McKinsey. (2018). *Digital insurance in 2018: Driving real impact with digital and analytics.* www.mckinsey.com/~/media/McKinsey/Industries/Financialpercent20Services. Accessed 10 May 2020.

[38] Nicastro, A. (2018). *Strategic alternative for banks to seize fintech revolution opportunities: Cases of successful M&As and alliances.*

their business models, placing the customers at the center of their strategies, and being active and not reactive to changes and innovations.[39]

Customer expectations are relevant components as drivers of disruption. Technology has had an impact on the so-called tech-barriers, which has lowered them and allows access to the insurance industry to several new players.[40] The diffusion of open-source frameworks, development, on-demand insurance, and cloud computing are other examples of technology facilitators for the new entrants. The results are causing unexpected disruptions and turbulence in the financial services market that was, by its very nature, stable and stationary in all its components.

Insurtech organizations have received a lot of attention from investors over the years.[41] The investments in companies building technology solutions for the insurance sector have been USD 18 bn. Interest has increased over the years, with a total of USD 7.1 bn invested in the insurtech organizations during 2019. This investment has been USD 2.7 bn more capital than deployed during 2018. The volume of deals has risen in sync with the amount of equity invested. In 2019, there were 261 insurtech organizations to close a funding round.

This section focuses on the application of the model presented in this book into this exciting sector.

Business Model of Insurtech Organizations

To define a business model of insurtech organizations, it is possible to start with the general model for insurance organizations presented in this book and make the necessary adjustments.[42] Every startup should address

[39] Kindström, D., & Kowalkowski, C. (2014). Service innovation in product-centric firms: A multidimensional business model perspective. *Journal of Business & Industrial Marketing*.

[40] Barry, C., Hogan, M., & Torres, A. M. (2011). Low-cost companies and high-tech barriers: User views on questionable web design practices in Ireland. *Irish Journal of Management, 31*(1), 43.

[41] member.fintech.global/2020/05/15/how-akur8-is-filling-the-gap-in-pricing-automation/. Accessed 30 May 2020.

[42] Nicoletti, B. (2017). *The future of fintech*. London, UK: Springer International Publishing. ISBN 978-3-319-51414-7.

its focus toward these essential components to effectively engage with today's knowledge-empowered policyholders[43]:

(a) Proposition of value—Focus on the right products that suit evolving needs and preferences across the customer lifecycle;
(b) Proximity to the customer—Focus on timely communication in such a way that customers perceive insurance as valuable; predicting customers' life situations and offering coverage when they need it most;
(c) Partition of the market—Focus on two essential factors that define customer behavior when it comes to buying insurance: social media behavior and shopping preferences[44];
(d) Place or channels—Focus on the right channels that customers prefer and access most. Define an omnichannel strategy;

(e) Platforms—Focus on solutions, not on technology;
(f) Processes—Focus on business process integration;
(g) Persons—Focus on new ways of working, new roles, and teamwork;
(h) Partnership and collaboration—Focus on financial requirements and the distribution network. Be part of an ecosystem to offer a full range of services;
(i) Pricing and revenue—Focus on customer lifetime value[45] and granular pricing,[46] based on better data capture;
(j) Payments on costs and investments—Focus on lean and digitize.[47]

This framework fits better with the new environment for a startup operating in the financial services industry. Considering different categories in insurtech initiatives, the difference would be the weight of the various items in the list and their specific aims and objectives. Regarding the

[43] Nicoletti, B. (2017). *The future of fintech*. London, UK: Springer International Publishing. ISBN 978-3-319-51414-7.

[44] worldinsurancereport.com/. Accessed 30 May 2020.

[45] Berger, P. D., & Nasr, N. I. (1998). Customer lifetime value: Marketing models and applications. *Journal of Interactive Marketing, 12*(1), 17–30.

[46] Seminar, G. I. *A practical guide to commercial insurance pricing*.

[47] Nicoletti, B. (2016). *Lean and digitize: An integrated approach to process improvement*. London, UK: Routledge.

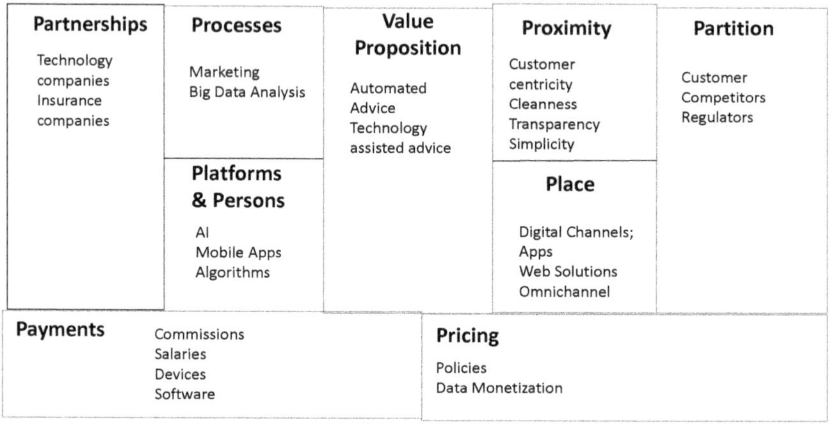

Fig. 15.4 Business Model Canvas for an insurtech organization (example)

"partnership and collaboration" area, for example, the weight of financial institutions is quite different if referred to an insurtech organization or an incumbent insurance company. Thus, the focus is not on "Financial institutions" but rather "Financial institutions and other strategic partners."

Insurtech organizations have targeted all parts of the value network of traditional companies as much as by other industry players.[48] Although these newcomers are populating every part of the value network, their focus to date has been on the more easily accessible parts of the value network: mainly distribution, in property and casualty insurance. Since innovation from insurtech organizations aims to contribute to the insurance value network (except distribution for large players), many insurance companies view possible partnerships with insurtech organizations as positive (Fig. 15.4).

Insurtech organizations adopt simple business models focused on specific areas and rich in technological aspects. Several of them use artificial intelligence, specifically machine learning. They possess a vast capacity for big data analysis and processing. Insurtech organizations can seize the

[48] Mair, J., & Schoen, O. (2007). Successful social entrepreneurial business models in the context of developing economies. *International Journal of Emerging Markets*.

opportunities offered by the market more swiftly than traditional companies thanks to their use of digitization and automation. They often have a culture that strives for and recognizes innovation, and a mentality that places them in pole position in sector change.[49]

It is interesting to analyze which type of organization mostly benefits from the business model presented in this book. Even though the application of this model in this chapter is mainly for new entrants, every organization that is performing its business in the insurance industry can benefit from the insights given in this chapter. Setting the stage for innovation and contextually being inspired by the change are components that must lead the mindset of each business organization, both startups, and incumbent companies. It is critical never to lose the overall view and not limit the transformation to one specific component.

Open Insuring Model

To understand the relevance of insurtech organizations, it is possible to transport in the insurance field the statement of Bill Gates for banks: "Banking is necessary, banks are not."[50] It is similar to state that insuring is necessary, but insurance companies are not. Insurtech organizations are playing a fundamental role in the development of solutions that address the sector's needs. Higher customer loyalty, new income sources, and more operational efficiency are just some of the benefits that make insurtech organizations attractive partners for incumbent companies.

In terms of technologies, most investments target insurtech organizations active in the artificial intelligence and mobile application fields. Compared to other sectors, these solutions help in facilitating value creation. They attract investors interested in new business models.[51] Other investments focus on big data analytics, cloud computing, the internet of things, and blockchain solutions.

[49] Catlin, T., & Lorenz, J. T. (2017, March). Digital disruption in insurance: Cutting through the noise. *Digital McKinsey*.

[50] Angelshaug, M. A. G. N. E., & Saebi, T. I. N. A. (2017). The burning platform of retail banking. *The European Business Review, 5*, 30–35.

[51] *NTT DATA: And Everis Publish InsurTech Outlook 2019*.... www.marketscreener.com/NTT-DATA-CORP-6491233/news/NTT-DATA-and-everis-Publish-InsurTech-Outlook-2019-29215636/. Accessed 10 May 2020.

Investment in AI-based startups is multiplying; during 2016–2018, investment levels in the artificial intelligence sector were 665 percent higher than during the last five years.[52] This investment focus underlines the importance to be a data-driven organization to construct personalized offers, attract and retain customers, and achieve more effective and efficient processes across all business lines.[53]

Mobile applications are becoming more essential. Their impact increases owing to their focus on personalization and the increased use of comparators or MSPs platforms. E-commerce is the most commonly used technology platform. It is more focused on cyber security due to the increase in risks perceived to bring.

Insurance companies are collaborating with insurtech organizations to face these technological challenges and benefit from these new opportunities. The vision does not always appear as positive: Nine out of ten companies consider insurtech organization activity as posing a risk to their existing business.[54] On the other hand, startups value the chance to get close to traditional companies, since accessing their customer databases, funding, and addressing compliance issues are critical factors in scaling their businesses.

The big five technology companies, Google, Amazon, Facebook, Apple, and Microsoft (GAFAM), are looking to innovate in the insurance sector by collaborating with several disruptive insurtech organizations to enter the health or small and mid-caps insurance markets. Their objective is to innovate in the vision, design, and commercial phases of insurance products to adapt to new living norms (connected homes, self-driving cars, sharing economy, and so on). They aim to connect them through their platforms, transforming the insurance distribution model. These companies might have a significant impact on the insurance market over

[52] www.nttdata.com/global/en/media/press-release/2019/september/ntt-data-and-everis-publish-insurtech-outlook-2019. Accessed 20 May 2020.

[53] *NTT DATA: And Everis Publish InsurTech Outlook 2019*.... www.marketscreener.com/NTT-DATA-CORP-6491233/news/NTT-DATA-and-everis-Publish-InsurTech-Outlook-2019-29215636/. Accessed 22 June 2020.

[54] www.nttdata.com/global/en/media/press-release/2019/september/ntt-data-and-everis-publish-insurtech-outlook-2019. Accessed 20 May 2020.

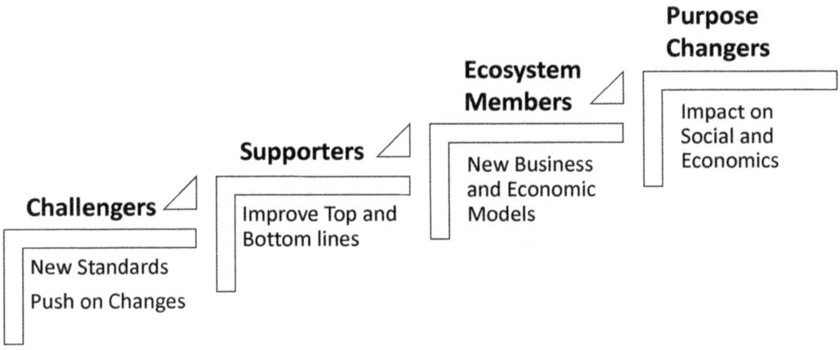

Fig. 15.5 Four waves of insurtech organizations (Adapted from https://www.digitalinsuranceagenda.com/thought-leadership/the-four-waves-of-insurtech/)

the coming years. Google and Amazon will have the most significant impact on technology and distribution, respectively.[55]

Big insurance companies confirm that insurtech organizations' value chain fragmentation is a critical point in their strategic plan. This situation will enhance the necessary evolution toward an open innovation model to maintain their relevance in the market.[56]

Development of Insurtech Organizations

It is possible to distinguish four waves in the development of insurtech organizations (Fig. 15.5).[57] In the first wave, around 2016, insurtech organizations were mostly challengers. New entrants were out attacking the established order. The mantra was disruption. The main driver for this first wave was eroding entry barriers thanks to new technologies. New entrants took the lead in the smart and innovative use of technology

[55] www.nttdata.com/global/en/media/press-release/2019/september/ntt-data-and-everis-publish-insurtech-outlook-2019. Accessed 20 May 2020.

[56] www.nttdata.com/global/en/media/press-release/2019/september/ntt-data-and-everis-publish-insurtech-outlook-2019-. Accessed 25 April 2020.

[57] Peverelli, R., & de Fenika, R. (2019). *The four waves of insurtech organization*. xprimm.com/The-Four-Waves-of-Insurtech-articol-117,149-13848.htm. Accessed 30 May 2020.

and data, designing new ways of working that solved the dissatisfactions of customers experienced when working with traditional companies. Their focus on fewer frictions and new service levels has changed the expectations of customers. New entrants set new standards.

This sense of urgency fueled the second wave. The value of the second wave, the enablers, is the impact on the top line and bottom line of incumbents. Many insurtech organizations explore the potential of new data streams to improve pricing, automate claims, and reduce fraud. They are also launching all sorts of new proactive services, especially in the online and mobile space. Many traditional companies realize that teaming up with insurtech organizations is vital to accelerate innovation.

The third wave can be labeled as ecosystems beyond insurance. This trend is important for the next few years. This trend is the key driver for the insurtech organizations third wave. More and more insurers realize that the most effective way to reach out to customers is to be part of relevant platforms and ecosystems. These platforms are not only platforms around the home, mobility, work, and health. They are also around significant life events such as study, weddings, birth, divorce, and retirement, in the case of individuals. It is around transportation, logistics, manufacturing, and so on for commercial insurance. They are events that require substantial financial and risk decisions. The third wave of Insurtech organization is about increasing relevancy and opening up new business models.

The fourth wave is one of the changers or disruptors. New technologies are critical to repositioning the industry as more customer-centric. They also offer companies the opportunity to increase their social and economic impact and position themselves as a Force for Good.[58] More and more insurtech organizations have the mission to tackle critical global challenges: applying new sustainable solutions, with significant social and economic impact. Examples are health insurers applying all types of connected devices and advanced algorithms to improve patient health care, while decreasing total healthcare costs, which is so relevant in, for instance, regions with an aging population. The added value of the fourth wave is again totally different. The possibilities to increase the social and economic impact of the insurance industry with new technologies seem almost endless. To be clear, most of the insurtech organizations are still

[58]Taddeo, M., & Floridi, L. (2018). How AI can be a force for good. *Science, 361*(6404), 751–752.

working on realizing the promise of the second wave. The status is that the tide is on the third and even the fourth wave.

Threats of the Insurtech Organizations

In the early stages of their market entry, the innovative business model of insurtech organizations raised concerns about whether they would constitute a threat to the incumbent companies due to their digital disruptors' characteristics.[59] The difficulties that insurtech found are several. Some initiatives in insurance will fail. Their challenges are limited financial resources available, inadequate knowledge and data availability of the market, lack of an appropriate business model, and a high level of compliance and competition in the insurance sector.

The internet is an open system. The low entry barriers for new vendors and sales channels are more comfortable to overcome. There is no need for resources such as an agency on the spot and employees since digital process can replace such tasks. This leads to new creative and innovative solutions that will open up opportunities. Insurtech organizations can win thanks to the innovation in customer experiences.[60] Insurtech organizations focus mostly on specific, little-regulated businesses. They target processes where the companies have the most significant ineffectiveness and inefficiencies. These processes are the ones primarily connected with customer proximity. This situation will not last long. The number of startups will rise, and the core business of traditional companies will be under attack. Also traditional companies are expected to invest in new business models. Companies who refuse these developments are putting in doubt their existence.

Insurtech organizations also threaten the traditional reinsurance business. New models and algorithms are sold to financially robust players in hedge funds and pension funds with a more aggressive pricing policy in the reinsurance market. In this case, it is both primary and reinsurance that are working together on new business potentials.

Insurtech organizations are now experiencing a significant shift in their environment. This shift involves the nature of the environment itself

[59] Naylor, M. (2017). *Insurance transformed: Technological disruption*. Cham, Switzerland: Springer.

[60] Hartung, T., & Rohatsch, N. (2018). *Einfluss der Digitalisierung auf die Unternehmensstrategie*. Munchen, Germany: München University.

(regulation, new entrants, and boundaries), the kind of risks, and the requirements of customers. Business organizations need adapt to the new rules. These rules are now part of the financial services. One of the essential changes is in the characteristics of customers. In particular, the internet of things stands as a new approach to the business. Customers and assets (for instance, vehicles) become always-connected. They continuously exchange information between each other, and demand more digitally sophisticated insurance products and services.

Insurtech organizations may benefit from IoT in several areas[61]:

- Innovation in the value proposition with new
  - Sources of revenues;
  - Customer services.
- Improving pricing and claims
  - Better risk management;
  - Less risky behavior (e.g., vehicle driving);
  - Better fraud detection.
- Innovation in prevention solutions
  - New ways for avoiding losses (e.g., alerts);
  - Advanced monitoring (e.g., on vehicle).

Insurtech organizations should develop a specific approach to "Improve and Expand."[62] The overall proliferation of data generated by that sensors and devices could support a more effective decision-making process, streamlining procedures, and operations.

Collaboration Between Insurtech and Incumbents

Insurance companies are beginning to consider the insurtech organizations not as market disruptors but rather as possible partners, just as traditional banks and fintech organizations are doing. Banks started working together with fintech organizations to offer the best possible

[61] Lee, I., & Lee, K. (2015). The Internet of Things (IoT): Applications, investments, and challenges for enterprises. *Business Horizons, 58*(4), 431–440.

[62] ebrary.net/79680/business_finance/internet_things. Accessed 10 May 2020.

customer experience to their customers, both in the relationship stage, carried out by the incumbent companies, and in the management of the customer-centric approach, brought by the innovators.

To improve their products and customer service and limit the damage coming from the new entrants, insurance companies have started integrating with insurtech organizations. The objective is to build profitable partnerships with new operators and defend and possibly increase their market share. These initiatives demonstrate that incumbent operators are beginning to understand the insurtech sector's potential and consider the digitization of their business model as essential and positive.[63]

Insurtech organizations attract traditional companies to buy their know-how. The partnerships with insurtech organizations allow the partners to extend and improve their insurance services and bring new competencies, value, effectiveness, and efficiency. This collaboration can reach faster results, create a research and development center quickly, and build a corporate culture of innovation, which otherwise would be costly and require time. The insurtech organizations are interested in collaborating with traditional companies because the latter has more experience in the industry, a large customer base, and the availability of financing.[64]

There is a robust tendency in a mixture of partnership and acquisition by insurance companies of insurtech organizations. An example of a partnership is the Insurtech hub in Munich, Germany.[65] There, many large insurance companies such as Munich Re and Generali, through research, science, industry, and effective governance, encourage startups and promote the industry and the location. Allianz has increased its stake

[63] Munich RE. (2016, January). *Reinventing insurance for the digital generation*. www.munichre.com/topics-online/en/html. Accessed 30 March 2020.

[64] Kumaresan, A., Saurav, S., & Raghunanda, K. (2017). *Top 10 trends in property & casualty insurance 2018*. www.capgemini.com/wpcontent/uploads/2017/12/property-and-casuality-insurance-trends_2018.pdf. Accessed 14 March 2020.

[65] Kanbach, D. K., & Stubner, S. (2016). Corporate accelerators as recent form of startup engagement: The what, the why, and the how. *Journal of Applied Business Research (JABR), 32*(6), 1761–1776.

in insurtech Simplesurance which offers to match online purchases insurance.[66] Ergo tried since 2017 with the online automotive vendors to start Nexible for all-in-one car insurance.[67]

From 2016 to 2018, the insurtech ecosystem attracted investments totaling USD 11.2 billion; more than double the USD 5.5 billion raised between 2010 and 2015.[68] The majority of investment in insurtech organizations is in more mature firms. There are regional differences, with the Western world executives express a preference for investing at an early stage, while in Latin America, the favorite is investing in a more advanced phase.

There are several forms of collaboration established between traditional insurance companies and startups that are sometimes present in a similar business model:

- Investments in venture capital funds. This type is the most common of partnership between incumbent companies and startups. It has the objective to buy insurtech shares, to acquire control over this sector, and to take advantage of the technological innovation developed;
- Entering into a strategic partnership with insurtech organizations. It aims at outsourcing or improving some stages of the value network;
- Configuring accelerators and business incubators to create and develop new technologies, promote innovative ideas and business models.

The insurance sector still needs to have a consistent approach to the insurtech disruption. It is the time for executives to think forward, inserting innovation at the heart of their strategies,[69] They need to decide

[66] www.allianz.com/en/press/news/financials/stakes_investments/160620-allianz-cooperates-with-simplesurance.html. Accessed 10 May 2020.

[67] coverager.com/munich-re-set-to-launch-all-in-one-car-insurance-in-germany/. Accessed 10 May 2020.

[68] www.nttdata.com/global/en/media/press-release/2019/september/ntt-data-and-everis-publish-insurtech-outlook-2019-. Accessed 25 April 2020.

[69] Cappiello, A. (2020). The digital (r)evolution of insurance business models. *American Journal of Economics and Business Administration, 12*(1), 1–13.

how, and not if or when, to participate in the insurtech ecosystem. To embrace insurtech initiatives, incumbents should take concrete steps[70]:

- Exploration. Traditional insurance companies should actively monitor new trends and innovations;
- Strategic partnerships. Incumbents should collaborate with startups and build pilot solutions to test in the market;
- Insurtech involvement. Traditional insurance companies' participation in startup programs such as incubators, accelerators, mechanisms to fund companies, and strategic acquisitions may result in companies' readiness to address specific problems, mainly those that otherwise not to be important in the short term;
- New product development. Involvement in insurtech initiatives can help traditional insurance companies to discover emerging coverage requirements and threats that require new or modified insurance products and services;

The insurance industry needs to work to develop proof-of-concept initiatives around innovative solutions to offer more customer insights. This way is the more effective insurance marketing and operations to start, for example, to engage millennials.

The expectation is that investments in the next few years in insurtech organizations to significantly outweigh investments in banking and capital markets, much of which has been compliance-driven.[71] Insurtech acquisitions by incumbent insurance companies have also taken place. In 2016, Allstate acquired SquareTrade, a startup offering policies covering customer electronics. Through these acquisitions now, Allstate plays an essential role in this sector. Investment strategies will move toward mergers and acquisitions in the short term, to pre-empt competitors and acquire better control over the technological innovation needed.[72]

[70] PwC. (2016, June). *Opportunities await: Global Fintech Survey*. www.PwC.com/gx/en/financial-services/assets/fintech-insurance-report.pdf. Accessed 15 July 2016.

[71] www.insurancenetworking.com/news/innovation/insurtech-companies-are-the-new-fintech-leaders-37470-1.html. Accessed 23 August 2016.

[72] Deloitte. (2018). *A catalyst for change: How Fintech has sparked a revolution in insurance*. www2.deloitte.com/content/dam/Deloitte/global/Documents/Financial-Services/gx-fsi-cataylst-for-change.pdf. Accessed 22 June 2020.

Insurance companies use different criteria to select the insurtech model in line with their strategic objectives[73]:

- Short- and medium-term evaluations are carried out by analyzing the value-added impact on customers, consequences on business lines, simplicity of integration, opportunity costs deriving from the failure to collaborate, and modular nature of offers;
- Long-term evaluation, on the other hand, adds the analysis of market potential, the ability to generate profit over time, to meet regulations, and to integrate into an ecosystem.

In a McKinsey research, there is apparent complementarity between incumbents and startups, inasmuch that less than 10 percent of insurtech organizations are now a disrupter of the traditional insurance model.[74] The real difficulty is finding the right combination of collaboration between these two types of businesses.

Future business models will likely have the characteristics of close partnerships, in which incumbents will focus their activity on customer proximity. At the same time, insurtech organizations, as innovators and carriers of new technologies and applications, will act on the value network. The result of this collaboration is a reorganization of the traditional insurance value network. The insurtech startup sector is demonstrating the same dynamic in the insurance sector as that which has affected the entire financial service industry.[75]

Most insurtech organizations' investments are in innovation for the non-life compartment, mainly in the health and motor segments. Diversification by area is growing. Stakes were primarily in marketing and distribution. That is still predominant. Now, investments aim to solutions in analytics, artificial intelligence, and underwriting on-demand. These are the specific activities of selection and risk assessment of policies sold

www2.deloitte.com/content/dam/Deloitte/global/Documents/Financial-Services.pdf. Accessed 20 March 2020.

[73] Capgemini & Efma. (2019). *World insurance report 2019*. www.efma.com/study/detail/30818. Accessed 20 March 2020.

[74] www.mckinsey.com/industries/financial-services/our-insights/insurtech-the-threat-that-inspires. Accessed 10 April 2020.

[75] Swiss Re Institute. (2017, June). *Technology and insurance: Themes and challenges*.

to policyholders. The trend is to intervene in all phases of the insurance value network and even different insurance sectors than the non-life compartment.[76]

The main differences between incumbent companies from the insurtech organizations are mainly attributable to the approach to the market, type of interaction between the policyholder and the insurance company, and characteristics of the service provided.[77] The marketing approach adopted by insurance companies is often product-oriented since they focus on offering a better product/pricing than their competitors. An indirect connection is between the seller and the customer. The service provision focuses mainly on product development and on its distribution.

The marketing objectives of insurtech organizations are process-oriented. The emphasis is on offering the best experience in the customer journey. The relationship with the customer is direct.[78] The automation of processes allows for higher connectivity: Distribution can also occur through chatbots and robo-advisors to optimize time, location, and customer needs and specially to reduce costs (and hence prices of the services). The development of alliances with insurtech organizations allows the incumbents to profit from the expertise, dynamics, and ways of doing business, which, by its very nature, the insurance industry has not developed. Big data analytics, artificial intelligence, and blockchain solutions are the most attractive developing areas in the medium term for the insurance sector.[79]

The service providers focus mainly on promoting the distribution of information about the product to the right prospects at the right time and place. Insurtech organizations adopt decision-making processes driven by data analysis to support innovative and customized products and services based on improved customer experience.

[76] Cappiello, A. (2020). *The European insurance industry: Regulation, risk management, and internal control*. New York, NY: Springer Nature.

[77] Svetlana, V. (2016). InsurTech: challenges and development perspectives. *International Journal of Innovative Technologies in Economy*, 3(5).

[78] Cappiello, A. (2020). The digital (r)evolution of insurance business models. *American Journal of Economics and Business Administration, 12*(1), 1–13.

[79] Braun, A., & Schreiber, F. (2017). The current InsurTech landscape: Business models and disruptive potential. *Institute of Insurance Economics*. St. Gallen, Switzerland: University of St. Gallen.

All stages of the customer's journey and the value network may be affected by the insurtech organizations. The macro trend of innovation is leading to a much more dynamic state in the sector. The value proposition can become the integration of a set of multiple modules belonging to different players in an insurance ecosystem. The boundaries are increasingly disappearing between the traditional roles of a distributor, partners (in some cases from another sector), companies, and reinsurers. The challenges in this collaboration are to the balance of power and in the share of the profit of the various participants.

Some surveys report that customers do not seem ready to leave traditional insurance providers. They consider them more reliable in security and protection against fraud. The customers attribute excellent value to brand reputation and personal interaction.[80] Radical disintermediation of insurance companies would imply profound innovation of the incumbent business models. This change is unlikely in the short-to-medium term (Fig. 15.6).[81]

Once, based on these components, the insurance company has opted for single or multiple partners, different scenarios are possible:

- The insurtech company has a leading position;
- The incumbent has a leading position;
- Creation of a joint venture.

This differentiation aims to explain the strategical rationale behind every choice.[82] There are several reasons why financial institutions and companies establish business relationships in each of the three scenarios.

Cooperation between financial institutions and insurtech organizations is a necessary step capable of bringing about significant benefits to both organizations:

[80] Capgemini & Efma. (2019). *World insurance report 2019*. www.efma.com/study/detail/30818. Accessed 30 May 2020.

[81] Braun, A., & Schreiber, F. (2017). The current InsurTech landscape: Business models and disruptive potential. *Institute of Insurance Economics*. St. Gallen, Switzerland: University of St. Gallen.

[82] Oliynyk, H., & Sabirova, A. (2013). Insurance company and bank partnership as a distribution channel of insurance products. *Economics & Economy, 1*(2), 131–141.

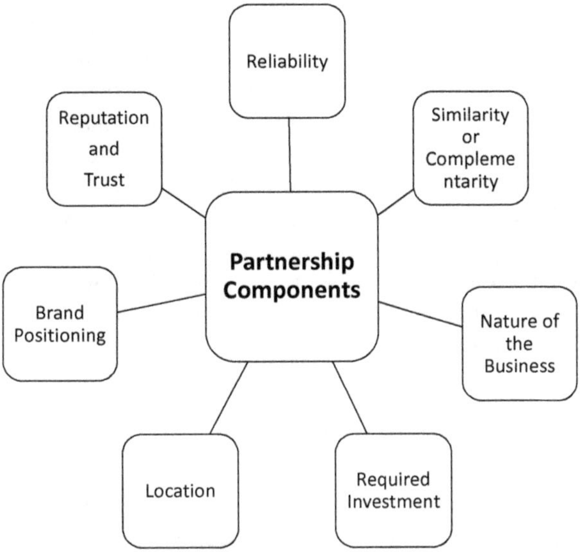

Fig. 15.6 Partnership components

- Economies of scale and costs reduction;
- Market share growth;
- Diversification;
- Synergies;
- Elimination of competitors in the same market.

Each one can cooperate or compete according to the context and the moment, becoming a so-called coopetitor.[83]

As far as collaboration is concerned, the consultancy company Ernst and Young suggests helping distribution partners to develop digital capability by sharing resources and expertise.[84]

[83] Bouncken, R. B., Gast, J., Kraus, S., & Bogers, M. (2015). Coopetition: A systematic review, synthesis, and future research directions. *Review of Managerial Science, 9*(3), 577–601.

[84] EY Report. (2013). *Insurance in a digital world: Time is now*. www.ey.com/Publication/vwLUAssets/EY_Insurance_in_a_digital_world:_The_time_is_now/$FILE/EY-Digital-Survey-1-October.pdf. Accessed 20 August 2016.

Insurtech initiatives should privilege customer-centricity in all aspects. All the contacts with customers should be better managed, integrated, and consistent. Agents and other intermediaries should then be provided with all the necessary analytics, tools, and services for making the customer experience unique and, consequently, to improve sales. All these actions should instill in the organization what McKinsey (2016) names "customer empathy."[85] This situation means that real empathy allows insurtech organizations to respond to actual underlying needs, not superficial, stated interests. By doing this, it spurs breakthrough innovation. This way is the only one an incumbent insurer can be sure of delivering more than a "me-too" customer experience.

Social Media

This section's suggestion is to establish different profiles in all leading social media sites, monitor them regularly, and promptly respond to any brand-damaging act from unsatisfied customers. It might be useful to consider guerrilla actions, mostly in the first phases of the company's life cycle.[86] Companies may consider posting articles to spread out the brand image they want to instill to customers. The benefits of social media might be several (Fig. 15.7).

Marketing campaigns through social media, if well planned and implemented, may be highly effective, mainly when unsatisfied or simply unreached customers do not know much about innovative and potentially disrupting products and services. It is critical to note that social media most used by customers, primarily millennials, change over time.[87]

[85] www.mckinsey.it/idee/transforming-life-insurance-with-design-thinking. Accessed 10 April 2020.

[86] Hutter, K., & Hoffmann, S. (2011). Guerrilla marketing: The nature of the concept and propositions for further research. *Asian Journal of Marketing, 5*(2), 39–54.

[87] It is necessary to take into account that social media most used by customers, mainly Millennials, change over time.

Fig. 15.7 Social media benefits

Amodo[88]

Telecom operators are offering their customers an increasing range of connectivity and IoT-related products and services, such as "connected home" and other solutions. Working with companies, they can branch out into insurance services as well. For companies, it becomes essentially a distribution channel.[89]

Amodo is a Croatian startup, active also in the USA and other countries. With Amodo's Connected Customer Platform, companies can adequately address the needs and lifestyle of the new connected generation. Amodo collects data from smartphones and several different connected customer devices to build holistic customer profiles, providing better insights into customer risk exposure and customer product needs.

[88]www.amodo.eu/. Accessed 30 May 2020.

[89]www.amodo.eu/. Accessed 30 May 2020.

Following the analysis, risk prevention programs, individual pricing, and personalized and "on the spot," insurance products can be offered to customers, increasing their loyalty and lifetime value. With these solution used throughout the entire process, companies have the means to engage their customers proactively. Customers enjoy a continuous positive experience with the company.

Regtech Organizations[90]

The term regtech (short for Regulatory Technology) refers to the technological solutions to support the processes of management and monitoring of regulatory compliance. This term also refers to the group of companies that develop these solutions. These are often startups characterized by lean operating models and the adoption of innovative technologies (e.g., cloud computing, big data, machine learning, and so on). Regtech organizations are part of a wider fintech world.[91] It has gradually gained an independent space in the market.

Regtech organizations emerged years ago. The British Financial Conduct Authority, for example, started to study this area back in 2015.[92] In that year, it launched the first operational programs on the subject. In other countries, the large consultancy companies have offered services in the sector for several years. What is surprising, however, is the speed with which the market has grown over the past years.

The sector most involved in the growth of regtech organizations is the banking sector. The insurtech sector is interested. In 2019, the Italian Banking Association started building the first website dedicated to this issue, to analyze the available technological solutions and related trends. Until now, however, the phenomenon has mostly affected large financial

[90] Nicoletti, L. (2020). *Regtech: la nuova frontiera della Compliance*. www.dedaload.it/2020/04/22/regtech-la-nuova-frontiera-della-compliance/. Accessed 10 May 2020.

[91] Nicoletti, B. (2017). *The future of fintech*. London, UK: Springer International Publishing. ISBN 978-3-319-51414-7.

[92] www.fca.org.uk/publication/call-for-input/regtech-call-for-input.pdf. Accessed 10 May 2020.

institutions or banking groups. Now, regtech organizations start to aim also to the insurance sector.[93]

Four main factors motivate the adoption (and costs) of these new technological solutions, and small or so-called minor institutions, which are estimated to support 26 percent of financial institutions in Italy.

1—The growing complexity of the legislation. Since the 2008 crisis, the regulatory requirements and controls for the financial sector have increased dramatically—both in volume (up to 1503 standards in one year) and in complexity. The MiFID II regulation, for example, is divided into 1400 measures, distributed over 7000 pages. Similar situation for Solvency II. Furthermore, regulations introduced stringent requirements regarding the content and frequency of mandatory reporting. The adoption of new technologies and new trends in a market in full transformation have contributed to this expansion (e.g. the legislation on outsourcing of cloud services). Small institutions are impacted proportionately more by new regulatory requirements. The effects of this growing regulatory complexity still have significant consequences on the operations of these actors since often they lack the possibility of investments and the availability of the necessary resources and competencies.

2—Costs related to compliance. Compliance costs are of two types. On the one hand, there are the costs associated with the monitoring and compliance adjustment activity, which is estimated to be around 10–15 percent of operating expenditure in the financial services. These costs are growing. In 2018, 89 percent of the compliance officers in the financial services forecasted an increase.[94] On the other hand, there are the growing costs due to sanctions, which have grown at the same time as the volume and complexity of the legislation. The new sanctioning regimes introduced for the banking sector, for example, extend the administrative sanctions' recipients, diversify the type of applicable penalties, and tighten the financial ones. This phenomenon is also evident in other regulatory areas, such as that of privacy (e.g. the sanctioning regime introduced with the GDPR and the CCPA).

3—Compliance as an enabling vehicle for business. The adoption and continuous updating of organization and control models in compliance

[93] Mulder, B. J. M. (2019). RegTech: Tackling regulation with innovation. *The RegTech Book*.

[94] www.finextra.com/blogposting/17167/4-trends-to-watch-in-regulatory-ai. Accessed 30 May 2020.

with the main corporate regulations (such as the Italian Legislative Decree 231 of 2001, Legislative Decree 262 of 2005, the European Data Protection Regulation, the adoption of a Legality Rating, and so on) no longer appear to be only a cost for the companies that invest in this area. It represents a capable vehicle for enabling business, allowing companies access to public tenders, on stock exchange listing operations, on the granting of public financing by public administrations, on facilitating access in the capital market, and on improving reputation towards all stakeholders. In this context, the technologies adopted for the implementation of the regtech model play a decisive role.

4—The diffusion of new technologies. The diffusion of new technologies has enabled the development of cheaper solutions. Technologies such as artificial intelligence and machine learning solutions are implemented in a synergistic and coordinated way. Today, these solutions allow automating activities that traditionally required significant use of resources and time, such as monitoring the legislation (analyze thousands of regulatory sources), risk analysis, up to the production of dedicated reports, and dashboards.

Large volumes of data from different sources can be harmonized and used more effectively and efficiently. The analyzes made possible by this harmonization offer more solid foundations for corporate decision making.

To date, in some countries, regtech still represents a challenge. This technology would require significant changes to the approach to compliance, as well as new challenges to technological capabilities. Furthermore, the real benefits of regtech solutions could disappear due to the high implementation and management costs. These considerations are particularly relevant for small- and medium-sized enterprises.

There is now the availability of automated, flexible, dynamic, and modular solutions according to financial institutions' needs. An example is CR.AA.M. (Compliance Risk and Audit Activity Management). This solution allows the management and monitoring of the compliance checks applicable to a company, automating the trend over time of the risk status.[95] The strength of this web-based application, however, is the reporting: CR.AA.M allows operators to configure and generate summary and analytical reports of a graphic, tabular, and descriptive type together

[95] www.ict-ss.net/?q=node/18. Accessed 10 May 2020.

with historical trend graphs on the state of compliance. Reports can be set according to specific organization requirements and generated in a short time.

Digital Wholesale Insurance

Wholesale financial services are mostly operators who provide coverage for risks outside of the risks covered by traditional companies or which provide specialized capabilities. The digital transformation is spreading around the world. Wholesale insurance is no exception. It is slowly moving toward insurance 4.0. Studies aim to create and describe a business model for digital insurance.[96] The spread of digital insurance follows the path of the so-called information and communication technologies (ICT) customerization.[97] In the past, businesses were the first to use ICT innovations. Nowadays, more and more customers get priority in introducing ICT innovation. This sequence took place with physical products, like smartphones and tablets. Initially, the target was the customer market. Later they expanded also in the businesses. Something similar is happening in financial services, like in banking, where mobile banking was initially introduced mainly in retail banking. Later were introduced solutions also for corporate and small- and medium-sized companies banking. It is now time to rethink this approach and understand how to use insurtech initiatives even for wholesale insurance services. Some insurtech organizations are moving in this direction. More and more will come.

To analyze how digital insurance could support this sector, it might be interesting to refer to a sentence of Rudyard Kipling in his book: *The Little Elephant*.[98] Kipling considered complete the description of a problem if it is possible to respond to six questions starting with an interrogative character: 5 W's and 1 H. In the case of digital wholesale insurance, this would mean to answer these questions:

[96] *Digital wholesale insurance—The future of FinTech*. ebrary.net/79683/business_finance/digital_wholesale_insurance. Accessed 20 May 2020.

[97] Nicoletti B. (2017). *The future of FinTech*. Cham, Switzerland: Springer.

[98] Kipling, R. (2013). *Just so stories*. Scotts Valley, CA: CreateSpace Independent Publishing Platform.

- Why: The reason to go digital could be defensive for wholesale companies. Insurtech organizations might be able to invade their markets and introduce disruptive innovations. To go digital could also help establish wholesale insurance players to become more active, productive, efficient, and economical;
- Where: Thanks to cloud computing, commercial insurance can expand the reach of concentrated markets quickly, undoubtedly fueling competition but also increasing the size of markets;
- What: Big data analytics can help to improve the analysis of the risks. It is also useful for capital markets, security, customer insight, channel marketing, and providing new data sets for risk-based pricing and assets monitoring and tracking;
- Who: Artificial intelligence and robotics can help in selecting the best alternatives. It is not easy to think about how social media, now spreading in financial services, could help with wholesale insurance. On the other hand, comparators websites could also help also business customers to pick up worldwide their most convenient insurer. The marketplace approach could also help in the wholesale insurance market to find the best solution for the requirements of a specific business customer;
- When: Mobile technologies can help reduce the time to decide and specially to make decisions when the customer wants;
- How: Another opportunity connected with new technologies is blockchain. It could change thoroughly also the wholesale insurance environment. Blockchain is a technology introduced with the virtual currency of bitcoin. It is an exciting technology in itself. Its base is an online, distributed ledger technology. Blockchain could help in setting up smart contracts with a distributed ledger solution. It could help in managing customer identities, reference data, and assets, increasing visibility securely. It can ensure a seamless, reliable, and uninterrupted messaging service to the insurance market, a cost-effective method of facilitating the availability and exchange of data between insurance business partners, and a trusted utility service that expands insurance market competitiveness. Price Waterhouse Coopers is working on a Long Finance research project into the potential of blockchain solution in wholesale insurance.[99]

[99] www.finextra.com/pressarticle/64838/PwC-preps-research-into-blockchain-tech-for-wholesale-procurement. Accessed 20 August 2016.

In this new insurtech ecosystem, there is a need for new business models. They could foster, for example, much closer collaboration and partnership between wholesale companies and brokers. The latter could substantially benefit from digital solutions. Brokers cannot invest in them, due to their small size or lack of the necessary technological expertise.

Sustainable Insurance

Sustainable insurance is a strategic approach where all activities in the insurance value network, including interactions with stakeholders, are done in a responsible and forward-looking way.[100] It is necessary to identify, assess, manage, and monitor risks and opportunities associated with environmental, social, and governance issues.[101]

Sustainable insurance aims to reduce risks, develop innovative solutions, improve business performance, and contribute to environmental, social, and economic sustainability; the so-called 3 Ps.[102]

- Planet—The environment and earth.
- Persons—Everyone inhabiting the earth, from domestic and offshore workers to families and children.
- Profit—The financial and overall long-term viability of the organization.

The insurance industry's core business is to follow, manage, and take care of the risks.[103] Through risk prevention, risk mitigation, and by sharing risks over many operators, the insurance industry helps protect society, fosters innovation, and supports economic development. These are critical contributions to a well-functioning and sustainable social insurance business.

Today, the world is facing increasing environmental, social, and governance (ESG) challenges. This changing risk environment is bringing to

[100] *PSI principles for sustainable insurance*. www.unepfi.org/fileadmin/documents/PSI_document-en.pdf. Accessed 10 May 2020.

[101] The Principles «UNEP FI Principles for Sustainable Insurance. www.unepfi.org/psi/the-principles/. Accessed 10 May 2020.

[102] www.e-education.psu.edu/ba850/node/643. Accessed 15 March 2020.

[103] *The insurance industry's core business is to understand*. www.coursehero.com/file/p3isrcee/. Accessed 10 May 2020.

diverse, interconnected, and complex risks. It presents new risks but also opportunities, which insurance 4.0 needs to take into account. The insurance industry needs to cope with the risk factors considered in managing its business. ESG issues are increasingly influencing new and traditional risk factors. They can have a significant impact on the industry's viability. A resilient insurance industry depends on integrated and far-sighted risk management with the consideration of ESG issues.[104]

Better management of ESG issues will support the insurance contribution to building a resilient, inclusive, and sustainable society. Many ESG issues are too big and complex. They need widespread action across society, innovation, and long-term solutions. It is necessary to build on the foundation the insurance industry has laid in supporting a sustainable community. The vision is a society in which persons are aligned and incentivized to adopt sustainable practices. For the implementation of this objective, it is necessary to use all intellectual, operational, and investment capacities to realize the principles for sustainable insurance (PSI) across spheres of influence, subject to applicable laws, rules, regulations, and duties owed to shareholders and policyholder. The principles were launched during Rio+20—This composition of the coalition is of most publicly traded companies, insurance industry associations, and United Nations' officials.[105] There are just four principles. A sustainable insurer should[106]:

- Embed in its decision making relevant Environmental, social, and governance (ESG) issues;
- Work with customers and business partners to raise awareness of ESG issues, manage risk, and develop solutions for risks;
- Work together with governments, regulators, and other critical stakeholders to promote wide-act across society on ESG issues; and

[104] Nogueira, F. O., Lucena, A. F. P., & Nogueira, R. (2017). Sustainable insurance assessment: Towards an integrative model. *The Geneva Papers on Risk and Insurance—Issues and Practice, 43*(2), 275–299. https://doi.org/10.1057/s41288-017-0062-3.

[105] Scordis, N. A., Suzawa, Y., Zwick, A., & Ruckner, L. (2014). Principles for sustainable insurance: Risk management and value. *Risk Management and Insurance Review, 17*(2), 265–276.

[106] www.unepfi.org/fileadmin/documents/PSI_document-en.pdf. Accessed 14 March 2020.

- Demonstrate accountability and transparency in regularly and publicly disclosure of the progress in the implementation of each of the preceding principles.

The PSI promote a strategic management of risk.[107] They encourage companies to identify future risks from environmental, social, and government sources. They use this new data to inform their processes. They also promote the development of products useful to manage uncertainty and finance macroeconomic risks. The PSI expand the practice of risk management as they encourage thinking in uncertainty and for the long term rather than in risks and for the short time.

Insurance has been increasingly aligned with sustainability goals. Organizations can gradually move toward the insurance 4.0 model to enhance resource conservation in support of circular economy efforts.[108] A study demonstrated that organizations with a robust insurance strategy and valid insurance 4.0 review processes are most able to optimize their insurance processes and attain improved circular economy performance.[109] The information processing capability, drawing on insurance 4.0 technologies, moderates the relationship between the insurance 4.0 performance review, and the intention to optimize. Organizations with an insurance 4.0 model are abler to leverage the performance review process and maximize their insurance processes. Insurance 4.0 applications can speed up insurance transactions by developing information processing capabilities to support organizational processing of information and data, aiding a more effective, efficient, ethical, and economic organization.

[107] Scordis, N. A., Suzawa, Y., Zwick, A., & Ruckner, L. (2014). Principles for sustainable insurance: Risk management and value. *Risk Management and Insurance Review, 17*(2), 265–276.

[108] Geissdoerfer, M., Savaget, P., Bocken, N. M., & Hultink, E. J. (2017). The circular economy—A new sustainability paradigm? *Journal of Cleaner Production, 143,* 757–768.

[109] Bag, S., Wood, L. C., Mangla, S. K., & Luthra, S. (2020). Insurance 4.0 and its implications on business process performance in a circular economy. *Resources, Conservation and Recycling, 152,* 104502.

An organization should focus on four areas to reach the targets of PSI[110]:

- Defining and implementing insurance 4.0 strategies for the development of their needed capabilities. Organizations need to strengthen collaborative relationships, share technical know-how with partners, adopt advanced processes and platforms, and improve transparency/traceability over value networks;
- Increasing insurance 4.0 awareness among employees and value network partners is necessary to improve their understanding of insurance 4.0 benefits and its importance in the circular economy;
- Reviewing insurance 4.0 is critical to assess the progress of its deployment and change insurance 4.0 strategies accordingly;
- Measuring performance also in the fields of sustainability, such as resource outputs, energy outputs, consumption of energy and water, solid waste recycling rate, waste water reuse rate in every stage of business process activity, can provide a real picture to the management.

Tokio Marine Group[111]
Tokio Marine Group is a Japanese insurance with subsidiaries around the world. It has planted over 18,000 acres of mangrove trees in Asian coastlines and the Fiji Islands. Mangrove trees absorb carbon dioxide, improve the health of coastal fisheries, and buffer coastal communities (where many policyholders live and file claims) from robust winds, high waves, and erosion.

[110] Bag, S., Wood, L. C., Mangla, S. K., & Luthra, S. (2020). Insurance 4.0 and its implications on business process performance in a circular economy. *Resources, Conservation and Recycling, 152,* 104502.

[111] www.tokiomarinehd.com/en/sustainability/theme2/productservice02.html. Accessed 16 March 2020.

Munich RE[112]
Munich RE for an upfront premium provides fast payments to the owners of solar panels from an insurer-certified manufacturer that does not perform within a margin of their stated capacity for 25 years from installation. Reducing uncertainty associated with the long-term success of a new technology encourages the adoption of the technology.

Conclusions

The future is uncertain. Still, there are some possible scenarios for the role of insurance and on the actions to take to improve the future standing of companies. Organizations will move more and more from a linear value chain to a value network, called an ecosystem. In other words, the role of insurance will be to build and coordinate an ecosystem composed of different actors with the partners' collaboration. It will not be an easy task, but it is an essential one.

The world, and the insurance, will continue to change. Because of the forecasts and the variability of the environment, the organization needs to plan carefully. It is, however, interesting to consider that "plans are made to change them." The secret for the organization's success in better insurance will be its agility and flexibility to adapt to change.

The role of insurance will grow, more and more out of the risk management activity into creation of alliances with partners and the customers. The latter will want to customize the products/services they buy. A key competence of partners will be in cognitive solutions.[113] They should create the environment and mobilize customers to generate value for themselves. Creating the settings will be possible due to self-service platform solutions, systems enabling the creation and development of artificial intelligence solutions and educational systems.

Due to the specificity of industry solutions and the need to adapt services to the specifics of the customers' activities, the partners will have

[112] Bleich, R. (2018). Corporate responsibility in business at Munich Re, Munich RE document, Frankfurt, Germany.

[113] Wodecki, A. (2018). *Artificial intelligence in value creation: Improving competitive advantage*. Cham, Switzerland: Springer.

to work out effective, efficient, ethical, and economical methods and tools for creating customized versions of their services.[114] The support will come from the ability to group customers into categories and identify the optimal services for a given customer category.[115]

According to the MECSPE Italian Observatory, related to the second half of 2018, eight organizations out of 10 believe that their digital transformation occurred in recent years and almost all (9 out of 10) believe they have a medium-high level of knowledge on the technology and digital opportunities on the market.[116] The future focus is in new enabling technologies, continuing in the direction toward ICT security (74 percent), connectivity (60 percent), cloud computing (33 percent), and collaborative robotics (28 percent), and at research and innovation: 61 percent will invest up to 10 percent of their turnover. Twenty-five percent will dedicate between 10 percent and 20 percent thereof. Targeted advice (51 percent), knowledge transfer (42 percent), confrontation with competing organizations (39 percent), workshops (21 percent), and the tutorship from a university (15 percent) are considered useful tools for this development process.

Insurtech organizations will not be the great disrupters of traditional insurance. The empirical evidence and academic studies tend toward relationships of synergy rather than competition between the two parties.[117] Several insurance companies are looking for new business and partnership models with insurtech organizations to innovate every phase of their value network.[118] The leading insurance companies have established solid partnerships with the top insurtech organizations. They have set up venture capital funds for their acquisition and to benefit from the solutions they are developing. They have increased innovation efforts and have

[114] Wodecki, A. (2018). *Artificial intelligence in value creation: Improving competitive advantage*. Cham, Switzerland: Springer.

[115] Wodecki, A. (2018). *Artificial intelligence in value creation: Improving competitive advantage*. Cham, Switzerland: Springer.

[116] www.mecspe.com/en/comunicati-stampa-en/osservatorio-mecspe-focus-nazionale/. Accessed 6 August 2019.

[117] Cappiello, A. (2020). The digital (r)evolution of insurance business models. *American Journal of Economics and Business Administration, 12*(1), 1–13.

[118] Cappiello, A. (2020). The digital (r)evolution of insurance business models. *American Journal of Economics and Business Administration, 12*(1), 1–13.

even created good contests, named hackathons, to obtain new collaborations.[119] Companies are now called upon to design digital infrastructure that improves customer engagement through distribution channels. The vision is to address them through a combination of internally driven innovation, joint ventures, and merger and acquisition activities.

It is critical to follow the development of bigtech and insurtech organizations.[120] The development of fintech organizations and the rate of creation of relevant innovative products and services depend upon the formation and efficient functioning of the appropriate ecosystem. The ecosystem should include a set of interrelated factors such as access to funding, regulation, technology, demand, and human capital, which are developing in parallel.[121] It seems rather unlikely that insurtech organizations will cause a significant change or disruption to the insurance industry (today and in the future). The reason is that the business model of insurtech organizations can be easily copied. Companies could easily acquire small insurtech organizations. Insurtech organizations are focused more on cooperation than rivalry with traditional companies. Regulations and lack of expertise serve as entry barriers when insurtech organizations want to expand their businesses.[122]

To end with another quote, this time attributed to Charles Darwin: "It is not the strongest of the species that survives, nor the intelligent, but the most open to change."[123] This message is also true for insurance companies.

[119] vc4a.com/the-hatch/insurtech-hackathon/. Accessed 10 May 2020.

[120] Eling, M., & Lehmann, M. (2018). The impact of digitalization on the insurance value chain and the insurability of risks. *The Geneva Papers on Risk and Insurance—Issues and Practice, 43*(3), 359–396.

[121] Nicoletti, B. (2017). *The future of FinTech: Integrating finance and technology in financial services*. London, UK: Palgrave Macmillan.

[122] Cappiello, A. (2020). The digital (r)evolution of insurance business models. *American Journal of Economics and Business Administration, 12*(1), 1–13.

[123] Girotto, V., Pievani, T., & Vallortigara, G. (2014). Supernatural beliefs: Adaptations for social life or by-products of cognitive adaptations? *Behaviour, 151*(2–3), 385–402.

CHAPTER 16

Conclusions

Organizations are increasingly aware of the importance of implementing innovative solutions. They are struggling to understand the scope of digital transformation. This situation is not limited to some organizations or certain business functions. It embraces almost every organization in its entirety.

The main driver that pushes organizations to evolve digitally is to provide a better customer experience. Customer expectations change faster than the solutions offered by the organizations. They are formed on the best experience of proven use, regardless of the industry. Even for what concerns communication, organizations must chase the new characteristics of digital customers. The interaction with the organization is increasingly in the hands of the customer. The image that he or she has of a product/service is formed more through casual chats on social networks rather than in channels controlled directly by marketing managers.

This landscape means that organizations must adapt to the changing times, reviewing their internal processes, and rethinking about their business models. They must adapt to the digital age and look for new solutions that are increasingly attractive to the market to reach a competitive advantage.

Decentralization of decision making and the implementation of a flat and agile structure facilitate team aggregation. It is a trend common to all sectors among innovating companies. Of course, they are applied differently in each industry and business.

B. Nicoletti, *Insurance 4.0*, Palgrave Studies in Financial Services Technology, https://doi.org/10.1007/978-3-030-58426-9_16

The innovation must be integrated among the functions and follow a strategy promoted by the top management covering the entire organization. Organizations in an initial stage of change tend to apply the new solutions according to the logic of improving current processes, often trying only to reduce costs. Organizations in an advanced innovation stage entirely rethink their business models around the digital opportunities and place their relationship with the customer at the center of their efforts, rather than doing only cost-cutting. Insurance 4.0 approach is an essential step for the innovation of insurance companies. To remain competitive in today's digital age, where the number of new competitors grows continuously, insurance organizations must act, and quickly. Agile and individual policies are a real added value for the customers. To offer this type of service, companies must know their customers better to propose customized policies, satisfying specific needs and gaining long-term confidence with their customers. Fast and efficient big data analysis can help insurance organizations to use the vast business potential of innovation in the best possible way. Many insurance organizations still adopt a traditional business model. They need to expand it by including an insurance 4.0 strategy.

One of this book's main topics is how to add value to the customer and how to distribute these improved services. Particular attention is devoted to the new type of distribution all-digital, born from the needs of customers and digital evolution. In the case of the distribution through agencies, the current situation is that there are long or multiple-stage distribution channels. The actors who stand between the organization and the customers are several, including commercial inspectors, insurance organizations, agents, subagents, brokers, and other financial institutions. For the organization, it is structurally difficult to place on the market effectively, efficiently, economically, and timeliness through the agential channel products, marketing initiatives, and business activities. The number of the actors, represented by legal entities, is a brake on the actual integration of the entire distribution chain.

The impressive sales rates of smartphones and tablets around the world give evidence of how already today, and more shortly, both customers and insurance organization partners must have fully embraced the logic of online and mobility. To take full advantage of innovation opportunities offered by mobility, organizations must define a clear picture of how they want it to be in the customer proximity. Based on this perspective, companies can design an operational distribution model and consequently develop marketing, sales, and after-sales consistently by deciding to invest resources in new solutions. In this field, the highest returns are economic satisfaction and customer and intermediary loyalty. Developing a tailored strategy allows making it online and mobile coherently with the structure and characteristics of the organization.

The future will revolutionize the management of insurance. Insurance 4.0 is an essential business model to make the future, described in the previous chapters, real. This book presents a business model that highlights the main components and solutions for effective, efficient, ethical, and economical insurance 4.0.

The results, included in this book, demonstrate that insurance 4.0 can bring many benefits, including supporting the organization's activities and daily administrative tasks to perform complex decision making, acquiring more focused strategic decisions and actions. There are barriers to the digitization of the insurance processes. These obstacles are in legacy procedures and systems, fragmented processes, current capacity, and mainly the availability of talents. This book discusses several enabling technologies for supporting transformation to insurance 4.0 and methods to overcome the challenges.

Cultural change is critical to the success of insurance 4.0.[1] Digital education at all levels is crucial. The transformation will be completed successfully by implementing the lean and digitize approaches that can speed progress and make the organizations agile. At the same time, companies need to focus on customers and cross-functional teams that pool specific types of expertise. Traditional companies should start looking for ways to attract brilliant and new talents to set up a proper team, considering that the competition for digital bright persons is high. Insurtech organizations are more attractive for talents for their characteristics.

Since innovation requires large amounts of money (e.g., Axa invested €950 million over just two years), investments have to be secured.[2]

Insurance 4.0 comes hand in hand with a customer-centric approach to implement across all the value network. To gain new support, incumbents should promote projects that deliver quick rewards at manageable risk.

[1] Thesis final. www.slideshare.net/AngelicaGreco/thesis-final-87203889.

[2] www.mckinsey.com/industries/financial-services/our-insights/the-age-of-innovation. Accessed 14 March 2020.

For example, in the customer service activities and the redesign of claim processes, it is crucial to building proper capabilities to modernize core operating platforms.

Long-term success will be dictated by the power, competencies, and know-how not of the company but of the ecosystem that companies need to build around them. Ecosystems will create the competitive benefits necessary to survive in the market. They will enable the reduction of the innovation gap between the current service offering and the possible competition by technology giants. Incumbents must learn new ways of working, such as the agile approach. They will also benefit from the power of new solutions and implement a proper digital culture.

The future of insurance will be a full immersion in the digital world. It will require to act on the entire business model. The innovation needs to overcome excessive regulation, companies' legacy, portfolios, and win customer loyalty.

The disruption of insurance 4.0 will result in a much more agile and effective business model that will meet customers' needs and capitalize on the evolving commercial opportunities in a much more effective, efficient, economical, and ethical way to the present and past times.

In conclusion, the future seems brighter for companies. They will have more opportunities to capture demand and evolve their service portfolio, delivering higher value to their customers. Crucial will be to establish the right partnership with the right partners within the ecosystem.

The spreading of data and information will enable insurance companies to analyze and turn them into smarter solutions for customers, which must be a winner in this transformation. Companies need to maintain integrity by protecting individuals from these innovations and by setting up the proper moral and ethical bounds around these innovations. Insurance has always been a representative and side player for regulation. It will be useful to keep on doing that during these times of crisis and changes.

> *This is the age of digital disruption. Across industries, insurgents with digitally enabled business models are challenging incumbents and their established business models. The incumbent has a choice: be disrupted or be the disruptor. Those that prosper in the digital future will be those that choose to be disruptors and invest in innovation today.*[3]

[3] www.mckinsey.com/industries/financial-services/our-insights/the-age-of-innovation. Accessed 14 March 2020.

The combination of all the nine components of the business model—provision of value, proximity to the customer, partition of the customers, places of the distribution, processes, platforms, persons, partnerships, pricing and payments for costs and investments—provides new opportunities for companies and ecosystem players.

The continuous evolution of the digital era means increasing customer expectations, both as service levels and as the customer journey, continually growing compared to what is offered by organizations. The message is that adopting a conservative strategy is a loss.

Few leadership principles need to consider when working for insurance 4.0[4]:

- Get the chief executive officer and board members to embrace the insurance 4.0 approach and become the ones that will push and motivate the company to evolve;
- Focus on solutions rather than technologies;
- Focus on critical values as a feature of new solutions, rather than as a problem;
- Empower the organization to manage new solutions and counter a fatalistic and deterministic view of the future;
- Prioritize futures by design rather than by default.

It is not easy to predict what the future holds. Insurance 4.0 is a revolution compared to the past. The blockchain, such as a digital trust mechanism, and the smart contracts, as self-executing contracts, are just some examples of future implementations. The new solutions will exceed the imagination.

There are still many questions not answered. Hopefully, new research will clarify them.[5] There has been little academic research on digitization in the insurance segment. This situation is surprising, given that digitization and big data offer enormous potential for empirical research.

[4] Schwab, K. (2016). *Four leadership principles for the Fourth Industrial Revolution*. www.weforum.org/agenda/2016/10/four-leadership-principles-for-the-fourth-industrial-revolution. Accessed 22 July 2019.

[5] Eling, M., & Lehmann, M. (2018). The impact of digitalization on the insurance value chain and the insurability of risks. *The Geneva Papers on Risk and Insurance—Issues and Practice, 43*(3), 359–396.

One example is the increasing use of telematics devices in motor insurance. How does telematics insurance affect driving behavior? If a risk reduction can be analyzed empirically, is it a result of less moral hazard or adverse selection? How is it possible to separate the two? The few academic studies done have not analyzed the impact of telematics insurance on moral hazard and adverse selection empirically to the best of our knowledge.[6]

The fourth industrial revolution will potentially shape insurance to new heights, enabling a fully autonomous value network with the power of technology advances.

The identification and evaluation of big data analytics and artificial intelligence open up a new research field, for example, from actuarial science (pricing telematics contracts). Bigtech organizations, like Apple or Google, have access to an enormous amount of data and information, how will they use them?[7] What is the role of insurance companies in such an environment? Which would be the implications on the possibility that mobile devices could track every moment of the life? Which would be the product variety to win in the competition? How privacy and data protection laws and regulations interact with big data analytics.

Regarding future research, the role of the insurance industry in ensuring the risks from the digital world is relevant. The world is moving quickly from physical to virtual assets. For example, can the availability of cyber risk insurance support investments in cyber risk protection? How can modeling and pricing of cyber risk be improved, given the lack of experience, continuous changes in this type of risks and complex correlation structures? Are transfer schema to the capital market (alternative risk transfer instruments such as insurance-linked securities) a viable solution for risk-bearing capacity for cyber risk to develop the cyber risk insurance market?

[6] Filipova-Neumann, L., & Welzel, P. (2010). Reducing asymmetric information in insurance markets: Cars with black boxes. *Telematics and Informatics, 27*(4), 394–403.

Hummel, T., Kühn, M., Bende, J., & Lang, A. (2011). Advanced driver assistance systems. *German Insurance Association Insurers Accident Research*. Available on www.udv.de, accessed at, *6*(1), 2015.

Bolderdijk, J. W., & Steg, L. (2011). *Pay-as-you-drive vehicle insurance as a tool to reduce crash risk.*

[7] *The impact of digitalization on the insurance value chain*.... slideheaven.com/the-impact-of-digitalization-on-the-insurance-value-chain-and-the-insurability-o.html. Accessed 20 June 2020.

In general, the link between new solutions and insurance will raise many research questions. For example, what should insurance characteristics look like in a world with autonomous-driving vehicles? What does pay-as-you-live or pay-as-you-drive mean for the insurance idea of providing mutuality? What if the individual risk profile is fully known to the insurance company (reversing information asymmetry)? What if mitigation and prevention reduce the loss exposure so much that the idea of insurance becomes un-useful (i.e., the utility gain from risk transfer insuring is too small to justify the insurance transaction costs)?[8]

The time intervals for moving to the next industrial revolution decrease over time. If this is confirmed, insurance 5.0 is not far in the future. It should be able to bring answers to all, or at least most of, the unanswered questions listed.

In the meantime, insurance 4.0 brings several opportunities and challenges to the organizations: significant financial investments, implementation and operational risks, strict infrastructure requirements, new levels of education and competencies of the persons involved, and so on. At the same time, this concept is dynamic since new technologies are continuously in development and new solutions available. Applying the insurance 4.0 concepts for the organizations is not a matter of choice (use it?) but a matter of time (when start?).

[8] *The impact of digitalization on the insurance value chain…*. slideheaven.com/the-impact-of-digitalization-on-the-insurance-value-chain-and-the-insurability-o.html. Accessed 20 June 2020.

Glossary[1]

Agility It is a metric to measure how quickly a solution responds to the customer's changes and resource load scales, allocating additional and different resources to the activity.

Algorithms They are an essential part of modern advanced applications. They are used for a certain number of tasks, from recommending books, movies, and music to automating the investments online. In stock markets, algorithms are connected directly into an electronic exchange, and trading happens without any person intervention. According to the BBC, they suggest where the most money can be made faster and more accurately than any human being.[2] Pedro Domingos offers a simple definition: "An algorithm is a sequence of instructions telling a computer what to do."[3] He goes on to explain, algorithms are reducible to three logical operations—AND, OR, and NOT. While these operations can chain together in complex ways, algorithms are built out of a simple rational at the core.

[1] These definitions are of necessity synthetic and not necessarily very accurate. Please refer to the text for a more proper presentation. This glossary includes a few terms based on the possible need to find a rapid clarification while reading this book. An useful reference is Glossary—link.springer.com. link.springer.com/content/pdf/bbm%3A978-3-319-61085-6%2F1.pdf. Accessed 10 May 2020.

[2] www.bbc.com/news/technology-14841018. Accessed 20 July 2019.

[3] Domingos, P. (2015). *The master algorithm: How the quest for the ultimate learning machine will remake our world*. New York, NY: Basic Books.

B. Nicoletti, *Insurance 4.0*, Palgrave Studies in Financial Services Technology, https://doi.org/10.1007/978-3-030-58426-9

App It is short for application. It is a program or piece of software, mainly as downloaded by a user into a mobile device.

Application It is software that a user can run on ICT resources to achieve a specific function related to the purposes of the user or the organization. These ICT resources could be programmable logic controllers, standard computers, and mobile devices or the cloud.

Application/App store It is the virtual location for the distribution of digital applications. It is available on mobile devices.

Application Programming Interfaces (API) An Application Programming Interface allows software programs to interact by exchanging data.[4] The data, in turn, can prompt certain actions such as making a transaction. There are four main categories of APIs: payment APIs, which help third parties create and receive payments; data APIs, which share individual (with proper customer consent) and aggregate data with third parties, enabling them, for example, to understand the risk profiles of individuals better; "ecosystem expansion" APIs, which allow loan origination or account creation; and "consent and identity" APIs, which facilitate Know your customer KYC, allow sharing of data and/or movement of money by third parties.

Artificial Intelligence It is a system that performs actions, reasoning, and behaviors that usually require the human being (learning, visual perception, speech understanding, linguistic translation, object management, decision-making ability).

Audit It is the process by which an internal or external auditor independently verifies financial records, business processes, and information systems.

Augmented Operator It is an employee in the smart office, who can better perceive and control the operational processes thanks to a (virtual) expanded view of the real office. It thus acts as a carrier of decisions and optimization processes.

Augmented Reality (AR) Augmented reality is the solution that allows enriching the perception of reality by superimposing on the vision of real environments information or virtual objects.

Authentication It is the verification of the identity of a user by a system or service.

[4] documents.worldbank.org. documents.worldbank.org/curated/en/130201561082549144/text/Fintech-The-Experience-so-Far-Executive-Summary.txt. Accessed 20 May 2020.

Authorization It is the procedure to check whether a customer or another person inside or outside the organization has the right to do a specific action, for example, to transfer funds or access sensitive data.

Automation It is the automated handling of services or goods. It is also the percentage of requests to the partner handled without any human intervention.

Availability It is the metric that measures the percentage, usually computed over a periodical (such as a month) basis and net of planned or unplanned service downtimes of service coverage.

Bancassurance It is the partnership or relationship between a bank and an insurance organization. The insurance organization uses the bank's sales channels to sell its insurance products.

Beacon Literally, "light signal" is a technology based on Bluetooth, through which the beacons transmit short messages within limited distances.

Benchmarking It is the comparison of processes and/or measures to other processes and/or measures implemented by well-organized entities or a large number of them.[5]

Beneficiary It is the person who, according to the designation made by the contractor, receives the benefits of the insurer.

Big Data It is a term for any collection of data sets so large and complex that it becomes difficult to process them using traditional data processing applications.[6] Big data has five Vs characteristics: Volume, Velocity, Variety, Veracity, and Value.

Biometrics It is the process to detect and possibly record a person's unique physical and other traits using an electronic device or system to confirm identity.

Bitcoin It is a cryptocurrency, a token of value exchanged between two parties.

Black Belt It is a term used to describe a level of expertise in the six sigma method. The black belt can help or direct a group that applies the method of six sigma and other process improvement initiatives. A typical black belt must have completed several training courses and at

[5] Benchmarking—Open Risk Manual. www.openriskmanual.org/wiki/Benchmarking. Accessed 20 May 2020.

[6] Top Fintech Terms You Should Know—Trulioo: Global. www.trulioo.com/blog/top-fintech-terms-know/. Accessed 30 May 2020.

least one significant project. In some organizations, there is a process of official registration. It is a full-time position.

Black Swan Event Events that come as a surprise, have a significant effect, and are often inappropriately rationalized with the benefit of hindsight.[7]

Block (in Blockchains) It is a recording of transactions validated by a set of cryptographic keys. Once completed, it goes into the blockchain as a permanent database. A block makes transactions recordable and trackable, representing the source of truth for the included operations.

Blockchain It is a distributed database where trust is established through mass collaboration. Each transaction is recorded continuously and sequentially on a public block creating a unique ongoing chain. The blockchain is the technology used for the first time by the Bitcoin transactions.[8] It can record cryptocurrency transactions. It operates like a distributed public ledger where information, once entered, cannot be modified. Blockchain solution has several possible applications, including smart contracts and the recording of digital assets. It can record data—a digital ledger of transactions, agreements, contracts or anything that needs to be independently recorded and verified as having happened. The blockchain solutions run across several, even thousands of computers in some applications. Every time a new batch of transactions is encrypted, it is added to the ledger "chain" as a "block." Its appeal stretches beyond fintech into government, trade, and other fields. The simplest definition is that the blockchain solution is a decentralized digital ledger. It records all digital transactions as a string of data stored on a global network of computers.

Blockchain-as-a-Service (BaaS) It is a new term, coined by William Mougayar of Virtual Capital Ventures in early 2015.[9] It means Blockchain as a Service. Equivalent terms include Ethereum Blockchain as a service (EthBaaS), or "blockchain-as-a-Platform" (BaaP). It refers to the growing number of services, based on blockchain solutions, available in cloud computing. This platform

[7] mitpress.mit.edu/books/war-weather. Accessed 20 June 2019.

[8] Karajovic, M. Narula, H. Pandya, K. Patel, J. and Warring, I. (2017). *Blockchain: A Manager's Guide*, A Report for OMIS 3710 Schulich School of Business York University Toronto, Ontario.

[9] www.slideshare.net/wmougayar/blockchain-2015-analyzing-the-blockchain-in-financial-services. Accessed 30 July 2016.

allows organizations to begin working with blockchain solutions without having to make significant investments in hardware or base software.

Bluetooth (BT) It is a connection protocol and wireless communication between devices, with data exchange via radio waves.

Bluetooth Low Energy (BLE) It is a Bluetooth feature for low-power applications, designed for wireless devices with a range of up to 50 meters. It is used for the internet of things (IoT).

Broad Network Access It facilitates network capabilities and their access through standard mechanisms. Heterogeneous thin or thick customer platforms promote the use of the platform. Notebooks, tablets, PDAs, smartphones, and others are the devices that can access the network.

Broadband It is internet access via networks implemented as DSL, TV cable, or wireless technology (UMTS, WLAN, LTE, satellite, and so on). In developed countries, 99.5 percent of households now have the option of using accesses with at least one megabit per second; 51 percent of households can already use bandwidths of at least 50 megabits per second.

Business Continuity An ongoing process to ensure that the necessary steps are taken to identify the impacts of possible losses and maintain viable recovery strategies, recovery plans, and continuity of services.[10]

Business Intelligence (BI) It is a broad category of applications and solutions for gathering, storing, analyzing, retrieving, and providing data to help users make better organization decisions. BI applications include activities such as decision support systems, querying and reporting, online analytical processing, statistical analysis, forecasting, and data mining. Analytics has generalized and extended business intelligence.

Business Model It is a simplified representation of a company and an abstraction of how its business and value creation ultimately make money. It describes the organization, cost structures, financial flows, value chain, and products of a company compactly. The process of defining a business model is part of the business strategy.

Business Model Canvas It is strategic management and entrepreneurial tool. It allows describing, designing, challenging, inventing, and

[10]NFPA 160. Accessed 20 June 2019. Business Continuity—About UC | University of Cincinnati. www.uc.edu/about/publicsafety/emergencymanagement/business-continuity.html-. Accessed 40 May 2020.

pivoting a business model. It was introduced by Osterwalder and Pigneur.[11]

Business-to-Business (B2B) It refers to organizations that relate to other organizations, rather than customers.

Business-to-Customer (B2C) It indicates the solutions from an organization for the customer.

Business Web It is the use of the internet by companies or organizations in general. The speed of change inherent to the internet and the existing international technical and semantic standards opens up innovation potential to all areas of a company, their organizational structures, and functions. This makes value-added networks flexible and secure. Concepts such as cloud computing and social media are used to support business webs.

Chatbot Artificial intelligence program (AI) simulates human conversations interactively, using pre-set sentences. It is used for assistance services (customer care) or marketing such as in the social network and instant messaging.

Cloud Computing It is a computing capability that provides convenient and on-demand network access to a shared pool of configurable computing resources.[12] These resources can be rapidly provisioned and released with minimal management effort or partner interaction. Cloud computing has six essential characteristics—pay-per-use, self-service, broad network access, resource pooling, rapid elasticity, and measured service. In general terms, cloud computing enables four possible modes—Infrastructure as a Service (IaaS), Platform as a Service (PaaS), Software as a Service, and Business Process as a Service (BPaaS). It can be public, private, or hybrid.

Cloud It is a metaphor for a global network or a synthetic expression for cloud computing. Initially, it referred to the telephone network. It now refers to the internet.

Cognitive Search It collects, analyzes, and gives meaning to different types of data using rule-based or machine learning algorithms often in a way that is similar to human cognition to make decisions in complex situations.

[11] Osterwalder, A., & Pigneur, Y. (2010). *Business model generation: A handbook for visionaries, game changers, and challengers*. Hoboken, NJ: John Wiley & Sons.

[12] Liu, F., Tong, J., Mao, J., Bohn, R., Messina, J., Badger, L., & Leaf, D. (2011). NIST cloud computing reference architecture. *NIST special publication*, *500*(2011), 1–28.

Collaboration Risks They are the risks arising from the legal structure of a joint venture; for example, in contrast, the finances of each partner in a joint venture might be robust, the joint venture vehicle itself may be poorly capitalized and carry a real risk of insolvency.

Compliance It is respect for the internal and external compulsory rules of the organization or of the governments.

Computer Vision It is the capability in support of a machine to see and visually sense the environment around it. Computer vision supports the automatic extraction, analysis, and understanding of useful information from a single image or a sequence of images.

Consensus Mechanism It is a mechanism that allows applications on computers to agree regularly on how to update the database, after which the modifications they have settled on are made unchangeable with the help of complex cryptography.[13]

Consent It is the decision-making strategy based on the conviction and approval by all the members who undertake to support the decision.

Continuous Improvement It is a structured method to improve the overall performance of the organization by using arrangements appropriate to its problems.[14] Its scope may be the quality or social responsibility of the organization. Continuous improvement is called *Kaizen* in Japanese.

Contractor (in Insurance) It is the person who stipulates the insurance contract with the insurer. Its primary obligation is to pay the premiums. Its essential right, typical in life insurances and accidents, is to designate the beneficiary.

Corporate Performance Management (CPM) It is the information system for the management of key business metrics.

Corporate Planning Level It includes ICT systems to use the resources available in a company in the form of capital, operating resources, or personnel as efficiently as possible for the operational processes and, thus, controlling business processes (for instance, policy, customer management, bookkeeping, purchasing, shipping) and optimize them.

Cps Platform It is the platform construct, the hardware, software, and communication systems with basic standardized Cyber-physical

[13] The blockchain in finance - Hype springs eternal | Finance .... www.economist.com/finance-and-economics/2016/03/19/hype-springs-eternal. Accessed 22 June 2020.

[14] Bessant, J., & Caffyn, S. (1997). High-involvement innovation through continuous improvement. *International Journal of Technology Management*, *14*(1), 7–28.

services (CPS) mediation, interoperability, and quality of services for the implementation and management of cyber-physical systems and their applications as well as their integration in value networks. CPS platform services with their basic functionality for the implementation, reliable operation, and evolution of cyber-physical systems are an integral part of domain-specific CPS application platforms. They secure the cross-domain and cross-company functionality and quality at the technical system level, for example, through quality of service-capable communication, services for ICT security or self-diagnosis, self-healing, and reconfiguration.

Crisis It is a situation formally declared as service interruption or the deterioration of one or more critical processes or as systemically essential because of incidents or disasters.

Crowdfunding It is the practice of funding a project or venture by raising money from a large number of persons. This transaction takes place most often via online platforms.[15] It can also take place through mail-order subscriptions, benefit events, and other methods.[16] Equity crowdfunding is the process whereby persons (the "crowd") invest, in an early stage, unlisted organization or initiative in exchange for shares in that organization. A shareholder has partial ownership of an organization and stands to profit should the organization perform well. The opposite is also exact, so if the organization fails, investors can lose some, or all, of their investment. Seedrs is an example of an equity-based crowdfunding platform in the UK.[17] Debt-based crowdfunding is when persons lend to an organization. The lenders earn a rate of return based on the interest charged on loan. Typically, loans are secured against assets, which provide investors with some protection should the borrower fail to repay. Donation-based crowdfunding is when persons donate money to a project. In return, backers may receive token rewards that increase in prestige as the size of the donation increases; for small sums, the funder may receive nothing at all. There are two types of crowdfunding—rewards-based crowdfunding and equity-based crowdfunding. The first relates to platforms

[15] Common Definitive Financial Technology (FinTech) Jargon. pupuweb.com/common-fintech-jargon-glossary-term/. Accessed 30 May 2020.

[16] Common Definitive Financial Technology (FinTech) Jargon .... pupuweb.com/common-fintech-jargon-glossary-term/. Accessed 22 June 2020.

[17] www.seedr.cc/. Accessed 22 April 2019.

like Kickstarter[18] or Indiegogo,[19] where startups raise pledges and, in return, offer buy-in incentives for anything they produce. Equity crowdfunding is where pledgers are investors that receive a small share in the business in return for their contributions.

Customer It is she/he who pays for the products, services, or activities, not necessarily the user of the product or the process or event. It can be external or internal to the organization. In the latter case, unless there is a system of internal prices, the internal customer does not pay the product, the service, or the activity but uses it.

Customer Due Diligence (CDD) It comprises the facts about a customer that should enable an organization to assess the extent to which the customer exposes it to a range of risks.[20] These risks include money laundering and terrorist financing.

Customer Relationship Management (CRM) It is an information system for managing the relationships with the customers. It can control the life cycle of the customer, the acquisition of new customers, more essential the increased customer proximity, and customer loyalty based on the relationships with the organization. It lowers transaction costs between customers and the organization and integrates the processes of customer management.

Customer Value Proposition They are the benefits a product or service holds for a customer. It is the reason why a customer might buy that product or service.

Cyber-Physical Systems (Cps) They encompass embedded systems, production, logistics, engineering, coordination, management processes, and internet services that directly capture physical data using sensors and act on physical processes using actuators, are connected using digital networks, use data and services available worldwide, and have multimodal person-machine interfaces. Cyber-physical systems are open socio-technical systems and enable several new functions, services, and properties.

Cybersecurity It is the set of solutions and services aimed at protecting computers, other connected devices, equipment, and ICT systems

[18] www.kickstarter.com. Accessed 20 July 2019.

[19] www.indiegogo.com. Accessed 20 July 2019.

[20] ING Know Your Customer (KYC): the hunt for 'detectives' | ING. www.ing.jobs/Netherlands/Expertise/Risk-Management/Know-Your-Customer.htm. Accessed 30 May 2020.

from attacks of several types (malware, viruses, trojans, ransomware, and so on), to prevent loss or compromise of data and information.

Data Collection It is the process of collecting the data to generate information that can be used to make decisions.[21] In manual data collection, persons use the so-called sheets check to collect data and provide for their initial classification.

Data Governance and Compliance It defines who is responsible for what, and the policies and procedures that persons or groups need to follow. Data governance requires governing the organization's infrastructure and the infrastructure that the organization does not control. Data governance has two critical components—understanding compliance and risk, healthy organization performance goals.

Data Protection It is the protection of the individual against impairment of his right about personal data.

Data Source It is a database of personal information used by identity verification/identity proofing services to validate an identity. Examples of data sources include credit bureau records, government records, property files, customer marketing data, and telephone/utility records.

Dataset or Database It is a collection of data usually from a common source and assembled for a particular business or another purpose. The term is generally used to define data that could historically have been brought together in a document, but in an automated process is stored as a dataset.

Defects They are the lack of fulfillment of customer expectations by a process or service.

Define, Measure, Analyze, Develop, and Verify (DMADV) It is the six sigma method for radical improvement of the processes.

Define, Measure, Analyze, Improve, and Control (DMAIC) It is the six sigma method for continuous process improvement. This structured process eliminates non-productive steps, focusing on new measurements, and applying solutions to improve.

Digital Currency It is a digital representation of either virtual currency (non-fiat) or e-money (fiat) and thus is often used interchangeably with the term "virtual currency."[22]

[21] Data Collection—Open Risk Manual. www.openriskmanual.org/wiki/Data_Collection. Accessed 30 May 2020.

[22] Crypto Currency / Virtual Currency / Digital Currency. arthapedia.in/index.php?title=Crypto_Currency_/_Virtual_Currency_/_Digital_Currency. Accessed 30 May 2020.

Digital Financial Inclusion It is the use of digital financial services to progress in financial inclusion.[23] It involves the deployment of digital ways to reach financially excluded and underserved populations with a range of financial services suited to their needs and delivered in a responsible way at a cost affordable to customers and sustainable for providers.[24]

Digital Financial Services (DFS) They are financial products and services, including payments, transfers, savings, credit, insurance, securities, financial planning, and account statements that are provided via digital technology such as e-money (initiated either online or on a mobile phone), payment cards, and a regular bank account.[25]

Digital Transformation It is a change in the business model. It is the set of social, cultural, and technological changes associated with the use of digital solutions.[26]

Disruptive Innovation It is an innovation that completely changes how persons do something (e.g., Amazon vs. in-store shopping).[27] It describes innovations that improve products or services in un-expected ways and change both how things are done and the market. The smartphone is an example of a disruptive innovation solution.[28] It has completely changed how users connect to ICT services. Disruptive innovations impact also on the society at large.

Distributed Ledger Technology (DLT) Distributed ledgers use independent computers (referred to as nodes) to record, share, and synchronize transactions in their respective electronic ledgers (instead

[23] G20 High-Level Principles for Digital Financial Inclusion. www.gpfi.org/sites/gpfi/files/G20%20High%20Level%20Principles%20for%20Digital%20Financial%20Inclusion.pdf. Accessed 30 May 2020.

[24] G20 High-Level Principles for Digital Financial Inclusion. www.gpfi.org/sites/gpfi/files/documents/G20%20High%20Level%20Principles%20for%20Digital%20Financial%20Inclusion%20-%20Full%20version-.pdf. Accessed 22 June 2020.

[25] G20 High-Level Principles for Digital Financial Inclusion. www.gpfi.org/sites/gpfi/files/documents/G20%20High%20Level%20Principles%20for%20Digital%20Financial%20Inclusion%20-%20Full%20version-.pdf. Accessed 22 June 2020.

[26] Matt, C., Hess, T., & Benlian, A. (2015). Digital transformation strategies. *Business & Information Systems Engineering*, *57*(5), 339–343.

[27] Disruptive Innovation— Open Risk Manual. www.openriskmanual.org/wiki/Disruptive_Innovation. Accessed 40 May 2020.

[28] Disruptive Innovation—Open Risk Manual. www.openriskmanual.org/wiki/Disruptive_Innovation. Accessed 22 June 2020.

of keeping data centralized as in a traditional environment).[29] Blockchain is one type of a distributed ledger that organizes data into blocks, which are chained together in an append-only mode.

Distributor It is a person or entity that supplies goods on a wholesale basis to retail outlets or organizations. It may be an organization entity, an arm of an organization entity, or an independent entity. It can be physical or virtual.

Ecosystem Participants They are a set of organizations or individuals that can work together to gain synergies.

Ecosystem It is a network of organizations, including partners, distributors, customers, competitors, government agencies, and others, involved in the delivery of a specific product or service through cooperation.[30] An ecosystem allows users to fulfill a variety of needs in one integrated experience.[31] Customer ecosystems are currently emerging around the world. They tend to concentrate on requirements such as travel, healthcare, or housing. Business-to-business (B2B) ecosystems generally revolve around a specific function, for example, marketing and sales, operations, procurement, or finance.[32]

Electronic Data Interchange (EDI) It is the computer-to-computer exchange of documents in a standard format between partners.

Embedded Systems They are hardware and software components that are integrated into a comprehensive system to implement system-specific functional features.

Encryption It is the process of encoding messages or coding to protect the customer's information assets. Encryption is vital to organizations, to the blockchain, and anything else that needs to be secure. Documents or data, like names and numbers, are turned into code using

[29] Blockchain & Distributed Ledger Technology (DLT). www.worldbank.org/en/topic/financialsector/brief/blockchain-dlt. Accessed 4 May 2020. Blockchain & Distributed Ledger Technology (DLT). www.worldbank.org/en/topic/financialsector/brief/blockchain-dlt. Accessed 22 June 2020.

[30] Anitha, C., & Reddy, D. Evolution and emerging role of MFIs in Indian microfinance sector. *Sumedha Journal of Management, 6*(4), CMR College of Engineering & Technology, October 2017, p. 87. Accessed 30 May 2020.

[31] Insuritas | NSC | NAFCU. www.nafcu.org/insuritas. Accessed 30 May 2020.

[32] www.mckinsey.com/industries/financial-services/our-insights/insurance-beyond-digital-the-rise-of-ecosystems-and-platforms. Accessed 10 January 2020.

algorithms (mathematical formulas). A key is required to turn that code back into readable, useful data (Decryption).

End User It is the end or final user of an application.

Engineering, System Engineering It is interdisciplinary approach to design, systematically develop, and implement complex technical systems according to requirements (industrial engineering: is based, for example, on specialized knowledge and skills in mathematics, physics, computer science, social sciences, etc., together with the principles and methods of technical analysis and design to implement or improve integrated systems of persons, technical components, materials, and information, as well as equipment and energy).

Enterprise Content Management (ECM) It is the management of all contents (data, unstructured documents, email, voice, video, and so on).

Enterprise Resource Planning It is the extension of the Manufacturing Resource Planning II to the organization's remaining functions, such as engineering, finance, and personnel administration and management.[33] Some components of an ERP are accounting, industrial accounting, HR management, payrolls, sourcing, warehouse management, operations, project control, sales, distribution, and facility maintenance.

Facilitator It is a person who helps a group to accomplish its full potential through the identification and removal of barriers. She/he leads the group to achieve its mission.

Federation In the context of federal CPS platforms, federation means that CPS platforms, services, and applications from different participants are used jointly for cooperative activities, but the individual component or context remains secured for each of the participants. Only the data and information that are necessary for joint actions are exchanged between the participants. The different parts can be accessed directly within the applications, services, or platform, without central, dominant control. The individual components remain in control of their data.

Financial Market Infrastructure It is a multilateral system among participating institutions, including the operator of the system, used

[33] Enterprise Resource Planning—Open Risk Manual. www.openriskmanual.org/wiki/Enterprise_Resource_Planning. Accessed 22 June 2020.

for clearing, settling, or recording payments, securities, derivatives, or other financial transactions.

Fintech It is the emerging financial technology sector whose name is composed of the words "finance" and "technology." It uses technological innovation to compete with traditional financial institutions.

Global Information Systems It is an organized collection of computer hardware, software, and geographic data designed to capture, store, update, process, analyze, and display all forms of geographically referenced information efficiently.[34]

Globalization It is a worldwide movement toward economic, financial, trade, and communications integration.[35]

Governance It refers to the controls and processes that ensure the effectiveness, efficiency, economics, and ethics of a sector.[36] The sector might refer to the entire organization or an organization unit, a process, or data.

Home Automation It is the set of technologies based on computer engineering and electronics, aimed at integrating devices capable of automating and simplifying the daily actions of a house or building. These technologies must be connected to a shared computer network, usually the internet, for using shared information.

Human-Machine Interaction/Man-Machine Interaction (Mmi)/ Human-Computer Interaction (Hci) It is part of computer science that deals with the user-friendly design of interactive systems and their human-machine interfaces. In addition to findings from computer science, those from psychology, ergonomics, cognitive science, ergonomics, sociology, and design are also used. Important sub-areas of human-machine interaction are, for example, usability engineering, interaction design, information design, and context analysis. The last aspect is vital for cyber-physical systems to ensure that the interaction is optimally adapted to the user in every situation.

Internet of Services It is the part of the internet that maps services and functionalities as granular, web-based software components. Providers make these available on the internet and offer their use on request. The

[34] mitpress.mit.edu/books/war-weather. Accessed 20 June 2019. What Is a GIS?—GISuser.com. gisuser.com/2012/03/what-is-a-gis-2/. Accessed 30 May 2020.

[35] businessdictionary.com. Accessed 20 June 2019.

[36] Governance—Open Risk Manual. www.openriskmanual.org/wiki/Governance. Accessed 30 May 2020.

individual software modules or services can be integrated via internet service technologies. Companies can orchestrate the different software components into complex, yet flexible solutions (service-oriented architecture). A large number of market players can quickly develop and offer internet-enabled services via cloud-based development platforms. Besides, service platforms are created on which customers can find a complete, need-based, or process-oriented offer instead of having to search, compare, and compile individual offers.

Identity Verification It is the identification of individuals by using their physical and behavioral characteristics to establish a mapping from a person's online identity to their real-life identity.[37]

Incident It is an event that is not part of the standard operation of a service and that causes or may cause an interruption to, or a reduction in, the quality of service.

Industrial Internet of Things Less known than the internet of things (IoT), it is an application of it in the context of industry 4.0. The industrial internet of things (IIoT) is linked to the enterprise and is applied in the factory, in the context of industry 4.0. The aim is to optimize the operational processes through the connection between machines, whose health and functioning status is checked in advance. An IIoT object also allows operators and professionals to develop data for analysis and to control operational times.

Industry 4.0 It is the operations and work organization's model that brings automation to a form of digital integration of all its components. The fourth industrial revolution is based on the adoption of enabling technologies that connect physical and digital systems, the analysis of information obtained from the network, and more flexible management of the operations cycle.

Information and Communication Technology (ICT) It is the combination of computers, storage, network, applications, and so on, that provides integrated computer-based services.

Input It is a resource introduced into the system or consumed in its operation, which helps in getting a result or output.

[37] Top Fintech Terms You Should Know—Trulioo: Global. www.trulioo.com/blog/top-fintech-terms-know/. Accessed 22 June 2020.

Insurance Agent A person licensed by a state and generally employed by an insurance organization to sell insurance policies on the organization's behalf.[38] The agent typically receives a commission for this service. She/he attempts to extract the maximum value for the insurance organization and the customer in all his/her dealings. An insurance agent should not be confused with an insurance broker or an insurance underwriter.[39]

Insurance Broker It is a person who sells insurance policies. An insurance broker does not work for an insurance organization but rather represents the buyer of the policy to ensure that she/he receives a fair and customized deal.[40]

Insurance Intermediaries They serve as a bridge between customers (seeking to buy insurance policies) and insurance organizations (trying to sell those policies).[41] They are contracted with multiple insurance organizations so that they can focus on their customers' needs. Examples are agents, brokers, and banks.

Insurance Organization (or company in this book) It is a business that provides coverage, in the form of compensation resulting from loss, damages, injury, treatment, or hardship in exchange for premium payments.[42] The organization computes the risk of occurrence then determines the cost to replace (pay for) the loss to determine the premium amount.[43]

Insurance Policy It is the document that proves the insurance and that the insurer is obligated to issue (bearing his/her signature) to the contractor. About the policy, the insurer is required to issue duplicates or copies on request and at the contractor's expense, with the right to be presented or returned by them the original. This document contains the identification of the contractor, of the persons or

[38] Insurance agent financial definition of Insurance Agent (IRDA). financial-dictionary.thefreedictionary.com/Insurance+agent. Accessed 30 May 2020.

[39] financial-dictionary.thefreedictionary.com/insurance+agent, Accessed 30 May 2020.

[40] financial-dictionary.thefreedictionary.com/insurance+broker. Accessed 30 May 2020.

[41] www.policyholder.gov.in/uploads/CEDocuments/Intermediariespercent20Handbook.pdf. Accessed 30 May 2020.

[42] Insurance agent financial definition of Insurance agent. financial-dictionary.thefreedictionary.com/Insurance+agent. Accessed 30 May 2020.

[43] www.businessdictionary.com/definition/insurance-organization.html. Accessed 30 May 2020.

the insured things and the conditions governing the insurance, the premium, the guarantee limits, and so on. It is signed by the insurer and the contractor.[44]

Insurance Premium It is the "price" of insurance. Usually, the first year is due in full even if divided into several payments.

Insurer It is the contractual subject whose specific characteristic is that of being finalized to the offering of insurance services and products.

Insurtech It is the fintech organization that specifically focuses on insurance. Insurtech encloses all initiatives to streamline the insurance value network through technology from actuarial modeling to brokerage.[45]

Integration It is the process of combining components or systems into one integrated entity.

Internet of Everything It is the internet of everything. It goes beyond the interconnection of devices involving everything: persons, objects, processes. It is the basis for a hyper-connected world that includes things, processes, data, and persons.

Internet of People It means the internet of human beings. It refers to direct or indirect interactions between devices and persons, generating a set of useful information to understand and improve persons' lives and work.

Internet of Things It is the set of components and devices (e.g., sensors) embedded in objects and machinery to create an interface between the physical and digital world. It allows communication between objects over the internet, allowing information to be exchanged, modified behavior based on input received, instruction memory, and learning from the interactions.

Internet Protocol It is the primary protocol for transmitting data or information over the internet.

Interoperability It is the ability of independent, heterogeneous systems to work together (as far as possible) seamlessly to exchange information in an efficient and usable manner, to cooperate, and to provide services to customers without the need for separate agreements between the systems.

[44] www.bppb.it/documents/10157/27937/bppb_glossario_termini_assic_2.pdf?version=1.0. Accessed 30 May 2020.

[45] Yoder, J., Rao, A., & Baixas, J. (2016). *InsurTech: A golden opportunity for companies to innovate.* Price Waterhouse Coopers.

Key Performance Indicators or Key Process Indicators It is the metrics (or measures) used within corporations to measure one department's performance against another concerning revenue, sales, lead conversion, costs, customer support, and so on.

Know Your Customer It is the process of an organization verifying the identity and the standing of its customers and the character of the business or transactions they generate. The term also refers to the legal regulations which govern these activities.

Lean and Digitize It is the method used to make the processes simultaneously lean and automated, wherever it is useful to improve the processes.[46] It aims to make the process automated and streamlined. The method is based on the re-engineering of the processes to make them lean and then automated where and when necessary.

Lean Six Sigma It is a method, complete, flexible, and highly structured, aimed at achieving, maintaining, and increasing customer value.[47]

Light Fidelity It is a technology that allows wireless communication between devices, using light to transmit high-speed data.

Logical Security It is a set of processes and activities aimed at obtaining confidentiality, integrity, and availability of data and information through the adoption of measures—techniques (system for access control, antivirus, firewalls, intrusion detection systems, and so on), organizational (definition of policies, safety standards, user profiling, and detailed ratings, and so on), and procedural (process definition).

Machine Learning It is a set of algorithms used to make a system artificially intelligent. It enables to recognize patterns from large datasets and apply past findings to new data.[48]

Maintainability It is a property of a system that can be changed or expanded. The purpose is to isolate and eliminate defects and shortcomings or set the system up for new requirements to work in a changing environment.

Management Process It is a method to optimize the organization as a system, determining what processes need improvement and/or

[46] Nicoletti, B. (2012), *Lean and digitize: An integrated approach to process improvement*. Farnham, UK: Gower Publishing. ISBN-10: 1409441946.

[47] Dahlgaard-Park, S. M., Andersson, R., Eriksson, H., & Torstensson, H. (2006). Similarities and differences between TQM, six sigma and lean. *The TQM Magazine*.

[48] Artificial-Intelligence-Sep2017.pdf—Artificial .... www.coursehero.com/file/43001568/Artificial-Intelligence-Sep2017pdf/. Accessed 22 June 2020.

control, defining priorities, and providing leadership to initiate and support efforts for improving processes. It is also the management of the information obtained because of these processes.

Marketing The American Marketing Association (AMA) defines the activity, set of institutions, and processes for creating, communicating, delivering, and exchanging offerings that have value for customers, partners, and the society.[49]

Maximal It is a sum indicated in the insurance contract representing the maximum amount given by the organization.

Metrics It is an index of the performance of an organization that wants to show whether it reaches a goal.

Micro-Insurance Agent It is a micro-insurance plan that provides protection to individuals who have little savings and is tailored specifically for lower valued assets and compensation for illness, injury, or death.[50]

Millennial (or Generation Y) It refers to the customer segment between 18 and 34 years. This segment is very active on the web, social media, and mobile phone. Generation Y represents a quarter of the world population. It is a significant challenge for insurance companies to try and conquer this market, as they are the customers of the future.

Mission It is how to proceed toward the vision.

Mixed Reality Mixed reality overlaps physical, virtual, and augmented reality (AR) devices for an observation of the world that offers useful information (in AR) and allows to interact with virtual objects within it (in virtual reality (VR)).[51]

Mobile Device It includes smartphones, feature phones, and tablet computers. The term "mobile device" is also used interchangeably with "mobile handset" or "handset."[52]

[49] www.ama.org/the-definition-of-marketing/. Accessed 30 May 2020.

[50] www.investopedia.com/terms/m/microinsurance.asp. Accessed 30 May 2020. Microinsurance—Investopedia. www.investopedia.com/terms/m/microinsurance.asp. Accessed 30 May 2020.

[51] www.forbes.com/sites/quora/2018/02/02/the-difference-between-virtual-reality-augmented-reality-and-mixed-reality. Accessed 12 August 2019.

[52] Mobile Device—Open Risk Manual. www.openriskmanual.org/wiki/Mobile_Device. Accessed 30 May 2020.

Mobile Money It is an electronic money product where the record of funds is stored on the mobile phone or a central computer system, and which can be drawn down through specific payment instructions to be issued from the bearers' mobile phone, also known as m-money.

Mode It is a simplified representation of a subject's characteristics, which is aimed at a specific goal, which facilitates an investigation or an investigation or makes it possible in the first place. Models are essential artifacts of engineering; they represent systems on different levels of abstraction (analysis, design, implementation), system parts or trades (process engineering, mechanics, electrical engineering, automation, ICT), issues (security, performance, resilience), and tasks (testing, deployment). There are a variety of modeling concepts; models are used for simulation.

National Institute of Standards and Technology (NIST) It is a US Department of Commerce agency which promotes also the effective and secure use of cloud computing within organizations.

Natural Language Processing It is the understanding and/or interacting in human language, including Natural Language Understanding (Sentimental Analysis, Conversational AI bots.) and Natural Language Generation.

Near Field Communication It is the technology that allows the exchange of data and information without wires, between very close devices.

Neural Networks It is a type of algorithms that is a subfield of machine learning using several layers of neural networks (algorithms that mimic the brain) and requires intensely supervised or unsupervised learning.

Node In this book, it is a component of the blockchain solution that receives/sends transactions.

Omnichannel It is a cross-channel content strategy that organizations use to improve their user experience and drive better relationships with their audience across different channels or points of contact. Communication The design of the channels and their supporting resources is able to support communication.[53]

[53] Beaudon, G., & Soulier, E. (2019, February). Customer experience analytics in insurance: Trajectory, service interaction and contextual data. In *International Conference on Information Technology & Systems* (pp. 187–198). Cham. Switzerland: Springer.

Open Banking It is the sharing and leveraging of customer-permissioned data by banks with third-party developers and businesses to build applications and services. These services include, for example, the provision of real-time payments, improved financial transparency options for account holders, marketing, and cross-selling opportunities.[54]

Open Source It is human-readable program code (source code) of software that can be viewed publicly and used, modified, and distributed under the conditions of open-source licenses.

Orchestration It describes the setup and networking of software services to form a business process. Internal and external services can be combined. Each service realizes only one specific activity within the business process. With conventional web services, a participant controls the process flow. In industry 4.0, business processes will emerge *ad hoc* and decisions made dynamically on the control of process flows. In this respect, the term orchestration is broader in this context than with conventional web services. It also refers to the setting up of federal services that can be used in several business process flows at the same time and thereby ensure the own context for each software process.

Organization This book includes companies, public institutions, either central or local, a department, or a nonprofit organization.

Output It is the result of a product or system processes. It can be a product or a service. It is the result produced by a system or process. The final output is usually a product, a service, or an initiative.

Outsourcing The term defines an operation whereby an organization relies on an outside partner to manage a specific process, sub-process, or activity already operational within the organization (usually non-core assets such as the procurement of indirect materials, administrative management, and so on). It is the acquisition from an external partner of products or services that are resulting from direct operations activities and internal management organization.

Over-the-Counter (OTC) Service It is a service in which a mobile money agent performs the transactions on behalf of the customer, who does not need to have a mobile money account to use the service.

Pandemic It is an epidemic of disease that has spread across a vast region, possibly globally.

[54] Emerging Payments Association Asia Outlines How Asia Can. www.jumpstartmag.com/emerging-payments-association-asia-outlines-how-asia-can-lead-innovation-in-open-banking/. Accessed 30 May 2020.

Platform A platform is a group of technologies used as a base upon which other applications, processes, or technologies are developed. In this book, the term indicates any information and communication system or automation support. Recently, this term is short for multi-service platform, which indicates a business model that allows multiple participants (producers and customers) to connect to it, interact with one another, and create and exchange value. The most successful companies in the digital era, including Alibaba, Amazon, and Facebook, were all designed on multi-service platform business models.

Policy In this book, it is a general term for an insurance contract.

Policyholder or Insured It is the subject of whose person the insurance is stipulated. There may be no coincidence between the same and the contractor. The benefits relating to insurances like personal and life damage may be paid to a person (the beneficiary) who, in specific cases, may coincide with the contractor or the policyholder or maybe a third person other than these two.

Portability It is the ability to run applications, components, or systems running on one implementation and deploy it on another one, for example, of a partner.

Predictive Analytics It combines data, statistical algorithms, and machine learning techniques to identify the likelihood of future outcomes based on historical data and improve the reliability of the predictions.

Problem It is the cause that creates an incident. Incidents not resolved due to the lack of an available solution, and repeated incidents related to a known issue ("known problem/error"), pass through problem management. A work-around could remediate the problem before finding the root causes and resolving them.

Process It is a set of interrelated activities that change a set of inputs on one or more results. Sometimes the process is identified with a system. It would be correct to regard it as a component of a system.[55]

Process Control System It is used to manage a production system. It typically consists of: (1) process-related components for controlling and regulating the technical process, for controlling actuators and for

[55] Process—Open Risk Manual. www.openriskmanual.org/wiki/Process. Accessed 33 June 2020.

recording the measured values via sensors; (2) operating and monitoring stations for system visualization, alarming the operator, and archiving of measured values; and (3) engineering components for the configuration of the entire process control system.

Process Improvement It is a continuous effort to learn the causes and effects in a process to reduce the complexity and the variations and shorten the times. The process gets better by removing incorrect root causes. Through the redesign of the process, it is possible to reduce the variations in common causes. It is a continuous effort to learn from the causes and effects in a process, aiming at minimizing the complexity, variation, and cycle time. Eliminating or reducing the impact of the root causes improves the processes.

Process Management It is a method to optimize the organization as a system, determine which processes need to be improved and/or controlled, define priorities, and encourage leadership to initiate and sustain process improvement efforts. It manages the information obtained in these processes.

Program It is a set of projects with similar objectives. An example is the set of projects for the improvement of systems installed at different subsidiaries of the same group.

Project Team It is a group of persons from the same sector or, better, from different fields (and in some cases, from various organizations) working for a certain period to improve the process or implement an output.

Quality Checks They are the tools and operational activities undertaken to meet the quality requirements.

Quality Plan A document or set of documents that describe the standards, quality practices, resources, and activities.

Quality It is not easily defined, because there are several variants, at times specified by an adjective or specification added to the name. In general, one can say that the quality is customer satisfaction profitably for the organization. There are many variations of the concept of quality, sometimes determined by an adjective or specifications.

Quick Response (QR) code It is a two-dimensional barcode that contains data that a customer or merchant can scan using the camera on the smartphones.

Reference Architecture (Architecture Framework) It is a concept and method structure that forms a uniform basis for the description and specifications of system architectures. The aim of reference architectures is, on the one hand, to create a standard structure and language for architectural stories. On the other hand, they provide a method to get a detailed structural description.

Regtech It is a startup that uses technology to facilitate and enhance regulatory compliance.[56]

Reporting It consists of supplying and updating representative data and indicators whose degree of details tends to vary depending on the person or organization for whom or for which they are intended. For sustainable development, tools such as the GRI (Global Reporting Initiative).[57] enable a standardized method agreed on at the international level. In a certain number of countries, all organizations beyond a certain size publish a corporate social responsibility or "sustainability" report.

Resilience It is the capability to anticipate risks, limit impacts, and bounce back rapidly through survival, adaptability, evolution, and growth in the face of turbulent changes.[58]

Resilient Design It is the design that exceeds the level of robustness and/or redundancy of the life code such that impact to facilities and associated systems from disruptive events is minimum.

Response It is an immediate and ongoing set of activities, tasks, programs, and systems to manage the effects of an incident that threatens life, property, operations, or the environment.[59]

Risk In this book, it is a condition for the existence and logical substantiation of the contract, which is void if the threat has never existed or has ceased. It is the effect of uncertainty on objectives often expressed

[56] Discussion Note From Spreadsheets to Suptech. documents.worldbank.org/curated/en/612021529953613035/pdf/127577-REVISED-Suptech-Technology-Solutions-for-Market-Conduct-Supervision.pdf. Accessed 30 May 2020.

[57] Willis, A. (2003). The role of the global reporting initiative's sustainability reporting guidelines in the social screening of investments. *Journal of Business Ethics*, *43*(3), 233–237.

[58] Community and Regional Resilience Institute (CARRI) (2013). Definitions of Community Resilience: An Analysis www.resilientus.org/wp-content/uploads/2013/08/definitions-ofcommunity-resilience.pdf. Accessed 30 July 2019. Infos Pro Solutions—Infos Pro Solutions. infoprosolution.com/. Accessed 40 May 2020.

[59] www.nfpa.org/codes-and-standards. Accessed 20 June 2019.

in a combination of the consequences of an event and the associated likelihood.[60]

Rule-Based Reasoning It is a set of algorithms used as a way to store and manipulate knowledge to interpret information in a useful way.

SaaS It is an acronym for Software as a Service. It is a way to use cloud computing, based on using the software as a service offered by a third party on their computers.

Safety Critical It is the property of systems to have a risk or hazard potential in operation and uses.

Semantic Technologies They are technologies that take the context (semantics) of terms, data structures, and writing conventions into account to carry out data exchange between organizations in integrated, media-free business processes efficiently and without misunderstandings.

Sensor It is a technical component that can qualitatively or quantitatively sense specific physical or chemical properties.

Service Vendor An organization such as a bank, a telecommunication organization, a merchant, and so on provides services to be integrated, for example, with near-field communication (NFC) mobile payments.

Service In computer science, it is the bundling of specialist functions of a program, in networks, the provision of an application on a server, and in telecommunications, data transmission. Services refer to the provision of services to meet a defined need.

Sharing Economy It is an economic model based on sharing, swapping, trading, or renting products and services, enabling access or use over ownership.[61] It is reinventing not just what is consumed but how it is consumed.

Short Message Service It is a system of communicating with short messages over the mobile telephone network. It can be somewhat secure if encrypted.

Sigma (σ) It is the eighteenth letter of the Greek alphabet. In the statistical theory, it is connected with the variance. It is a metric based on the number of defects that occur per million opportunities.

[60] www.iso.org/iso/catalogue_detail?csnumber=44651. Accessed 20 June 2019.

[61] Geissdoerfer, M., Savaget, P., Bocken, N. M., & Hultink, E. J. (2017). The circular economy—A new sustainability paradigm? *Journal of Cleaner Production*, *143*, 757–768.

Single Point of Failure It is a component or part of a system for which no backup exists and a failure disable the entire system.[62]

Six Sigma It is a method and a performance goal.[63] The method is a structured approach to continuous process improvement. The goal is to measure and improve the performance of a process defined as the number of defects per million opportunities. It is a philosophy and a performance objective. It is a structured method for the continuous improvement of processes. The goal is a measure of process performance defined in defects, with 3.4 defective parts per million opportunities.

Smart Contracts It is a computer program that automatically executes a contract or part of it. These are automated and often blockchain-based contracts. They could save time and reduce costs in standard transactions. Smart contracts are computer protocols that facilitate, verify, or enforce a digital agreement. The idea is that these programs potentially replace notaries, lawyers, and financial institutions when handling standard legal and business transactions. Technically, it is a piece of code stored on a blockchain, triggered by blockchain transactions, and reads and writes data in that blockchain database.

Socio-Technical System It is the interaction of employees, technologies (machines, plants, systems), and work organization to carry out a task.

Software as a Service It is a software distribution model in which applications are hosted by a partner or service partner and made available to customers over a network, typically the internet. Many fintech startups use this software distribution model. It refers to applications hosted by a partner on the cloud. The users can access them online for a subscription fee, as opposed to users procuring the license of software outright in a hard or soft format like a tape or a CD. Software as a Service is a standard tool utilized particularly by startups. A partner sells the service of hosting applications on a cloud for users to access online, normally via internet.

Sponsor It is a person in the organization, usually at a high level that sponsors the project or an initiative, having the necessary authority

[62] businessdictionary.com. Accessed 20 June 2019. Leadership Spotlight: Single Point of Failure—LEB. leb.fbi.gov/spotlights/leadership-spotlight-single-point-of-failure. Accessed 30 May 2020.

[63] Schroeder, R. G., Linderman, K., Liedtke, C., & Choo, A. S. (2008). Six Sigma: Definition and underlying theory. *Journal of Operations Management*, *26*(4), 536–554.

and power. It is typically a member of the executive. It is an essential success factor for a project.

Stakeholder It is an individual, group, or organization that is likely to be affected, directly or indirectly, by an activity, a program, or a particular arrangement of an organization. Stakeholders include all those groups that participate or are otherwise involved in its economic life (employees, customers, partners, shareholders), those who observe the organization (unions, nongovernmental organizations), and those that it affects either directly or indirectly (civil society, local authorities, and so on).

Standards They are indications of voluntary or compulsory standardization.

Steering Committee It is a group that assembles periodically. It includes representatives of the executive, the project leader, and the facilitators. Its primary responsibilities are the management of the efforts of the improvement process, the assessment of the needs and overseeing the support and training within its area of responsibility, the communication of the progress to all stakeholders, and agreement on the direction and mission of the efforts.

Straight-Through Processing It is the implementation of a system that requires no personal intervention for the approval or processing of a customer application or transaction.

Suptech The use of technology to facilitate and enhance supervisory processes from the perspective of supervisory authorities. This organization differs from Regtech, as Suptech organizations are not focused on assisting with compliance with laws and regulations, but on supporting supervisory agencies in their assessment of that compliance.

SWOT Analysis It is a structured planning method used to evaluate the strengths, weaknesses, opportunities, and threats involved in a project, an initiative, or an organization or a part of them.

System It is a network of interacting components that cooperate to achieve the objectives of the system.[64]

Tablets It is a general-purpose computer contained in a single panel, with a touch screen as the input device.

[64] Deming, W. E. (1994). *The new economics for industry, government, education*. Boston, MA: MIT Press.

Task Order It is a supplemental contractual and obligatory document that usually includes the description of the tasks.[65]

Telematics It is the set of technical and methodological solutions adopted to allow the processing of remote data or to communicate with applications residing on remote computing systems and connected. It denotes the synergy between telecommunications and informatics. In this book, it is indicated as ICT.

Threat It is an adverse event that can cause a risk to become a loss. A threat may be a natural event such as an earthquake, flood, storm, or a human-made incident such as fire, power failure, sabotage, and so on.[66]

Throughput It is a metric on how quickly the service responds.

Time to Market In the process of development of new products, it is the time that elapses between the first phase of the concept of the new product and its launch on the market.

Total Cost Management (TCM) It is a business philosophy of managing the entire organization resources arid the activities that consume those resources. Operating costs in a TCM approach means focusing on the activities and the events, the circumstances, or the conditions that cause or drive these cost-consuming actions.

Total Cost of Ownership It is a metric taking into account the costs, all along with the lifecycle of a solution. Typically, it includes procurement costs, installation, testing, maintenance, use, and disposal at the end of the useful life.

Transaction It is the action of executing a function or an application. An example of a transaction is the execution of the purchase at a point of sale and the processing of authorization and clearing messages.

Trust It is the ability of two parties to define a positive relationship with a formal authentication of the two parties.

Ubiquitous Computing It is the omnipresence of computer-aided information processing. Information processing is integrated into everyday objects and activities far beyond personal computer and laptop and the paradigm of person-machine interaction there; Via the internet of things, persons are sometimes imperceptibly supported in their operations.

[65] businessdictionary.com. Accessed 20 June 2019.

[66] businessdictionary.com. Accessed 20 June 2019.

Validation It is a method to provide specific personal information to prove ownership of the identity for identity verification.

Value The end user defines the value. Conceptually, it is the relationship between benefits and cost/damage to a product or service. It is expressed in a product/service able to meet the customer's needs at a given price and at a given time.[67] It is also possible to talk about the value perceived by the customer as all the features of the product/service that the customer deems necessary and valuable. Any activity that consumes resources (including time) and does not create value is a waste (*muda* in Japanese).

Value-Added Network It is a decentralized polycentric network, which is characterized by complex mutual relationships between autonomous, legally independent actors. It forms an interest group of potential value creation partners who interact in standard processes if necessary. The creation of value creation networks is geared toward sustainable economic added value. Particular forms of value creation networks are referred to as business webs.

Value-Added System It is an association of companies that are in service relationships and exchange goods, information, services, and money with each other.

Value Chain It is a model of added value as a sequential, graded series of activities or processes, from development through production to marketing and services.

Value Engineering It is a systematic approach to reducing costs without reducing functions.

Value Network Mapping It is the identification and subsequent graphical representation of all the activities that are performed in the value network for a product/service or a family of products/services.

Value Network It is the process used to deliver a good or service. It is a set of activities required to design, order, manufacture, and supply (or provide in the case of a service) a given product or service. These activities cover the entire cycle of the product/service organization up to the end customer. An objective analysis of the value network is to classify tasks. The value network is the sequence of activities that brings value to the customer (and indirectly to the organization).

[67] Value Proposition—Open Risk Manual. www.openriskmanual.org/wiki/Value_Proposition. Accessed 30 May 2020.

Variance In statistics, it is the average of the squared deviations. It is a dispersion index.

Variations They are changes in the quantity or time value between cases caused by acts and not predictable.

Vertical and Horizontal Integrations Vertical integration is the implementation of information and management systems capable of interacting and exchanging information between subjects in the operational chain. Horizontal integration is the implementation of systems capable of interacting organizations, distributors, and partners of the same value network.

Virtual Reality It is a solution that simulates reality, replacing it with a digital environment, whose input is made possible by unique accessories that allow an operator to interact within virtual reality.

Virtualization It is the production of a virtual (instead of an actual) version, detached from the specific resources, such as a hardware platform, an operating system, a storage medium, or network resources.

Vision It is the expression of what would represent a success for the organization. The goal is to produce a mental image to strive to make sure that the organization provides the creative tensions between the current reality and the vision. Mission is how the organization must make progress toward the vision. Vision is an expression of what would represent a success for the organization. To be valuable, the whole organization should know and accept the vision. To implement the vision normally requires much effort and patience.

Visualization It is the representation of abstract data arising in administrative and production processes. Numbers are displayed in their context and a suitable visual form, for example as a graphic. This contextual representation is based on prioritization, which means that less meaningful data are omitted in the given context.

Voice of the Customer It is the customer's voice, or the voice of the citizen, in the case of public organizations.

Vulnerability They are the intrinsic properties of a system resulting in susceptibility to a risk that can lead to an event.

Wearable technologies They are solutions, developed based on the human body, which becomes natural support to make them work. These technologies detect and monitor the biological signals of the body and the emotional ones. This solution is valid for personal needs.

Working Capital It is the set of the financial resources invested by an organization in financing its current trading operations. They are usually expressed as the difference between current assets (receivables, inventory, and operating cash balances) and current liabilities (payables and short-term debt).[68]

Zero-Notice Event An event that cannot be forecasted so that preparations can be made before its impact. For example, an earthquake is a zero-notice event.

[68] Working Capital—Open Risk Manual. www.openriskmanual.org/wiki/Working_Capital. Accessed 30 May 2020.

References

Abdi, F., Shavarini, S., & Hoseini, S. (2006). Glean lean: How to use lean approach in services industries? *Journal of Services Research* [Special issue], *6*, 191–206.

Accenture. (2017). *The future of insurance distribution: New models for a digital customer* (Accenture Papers).

Accenture.com. (2018). *Identifying disruptive opportunities in insurance distribution* | Accenture. www.accenture.com/us-en/insight-insurance-distribution-marketing-consumer-study. Accessed 8 March 2020.

Afflerbach, P., Kastner, G., Krause, F., & Röglinger, M. (2014). The business value of process flexibility: An optimization model and its application in the service sector. *Business & Information Systems Engineering, 56*(4), 203–214. https://doi.org/10.1007/s10796-016-9678-2.

Ågerfalk, P. J. (2014). Insufficient theoretical contribution: A conclusive rationale for rejection? *European Journal of Information Systems, 23*(6), 593–599. https://doi.org/10.1057/ejis.2014.35.

Aggogeri, F., & Gentili, E. (2006). *Lean Six Sigma: la nuova frontiera per la qualità. La sinergia tra six sigma & lean production per un innovativo metodo di gestione & miglioramento dei processi industriali*. FrancoAngeli, Milan, Italy.

Agostini, L., & Filippini, R. (2019). Organizational and managerial challenges in the path toward Industry 4.0. *European Journal of Innovation Management, 22*, 406–421.

Ahmed, E. et al. (2017). The role of big data analytics in Internet of Things. *Computer Network.*

B. Nicoletti, *Insurance 4.0*, Palgrave Studies in Financial Services Technology, https://doi.org/10.1007/978-3-030-58426-9

Akroush, M., & Mahadin, B. (2019). An intervariable approach to customer satisfaction and loyalty in the internet service market. *Internet Research, 29*, 772–798.

Albrecher, H., Filipović, D., Koch-Medina, P., Schmeiser, H., & Loisel, S. (2019). *Insurance: Models, digitization and data science*. Research Paper Series. Swiss Finance Institute.

Albrecht, C., Dean, D., & Hansen, J. (2005). Marketplace and technology standards for B2B e-commerce: Progress, challenges, and the state of the art. *Information and Management*, 42.

Albrecht, P. (2017). Bedroht Big Data Grundprinzipien der Versicherung? (II.). *Zeit-schrift fuer Versicherungswesen* (6).

Allianz. (2016). *Blockchain technology successfully piloted by Allianz Risk Transfer and Nephila for catastrophe swap*. www.agcs.allianz.com/about-us/news/blockchain-technology-successfully-piloted-by-allianz-risk-transfer-and-nephila-for-catastrophe-swap. Accessed 30 May 2020.

Allianz. (2017). Allianz global automotive offers specific insurance products for the new BMW 5 series. *Allianz Press Release*. www.allianz-worldwide-partners.de/business/images/Pressemitteilung_Allianz_BMW5er_Launch_Paket-en.pdf. Accessed 10 July 2019.

Allianz. (2017). *Bits on bytes*. www.allianz.com/en/press/news/business/news_to_use/171009-bits-on-bytes.html. Accessed 10 July 2019.

Almoatazbillah, H. (2012). The value proposition concept in marketing: How customers perceive the value delivered by firms. A study of customer perspectives on supermarkets in Southampton in the United Kingdom. *International Journal of Marketing Studies, 4*(3), 68.

Altuntas, M., & Uhl, P. (2016). *Industrielle Exzellenz in der Versicherungswirtschaft*. Wiesbaden, Germany. Fachmedien: Springer. https://doi.org/10.1007/978-3-658-12033-7.

Amit, R., & Zott, C. (2012). Creating value through business model innovation. *MIT Sloan Management Review, 53*(3), 41–49.

Anchen, J., & Dowe, A. (2019). Advanced analytics unlocking new frontiers in P&C insurance. *Sigma, 4*, 2–30.

Anchen, J., Frey, A., & Kirova, M. (2015). *Life insurance in the digital age: Fundamental transformation ahead*. Swiss Re sigma No. 6/2015. media.swissre.com/documents/sigma6_2015_en.pdf. Accessed 26 January 2017.

Anon. (2016). *Innovation in insurance: How technology is changing the industry*. www.iif.com/system/files/32370132_insurance_innovation_report_2016. Accessed 8 March 2020.

Antony, J. (2006). Six Sigma for service processes. *Business Process Management Journal., 12*(2), 234–248.

Antony, J., Kumar, M., & Byung, R. C. (2007). Six sigma in service organizations. Benefits, challenges & difficulties, common myths, empirical observations & success factors. *International Journal of Quality & Reliability Management, 24*(3): 294–311.

Armbrust, M. et al. (2009). *Above the Clouds: A Berkeley view of Cloud Computing* (Technical Report No.UCB/EECS-2009-28).

Armbrüster, C. (2020). New technologies. Political, legal, economic and factual impact in Germany. *ZVersWiss*. https://doi.org/10.1007/s12297-020-00460-2. Accessed 30 May 2020.

Armrobust, M. (2006). Competition in two-sided markets. *RAND Journal of Economics, 37*(3), 668–691.

Arnold, U. (1997). *Beschaffungsmanagement*. Stuttgart, Germany: Schäffer-Poeschel Verlag.

Ashton, K. (2009). That 'internet of things' thing. *RFID Journal, 22*(7), 97–114.

Asian Insurance Review. (2016, June). How new technology is shaping the future of underwriting and underwriters. *Asian Insurance Review*, 76–77.

Atlas-mag.net. (2017). *Insurance fraud detection and cost to industry*. www.atlas-mag.net/en/article/insurance-fraud-detection-and-cost-to-industry. Accessed 8 March 2020.

Aymerich, F. M. Fenu, G., & Surcis, S. (2008, August). An approach to a cloud computing network. In *2008 First International Conference on the Applications of Digital Information and Web Technologies* (ICADIWT) IEEE, 113–118.

Back, A. Berghaus, S., & Kaltenrieder, B. (2016). *Digital Maturity and Transformation Report 2016*. IWI-HSG & Crosswalk. Accessed 30 May 2020.

Badoc, M. (1986). *Marketing pour le banque et l'assurance europeennes*. Paris, France: Les Editions d'Organization.

Baecke, P., & Bocca, L. (2017). The value of vehicle telematics data in insurance risk selection processes. *Decision Support Systems, 98*, 69–79. https://doi.org/10.1016/j.dss.2017.04.009.

Baesens, B., Bapna, R., Marsden, J. R., Vanthienen, J., & Zhao, J. L. (2016). Transformational issues of big data and analytics. In M. J. Baker & B. Nicoletti. et.al. (1988). *L'impresa mondiale: Nuove strategie di produzione*. FrancoAngeli, Milano, Italy.

Bakos, Y., & Katsamakas, E. (2008). Design and ownership of two-sided networks: implications for internet platforms. *Journal of Management Information Systems, 25*(2), 171–202. https://doi.org/10.2753/MIS0742-1222250208.

Barile, S., Lusch, R., Reynoso, J., Saviano, M., & Spohrer, J. (2016). Systems, networks, and ecosystems in service research. *Journal of Service Management, 27*(4), 652–674. https://doi.org/10.1108/JOSM-09-2015-0268.

Bartikowski, B., & Walsh, G. (2014). Attitude contagion in consumer opinion platforms: Posters and lurkers. *Electronic Markets, 24*(3), 207–217. https://doi.org/10.1007/s12525-013-0149-z.

Barwitz, N., Maas, P., Block, D., & Nu¨tzenadel, C. (2016). *Die customer journey in einer multioptionalen Welt.* I.VW-HSG & Synpulse Schweiz AG.

Basole, R. C., & Karla, J. (2011). On the evolution of mobile platform ecosystem structure and strategy. *Business & Information Systems Engineering, 53*(5), 313–322. https://doi.org/10.1007/s12599-011-0174-4.

Bauer, A., Groninger, Y., Scheidt, J., Garcia, R., & Rimpo, E. (2016). *Dying, surviving or thriving: Strategic analysis of the future Swiss Insurance Market.* EY, swissfinte.ch/wp-content/uploads/2016/07/dying-surviving-or-thriving-english-study-1.pdf. Accessed 3 October 2016.

Bauer, W., Schlund, S., Marrenbach, D., & Ganschar, O. (2014). *Industrie 4.0: Volkswirtschaftliches Potenzial für Deutschland.* Berlin: BITKOM.

Baumöl, U., Hollebeek, L., & Jung, R. (2016). Dynamics of customer interaction on social media platforms. *Electronic Markets, 26*(3), 199–202. https://doi.org/10.1007/s12525-016-0227-0.

Becker, L., & Pousttchi, K. (2013). Requirements for personalized m-commerce—What drives consumers' use of social networks? *Journal of Electronic Commerce in Organizations, 11*(4), 19–36.

Beimborn, D., Miletzki, T., & Wenzel, S. (2011). Platform as a Service (PaaS). *Business & Information Systems Engineering, 53*(6), 313–322. https://doi.org/10.1007/s12599-011-0183-3.

Belk, R. W. (2013). Extended self in a digital world. *Journal of Consumer Research, 40*(3), 477–500. https://doi.org/10.1086/671052.

Belozyorov, S., Sokolovska, E., & Kim, Y. (2020). Fintech as a precondition for transformations on global financial markets. *Foresight and STI Governance, 14*(2), 23–35. https://doi.org/10.17323/2500-2597.2020.2.23.35.

Benbasat, I., Goldstein, D. K., & Mead, M. (1987). The case research strategy in studies of information systems. *MIS Quarterly, 11*(3), 369–386. https://doi.org/10.2307/248684.

Benlian, A., Hilkert, D., & Hess, T. (2015). How open is this platform? The meaning and measurement of platform openness from the complementors' perspective. *Journal of Information Technology, 30*(3), 209–228. https://doi.org/10.1057/jit.2015.6.

Berger, D., Broer, P., & Pankoke, D. (2016). Digitization in life insurance: A prerequisite for success in spite of low interest rates. *I. VW HSG Trendmonitor, 1*, 15–19.

Berger, D., Broer, P., & Pankoke, D. (2016). Digitization in life insurance: A prerequisite for success despite low interest rates. *I. VW HSG Trendmonitor, 1*, 15–19.

Berliner, B. (1982). *Limits of insurability of risks*. Upper Saddle River, NJ: Prentice Hall.

Berman, B. (2012). 3-D printing: The new industrial revolution. *Business Horizons, 55*(2), 155–162.

Bertels, T. (2003). *Rath & Robust's six sigma leadership handbook*. Hoboken, NJ: John Wiley & Sons.

Besnik Zekaj, B. (2016). Marketing in insurance industry, marketing functions in insurance industry. *European Journal of Multidisciplinary Studies, 1*(5), 33–39.

Bharadwaj, A., El Sawy, O. A., Pavlou, P. A., & Venkatraman, N. (2013). Digital business strategy: Toward a next generation of insights. *MIS Quarterly, 37*(2), 471–482. https://doi.org/10.25300/MISQ/2013/37:2.3. Accessed 4 May 2020.

Bialek, C. (2018). Deutsche Firmen wollen mit dem Facebook-Button konkurrieren. *Handelsblatt*. www.handelsblatt.com/unternehmen/it-medien/generalschluessel-fuer-das-internet-deutsche-firmen-wollen-mit-dem-facebook-button-konkurrieren/21101098.html. Accessed 10 July 2019.

Bieck, C., Marshall, A., & Patel, S. (2014). *Digital reinvention: Trust, transparency and technology in the insurance world of tomorrow*. IBM Institute for Business Value, public.dhe.ibm.com/common/ssi/ecm/gb/en/gbe03589usen/GBE03589USEN.PDF. Accessed 20 March 2020.

Bieck, C., & Tjioe L.-H. (2015). *Capturing hearts, minds and market share: How connected companies are improving customer retention*. IBM Institute for Business Value. www-935.ibm.com/services/us/gbs/thoughtleadership/insuranceretention/. Accessed 20 March 2020.

Bieger, T., & Krys, C. (2011). Die Dynamik von Geschaftsmodellen. In T. Bieger, D. zu Knyphausen-Aufsess & C. Krys (Eds.), *Innovative Geschaftsmodelle*. 19. Berlin, Germany: Springer.

Bieger, T., & Reinhold, S. (2011). Das wertbasierte Geschaftsmodell — Ein aktualisier-ter Strukturierungsansatz. In T. Bieger, D. zu Knyphausen-Aufsess, & C. Krys (Eds.), *Innovative Geschaftsmodelle* (pp. 13–70). Berlin, Germany: Springer.

Biener, C., & Eling, M. (2012). Insurability in microinsurance markets: An analysis of problems and potential solutions. *The Geneva Papers on Risk and Insurance—Issues and Practice, 37*(1), 77–107.

Biener, C., Eling, M., & Wirfs, J. H. (2015). Insurability of cyber risk: An empirical analysis. *The Geneva Papers on Risk and Insurance—Issues and Practice, 40*(1), 131–158.

Biihler, P., & Maas, P. (2017). Transformation von Geschaftsmodellen in einer digitali-sierten Welt. In M. Bruhn & K. Hadwich (Eds.), *Dienstleistungen 4.0. Geschaftsmodelle — Wertschopfung - Transformation*. Band 2. (pp. 43–70). Wiesbaden, Germany: Springer Gabler.

Bijmolt, T. H. A., Leeflang, P. S. H., Block, F., Eisenbeiss, M., Hardie, B. G. S., Lemmens, A., et al. (2010). Analytics for customer engagement. *Journal of Service Research, 13*(3), 341–356. https://doi.org/10.1177/1094670510375603.

Bitkom & KPMG (2016) *Mit Daten Werte schaffen.* cdn2.hubspot.net/hubfs/571339/LandingPages-PDF/kpmg-mdws-201-sec.pdf. Accessed 30 May 2020.

Bolderdijk, J. W., Knockaert, J., Steg, L., & Verhoef, E. (2011). Effects of Pay-As-You-Drive vehicle insurance on young drivers' speed choice: Results of a Dutch field experiment. *Accident Analysis and Prevention, 43*(3), 1181–1186.

Bonisone, P. P., Subbu, R., & Aggour, K. S. (2002, May). Evolutionary optimization of fuzzy decision systems for automated insurance underwriting. In 2002 IEEE World Congress on Computational Intelligence. *2002 IEEE International Conference on Fuzzy Systems. FUZZ-IEEE'02. Proceedings* (Cat. No. 02CH37291), Vol. 2, 1003–1008. IEEE.

Boston Consulting Group. (2017, July). Beyond the hype. www.bcg.com/publications/2017/technology-digital-beyond-hype.aspx. Accessed 20 June 2020.

Botthof, A. (2015). Zukunft der Arbeit im Kontext von Automatik und Industrie 4.0. In A. Botthof & E. A. Hartmann (Eds.), *Zukunft der arbeit in industrie 4.0* (pp. 3–8). Berlin, Germany: Springer.

Boucher, J., & Inoussa, R. (2014). A-posteriori ratemaking with panel data. *ASTIN Bulletin, 44*(3), 587–612. https://doi.org/10.1017/asb.2014.11.

Boudreau, K. J. (2010). Open platform strategies and innovation: Granting access vs. devolving control. *Management Science, 56*(10), 1849–1872. https://doi.org/10.1287/mnsc.1100.1215.

Bovaird, T. (2016). The ins & outs of outsourcing & in procurement: What have we learnt from the past 30 years? *Public Money & Management, 36*(1), 67–74.

Boyer, M., & Nyce, C. M. (2011). Market growth and barriers to entry: Evidence from the title insurance industry. *Insurance Risk Management., 78,* 283–315.

Boyer, M. M., Jacquier, E., & van Norden, S. (2012). Are underwriting cycles real and forecastable? *The Journal of Risk and Insurance, 79*(4), 995–1015. https://doi.org/10.1111/j.1539-6975.2011.01458.x.

Brandon-Jones, A., & Kauppi, K. (2018). Examining the antecedents of the technology acceptance model within e-procurement. *International Journal of Operations & Production Management, 38*(1), 22–42.

Brat, E., Clark, P., Mehrotra, P., Stange, A., & Boyer-Chammard, C. (2014). *Bringing big data to life: four opportunities for companies.* The Boston Consulting Group, www.bcgperspectives.com/content/articles/insurance_digital_economy_bringing_big_data_life/. Accessed 30 May 2020.

Braun, A., & Schreiber, F. (2018). *The current InsurTech landscape: Business models and disruptive potential.* www.ivw.unisg.ch/. Accessed 8 March 2020.

Braunwarth, K., Kaiser, M., & Müller, A. (2010). Economic evaluation and optimization of the degree of automation in insurance processes. *Business & Information Systems Engineering, 52*(1), 29–39. https://doi.org/10.1007/s12599-009-0088-6.

Breading, M. (2012). *The drive to digitization in insurance: Turning big paper into big profit.* SMA. www.the-digital-insurer.com/wp-content/uploads/2014/05/183-The-Drive-to-Digitization-in-Insurance.pdf. Accessed 3 October 2016.

Brealey, R. A., Myers, S. C., Allen, F., & Sandri, S. (2007). *Principi di Finanza Aziendale.* Milano, McGraw-Hill: Quinta edizione.

Brousseau, E., & Penard, T. (2007). The economics of digital business models: a framework for analyzing the economics of platforms. *Review of Network Economics, 6*(2), 81–114. https://doi.org/10.2202/1446-9022.1112.

Bughin, J., LaBerge, L., & Mellbye, A. (2017). The case for digital reinvention. *McKinsey Quarterly.* https://goo.gl/iqb7rJ.

Burgelman, R., Christensen, C., & Wheelwright, S. (2008). *Strategic management of technology and innovation* (5th ed.). New York, NY: McGraw-Hill/Irwin.

Cant, B., Khadikar, A., Ruiter, A., Bronebakk, J. B., Coumaros, J., Buvat, J., & Gupta, A. (2016). *Smart contracts in financial services: Getting from hype to reality.* Capgemini Consulting. www.capgemini-consulting.com/resource-file-access/resource/pdf/smart-contracts.pdf. Accessed 30 May 2020.

Capgemini, M. E. H., & Efma, A. Q. (2018). World insurance report 2018. Available online at https://www.worldinsurancereport.com/wp-content/uploads/sites/6/2018/10/World-Insurance-Report_2018.pdf. Accessed 10 July 2019.

Cappiello, A. (2018). *Technology and the insurance industry: Re-configuring the competitive landscape* (1st ed, pp. 119). Cham: Springer. ISBN-10: 3319747118.

Cappiello, A. (2020). The digital (r)evolution of insurance business models. *American Journal of Economics and Business Administration.* https://doi.org/10.3844/ajebasp.2020.

Cash. (2016). *Helvetia Ubernimmt 70 percent am Hypothekenvermittler Moneypark.* www.cash.ch/news/boersenticker-firmen/helvetia-ubernimmt-70-am-hypothekenvermittler-moneypark-522954. Accessed 30 May 2020.

Cassab, H., & MacLachlan, D. L. (2009). A consumer-based view of multichannel service. *Journal of Service Management, 20*(1), 52–75. https://doi.org/10.1108/09564230910936850. Accessed 40 May 2020.

Catlin, T., & Lorenz, J. (2017). *Digital disruption in insurance: Cutting through the noise.* Mckinsey.com. www.mckinsey.com/~/media/McKinsey/Indust

ries/Financialpercent20Services/Ourpercent20Insights/Timepercent20forpercent20insurancepercent20companiespercent20topercent20facepercent20digitalpercent20reality/Digital-disruption-in-Insurance.ashx. Accessed 8 March 2020.

Catlin, T., Hartmann, R., Segev, I., & Tentis, R. (2015). *The making of a digital insurer: The path to enhanced profitability, lower costs and robuster customer loyalty*. McKinsey & Company. www.mckinsey.com/industries/financial-services/our-insights/the-making-of-a-digital-insurer. Accessed 30 March 2020.

Catlin, T., & Lorenz, J. (2016). *Digital disruption in insurance: Cutting through the noise*. McKinsey Digital. www.mckinsey.com/~/media/McKinsey/Industries/Financial%20Services/Our%20Insights/Time%20for%20insurance%20companies%20to%20face%20digital%20reality/Digital-disruption-in-Insurance.ashx. Accessed 10 July 2019.

Catlin, T., Lorenz, J., Nandan, J., Sharma, S., & Waschto, A. (2018). *Insurance beyond digital: The rise of ecosystems and platforms*. McKinsey & Company. www.mckinsey.com/industries/financial-services/our-insights/insurance-beyond-digitalthe-rise-of-ecosystems-and-platforms.

Catlin, T., McGranahan, D., & Ray, S. (2013). *Winning share and customer loyalty in auto insurance*. McKinsey & Company. de.scribd.com/document/306175438/Winning-Share-and-Customer-Loyalty-in-Auto-Insurance. Accessed 8 March 2020.

CB Insights. (2016). *Google Insurance Tech investments*. goo.gl/dkTfFm.

CB Insights. (2017). Oscar health insurance strategy teardown. goo.gl/zx6R5i.

CB Insights. (2017, January). *Insurance tech startups raise $1.7B across 173 deals in 2016*. www.cbinsights.com/research/2016-insurance-tech-funding/d. Accessed 8 March 2020.

CB Insights. (2018). *How blockchain could disrupt insurance*. www.cbinsights.com/research/blockchain-insurance-disruption/. Accessed 8 March 2020.

CB Insights Research. (2018). *How blockchain could disrupt insurance*. www.cbinsights.com/research/blockchain-insurance-disruption/. Accessed 8 March 2020.

Ceccagnoli, M., Forman, C., Huang, P., & Wu, D. J. (2012). Cocreation of value in a platform ecosystem: the case of enterprise software. *MIS Quarterly, 36*(1), 263–290.

Charlotte, M. (2018). *Un bilan de la loi Hamon 2 ans après -CSCA*. CSCA. www.csca.fr/webzine/actualites/le-secteur/un-bilan-de-la-loi-hamon-2-ans-apres. Accessed 8 March 2020.

Chathoth, P. (2007). The impact of information technology on hotel operations, service management and transaction costs: A conceptual framework for full-service hotel firms. *International Journal of Hospitality Management, 26*(2), 395–408.

Chen, D., Preston, D., & Swink, M. (2015). How the use of big data analytics affects value creation in supply chain management. *Journal of Management Information Systems, 32*(4), 4–39. https://doi.org/10.1080/07421222.2015.1138364. Accessed 8 March 2020.

Chen, J., Tsou, H., & Huang, A. (2009). Service delivery innovation: Antecedents and impact on firm performance. *Journal of Service Research, 12*(1), 36–55. https://doi.org/10.1177/1094670509338619. Accessed 8 March 2020.

Chester, A., Clarke, R., & Libarikian, A. (2016). *Transforming into an analytics-driven insurance carrier*. McKinsey & Company. www.mckinsey.com/industries/financial-services/our-insights/transforming-into-an-analytics-driven-insurance-carrier. Accessed 8 March 2020.

Chester, A., Hoffman, N., Johansson, S., & Braad Olesen, P. (2018). *Digital insurance. Commercial Lines InsurTech: A pathway to digital*. McKinsey & Company.

Chiesa, G. (2017, December). Switch — On. Bereit fur die digitale Therapie?. *Vortrag anlasslich der 6. Jahrestagung des Luzerner Kongress Gesellschaftspolitik*. Luzern.

Chishti, S., & Barberis, J. (2016). *The FinTech book: The financial technology handbook for investors, entrepreneurs and visionaries* (1st ed., pp. 312). Chichester, UK: John Wiley and Sons Ltd. ISBN-10: 1119218888.

Christl, W., & Spiekermann, S. (2016). *Networks of control: A report on corporate surveillance, digital tracking, big data & privacy*. Vienna: Facultas. www.wu.ac.at/fileadmin/wu/d/i/ec/Press___Events/Books-Press_Release/Networks_of_Control.pdf. Accessed 10 July 2019.

Cisco. (2017). *Digital transformation for the insurance industry*. goo.gl/yUbCAE.

Clarke, I., & Flaherty, T. (2003). Web-based B2B portals. *Industrial Marketing Management, 32*, 15–23.

Coelho, F., & Easingwood, C. (2005). Determinants of multiple channel choice in financial services: An environmental uncertainty model. *Journal of Services Market., 19*, 199–211. https://doi.org/10.1108/08876040510605235.

Coelho, F., & Easingwood, C. (2008). An exploratory study into the drivers of channel change. *European Journal Market., 42*, 1005–1022. https://doi.org/10.1108/03090560810891118.

Coelho, F., Easingwood, C., & Coelho, A. (2003). Exploratory evidence of channel performance in single vs multiple channel strategies. *International Journal of Retail Distribution Management, 31*, 561–573. https://doi.org/10.1108/09590550310503294.

CoinDesk. (2018). *A (short) guide to blockchain consensus protocols*. CoinDesk. www.coindesk.com/short-guide-blockchain-consensus-protocols/.

Constantiou, I. D., & Kallinikos, J. (2015). New games, new rules: big data and the changing context of strategy. *Journal of Information Technology, 30*(1), 44–57. https://doi.org/10.1057/jit.2014.17. Accessed 8 March 2020.

Corlosquet-Habart, M. & Janssen, J. (2018). *Big data for insurance companies*. https://www.books.google.it/books?isbn=9781786300737. Accessed 8 March 2020.

Corten, P. A. (2018). *Implementation of blockchain powered smart contracts in governmental services. Master of science in complex systems*. Engineering and Management. Faculty of Technology, Policy and Management.

Cox, J. (2017). The sharing economy is failing because people can't be trusted. *The Independent*. www.independent.co.uk/voices/uber-airbnb-sharing-economy-people-cant-be-trusteda7867301.html. Accessed 8 March 2020.

Crawford, M. (2017). The insurance implications of blockchain. *RM Magazine Online*. www.rmmagazine.com/2017/03/01/the-insurance-implications-of-blockchain. Accessed 10 July 2019.

Crosby, M., Nachiappan, Pattanayak, P. Verma, S., & Kalyanaraman, V. (2016). Blockchain technology: Beyond bitcoin. *Applied Innovation Review 2*. scet.berkeley.edu/wp-content/uploads/AIR-2016-Blockchain.pdf. Accessed 30 May 2020.

Cukier, K., & Mayer-Schenberger, V. (2013). The rise of big data: How it's changing the way we think about the world. *Foreign Affairs, 92*, 28–40.

Cusano, J. (2016, September 7). Intelligent automation is set to transform insurance underwriting. insuranceblog.accenture.com/intelligent-automation-is-set-to-transform-insurance-underwriting. Accessed 8 March 2020.

Cutter.com. (2018). *Insurtech: Reinventing the insurance industry—Opening statement | Cutter Consortium*. www.cutter.com/article/insurtech-reinventing-insurance-industry-opening-statement-497341. Accessed 08 March 2020.

Dai, H., & Salam, A. F. (2014). Does service convenience matter? An empirical assessment of service quality, service convenience and exchange relationship in electronic mediated environment. *Electronic Markets, 24*(4), 269–284. https://doi.org/10.1007/s12525-014-0170-x.

Dai, J., & Vasarhelyi, M. (2017). Toward blockchain-based accounting and assurance. *Journal of Information Systems, 31*(3), 5–21.

Daniel, T. (2018). *Interner Runoff: Ergo verwaltet mit IBM seine Altpolicen. Versicherungswirtschaft Heute*. versicherungswirtschaft-heute.de/unternehmen-management/interner-run-off-ergo-verwaltet-mit-ibm-seiner-altpolicen/. Accessed 10 July 2019.

Danny, V. (2016). *Disruption in insurance*. Cisco. goo.gl/rxj8oW.

Dans, E. (2015, August, 18). Internet of things, sector seguros y la confianza del customere. www.enriquedans.com/2015/08/internet-of-things-sector-seguros-y-la-confianza-del-customere.html. Accessed 8 March 2020.

Davenport, T. H., & Dyché, J. (2013). Big data in big companies. *International Institute for Analytics, 3*.

Davenport, T. H., & Harris, J. G. (2007). *Competing on analytics: The new science of winning*. Cambridge, MA: Harvard Business School Press.

Davis, F. D. (1989). Perceived usefulness, perceived ease of use, and user acceptance of information technology. *MIS Quarterly, 13*(3), 319–340.

de Reuver, M., Sørensen, C., & Basole, R. C. (2018). The digital platform: A research agenda. *Journal of Information Technology, 33*(2), 1–12. https://doi.org/10.1057/s41265-016-0033-3. Accessed 8 March 2020.

Dehning, B., Richardson, V. J., & Zmud, R. W. (2003). The value relevance of announcements of transformational information technology investments, *MIS Quarterly*.

Deloitte. (2014). *Industry 4.0: Challenges and solutions for the digital transformation and use of exponential technologies*. www2.deloitte.com. Accessed 18 December 2018.

Deloitte. (2016). Companies on the brink—Disrupt or be disrupted. www2.deloitte.com/content/dam/Deloitte/ke/Documents/financial-services/FSI-Insurance%20Final.pdf. Accessed 10 July 2019.

Deloitte. (2018). *A catalyst for change: How Fintech has sparked a revolution in insurance*. www2.deloitte.com/content/dam/Deloitte/global/Documents/Financial-Services/gx-fsi-cataylst-for-change.pdf. Accessed 8 March 2020.

Deloitte. (2018). www.2.deloitte.com/content/dam/insights/us/articles/innovation-in-insurance-iot/DUP2824_IoT_Insurance_vFINAL_6.6.16.pdf. Accessed 8 March 2020.

Deloitte Malta. (2018). *Blockchain: A game changer for audit processes?* | Deloitte Malta | Audit & Assurance. www.2.deloitte.com/mt/en/pages/audit/articles/mt-blockchain-a-game-changer-for-audit.html?id=gx:2sm:3li:4gx-blockchain-np::6Audit:20180703170500:Global&linkId=53758389. Accessed 8 March 2020.

Derikx, S., de Reuver, M., & Kroesen, M. (2016). Can privacy concern for insurance of connected cars be compensated? *Electronic Markets, 26*(1), 73–81. https://doi.org/10.1007/s12525-015-0211-0.

Dietl, H. (2010). Erfolgsstrategien im Plattformwettbewerb. *Zeitschiftfür betriebswirtschaftliche Forschung, Special Issue, 62*, 63–83.

Discovery. (n.d.). *Save on your insurance costs by driving well*. www.discovery.co.za/car-and-home-insurance/vitalitydrive-rewards. Accessed 8 March 2020.

Dobrin, C. (2014), Industry 4.0, M2m, Iot&S—All equal? *Acta Universitatis Cibiniensis*. Technical Series, v 64, n 1, 40-5, Nov. 2014; ISSN: 1583-7149; https://doi.org/10.2478/aucts-2014-0008; De Gruyter Open, Romania.

Doerner, K., & Edelman, D. (2015). *What 'digital' means*. McKinsey & Company. www.mckinsey.com/industries/high-tech/our-insights/what-digital-means. Accessed 30 March 2020.

Doherty, N., & Posey, L. (1998). On the value of a checkup: Adverse selection, moral hazard and the value of information. *The Journal of Risk and Insurance, 65*(2), 189–211.

Donham, P. (2007). *Aligning IT to business processes: How BPM is complementing ERP & custom applications*. Aberdeen Group. www.aberdeen.com/summary/report/benchmark/4097-RA-Align-Business.asp. Accessed 20 January 2019.

Donnelly, J., Berry, L. L., & Thompson, T. W. (1985). *Marketing financial services: A strategic vision*. New York: Dow Jones Irwin.

Drath, R. (2014). Industrie 4.0. *Eine Einführung. Open Automation, 3,* 2–7.

Drummer, D., Jerenz, A. P., Siebelt, P., & Thaten, M. (2016). *FinTech: Challenges and opportunities-how digitization is transforming the financial sector*. Dusseldorf, Germany: McKinsey & Company.

Dumm, R., & Hoyt, R. (2002): Insurance distribution channels: Markets in transition. *38th Annual Seminar of the International Insurance Society 2002*, Singapore.

Durgesh, P., & Sharma, M. K. (2009). Cloud Computing. *CSI Communication, 32*(10), 10–13.

Eckstein, A., & Liebetrau, A. (2019). *Insurance & Innovation 2019*. Karlsruhe, Germany: VVW GmbH; Auflage.

Egan, R., Cartagena, S., Mohamed, R., Gosrani, V., Grewal, J., et al. (2019). Cyber operational risk scenarios for insurance companies. *British Actuarial Journal, 24,* 1–34. https://doi.org/10.1017/S1357321718000284.

Eiglier, P., & Langeard, E. (1987). *Servuction: le Marketing des Services* (1st ed., pp. 205). Paris FR: McGraw-Hill. ISBN-10: 2840740338.

Eisenhardt, K. M. (1989). Building theories from case study research. *The Academy of Management Review, 14*(4), 532–550.

Eisenmann, T., Parker, G., & Alstyne, M. W. V. (2006). Strategies for two-sided markets. *Harvard Business Review, 84*(10), 1–11.

El Sawy, O. A., & Pereira, F. (2013). *Business modelling in the dynamic digital space, an ecosystem approach*. New York, NY: Springer.

Eling, M. (2016). *Gesundheit 2020+: Aktuelle strategische Herausforderungen und Handlungsfelder in der sozialen Krankenversicherung*. St. Gallen: Institut filr Versicherungswirtschaft der Universitat St. Gallen.

Eling, M., & Lehmann, M. (2018). The impact of digitization on the insurance value chain and the insurability of risks. *The Geneva Papers on Risk and Insurance-Issues and Practice, 43,* 359–396. https://doi.org/10.1057/s41288-017-0073-0.

Eling, M., & Schmeiser, H. (2012). Schaden- und Leistungsmanagement. In W. Ackermann, & H. Schmeiser (Hrsg.), Versicherungswirtschaft & Versiche-rungsmanagement (pp. 125–157). *Berufsbildungsverband der Versiche-rungswirtschaft*. Bern, Switzerland.

Eling, M., & Schnell, W. (2016). What do we know about cyber risk and cyber risk insurance? *The Journal of Risk Finance, 17*(5), 474–491.

Elliott, A. (2017, December). *The Internet of Things is changing the way we view the world*. www.zurich.com/en/knowledge/articles/2017/12/the-internet-of-things-is-changing-the-way-we-view-the-world.

Eminente, G., & Nicoletti, B. (1985). *Strategia organizzazionale & sviluppo tecnologico*. Bologna, Italy: Il Mulino.

Eric W., & Sleigh, E. W. (2018, May 25). After GDPR, what's next for technology companies? *Thomson Reuters*.

Erixon, F., & van der Marel, E. (2011). *What is driving the rise in health care expenditures? An inquiry into the nature and causes of the cost disease* (ECIPE Working Paper 5).

EU – European Union. (2009). Directive 2009/138/EC of the European Parliament and of the Council of 25 November 2009, Section 3, "Own Funds." https://eur-lex.europa.eu/LexUriServ/LexUriServ.do?uri=OJ:L:2009:335:0001:0155:en:PDF. Accessed 10 July 2019.

European Commission Justice. (2016). *Protection of personal data*. https://ec.europa.eu/justice/data-protection/index_en.htm. Accessed 30 March 2020.

Evans, D. S. (2003). Some empirical aspects of multi-sided platform industries. *Review of Network Economics, 2*(3), 191–209.

Evans, D. S., Hagiu, A., & Schmalensee, R. (2006). *Invisible engines: How software platforms drive innovation and transform industries*. Cambridge, MA: MIT Press.

Evers-Wolk, M., Jacobs, M., & Oertel, B. (2018). Wirtschaftliche Aspekte. In U. Meidert et al. (Hrsg.), *Quantified Self — Schnittstelle zwischen Lifestyle und Me-dizin* (pp. 151–175). Ziirich: vdf Hochschulverlag AG.

EY. (2015). *Mobile technology in insurance*. goo.gl/MPXdDh.

EY. (2015). *The future of health insurance*. goo.gl/28MsfN.

EY. (2016). *PAYL—Wearable trends*. goo.gl/86Km45.

EY (2017). *Digital transformation in insurance*. goo.gl/JwFJyW.

EY. (2017). *The evolution in self-driving vehicles*. goo.gl/YJCSGP.

EY (2018). *Can commercial companies transform, cut costs and accelerate growth?*

Farnung, A. (2014). *Die Folgen der Digitalisierung in der Versicherungsbranche*. 3C Dialog. www.vbw-bayern.de/Redaktion/Frei-zugaengliche-Medien/Abteilungen-GS/Planung-und-Koordination/2017/Downloads/Digitalisierung-in-der-Versicherungswirtschaft.pdf. Accessed 10 July 2019.

Farny, D. (2005). *Versicherungsbetriebslehre*. Karlsruhe: Versicherungswirtschaft., Karlsruhe, Germany.

Farny, D. (2011). *Versicherungsbetriebslehre* (5th ed.). Karlsruhe, Germany: Verlag Versiche-rungswirtschaft GmbH.

Fayyad, U., Piatetsky-Shapiro, G., & Smyth, P. (1996). From data mining to knowledge discovery in databases. *AI Magazine, 17*(3), 37–54.

Fearon, C., & Philip, G. (2005). Managing expectations and benefits: A model for electronic trading and EDI in the insurance industry. *Journal of Information Technology, 20*(3), 177–186. https://doi.org/10.1057/palgrave.jit.2000036. Accessed 08 March 2020.

Federal Bureau of Investigation. (2017). *Insurance fraud*. www.fbi.gov/stats-services/publications/insurance-fraud. Accessed 8 March 2020.

Filali, N., & Benichou, L. (2016). Blockchain: « L'assurance traditionnelle pourrait être menacée par de nouveaux entrants ». *L'Argus de l'Assurance.*

Filipova-Neumann, L., & Welzel, P. (2010). Reducing asymmetric information in insurance markets: Cars with black boxes. *Telematics and Informatics, 27*(4), 394–403.

Finaccord. (2013). *Aggregation metrics: Consumer approaches to insurance comparison sites in Europe*. www.finaccord.com/press-release_2013_aggregation-metrics_consumer-approaches-to-online-insurance-comparison-sites-in-europe_channels-used-to-buy-insurance.htm. Accessed 30 March 2020.

Fjeldstadt, Ø. D., & Ketels, C. H. M. (2006). Competitive advantage and the value network configuration: making decisions at a Swedish life insurance company. *Long Range Planning, 39*(2), 109–131. https://doi.org/10.1016/j.lrp.2006.05.001. Accessed 8 March 2020.

Fleisch, E., Weinberger, M., & Wortmann, F. (2015). Geschäftsmodelle im Internet der Dinge. *Zeitschrift für Betriebswirtschaftliche Forschung, 67*(4), 444–464.

Fonseca, L. M. (2018). Industry 4.0 and the digital society: Concepts, dimensions and envisioned benefits, *Sciendo, 12*(1), 386–397.

Foster, M. (2019, January). *The cognitive enterprise: Part 1—The journey to AI & the rise of platform-centric business architectures*. IBM Institute for Business Value. https://www.ibm.com/business/value/cogentpart1. Accessed 30 June 2019.

Freysoldt, T., Johansson, S., Korwin-Szymanowska, C., Münstermann, B., & Vogelgesang, U. (2018). *Evolving insurance cost structures. How incumbents can adapt and save to remain competitive in the digital age. Insurance practice.* McKinsey & Company.

Fricke, T. (2019). *Insurance 4.0. Chancen und Herausforderungen für die Versicherungswirtschaft durch die Digitalisierung*. GRIN Verlag, Munich, Germany.

G7-10 WG. (1997, April). *Electronic commerce better practice, case study book of the G7 Global Marketplace for SMEs Pilot Project* (1st ed.).

Gandomi, A., & Haider, M. (2015). Beyond the hype: Big data concepts, methods, and analytics. *International Journal of Information Management, 35,* 137–144.

Garimella, K. K. (2006). *The power of process*. Tampa, FL: Meghan-Kiffer Press.

Gartner. (2018). *Dark data*. www.gartner.com/it-glossary/dark-data. Accessed 19 March 2020.

Gassmann, O., Frankenberger, K., & Csik, M. (2017). *Geschäftsmodelle entwickeln. 55 innovative Konzepte mit dem St. Galler Business Model Navigator*. 2. Auflage. Carl Hansen, München, Germany.

Gatteschi, V., Lamberti, F., Demartini, C., Pranteda, C., & Santamaría, V. (2018). *Blockchain and smart contracts for insurance: Is the technology mature enough?*

Gatzert, N., Schmit, J. T., & Kolb, A. (2016). Assessing the risks of insuring reputation risk. *The Journal of Risk and Insurance, 83*(3), 641–679. https://doi.org/10.1111/jori.12065. Accessed 19 March 2020.

Gaudeul, A., & Jullien, B. (2001). E-commerce: Quelques éléments d'économie industrielle. *Revue Economique, 52,* 97–117.

Giudici, G. (2008). *Intermediazione Assicurativa e Mercato*. Milano, Italy: FrancoAngeli.

Glaser, F. (2017). *Pervasive decentralisation of digital infrastructures: A framework for blockchain enabled system and use case analysis*. Frankfurt, Germany: Goethe University Frankfurt.

GlobalData Plc. (2017). *After Guevara's collapse, is the industry ready for P2P insurance?* | GlobalData Plc. www.globaldata.com/guevaras-collapse-industry-ready-p2p-insurance/. Accessed 8 March 2020.

GmbH, A. (2018). *Friendsurance*. www.friendsurance.com.au/. Accessed 8 March 2020.

Goldman Sachs. (2014). *The Internet of Things: Making sense of the next mega-trend*. goo.gl/J656qk.

Goldratt, E. M., & Cox, J. (2004). *The goal: A process of on-going improvement* (2nd ed.). Great Barrington, MA: North River Publishing Corporation.

Gondring, H. (2015). *Versicherungswirtschaft. Handbuch für Studium und Praxis*. 1. Auflage. Verlag Franz Vahlen GmbH, München, Germany.

Gonzalez, R., Gasco, J., & Llopis, J. (2005). Information systems outsourcing risks: A study of large providers. *Industrial management & Data systems, 105*(1), 45–62.

Gordijn, J., Akkermans, J. M., & van Vliet, J. C. (2000). What's in an electronic business model? In R. Dieng & O. Corby (Eds.), *Knowledge engineering and knowledge management: Methods, models and tools*. 12th International conference EKAW 2000, Juan-les-Pins (pp. 257–273). Berlin, Germany: Springer.

Gore, A., Harmer, P., Pfitzer, M., & Jais, N. (2017). Can insurance companies incentivize their customers to be healthier? *Harvard Business Review*, 3.

Granados, N., & Gupta, A. (2013). Transparency strategy: Competing with information in a digital world. *MIS Quarterly, 37*, 637–641.

Grochla, E., & Schönbohm, P. (1980). *Beschaffung in der Unternehmung*. Stuttgart, Germany: Poeschel.

Gröger, A. C. (2014). Insurance deductions for using health-monitoring apps, risks and rewards. *Worldcrunch*, 21. goo.gl/hb6Y56.

Grossman, R. L. (2009), *The case of cloud computing, IEEE-2009, Cloud Computing*: First International Conference, CloudCom 2009, Beijing, China.

Grover, V., & Kohli, R. (2013). Revealing your hand: Caveats in implementing digital business strategy. *MIS Quarterly, 37*(2), 655–662.

Grzadkowska, A. (2018). Measuring the scale of Amazon's threat to the insurance industry. *Insurance Business America*. www.insurancebusinessmag.com/us/news/technology/measuring-the-scale-of-amazons-threat-to-the-insurance-industry-116810.aspx. Accessed 10 July 2019.

Guo, Y., & Liang, C. (2016). Blockchain application and outlook in the banking industry. *Financial Innovation,* 2.

Guyer, A., & Reding, M. (2016). My Zurich: Daten und Know-how nutzen. In O. Gassmann, & P. Sutter (Hrsg.), *Digitale Transformation im Unternehmen gestalten* (pp. 201–205). München, Germany: Carl Hanser Verlag.

Gyorffi, M. (2017). Digitising industry (Industry 4.0 and cybersecurity). *European Parliament. Industry, Research and Energy (ITRE).*

Haapio, H., de Rooy, R., & Barton, T. D. (2018). New contract genres. In E. Schweighofer et al. (Eds.), *Data Protection/LegalTech. Proceedings of the 21th International Legal Informatics Symposium IRIS 2018*, Editions Weblaw, Bern 2018, 455–460.

Haas, A., & Hofmann, A. (2014). Risiken aus der Nutzung von Cloud-Computing-Diensten: Fragen des Risikomanagements und Aspekte der Versicherbarkeit. *Zeitschrift für die gesamte Versicherungswissenschaft, 103*(4), 377–407.

Hagiu, A. (2006). *Multi-sided platforms: From microfoundations to design and expansion strategies* (Harvard Business School Strategy Unit Working Paper). www.hbs.edu/faculty/Publication%20Files/07-094.pdf. Accessed 10 July 2019.

Hagiu, A. (2006). Pricing and commitment by two-sided platforms. *The RAND Journal of Economics, 37*(3), 720–737.

Hagiu, A. (2009). Two-sided platforms: Product variety and pricing structures. *Journal of Economics and Management Strategy, 18*(4),

Hagiu, A., & Wright, J. (2011). *Multi-sided platforms* (HBS Working Paper).

Hagiu, A., & Wright, J. (2015). Multi-sided platforms. *International Journal of Industrial Organization, 43,* 162–174. https://doi.org/10.1016/j.ijindorg.2015.03.003.

Hall, P., Phan, W., & Whitson, K. (2016). *The evolution of analytics: Opportunities and challenges for machine learning in business*. Sebastopol, CA: O'Reilly Media.

Haller, M. (1997). *Von Assekuranz 2000 Versicherung im Netzwerk 2.007*. I.VW HSG. www.risiko-dialog.ch/images/RD-Media/PDF/Team/Publikationen_MH/1997-01_von_assekuranz_2000_zur_versicherung_im_netzwerk_2_007.pdf. Accessed 19 March 2020.

Haller, M., & Holenstein, M. (2017). Big Data und Versicherung. In K. Hummler & F. Schonenberger (Hrsg.), *Total data—Total control* (pp. 143–164). NZZ, Zurich, Switzerland.

Halverson, M., & Malhotra, R. (2015). *Beyond insurance: Embracing innovation to monetize disruption*. Accenture. goo.gl/Ly5Nbk.

Hamel, F., Herz, T. Ph., Uebernickel, F., & Brenner, W. (2012). Managing costs and performance of IT in business groups: Towards a performance measurement model for global insurance business groups. *18th Americas Conference on Information Systems*, Seattle.

Hanninen, N., & Karjaluoto, H. (2017). The effect of marketing communication on business relationship loyalty. *Marketing Intelligence & Planning, 35,* 458–472.

Hans, R., Rizk, A., Zubr, H., & Steinmetz, R. (2017). Blockchain and smart contracts: Disruptive technologies for the insurance market. *23rd Americas Conference on Information Systems*, Boston.

Hedman, J., Sarker, S., & Veit, D. (2016). Digitization in business models and entrepreneurship. *Information Systems Journal, 26*(5), 419–420.

Hegmann, G. (2016). *Allianz wird zum Amazon des Gebrauchtwagenhandels*. Die Welt. www.welt.de/wirtschaft/article158841373/Allianz-wird-zum-Amazon-des-Gebrauchtwagen-handels.html. Accessed 30 May 2020.

Heide, D. (2015). *DAX-Firmen gründen Digitalinstitut*. Handelsblatt. www.handelsblatt.com/unternehmen/it-medien/basf-und-allianz-gute-forschung-braucht-viel-geld/12427404-2.html?ticket=ST-5225230-gn52i1bUDSzg6g2bo2oA-ap1. Accessed 10 July 2019.

Heinhuis, D., & De Vries, E. J. (2008, December). Modelling customer behaviour in multi-channel service distribution. In *International Workshop on Enterprise Applications and Services in the Finance Industry* (pp. 47–63). Berlin, Heidelberg, Germany: Springer.

Heinrich, B., Zellner, G., & Leist, S. (2011). Service integrators in business networks–the importance of relationship values. *Electronic Markets, 21*(4), 215–235. https://doi.org/10.1007/s12525-011-0075-x.

Helfferich, C. (2011). *Die Qualität qualitativer Daten. Manual fiir die Durchführung qualitativer Interviews*. 4. Auflage. VS Verlag fiir Sozialwissenschaften, Wiesbaden, Germany.

Henriette, E., Feki, M., & Boughzala, I. (2015). Information systems in a changing economy and society. *MCIS Proceedings*.

Herz, T. Ph., Hamel, F., Uebernickel, F., & Brenner, W. (2012). IT multisourcing in international insurance companies. *18th Americas Conference on Information Systems (AMCIS),* Seattle, WA.

Hess, T., Matt, C., Benlian, A., & Wiesböck, F. (2016). Options for formulating a digital transformation strategy. *MIS Quarterly Executive, 15*(2), 123–139.

Hevner, A. R., March, S. T., Park, J., & Ram, S. (2004). Design science in information systems research. *MIS Quarterly, 28*(1), 75–105.

Hiendlmeier, S., & Hertting, M. (2015). *The impacts of digitization on the management of insurance companies: Steering business in a digital world*. Horváth & Partners. www.horvath-partners.com/fileadmin/horvath-partners.com/assets/05_Media_Center/PDFs/englisch/WP_Insurance_Digital_web_g.pdf. Accessed 3 October 2016.

Higginbotham, S. (2016, December). Why insurance companies want to subsidize your smart home. *MIT Technology Review*.

Hirt, T. (2006). *Allgemeine Kenntnisse der Versicherungswirtschaft* (1st ed.). Verlag SKV, Zurich: Switzerland.

Hofmann, M., Neukart, F., & Bäck, T. (2017). Artificial intelligence & data science in the automotive industry. *Data Science Blog, 489,* 484–489.

Honka, E., & Chintagunta, P. (2016). Simultaneous or sequential? Search strategies in the USA auto insurance industry. *Marketing Science, 35*(4), 21–42. https://doi.org/10.1287/mksc.2016.0995.

Hood, J., & Stein, W. (2003). Outsourcing of insurance claims: A UK case study. *Geneva Paper Risk Insurance Issues and Practice, 28,* 510–520.

Hook, L. (2018). How can the insurance industry prepare for Amazon's arrival? *Insurance Business Magazine*. www.insurancebusinessmag.com/uk/news/technology/how-can-the-insurance-industry-prepare-for-amazons-arrival-88920.aspx. Accessed 10 July 2019.

Hoy, M., & Ruse, M. (2005). Regulating genetic information in insurance markets. *Risk Management and Insurance Review, 8*(2), 211–237.

Huckstep, R. (2017) *Chatbot & the rise of the automated insurance agent*. Accessed 19 March 2020.

Hummel, T., Ku¨hn, M., Bende, J., & Lang, A. (2011). *Advanced driver assistance systems: An investigation of their potential safety benefits based on an analysis of insurance claims in Germany*. German Insurance Association—Research Report FS 03.

Hurley, R., Evans. P., & Menon, A. (2015). Insurance disrupted. General insurance in a connected world. Deloitte.

Hussain, K., & Prieto, E. (2016). Big data in the finance and insurance sectors. In J. M. Cavanillas, E. Curry, & W. Wahlster (Eds.), *New horizons for a data-driven economy—A roadmap for usage and exploitation of big data in Europe* (pp. 209–223). https://www.springer.com/book/10.1007percent2F978-3-319-21569-3. Accessed 30 March 2020.

IAIS. (2017). *FinTech developments in the insurance industry*. Basel, Switzerland: International Association of Insurance Supervisors.

Iansiti, M., & Lakhani, K. R. (2017). The truth about block chain. *Harvard Business Review*.

IHS Markit. (2016). *Usage-based insurance expected to grow to 142 million subscribers globally by 20232* (Italian Axa Paper, 2016). corporate.axa.it/documents/715596/722400/IITALIAN+AXA+PAPER+N.+8.pdf/fc949063-b0c6-31ba-4c3d-036dbe691c32. Accessed 30 March 2020.

Ingleton, R., Ozler, Y., & Thomas, P. (2011). *The digitization of everything: How organizations must adapt to changing consumer behavior*. EY. www.ey.com/Publication/vwLUAssets/The_digitisation_of_everything__How_organizations_must_adapt_to_changing_consumer_behaviour/percent24file/EY_Digitisation_of_everything.pdf. Accessed 5 June 2020.

Insurance 2020 & beyond: Necessity is the mother of reinvention. (2015). [ebook] pwc. www.pwc.com/gx/en/insurance/publications/assets/pwc-insurance-2020-and-beyond.pdf. Accessed 8 March 2020.

Insurance Europe. (2015). *European insurance in figures*. goo.gl/s9SUH9.

Insurance Europe. (2016). *European insurance—Key facts*. goo.gl/1bsR5U.

Jara, M., & Zinsli, J. (2012). Schaden- und Leistungsmanagement. In W. Ackermann & H. Schmeiser (Hrsg.), *Versicherungswirtschaft & Versicherungsmanagement* (pp. 245–265). Bern: Berufsbildungsverband der Versicherungswirtschaft.

Jeansson, J., Nikou, S., Lundqvist, S., Marcusson, L., Sell, A., & Walden, P. (2017). SMEs' online channel expansion: Value creating activities. *Electronic Markets, 27*(1), 49–66. https://doi.org/10.1007/s12525-016-0234-1.

Jergler, D. (2016). Insurance industry analyzes Google's failed online insurance experiment. *Insurance Journal*. www.insurancejournal.com/news/national/2016/02/23/399632.htm. Accessed 30 March 2020.

Jeston, J., & Nelis, J. (2006). *Business process management*. Amsterdam, Netherlands: Elsevier Science B.V.

Jim. (2014). *Disrupting insurance with Friendsurance*. goo.gl/LDhmsb.

Johannsen, F., & Leist, S. (2009). A Six Sigma approach for integrated solutions. *Managing Service Quality, 19*(5), 558–580.

Johansson, S. & Vogelgesang, U. (2015) *Insurance on the threshold of digitization: Implications for the life and P&C workforce*. McKinsey & Company. www.mckinsey.com/industries/financial-services/our-insights/insurance-on-the-threshold-of-digitization. Accessed 30 March 2020.

Johne, A. (1993). Insurance product development: Managing the changes. *International Journal of Bank Marketing, 11*(3), 5–14. https://doi.org/10.1108/02652329310027693.

Johnson, B. (n.d.). The Great Fire of London, Historic UK Ltd. Company Registered in England No. 5621230. www.historic-uk.com/HistoryUK/HistoryofEngland/The-Great-Fire-of-London/. Accessed 30 May 2020.

Johnson, L. G. (2017). Blockchain solution and the insurance industry. *In-House Defense Quarterly*.

Jones, D. T., & Womack, J. P. (2006). *Lean thinking. Come creare valore & bandire gli sprechi*. Guerini, Milano. Italy.

Jones, M. (2016). *Anything you can do, AI can do better: Machine learning and artificial intelligence in insurance*. Insurance Nexus. www.insurancenexus.com/analytics/anything-you-can-do-ai-can-do-better-machine-learning. Accessed 19 March 2020.

Jost, J. (2019). *Im Wandel der Digitalisierung*. Thesis Hochschule Furtwangen, Germany.

Jullien, B. (2005). Two-sided markets and electronic intermediaries. *CESifo Economic Studies, 51*(2–3), 235–262.

Kabadayi, S. Y., Loureiro, Komarova, & Carnevale, M. (2017). Customer value creation in multichannel systems. The interactive effect of integration quality and multichannel complexity. *Journal of Creation of Value, 3,* 1–18.

Kaczmarek-Heß, M., & de Kinderen, S. (2017). A multilevel model of it platforms for the needs of enterprise it landscape analyses. *Business & Information Systems Engineering, 59*(3), 315–329. https://doi.org/10.1007/s12599-017-0482-4. Accessed 19 March 2020.

Kaesler, S. (2019). *A new industry model for InsurTech*. McKinsey & Company.

Kaewsawad, S., & Li, Z. (2018). The effects of service quality of customer service on total customers' satisfaction in case of buying life insurance via online channel. *Proceedings of the 2nd International Workshop on Entrepreneurship in Electronic and Mobile Business, (EMB' 18)*, Publiqation, Germany.

Kagermann, H. (2015). Change through digitization: Value creation in the age of industry 4.0. In H. Albach, A. Meffert, H. Pinkwart, & R. Reichwald (Eds.), *Management of permanent change* (pp. 23–45). Wiesbaden, Germany: Springer Gabler.

Kagermann, H., Wahlster, W., & Helbig, J. (2013). Umsetzungsempfehlungen für das Zukunftsprojekt Industrie 4.0. *Abschlussbericht des Arbeitskreises Industrie, 4*(5).

Kaiser, R. (2014). *Qualitative Experteninterviews. Konzeptionelle Grundlagen und praktische Durchführung. 1. Auflage*. Wiesbaden, Germany: Springer.

Kaiser, U., & Wright, J. (2006). Price structure in two-sided markets: Evidence from the magazine industry. *International Journal of Industrial Organization, 24*(1), 1–28.

Kamble, S. S., Gunasekaran, A., & Gawankar, S. A. (2018). Sustainable Industry 4.0 framework: A systematic literature review identifying the current trends and future perspectives. *Process Safety and Environmental Protection, 117*, 408–425.

Kane, G., Palmer, D., Phillips, A., Kiron, D., & Buckley, N. (2015). *Strategy, not technology, drives digital transformation—Becoming a digitally mature enterprise*. MIT *Sloan Management Review* and Deloitte. sloanreview.mit.edu/projects/strategy-drives-digital-transformation. Accessed 30 March 2020.

Kaplan, J. M., Bailey, T., O'Halloran, D., Marcus, A., & Rezek, C. (2015). *Beyond cybersecurity: Protecting your digital business*. Hoboken, NJ: John Wiley.

Kaplan, S, & Sawhney, M. (2000). E-hubs: The new B2B marketplaces. *Harvard Business Review*, May–June, 97–103

Kaptein, M., & Parvinen, P. (2015). Advancing e-commerce personalization: process framework and case study. *International Journal of Electronic Commerce, 19*(3), 7–33. https://doi.org/10.1080/10864415.2015.1000216.

Karten, W., Nell, M., Richter, A., & Schiller, J. (2018). *Risiko und Versicherungstechnik. Eine ökonomische Einführung. 1. Auflage*. Wiesbaden, Germany: Springer Gabler.

Kastner, P. S. (2006). *The Business Process Management Benchmark Report*. Aberdeen Group.

Kaufman, J., & Sato, Y. (2005). *Value analysis tear-down: A new process for product development & innovation*. New York, NY: Industrial Press Inc.

Kazan, E., & Damsgaard, J. (2016). Towards a market entry framework for digital payment platforms. *Communications of the Association for Information Systems, 38*(1), 761–783. https://doi.org/10.17705/1CAIS.03837.

Kazan, E., Tan, C., Lim, E. T. K., Sørensen, C., & Damsgaard, J. (2018). Disentangling digital platform competition: The case of UK mobile payment platforms. *Journal of Management Information Systems, 35*(1), 180–219. https://doi.org/10.1080/07421222.2018.1440772.

Keen, P., & McDonald, M. (2000). *The eProcess edge: Creating customer value & business in the Internet Era*. New York, NY: Osborn/McGraw-Hill.

Keerati, R. (2018). *Preparing for blockchain challenges and alternatives for financial regulators*. Berkeley, CA: Center for Technology, Society and Policy (CTSP), University of California: 7, 8, 9.

Keller, B. (2018). *Big data and insurance: Implications for innovation, competition and privacy*. Zurich, Switzerland: Geneva Association.

Keller, A., & Transchel, F. (2016). *Telematics: Connecting the dots*. Swiss Re. www.swissre.com/library/archive/Telematics_connecting_the_dots.html. Accessed 30 March 2020.

Kenneth, F. C. Gupta, A., & Sommer, D. (2015). *Maverick research: Surviving the rise of 'smart machines,' the loss of 'dream jobs' & '90 percent unemployment.* Gartner Maverick Research. 23 September 2013, refreshed 6 January 2015.

Kerber, T. (2016). IoT: Smart home business models. Parks Associates.

Kimberley, J. & Minvielle, E. (2000). *The quality imperative: Measurement & management of quality in healthcare* (1st reprint). London, UK: Imperial College Press.

Kitchens, F. (n.d.). Financial implications of artificial Neural Networks in automobile insurance underwriting. *International Journal of Electronic Finance, 3*, 311–319. https://doi.org/10.1504/IJEF.2009.027853.

Kloppenborg, T. J., & Petrick, J. A. (2002). *Managing project quality.* Vienna, VA: Management Concepts.

Klotzki, U., Gatzert, N., & Münstermann, B. (2017). The cost of life distribution in Europe. *Geneva Papers on Risk and Insurance*, 42(2), 296–322. https://doi.org/10.1057/s41288-016-0036-x. Accessed 19 March 2020.

Klumpes, P. J. M., & Schuermann, S. (2011). Corporate, product and distribution strategies in the European life insurance industry. *The Geneva Papers, 36*(1), 50–75. https://doi.org/10.1057/gpp.2010.38. Accessed 19 March 2020.

Koch, S., & Bierbamer, M. (2016). Opening your product: Impact of user innovations and their distribution platform on video game success. *Electronic Markets, 26*(4), 357–368. https://doi.org/10.1007/s12525-016-0230-5. Accessed 19 March 2020.

Koehler, P., Six, B., & Michels, J. S. (2015). Industrie 4.0: Ein Überblick. In C. Koehler-Schute (Ed.), *Industrie 4.0: Ein praxisorientierter Ansatz* (pp. 17–39). Berlin, Germany: KS-Energy.

Köhler, O., & Skorna, A. (2016). *Insurance 4.0: Die digitale Revolution in der* Versicherungswirtschaft. Online verfügbar unter. www.researchgate.net/publication/306118545_.

Köhler, O., & Skorna, A. (2016). Insurance_4.0_Die_digitale_Revolution_in_der_ Versicherungswirtschaft, zuletzt geprüft am. In A. Liebetrau, A. Funk-Münchmeyer, & A. Eckstein. *Insurance & Innovation 2016.* Karlsruhe, Germany: Verlag Versicherungswirtschaft.

Köhler, O., & Skorna, A. (2016, December). Industrie 4.0 – Auswirkungen auf das Risikomanagement von Produktion und Lieferkette. In *Österreichisches Jahrbuch für Risikomanagement* 2017. Wien, Austria: TÜV Österreich.

Köhne, T. (2006). *Marketing im strategischen Unternehmensnetzwerk.* Wiesbaden, Germany: Gabler/Deutscher Universitätsverlag.

Kolmar, M. & Booms, M. (2016) *Autonome Autos: Keine Algorithmen fu¨r ethische Fragen.* Neue Zu¨rcher Zeitung. www.nzz.ch/meinung/kommentare/keine-algorithmen-fuer-ethische-fragen-ld.4483. Accessed 30 March 2020.

Kolodner, J. (2014). *Case-based reasoning*. Burlington, MA: Morgan Kaufmann.

Korhonen, P., & Voutilainen, R. (2006). Finding the most preferred alliance structure between banks and insurance companies. *European Journal of Operational Research, 175*(2), 1285–1299.

Kosoff Maya. (2015). Google just invested $32 million in Oscar, a billion-dollar startup that wants to shake up healthcare, *Business Insider*. goo.gl/Jk2s5V.

Kotler, P. (2001). *A framework for marketing management* (1st ed.). Upper Saddle River, NJ: Prentice Hall.

Kotler, P. (2002). *Marketing management*. Upper Saddle River, NJ: Prentice Hall.

Kottmann, D., & Do¨rdrechter, N. (2016). *Zukunft von Insurtech in Deutschland—Der Insurtech Radar*. Oliver Wyman and Policen Direkt. www.oliverwyman.de/content/dam/oliver-wyman/europe/germany/de/insights/publications/2016/jul/Oliver_Wyman_Policenpercent20Direkt_Insurtech-Radar.pdf. Accessed 30 March 2020.

KPMG & CBInsights. (2016). *The pulse of Fintech Q2 2016: Global analysis of Fintech venture funding*. home.kpmg.com/xx/en/home/insights/2016/11/the-pulse-of-fintech-q2-2016.html. Accessed 30 March 2020.

KPMG & H2 Ventures. (2015). *Fintech 100: Leading Global Fintech Innovators Report 2015*. fintechnews.ch/fintech/top-10-fintech-startups/2454/. Accessed 30 March 2020.

KPMG. (2019). *Insurtech 10: Trend for 2019* (Kpmg Paper).

Krotoszynski, R. J., Jr. (2015). Reconciling privacy and speech in the era of big data: A comparative legal analysis. *William & Mary Law Review, 56*(4), 1279–1338.

Kuechler, W., & Vaishnavi, V. (2012). A framework for theory development in design science research: Multiple perspectives. *Journal of the Association for Information Systems, 13*(6), 395–423.

Kunreuther, H., & Heal, G. (2004). Interdependent security: The case of identical agents. *Journal of Risk & Uncertainty, 23*(2), 103–120.

Kwak, Y. H., & Anbari, F. T. (2006). Benefits, obstacles, & future of six sigma approach. *Technovation, 26*(1), 708–715.

Kwon, H. E., Oh, W., & Kim, T. (2017). Platform structures, homing preferences, and homophilous propensities in online social networks. *Journal of Management Information Systems, 34*(3), 768–802. https://doi.org/10.1080/07421222.2017.1373008. Accessed 19 March 2020.

Laffey, D., & Gandy, A. (2009). Applying Stabell and Fjeldstad's value configurations to E-commerce: A cross-case analysis of UK comparison websites. *The Journal of Strategic Information Systems, 18*(4), 192–204. https://doi.org/10.1016/j.jsis.2009.10.002. Accessed 19 March 2020.

Lamberti, F., Gatteschi, V., Demartini, C., Pranteda, C., & Santamaria, V. (2017). Blockchain or not blockchain, that is the question of the insurance and other sectors. *IT Professional* 2017, https://doi.org/10.1109/MITP.2017.265110355. Accessed 8 March 2020.

Lambrecht, A., & Tucker, C. (2013). When does retargeting work? Information specificity in online advertising. *Journal of Marketing Research, 50*(5), 561–576.

Larsson, A., & Broström, E. (2019). *Ensuring customer retention: companies' perception of customer loyalty*. Market: Inteligence. Planning. https://doi.org/10.1108/MIP-02-2019-0106.

Lascelles, D., & Keyur, P. (2017). *Insurance banana skins* (Price Waterhouse Coopers Paper). goo.gl/mjaDz4.

Lasi, H., Kemper, H.-G., Fettke, P., Feld, T., & Hoffmann, M. (2014). Industry 4.0. *Business & Information Systems Engineering, 6*(4), 239–242.

Legifrance.gouv.fr. (2018). *Décret n° 2014-1685 du 29 décembre 2014 relatif à la résiliation à tout moment de contrats d'assurance et portant application de l'article L. 113-15-2 du code des assurances | Legifrance*. www.legifrance.gouv.fr/eli/decret/2014/12/29/FCPT1410391D/jo/texte. Accessed 8 March 2020.

Legoff, E. (2017). *Zoom sur 14 insurtech qui veulent transformer l'assurance*. L'Argus de l'assurance. www.argusdelassurance.com/acteurs/zoom-sur-14-insurtech-qui-veulent-transformer-l-assurance.116778. Accessed 8 March 2020.

Lehrer, C., Wieneke, A., vom Brocke, J., Jung, R., & Seidel, S. (2018). How big data analytics enables service innovation: Materiality, affordance, and the individualization of service. *Journal of Management Information Systems, 35*(2), 424–460. https://doi.org/10.1080/07421222.2018.1451953. Accessed 19 March 2020.

Lehtonen, T., & Liukko, J. (2015). Producing solidarity, inequality and exclusion through insurance. *Res Publica, 21*(2), 155–169.

Levy, F., & Murnane, R. (2005). *The new division of labor: How computers are creating the next job market*. Princeton, NJ: Princeton University Press.

Lezzi, M., Lazoi, M., & Corallo, A. (2018). Cybersecurity for industry 4.0 in the current literature: A reference framework. *Computers in Industry, 103*, 97–110.

Lima, T., & Santos, B. (2018). Indústria 4.0: Desafios e Oportunidades. *Revista Produção e Desenvolvimento, 4*(1), 111–124.

Linderman, K., Schroeder, R. G., Zaheer, S., & Choo, A. S. (2003). Six Sigma: A goal-theoretic perspective. *Journal of Operations Management, 21*(1), 536–554.

Lluis de la Rosa, J., Torres-Padrosa, V., el-Fakdi, A., Gibovic, D., O, H., Maicher, L. & Miralles, F. (2017). A survey of blockchain technologies for open innovation. In *World Open Innovation Conference 2017*, Technology Transfer Research Group. San Francisco, CA.

Loebbecke, C., & Picot, A. (2015). Reflections on societal and business model transformation arising from digitization and big data analytics: A research agenda. *Journal of Strategic Information Systems, 24*(3), 149–157.

Lombardi, R. (2019). Knowledge transfer & organizational performance & business process: Past, present & future research. *Business Process Management Journal, 25*(1), 2–9.

Lorenz, J., Münstermann, B., Higginson, M., Olesen, P., Bohlken, N., & Ricciardi, V. (2016). *Blockchain in insurance—Opportunity or threat?* www.mckinsey.com/~/media/McKinsey/Industries/Financialpercent20Services/Ourpercent20Insights/Blockchainpercent20inpercent20insurancepercent20opportunitypercent20orpercent20threat/Blockchain-in-insurance-opportunity-or-threat.ashx. Accessed 8 March 2020.

Loucks, J., Davenport, T., & Schatsky, D. (2018). State of AI in the enterprise: 2nd Edition: Early adopters combine bullish enthusiasm with strategic investments, *Deloitte Insights*.

Lowry, P., Wells, T., Moody, G., Humpherys, S., & Kettles, D. (2006). Online payment gateways used to facilitate e-commerce transactions and improve risk management. *Communications of the Association for Information Systems, 17*(1), 123–151. https://doi.org/10.17705/1CAIS.01706.

Lucas, A. (2016). *Vorlesungsskript Einführung Risk & Insurance. Fraling Semester 2016*. ZHAW School of Management and Law. Winterthur, Germany.

Lucas, H. C., Agarwal, R., Clemons, E. K., El Sawy, O. A., Weber, B. (2013). Impactful research on transformational information technology: An opportunity to inform new audiences. *MIS Quarterly, 37*, 371–382.

Lucking-Reiley, D., & Spulber, D. F. (2001). Business-to-business electronic commerce. *Journal of Economic Perspectives, 15*(1), 55–68.

Lunn, V. (2018). Blockchain catastrophe swaps and the unbundling of insurance. *Daily Fintech*. dailyfintech.com/2016/09/15/blockchain-catastrophe-swaps-and-the-unbundling-of-insurance/. Accessed 8 March 2020.

Lupi, C. (2007, May), Una intervista a Bernardo Nicoletti: Lean Six Sigma: Un percorso di successo. *Sistemi & Impresa*, N. 4.

Lusvarghi, V. (1990). *La gestione dell'impresa di assicurazione*. Padova, Italy: Cedam.

Lyytinen, K., Yoo, Y., & Boland, R. J., Jr. (2016). Digital product innovation within four classes of innovation networks. *Information Systems Journal, 26*(1), 47–75.

Maarse, H., & Paulus, A. (2003). Has solidarity survived? A comparative analysis of the effect of social health insurance reform in four European countries. *Journal of Health Politics, Policy and Law, 28*(4), 585–614.

Maas, P., & Buehler, P. (2015). *Industrialisierung der Assekuranz in einer digitalen Welt*. I.VW-HSG and Adcubum, St. Gallen. www.ivw.unisg.ch/—'/media/internet/content/dateien/instituteundcenters/ivw/studien/industrialisierung digital2015.pdf. Accessed 30 March 2020.

Maas, P., & Milanova, V. (2014). Zwischen Verheißung und Bedrohung — Big Data in der Versicherungswirtschaft. *Die Volkswirtschaft, 2014*(5), 23–25.

Maas, P., & Miler, P. (2015). *Industrialisierung der Assekuranz in einer digitalen Welt*. St. Gallen, Switzerland: Institut fiir Versicherungswirtschaft I.VW-HSG.

Maas, P., & Steiner, P. (2012). *Schaden- und Leistungsmanagement*. In W. Acker-mann & H. Schmeiser (Hrsg.), *Versicherungswirtschaft & Versicherungsmanagement* (pp. 177–231). Bern, Switzerland: Berufsbildungsverband der Versicherungswirtschaft.

Maas, P., Buhler, P., & Fleischer, M. (2017). Digitale Disruption in der Versicherungswirtschaft: Von der Verteidigung des Geschäftsmodells bis zur Auflosung der Branche. In A. Widmer (Hrsg.), *Der rasante technologische Wandel — Überforderung der Gesellschaft?* (pp. 93–110). Zurich, Switzerland: Dike Verlag.

Maas, P., Graf, A., & Bieck, C. (2008). *Trust, transparency and technology: European customers' perspectives on insurance and innovation*. I.VW-HSG and IBM Institute for Business Value. www-935.ibm.com/services/us/gbs/bus/pdf/gbe03008-usen-02-insurancet3.pdf. Accessed 30 March 2020.

Mackenzie, A. (2015). The Fintech revolution. *London Business School Review, 26*, 50–53.

Maeder, P. (2016). *The smart insurer: More than just big data*. Bearing Point Institute. goo.gl/DcgYpN.

Maissin, J. P., & Flamand, T. (2014). *When digital changes the way insurance works Deloitte*. goo.gl/XxfhHm.

Maletski, G., & Delman, Z. (2017). *Blockchain's benefits for companies begin planning for the next blockbuster technology*. www.sapiens.com. Accessed 8 March 2020.

Mani, D., & Barua, A. (2015). The impact of firm learning on value creation in strategic outsourcing relationships. *Journal of Management Information Systems, 32*(1), 9–38.

Mantena, R., & Saha, R. L. (2012). Co-opetition between differentiated platforms in two-sided markets. *Journal of Management Information Systems, 29*(2), 109–140. https://doi.org/10.2753/MIS0742-1222290205.

Marabelli, M., Hansen, S., Newell, S., & Frigerio, C. (2017). The light and dark side of the black box: Sensor-based technology in the automotive industry. *Communications of the Association for Information Systems, 40*(5), 351–374. https://doi.org/10.17705/1CAIS.04016.

March, S. T., & Storey, V. C. (2008). Design science in the information systems discipline: An introduction to the special issue on design science research. *MIS Quarterly, 32*(4), 725–730.

Markus, M. L., & Loebbecke, C. (2013). Commoditized digital processes and business community platforms: new opportunities and challenges for digital business strategies. *MIS Quarterly, 37*(2), 649–653.

Matt, C., Hess, T., & Benlian, A. (2015). Digital transformation strategies. *Business & Information Systems Engineering, 57*(5), 339–343. https://doi.org/10.1007/s12599-015-0401-5.

Mayring, P. (2010). *Qualitative Inhaltsanalyse. Grundlagen und Techniken*. 11. Auflage. Weinheim und Basel, Switzerland: Beltz Verlag.

McCarthy, J. (2007). *What is artificial intelligence?* www-formal.stanford.edu/jmc/whatisai.pdf. Accessed 30 March 2020.

McCurry, J. (2017). Japanese company replaces office workers with Artificial Intelligence. *The Guardian*. www.theguardian.com/technology/2017/jan/05/japanese-company-replaces-office-workers-artificial-intelligence-ai-fukoku-mutual-life-insurance. Accessed 30 March 2020.

McKinsey & Company. (2017). *Blockchain in insurance–Opportunity or threat?* www.mckinsey.com/industries/financial-services/our-insights/blockchain-in-insurance-opportunity-or-threat. Accessed 8 March 2020.

McKinsey. (2016). *Making digital strategy a reality in insurance*. McKinsey & Company.

McKinsey. (2017). *Digital disruption in insurance: Cutting through the noise*. McKinsey & Company. goo.gl/9Cd9BC.

McKinsey. (2018). *Digital insurance in 2018: Driving real impact with digital and analytics*. McKinsey & Company.

McKinsey. (2019). www.mckinsey.com/industries/financial-services/our-insights/insurance-blog/a-new-industry-model-for-insurtech. Accessed 30 March 2020.

Medici. (2018). *31 P2P Insurance startups capitalizing on the power of virtual communities*. gomedici.com/31-p2p-insurance-startups/. Accessed 8 March 2020.

Meidert, U., Scheermesser, M., Prieur, Y., Hegyi, S., Stockinger, K., Eyyi, G., et al. (2018). *Quantified Self—Schnittstelle zwischen Lifestyle und Medizin* (1st ed.). Zurich, Switzerland: Hochschul-verlag AG.

Meier, A., & Stormer, H. (2009). *eBusiness and eCommerce: Managing the digital value chain* (1st ed., pp. 222). Berlin: Springer. ISBN-10: 3540893288.

Menon, N. M. (2018). *Information spillover and semi-collaborative networks in insurer fraud detection*. Misq.org. misq.org/information-spillover-and-semi-collaborative-networks-in-insurer-fraud-detection.html. Accessed 8 March 2020.

Menon, N. M. (2018). *Information spillover and semi-collaborative networks in insurer fraud detection*. Misq.org. misq.org/information-spillover-and-semi-collaborative-networks-in-insurer-fraud-detection.html. Accessed 30 May 2020.

Mesropyan, E. (2016) *101 Insurtech startups revolutionizing the $4.5-trillion-dollar insurance industry*. letstalkpayments.com/101-insurtech-startups-revolutionizing-the-4-5-trillion-dollar-insurance-industry/. Accessed 30 May 2020.

Mihler, P., & Mass, P. (2016). *Kunden transformieren die Versicherungsmärkte*. In O. Gassmann & P. Sutter (Hrsg.), *Digitale Transformation im Unternehmen gestalten* (pp. 99–114). München, Germany: Carl Hansen.

Miles, I. (2007). Research and development (R&D) beyond manufacturing: the strange case of services R&D. *R&D Management, 37*(3), 249–268. https://doi.org/10.1111/j.1467-9310.2007.00473.x.

Mohamed, M. (2018). Challenges and benefits of Industry 4.0: An overview. *International Journal of Supply and Operations Management., 5*, 256–265.

Moneta, A. (2014). *The customer-centric insurer in the digital era*. Accenture. www.accenture.com/t20150523T033833__w__/sg-en/_acnmedia/Accenture/Conversion-Assets/DotCom/Documents/Global/PDF/Dualpub_9/Accenture-The-Customer-Centric-Insurer-In-The-Digital-Era.pdf. Accessed 30 March 2020.

Moore, M. (2018). *World insurance report 2018: Digital agility is key for companies as BigTechs ponder entering the market*. www.capgemini.com/news/world-insurance-report-2018-as-more-customers-buy-insurance-from-bigtechs-digital-agility-is-key-for-traditional-companies/. Accessed 10 July 2019.

Moreau, F. (2013). The disruptive nature of digitization: The case of the recorded music industry. *International Journal of Arts Management, 15*(2), 18–31.

Morgan Stanley. (2015). *Insurance Tech Ecosystems*. goo.gl/N3QH45.

Morgan, J. (2014). A simple explanation of the 'Internet of Things'. *Forbes*. goo.gl/AprcVV.

Morgan, L., Feller, J., & Finnegan, P. (2013). Exploring value networks: Theorising the creation and capture of value with open source software. *European Journal of Information Systems, 22*(5), 569–588. https://doi.org/10.1057/ejis.2012.44.

Moro, O. (1997). *I flussi finanziari nelle imprese di assicurazione: aspetti gestionali*. Milano, Italy: Egea.

Mougayar, W. (2016). *The business blockchain*. Hoboken, NJ: John Wiley.

Mougayar, W., & Buterin, V. (2016). *The business blockchain: A primer on the promise, practice and application*. Hoboken, NJ: John Wiley & Sons.

Mueller, F., Naujoks, H., Singh, H., Schwarz, G., Schwedel, A., & Thomson, K. (2015). *Global Digital Insurance Benchmarking Report 2015*. Bain & Company, www.bain.com/Images/GLOBAL-DIGITAL-INSURANCE-2015.pdf. Accessed 30 March 2020.

Muhuri, P., Shukla, A., & Abraham, A. (2019). Industry 4.0: A bibliometric analysis and detailed overview. *Engineering Applications of Artificial Intelligence., 78*, 218–235. https://doi.org/10.1016/j.engappai.2018.11.007.

Myers, M. D. (1997). Qualitative research in information systems. *MIS Quarterly, 21*(2), 569–588. misq.org/skin/frontend/default/misq/MISQD_isworld/index.html. Accessed 10 July 2019.

Nakamoto, S. (2008, October 31). *Bitcoin: A peer-to-peer electronic cash system*. Satoshi Nakamoto Institute.

Nationaler Ethikrat Deutschland. (2007). *Pradikative Gesundheitsinformationen bei Einstellungsuntersuchungen: Stellungnahme*. www.ethikrat.org/dateien/pdf/praediktive-gesundheitsinformationen-bei-einstellungsuntersuchungen.pdf. Accessed 30 May 2020.

Naujoks, H., & Sherer, L. (2016). *How companies can invest in big data analytics to improve decision making*. Bain & Company. www.bain.com/Images/bain_brief_Insurance_Analytics.pdf. Accessed 30 March 2020.

Naujoks, H., Brettel, T., Singh, H., Darnell, D., & Schwedel, A. (2014, September). *Customer behavior and loyalty in insurance*. Global Edition 2017. Bain & Company.

Naujoks, H., Schwarz, G., Matouschek, G., & von Hu¨lsen, B. (2013). *Versicherungen: Die digitale Herausforderung*. Bain & Company. www.bain.de/Images/BainBrief_Versicherungen_Die-digitale-Herausforderung_FINAL.pdf. Accessed 30 March 2020.

Naujoks, H., Mueller, F., Darnell, D., & Singh, H. (2017, September). *Ecosystems: How companies can reinvent customer relationships*. Bain. www.bain.com/insights/ecosystems-how-insurers-can-reinvent-customer-relationships/J. Accessed 21 March 2020,

Naydenov, R., Liveri, D., Dupre, L., & Chalvatzi, E. (2015). *Secure use of cloud computing in the finance sector*. European Union Agency for Network and Information Security. www.enisa.europa.eu/publications/cloud-in-finance. Accessed 30 March 2020.

Naylor, M. (2016). A perfect storm in insurance: How to survive the looming waves of disruptive technology. *SSRN Electronic Journal*.

Naylor, M. (2017). *Insurance transformed: Technological disruption*. Cham, Switzerland: Springer.

Networks, E., & Monitoring, P. (2018). *Future Internet*. Mdpi.com. www.mdpi.com/journal/futureinternet.

Ngai, E., Hu, Y., Wong, Y., Chen, Y., & Sun, X. (2011). The application of data mining techniques in financial fraud detection: A classification framework and an academic review of literature. *Decision Support Systems, 50*(3), 559–569. https://doi.org/10.1016/j.dss.2010.08.006.

Nguyen, T., & Romeike, F. (2013). *Versicherungswirtschaftslehre – Grundlagen für Studium und Praxis*. Wiesbaden, Germany: Springer Gabler.

Nicoletti, B. (2008, October 10–13). Project Management 2.0. *IPMA Congress*, Rome, Italy.

Nicoletti, B. (2012). *The method of lean & digitize*. London, UK: Gower.

Nicoletti, B. (2016). *Digital insurance*. Houndmills, UK: Palgrave-MacMillan (also translated in Chinese). https://doi.org/10.1057/9781137553270_8.

Nicoletti, B. (2017). *The future of FinTech*. London, UK: Springer.

Nightingale, P. (2003). Innovation in financial services infrastructure. In L. V. Shavinina (Ed.), *The international handbook on innovation* (pp: 529–547). Oxford, UK: Elsevier Science Ltd. ISBN-10: 008044198X.

Noack, S., & Illguth, V. (2016) *Insurtech U¨bersicht DACH*. New Players Network.

Noack, S., Vogel, M., Kühne, M., Staack, L., & Rieckhoff, R. (2017). *Insurtech-Übersicht 2017*. New Players Network. newplayersnetwork.jetzt/wp-content/uploads/2017/07/Insurtech-%C3%9Cbersicht-2.3.-final.pdf. Accessed 10 July 2019.

Normann, R. (2001). *Service management: Strategy and leadership in service business* (pp. 256, 3rd ed.). New York, NY: John Wiley and Sons. ISBN: 0471494399.

O'Reilly, P., & Finnegan, P. (2005). Intermediaries in inter-organizational networks: Building a theory of electronic marketplace performance. *European Journal of Information Systems, 19*(4), 462–480. https://doi.org/10.1057/ejis.2010.12. Accessed 30 May 2020.

Oakland, J. S. (2003). *TQM: Text with cases*. Oxford, UK: Elsevier.

OECD. (2010). *The economic and social role of intermediaries*. goo.gl/MT6PGQ.

Oecd.org. (2016). *OECD Insurance—OECD*. www.oecd.org/pensions/oecdinsurancestatistics.htm. Accessed 8 March 2020.

Oecd.org. (2018). *Improving the role of insurance in cyber risk management—en—OECD*. www.oecd.org/publications/improving-the-role-of-insurance-in-cyber-risk-management-9789264282148-en.htm. Accessed 8 March 2020.

Ondrus, J., Gannamaneni, A., & Lyytinen, K. (2015). The impact of openness on the market potential of multi-sided platforms: A case study of mobile payment platforms. *Journal of Information Technology, 30*(3), 260–275. https://doi.org/10.1057/jit.2015.7.

Orlikowski, W. J., & Baroudi, J. J. (1991). Studying information technology in organizations: Research approaches and assumptions. *Information Systems Research, 2*(1), 1–8. https://doi.org/10.1287/isre.2.1.1.

Osei-Bryson, K. M., & Ngwenyama, O. K. (2006). Managing risks in information systems outsourcing: An approach to analyzing outsourcing risks & structuring incentive contracts. *European Journal of Operational Research, 174*(1), 245–264.

Osmonbekov, T., & Johnston, W. J. (2018), Adoption of the Internet of Things technologies in business procurement: Impact on organizational buying behavior. *Journal of Business Industrial Marketing, 33*, 781–791.

Osterwalder, A., & Pigneur, Y. (2010). *Business model generation: A handbook for visionaries, game changers, and challengers*. Chichester, UK: John Wiley & Sons.

Paefgen, J., Fleisch, E., Ackermann, L., Staake, T., Best, J., & Egli, L. (2013). *Telematics strategy for automobile companies* (I-Lab Whitepaper). www.alexandria.unisg.ch/223402/1/Telematicspercent20Strategypercent20forpercent20Automobilepercent20Companiespercent20(I-Labpercent20Whitepaper).pdf. Accessed 30 March 2020.

Pagani, M. (2013). Digital business strategy and value creation: Framing the dynamic cycle of control points. *MIS Quarterly, 37*(2), 617–632.

Pain, D., Tamm, K., & Turner, G. (2014). *Digital distribution in insurance: A quiet revolution*. Swiss Re sigma.

Pant, V., & Yu, E. (2018). Modeling simultaneous cooperation and competition among enterprises. *Business & Information Systems Engineering, 60*(1), 39–54. https://doi.org/10.1007/s12599-017-0514-0.

Parker, G., & Van Alstyne, M. W. (2014, April). *Platform strategy* (Boston University School of Management Research Paper No. 2439323), 14.

Parker, G., & Van Alstyne, M. W. (2005). Two-sided network effects: a theory of information product design. *Management Science, 51*(10), 1494–1504. https://doi.org/10.1287/mnsc.1050.0400.

Parker, G. G., Van Alstyne, M. W., & Jiang, X. (2017). Platform ecosystems: how developers invert the firm. *MIS Quarterly, 41*(1), 255–266.

Peppard, J., & Rylander, A. (2006). From value chain to value network: lessons for mobile operators. *European Management Journal, 24*(2), 128–141. https://doi.org/10.1016/j.emj.2006.03.003.

Pereira, T., Barreto, L., & Amaral, A. (2017). Network and information security challenges within industry 4.0 paradigm. *Procedia Manufacturing, 13*, 1253–1260.

Perez, S. (2017, November). *Amazon sold millions of Alexa devices over the holiday shopping weekend*. TechCrunch.

Perissinotto, G. (2003). The creation of value through a specialized distribution network. *Geneva Papers on Risk & Insurance—Issues & Practice, 28*(3), 495–501.

Perrin, G. (2017). *Insurtech: les principales startup à l'assaut de l'assurance*. L'Argus de l'assurance. www.argusdelassurance.com/acteurs/insurtech-les-principales-startup-a-l-assaut-de-l-assurance.120997/. Accessed 8 March 2020.

Peverelli, R., & de Feniks, R. (2018). *Amodo: Mobility platform enabling new products and services*. Digital Insurance Agenda. www.digitalinsuranceagenda.com/227/amodo-mobility-platform-enabling-new-products-and-services/. Accessed 10 July 2019.

Piercy, N., & Rich, N. V. (2008). Lean transformation in the pure service environment: The case of the call service centre. *International Journal of Operations & Production Management, 29*(1), 54–76.

Pires, C. P., Sarkar, S. & Carvalho, L. (2008). Innovation in services-how different from manufacturing? *Service Industries Journal, 28*, 1339–1356. https://doi.org/10.1080/02642060802317812.

Pisoni, G. (2020). Going digital: Case study of an Italian insurance company. *Journal of Business Strategy*, ahead-of-print. https://doi.org/10.1108/JBS-11-2019-0225.

Plaster, G. A., & Alderman, J. D. (2006). *Beyond Six Sigma: Profitable growth through customer value creation*. Hoboken, NJ: John Wiley & Sons.

Polo, Y., & Sese, F. J. (2016). Does the nature of the interaction matter? Understanding customer channel choice for purchases and communications. *Journal of Service Research, 19*(3), 276–290. https://doi.org/10.1177/1094670516645189.

Ponsignon, F., Durrieu, F., & Bouzdine-Chameeva, T. (2017). Customer experience design: A case study in the cultural sector. *Journal of Service Management, 28*(4), 763–787. https://doi.org/10.1108/JOSM-01-2017-0016.

Ponsignon, F., Klaus, Ph, & Maull, R. S. (2015). Experience co-creation in financial services: An empirical exploration. *Journal of Service Management, 26*(2), 295–320. https://doi.org/10.1108/JOSM-10-2014-0277.

Porter, M. E. (1985). *The competitive advantage: Creating and sustaining superior performance* (1st ed., pp. 557). New York, NY: The Free Press. ISBN-10: 0029250900.

Poole, M. S., & van de Ven, A. H. (1989). Using paradox to build management organization theories. *The Academy of Management Review, 14*(4), 562–578.

Porter, M. E., & Heppelman, J. E. (2014). How smart, connected products are transforming competition. *Harvard Business Review, 92,* 11–64.

Porter, M. E. (1990). The competitive advantage of nations. *Harvard Business Review, 68*(2), 73–93.

Pousttchi, K. (2005). *Mobile Payment in Deutschland – Szenarienübergreifendes Referenzmodell für mobile Bezahlvorgänge*. Wiesbaden, Germany: Gabler/Deutscher Universitätsverlag.

Pousttchi, K. (2008). A modeling approach and reference models for the analysis of mobile payment use cases. *Electronic Commerce Research and Applications, 7*(2), 182–201.

Pousttchi, K. (2017). Digitale transformation. In N. Gronau, J. Becker, N. Kliewer, J. M. Leimeister, & S. Overhage (Eds.), *Enzyklopädie der Wirtschaftsinformatik* [*Encyclopedia of Business Informatics*]. www.enzyklopaedie-der-wirtschaftsinformatik.de/lexikon/technologien-methoden/Informatik%2D%2DGrundlagen/digitalisierung/digitale-transformation/digitale-transformation. Accessed 10 July 2019.

Pousttchi, K., & Dehnert, M. (2018). Exploring the digitalization impact on consumer decision-making in retail banking. *Electronic Markets, 28*(3), 265–286. https://doi.org/10.1007/s12525-017-0283-0.

Pousttchi, K., & Gleiss, A. (2019). Surrounded by middlemen—How multi-sided platforms change the insurance industry. *Electronic Markets, 29*(4), 609–629. https://doi.org/10.1007/s12525-019-00363-w.

Pousttchi, K., & Goeke, L. (2011). Determinants of customer acceptance for mobile data services: An empirical analysis with formative constructs. *International Journal of Electronic Business, 9*(1–2), 26–43.

Pousttchi, K., & Hufenbach, Y. (2011). Value creation in the Mobile market—A reference model for the role(s) of the future mobile network operator. *Business & Information Systems Engineering, 53*(5), 300–311.

Pousttchi, K., & Hufenbach, Y. (2014). Engineering the value network of the customer interface and marketing in the data-rich retail environment. *International Journal of Electronic Commerce, 18*(4), 17–41. https://doi.org/10.2753/JEC1086-4415180401.

Pousttchi, K., Gleiss, A., Buzzi, B., & Kohlhagen, M. (2019, July). Technology impact types for digital transformation. In *2019 IEEE 21st Conference on Business Informatics (CBI)* (vol. 1, pp. 487–494). IEEE.

Pousttchi, K., Tilson, D., Lyytinen, K., & Hufenbach, Y. (2015). Introduction to the special issue on Mobile commerce: Mobile commerce research yesterday, today, tomorrow—What remains to be done? *International Journal of Electronic Commerce, 19*(4), 1–20. https://doi.org/10.1080/10864415.2015.1029351.

Pretty, R. (2017). *Innovations in life insurance: Research & development*. SCORviews Knowledge Center. www.scorgloballifeamericas.com/en-us/knowledgecenter/innovations-in-life-insurance-r-d. Accessed 10 July 2019.

Price Waterhouse Coopers. (2014). In-depth. A look at current financial reporting issues reimagining customer relationships—Key findings from the EY Global Consumer Insurance Survey.

Price Waterhouse Coopers. (2014). *Industrie 4.0: Chancen und Herausforderungen der vierten industriellen Revolution*. Munich: GRIN Verlag.

Price Waterhouse Coopers. (2015). *The sharing economy*. Consumer Intelligence Series. www.pwc.com/us/en/industry/entertainment-media/publications/consumer-intelligence-series/assets/pwc-cis-sharing-economy.pdf. Accessed 30 March 2020.

Price Waterhouse Coopers. (2015). *Disruption is the new reality in the global insurance industry*. goo.gl/oh8Htt.

Price Waterhouse Coopers. (2016). *AI in insurance: hype or reality?* www.pwc.com/us/en/insurance/publications/assets/pwc-top-issues-artificial-intelligence.pdf. Accessed 30 March 2020.

Price Waterhouse Coopers. (2016). *The $5 billion opportunity for reinsurers*. www.pwc.com/insurance. Accessed 08 March 2020.

Price Waterhouse Coopers. (2017). *A marketplace without boundaries? Responding to disruption*. goo.gl/p8Hs9b.

Price Waterhouse Coopers. (2018). *Blockchain, a catalyst for new approaches in insurance*. www.pwc.com/gx/en/industries/financial-services/publications/blockchain-a-catalyst.html. Accessed 8 March 2020.

Price Waterhouse Coopers. (2018). *Chain reaction: How blockchain solution might transform wholesale insurance*. www.pwc.com/gx/en/industries/financial-services/publications/blockchain-technology-might-transform-wholesale-insurance.html. Accessed 8 March 2020.

Prieto, B., Plumbee, J., Vaughn, D., & Vaughn, J. (2015). Resilience: Managing the risk of natural disaster, Fluor, *Proceedings of the 3rd International Conference on Theory and Practice of Electronic Governance*, Bogota, Colombia, 10–13 November, 409–410

Puschmann, T. (2017). Fintech. *Business & Information Systems Engineering, 59*(1), 69–76. https://doi.org/10.1007/s12599-017-0464-6.

Puschmann, T., & Alt, R. (2016). Sharing economy. *Business & Information Systems Engineering, 58*(1), 93–99. https://doi.org/10.1007/s12599-015-0420-2.

Pyzdek, T. (2003). *The Six Sigma handbook*. New York, NY: McGraw-Hill.

Rahlfs, C. (2007). *Redefinition der Wertschöpfungskette von Versicherungsunternehmen* (Gabler Wirtschaft ed.). Wiesbaden, Germany: Deutscher Universitäts-Verlag.

Rainie, L. (2018). *Americans' complicated feelings about social media in an era of privacy concerns*. Pew Research.

Rajput, S., & Singh, S. P. (2018, March). Identifying Industry 4.0 IoT enablers by integrated PCA-ISM-DEMATEL approach. Management Decisions.

Rayport, J., & Sviokla, J. (1995). Exploiting the virtual value chain. *Harvard Business Review., 73,* 75–85.

Razo-Zapata, I. S., Gordijn, J., de Leenheer, P., & Wieringa, R. (2015). e3 service: a critical reflection and future research. *Business & Information Systems Engineering, 57*(1), 51–59. https://doi.org/10.1007/s12599-014-0360-2.

Reichel, L., & Schmeiser, H. (2017). Digitales Monitoring in der Assekuranz. In: Institut für Versicherungswirtschaft (Hrsg.), *Assekuranz 2025: Quo vadis?*. 85102. St. Gallen: Verlag Institut für Versicherungswirtschaft der Universität St. Gallen.

Reichheld, F. F. (1996). *The loyalty effect* (1st ed., pp. 323). Boston: Harvard Business School Press. ISBN-10: 0875844480.

Ringel, J., & Rosenbaum, M. (2016, May). *Ein Netzwerk. Vielfältige Leistungen. Presentation at Versicherungsforen*. Leipzig, Germany. docplayer.org/20068468-Ein-netzwerk-vielfaeltige-leistungen.html. Accessed 10 July 2019.

Ritchey, T. (2013). *General morphological analysis—A general method for non-quantified modelling*. Swedish Morphological Society. www.swemorph.com/pdf/gma.pdf.

Robertshaw, G. S. (2012). Online price comparisons sites: How technology has destabilized* and transformed the UK insurance market. *Journal of Revenue and Pricing Management, 11*(2), 137–145.

Rochet, J.-C., & Tirole, J. (2003). Platform competition in two-sided markets. *Journal of the European Economic Association, 1*(4), 990–1029. https://doi.org/10.1162/154247603322493212.

Rochin Demong, N. A., Othman, A. K., Hj Yunus, N., & Wan Amran, N. A. (2019). Service quality factors and customer satisfaction on life insurance services. *Journal Islamic Management. Studies, 2*, 22–31.

Roden, S., Nucciarelli, A., Li, F., & Graham, G. (2017). *Big data & the transformation of operations models: A framework & a new research agenda*. Production Planning Control.

Rogers, D. L. (2016). The digital transformation playbook: Rethink your business for the digital age.

Roland Berger. (2015). *Internet of Things and insurance*. goo.gl/h4pCys.

Roland Berger. (2016). *Digital and disrupted: All changes for healthcare*. goo.gl/i1PxkY.

Ross, J. W., Sebastian, I. M., Beath, C., Mocker, M., Moloney, K. G., & Fonstad, N. O. (2016). Designing and executing digital strategies. In *37th International Conference on Information Systems (ICIS)*, Dublin, Ireland.

Rossbach, S., & Hilberg, L. (2016). *InsurTech: Wie Startups die Wertschöpfungskette der Versicherungen revolutionieren* (TME Whitepaper). www.tme-ag.de/fileadmin/customer/documents/2016-08_TME-Whitepaper_-_InsurTech.pdf. Accessed 10 July 2019.

Rother, M., & Harris, R. (2006). *Creating Continuous Flow: una guida all'azione per manager, ingegneri & direttori di produzione*. Milano, Italy: The Lean Enterprise Institute.

Rother, M., & Shook, J. (2003). *Learning to See, la mappatura del flusso del valore per creare valore & eliminare i muda*. Milan, Italy: The Lean Enterprise Institute.

Rottker, C. (2016). Wenn der Schrittzähler die Prämie senkt. *Bilanz., 26*(10), 2016.

Rottker, C. (2017). Das Problem mit der individuellen Versicherung. *Bilanz., 07*(03), 2017.

Rupawala, H. (2018, December). *Homeowners loss ratios improve, premiums increase in Q3*. S&P Global Market Intelligence.

Rust, R., & Huang, M. (2014). The service revolution and the transformation of marketing science. *Marketing Science, 33*(2), 206–221. https://doi.org/10.1287/mksc.2013.0836.

Saarijärvi, H., Grönroos, C., & Kuusela, H. (2014). Reverse use of customer data: Implications for service-based business models. *Journal of Services Marketing, 28*(7), 529–537. https://doi.org/10.1108/JSM-05-2013-0111.

Salcedo-Sanz, S., Cuadra, L., Portilla-Figueras, A., Jiménez-Fernández, S., & Alexandre, E. (2013). A review of computational intelligence algorithms in insurance applications. In *Statistical and soft computing approaches in insurance problems*. Commack, NY: Nova Science Publishers, Inc.

Santos, C., Mehrsai, A., Barros, A. C., Araujo, M., & Ares, E. (2017). Towards Industry 4.0: An overview of European strategic roadmaps. *Procedia Manufacturing, 1*(3), 972–979.

SAS. (2017). *Data mining—What it is and why it matters*. www.sas.com/en_us/insights/analytics/data-mining.html. Accessed 30 May 2020.

Sawers, P. (2018). *P2P insurance firm Lemonade launches out of stealth, powered by chatbots, morals, and big bucks*. VentureBeat. venturebeat.com/2016/09/21/lemonade-insurance-social-good-p2p/. Accessed 8 March 2020.

Sayegh, K., & Desoky, M. (2019). *Blockchain Application in insurance and reinsurance*. France: Skema Business School. www.researchgate.net/publication/327987901_Blockchain_Application_in_Insurance_and_Reinsurance. Accessed 30 May 2020.

Scardovi, C. (2017). *Digital transformation in financial services*. Cham: Springer International Publishing.

Scarfo, A. (2011). *Insurance distribution in Italy: Post-downturn scenarios*. Value Partners.

Scheuermann, A. (2017). *Versicherer vergleichen sich selbst*. Hannoversche Allgemeine Zeitung. www.haz.de/Nachrichten/Wirtschaft/Niedersachsen/Hannoversches-Unternehmen-Concordia-finanziert-Online-Vergleich. Accessed 10 July 2019.

Scheuffel, P. (2016). Taming the beast: A scientific definition of Fintech. *Journal of Innovation Management, 4*, 32–54.

Schlenk, C. T. (2017). *Das wertvollste Unternehmen in 15 Jahren wird eine Versicherung sein*. Gründerszene. www.gruenderszene.de/allgemein/wefox-julian-teicke-plaene-one. Accessed 10 July 2019.

Schmeiser, H. (2016). Schafft sich die Assekuranz ab? *Schweizer Versicherung, 2016*(7), 31.

Schmid, C. N. (2015). *Referenzprozessmodell zur Steuerung der Entwicklung von IT-enabled Business Innovations in der Versicherung*. Wiesbaden, Germany: Springer Gabler.

Schmidt, C. (2018). *Insurance in the digital age*. Zurich: The Geneva Association, 1–20.

Schmidt, R., Möhring, M., Härtling, R. C., Reichstein, C., Neimaier, P., & Jozinovic, P. (2015). Potentials for creating smart products: empirical research results. In W. Abramowicz (Ed.), *Business information systems* (pp. 16–27). Springer: Cham, Switzerland.

Schroeder, R. G., Linderman, K., Liedtke, C., & Choo, A. S. (2008). Six Sigma: Definition & underlying theory. *Journal of Operations Management, 26*(4), 536–554.

Schwab, K. (2017). *A Quarta Revolução Industrial. Edição: Levoir, Marketing e Conteúdos*. S.A. Lisbon, Portugal: Multimédia.

Schwarz, G. et al. (2014). Customer loyalty and the digital transformation in P&C and life insurance.

Schweri, S., Greber, D., Frick, P., & Erny, M. (2015). *Die Schweizer Versicherungsbranche 2015*. Entwicklungen und ihre Auswirkungen auf die Soil-Kompetenzen. Zhaw School of Management and Law Winthertur, Switzerland.

Seddon, P. B., Constantinidis, D., Tamm, T., & Dod, H. (2017). How does business analytics contribute to business value? *Information Systems Journal, 27*(3), 237–269. https://doi.org/10.1111/isj.12101.

Seebacher, S., & Schüritz, R. (2018). Blockchain technology as an enabler of service systems: A structured literature review.

Segev, I., & Vickers, A. (2017). *What the new world of insurance could look like*. McKinsey and Company.

Selke, S. (2016). Lifelogging zwischen disruptiver Technologie und kulturellem Wan-del. In S. Selke (Hrsg.), *Lifelogging. Digitale Selbstvermessung und Lebenspro-tokollierung zwischen disruptiver Technologie und kulturellem Wandel* (pp. 1–24). Wiesbaden: Springer VS.

Selleri, L. (2003). *Impresa di assicurazione e strategia del valore*. Milano, Italy: Etas.

Severeijns, L. (2017). *What is blockchain? How is it going to affect business?*. Amsterdam, Netherlands: Vrije Universiteit Amsterdam.

Seville, E. (2016). *Resilient organizations: How to survive, thrive and create opportunities through crisis and change*. London, UK: Kogan Page Publishers.

Shapiro, C., & Varian, H. (1998). *Information rules: A strategic guide to the network economy*. Boston: Harvard Business Press.

Sharples, M., & Domingue, J. (2016). The blockchain and kudos: A distributed system for educational record, reputation and reward. In K. Verbert, M. Sharples, & T. Klobučar (Eds.), *Adaptive and Adaptable learning. EC-TEL 2016. Lecture Notes in Computer Science*, 9891. Springer: Cham, Switzerland. https://doi.org/10.1007/978-3-319-45153-4_48.

Shubber, K. (2014). Guevara wins Wired Money's startup competition. *Wired*, goo.gl/zt5Fhu.

Shurter, S., & Towers, S. (2002). *Customer expectation management & successful customer outcomes*. Tampa, FL: Meghan Kiffer Press.

Siering, M., Koch, J. A., & Deokar, A. V. (2016). Detecting fraudulent behavior on crowdfunding platforms: The role of linguistic and content-based cues in static and dynamic contexts. *Journal of Management Information Systems, 33*(2), 421–455.

Silverstein, D., Samuel, P., & DeCarlo, N. (2009). *The innovator's toolkit*. Hoboken, NJ: John Wiley.

Singh, A., & Akhilesh, K. B. (2020). The insurance industry-cybersecurity in the hyper-connected age. In K. Akhilesh & D. Möller (Eds.), *Smart technologies* (pp. 201–219). Singapore: Springer.

Sinha, M. N. (2018). Selected papers from 9th Canadian Quality Congress. *Business Process Management Journal, 24*(6), 1286–1288.

Skalle, Ramachandran S., Schuster, M., Szaloky, V., & Antoun, S. (2009). *Aligning business process management, service-oriented architecture, & lean six sigma for real business results*. Armonk, NY: IBM Redbooks.

Slusarczyk, B. (2018). Industry 4.—Are we ready? *Polish Journal of Management Studies, 17,* 232–248.

Smit, J., Kreutzer, S., Moeller, C., & Carlberg, M. (2016). *Industry 4.0*. European Parliament. Study for the ITRE Committee.

Smith, H., & Fingar, P. (2003). *Business process management, the third wave*. Tampa, FL: Meghan-Kiffer.

Smith, H., & Fingar, P. (2003). *It doesn't matter—Business processes do*. Tampa, FL: Meghan-Kiffer.

Snee, R. D., & Hoerl, R. W. (2003). *Leading Six Sigma. A step-by-step guide based on experience with GE & other Six Sigma companies*. Upper Saddle River, NJ: Pearson Education.

Son, J., Kim, S. S., & Riggins, F. J. (2006). Consumer adoption of net-enabled infomediaries: Theoretical explanations and an empirical test. *Journal of the Association for Information Systems, 7*(7), 473–508.

Song, P., Xue, L., Rai, A., & Zhang, C. (2018). The ecosystem of software platform: A study of asymmetric cross-side network effects and platform governance. *MIS Quarterly, 42*(1), 121–142. https://doi.org/10.25300/MISQ/2018/13737.

Sousa, R., & Voss, C. (2002). Quality management re-visited: A reflective review & agenda for future research. *Journal of Operations Management, 20*(1), 91–109.

Spagnoletti, P., Resca, A., & Lee, G. (2015). A design theory for digital platforms supporting online communities: A multiple case study. *Journal of Information Technology, 30*(4), 364–380. https://doi.org/10.1057/jit.2014.37.

Spekman, R. (1979). Influence & information: An exploratory investigation of the boundary role person's basis of power. *Academy of Management Journal, 22*(1), 104–117.

SrinSoft. (2018). IoT (Internet of Things) Solutions & Services. www.srinsofttech.com/iot-solutions-internet-of-things.html. Accessed 19 December.

Sriram, S., Manchanda, P., Bravo, M. E., Chu, J., Ma, L., Song, M., et al. (2015). Platforms: a multiplicity of research opportunities. *Marketing Letters, 26*(2), 141–152. https://doi.org/10.1007/s11002-014-9314-1.

Stamison C. M., Campbell, A., & Winkler, M. (2011). Beyond EDI: An Agent's Role in the Cloud Proceedings of the Charleston Library Conference.

Statista. (2019). www.statista.com/topics/4116/insurtech/.

Staykova, K., & Damsgaard, J. (2014). A model of digital payment infrastructure formation and development: The EU regulator's perspective. In *13th International Conference on Mobile Business (ICMB 2014)*. London, UK.

Staykova, K., & Damsgaard, J. (2015). A typology of multi-sided platforms: The core and the periphery. *23rd European Conference on Information Systems (ECIS),* Münster, Germany.

Stepanek, L., & Roman, P. (2017). Urban insurance industry ideas of second millennium. *Ecoforum. Swiss Re Institute (2017). Technology and insurance: Themes and challenges.*

Stephenson, D. (2013). *7 Big data techniques that create business value.* www.firmex.com/thedealroom/7-big-data-techniques-that-create-business-value/. Accessed 30 March 2020.

Steven, M., & Klünder, T. (2018). Nachhaltigkeit schlanker Industrie 4.0-Netzwerke. In A. Khare, D. Kessler, & J. Wirsam (Eds.), *Marktorientiertes Produkt- und Produktionsmanagement in digitalen Umwelten* (pp. 201–221). Wiesbaden, Germany: Springer Gabler.

Stevens, E., & Dimitriadis, S. (2004). New service development through the lens of organizational learning: Evidence from longitudinal case studies. *Journal of Business Research, 57*(10), 1074–1084.

Swiss RE. (2016) *Companies and reinsurers launch blockchain initiative.* www.swissre.com/reinsurance/companies_and_reinsurers_launch_blockchain_initiative.html. Accessed 30 May 2020.

Tan, B., Pan, S., Lu, X., & Huang, L. (2015). The role of is capabilities in the development of multi-sided platforms: The digital ecosystem strategy of

Alibaba.com. *Journal of the Association for Information Systems, 16*(4), 248–280. https://doi.org/10.17705/1jais.00393.
Tanguy, C., & Lorenz, J. T. (2017). InsurTech—The threat that inspires.
Thornton, J. & L. White, 2001. Customer orientations and usage of financial distribution channels. *Journal of Services Market., 15,* 168–185. https://doi.org/10.1108/08876040110392461.
Tanushree, S., & Deepanshu, Y. (2017). *Digital disruption in the insurance industry*. KPMG. goo.gl/k8wb4s.
Täuscher, K., Hilbig, R., & Abdelkafi, N. (2017). Geschäftsmodellelemente mehrseitiger Plattformen. In D. Schallmo, A. Rusnjak, J. Anzengruber, T. Werani, & M. Jünger (Eds.), *Digitale Transformation von Geschäftsmodellen – Grundlagen, Instrumente und Best Practice* (pp. 179–212). Wiesbaden, Germany: Springer Gabler.
Teambrella.com. (2018). *Teambrella: A peer to peer insurance system.* teambrella.com. (WhitePaper). Accessed 8 March 2020.
Telukdarie, A., Buhulaiga, E., Bag, S., Gupta, S., & Luo, Z. (2018). Industry 4.0 implementation for multinationals. *Process Safety and Environmental Protection, 118,* 316–329.
Ter Meulen, R., Arts, W., & Muffels, R. (2010). Solidarity, health and social care in Europe. Introduction to the volume. In: R. ter Meulen, W. Arts, & R. Muffels (Hrsg.), *Solidarity in health and social care in Europe* (S. 1–12). Dordrecht: Kluwer Academic Publishers.
Tessarini, G., & Saltorato, P. (2018). Impactos da indústria 4.0 na organização do trabalho: uma revisão sistemática da literatura. *Revista Produção Online, 18*(2), 743–769.
Thakur, S., & Kulkarni, V. (2017). Blockchain and its applications—A detailed survey. *International Journal of Computer Applications, 180*(3), 29–35.
The IoT Insurance Consumer Insurance Survey. (2016). *IoT insurance observatory.*
The Smart Home Startups Companies Have Invested In. *CB Insights Research,* 5 Marh. 2018. www.cbinsights.com/research/smart-home-insurance-investment/.
Tierney, K., & Bruneau, M. (2007, May–June). Conceptualizing & measuring resilience: A key to disaster loss reduction. *TR News*, No. 250, 14–16.
Timmers, P. (1998, September 9). *Business models for electronic markets.* CommerceNet Research Report.
Tischhauser, P., Naumann, M., Candreia, A., Treier, S., & Senser, J. (2016) *Digitalisierung: Der Schweizer Versicherungssektor im Umbruch.* The Boston Consulting Group. image-src.bcg.com/BCG_COM/Report_Digitalisierung_tcm20-40440.pdf. Accessed 30 March 2020.
Tjahjono, B., Esplugues, C., Ares, E., & Pelaez, G. (2017). What does industry 4.0 mean to supply chain? *Procedia Manufacturing, 13,* 1175–1182.

Townsend, A. (2014). *Re-programming mobility: The digital transformation of transportation in the United States*. New York, NY, USA: Rudin Center for Transportation Policy and Management.

Treacy, M., & Wiersema, F. (1995). *The discipline of market leaders: Choose your customer, narrow your focus, dominate your market*. Boston, MA: Addison-Wesley Pub Co.

Turban, E. (2008). *Information technology for management: transforming organizations in the digital economy* (6th ed.). Hoboken, NJ: John Wiley & Sons.

Uday, M. A., & Chon, G. (2004). Applying lean manufacturing principles to information intensive services. *International Journal of Services Technology & Management, 5*(5–6), 488–506.

Ulrich, D., Kerr, S., & Ashkenas, R. (2002). *The GE work-out: How to implement GÈ's revolutionary method for busting bureaucracy & attacking organizational—Fast*. New York, NY: McGraw-Hill.

Vaia, G., Carmel, E., DeLone, W. H., Trautsch, H., & Menichetti, F. (2012). Vehicle telematics at an Italian insurer: New auto insurance products and a new industry ecosystem. *MIS Quarterly Executive, 11*(3), 113–125.

Vaidya, S., Ambad, P., & Bhosle, S. (2018). Industry 4.—A glimpse. *Procedia Manufacturing, 20*, 233–238.

Van Doorn, J., Mende, M., Noble, S. M., Hulland, J., Ostrom, A. L., Grewal, D., & Petersen, J. A. (2017). Domo arigato Mr. Roboto: Emergence of automated social presence in organizational frontlines and customers' service experiences. *Journal of Service Research, 20*(1), 43–58. https://doi.org/10.1177/1094670516679272.

van Rossum, A., de Castries, H., & Mendelsohn, R. (2002). The debate on the insurance value chain. *The Geneva Papers on Risk and Insurance, 27*(1), 89–101.

Various Authors. (2007). *Rath & Robust's Integrated Lean Six Sigma pocket guide*. Lexington, MA: Rath & Strong.

Vellinga, N. E. (2017). From the testing to the deployment of self-driving cars: Legal challenges to policymakers on the road ahead. *Computer Law & Security, 33*(6), 847–863. https://doi.org/10.1016/j.clsr.2017.05.006.

Vendrell-Herrero, F., Bustinza, O. F., & Parry, G. (2017). Servitization, digitization and supply chain interdependency.

Volosovich, S. (2016). InsurTech: Challenges and development perspectives. *International Journal of Innovative Technologies in Economy, 3*, 39–42.

Voss, C., Tsikriktsis, N., & Frohlich, M. (2002). Case research in operations management. *International Journal of Operations & Production Management, 2*, 195–219.

Vrobel, E., & Donohue, E. (2016). Generali and progressive announce telematics R&D agreement. *Generali Press Release*. www.generali.de/ueber-gen

erali/presse-medien/pressemitteilungen/generali-and-progressive-announce%2D%2Dtelematics-r-d-agreement-11382/. Accessed 10 July 2019.

Wade, R. M. (2015). *The battle for digital disruption: startups vs incumbents*. IMD. goo.gl/du9xYU.

Wagelaar, D., & Van Der Straeten, R. (2007). Platform ontologies for the model-driven architecture. *European Journal of Information Systems, 16*(4), 362–373. https://doi.org/10.1057/palgrave.ejis.3000686.

Waller, M. A., & Fawcett, S. (2013). Data science, predictive analytics, and big data: a revolution that will transform supply chain design and management. *Journal of Business Logistics, 34*(2), 77–84.

Walser, E. (2008, June). *Versicherungswirtschaft im Spannungsfeld zwischen Solida-Halt und Eigenverantwortung*. Vortrag anlässlich der Generalversammlung des Schweizerischen Versicherungsverbandes, Zurich. Switzerland.

Wang, P., Xiong, Z., Wang, W., Niyato, D., & Feng, S. (2018). *On cyber risk management of blockchain networks: A game theoretic approach*. Singapore: Nanyang Technological University.

Ward, A. C. (2007). *Lean product & process development*. Cambridge, MA: Lean Enterprise Institute.

Weber, T. A. (2014). Intermediation in a sharing economy: insurance, moral hazard, and rent extraction. *Journal of Management Information Systems, 31*(3), 35–71.

Webster, J., & Watson, R. T. (2002). Analyzing the past to prepare for the future: writing a literature review. *MIS Quarterly, 26*(2), xiii–xxiii.

Weidmann, M., Renner, T., & Rex, S. (2010). Cloud Computing in der Versicherungsbranche: It-Trends im Internet der Dienste aus der Sicht von Anwendern und Anbietern. Fraunhofer IAO*: IT-Trends in der Versicherungsbranche*. wiki.iao.fraunhofer.de/images/studien/cloud-computing-in-der-versicherungsbranche.pdf. Accessed 10 July 2019.

Weinmann, M., Schneider, C., & vom Brocke, J. (2016). Digital nudging. *Business & Information Systems Engineering, 58*(6), 433–436. https://doi.org/10.1007/s12599-016-0453-1.

West, D. M., & Allen, J. R. (2018). *How artificial intelligence is transforming the world*. Washington DC: Brookings Institution.

Wiener, K. & Theis, A. (2017). *InsurTech(s): Zwischen Konkurrenz und Partnerschaft*. GDV—Makro und Märkte kompakt 9. www.gdv.de/2017/02/schumpeterscher-moment-fuer-die-versicherungsbranche/. Accessed 30 March 2020.

Williams, R. (2006). eneralized ordered logit/partial proportional odds models for ordinal dependent variables. *The Stata Journal, 6*(1), 58–82.

Willing, C., Brandt, T., & Neumann, D. (2017). Electronic mobility market platforms—A review of the current state and applications of business analytics. *Electronic Markets, 27*(3), 267–282. https://doi.org/10.1007/s12525-017-0257-2.

Willis Tower Watson, & CB Insights, (2017). New horizon: How diverse growth strategies can advance digitization in the insurance industry. *Quarterly InsurTechs Briefing* Q1 2017. goo.gl/Hcj5vH.

Wills, G. (2017). B3i stellt funktionsfähigen Prototypen für Rückversicherung vor. *Allianz Pressemitteilung*. www.allianz.com/de/presse/news/engagement/sponsoring/170910-B3i-stellt-funktionsf%C3%A4higen-Prototypen-vor/. Accessed 10 July 2019.

Wilson, J. D., Jr. (2017). *Creating strategic value through financial technology*. Hobokine, NJ: John Wiley & Sons.

Wns.com. (2018). *Article: Cashing in on IoT: Time for companies to change the blueprint?* www.wns.com/insights/articles/articledetail/516/cashing-in-on-iot-time-for-companies-to-change-the-blueprint. Accessed 8 March 2020.

Womack, R., & Trish, R. (2013). Google's Schmidt: Insurance about to 'explode' with uses of big data. goo.gl/1ZWeNf.

Wüllenweber, K., & Weitzel, T. (2007). An empirical exploration of h240c-240cow process standardization reduces outsourcing risks. *System Sciences, IEEE*, January, 240–250

Yates, J. (2005). *Structuring the information age—Life insurance and technology in the twentieth century*. Baltimore: John Hopkins.

Yin, R. K. (2003). *Case study research: Design & methods* (3rd ed.). *Applied Social Research Methods Series*. Beverly Hills, CA: Sage.

Yin, R. K. (2009). *Case study research: Design and methods*. Newbury Park, CA and Thousand Oaks: Sage.

Youseff, L., Butrico, M., & DaSilva, D. (2008). Towards a unified ontology of Cloud Computing. *Grid Computing Environments Workshop, GCE08*, 1–10.

Yue, X., Wang, H., Jin, D., Li, M., & Jiang, W. (2016). Healthcare data gateways: Found healthcare intelligence on blockchain with novel privacy risk control. *Journal of Medical Systems, 40*(10), 218.

Zhang, S., Zhang, S., Chen, X., & Huo, X. (2010). Cloud Computing research and development trend. *2010 Second International Conference on Future Networks*.

Zhao, X., Xue, L., & Whinston, A. B. (2013). Managing interdependent information security risks: Cyberinsurance, managed security services, and risk pooling arrangements. *Journal of Management Information Systems, 30*(1), 123–152.

Zhu, Y., & Chang, Y. (2016). The key role of relevance in personalized advertisement: examining its impact on perceptions of privacy invasion, self-awareness, and continuous use intentions. *Computers in Human Behavior, 65*, 442–447. https://doi.org/10.1016/j.chb.2016.08.048.

Zott, C., Amit, R., & Massa, L. (2011). The business model: Recent developments and future research. *Journal of Management, 37*(4), 1019–1042. https://doi.org/10.1177/0149206311406265.

Zurich, GfK & Google. (2016). *ROPO Studie fu¨r Versicherungsprodukte in Deutschland—Kernergebnisse*. www.zurich.de/de-de/ueber-uns/presse/aktuell/gfk-studie. Accessed 30 March 2020.

Zwicky, F. (1966). *Entdecken, Erfinden, Forschen im Morphologischen Weltbild*. München, Germany: Knaur-Droemer.

Sitography

blog.axa.ch
blogs.microsoft.com
cfos.ch
data.gov.uk
emeia.ey-vx.com
fintechnews.ch
home.kpmg.com/content
industry4.hu
leanforum.se
myhippo.com
openparliament.ca
searchmanufacturingerp.techtarget.com
ssrn.com
www.3isite.com
www.aaai.org
www.aberdeen.com
www.accountingtools.com
www.advisorevolved.com
www.agcs.allianz.com
www.agendadigitale.eu/cloudmate.com/about
www.allianz.com
www.altimate.ca
www.americanexpress.com
www.amfam.com
www.amodo.eu
www.assicurazione.it
www.assinews.it
www.axa.com
www.bain.com
www.bernardonicoletti.com
www.bershka.com
www.bppb.it
www.briansolis.com
www.businessdictionary.com

www.canon.it
www.capgemini.com
www.carriermanagement.com
www.ceclass.com/
www.chaseperformance.com
www.cii.co.uk
www.cloudmate.com
www.cnipa.it
www.consult.it
www.con-way.com
www.cordis.lu
www.corrierecomunicazioni.it
www.cscmp.org
www.data.com
www.dcvelocity.com
www.docplayer.it/
www.dylog.it
www.eccellere.com
www.econ.uniurb.it
www.economyup.it
www.ecostat.unical.it
www.en.wiktionary.org
www.esisinc.com
www.europarl.europa.eu/
www.expansion.com
www.ey.com
www.financial-dictionary.com
www.fostec.com
www.fraunhofer.de
www.freedomdefined.org
www.fujutsu.com
www.generali.com
www.georgia-associates.com
www.gformula.com
www.grin.com
www.hem.com
www.hp.it
www.hrpub.org
www.hyphen-italia.com/
www.i4punto0.it
www.ibm.com
www.idtech.it

www.ieee.com
www.iged.it
www.ilpuntopensionielavoro.it
www.ilsole24ore.com
www.impind.de
unifi.it
www.impresaestesa.it
www.impresaprogetto.it
www.inditex.com
www.industriequattropuntozero.it
www.industryweek.com
www.institute.swissre.com
www.insuranceeurope.eu
www.insurancequotes.org
www.investopedia.com
www.iotinsobs.com/.
www.isixsigma.com
www.ispo.cec.be/ecommerce/.
www.istitute-of-logistics.org.uk
www.iungo.it
www.ivass.it
www.kin.com
www.kpmg.com
www.laserfiche.com
www.leancenter.it
www.leancompany.it
www.Lean-digitize.com
www.leanmanufacturing.it
www.logility.com
www.ltdmgmt.com
www.luzerner-forum.ch
www.managementstudyguide.com
www.massimodutti.com
www.mckinsey.com
www.mckinseyquarterly.com
www.metromile.com
www.microsoft.com
www.newagepublishers.com
www.novell.com
www.ohio-state.edu/index.php
www.opendefinition.org
www.openwork.it

www.optimialelectronics.com
www.organizzazioniaziendali.it/index.asp
www.oysho.com
www.pacificlifere.com
www.panorama.it
www.pewresearch.org
www.policyholder.gov.in
www.prophet.com/
www.pullandbear.com
www.qualityi.it
www.queoconsulting.it
www.qurius.it
www.reggiani.it
www.rgare.com
www.ryder.com
www.sas.com
www.sciencedirect.com
www.scmr.com
www.scodanibbio.com/site/access/homeaccess/65.html
www.sistemamodaitalia.it
www.skillprofiles.eu
www.stradivarius.com
www.strategyzer.com
www.supply-chain.org
www.svv.ch
www.thebalancesmb.com
www.the-digital-insurer.com
www.theinstitutes.org
www.theinsurance.it
www.timreview.ca
www.toshiba.it
www.tso.it
www.unifi.it
www.unioncamere.it
www.unitec.it
www.uterque.es
www.uwplatt.edu
www.xerox.it
www.zara.com
www.zarahome.com
www.zenshare.it
www2.deloitte.com

Webplaces of business cases

manulife.ca
www.crunchbase.com
gusto.com
heyguevara.com
www.hioscar.com
www.lemonade.com
statista.com
www.shopify.com
www.friendsurance.com

Index

A
Africa
  North Africa, 119
  South Africa, 141
America
  Latin America
    Brazil, 108
    Chile, 90
    Colombia, 90
    Mexico, 90
    Panama, 90
    Peru, 90
  USA
    American Marketing Association, 459
    California, Silicon Valley, 367
    Florida, Miami, 237
    New York, 232
    Ohio, 244
Asia
  China, 108, 282
  East Asia, 119
  India, 119
  Japan, 209
  Malaysia, 108
  Middle East, 401
Authors
  Aksin, O.Z., 115, 116, 118, 119, 133
  Anton, J., 118
  Balbinot, S., 362
  Baudry, M., 228
  Bharal, P., 219
  Chandler Jr., A.D., 122, 138
  Chesbrough, H., 44
  Crane, M., 86
  Darwin, C., 11, 64, 431
  Deming, W.E., 467
  Domingos, P., 441
  Drucker. P., 42, 44, 45, 61, 70, 130
  Gates, Bill, 405
  Gold, J., 86
  Gronroos, C., 118
  Halfon, A., 219
  Kipling, R., 322, 423
  Leavitt, H.J., 122, 127, 138
  LeBoeuf, M., 60
  Lehtinen, J.R., 118

B. Nicoletti, *Insurance 4.0*, Palgrave Studies in Financial Services Technology, https://doi.org/10.1007/978-3-030-58426-9

Lehtinen, U., 118
Magretta, J., 44
Moss, P., 119
Osterwalder, A., 41, 46, 446
Parasuraman, A., 2, 130, 131
Pfeffermann, M., 41
Pigneur, Y., 446
Porter, M., 61–63, 331, 347, 353
Rappa, M., 43
Robert, C.Y., 228
Rosenbloom, R.S., 44
Stephens, J., 250
Valverde, R., 250
von Bismarck, O., 27
Watt, J., 26

C

Compliance
Regulations
Basel, 282, 290
California Consumer Privacy Act (CCPA), 253, 254, 421
EC 261-2004, 278
General Data Protection Regulation (GDPR), 73, 253, 254, 421
IFRS, 350
Insurance Distribution Directive, 168
MiFID II, 421
National Insurance Act, 27
Solvency II, 98, 421
US Gaap, 350
Regulators
Bima, 246
British Financial Conduct Authority, 420
Chartered Institute of Insurance and Supply (CIPS), 281
Federal Aviation Authority (FAA), 240
Ivass, 387
National Association of Insurance Commissioners, 254
NIST, 460
NRMA (National Roadmap Motorist Assurance) Insurance, 248
Securities and Exchange Commission, 341
Consultants and Advisory
Accenture, 72, 103, 157, 161, 363, 367
Altimeter Group, 366
Bain & Company, 362
Boston Consulting Group (BCG), 167, 173
Capgemini, 97, 216, 414, 416
Deloitte, 2, 5, 16, 82, 94, 165, 187, 269, 274, 339, 413
DXC Technologies, 335
Ernst & Young (EY), 105
Fujitsu Consulting, 74
Gartner, 103, 114, 183, 254, 349
IDC, 205, 214
IHS Markit, 191
KPMG, 82, 313, 375
McKinsey & Company, 200, 274
MECSPE Italian Observatory, 430
Pew Research Center, 108
Price Waterhouse Coopers (PWC), 21, 160, 200, 202, 217, 271, 274, 349, 350, 400, 424
Simon-Kutchner & Partners, 351
Talent Risk Framework, 313
Customer
customer acquisition costs, 84
customer experience (CX), 49, 60, 70, 98, 112, 116, 117, 120, 121, 129, 131, 138, 148, 220,

231, 233, 239, 384, 409, 411, 415, 418, 433
customer relationships point, 120
Know Your Customer (KYC), 207, 258, 442, 458
one-customer segment, 52, 65, 82, 140, 143, 156, 187, 339, 459
value
customer value proposition, 48, 70, 96, 449
supply chain, 12, 32, 34, 267, 377
value chain, 12, 31, 42, 68, 71, 221, 258, 306, 347, 351, 376, 387, 393, 407, 429, 431, 437, 445, 469
value network, 3, 12, 15, 16, 21, 32–34, 36–38, 42, 69, 71, 72, 88, 94, 150, 172, 178, 182, 197, 200, 214, 232, 250, 258, 309, 322, 329, 331, 334, 342, 345, 347, 375, 387, 390, 394, 395, 401, 404, 414–416, 425, 429, 430, 435, 438, 448, 457, 469, 470

D

Distribution
Bancassurance, 443
channel, 4, 8, 29, 49, 52, 53, 65, 139, 147, 150, 152, 153, 155, 156, 165, 232, 387, 419, 431, 434
direct insurance channel, 149, 150, 160
e-Commerce
Alibaba, 181, 395, 462
Amazon, 74, 181, 218, 395, 401, 407, 451, 462
eBay, 181
insurance, 29, 164, 168, 314, 330
intermediaries
agencies, 49, 104
banks, 104, 149, 160
brokers, 104, 160, 330, 387
Price Comparison Websites, 165
Value Comparison Websites, 165
omnichannel, 150, 158, 394, 460
relationships
B2B, 245, 344, 395, 446, 452
B2C, 446
P2P, 78, 83
Research Online Purchase onsite (ROPO), 167

E

Ecosystem, 3, 6, 9, 12, 13, 16, 19, 31, 32, 39, 71, 76, 84, 87, 88, 94, 95, 106, 178, 184, 193, 194, 196, 197, 245, 250, 258, 262, 263, 288, 292, 296, 301, 305, 310, 330, 332, 334, 336–340, 342, 347, 348, 365, 373, 375, 380, 384, 385, 390, 395, 397, 398, 408, 412–414, 416, 425, 429, 431, 436, 437, 452
Europe
EMEA, 2, 401
European Union, 73, 254
France, 97, 141, 164
Germany
Fraunhofer Gesellschaft, 325
Koblenz, 345
Munich, 411
Italy
Italian Banking Association (ABI), 420
Lithuania, 234
Spain, 164
Sweden, 246
Switzerland, 74, 191, 398

- the Netherlands, 164
- UK
  - BBC, 441

F

Financial Institutions
- AB Kinnevik, 247
- Astorya VC, 233
- Credit Agricole, 97
- Leapfrog Investment, 247
- Millicom, 247
- Santander, 236
- Solidum Partners, 202

Function
- Asset Investment, 99, 236
- call center, 49, 114–123, 126–129, 131, 133, 134, 137, 138
- claim management, 227, 231, 234, 352, 353
- Human Resources (HR), 312
- information and communication technology (ICT), 11, 75, 84, 86, 115, 145, 152, 178, 252, 343, 455
- insurance finance, 332
- marketing, 32, 55
- pricing, 285, 351
- Research and Development (R&D), 312
- risk management, 281, 282
- underwriting, 280

G

Generation
- Generation Y, 65, 143, 459
- Generation Z, 311
- millennial, 65, 143, 311, 459

I

Industry 4.0
- First Industrial Revolution, 25
- Fourth Industrial Revolution, 30
- Insurance 4.0 Success Factors
  - cognition, 37
  - collaboration, 299
  - communication, 35
  - condivision, 21, 197
  - confidence, 21, 50, 197
  - connection, 36
  - controllership, 18
  - cybernetics, 18, 34
- Insurance 5.0, 399, 439
- Second Industrial Revolution, 27
- Third Industrial Revolution, 28

Insurance
- Insurance Companies
  - Aegon, 201, 206
  - AIG, 300
  - Allianz, 201, 206, 208, 209, 300, 411
  - Allstate Business Insurance, 51
  - American Family, 95, 96, 263, 354
  - Assicurazioni Generali, 213
  - Aviva, 206
  - Axa, 248, 278, 435
  - CCRIF SPC, 90
  - Code of Hammurabi, 25
  - Debeka, 345
  - Discovery, 141
  - Groupama, 212, 213
  - Liberty Mutual, 248
  - Munich Re, 201, 206, 411, 429
  - Ping An Insurance, 334, 340
  - Progressive Insurance, 341
  - Railways Passengers Assurance Company, 26
  - Swiss RE, 107, 201, 206
  - Tokio Marine Group, 428

Universal Casualty Compensation Company, 26
US Geico Insurance, 113
Zurich Insurance, 108, 248
Insurance Products
Bought By Many, 167
Business Interruption, 90
Car Digital Dossier, 399
co-insurance, 357
Cyber Insurance, 84
Dacadoo, 251
Fizzy, 277, 278
G-Evolution, 213, 214
Insurance based Investment Products, 169
Insurance-linked Securities, 202, 438
life, 98, 99, 149
Lings, 251
on-demand, 82, 144, 151, 251
other services, 91
parametric, 88
pay-as-you-drive, 82
peer-to-peer, 83
Product Oversight Governance, 169
Property & Casualty (P&C), 23
re-insurance, 146
retrocession, 207, 357
sustainable insurance, 425
Trov, 114, 144, 251
unit-linked, 82, 98, 154, 356
usage-based, 82, 83, 188, 189, 192, 215
vehicle insurance, 4, 144, 154, 160, 164, 189, 275, 314, 398
Vitality, 140, 141
wholesale insurance, 423
Insurance Support Organization
Compliance Risk & Audit Activity Management (CR.AA.M.), 422
ecosystem, 6, 12, 31, 32, 39, 84, 292, 305
McKennon, 37
Oxbotica, 196
SDA SE, 345
Tradle, 207, 208
Insurtech
Amodo, 193, 419
Assurely, 91
Bima, 246
BudgetChain, 208
Claims Control, 234
CosmosDirekt, 111
Cove, 232
Dynamis, 277
Everledger, 203
Fukoku Mutual Life Insurance, 230
Indiegogo, 449
InsurETH, 276
Kickstarter, 449
Ladenburg Thalmann Financial Services, 237
Lemonade Insurance Company, 232
Mattereum, 179
Nexecur, 97, 98
Openclaims, 234
Oscar Health, 112
Rightindem, 233
Safeshare Insurance, 203
SCOR, 208
Shift Technologies, 234
spixii, 113, 232
ThinxNet, 191
Tradle, 207
Wekeep, 271
Zelros, 233
Zubie, 341
International Organizations

Organization for Economic Co-operation and Development (OECD), 163
United Nations (UN)
Environmental, Social, and Governance (ESG), 425, 426
World Economic Forum, 85
World Health Organization (WHO), 91
Investment vehicles
lines of credit, 54
Merger & Acquisition (M&A), 3
mutual funds, 171
options, 63, 296
stocks, 54

M
Management
Chief Digital Officer (CDO), 321
Chief Executive Officer (CEO), 437
Chief Information Officer (CIO), 396
Chief Information Security Officer (CISO), 396
Models
business model canvas, 6–8, 41, 45–47, 59, 64, 66, 68, 146, 171, 263, 445
business model innovation, 41
marketing mix, 264, 390
Technology Acceptance Model, 376

O
Oceania
Australia, 248
Fiji Islands, 428
New Zealand, 232

P
Pandemic
COVID-19, 398
remote working, 315, 356
Severe Acute Respiratory Syndrome (SARS), 90
Partnerships
general partnership, 57
groupware, 315, 343
joint venture, 57, 416, 431, 447
limited liability partnership, 57
limited partnership, 57
teamwork, 343
Profile
data scientist, 317
On-going Support and Maintenance Staff, 319
process architect, 318
technologist, 319

Q
Quality
agile management, 6
critical success factors, 8, 34, 37, 196, 226
ISO 9000, 372
Key Performance Indicator (KPI), 297, 305, 458
lean and digitize, 128, 130, 180, 309, 358, 359, 435, 458
SERVQUAL, 130, 131

R
Regtech
Friendsurance, 204
Suptech, 467
Trov, 114, 144, 251
Resilience
graph of resilience, 297

S
Schools
ETH University, 253

Osservatorio del Politecnico di Milano, 327
University of New Orleans, 60
Shared economy
multi-side platform (MSP), 393, 394, 406
Social network
Facebook, 113, 159, 395, 401, 462
LinkedIn, 159, 277
WhatsApp, 113

T

Technologies
artificial intelligence
chatbot, 16, 113, 114, 446
cognitive search, 224, 446
cognitive technologies, 16, 145, 210
computer vision, 224, 447
machine learning, 16, 223, 224, 229, 233, 235, 287, 404, 422, 458
natural language processing, 210, 224, 460
neural networks, 210, 224, 225, 460
predictive analytics, 210, 215, 224, 462
rule based reasoning, 224
augmented reality, 247, 442, 459
automation
intelligent automation (IA), 210
robo-advisor, 33, 127, 161, 164, 235, 236, 258, 415
robotic process automation, 174, 211, 234–237, 255
virtual reality, 228, 470
cloud computing
Business Process as a Service (BPaaS), 243, 446
Cloud BB, 245, 344
Infrastructure as a Service (IaaS), 446
Platform as a Service (PaaS), 241, 446
Software-as-a-Service, 234, 466
Contract Lifecycle Management
Smart Contracts, 266
Smart Contracts Alliance, 267
data management
application programming interface (API), 232, 442
big data analytics, 16, 20, 37, 38, 68, 80, 137, 214, 221, 300, 353, 415, 438
business intelligence, 128, 301, 445
data governance, 216, 218, 255, 450
data-driven, 303
Electronic Data Interchange (EDI), 29, 452
integrated analytics, 215
Linked Data, 22
operational data analytics, 127–129
web service, 461
distributed ledger protocol
blockchain, 80, 197, 424, 444
Blockchain-as-a-Platform, 444
Blockchain as a Service, 444
Blockchain Insurance Industry Initiative (B3i), 203, 206
Documentation
Content Service Platform (CSP), 229
Extensible Markup Language (XML), 29
Information and Communication Technology
Customer Relationship Management (CRM),

- 109–111, 137, 140, 233, 236, 303, 449
  - Enterprise Content Management (ECM), 453
  - Enterprise Resource Planning (ERP), 18, 236, 303
  - Straight Through Processing (STP), 35, 73
- network
  - Bluetooth, 184, 443, 445
  - Global Positioning System (GPS), 191, 192, 213, 250, 276, 341
  - instant messaging, 304, 446
  - Internet of Everything (IoE), 19, 30, 33, 457
  - Internet of Services (IoS), 21, 454
  - Internet of Things (IoT), 3, 4, 12, 16, 19, 30, 80, 139, 146, 182–185, 242, 250, 330, 362, 405, 445, 457
  - Internet Protocol (IP), 183, 457
  - mobile, 4, 12, 30, 65, 83, 121, 144, 424
  - Real Feeding Identification Device (RFID), 177
  - Short Message Service (SMS), 246, 465
  - Subscriber Identity Module (SIM), 184
- operating systems
  - Linux, 244
- operational technology (OT), 11, 17, 84, 178
  - proof of concept, 40, 208
  - security
    - cyber risk, 73, 85, 87, 251, 252, 291, 306, 438
    - cybersecurity, 178, 241, 248, 449
    - DDoS attacks, 87
    - encryption, 452
    - ISO 27000, 372
- Technology Company (BigTech)
  - Alphabet, 112
  - Apple, 194, 438
  - Facebook, 74, 113, 159, 395, 401, 462
  - Google, 74, 112, 167, 218, 401, 407, 438
  - IBM, 114
  - Microsoft, 95
- Telecom operators
  - Amodo, 193, 419
- Transport
  - drones, 237–239
  - Maersk Cargo, 336
  - Unmanned Aircraft System (UAS), 240
  - vehicle
    - advanced driver assistance system (ADAS), 189
    - autonomous driving vehicle, 18, 191, 193
    - Tesla Motors, 194
    - Toyota, 194

V

- Virtual currency(ies)
  - Bitcoin, 198, 443
  - Ethereum, 276–278, 444